ALSO BY GEORGE STEVENS, JR.

Conversations with the Great Moviemakers of
Hollywood's Golden Age at the American Film Institute

CONVERSATIONS
at the AMERICAN
FILM INSTITUTE
with the GREAT
MOVIEMAKERS

CONVERSATIONS
at the AMERICAN
FILM INSTITUTE
with the GREAT
MOVIEMAKERS

The Next Generation

—◆—

George Stevens, Jr.

ALFRED A. KNOPF　　NEW YORK　2012

THIS IS A BORZOI BOOK
PUBLISHED BY ALFRED A. KNOPF

Copyright © 2012 by the American Film Institute
All rights reserved. Published in the United States by Alfred A. Knopf,
a division of Random House, Inc., New York, and in Canada
by Random House of Canada Limited, Toronto.
www.aaknopf.com

Knopf, Borzoi Books, and the colophon are registered trademarks
of Random House, Inc.

LIBRARY OF CONGRESS CATALOGING-IN-PUBLICATION DATA
Conversations at the American Film Institute with the great moviemakers :
the next generation / edited and with an introduction by George Stevens, Jr.—1st ed.
p.   cm.
Includes bibliographical references and index.
Includes filmographies.
ISBN 978-0-307-27347-5
1. Motion picture producers and directors—United States—Interviews.
2. Motion pictures—Production and direction.   I. Stevens, George, Jr., 1932–
II. American Film Institute.
PN1998.2.C613 2012
791.4302'32092—dc23   2011043741

Jacket design by Abby Weintraub

Manufactured in the United States of America

FIRST EDITION

For

Elizabeth Stevens

Contents

Preface

On September 1, 2010, the American Film Institute welcomed the forty-first class of the AFI Conservatory. This opening day for America's future storytellers included the screening of a new film, *Love and Other Drugs,* and when the lights came up, the creative ensemble—all of whom are AFI alumni—took to the stage: Ed Zwick, director, producer, writer ('75); Marshall Herskovitz, producer, writer ('75); Pieter Jan Brugge, producer ('79); Steven Rosenblum, editor ('76); and Steven Fierberg, cinematographer ('95).

The view from the audience was seminar enough—that the tradition captured in these pages had been reborn in a new generation. It was not lost upon the filmmakers that their move from the audience to the stage was a seed planted years ago at AFI.

These treasures are preserved and presented here through the passion of George Stevens, Jr., the founding director of the American Film Institute, who continues to support the organization's mandate by bringing the words and the wisdom of our nation's storytellers to all who love the movies. A light should also shine on the contributions of Jean Picker Firstenberg, who served as director of AFI for over twenty-seven years. In her first year of this extraordinary tenure, Jeannie created a permanent home for AFI high in the hills of Hollywood. And, finally, I would like to acknowledge the trustees, faculty and staff of AFI, each and all who believe in the singular power of the moving image: that it is more than amusement or amazement, but an art form—one that records America's cultural legacy.

Bob Gazzale
President and CEO, American Film Institute

Introduction

We are beginning here today a Center for Advanced Film Studies
that will entrench itself in the film present and provide new talent
for the film future . . . I believe that while it may not be possible to
train people to make films, it is possible to create a climate in which
people can learn to make films, where aspiring artists can absorb, in
a relatively short, intensive period, insight that others have wrested
from the experience of an entire career.

—George Stevens, Jr.
September 29, 1969

In 1970 Arthur Schlesinger, Jr., the eminent historian who was a founding
trustee of the American Film Institute, described the place of motion pictures
among the arts in America in this way: "Film is the only art in which the
United States has made a real difference," he wrote. "Strike the American
contribution from drama, painting, music, sculpture, dance, even possibly
from poetry and the novel, and the world's achievement is only marginally
diminished. But film without the American contribution is unimaginable."
Schlesinger's thesis crystallized the feelings that led me to invest myself in
AFI's founding. It was a reminder that the motion picture had been the most
potent vehicle of the American imagination and deserved to be preserved and
nurtured in the country of its birth.

The men who made the movies that inspired Schlesinger were pioneers
who came to the new medium with no models to look to and no formal
training for the tasks at hand. D. W. Griffith, Buster Keaton, Charlie Chap-

Greystone in Beverly Hills, California, was the home
of the AFI Conservatory from its opening in 1969 until
1981, when AFI acquired land and moved to a
permanent campus in Hollywood.

lin, King Vidor and their contemporaries came to moviemaking with experience in the theater or vaudeville, or in some cases with no dramatic experience at all, and they figured out how to use cameras and film to tell compelling stories. It was an era of breathtaking innovation, and the people who worked alongside these men in a thousand apprenticeships were to become the directors, writers, cameramen and technicians who would be the mainstays of a burgeoning new art, telling stories and exploring the mysteries of American life.

Woodrow Wilson was the first president to screen motion pictures in the White House, and in 1915 when he saw D. W. Griffith's epic *The Birth of a Nation,* he observed, "It is like writing history with lightning."

Half a century later, on September 29, 1965, another American president, Lyndon Johnson, stood in the Rose Garden of the White House and declared, "We will create an American Film Institute that will bring together leading artists of the film industry, outstanding educators and young men and women who wish to pursue this twentieth-century art form as their life's

The founders of the American Film Institute at Greystone
in 1969. Roger L. Stevens, founding chairman of the National
Endowment for the Arts; George Stevens, Jr., founding director
of AFI; Gregory Peck, founding chairman;
and Sidney Poitier, vice chairman.

work." I watched that day as Johnson put his pen to the law that established the National Endowment for the Arts, the organization that would foster the creation of the American Film Institute.* As founding director of AFI, I shared with my fellow trustees the dream of creating a conservatory that would be a bridge between the study of film and the filmmaking profession.

On the night we opened the Center for Advanced Film Studies in 1969, Harold Lloyd screened his classic comedy *The Freshman,* then met with the "fellows" who had come to AFI to learn filmmaking. Lloyd's seminar was an historic first step toward a tutorial tradition at AFI in which master filmmakers would pass their knowledge and experience to the next generation. The setting was the stately stone mansion in Beverly Hills called Greystone, which had been the home of E. L. (Ned) Doheny, Jr., son of E. L. Doheny, the oil baron who was involved in the Teapot Dome bribery scandal of the 1920s. The younger Doheny and his secretary-chauffeur were found dead in one of the bedrooms in what was reported as a murder-suicide, a tale of intrigue worthy of a school for storytellers.

Lloyd was accompanied by his close friend King Vidor, and that night

*In his remarks Johnson also called for a National Theater, a National Opera Company and a National Ballet. The American Film Institute was the only one of these ideas to become a reality.

these accomplished and gracious men in their seventies set the tone for the AFI series that continues today as the Harold Lloyd Master Seminar Program. In the audience that night were young people in their twenties, the first class of eighteen AFI fellows, which included Terrence Malick, Paul Schrader and Caleb Deschanel, who would soon embark on film careers of their own.

James Powers, a correspondent for the *Hollywood Reporter,* described that first night in an article, "Film Institute Bows with Harold Lloyd and *The Freshman*":

> It is as old as Socrates, of course, the method that Stevens and the institute have chosen to preserve and regenerate the most American of arts. The institute calls it a "tutorial" system. Most of the young filmmakers are already expert in the technical aspects of their craft. By exposure to the great figures of Hollywood film, they will be inspired and propelled into doing something with that craft.

Jim Powers' enthusiasm for the concept led me to hire him to head the seminar program. You will see Jim's name listed as the moderator of many of the seminars.

This book follows an earlier volume, *Conversations with the Great*

Federico Fellini (left) came to AFI to discuss *Fellini Satyricon* on January 12, 1970. He was joined by Anthony Quinn, who starred as Zampano, the brutish circus performer in *La strada,* and seminar host, George Stevens, Jr.

Frank Capra answers questions by AFI fellows in the main seminar room
at Greystone, May 1978.

Moviemakers of Hollywood's Golden Age at the American Film Institute, published by Knopf in 2006, in which we presented the seminars of Lloyd and Vidor, as well as Hitchcock, Hawks, Huston, Walsh, Wyler, Wilder, Stevens, Lean, Capra and others of what might be called filmmaking's first generation. Martin Scorsese described the book as invaluable for those "who want to learn about movies and to those of us who may want to recharge our batteries and look to the masters for inspiration." The director Alexander Payne was at AFI in 2011, and halfway through his seminar he took a copy of *Golden Age* from a bag beside his chair, saying to the fellows, "The most valuable thing I can say here today is read this book. I turn to it constantly. You learn film history and film technique from the true giants."

I decided to do *Conversations at the American Film Institute with the Great Moviemakers: The Next Generation* because so many found the first book valuable. With this volume we move beyond the formative era of the golden age into a generation of filmmakers whose careers began in the second half of the twentieth century, and in many cases extend into the new millennium. The first book was confined to directors, cameramen, two screenwriters and a producer. This volume includes directors, producers, writers, actors, cinematographers, a composer, an editor, an experimental filmmaker and a film

George Stevens, Jr., in the entry staircase of Greystone in 1976
with producer Martin Manulis, who served as director
of AFI West from 1974 to 1977.

critic, reflecting the range of creators who have participated in more than
2,500 seminars at AFI over the past forty years.

One reason why these seminars are so informative and stimulating is
because at the AFI Conservatory the questions are asked by aspiring filmmakers who intend to spend their lives making films. Their curiosity bends
toward craft—they are more interested in how things are made than in what
things mean. Picasso said that when critics sit around they talk about aesthetics, but when artists sit around they talk about turpentine. Turpentine is the

topic at AFI. Walter Gropius, the founder of the famed Bauhaus school of design in Germany, declared that "the artist is the climax to the craftsman." Although the fellows at the Conservatory aspire to be artists, their training is focused on craft.

When the pioneers of the Golden Age were growing up, there were few films to watch and certainly no film schools, and when feature films burgeoned they were silent—stories told with pictures and no dialogue. So each of these storytellers came to moviemaking knowing that story and character must be revealed visually. When sound came along, Hitchcock offered his famous complaint that most talkies were "simply photographs of people talking."

The men and women you will meet in this book grew up watching movies with sound. They studied motion pictures, seeing them first in theaters, and then—many of them—in film school. They were influenced by the films and filmmakers that preceded them in a way that the earlier generation was not, and in recent years they have had unimpeded access to the full spectrum of world cinema on video and DVD.

The most valuable learning experience in the early years of the AFI Conservatory took place in two screening rooms at Greystone, where 35mm prints were shown daily, providing fellows the opportunity to view films as they were intended to be seen. One week it would be the work of Preston Sturges and the next the films of Jean Renoir, or a series of Howard Hawks pictures shown before the man himself gave a seminar. "I thought for sure I'd died and gone to heaven," David Lynch wrote of the experience. "At AFI all day the greatest cinema played in the Great Hall. And we listened to filmmakers—foreign voices along with powerful American voices." All these years later I still recall those screenings and the vitality of the discussions with the fellows afterward. It was instructive and inspiring to study the best work from the past, classic films not yet accessible on video and DVD.

There is a significant difference between seeing a masterwork on a large screen in a room with others and seeing it alone on a television monitor or a laptop, and it is unfortunate that today so many people gain their first impression of films on a small screen rather than from the larger-than-life experience in a theater. When one studies the appraisals of vintage films by film critics, or tracks reviews in the blogosphere, I often wonder if the writers have ever seen the film they are describing as it was designed to be presented. Peter Bogdanovich believes that many young people don't appreciate films made before the sixties because they've never had a proper look at them. "If you don't see a film on a big screen you haven't really seen it," he wrote. "You've seen a version of it, but you haven't seen it." Manohla Dargis, a film critic of *The New York Times,* reported how one observer characterized the sensation of seeing films at the 2010 Cannes Festival: "The projection alone can seem worth the trip, and usually on screens so large they remind you of when movies were bigger than you, bigger than life."

THE NEXT GENERATION

I wrote a paper in grammar school on Eadweard Muybridge, the nineteenth-century British photographer who presented successive still photos of a running horse to create motion, an illusion that relied on the concept of "persistence of vision" that led to moving pictures being projected at twenty-four frames a second so the viewer would perceive continuous motion. As I studied the men and women in this book it occurred to me that persistence of vision is a shared quality that has enabled them to sustain long and distinguished careers. They worked in challenging times when film studios were losing their dominant position and moviemakers were forced to set up pictures independently. The directors in this book were often, or always, also producers of their films—responsible for creating their own opportunities, making deals, managing their productions and enlisting actors who would attract financing. Many of the actors started independent production companies. In the golden age, the studios had stables of stars under contract, so that actors had less control over their careers and it was much easier to cast leading roles. If Jimmy Stewart wasn't available, there was Fonda or Cooper or Wayne or Cagney or Bogart or Tracy or Gable, all of whom were making several pictures every year.

I remember when my father was about to begin shooting *Shane* with Montgomery Clift and William Holden in the leading roles, Clift suddenly bowed out, followed by Holden. Paramount was all set to postpone the picture when my father went to studio head Y. Frank Freeman's office and asked to see the contract list he kept in his left-hand drawer. Dad glanced at it and said, "You have a commitment with Alan Ladd. He'll be fine as Shane. And you have pictures with Van Heflin, he can play the Holden part. And Jean Arthur has always been good for me. She can play the woman." The picture was cast in ten minutes and shooting started several weeks later.

By the seventies, not only had the studio contract system disappeared, but actors like Beatty, Eastwood and Redford, and later Costner, Gibson and Clooney, who had the star power to get pictures financed, decided to become director-producers, making one picture every two or three years and taking themselves off the market for other directors. Robert Towne describes in his seminar the value of movie stars in getting quality films launched and overcoming studio interference. Speaking of his long association with Warren

Beatty, Towne observed, "You could be even bolder because you were backed by movie stars who were invested in the movie getting made. As long as they were on board, the film would get done."

I hope aspiring filmmakers find that the knowledge offered in this book removes some of the mystery about the process and will inform their own work. AFI encourages collaboration, and many graduates find that the relationships they develop with colleagues at the Conservatory continue throughout their careers. Many of the people in this book are linked by intersecting paths and describe working with one another. Peter Bogdanovich, John Sayles and Robert Towne all got their first jobs with Roger Corman, and Bogdanovich formed a film company with Billy Friedkin. Towne was on the set with Arthur Penn on *Bonnie and Clyde,* and Meryl Streep worked with Alan Pakula, Sydney Pollack and Nora Ephron.

A major evolution in American motion pictures was sparked by two of the directors in this book who were frequent collaborators. When *Jaws* opened in 1975, Steven Spielberg gave us the summer blockbuster, with Universal shipping hundreds of prints around the country backed by a huge national marketing campaign. And when George Lucas launched *Star Wars* two years later, the tentpole concept was born, which led studios to look for pictures that could be serialized and provide opportunities for merchandising and the creation of theme parks, which in turn led to the arrival each summer of successive versions of comic-book-based action franchises, effects-driven fantasies and animated films for families. Soon box-office reporting, for which *Variety* had always been the source, became a regular feature in *The New York Times* and other major newspapers. And as the stock prices of major entertainment companies become ever more dependent on summer blockbusters with global appeal, the funding of mainstream films for adults becomes more problematic.

I find common cause between the filmmakers of the Golden Age and those presented here. The art and craft of telling compelling stories on the screen have not changed. We discover in these seminars the ways in which some of the foremost contributors to modern filmmaking created their most appreciated and enduring works. A young filmmaker who digests these concepts and insights will develop a solid understanding of the creative process, one drawn not from theory but from practical and proven experience. Veteran director Robert Altman suggests the job of the director is to establish an atmosphere where the actor feels safe, an objective echoed by newcomer Darren Aronofsky, as well as by actors Jack Lemmon, Gregory Peck and actor-director Sidney Poitier. Poitier makes a point of never giving an actor instructions within earshot of the other performers. Peck says the head should control the heart, while Lemmon seeks a spontaneous environment on the set where everything is up for interpretation guided by a director who is open to suggestions. Peck wasn't bothered when William Wyler demanded forty takes on a scene, but Morgan Freeman says that if a director wants more than three takes he should tell him what's wrong. Penn, Pollack and Sayles all urge aspiring directors to study acting to better understand the needs of the actor. And while the films of Sayles and Neil Simon couldn't be more different, both read the lines of each character aloud while writing their screenplays. Penn, Pollack and Alan Pakula, men whose careers began in and around the theater in New York, place an emphasis on the psychological inner lives of their characters and expect considerable character development during shooting. Pakula says he loves surprises on the set, while Penn looks for "controlled accidents" that will enhance the film.

Robert Towne's key for lucid dramatic narrative is a simple one: "You need to know what those characters want and what they don't want, what they're afraid of and what they're not afraid of." Paul Schrader advises aspiring writers to return to the campfire and learn to tell the story of their screenplay in conversation, alert to the response of listeners, so that in each iteration the story will become sharper and more dramatic. He looks for that complicating "piece of sand in your oyster" that can be transformed into cinematic metaphor, while Nora Ephron speaks of the "little ghost that flies away" to explain how the idea in the writer's head is displaced in a blink of the eye by the reality of actors on the set.

A motion picture is a shotgun wedding between art and commerce, a theme that emerges in many of the seminars. Penn, Pakula, Pollack, Bogdanovich, Sayles and writer-producer Larry Gelbart talk about the tension between filmmaker and studio, with each one stressing the importance of maintaining control over the screenplay, shooting and editing. Penn urges the fellows to break the rules and put a personal stamp on their work. Spielberg's seminars at AFI took place early in his career and he provides a fascinating perspective on how a young filmmaker builds a career, which in his case turned out to be one of the most illustrious in cinema history.

Shirley Clarke and Ed Emshwiller represent filmmakers who worked apart from the organized industry, creating films very personal to themselves. They describe the burden of financing one's own work and the satisfaction of having complete control of the result. But it is, perhaps, from George Lucas that we learn the most basic lessons: believe in your own ideas, ignore the critics and never give up sequel or merchandising rights.

Former fellows who once listened to and questioned the AFI seminar guests are now making films of their own, and many of them speak of the

Robert De Niro talks with AFI fellows at Greystone, November 1980.

insights offered and the lessons learned from the seminars. Many of today's best cinematographers are AFI alumni, including Janusz Kaminski, whose seminar is in this book, and Robert Richardson, Juan Ruiz Anchía, Wally Pfister, Matt Labatique and Caleb Deschanel. Directors from the AFI Conservatory include David Lynch, Darren Aronofsky and Paul Schrader, who are in the book, as well as Edward Zwick, Carl Franklin, Terrence Malick, Marshall Herskovitz, Leslie Linka Glatter, Mimi Leder, Todd Field, Patty Jenkins and Rodrigo García. Their achievement is part of the harvest of the tutorial idea encompassed in the Harold Lloyd Master Seminar program.

Credit for AFI's success and the success of AFI graduates is widely shared among many people who devoted themselves to making the Conservatory a vibrant place to learn about filmmaking. One man, however, merits special mention. Toni Vellani served AFI from 1968 until his death in 1989, and he more than anyone else shaped our training concept. Many AFI graduates credit Toni with their understanding of how to tell a story and still live by his rigorous demand that they define and understand the "premise" of their films. One fellow recalled, "The question I dreaded hearing from Toni Vellani was, 'What is the premise of your story?' That question meant that on some fundamental level my film had failed. It failed because, in Mr. Vellani's opinion, I hadn't conveyed to the audience what was driving my story, or why the audience should care." Toni died too young, but not before nourishing a generation of fine filmmakers.

Antonio Vellani joined AFI in 1968 and served as
associate dean of the Conservatory beginning in 1971
and later as its director until his death in 1989. The
fellows valued him as a mentor who understood
the craft of narrative storytelling.

Other members of the faculty in my era at the American Film Institute
were James Blue, Frank Daniel, Jan Kadar, Martin Manulis, Jim Silke, and
Bob Blumofe. Later, under Jean Firstenberg's leadership, Frank Pierson was a
mainstay and Robert Mandel, an AFI graduate, became dean and still serves
in that capacity under AFI's new president, Bob Gazzale.

At AFI we have always emphasized the art of film, while recognizing that
it is also a business. Many of the artists in this book have succeeded financially, but not all. When Orson Welles received the AFI Life Achievement
Award in 1975, he had fallen on hard times. He was broke, with several films
incomplete or abandoned. In presenting the award to Orson, I quoted John
Ruskin, who observed a hundred years earlier that many of the most enduring works of art and literature are never paid for. "How much," Ruskin asked,
"do you think Homer got for his *Iliad*? Or Dante for his *Paradise*? Only bitter bread and salt and walking up and down other people's stairs." This too is
part of AFI's teaching. In the final analysis, it's the work that counts—and

Orson Welles accepting the AFI Life Achievement Award, 1975.

may every AFI fellow aspire to a legacy as rich and lasting as that of Orson
Welles.

I offer my heartfelt thanks to the men and women whose seminars are in
this book for their generous commitment of time and energy in coming to
AFI to meet with the fellows, and for the many pleasures their films have
brought to me and so many others around the world.

CONVERSATIONS *at the* AMERICAN FILM INSTITUTE *with the* GREAT MOVIEMAKERS

My films are scripted. I use improvisation as a tool during the rehearsal period before we shoot, but basically, once we start shooting it's a very set thing. Improvisation is misunderstood. We don't just turn people loose.

ROBERT ALTMAN
(Born in Kansas City, Missouri, 1925—Died 2006)

Robert Altman became one of the most accomplished filmmakers of his generation, but his pathway to making features was a long and winding one. After flying fifty bombing missions as a B-24 co-pilot in the Army Air Corps, he returned to his native Kansas City, where his father was a prosperous insurance man and amateur gambler. He spent the next decade shooting documentaries for a local industrial company before heading for Hollywood in 1955, where he made *The Delinquents* in 1957. He spent another decade directing television shows, including *Maverick, Peter Gunn, Route 66, Bonanza* and *Alfred Hitchcock Presents,* before making *Countdown* in 1968, a low-budget story of the first flight to the moon starring James Caan and Robert Duvall.

Once Altman started making features, the skills he acquired on television sound stages enabled him to become one of Hollywood's most prolific directors, displaying the widest range of subject matter and style. *That Cold Day in the Park* with Sandy Dennis in 1969 wasn't well received, and his career had stalled when he was offered *M*A*S*H,* a script that had been passed over by many leading directors. Altman, at age forty-five, placed his stamp on the story of an army field hospital during the Korean War, creating a box-office hit and capturing the Palme d'Or at Cannes, five Oscar nominations, and Best Picture of the Year recognition from the National Society of Film Critics.

Altman liked to have several stories moving at the same time. He favored overlapping dialogue and he was more interested in characters than plot. "I look at film as closer to painting or a piece of music," he once explained. "It's an impression of character and total atmosphere—an attempt to enlist an audience emotionally, not intellectually." He followed *M*A*S*H* with hits and misses like *Brewster McCloud, McCabe & Mrs. Miller, Images, The Long*

Robert Altman on location in Vancouver
for *McCabe & Mrs. Miller* in 1971.

Goodbye, Thieves Like Us, California Split and then, in 1975, one of his career triumphs, *Nashville*. Set during the last five days of a fictional presidential primary, *Nashville* interwove the stories of twenty-four characters in the music business and showed off many of Altman's favorite performers, including Elliott Gould, Lily Tomlin, Julie Christie, Shelley Duvall and Keith Carradine. Roger Ebert wrote that after seeing the film, "I felt more alive, I felt I understood more about people, I felt somehow wiser."

Between 1976 and 1990, Altman made fourteen pictures including *Buffalo Bill and the Indians, 3 Women, Popeye, Come Back to the Five and Dime, Jimmy Dean, Jimmy Dean,* and *Vincent and Theo.* His career received a shot in the arm with *The Player,* the sardonic look at Hollywood based on Michael Tolkin's novel, a film that earned him his third Oscar nomination for Best Director and the award for Best Director at Cannes. It was followed by *Short Cuts,* for which he took Raymond Carver's writings as a point of departure and earned a fourth Oscar nomination. Then came seven films in six years,

Altman applies makeup to Keith Carradine on the set of *Thieves Like Us* (1974).

including *Prêt-à-Porter, The Gingerbread Man* and *Dr. T and the Women,* none of which matched his most admired work.

Throughout his career Altman jousted with studios and sometimes with collaborators. He angered screenwriters when he said: "Many writers have hard feelings about what I do to their scripts, but my idea is, it's not their script. Their script is my tool to work with—I don't owe them an apology."

Altman had to fight to get his films financed, often pressing his vision in ways that put his career at risk. He was known for his irascibility and hard drinking and found it difficult to convey his concepts to studio heads. "When I explain what I want to do," he told *The Washington Post,* "they can't see it, because I'm trying to deliver something they haven't seen before."

Hollywood honored the iconoclastic director with an honorary Oscar in 2006. In accepting it on national television he revealed for the first time that he had received a heart transplant ten years earlier.

In 2001, Altman made *Gosford Park,* an elaborate, multilayered murder mystery filmed in an elegant English manor house with an ensemble cast of England's finest actors. It was the third-best box-office outing of his career and earned seven Oscar nominations, including Best Director and Best Picture. He received the Golden Globe for directing *Gosford Park.*

Altman came to AFI and spoke with the fellows following a screening of *Gosford Park.*

ROBERT ALTMAN

—◆—

December 18, 2001*

I saw in the Gosford Park *production notes that you passed out etiquette books to the upstairs people.*

We had three technical advisors. We had a butler, a housemaid and a cook who were all in their mid-to-late eighties and who, during the period of our film, which is set in the early thirties, had all worked in service. The maid, a woman named Violet, had worked at Chequers, which is the prime minister's residence, and also for Bernard Shaw. They were there to assist the actors. I'm a foreigner making a film about English manners, which is a little presumptuous and arrogant of me, so I wanted to be sure that we got it right. And the actors all wanted to get it right. We found out in doing this that most of these films you see from England about this sort of thing aren't right at all. In the first half of the twentieth century you had these estates with maybe forty servants for a family of six. You had these two totally separate societies going on. That's really the reason we made the film.

What we found is that most of these people worked in an average of two households their entire life, and none of these houses were run in the same way. There were certain protocols that were similar, but when somebody would say, "Oh no, they never served this with so-and-so," it became clear that in another house they did things completely differently.

*Carolyn Pfeiffer moderated this seminar. The transcript also contains segments from seminars Robert Altman gave at the American Film Institute on December 4, 1974, and September 8, 1999.

Except for cigars and brandy after dinner?

That's always the same. And get the women out of the room.

I wonder if there is any particular reason why you're drawn to stories with large ensemble casts.

It's a caprice of mine. I can give you a lot of quick answers. I made a film called *Secret Honor* which had one character, Richard Nixon. I've made films with only a few characters. *3 Women* comes to mind. But generally I like to see a lot of stuff going on. A glib answer I have, which is true, is that if a scene doesn't work I can always cut away and go to something else. I'm finding that large casts seem to hurt a film commercially. These are not date films. It's not Julia Roberts and Richard Gere and a few people, which is what I think most people want in a film.

Did you find it different working with British actors as opposed to working with an American ensemble?

Yes. I never saw an agent. Nobody ever came and argued about how big somebody's trailer was. They all got paid the same. They all had a great time doing it. It was the best experience of my life. An actor like Alan Bates, who worked ten weeks on the film, was there an average of four and a half days a week for the first six weeks. He was standing way in the background in every shot. I don't think he had a scene. It was the same with Derek Jacobi, who played a really small part. He was there for all that time. That kind of thing couldn't happen in America.

Was it more fun working "upstairs" or "downstairs"?

I enjoyed both equally. They divided themselves into two groups and kept themselves kind of automatically separated. It was a lot of fun.

Could you describe the process you use with actors as you work on their performances?

Well, I don't have much to do with the actor's performance. When I cast a film, most of my creative work is done. I have to be there to turn the switch on and give them encouragement as a father figure, but they do all the work. If an actor comes to me and asks, "What exactly should I do when I come in that door?" I'll say, "Have you thought about wearing cowboy boots instead of those slippers?" I'll say anything except answer their question directly, because the minute I've narrowed the 360-degree possibility down, they're not creating things themselves, and I'm doing the work. I want to see *them* do the work. All I'm trying to do is make it easy on the actor, because once you start to shoot, the actor is the artist. I don't say, "Here's the way I want it done," because I want to see something I've never seen before. How can I say what that is? I've got to let them know that if they stretch and they do something that's bad, I'm not even going to show it in dailies. The actors in *Gosford Park* all took care of themselves.

As a director, I have to give them confidence and see that they have a certain amount of protection so they can be creative. The actors know that even though they don't get paid well, they trust that I'll let them do the creative work. I let them do what they became actors for in the first place: to create. And I not only let them do it, I insist that they do it. That's what I do in setting the thing up, and they do the rest. Actors tend to police themselves. The more of them there are, the easier it is to manage. If there are six actors, one of them isn't going to come in and misbehave, because the other five are going to beat him up. I work hard to try and create a family atmosphere. The first thing I do is get a place to see the

Altman (right) with Michael Gambon (far left) and Emily Watson, shot *Gosford Park* (2001), often using multiple cameras in manors in England and at Shepperton Studios.

dailies. I encourage everyone to watch them. You find that the actors start rooting for each other when they find out they're not in competition.

Did you have any rehearsal time on Gosford Park?

I never had a full quorum together, but I would meet with the actors and offer all this research and the technical advisors we had available, and encourage them to do as much work as they wanted to.

Where did the idea for the film come from?

Bob Balaban has been a friend of mine for many years. He's sort of a Renaissance man. He's an actor, a director, a producer. He does everything, and he and I were talking one day. He said, "I wish we could do something together. Could my company develop something for you?" And I said, "Well, I've never done a whodunit." I'm not very original. I mean, I'll take a genre that's comfortable and then go in and just kind of tilt it a little bit. Bob said, "What do you mean?" I said, "You know, the big house and all the people coming to shoot pheasants, and there's a murder and the like." We started describing the film as *Ten Little Indians* meets *Rules of the Game,* and then got Julian Fellowes to write a script. The next thing I know we're shooting it.

I'm curious about the process in the larger scenes when there's so much action in both the foreground and the background. Are you using two cameras?

I used two cameras almost all the time except when the room was so small we couldn't get two cameras in. I arbitrarily had them moving, with no particular purpose. That wasn't new. I lifted it from myself, from *The Long Goodbye* where the camera was always moving without purpose. I did it in *Gosford Park* because these wonderful English period films like *Brideshead Revisited* or the Merchant-Ivory films are so formal and their speech is all so precise. I thought, "You know, I don't believe that's the way people really behaved." I just wanted to make it sloppy. I didn't want to have nice formal two-shots and singles and that sort of thing, so we just kept the camera moving. The standard thing with a film like this is a guy sitting watching television who gets up to go open a beer, and then comes back and he says, "Did she kill him yet?" He knows he'll be shown the important stuff in close-up three times. But I wanted to put the audience on notice, right off the bat, that they have to pay attention or they're going to miss something. Some of the punchlines are done on the backs of people when they're leaving the room, like Maggie Smith when she says, "I haven't got a snobbish bone in my body." The more people I had in the scene, the easier it was for me to orchestrate, because all those actors could take care of themselves. We'd say, "Everybody just get in the room and go where you think you would be," and they'd just start moving. The more of that kind of thing I had to do, the more of it was done for me by the actors and the easier it was. We have created this film in a way that if you like it, you really have to go back and see it again and you'll see a different film. Once you know all of the mandatory things about who did it or who didn't do it, it becomes not so much a whodunit as a why-didn't-they-do-it-earlier. Or who-cares-who-did-it. I just really wanted the audience to have to turn their necks and work rather than serving it all up for you.

Is the overlapping dialogue also something you leave to the actors?

If you've got fourteen people at a dinner table, it seems to me it's pretty unlikely that only two of them are going to be talking.

Can you talk a little bit about the casting process?

For a film like this I had to have half the actors be people you recognize so you could tell them apart. If I had the finest talent in the world and you had never seen any of these people before, twenty minutes into the film you'd say, "I can't stay with this. Who's who?" Even now it's hard to keep the upstairs people really separate and know exactly what their relationships are. But it's not really that important. Hopefully you'll say, "Ah, there is a story going on between these people," and you kind of figure it out, much like if you go to a party. You spend four hours at a party with twenty people, sixteen of whom you've just met for the first time. Then you go home and say, "What did he really do?" "Which one?" "The tall guy smoking a cigar . . ." I know that's not the way to make a hit picture, but I say this truthfully: I'm not interested in making a hit picture. I'm interested in making the picture I made, and I hope people respond to it. I think I'd be late for work if I started doing one of these things that was all laid out for you.

Did you have specific actors in mind when the script was being written?

No, but the casting process took a long time because I was careful that if I got a tall guy, I also got a short guy. If I got a heavyset woman, I also got a skinny woman. I wanted to be able to tell them apart. We did go after people like Maggie Smith. When you see Maggie Smith you invest your own knowledge of her. You know that this is Maggie Smith. It helps the audience keep track.

Could you talk about the process of adapting literary works for the screen? The Long Goodbye *and* Short Cuts *are especially interesting in terms of both the faithfulness to the text and where they veer off from the original.*

The Long Goodbye was from a script by Leigh Brackett. It was presented to me but I said, "I'm not going to do Raymond Chandler and Philip Marlowe." They kept pressing me on it so I read the script. At the end of it, Philip Marlowe pulls out a gun and blows Terry Lennox away and walks off down the road. I said, "Okay. I'll do this, but I want in the contract that the studio can't change this ending." We shot the structure of Leigh Brackett's script, but the dialogue became something the actors pretty much improvised as we went along. The credit on *Short Cuts* says, "Based on the stories of Raymond Carver." We took great liberties with that. His

Cinematographer Vilmos Zsigmond and Nina Van Pallandt
with Altman filming *The Long Goodbye* in 1973.

widow, Tess Gallagher, worked on the film with us and it's just thick with Raymond Carver. And yet there's only one story that's really his, the one about the little kid getting hit by the car and dying. That was the closest to any of his stories, though there were pieces of the others everywhere. There's a scene where there's a guy with his kid walking down the street pushing a bicycle and he's been beat up. Nobody focused on it, it's just background action, but it's one of Carver's stories. We got a lot of heat from Raymond Carver fans just as we had done from Raymond Chandler fans who said, "You changed the book." Well, we didn't change the book. We made a film that was inspired by those things.

You have a reputation for being totally improvisational and just making it up as you go along.

Let me clarify what I just said. My films are scripted. I use improvisation as a tool during the rehearsal period before we shoot, but basically, once we start shooting it's a very set thing. Improvisation is misunderstood. We don't just turn people loose.

I had this project called *The Chicken and the Hawk,* which was about World War I flying. It was a comedy with a big ensemble cast. It would have been incredibly expensive and nobody really responded to it. I think I was the fifteenth director they offered *M*A*S*H* to. I didn't think the script was very good but saw I could take this attitude I wanted to use in *The Chicken and the Hawk* and put it into *M*A*S*H.* So I said okay. I went up to San Francisco where there was an improvisational theater group I knew about, with a bunch of crazy people on the stage doing whatever they wanted to do. I hired them all as extras before finding out you can't hire extras for a studio film unless each one has a proper character name. So I rewrote the script so that each one of these people had one line, which qualified them as actors. If you ever look at *M*A*S*H* you'll see in the opening credits it names Donald Sutherland and so forth, and then it says "And introducing," followed by about twenty-five names. They became the core background to the film, and that's where the improvisation happened.

Over the years you have moved further and further away from linear plots.

I do that purposely. I'm more interested in the impression of a character and the atmosphere than what actually happens. I want to make films that the audience can respond to emotionally, but not articulate anything like, "I don't think that guy would have done that under these circumstances." I don't want to deal with that. I think the reason may be the length of time I spent in television dealing with hundreds and hundreds of stories. Boy, you just knew why everybody did everything.

How do you keep your spirits up on the set?

I like what I do and it's never a chore. I'm always excited by it. I would rather be doing that than anything I can think of. So I'm having fun, and that really is the word for it.

When you see one of your pictures today and you've got some distance from it, is there anything you want to change?

No. It's like having a child. Sometimes you wish that he were a little taller or not quite so fat or those kind of things, but you tend to love your least successful children the most. I love every film I've made, and when people say, "Jesus, that wasn't a very good one," I say, "It all depends on how you look at it." I'm always shocked when I finish a film and show it and they don't make me king of the world. But then recently when I saw who they did make king of the world I said, "Thank God for that. I don't ever want to make that picture."

Your films have a light touch, but at the same time tell dark stories. Is that hard for the audience?

I know that the commercial problem with the films I make is that you've got to see them twice. The first time you're doing the whodunit thing. You're saying, "Oh, I betcha she's going to go in there! Oh, she didn't go in that door!" So you're missing a lot of the details. The second time you know whodunit, so you're able to look in the corners. It becomes a much better piece of work.

I would think that would give your pictures a long life.

The marketplace is almost impossible for me now because everybody reports how much money a film made. I find it just mind-boggling that such things are talked about.

At least it ought to be in the business section, not on the arts pages.

That's exactly right. It's really hard to get an adult audience out to the theater. Most adults say, "Oh, God, I hear that's pretty good. I'll wait until it comes out on video." And that's really what we're facing now. The release of the film is a trailer for the video sales.

And there is tremendous emphasis on youth. Do you think that the pendulum's going to swing back?

I don't think there's a prayer. It's too easy to see a film at home. Why should an adult couple get in their car and drive? They can just say, "Oh, what will we rent tonight?" And the video store orders are in direct ratio to how much money the film made. I did a film, *The Gingerbread Man,* and it didn't gross anything, so they didn't produce many copies to go into the stores. But they stock lots of copies of Tom Cruise's *Top Gun,* which did an enormous amount of money. If you come in and say, "I want *The Gingerbread Man,*" they say, "We're out of it." That store knows that you're going to pick up something else so they don't care that they don't have it.

What would you say are important films for us to watch?

An important film is one that affects me at a certain time in my life. The first film I saw that suddenly made the difference to me between "movies" and "film" was David Lean's *Brief Encounter.* I saw it and I thought, "Wait a minute. What am I doing here, in love with a girl who wears sensible shoes?" And I suddenly realized the power of it. It just hits you. And *The Treasure of the Sierra Madre.* I was just gaga over that film. So you'll see things during your life as your mind is growing and you'll go, "Wow. This is really something." They literally change your life, because they alter your attitude. If you look at one of these films forty years from now, it will still have an effect on you.

To me it's the process that's most important. It's the experience of getting a bunch of friends building this incredible sand castle. You finish it and have a beer and watch the tide come in and pretty soon it's all gone. But it remains in your mind, so you go home and say to your friends, "Come back next Saturday and we'll build another one." There's a lot of grumbling and one guy says, "Well, next time I'm not doing towers. I'll do the moat." But that work you did—the construction of whatever it was—endures only in the minds of people. Mainly yourself.

That's fairly Eastern. Very mystical.

Eastern United States . . . New York.

One of the advantages of working with a studio is that you have all the things you need to get into production. But you're kind of out there on your own. How do you do it?

Well, I've been doing this for a long time and, for some reason, I've just always operated this way. I run into people who say, "You really had some tough times and it's really difficult for you." But I don't think there's a filmmaker alive, or who ever lived, who's had a better shake than I've had. I've never been without a project and it's always been a project of my own choosing. So I don't know how much better it could be. I have not become a mogul, I don't build castles and I don't have a vast personal fortune, but I have been able to do what I've wanted to do and I've done it a lot.

What is your advice for us young filmmakers going out into the world?

I'll give you the same advice I gave my children: never take advice from anybody.

I noticed you had to have a backup director for Gosford Park.

Stephen Frears was gracious enough to back me up, though he was never on the set. At my age they won't let me make a film unless there's somebody that will back me up because they think I'm going to croak on the set.

And Bob, by the way, that's probably how you're going to go.

I hope so.

◆━━▶

Films as Director

1957 *The Delinquents* (also producer and screenplay)	1970 *M*A*S*H* *Brewster McCloud*
1968 *Countdown*	1971 *McCabe & Mrs. Miller* (also
1969 *That Cold Day in the Park*	screenplay)

1972 *Images* (also screenplay)
1973 *The Long Goodbye*
1974 *Thieves Like Us* (also screenplay)
     California Split (also producer)
1975 *Nashville* (also producer)
1976 *Buffalo Bill and the Indians, or Sitting Bull's History Lesson* (also producer and screenplay)
1977 *3 Women* (also producer and screenplay)
1978 *A Wedding* (also producer and screenplay)
1979 *Quintet* (also producer and screenplay)
     A Perfect Couple (also producer and screenplay)
1980 *HealtH* (also producer and screenplay)
     Popeye
1982 *Come Back to the 5 & Dime, Jimmy Dean, Jimmy Dean*
1983 *Streamers* (also producer)

1984 *Secret Honor* (also producer)
1985 *O.C. and Stiggs* (also producer)
     Fool for Love
1987 *Beyond Therapy* (also screenplay)
     Aria (also screenplay)
1990 *Vincent and Theo*
1992 *The Player*
1993 *Short Cuts* (also screenplay)
1994 *Prêt-à-Porter* (also producer and screenplay)
1996 *Kansas City* (also producer and screenplay)
1998 *The Gingerbread Man*
1999 *Cookie's Fortune* (also producer)
2000 *Dr. T and the Women* (also producer)
2001 *Gosford Park* (also producer and screenplay)
2003 *The Company*
2006 *A Prairie Home Companion* (also producer)

Altman also directed documentaries, movies for television and episodes of television series, including *Alfred Hitchcock Presents*, 1957–58; *Whirlybirds*, 1959; *The Millionaire*, 1959; *U.S. Marshall*, 1960; *Bonanza*, 1961; and *Combat*, 1962–63.

I guarantee actors that they'll never be embarrassed. They may see really potentially ugly parts of themselves, but they'll be incredibly truthful. Once you have that trust they will give it to you.

DARREN ARONOFSKY
(Born in New York City, 1969)

After studying at Harvard University and the AFI Conservatory, Darren Aronofsky embarked on a course of independent filmmaking in 1993 that eventually led to *The Wrestler* and *Black Swan*—films that earned critical acclaim for him as a director and major awards for Mickey Rourke and Natalie Portman. Aronofsky, who was raised in a Conservative Jewish family in Brooklyn and studied anthropology and biology before settling in to pursue his interest in motion pictures. He received his MFA from AFI and was later awarded the institute's Franklin J. Schaffner medal for his professional achievements.

Darren Aronofsky with Ellen Burstyn on the set of *Requiem for a Dream* (2000).
Burstyn received a Best Actress Oscar nomination for her performance.

His early films were personal quests, with years spent securing funding from friends and investors, a process through which he gained control over his work. His first full-length film, *Pi*—a thriller centered on a paranoid mathematician who believes he has discovered a numerical code that can explain everything in creation—was financed to a large extent with hundred-dollar donations. It was shown at Sundance in 1999, where Aronofsky received the directing award for a dramatic film. He next worked with author Hubert Selby, Jr., on a screenplay from his novel of love and addiction, *Requiem for a Dream,* which became a film starring Jennifer Connelly, Jared Leto, Marlon Wayans, and Ellen Burstyn, who received an Academy Award nomination for Best Actress. Aronofsky said that what he saw in Selby's work was a story that is completely human but takes you to the darkest place imaginable. With *The Fountain* he set out to create an allegory of eternal life, a love story spanning ten centuries for which he set "the ridiculous goal of making a film that would reinvent space without using CGI." Brad Pitt was set to play the lead in a $70,000,000 Warner Bros. production but dropped out when Aronofsky refused to rewrite the script. After a long hiatus Hugh Jackman and Rachel Weisz came on board in a more modestly budgeted production to portray lovers whose devotion spans a millennium. Aronofsky's longtime cinematographer, Matthew Libatique, believes that the lower budget produced a better result: "I think the streamlining of the film helped

Aronofsky with Mickey Rourke on the set of *The Wrestler* (2008). "Mickey Rourke doesn't rehearse. I mean, between 'Action' and 'Cut' we had a great time—it was getting Mickey to 'Action' that was the real work."

us tell the story more effectively. It's been stripped down to its core, to what it's really about: a search for immortality, when the truth of life is mortality."

Aronofsky engaged Robert Siegel to write *The Wrestler*, about an over-the-hill wrestler with a hearing aid and a steroid habit, Randy "the Ram" Robinson, who undergoes a life crisis when he suffers a heart attack. He bypassed major stars who were interested in playing the leading role, insisting on using Mickey Rourke even though it made production financing more difficult. He guided Rourke through a performance with co-star Marisa Tomei that earned both actors Golden Globe and Oscar nominations. Rourke won the Golden Globe, and *The Wrestler* was awarded the Golden Lion at the Venice Film Festival.

In 2010, after years of false starts, Aronofsky filmed *Black Swan*, which received five Academy Award nominations, earned him a nomination for direction, and provided Natalie Portman with an Oscar for Best Performance by an Actress in a Leading Role. Both *The Wrestler* and *Black Swan* featured characters who seek perfection using their bodies, placing unusual physical burdens on the actors. Aronofsky saw similarities in the roles, saying, "Whether you're an aging fiftysomething-year-old wrestler at the end of your career or an ambitious twentysomething-year-old ballet dancer, if the characters are truthful to who they are the audience will connect." He says he learned a great deal from the actors about "opening yourself up to the kind of discoveries that can only happen when you've accepted the chaos of their artistic process and the chaos of your own process."

Aronofsky was influenced by Scorsese, Coppola, Friedkin and Bogdanovich—directors he refers to as his icons and whom he credits with changing the way films were made in the 1970s. He has surrounded himself with a close-knit team of colleagues on most of his films, including Libatique, and producing partner Eric Watson, both of whom he met at AFI, and composer Clint Mansell.

He came to the Conservatory to discuss *The Wrestler* in a seminar conducted by one of his AFI mentors, Jim Hosney.

DARREN ARONOFSKY

—◆—

November 5, 2008*

It's a pleasure to welcome a former AFI fellow back to the campus. Darren was in the class of 1992. Could you talk about how The Wrestler *came about? When I first heard about it I believe Nicolas Cage was attached to the movie.*

In 2002 I got a call from Sylvester Stallone asking if I wanted to meet him. Of course! So I went up to his house and hung out and started to think it would be cool to bring Sly back to the ring. But then he started work on another *Rocky* film which meant we had to think of other people. Whoever played the part needed the physicality of a wrestler and the emotional surprise you always want from an actor so it's not the same old thing you've seen before. I met with Mickey and he told me he'd done twelve years of therapy. It was clear to me that he was self-aware and knew where he was in the world. I trusted that he would be okay. When it became difficult to raise money with Mickey, there was a brief tango with Nic Cage. The way independent film is done in today's messed-up world of filmmaking politics is that you have to cast a movie star, and then you go to these foreign-sales people who give you estimates, and then you go to a bank and get a loan. So it's all about how much value a person has. And Mickey Rourke had none. In fact he might have had negative value, so it took a very long time to find the money and there was this brief window with Nic. But it was always meant to be Mickey's role, and eventually we figured out a way to do it.

*Jim Hosney moderated this seminar.

Aronofsky with Vincent Cassel on the set of *Black Swan* (2010).

I was fascinated by the look of the film. I know your cinematographer, Maryse Alberti, had done documentaries, but she also did Todd Haynes' Poison and Velvet Goldmine, which are so incredibly stylized. How did you work with her?

I wanted someone who could give me a documentary feel. When I was here at AFI, Stuart Rosenberg, who directed Mickey in *The Pope of Greenwich Village,* was my teacher. He used to talk about how there was only one place to stick the camera, how you knew where to put the camera by what the story of the scene was. That stayed with me as I worked on *Pi, Requiem for a Dream* and *The Fountain.* Let the story drive what the camera was doing. I could have shot *The Wrestler* many different ways, but I wanted to build a visual language out of Mickey Rourke and allow him to be free. So this whole idea of a cinéma-vérité, documentary feel emerged. It was radically different from anything I'd done before, and I was excited by it. We shot everything in thirty-five days in February and March of this year [2008] in the beautiful, glorious state of New Jersey. We edited through the summer and finished two days before the Venice Film Festival. It was a quick one. We were the last film of the festival.

It looks perfect. Just seeing those close-ups of Mickey's face you have these memories of what this guy once looked like. I was surprised by the editing of the sequence where you think, "He spared us the violence." Then it says, "fourteen minutes earlier," and you really get the violence.

I had just two days to shoot that scene. It would have taken too much time to track the blood as the wounds happened. There was no way to shoot it consecutively, so I decided to go for snippets, and from that came the idea of doing these flashbacks. I'll be honest because you're film students, so don't repeat it outside this room. Originally he had the heart attack in the ring and all these wrestlers come out and have a hard time carrying him. But there was just no way to control a crowd that much. We couldn't afford SAG actors, so those were real live wrestling promotions with real wrestlers and real fans. It was like controlling a mob.

The thing with wrestlers is that they're actors.

They were better than a lot of the day players we had. They've done so much acting that it was natural for them. I just had to get them to relax and have fun. Mickey helped a lot because he's a gym rat, so he could hang out with these guys and talk shop. He was a pretty successful boxer, three fights away from a title, but he got hit in the face too many times so he quit.

How much time did you spend rehearsing with Mickey?

Mickey Rourke doesn't rehearse. I mean, between "action" and "cut" we had a great time—it was getting Mickey to "action" that was the real work. He's just so talented—used to coasting with his feet up on the desk—that he doesn't really like to work. He just likes to hang out, and he's so good that he can do that. Mickey did do a lot of preparation, a lot of training and complaining, and in the end put on thirty pounds of muscle. The thing I like to do that I've done with every single character I've directed is go through the script line by line with the actor—every single line, no matter how tedious it is. Mickey would rephrase it, because that was part of his process. He's kind of a writer. He wants to make it come out of his own mouth and out of his own being and out of his own soul. I went over every line, line by line, with Marisa Tomei. On my past films I've done tremendous amounts of rehearsal, and on all my cycle films* I did a lot of rehearsal.

A lot of the dialogue seems so natural. Was there much improvisation?

---

*Films made by fellows at the AFI Conservatory are referred to as "cycle films."

Endless. Mickey never quite says the same line twice. He's always feeling it out, like a jazz musician surfing around the notes.

There seems to be something so human in Mickey's eyes.

I think it's all about trust between an actor and a director. If they trust you, they'll give it. You've got to prove to them that you're not going to leave them out to dry. The worst thing in the world is when you see an actor working his heart out and a film not supporting him. Then they close up and are scared the next time, so that as a director you have to undo it. You get a lot of great actors, really famous actors, and they're terrified. You hear all these stories about people not getting out of their trailers, they're terrified that they're just going to be abused, because they get abused all the time. I guarantee actors that they'll never be embarrassed. They may see really potentially ugly parts of themselves, but they'll be incredibly truthful. Once you have that trust, they will give it to you.

I was interested in your use of music, because sometimes it's coming from a source within the movie, and yet there's also a score.

It was complicated. It's the first time I worked with source music, so it was a new challenge. The writer had a really great sense of the music and of that world. It added a lot of humor. I didn't know heavy metal at all. I had to learn all that stuff. I grew up in Brooklyn in the eighties, so it was all hip-hop. But every once in a while you find a gem, like "Balls to the Wall." It was really an education. I just looked for lyrics that kind of lined up with stuff. It was tough working with my composer, Clint Mansell, because if the music was sappy in any way the film just became really cheesy. Clint had to create genuinely atmospheric music. I can't take any credit for the Bruce Springsteen song at the end. It was all because Bruce was a fan of Mickey Rourke's and he said he just wanted to help out Mickey. That's why he did the song.

I thought it was fascinating that you didn't turn the ending into melodrama, like Rocky, *where he triumphs.*

I guess if we'd stuck the heartbeat in there it would have been melodrama—you know, the boom-boom-boom-boom. I always knew how the film was going to end, because if you're doing a wrestling picture you've got to have the guy jumping off the top rope at the end. It's obvious. I just didn't know how we would earn it. One of my favorite moments while making the film was that I had no idea what Mickey was going to do on the top rope, that close-up at the end of the film. We had "Sweet Child O' Mine" blasting because that was his song. Whenever we needed Mickey to get emotional, we just put on "Sweet Child O' Mine" and he'd cry. I was screaming stuff at him and he just kept sobbing for each ten-minute take, until he was dry. I wanted it to be tragic and glorious at the same time.

Could you just talk a little bit about your writing process?

I think Christopher Vogler's book *The Writer's Journey* is the best screenplay book out there. It's based on Joseph Campbell's ideas of the hero's journey. Rob Siegel had written a great screenplay. I spent a lot of time with Rob. If you look at *The Wrestler*, it's the hero's journey, beat by beat. If you have that backbone, you can get weird in other ways. Cast Mickey Rourke and you've got enough weirdness for a while, but it's good to have a solid structure at the core. Ideas kept coming up. The idea that wrestling's fake, yet this is his real world, was an interesting idea. Then there are the parallels between the stripper and the wrestler. I didn't want to do a film with a stripper because it's such a cliché of independent film, but I thought it was an original take on a wrestling story. There was a lot of rewriting. Rob Seigel must have done fifteen drafts.

Since you're a writer-director, I wondered if it was hard for you to work with a writer, and if it's something you might do in the future.

I think it's great. It's another way to expand the collaboration. It's getting another artist involved. I think as a director you almost have to be a writer even if you haven't written it, in the sense that you've got to understand everything that the writer intended, so when it's your time to direct you know what the words mean. You've got to get deep in there, and it's definitely not as hard, because you have someone doing a lot of the heavy lifting for you. I would love to do it again.

How was it working with a new cinematographer?

It was great. The whole team was new. My first three films were very much a chapter, and a lot's changed in my life and in the lives of all those people who made those films. So it was exciting to work with a new team. I was always kind of afraid to do it. You tend to get into a groove with people so that you think you can't do it without them. It was liberating just to try and do it with new people. For me it was a real growth.

You don't have any glorious dolly moves or anything that calls attention to the camera.

It could have been shot in a lot of ways, but when I choose a visual language it turns out there's only one place to put the camera. I think what Stuart Rosenberg was trying to teach is that before you figure out where the camera goes, you have to understand what the scene's about and, ultimately, what the film's about, and then how the scene fits into the film. You're trying to tell a story, so hopefully you can come up with more creative things than just going from a master into close-ups. I so loved this documentary style, and it worked so well with Mickey because it allowed him freedom to move. He's such a physical guy, always moving. I didn't want to hold him still. I wanted to see him wobbling through this world. I framed my other films. I got more and more exact from *Pi* through *Requiem for a Dream* to *The Fountain,* where the frames were so orchestrated, so I wanted to do something very different with *The Wrestler* and try it old-school style. I hired a good camera guy and a good DP, and watched them and could see what they were photographing, but I didn't really know what I had until I saw the dailies.

You want to push things all the way to the edge of your comfort zone. But I was never unprepared. I didn't have a shot list, but I always knew what the scene was about and what I needed to get. I just went in and saw what Mickey was doing, and would say, "Hey, Mickey, stand over there." I'd tell the camera guy to go there and I'd say, "See what happens." Then by take three we would figure out what was going on, so it was an experiment. The nice thing was that it was a tiny film, six million dollars. I knew that even if I fucked it up it would be an interesting experiment, because Mickey was interesting. That was my comfort zone. I knew that I was taking a chance with everything, but I didn't really care.

How difficult was it to get this made after The Fountain?

Amazingly it was only difficult because of Mickey Rourke. People loved the script, but no one believed that Mickey could hold a film for a hundred minutes. No one thought he could be sympathetic. I run into the same problem every time. *Pi* was done for no money, then everyone said, "What the hell do you want to do next? I'll give you money." Then we showed them *Requiem for a Dream* and no one returned our calls. We made *Requiem* and then it took us seven years to make *The Fountain,* and then no one wanted to make this film. I think any time you try to do something that's not a genre film—outside the box—it's tough. I think the same thing's going to happen to me when I try to make my next film.

It seems you've had to fight to make each of your films, but you've been very successful. What keeps you going?

I was thinking about that. I'm a stubborn bastard. It's very tough, as you guys will see. Even here at AFI it's tough. You've got to be very stubborn because persistence is nine-tenths of the game. The only thing you can offer is your own stories—and that's the beauty as well. If you go out there and just want to make the same crap, then God bless you and you may have tremendous success. But I think the exciting thing about film school is that you have a chance to experiment and try to develop a voice and then, hopefully, you'll root into some type of passion that will carry you through the years. For me the only thing that gets me through is that I'm telling things that only I, and maybe a few other people, can tell.

In reflecting on your time here at AFI, what stands out most for you?

The most important thing about AFI is to make as many connections as you can. Just remember: all of your cycle films suck. I promise you. So take chances with them and don't care about how well they do. Just take as many risks as you can—don't work in your safe zone. Really push yourself. The best thing that came out of AFI for me, besides Jim Hosney and Stuart Rosenberg as teachers, is the people I met. Matty Libatique, my DP, and Eric Watson, my producing partner—I met them both here. The reason I got to make *Pi* was because another directing fellow, Scott Silver, knew some rich people that made his film, and then passed them on to a guy named Mark Waters who passed them on to me. I'm still friends with six or seven directing fellows from my year. You make a network of people because you can't do it on your own.

You were talking about telling the stories you want to tell. You worked with Frank Miller on a Batman script, but then you turned down Batman Begins.

I was never really interested in doing *Batman.* I was trying to make *The Fountain* and was trying to convince them to give me a lot of money for an expensive art film, so when they offered me to work on *Batman,* my strategy was like, "If I develop this then maybe they'll perceive me as special." Now every Sundance director makes a superhero film, so it's old hat, but back then that really wasn't going on. There wasn't that crossover line. It was just a ruse to get going. But I liked the material and I wanted to collaborate with Frank, so it was a good opportunity to do that. I wanted to make *The Fountain* and then I wanted to make *The Wrestler.* So I'm doing fine, but not as well as I could have been doing. Not as well as Chris Nolan's doing right now.

If the only stories to tell are your own stories, then how is The Wrestler *your own story?*

That's for you to figure out. I think there are themes. Wrestling can be anything—it could be about any athlete, it could be about any artist. You could transplant this story to make him a filmmaker that's blown off his life.

Can you tell us a little bit about what your typical day is like when you're writing?

I've developed a lot of tricks over the years, ways to keep engaged with a script. I totally believe in procrastination. I think walking around and doing activities that are related, like going to a museum or an art show, will help you find important moments. It's about collaboration with other people, just throwing ideas around. I like having a bunch of different brains thinking together. Eventually things stick and get better and better. That's when you sit in the room and just try and plow through it, and hopefully get some moments of inspiration. Then let everyone read it and get feedback. And do it again. Just keep doing it over and over and over again.

———◀▶———

Films as Director

1998 *Pi* (also screenplay)

2000 *Requiem for a Dream* (also
    screenplay)

2006 *The Fountain* (also screenplay)

2008 *The Wrestler*

2010 *Black Swan*

As Renoir once said in an interview with Jacques Rivette, "When we have achieved total realism, we will have achieved total decadence." My interpretation of that is that today, with special effects, you can do anything on film. But who cares? The magic is gone. The audience knows it's all just one big expensive box of tricks.

PETER BOGDANOVICH
(Born in Kingston, New York, 1939)

Peter Bogdanovich's contribution to cinema would be significant if he had never made a film. His youthful obsession for seeking out and interviewing great directors like Howard Hawks, John Ford, Fritz Lang, Leo McCarey, Allan Dwan and George Cukor provided the world with a firsthand history of moviemaking in America that wouldn't otherwise exist. Bogdanovich's intimate knowledge of the work of these directors—in some years he saw four hundred movies—provoked detailed and fascinating recollections that appear in his book *Who the Devil Made It.*

The son of a Serbian painter, Bogdanovich wrote for magazines in New York in the 1960s, studied acting in the 1950s with Stella Adler and organized retrospectives on Orson Welles and Howard Hawks at the Museum of Modern Art. Influenced by Truffaut and the other French critics who were becoming directors, Bogdanovich set his heart on becoming a filmmaker. In 1961 he and his wife, Polly Platt, set out for Hollywood in a 1951 Ford convertible with her one-eyed spaniel and a black-and-white TV set in the backseat. His first break came when Roger Corman took him on as an assistant on *Wild Angels,* then let him shoot and edit the second-unit work. It was Bogdanovich's first production experience and he took it all in. Corman then backed him on *Targets,* a low-budget effort that starred Boris Karloff. Platt was his most valuable collaborator during that period. She read Larry McMurtry's novel *The Last Picture Show* and encouraged Peter to make a film of it. Bogdanovich insisted on shooting it in black and white, and with Platt helping with the story and finding locations and designing the sets, he came up with a film that to this day is admired by critics and enjoyed by audiences. In 2011, forty years after the release of *The Last Picture Show, The New York Times* described it as "a perfect film whose cosmic sadness makes it feel timeless."

Peter Bogdanovich at Greystone in 1975.

On location the director fell in love with the film's star, newcomer Cybill Shepherd. His career was affected both by losing his collaborator wife and by allowing Shepherd's career to shape his own.

Bogdanovich received an Academy Award nomination for Best Director and Best Screenplay for *The Last Picture Show,* which also was nominated for Best Picture. He was suddenly golden in Hollywood. Barbra Streisand wanted to work with him, so he wrote a screwball comedy, *What's Up, Doc?,* with Buck Henry, Robert Benton and David Newman, for her and Ryan O'Neal. It was his second consecutive success. *Paper Moon,* an exuberant Depression-era story of a con artist and the young girl he can't shake off, featured O'Neal and his daughter, Tatum, whose performance made her the youngest actor ever to win a competitive Academy Award. Bogdanovich then made two consecutive pictures with Shepherd: *Daisy Miller,* based on the Henry James novella, and *At Long Last Love,* a musical that featured songs by Cole Porter and Burt Reynolds as Shepherd's leading man. Neither picture matched his earlier successes, nor did *Nickelodeon,* a homage to the silent-film days that he desperately wanted to release in black and white, an idea the studio rejected. In 2009 he was finally able to have a black-and-white version issued on DVD.

Bogdanovich's troubles were compounded in 1980 with the murder of his girlfriend, Playboy Playmate Dorothy Stratten, who appeared in his film *They All Laughed.* It would be four years until he made *Mask,* starring Cher. Since then Bogdanovich has had success as a character actor, notably as a psychiatrist in *The Sopranos* on HBO. He's written books, directed television and the occasional film, including *Texasville,* a sequel to *The Last Picture Show,* and in 2001 *The Cat's Meow,* a clever reincarnation of old Hollywood in a story about a mysterious death on the yacht of William Randolph Hearst. His book *Who the Hell's in It,* published in 2004, adds to his legacy of chronicling motion-picture history with chapters on James Stewart, Henry Fonda, Humphrey Bogart, Cary Grant, Marlene Dietrich and James Cagney.

PETER BOGDANOVICH

—◆—

July 28, 1977*

How did you become a director?

I started acting in New York in stock theater and television between the ages of fifteen and nineteen. I worked for the New York Shakespeare Festival and Joe Papp in 1957 as a spear carrier in *Othello.* I was also studying acting with Stella Adler at the time. At a certain point, some time before I was eighteen, I decided that I'd just as soon not be an actor, that I'd rather direct. It was a big mistake, because actors don't have to work as hard and get paid more money.

The first thing I did as a director was an Off-Broadway production of *The Big Knife* by Clifford Odets, when I was about nineteen or twenty. Odets was the first person to give me a chance to direct professionally. I did another play Off-Broadway about four years later, Kaufman and Hart's *Once in a Lifetime.* During that time I was also writing about movies, because I didn't have any money and wanted to see them for free. There was a time when I was on every screening list in New York, and I also got all these books from publishers that I couldn't possibly read. I only had a small room and it was filled with books. I was writing for a strange little magazine called *Ivy* that appeared about six times a year, and then eventually hit the big time and wrote some pieces for *Esquire.*

At some point the director Frank Tashlin came to New York. I'd met him in Hollywood when I was doing an *Esquire* piece about Jerry Lewis.

*James Powers moderated this seminar. The transcript also contains segments from seminars Peter Bogdanovich gave at the American Film Institute on May 27, 1975, January 15, 1986, and March 4, 1992, and from an interview conducted in summer 2009.

He said, "What are you doing in New York? Don't you want to direct movies?" I said, "Yes." He said, "Well, they make them in California." So a few months later my former wife, Polly Platt, and I were in a car driving west. Soon afterwards I was at a movie screening and Roger Corman was sitting there. He said, "You write for *Esquire,* don't you? I've read your stuff. Would you ever consider writing screenplays?" I said, "Sure." He said, "Why don't you write a screenplay for me? I want something that's a kind of a combination of *Bridge on the River Kwai* and *Lawrence of Arabia.* But cheap." So Polly and I wrote a script called *The Criminals,* which was never produced. Right around that same time Roger was doing a motorcycle picture called *The Wild Angels* and he asked if I would like to work on this picture. I said, "Doing what?" He said, "I don't know. Just come on down and be with me. We're having problems with the film. It's a short shooting schedule, only three weeks, and the script needs a polish. I'll pay you $125 a week now, and when we're in production $150."

I read the script. It was really bad, sort of like a Disney picture. There were things in it like: "The motorcycles roar by. Cut to frog's POV of motorcycles going by." There was another scene with a horse and it said, "Cut to horse. Horse looks. Cut to horse's point of view of fight." Roger said, "We're going to start shooting in about a week. We need the script rewritten." I remember he had a yellow legal pad where he had written about forty pages of notes on the script. He called the writer and said, "Now, Chuck, on the first page there's a problem about . . ." And he was interrupted, listened for about ten minutes and said, "I'll get back to you, Chuck." Roger then turns to me and says, "He doesn't like my first note. Why don't you rewrite it?" So in about five or six days I rewrote the whole script, for which I didn't receive any credit, not that I asked for it. I helped cast it because George Chakiris, who was going to be in it, quit when he got the script. He said it was 'immoral.' Roger had to figure out who was going to play the part and decided that maybe Peter Fonda could do it. I remembered him looking very preppy in *Lilith* and wondered if he could play this biker guy, but he came into the office wearing aviator sunglasses and I thought he really looked fabulous. We gave him the part and I made sure he wore the glasses in almost every shot.

We shot for about three weeks. I did almost everything you could do on a picture. I got the laundry, made sure the lunch was there, helped find locations. We had real Hells Angels on the picture. Roger said, "Be sure you know before you get the setup where your next shot is, because the minute you have to think the crew will fall apart. Don't think—just go! When you finish a shot, just turn to them and say, 'Okay, we're over here.'

Even if you don't know where the hell you're going, just pretend. It keeps everybody on their toes, and keeps morale up." Meanwhile, the Hells Angels didn't feel like hurrying up so much. Roger would say, "Let's start the bikes now. All the bikes down the road!" and they'd just sort of leisurely kick over their engines, and after a couple tries someone would turn around and say, "It doesn't start, man." So then it would be a half-hour while we waited for them to get the bikes going, and we kept falling further and further behind schedule.

The last couple days we were doing a fight scene between the townies and the Angels. We didn't have any extras, so I played one of the townies. Roger said, "Run in there." Now, they had seen me standing next to Roger, whom they hated. Both of us wore sunglasses and they thought: sunglasses, sonofabitch director and all that. So I run in there and they just about killed me. They were kicking me, and I never prayed so much for a director to call "Cut." After about three days of shooting the guy who was the ringleader came over to me and said, "Hey, man, I'm sorry about hassling you before." I said, "That's all right." He said, "We thought you were a shit, you know, but you're all right." That was my first review. They've gotten progressively worse.

A few days before we were supposed to finish, Roger said, "We're going to have to throw out the rest of the script and just piece it together." I said, "Roger, we've only got about half the picture." He said, "No, we've got three-quarters of it." I said, "What about the other quarter?" "We'll just have to get a second unit to go out and shoot this junk. I can't do it. I'm not going to spend any more money." I said, "I'd love to do the second unit." He said, "My secretary or you, it doesn't make any difference." He wrapped the shoot and we went back to Los Angeles. He called me and said, "Okay, I want you to do the second unit."

I went out and shot for a week with a full crew, then for another week with a smaller crew, and then finally the last week with just me and a cameraman, one actor and a bike. Actually for a while we were first unit, because we had Peter Fonda and Nancy Sinatra. I did a whole sequence with Bruce Dern where he gets killed up in the mountains. The only thing Roger said was, "You know how Hitchcock works." I said, "What do you mean?" He said, "He plans everything." I said, "Yeah." He said, "You know how Howard Hawks works." I said, "Yeah." He said, "He never plans anything." I said, "Right." He said, "On this one be Hitchcock." I said, "Okay." I had a couple fights with the cinematographer who knew that I hadn't done anything and wanted to take advantage of it. I learned a lesson because I said, "I want to shoot over there." He said, "You can't shoot over there, the sun's not there." I said, "Well, will it ever be there?" He looked up and said, "No." I believed him. Twenty minutes later I look over and say, "Hey, there's sun over there." But it was too late because we'd already got the shot somewhere else, and I figured this guy didn't know what the hell he was doing, either. So that's how I learned to direct pictures. When I finished shooting the stuff, Roger said, "The cutter's got too much to do. You'll have to cut your own material together." I didn't have any idea how to cut, so we got a machine and a guy who knew something about it, and I started to cut. I worked twenty-two weeks on the picture, from preproduction, shooting, second unit, everything, and it was a twenty-two-week course in picture making. I haven't learned as much since.

The Wild Angels became a very big success. It cost about $300,000 and grossed about $5 million. It was Roger's most successful movie at that time, and he asked me if I wanted to direct my own picture, and that's how Targets came about. Roger said, "I'll pay $6,000 for you and your wife, but before that I want you to fix up another picture for me, same price. It's a little Russian picture I've got called Storm Clouds of Venus. It's got the greatest special effects, rocket ships taking off and landing on Venus and space stations. It's great stuff, but there's one problem with it. There's no girls in it. It's just a bunch of guys wandering around." I said, "What do you want me to do?" He said, "I can sell it if you can put some girls in it. You can go shoot with Mamie Van Doren but I can't afford sound." He told me to go down to Malibu to match the existing footage. Well, you all know what Malibu looks like. It does not look like the Black Sea, which was where the Russians shot their Venus.

We went to Malibu. There were a lot of rocks in one particular place, so we shot all this stuff on the rocks. We had seven girls. I don't know why, but I thought if they're on Venus they have to be blond. Some of them weren't blond but we gave them wigs. Polly designed gills of some kind because I thought they ought to be mermaids. Then I wondered how they were going to walk on the rocks. The costumes were tights with rubber things sticking off them and when they got wet they started to droop. You never saw such a group of saggy-assed sirens walking across the rocks. It was an unbelievable picture. We shot five days on the rocks. There was no dialogue, because we had no sound. We said, "How are they going to communicate?" I thought, "Telepathy!" So Mamie Van Doren would look meaningfully at one of the other girls and they would go get some fish or whatever. When all this was cut together it was totally impossible to understand, so Roger said to me, "You'll have to put in some narra-

Bogdanovich (right) with Boris Karloff during the shooting of *Targets* (1968).
Karloff owed Roger Corman two days' work. Corman told Bogdanovich
to shoot twenty minutes with Karloff for *Targets,* adding,
"I've shot whole pictures in two days."

tion." This went on for months. Eventually we finished the film, which
was called *Voyage to the Planet of Prehistoric Women.* It's a ridiculous
movie. I directed ten minutes of it, that's all.

Anyway, back to *Targets.* Roger said, "Boris Karloff owes me two days'
work. I made a picture with Boris and Jack Nicholson called *The Terror.* I
want you to take about twenty minutes of Karloff footage from *The Terror*
and shoot twenty more minutes with Karloff. You'll be able to shoot
twenty minutes in two days. I've shot whole pictures in two days. Then
get a bunch of other actors and shoot another forty minutes in ten days
and we've got an eighty-minute Karloff picture. Are you interested?"
Being twenty-six and interested in almost anything which would give me
a chance to direct, I said yes. I looked at the footage from *The Terror* and
wondered what I was going to do with this footage of Karloff skulking
around this mansion. I didn't want to make that kind of movie. Boris
didn't even scare me very much, so I figured, "I'll make him an actor in
this film." I was going to begin the picture in a projection room with
scenes from *The Terror.* The lights come up and there's Boris sitting there
with Roger Corman, and Boris turns to Roger and says, "It really was a
dreadful movie, wasn't it?" Roger turns and mumbles something. I figured
it wasn't a bad idea, because if he's a disgruntled actor then I have an alibi
for all this lousy footage. That was how the film started. Then Polly said,

"Why don't we write a story about the guy who shot those people in Austin, Texas?" I don't know if any of you remember, but in 1966 there was a guy named Charles Whitman in Texas who killed his wife and his mother and then went up that tower in Austin with a rifle and randomly killed a bunch of people for apparently no reason.

So we crosscut that with a story about an aging movie star who played in a lot of horror pictures who feels he's all washed up and has decided he's going to quit the business because the horror of the modern age is much worse than any Victorian horror. The tension between those two stories was what we ended up working on. It's a bit *manqué,* as the French would say, but it kind of worked. We had to kill Karloff off about halfway through the picture because I only had him for two days. I showed the outline to Sam Fuller and he said, "Why did you kill Karloff off in the middle of the picture, kid?" I said, "I've only got him for two days." "Don't think about that! Ignore that! He's the star of the picture. You can't kill him off in the middle." I said, "But Roger won't give me the time." "Ignore that!" he said. "Write the script like you got him for the whole picture. Never worry about anything practical when you're writing a picture. When you're directing it, that's another problem, but right now you're writing it." In three hours Sam proceeded to rewrite it, quite brilliantly. After I looked at the changes I said, "But Sammy, this is a complete rewrite. I've got to give you credit." He said, "Naw. If you give me credit they'll just think I wrote the whole thing."

I rewrote the script again and gave it to Roger, who said, "How are you going to shoot all this stuff with Karloff in two days?" I said, "I can't." He said, "Peter, I'm not going to pay for any more time." So I called up Karloff's agent and we tried several things. Luckily Karloff loved the script. I said, "I need five days." It was a big deal and cost Roger a little extra money, but we finally got Karloff for five days and shot all the stuff you see in the film. Then we shot with other people for about twenty days. It was really about fifteen days of principal photography and ten days of second unit, which was only five people: me and László Kovács and a couple other people. We stole all the shots on the freeway. We didn't even ask permission, because we knew they would turn us down. When the sniper is shooting the cars on the freeway, we had two cameras and a walkie-talkie system. I had some of my neighbors in cars. They said, "All right, we're coming on the Burbank on-ramp." I said, "Okay, okay, I see you. Okay, get ready, here we go." And as they came by the camera I would say, "Bang!" over the walkie-talkie and they would react to the shot. László asked, "What happens if we see a cop?" I said, "Film him."

The shots of the police you see in the picture are real police. They didn't know they were in the shot.

All together the film cost $130,000, including $22,000 for Boris. We finished it and every studio turned it down. They didn't think it was very good or maybe they thought it was too violent. God knows what they thought, they just weren't interested in it, except for Paramount, which sort of liked it but not enough to put up any money. Roger wanted the $130,000 that he had put out. We did a screening at Arthur Knight's USC cinema class and invited the trade press. I said, "If you like it, please review it." Well, they happened to like it, so they wrote reviews in the trades, and the next day Paramount called and said, "We're still interested. Have you sold it yet?" I said, "Yep, we've got a deal, but it hasn't really been closed yet." Paramount says, "What's the deal for?" and I say, "$130,000." They said, "Well, we'll make it $150,000," and they bought it. Then there was a big internal struggle at the studio. Bob Evans and Charlie Bluhdorn were the ones who really liked it, but almost nobody else at the studio did, so it wasn't well distributed and nobody really saw the film. The timing wasn't great, either. You might think people would be interested in seeing a picture about random violence after two assassinations—Martin Luther King and Bobby Kennedy—but they weren't. We finished shooting just before King was assassinated, and the guy who shot him used a 30.06 rifle, just like the one we used in the picture, and drove a white Mustang, which the boy does in the film.

Do you think you'll work with Corman again?

It was a marvelous way to start, because you learn a certain discipline that you never lose. Guerrilla filmmaking is something you should all learn. You steal, cheat, lie and do anything you can to get the scene. I think that's why many of the older directors were so good, because they had a discipline that was imposed from outside. That's the terrible thing about having too much freedom, particularly at the start of a career. I think there's nothing better than being told, "Look, you've got to do it in three days. You've only got this much money, so do it this way or you're not going to get it done." In the old days, somebody like John Ford had only so much film and that's all. It wasn't that he wanted to be economical. The guys in the front office said, "That's it. That's all you've got." At Columbia for years they wouldn't let you print more than one take. And the whole idea of "Let's go" is important. Get the crew going. "We got this shot over here, now we're over here." Keep it moving, because there's a terrible kind of lethargy and boredom that sets in on a crew. Making pictures is boring for everybody except the director, and sometimes even for him. But the more you get everybody going, the less boring it is. I was happy working for Roger. I loved it. He gave me the ground rules and then left me alone. He also loved the picture when it was finished. He didn't give me much money, but so what?

Where did The Last Picture Show *come from?*

What I think *Targets* lacked was a sense of the performances. I began as an actor at age fifteen, and when I'm on the set I still approach everything from the actor's point of view. Karloff was good in *Targets* and the boy in it was also good, but everybody else could have been better. What I really wanted to do on *The Last Picture Show* was concentrate on the actors, to really get good performances out of them. One other reason why I wanted to make the picture was because after reading the novel by Larry McMurtry I didn't know how to film it. Solving the problem of how to turn this story into a film was very intriguing to me. I liked the fact that it was about a world I knew nothing about. It was quite a challenge to make a film about what was, basically, a foreign country to me.

People kept giving me Larry's book to read and I never read it. Sal Mineo, a sweet, dear friend, gave it to me, as did two or three other people. I finally read it about two years later and liked it very much. I wanted to do it but I couldn't get the rights. The producer Bert Schneider, who had liked *Targets,* said to me once, "If you ever want to do a picture, let me know." A lot of people say that, so I didn't believe it, but I called him up and said, "Hey, were you on the level about wanting to do a picture?" He said, "Yeah." I said, "Well, I read a book I liked called *The Last Picture Show* by Larry McMurtry. Go get it and read it." I wanted to see if he was really on the level. About a week later he called and said, "Well, I read the book. Let's make it." I said, "Fine, except this other guy owns the rights and I think he's got some pretty bad ideas how to make this thing." Bert said, "How do you want to make it?" I said, "I just want to make the book." He said, "That's what we all like, isn't it?" So he got the rights and we made it. It was really pretty simple.

Larry wrote a draft, which I rewrote. The trouble with Larry was that he really didn't like his book as much as I did. He kept changing the script. I would say, "Larry, this wasn't in the book." He said, "No, it's better." I said, "No, it's worse," and I would change it back to the book. It's funny correcting the writer himself. He had written the book in five

Bogdanovich and Cybill Shepherd on *The Last Picture Show* (1971). Her
photo on the cover of *Glamour* magazine led to her being cast as Jacy.

weeks out of a kind of anger, and I don't think he felt the same thing I did
coming fresh to it. The script really was pretty much the book with parts
cut out. We really could have made the picture another hour longer.

How did you come to cast Ben Johnson in the film?

I couldn't think who could play the part of Sam the Lion. I went to
Nashville and interviewed old country-and-western singers, thinking
maybe I'd find some great old faces there. Then one day I thought, "Ben
Johnson!" But he didn't want to do it. He said, "Peter, there are too many
words. I can't say all those words." So I called John Ford and said, "I've got
this wonderful part for Ben and he doesn't want to do it. He says there's
too many words." "Oh, Christ," he says. "Ben's always been like that.
When we were shooting *Yellow Ribbon* Ben would come on the set and go
over to the script girl and ask, 'I got any words today?' If she said yes, he'd
go and sulk. If she said no, he was happy. All he had to do was ride." Ford
says, "Where is he? I'll call him." So about an hour later Ford calls me
back and says, "He'll do it." Then Ben calls and he says, "Christ, you got
the old man on me." I said, "Well, I just want you to do this picture." So
he came in about three or four days later and sat down in the office. He
had the script in his hand and said, "Pete, I just don't think I can do this

for you, boy." I said, "Ben, you've got to do it." He says, "Why do you keep saying that?" I said, "Because there's nobody else that could do it." He said, "Oh, shit, you can get ten other guys." I said, "No. You play this part and you'll win the Oscar." Finally he slammed the script shut and said, "All right, I'll do the goddamned thing." I said, "Look, we're going to start rehearsing Thursday." He said, "What have I gotta do?" I said, "You don't have to do anything but read through the scenes. I'd like the cast to meet you more than anything else." So on Thursday I introduce him to everybody and say, "Let's just read your scene." So we start to read and he's got the script closed. He doesn't open it because he already knows every line he's got in the thing, letter perfect. We finish and I say, "You know, you're a sonofabitch." He says, "Why?" I say, "What the hell do you mean, telling me you don't know how to read words? You didn't have to learn the lines by now." He said, "Well, Pete, I'm not too good at reading, so I just figured I'd better know 'em." Anyway, he did win the Oscar. The topper is that three years later I'm talking to him about a picture we wanted to do with Duke Wayne and Jimmy Stewart, and he says, "I like it, but there's not too many words in there for me."

Can I ask you a blunt question? You've worked with a lot of very good actors. Was Cybill Shepherd hired on the basis of her looks?

No, she wasn't hired on the basis of her looks. I was in New York casting and she came in and took off her shoes and sat on the floor next to a kind of a pot with a couple flowers sticking out of it. I said, "What do you do?" She said, "I go to college." "Where do you go to college?" "I go to Hunter." "Well, what are you taking?" "English literature." She's behaving like she doesn't give a damn about being there, and I asked her which authors she likes, and she says, "Dostoevsky." "What have you read of his?" Long pause. "I can't think of anything right now." But as she said it she played with a flower. There wasn't any kind of feeling that she had been caught short. It was as if I was the dummy for asking such a stupid question. It was the most wonderful reading I've ever heard. It turned out she was just nervous and that's the way she acts in those situations. She gets rather quiet and shy but it comes out as very cool. But when she touched that flower I expected it to wilt, and I thought to myself, "That's the character!" I hadn't understood the character until that moment. Jacy should be a girl who's kind of destructive to men, but not on purpose. She just flits from flower to flower and they wilt in her wake, but it's not like she goes out and says, "I'm going to kill that guy." That's the character we evolved, but she gave it to me just by touching the flower in the audition.

I think one of the finest moments in The Last Picture Show *is the last shot with Cloris Leachman just before you dissolve to the pan.*

You mean when she's trying to talk to him and she can't quite get anything out? Essentially, she had some answers to this situation. She seemed to glimpse the sun through a cloud and was trying to find the words to say it. This character is not an eloquent woman, so she lost the words. But she knew that it would all be okay. I was telling her all this as we were doing it. She was great, though the producers wanted me to cut the whole last sequence with Cloris and Tim. They thought the picture should end on the road. I said, "I only made the picture so I could have that scene." It's the best scene in the picture. I had to cut some other things as a sacrifice. You have to give them something so you can keep the stuff you like. That's true in life too.

You spoke earlier of studying with Stella Adler. Can you say what she taught you?

I was involved in many theater productions as an actor and stagehand and dresser, perhaps forty of them, before I ever directed. Everything I know about communicating with actors I learned from Stella, things I could fall back on when my instinctual approach failed me. Instinct will take you only so far. Because she taught acting in such a complete way, she was also talking about directing. I found the first six months of her class fascinating but just didn't understand what she was talking about. You needed to be eighteen to get into the class but I lied because I was only sixteen. After a few months, it all clicked into place and the basic idea of what theater and acting are—this heightened reality rather than mundane naturalism—really began to make sense to me.

Directing actually started for me because I was sitting around with five actors from Stella's class and I said, "Why don't I direct you guys in a scene?" Usually scene class would be a two-character scene or a mono-logue, so having five actors in a scene all interacting was unusual. We put it on for the class and when it was over Stella stood up and said, "Bravo darlings! But you've been directed. Who directed you?" They all pointed at me at the back of the room. She turned to me and said, "Brilliant, Peter!" So I figured I wasn't bad at this.

Did you have any contact with Sanford Meisner or Lee Strasberg?

I was in Strasberg's class once, but that's about it. I'm not a big fan of his. I'm very much from the Adler school, and Stella didn't think Strasberg was a good teacher. Strasberg was a perversion of the Stanislavsky method, and Stella would be the one to know because she's the only person in the United States who actually studied with the man himself. She heard it from the horse's mouth. Stanislavsky said that acting is fifty percent external and fifty percent internal. Strasberg completely eliminated the external and was interested exclusively in the internal, which is not a good thing for acting.

Did your time as an actor help you as a screenwriter?

Acting is very much a part of writing. With some scenes I'll act out the parts myself and transcribe what I say.

Was the idea for the slapstick What's Up, Doc? *your own?*

Warner Bros. came to me and said, "Would you make a picture with Streisand?" They had a script they wanted me to do called *A Glimpse of Tiger,* but it wasn't the kind of film I wanted to make. *Picture Show* hadn't even opened at that point and only two people had seen it. One was Steve McQueen, who wanted me to make *The Getaway.* He came into my office after seeing the film and said, "I'm just an actor, man, but you're a filmmaker. You only made one mistake in that picture." I said, "What was that?" He said, "You never should have cut away from the diving board." If you remember, there's a scene in *Picture Show* when Cybill strips at the swimming pool.

The other was Barbra Streisand and she wanted to work with me, so John Calley, the head of Warner Bros., said, "So you don't like this script. What would you like to make?" I said, "A screwball comedy, like *Bringing Up Baby,* with Barbra. A square professor and a daffy dame who breaks him down live happily ever after." He said, "Do it. Who do you want to write it?" I said, "Well, I worked with Benton and Newman at *Esquire.*" Calley said, "Great, they just did a picture for us." I called them and they explained they were starting another film in three weeks. I said, "If Ben Hecht and Howard Hawks can do *Scarface* in eleven days, we can do this in three weeks." We worked for three weeks and ended up with a draft that needed a lot of work. I rewrote it a little and had a reading with Ryan and Barbra. I read all the other parts and talked my way through all the action sequences, and at the end of it they both committed to it. John Calley suggested we bring in Buck Henry to rewrite it, who said, "You're going to hate me but I don't think it's complicated enough. You need another suitcase." So we added the whole Top Secret suitcase which was inspired by the Pentagon Papers story. That's actually why we cast Michael Murphy, because he looked a bit like Daniel Ellsberg. Buck rewrote the script, which is more or less what we shot. We made up some of the jokes as we were planning and shooting it. For the party scene in the million-aire's house, all Buck wrote in the script was: "There is now a fight which will be brilliantly staged by the director." That was it. Thanks a lot, Buck.

The film ended up being the second-biggest hit of the year, after *The Godfather,* which actually I turned down because I didn't want to make a Mafia film. There was an early, glitzy screening of *What's Up, Doc?* and the audience seemed to be resisting it. They weren't loose enough for a film like that. It's like everyone was sitting there asking themselves, "What is

Bogdanovich and Barbra Streisand on the set of *What's Up, Doc?* (1972).

this?" There had been some laughs but it wasn't as warmly received as it would later be by the public. About ten minutes in, John Cassavetes stands up, in the middle of the picture, turns to the audience and shouts, very loudly, "I can't believe he's doing this!" The place broke up, and from then on they loved it. John and I became friends after that. It's my favorite review of any film of mine.

It looks like you had fun making What's Up, Doc?

What's Up, Doc? was the most fun of any picture I've ever made. It was absolute heaven from beginning to end. I didn't give a damn if we ever made the picture, an enviable position to be in. This hasn't been the case on every picture I've made, but you must never give a damn if the whole thing falls apart. "It doesn't matter—we'll do something else": that's the only way to do pictures, because when you start caring they kill you. When you start saying, "If I don't make this picture I'm going to die," they will make you pay.

I remember Barbra Streisand told me before we did the picture, "I've never been directed. Nobody's ever directed me in a picture." I said, "Well, you're about to be directed," and I directed the hell out of her. She wouldn't listen to me a lot of times. She wouldn't cut her nails, for instance. I said, "Barbra, this girl is a college kid and she wouldn't have these movie-star nails." She said, "I'm not going to cut my nails." I said, "Jesus, first of all, your hands look better without the long nails." She said, "No, they don't. I have stubby fingers." I said, "You don't have stubby fingers." She happens to have very nice hands and her fingers don't look stubby at all. But she has these silly long nails, so I made her carry something all the way through the picture. She's got a suitcase or a coat over her arm or something so I wouldn't see her goddamn nails. But generally we really got along and worked well together. The director is an actor's first audience and she wanted to please me. She knew exactly what I wanted.

We took over San Francisco and wrecked a couple of streets and got in a lot of trouble. We had a hell of a scene when all the cars go into the water at the end. The first guy that went in was the Volkswagen. They told me Volkswagens float, but it ain't so. This thing went down like a stone, and it was very deep. The guy drove in at about seventy miles an hour without an oxygen tank. We were all standing there dying because the guy didn't come up for a minute, two minutes. Finally he comes up having escaped through the windshield which luckily came in on him, because he couldn't get the door open. We had seven or eight cameras on those particular shots, so if one camera malfunctioned we would still get it.

John Ford gave me a very good piece of advice. He said, "Never rehearse action." I said, "Why not?" He said, "Somebody could get hurt." It's a cryptic remark, as all of Ford's remarks were, but it makes sense. What you do is discuss everything that can possibly happen and what you want and what you'll take if you don't get that, and then you do it. Usually you get elaborate pieces of action on the first take because nobody wants to do it again, and they all work like hell to get it right. One of the last shots in *The Last Picture Show* is where all the guys are standing around the truck and the kid is lying on the ground dead, and it builds until Tim Bottoms yells out, "He was sweeping, you sons of bitches!" He picks up the body and carries it to the marquee of the theater. I wanted it to be without a cut. I didn't want the camera to leave him from the moment he said "He was sweeping" to the time he carries the body over and walks away. It was about fifty feet from there to the theater, so he had to pick up the body and carry it, and the camera was on a truck. It was a complicated shot for the actor because of the emotion and very complicated for the crew because there was a zoom involved which I wanted to hide. We set it up before lunch and I talked to Tim all through lunch. I was trying to find out what he was going to do without telling him what to do. This was a line that I wouldn't let him rehearse. I knew it was a line I only wanted to hear once. That's a movie-acting thing. It's not true on the stage, but there are certain lines in a movie that should only happen once, because the minute you have to do it again it becomes mechanical. That first emotion is very important for certain moments. The crew came back from lunch and I said, "We are not getting a shot of a guy carrying a body across the street. We are shooting a bridge being blown up. There is only one camera and we've only got one bridge. I don't want any mistakes from you guys. No excuses." So we did the shot and we got it, thank God. Luckily Tim was superb and the crew was superb. As a matter of fact, to prove my point we actually did the shot twice. The second one was technically better—but the performance wasn't there. The first one broke your heart. It's the only time I've ever been moved to tears on a set by an actor.

What did Barbra Streisand mean when she said that she hadn't ever been directed before?

Most directors have no idea how to direct actors. It's rare that they do. William Wyler would just say, "Do it again." Very few of the older guys had any theatrical experience, but they did have a sense of what they wanted.

Did you write the script of Paper Moon?

I was sent a script called *Addie Pray* which was based on a book. It wasn't too good but there were two scenes in it that were wonderful: the café scene and the scene on the hill with Trixie. Those two scenes were the only two scenes that remained after the rewriting. But they were so damned good that I said to myself, "Jesus, I could do something with this." I saw the whole thing as some kind of anti–Shirley Temple movie. I read the book and there were some things that weren't in the script that I put back in and some things that I took out. We didn't come up with an ending until we shot it. I finally came up with it the night before we shot it. We had that great location, that wonderful road, and we knew she was going to come after him but we weren't sure how, so I came up with that line about the $200, which got me out of a lot of trouble.

I came up with the title *Paper Moon,* which nobody at Paramount liked. I thought *Addie Pray* sounded like a snake or a lizard or something. They all said, "Why do you want to call it *Paper Moon*? What's it got to do with the picture?" I said, "What the hell does it matter what it has to do with the picture? It's a good title." I said to the writer, "We've got a problem. You know those paper moons that you sat in at carnivals and they took your picture? We've got to put a scene in so they'll think there's a reason for the title." I called up Orson Welles who was in Rome and said, "Hey, what do you think of this title?" Because this is long distance to Rome and I wanted to make sure he understood, I said, very loudly, "*Paper Moon.*" There was a long pause, and he says, "That title is so good you shouldn't even make the picture. Just release the title."

How did you work with Tatum O'Neal in Paper Moon?

With great difficulty.

Did you have to overcome some difficulty with her father?

Jesus no, I had to keep Ryan from killing her. "Goddammit, Tatum, would you learn your lines? Goddammit, I'm not going to do it again with her! Shit, we've done it twenty-eight times! Get the lines right, Tatum! Peter, I can't do it again. I did *Peyton Place* five thousand times and

I never went through anything like this!" This is on a road in the middle of Kansas with nothing anywhere but Kansas and the car and this rig that we had pulling the car with the camera on it and twelve people hanging around. It was a scene between Ryan and Tatum which played without a cut, and it was the end of the first act where they have this big argument about the Bibles. It's really the scene where they sort of admit that they care about each other without saying it or admitting they're going to stay together. It's one of those scenes where they don't say what they mean but hopefully you get the point. I wanted it to be without a cut with them driving along, so we figured the scene would take about a mile and a half to play, and we only had about a mile and a half where the road was good because after that you started seeing something that wasn't of the period. Two miles down the road there was a place where we could turn around and come back, but turning around took five or six minutes because the road was so narrow. So since it had to be without a cut, if they started down the road and after about three lines somebody blew it we'd have to go two miles and then turn around and go back. We did it twenty-five times the first day. I remember putting my arm around Ryan and walking up the road while I calmed him down. I got him to do it another few times and we still didn't get it. The next day it rained, and the day after it rained and we shot some other stuff, and a few days later we came back and did it again. We got it the second day on something like the sixteenth take.

Tatum was eight years old and didn't have any idea what the hell we were doing, and she sort of cared less. She'd never had any discipline in her life. She was in a world of her own, and sometimes her world and the one we were trying to create on screen didn't necessarily mesh, like the time we were shooting the carnival scene. It was a night scene so it took us about three hours to light it. Tatum got there about five o'clock and did what any kid would do. She started riding the Ferris wheel, eating popcorn, eating candy corn, eating peanuts, and by the time we were ready to shoot she was sick. She was on the floor. "I told you not to eat," said Ryan. "I told you, you idiot." "Oh, Daddy!" "Get up!" Ryan and I sort of alternated on who was going to be yelling at her. You had to scare her into doing it right. After about five weeks she really got into it and started to enjoy the shooting and was much better.

When Ryan's character says, "I ain't your pa," I always figured from the first frame he really was her father. He's just not going to cop to it. When we were casting the film, Paramount told me John Huston had wanted to make it with Paul Newman and his daughter. Polly said, "What about Ryan's daughter?" But Paramount said they wouldn't use Ryan under any circumstances because he'd had an affair with Ali MacGraw on *Love Story* when she was married to Bob Evans, who was head of the studio. I said, "I won't make it with anyone else." *What's Up, Doc?* was still playing in theaters and was a big hit, so I forced the issue with Paramount. It wouldn't have been good for their stockholders to turn the film down.

How did you come to make Daisy Miller*?*

I read a script of *Daisy Miller* that was pretty bad, but when I got to the end and all of a sudden she died I was very moved. So I read the original Henry James story and thought, "I ought to make this." In other words, the ending of the story made the whole thing really mean something. That's the case with most stories: it's how it finishes that matters. What does it all add up to? Deciding to do something really comes down to whether it moves me emotionally, or whether it makes me laugh. I made *Daisy Miller* because it moved me. What persuaded me to do it is the complete misunderstanding of Daisy Miller by the young man. He's so in love with her but absolutely doesn't get her. He judges her. It's why he's named Winterbourne. He's as cold as ice, certainly when compared to her vibrancy. It seems to me that one of the prevalent problems in society is that men don't understand women. Men trust what they shouldn't and don't trust what they should. Winterbourne is also a complete jerk who thinks he's superior to this young American girl who is shameless and stubborn, but also a quite innocent flirt. The line on the poster was "She Did as She Pleased." Daisy flaunts Italian custom by being seen walking in public with this man, but he just doesn't understand where she's coming from. James puts it very well when he has Winterbourne say at the end of the story, "I have lived too long in foreign parts."

We had Freddie Raphael write another version of the script based on a few conversations we had about making it darker, more dramatic. But that was a mistake, because Freddie wrote a Dostoevsky version and it just didn't work. So I went back to the book and rewrote every scene, and ended up keeping only a couple of his ideas, like setting the tea scene in the baths. The script went to arbitration and he ended up getting credit on the film. They offered me "Additional Dialogue" and I said, "I'm not going to be the Sam Taylor of my generation." Sam Taylor was the guy who took credit on a version of *The Taming of the Shrew*. After "Based on the play by William Shakespeare" it said "Additional Dialogue by Sam Taylor." My original plan was to play Winterbourne myself and have Orson direct, but he didn't want to do it.

Why do you think the film was so badly received?

I don't know. I'm very proud of it, and I think everybody is good in it. I think it's beautifully shot. I think the script is very faithful to the book and I think the book is wonderful. People don't realize that almost all the dialogue in the picture is by Henry James. I would just change certain words that were a little bit too formal, things like "I shouldn't think so" instead of "I wouldn't think so," because Daisy wouldn't say "I shouldn't." There were extraordinary words that came up in the dialogue that you thought wouldn't be used during that period. At one point she says, "Did you ever see anything so cool?" That's such a fifties or sixties expression, but she said it. It's in the book from 1875.

People find it difficult to accept a character like Daisy Miller in that milieu. I could tell a western with the same basic plot: an Eastern girl comes to the West and doesn't understand the codes of the West. If you put her into a western nobody would have any difficulty believing that character. But the minute you put her into a European milieu, which is sort of sophisticated and highbrow and artistic, people find it hard to believe that anybody could be that crude. But that's the point of the story, and if you read it again you'll find she's described as crude, vulgar and annoying. She was supposed to be that way, yet you were supposed to like her anyway. If you don't, I've failed in some way. But I do think that in ten years you'll like it better, when you forget about who Cybill Shepherd is, when you forget about the fact that she's my girlfriend, when you forget about the fact that she was a cover girl.

It's amazing, when you see movies again, how they change. I've seen pictures that I adored ten years ago and now think are crap, and pictures that I hated ten years ago and now think are masterpieces. Actually, what changes is you. But it is true that pictures have a way of changing their shape and color. That's why it's so difficult to be a critic. It's almost impossible to guess what's going to last. It sounds like I'm being very defensive, but really I'm talking here today about my films as though somebody else had made them. We're sitting here looking at *Daisy Miller* in terms of what the director intended to convey and what he achieved. When five or six years have passed I might go back and look at a film I made, and it either works for me or it doesn't, just like I might run a picture by Mizoguchi or John Ford or Lubitsch or Billy Friedkin.

With Daisy Miller, *which I think is one of the most beautiful films I've ever seen, were you influenced by anyone when it came to your camera setups and the color and the composition?*

Mainly my father, who was a painter. He worked at home because he couldn't afford a studio, so from the moment I was born I was surrounded by composition and color and images. It must have had a profound effect on me. He was influenced by the postimpressionists, but because of his Serbian heritage his work had some kind of Byzantine overlay, which meant the colors were brighter. *Daisy Miller* is one of the few pictures of mine I can look at and not feel like I actually had anything to do with it, which is nice. Looking at your own work is like looking in the mirror. I was in the Plaza Hotel some years ago with Ryan O'Neal. We were both staggering out in the morning for some sort of interview, and there was a mirror next to the elevators to let you know how you look. Ryan was already standing there looking in the mirror. I came running up and said, "Oh, shit," and he said, "What's the matter?" I said, "I always think it's going to be better." He said, "That's funny. I'm always pleased at how much better it is." That's an essential difference between actors and directors.

You had the great fortune of knowing Fritz Lang and John Ford. Do you think those relationships helped you with your own filmmaking?

There's a fine line between being influenced by these guys and stealing outright from them. All directors steal from each other. I was talking to Howard Hawks about the shot in *Red River* when the cloud comes in and covers the funeral. I said, "That's a hell of a shot." He said, "Well, you know, sometimes you get lucky and get one of those great Ford shots." I said, "Do you mean you thought of it as a Ford shot then?" He said, "Oh, sure. We all said, 'Let's get that Ford shot.' " I asked him if Ford had influenced his westerns and he said, "Well, Jesus Christ, Peter—I don't see how you can make a western and not be influenced by John Ford!"

I was fortunate because I got out to Los Angeles in 1961. Many of the great directors of the early period were still alive then, and some of them were even still working. I tracked them down and asked them as many questions as I possibly could. John Ford once yelled at me and said, "Jesus, can't you end a sentence with a period? Have you ever uttered a declarative sentence?" Almost all of them enjoyed talking about their work, even someone as recalcitrant as Ford. He could really talk once you got him going. It must have been gratifying that such a young guy was asking them so many questions. They were all aware that even though I was writing for *Esquire* I was actually a theater director and an actor. This was the trick to it all, that they knew I wasn't a real journalist but that I was in the business.

It was like putting myself through a unique film school that had as its faculty all the great directors. Almost all of them began in the silent era. I think one of the biggest problems facing movies today is that we've lost touch with silent cinema. They are the foundation of everything that came afterwards. One of the main things I learned from the older directors is not to let the dialogue dictate how you make the picture. Hitchcock said most pictures are simply pictures of people talking, and that's become more and more the case. I like what Allan Dwan said, that when we switched from silent pictures to sound, the whole artistry was gone. He said, "Every time I finished a talking picture I'd run it silent. If I could pretty much follow the plot, I figured I'd done a good job." Chaplin has a great line about this: "Just when we were getting it right, it was over." It's true that around the time silent cinema ended, they were becoming flawless at telling stories visually.

For me, the material, the story being told, dictates the style. I feel that one of the dangers in picture making is that style has become more important than content. On the other hand, if the content is very good and the style is no good, it's still no good. If there's no substance, a film will always be shallow. But substance with no craft is equally problematic.

Was it you who pioneered the idea of going back and interviewing the old directors?

The French did it first. Chabrol, Truffaut, Rohmer, Rivette and Godard were all interviewing the old-time American directors for *Cahiers du Cinéma*. I read the magazine in the late fifties and early sixties, and it seemed perfectly natural to go and interview those people I was interested in.

Did you ever think about going to Europe and doing for French and English directors what you were doing for American filmmakers?

My focus was on American movies and directors because I was going to make American films. I went to see Bergman and Antonioni, but that wasn't my predilection. I think something that has hurt American cinema of late is that younger filmmakers have gone after Antonioni and Fellini. Such pretension! Where's Raoul Walsh when we need him?

Had you really seen all the films you discussed with the directors you interviewed?

I think I saw all but one of Hawks' films, and I think I saw all of Hitchcock's films, but with someone like Ford a lot of his films are lost. I certainly didn't see all of Allan Dwan's films, because he made so many. But remember that film culture in New York in the fifties and sixties was a vibrant one, and there were a lot of opportunities to see rare films back then. People were starting to take film very seriously. I was marginally involved with a group of filmmakers and avant-garde artists that became known as the New American Cinema group, people like Lionel Rogosin and Jonas Mekas. Adolfas Mekas asked me to be in his film *Hallelujah the Hills,* but I turned him down because of the nudity. I didn't want my ass all over the screen. I was interested in seeing avant-garde films, but knew that wasn't the kind of work I wanted to make myself. By the time I was about twenty I had sketched an idea for a film I wanted to make called *The Land of Opportunity,* about a young couple in New York who get everything for free. They either steal it or somehow promote it for free. I just had the idea, and never even wrote the script. Years later I ended up using some of those ideas in *What's Up, Doc?*

I would go to Amos Vogel's film club Cinema 16 all the time and remember vividly seeing some memorable movies there, like *Gold Diggers of 1933* and Hawks' *Twentieth Century,* for the first time. I worked for Dan Talbot for a couple of years at the New Yorker Theater on the Upper West Side, which could hold something like a thousand people. Dan was the first person to show classic American films rather than foreign films, which the Thalia and most of the art houses were doing. He was following the *Cahiers* lead and started an American revival house which was a very influential theater for a number of years. I advised him somewhat on which pictures to book, and curated a number of shows like The Forgotten Films, where we ran fourteen double bills in two weeks—twenty-eight pictures in fourteen days which hadn't been seen on the big screen for thirty years. I had help from Andrew Sarris and Eugene Archer, and wrote all the program notes. In the program note I did when Dan revived

Orson's *Othello,* which had hardly been seen in New York at all, I called the film "the best Shakespeare film ever made." This was hardly the conventional wisdom at the time, and I got a call from Richard Griffith, head of the Museum of Modern Art film library, who asked me if I wanted to curate the first-ever American retrospective of Orson's work at the museum and write the accompanying monograph. I said, "Why me? Why don't *you* do it?" He said, "I don't really like Orson Welles very much, but we have many friends and colleagues who do and feel the museum should do this. We think you would be the right person to organize the retrospective." That became *The Cinema of Orson Welles,* my first book.

Why didn't you interview him at that time?

He was in Europe shooting *The Trial.* I sent two copies off to some address in Europe and didn't hear a thing for seven years, not until 1968, after I'd directed *Targets.* After the film had opened I get a phone call. "Hello, this is Orson Welles. I can't tell you how long I've wanted to meet with you." I said, "Hold on, that's my line. Why did you want to meet me?" He said, "Because you have written the truest words ever published about me." He paused for a few seconds and added, "In English." Then he said, "Meet me at the Beverly Hills Hotel tomorrow."

Your written work seems almost anti-academic.

I'm not consciously anti-academic, it's just not in my nature. Only occasionally do I explain what a film "means." I don't like to get philosophical about any films, even my own. I'm much more of an instinctual artist than people give me credit for, because they think I'm paying homage to various things with my films. One critic said that *Paper Moon* is a homage to thirties filmmaking. What nonsense! The film is set in the thirties, but I never saw a single film like that made in the thirties. I was in London a while ago and a taxi driver said, "I love *Paper Moon.* It's such a celebration of family." Well, that's not what I intended at all, but I'm not going to tell him that and disappoint him. His point of view is entirely valid. There was a Renoir series a few years ago here in town. I went over to his house afterwards and said, "Jean, I saw *Boudu Saved from Drowning.* What a wonderful film that is!" He was such a humble and generous man, and he said, "Oh, thank you very much. You're very kind." I said, "Do you like the film?" He said, "Well, you know it was made in the early days of sound, and some of the sound is not so good. The music recording is not so good. We had no money and had to buy film stock as we went along, so some of the picture doesn't match from shot to shot. Sometimes the cutting is a little too fast, and sometimes the cutting is a little too slow." He went on and on. "But I think that perhaps it's my best film."

As Renoir once said in an interview with Jacques Rivette, "When we have achieved total realism, we will have achieved total decadence." My interpretation of that is that today, with special effects, you can do anything on film. But who cares? The magic is gone. The audience knows it's all just one big expensive box of tricks. It used to be exciting when Douglas Fairbanks jumped up onto a table. The whole idea of suspension of disbelief has evaporated. Buster Keaton and Harold Lloyd did all their own stunts, which is what makes them so brilliant. Someone once complained to Chaplin that his camera angles weren't interesting. He said, "They don't have to be. I'm interesting." If you watch Astaire and Rogers dancing, there's hardly a cut. Long takes. Part of the greatness of movies is showing something happen in real time. Today special effects are getting so good that who knows what's real? And all the cutting and hand-held camera that goes on just makes you aware of the process. What does it add? Certainly not realism.

What do you make of Easy Rider? *It seems to be the antithesis of your own work, which looks quite conservative in comparison.*

I don't think "conservative" is the right word. I'm more of a classicist. But don't forget that *The Last Picture Show* had nudity and showed teenage sex in a way that had never been shown before. It was quite a radical film for its time even though the story was told in a classical style. *Easy Rider* really began with *The Wild Angels*. Peter Fonda basically plays the same character in both films. Brando in *The Wild One* hadn't done well, and *The Wild Angels* was the first really successful biker picture. It started a whole genre and without it there would be no *Easy Rider*. Peter and Dennis Hopper came to Roger Corman and asked if he wanted to make *Easy Rider*, but Roger turned it down because they wanted half a million dollars. Of course the two of them ended up winning the prize at Cannes and making a fortune.

Did you come up with the original idea for Nickelodeon?

It was a pet project of mine because I found the whole silent era so fascinating. Film is the only art form that was born within our lifetime. It's a complicated, wonderful and horrible medium, and I wanted to tell a story about how and when it all started. It's a moment full of great innocence, something I think is reflected in the film. All the stories in *Nickelodeon* are largely true because they were told to me by the directors who had been making films back then, people like Leo McCarey, Allan Dwan and Raoul Walsh. For example, Ryan O'Neal becoming a director comes directly out of what happened to Allan Dwan. A director went missing, so Dwan sent a telegram to his boss explaining what had happened, and received a reply telling him that he was the new director.

To be honest, I don't much like the film. It wasn't the picture we wanted to make. Too many compromises, like having to make it in color, and the casting. I wanted a younger cast, but the studio wanted big star names.

What are your thoughts on music in films?

I think that essentially I'm cheating if the music in a film accentuates or embellishes the action. It seems to me that the visuals should do absolutely everything. Too many movies today are told through the music. What I do like is when the music plays against the visuals, like if you have fast-paced images and something going on musically which acts as a counterpoint, or somebody playing a funny song in a sad scene.

It sounds as if the singing in At Long Last Love *was recorded live.*

That was a folly of mine. It was an ambitious but flawed film for which I can only blame myself. My favorite musicals are the Lubitsch films of the late twenties and early thirties. I fell in love with those pictures, and along with a book that Cybill gave me, a collection of Cole Porter lyrics, they're the reason I made *At Long Last Love*. One of the things that made *The Love Parade* and *The Smiling Lieutenant* so exciting was that you knew they were singing live. The orchestra was right off-camera. They couldn't mix sound in those days, so they had to record everything at the same time. I remember Hitchcock telling me he shot an insert of a radio and there was an orchestra playing off-camera because they didn't have the ability to record it later and mix it in. He might have been exaggerating, but for me it made sense not to postsynch, because the immediacy of the whole thing would be lost. I couldn't stand the thought of recording the singing first and playing it to the actors as they're being filmed. I wanted to make a musical where they were acting the songs and singing them live. Everybody thought this was crazy, but I was riding high at the time.

It became a huge problem, because we couldn't afford an orchestra on the set, so Fox spent quite a lot of money to develop a tiny speaker that fit into the actor's ear. They each had an antenna combed into their hair that could pick up an electric signal sent from an electric piano, so on the set the actors were hearing the music. Actually, none of them were really singers, although that was the fun of it. Remember the scene with Burt Reynolds and Cybill in the swimming pool when she laughs so hard she can't sing? That's just what I wanted. The point is that these people are superficial. They can't speak, which is why they're always singing. It's not an Astaire/Rogers homage, it's about people who aren't singers and dancers but would like to be, just like me. They can only express themselves through songs written by someone else. I often sang to girls because I didn't know how to put it into words of my own. It sounds corny to say "I love you," so why not sing instead [*singing*] "I've got a crush on you, sweetie-pie"? So it was a rather personal film for me, and the Cole Porter song that made me want to make the movie is the first scene I wrote but is one of the last scenes in the film [*singing*]:

> I loved him but he didn't love me
> I wanted him but he didn't want me
> Then the Gods had a spree and indulged in another whim
> Now he loves me but I don't love him.

I read that lyric before I knew the tune and said, "That's the movie I want to make."

What was the concept behind the Directors Company?

I got a call from Francis Coppola saying that Charlie Bluhdorn of Gulf + Western had the idea that we three—Coppola, Friedkin and I—get together and make a bunch of pictures and then go public and make a lot of money. Francis, Bill and I flew to New York and had a meeting with Bluhdorn. I remember that Frank Yablans, the head of Paramount, walked in and hated the whole idea. "Why don't you just give them the studio?" he said. For any picture that cost up to three million dollars we could make anything we wanted. We didn't even have to ask the studio or tell them what it was. For a million and a half or under we could produce a film directed by someone else. Again, we didn't have to tell them what it was. To put things in perspective, *Paper Moon* cost $2.8 million and *The Last Picture Show* cost $1.3 million, so I didn't think we needed much more. The other thing was that our contract said we didn't have to cut the films for television, which was important to us.

I was looking forward to making all kinds of films, including one with King Vidor called *The Extra* about James Murray, the actor in his film *The Crowd,* and a film with Orson based on a Joseph Conrad novel. The whole thing really was a great idea on paper, and we should have made a lot of pictures, but Francis and Billy ended up wanting more money up front. The back end was great but the money up front wasn't. I think there was a limit of $300,000 per film for the director, and because of that the whole thing fell apart fairly quickly. Everyone in the company ended up doing well on *Paper Moon,* which was the only picture that made money, because I threw the film into the mix to jump-start the company. I had a deal to make that film long before we formed the Directors Company but thought it would be a good idea to sweeten the pot for everyone. That was a big error on my part, because I ended up losing a lot of money.

Do you shoot lots of cutaways for protection?

Probably the central thing I heard from almost all the old directors I spoke to—Ford, Hawks, Hitchcock, Lang, Dwan, McCarey—was that they basically cut in the camera. Generally the old masters didn't shoot coverage. I saw Ford put his hand over the camera lens one time as if to say "That's enough." These guys knew where they were going to cut when they were shooting the scene. Being young in the business, I assumed that was the way everybody did it, but found out later that some directors, like Capra and Stevens, would shoot a lot of coverage. I learned from Ford, who said, "Just shoot what you need, kid, and don't give 'em anything they don't need and that you don't need." Ford was shooting *How Green Was My Valley* and there's a great shot during the marriage scene. Maureen O'Sullivan's character is marrying someone she's not in love with, and they ride off in a carriage. It's a long shot, and the camera pans them off and holds on the minister, Walter Pidgeon, standing under a tree. This is the man she's really in love with. It's a long shot, and the cameraman said to Ford, "Jack, do you think we should grab a close-up of Walter under the tree?" Ford said, "Oh no, Jesus—I mean, they'll just use it!" He meant that the editor, who he had no control over, would use the shot just because it was there. Part of my training was to think only in terms of what is needed. The time to make up your mind about what the scene is about, and how and where it should be played, is on the set during filming and not in the cutting room, otherwise you're wasting time shooting things you're not going to need. You can cut almost anything together in thirty different ways if you have enough footage, but that doesn't mean it's the right way to play the scene. The one thing that the old-timers spoke about most often was their pride in being able to make films quickly and economically.

I shoot very tight, and because of that editing goes very quickly. We showed *What's Up, Doc?* to the studio three weeks after we wrapped. It was the same thing with *Paper Moon* and *Daisy Miller.* "Protection" is a dirty word. I think running around covering things from every angle can ruin the morale on a set, particularly when you have a big, complicated setup and everybody has to work like a sonofabitch to get it right. Maybe it's a whole scene without a cut, like the shots we did in *Daisy Miller* which were fifteen pages without a cut, five minutes. You work at it for days and then you get it and everybody cheers, and then you say, "Now, we need a little protection here in case it doesn't work." Well, they'll kill you.

With scenes where you have to do several takes to get it right, do the performances ever change?

In movies something happens and it only happens once. That's the difference between movie acting and stage acting. There are very few moments in my pictures that I can say are perfect, but if there are any, it's little things, like a look between two people or a line. It's nothing I could ever have planned, and usually happens in a close-up. Almost everything I'm happiest with in the pictures I've done were first takes. There's always a bit of luck in any shot. You're hoping that something will go wrong that will make it great, a lucky accident of sorts. John Ford said that he thinks the best things in pictures happen by accident. Orson Welles said to me, "A director is essentially a man who presides over accidents." What you're really trying to do when you direct a picture is create an atmosphere in which accidents will happen. Things will go a little bit wrong and you'll say, "That's great. That's the one." Who knows why it's the one? Something was going through the actor's mind, or a cloud moved in at a certain point. Henry Fonda told me this story about Ford directing *Mister Roberts.* He said, "We were shooting a scene with William Powell. He was kind of shaky and nervous. It was a long scene, about four or five pages, and Ford set up the camera, and we started to roll—it was outside on a ship—and Jesus, Bill was just terrible. His hands were shaking and he could barely remember his lines. I was thinking, 'When is he going to cut?' But I went on playing the scene and we went on and on, and the scene was over and Ford said, 'Cut! Print! Did you see that cloud move in there? Jesus, wasn't that a hell of a thing? What a hell of a shot that was!' "

You said that the time to make up your mind about what the scene is about is when you're shooting it. But aren't some of those decisions also to be made in the script?

No. I don't like scripts to overly define the mechanics of the film. You might indicate certain things that jump out at you, like a close-up or an establishing shot, but I don't make decisions as to where the camera is going to be until the last moment. It's important to keep yourself fresh and open to ideas, like the actor suggesting something. But basically I know what the scene is about and how many angles I need to cover it. If you have a scene that plays well in a single shot, then just leave it alone. Maybe shoot four or five takes, but forget about coverage. Ford told me about a scene with two actors he held for a long time, and he said, "Well, you can see their faces and hear what they're saying. No reason to cut." I asked Orson how he would define the difference between shooting a scene in one shot or cutting it up into many pieces. He said, "That was what we used to say separated the men from the boys." Joseph H. Lewis was shooting a bank robbery and got it only with a single camera from inside the car. I asked him about this entire ten-minute shot. Did he get any coverage? He said, "No, a man must have courage."

Can you say anything about casting?

I once asked Hitchcock about the difference between casting an unknown actor and a star in a picture. He said, "You're driving along the street and there's an accident up ahead. You slow up as you go by the accident and see somebody. You don't know who it is and you say, 'Oh, tsk, tsk. Too bad,' and you drive on. Now," he said, "the same scene. You're driving along, you look to see who it is and, my god, it's your brother. That's the difference between casting an unknown and Cary Grant." You know and care about Cary Grant. You don't have to set it up. He just walks on the screen. That instant familiarity is what you are paying him for.

Have you ever run into any problems with actors?

I think you have to be some kind of actor to be a good director, because essentially you have to hear the words in your mind. It's like how a conductor hears a score. He doesn't necessarily need to have the musicians there to know how it ought to sound. In fact, what he's trying to do is get all the musicians to sound like what he hears. When I'm working on a script I hear it a certain way, and then it's a question of getting the actors to sound the same way. Sometimes they do something interesting that's different and I say, "Hey, I like that. That's nice. Keep that." But generally speaking you're trying to get them to do it more or less the way you're hearing it. Of course there are a million ways to do that. In fact, there are as many ways to do that as there are actors, because every actor is different. You beat Tatum O'Neal on the head or scare her, you indulge Burt Reynolds because he's nervous, but essentially I show them what I want by either saying the line the way I think they ought to say it or getting up and acting it out. I don't do it out of any kind of particularly egotistical desire to be a ham, but because I don't know how else to describe it.

Some actors are threatened by this, and if they don't like it then I don't do it. Usually it isn't a problem. Some directors did all the time. Lubitsch, for example, acted out every role: the maids, the butlers, every role. I asked Jack Benny once—he was the only actor I ever met who'd worked with Lubitsch—"Did he act out all the parts?" "Yeah, all the parts. It was a little broad but you got the idea." That's the thing: you got the idea. I got encouragement with this method of directing from James Cagney. I asked him at a dinner party, "What's a good director to you?" He said, "Kid, I've only worked with five." I said, "How many directors have you worked with in your life?" "Eighty-five. But only five are really directors." So I said, "What does a real director do?" He said, "A director to me is a man who, if I don't know what the hell to do, can get up and show me."

Is it easier to do six less expensive pictures than one expensive one?

Making an expensive film is the worst thing in the world. When I was sort of a half-assed critic I wrote once about *My Fair Lady* and said that George Cukor had made a very good picture considering the limitations of $15 million. I found when I had $6 or $9 million, which I had on two pictures, that I was right. It's a hell of a limitation. Things gets bigger and bigger and finally you've got all these people who don't do anything, and you're carrying them around with you. It's like a goddamned army. You can't just say, "Let's not shoot this today. Let's go over there." It's like saying, "We're not going to invade at Normandy. We're going to invade the Sea of Japan." Somehow the freedom goes, and at the same time so does the fun.

I've always thought that making a film is fun only when you feel that what you're doing is sort of a crime. What you're saying is, "Nobody knows what we're really doing." Jean Renoir once said that when you're making a picture you should have conspirators around you, as opposed to associates. That's why I love shooting at night. It's the best time to shoot because everybody else is asleep and you're really doing this terrible thing—you're making this movie—and nobody knows what you're doing. You've got to maintain that larcenous quality to your work as a director, and that's what's the matter with making big pictures.

What has it been like working with László Kovács as your cinematographer?

László had shot a bunch of nudie pictures before he did *Targets* and he'd never done what he thought was a good picture. In fact, his name on those had been Leslie Kovacs. His real name was László and he changed his name to fit more with an American image. I said, "Why in hell are you calling yourself Leslie? László Kovács is a beautiful name. It's classical." He said, "Okay, on this picture I'm going to put László. It's the first picture I'm proud of."

Otto Preminger once said to me that there were two kinds of good cameramen. "There's the good cameraman who'll give you what you want but doesn't know why you want it, and there's the other kind who can give you what you want and knows why you want it. Of course, it's much more fun to work with the second type." László's the second type. I remember one shot we had on *Paper Moon,* in the café scene when Tatum says, "I want my $200." The last setup in that sequence is a face-off between the two of them and the waitress comes up and says, "Hi there, precious." He says, "Her name ain't Precious." We ended up shooting with a slightly low angle, which is exactly what I had in mind but didn't know how to explain it to László. I just said, "Look, here's what I want. It's the last shot in the sequence and I want to get a kind of feeling like a Mexican standoff." He said, "What's that?" I said, "Give the impression of these two people opposing each other but we don't know which way it's going to go." He said, "Well, maybe if we shoot low," and I said, "That's good."

When we started work on *Paper Moon* it was going to be in color. I sent Polly to look for locations and take photos. She drove all over the South, in Tennessee and Georgia, before we decided on Kansas. She brought the pictures back and maybe half were in color and half were black and white. I looked at them and said, "Jesus Christ, we ought to do this in black and white. It looks wonderful." There were all these things that were anachronisms. The film was set in the thirties and here were all these black-and-white pictures with modern cars, with motorcycles, with modern signs, but in black and white it still looked like it was the thirties. I said, "Imagine if you take all the anachronisms out and we do it in black and white." In black and white you just get the feeling of the period right away, and suddenly I realized that all the great photographs I've ever seen of the Depression—Walker Evans is a perfect example—are in sharp black and white. I also thought the film would be too cute in color, with these two attractive, blue-eyed blond people. It would have looked like a Disney picture.

I said to László, "There's a quality I wanted in *Picture Show* which I never really achieved. I want *Paper Moon* to be very sharp-focus and as contrasty as possible, so we'll use a red filter." Orson Welles told me about that. He said, "Use a red filter. That's what Ford always did. That's what I did in *Chimes at Midnight*," which was a marvelous black-and-white picture. Filters like that emphasize the contrast between light and dark. László experimented for three or four days and we shot it all with a red filter. The use of black and white was kind of revived for a while, because Mel Brooks did *Young Frankenstein* and Fosse did *Lenny.* It's one of the great tragedies that black and white is no longer part of the filmmaker's palette.

Is your relationship with Verna Fields, who has edited several of your films, important to you?

Verna is originally a sound editor. I remember showing her *Targets,* much of which was shot silent. She said, "This is very well edited. Who cut it?" I told her, "I did. Can you do the sound?" She did a brilliant job. Verna's a real stickler and very intuitive, which is how editors should be. I asked her to cut *The Last Picture Show* but she was busy so I ended up cutting the whole thing myself. Donn Cambern is credited on the picture, but all he did was order the opticals from the lab and make sure they looked okay. We had problems with the union, which meant I couldn't take an editing credit. At the time Donn was editing *Drive, He Said* next door, so we gave him the credit. When it came to *What's Up, Doc?* I asked Verna if she would cut it. She said, "You know I've never cut a big feature before. Are you sure you want me to do this?" I said, "Yes. You're not going to touch it until I've marked it up anyway." That's how I work with Verna. I'm so used to editing my own stuff that I can't stand to look at someone else's cuts until I've made my own, which can then be refined. What I do is sit with the editor and look at the dailies and pick the takes I want. An editor is not allowed any leeway the first time through, because if they don't cut it my way the first time and it's not right, I go mad. I think it's my fault and that I've screwed up, so it's better if I just work on it myself until I get familiar with the material. Verna is always saying that she's not actually doing anything, but of course she's made some very valuable contributions, and at least once on every picture we've done together Verna has worked out how to fix something that no one else could solve. She earns her entire salary at moments like that.

What do you think is the most important tool that a director needs?

Good actors.

And the most important skill?

The ability to speak to actors and get performances from them. The second most important thing is a sense of where the hell to put the camera. The third most important thing is to know when to cut. Some directors know how to talk to actors and don't know where the hell to put the camera. That's not so bad, because somebody will tell them where to put the camera, and eventually it'll end up near where it ought to be. Some directors know how to cut and know how to deal with the camera but have no idea how to talk to the actors, so you have very interesting camerawork and good cutting and you have an interesting picture from a formal point of view, but the heart is missing. Some people know all three, and they make pretty good pictures.

Where do you put the camera?

I think there is one ideal place where the camera should be at any one time, and the job of the director is to find it. I usually map it out before I get on the set, just notes for myself, so I know how many setups I'm going to need for each given scene. That said, the best piece of advice I can offer is from Orson Welles, who once said to me, "If you really don't know where to put the camera, then you really don't know what to do in the scene."

Hitchcock always insisted that every scene should have a point of view. He didn't necessarily mean that the director should have a particular attitude toward it. Hitchcock had a great ability to jump from the subjective point of view of a character to an objective point of view. At times the audience is in the head of the character and at other times not. It's all done with camera angles and use of lenses and framing. Much of *Rear Window* is told from Jimmy Stewart's point of view as he looks out over at the buildings opposite. But at other times, at key moments, Hitchcock shifts to an objective point of view where he purposely shows you that Stewart is asleep and clearly doesn't see certain things. It helps build the tension because the audience says, "Aha! He didn't see that!" A shift like that is often done very subtly, without the audience even noticing, but the question is always the same: from whose point of view is the audience seeing the scene? For example, if you have a close-up of me and a wide shot of you, it's obviously my point of view. If I have you sitting there, and we start with a close-up of you and then cut to a shot of me from where you're sitting, it's obviously your point of view. It's really important to remember when you're writing a script or directing, because it affects everything in terms of the framing, the size of the image, the way you move the actors within the shot and how they interact with each other. Hitchcock did it wonderfully. It's absolutely a forgotten art. Most films don't have a point of view, they just have shot after shot. Always ask yourself: precisely which part of the story am I telling with this shot?

Do you rehearse your actors?

Always—for at least two weeks, if not more. For some scenes, the more the better, up to a point, because it's possible to overrehearse. You have to rehearse to the point where nobody knows exactly what they're going to do but they think they know approximately what they're going to do. Then it's time to shoot.

When you get to a location do you rehearse the actors before you light it and set your camera position?

While I'm rehearsing, I usually have an idea or two about shots and get a sense of exactly where the camera ought to be for each moment in the scene. When I read a well-written scene, it jumps out at me where the cuts need to be: "No cut . . . no cut . . . no cut . . . cut here . . . close-up here." If I don't see a cut, I get it in a single shot. Before I come on the set I sketch out exactly how many setups I need. You're usually shooting completely out of continuity. You're shooting the beginning last and the last first, but that's why the rehearsal has been valuable, because the actors know the scene, so even if you start in the middle they know more or less where they are, because they've rehearsed it all the way through.

Is there a way of building a joke so there might be one payoff followed by a bigger one?

Oh yes, that's essential. That's what's called the topper. You've usually got to have two jokes and then a third that's funnier than the previous two. It's bump, *bump,* BUMP! You'll find that if you don't give an audience the topper they slightly resent you. The comedy in *What's Up, Doc?* works on this principle of threes. You set up something with a laugh, you get another laugh with it, then you top it. There's a scene where there are cars all making a U-turn and they each smash into this Volkswagen bus which is parked along the curb. Each time it gets a bigger laugh. The topper is when the guy who obviously owns the bus runs out from his house, opens the door of the thing and the whole bus falls over into the street. That's the big laugh. The trouble with so many comedies today is that nobody understands the principle of topping a joke.

Do you think there's a market for the kind of slapstick Keystone Kop kind of thing that you have in What's Up, Doc?

It's not Keystone. It's not Mack Sennett. Look at Mack Sennett. He's not very funny. The chase in *What's Up, Doc?* is really Buster Keaton. There have really been only two great comedy directors: Buster Keaton and Ernst Lubitsch. Keaton for chases, Lubitsch for everything else. If you look at Keaton's pictures you'll see the impeccable placement of camera, cutting, timing. He was dancing, flying, doing pirouettes. When it comes to visual comedy, there was nobody else. The Keystone Kops and all of that is very primitive, grotesque running around. It was funny to people back then, but I don't find it funny today.

When you read a comedy script, how do you know whether it's funny?

That's hard. The toughest thing in the world is to do comedy. You know, Edmund Gwenn was gravely ill. Somebody came to see him, and they said, "How is it, Edmund?" He said, "It's rough. But not as rough as playing comedy."

Is genre an important starting point for you as a director?

Genre is a way of cloaking a personal film. I think a lot of the American filmmakers worked this way. Hawks' *Rio Bravo* is a perfect example. This whole issue is bound up in the so-called auteur theory, which by the way was never a theory. In France it was a political statement: *la politique des auteurs.* It was meant to kill off what they called *le cinéma de papa,* the old-fashioned French well-made film. For them, Hawks was a greater director than Fred Zinnemann, and Hitchcock was greater than David Lean. The idea, as stated by various French New Wave critics like Truffaut, Godard, Chabrol and Rohmer, was that despite the impositions of the studio system, the personality of certain directors would show through no matter who wrote it, who shot it or who was in it. Their points of view triumphed over the multiplicity of restrictions that might have existed. According to these critics, Zinnemann and Lean made films without much of their own personality in them. For them, clearly Hawks, Hitchcock, Ford and others were the governing force behind the films they put their name to as director, but the fact that these directors rarely took writing credit doesn't mean they didn't make enormous contributions to the screenplays of their films, both before and during production. It means looking at a director's body of work rather than an individual film.

What does this say about the obvious input of the writer on a film?

In many cases, the director worked closely with the writer, even if he got no credit. Hitchcock sat in the room with his writers for months. They structured the films together, then the writer would go off, write the dialogue and present Hitch with pages. I watched Hawks rewrite scenes on the set of *El Dorado.* I saw Ford ad-lib whole scenes on the set. Hawks too. The best example is probably Ernst Lubitsch. He rarely took credit for screenwriting, but as his frequent collaborator and screenwriter Samson Raphaelson explained, Lubitsch was there through the entire scripting process.

What do you think of film schools?

A lot of what I know I learned through osmosis. I never even graduated high school. I didn't study painting and yet I know a lot about it just by being around my father. I grew up looking at art and was surrounded by composition and color as a child. He took me to galleries and the Museum of Modern Art to see silent films all the time. I must have seen four hundred stage productions when I was growing up in New York. It's the same thing with movies. I never studied how to make them as such, I just watched a lot of them and asked a lot of questions. Sometimes I would sneak into Cecile Starr's class at Columbia University and watch a film, but generally I find film schools to be disappointing. They spend far too much time on production and not enough time showing the right films to students. Students need to see classics. We're talking about the foundation of the medium and that includes silent cinema. I taught a class at UCLA in 1969 about Howard Hawks. Ten weeks of his movies. I wasn't interested in the students' opinions. "I'm here to show you the movie and tell you what he said about it. I really don't care what you think."

A lot of directors who speak at these seminars are very reserved. You've been the most open person I've heard speak here at the AFI.

Really? Well, I think if I'm going to talk to people, I don't see why I should lie or hide anything. Actually, it's probably more instructive for me than for anyone. I'm not talking about my private life, I'm talking about making pictures, and maybe somebody can learn from something I've said, though I don't really believe that. I don't think I've learned anything from the things I've read. I learned from doing things, because everybody makes their own mistakes. You make a mistake and three years later you say, "Jeez, I read about that. I should have known better."

Do you think people will be laughing at What's Up, Doc? *thirty years from now?*

I don't see why not. Kids laugh at it and older people laugh at it, and I get letters from people who have seen it fifty times, so it must be funny if they see it that many times. I don't think there is anything dated about it. There are no topical jokes or references to specific things, like Jimmy Carter or last night's Johnny Carson show.

We showed a Buster Keaton film a couple of weeks ago and everyone thought it was very funny.

They screened *Nickelodeon* at the film festival in Berlin and asked me, "What would you like to see while you're in Berlin?" I said, "I think you've got some silent Lubitsch films here, and I want to see them." So they looked through the archives and found seven silent Lubitsch movies, from about 1918 to about 1923, none of which I'd seen. They said, "We have a problem. We can only get the projection room for one day, and we'll have to run all the pictures on this day." I said, "Seven pictures in one day? I'll start at noon," because I don't like to get up too early and the night before I had to go see Truffaut's new picture. So the next day at noon we go out somewhere far away and start looking at Lubitsch. Cybill is with me, she loves Lubitsch. The first one is *Madame Dubarry* with Pola Negri, one of the best costume pictures I've ever seen in my life. The second one was a comedy called *Die Bergkatze,* again with Pola Negri, which was never released in America because it came out after the war—it was sort of an anti-militarist movie—and it was one of the funniest movies I've ever seen. It's funnier than *The General.* I was just sick from laughing. The third picture was *Die Puppe,* also one of the funniest movies I've ever seen. So now I'm sick. Three movies. It's like eating a ten-course dinner. I said, "Stop a minute." The guy says, "But we have to run all the pictures today." I said, "Could you bring us something to eat?" Cybill is also exhausted. They bring us sandwiches and I'm sticking toothpicks into Cybill trying to keep her awake. "You're not going to get a chance to see this stuff anywhere else. Wake up." "I don't care. I've got to have some sleep." I can't say how many of the seven films I saw because I passed out.

It never ceases to amaze me how many treasures there are buried in those fourteen short years between 1915 and 1929, when sound came in and ruined everything. Mary Pickford once said, "If you look at the history of motion pictures, silent pictures and then talkies, and see the difference in terms of visual quality between the silent pictures and the talking pictures, somehow you'd think that they had evolved the other way." Isn't that great? That sort of sums up what I think about cinema.

Films as Director

1966 *Voyage to the Planet of Prehistoric Women* (as Derek Thomas)

1968 *Targets* (also producer and screenplay)

1971 *The Last Picture Show* (also screenplay)

1972 *What's Up, Doc?* (also producer and screenplay)

1973 *Paper Moon* (also producer)

1974 *Daisy Miller* (also producer)

1975 *At Long Last Love* (also producer and screenplay)

1976 *Nickelodeon* (also screenplay)

1979 *Saint Jack* (also screenplay)
1981 *They All Laughed* (also
         screenplay)
1985 *Mask*
1988 *Illegally Yours* (also producer)

1990 *Texasville* (also producer and
         screenplay)
1992 *Noises Off* (also producer)
1993 *The Thing Called Love*
2001 *The Cat's Meow*

Bogdanovich also directed documentaries and television including *The Great Professional: Howard Hawks,* 1967; *Directed by John Ford,* 1971; *Picture Windows,* 1995; *Fallen Angels,* 1995; *To Sir, with Love II,* 1996; *The Price of Heaven,* 1997; *Rescuers: Stories of Courage: Two Women,* 1997; *Naked City: A Killer Christmas,* 1998; *A Saintly Switch,* 1999; *The Mystery of Natalie Wood,* 2004; *The Sopranos,* 2004; *Hustle: The Pete Rose Story,* 2004; and *Tom Petty and the Heartbreakers: Runnin' Down a Dream,* 2007.

I wish there were more people in this town who would take me or any other critic to task and point out not that we are congenital idiots, but that there is another way to look at the film in question. I have never claimed infallibility, only honesty.

CHARLES CHAMPLIN
(Born in Hammondsport, New York, 1926)

Charles Champlin was named entertainment editor and principal film critic of the *Los Angeles Times* in 1965, when Otis Chandler, the scion of the powerful Chandler family and newly its publisher, decided to shake up the staid old paper. For the next twenty-six years, Champlin had the delicate task of reviewing movies in the company town where he would be mixing socially with the people upon whom he was passing judgment.

Champlin was one of many critics who came to the AFI to meet with the fellows. When the conservatory opened in 1969, we included several "research fellows," testing the concept of aspiring critics interacting with the filmmaking fellows. The concept proved unwieldy and at times unfriendly, and was abandoned after a few years, although one of the original research fellows, Paul Schrader, became a successful writer and director after leaving AFI.

Champlin was raised in upstate New York, where his family was involved in the wine industry. He served in the infantry in Europe during World War II and was awarded the Purple Heart and battle stars after being wounded in combat near the Remagen Bridge. Returning to civilian life, he graduated from Harvard and in 1948 got a job at *Life* magazine.

Champlin was with *Life* in its heyday, the era of its founder, Henry Luce. After many years reporting in various parts of the United States, he was assigned to London during the sixties, where he was an early observer of a young British rock group from Liverpool. He sent urgent telegrams to headquarters in New York heralding the new band. A reply finally arrived: "*Time* passing on obscure Liverpool group." While in the United Kingdom he interviewed Peter O'Toole, John Schlesinger, Julie Christie and David Lean, and reported on the creative ferment of that decade.

Charles Champlin discussed film criticism with the fellows at Greystone,
October 31, 1979.

"The profound difference between American movies up through the early
Sixties and American movies since then," he observed in his memoir *Back
There Where the Past Was: A Small-Town Boyhood*, "is that they formerly spoke
with one voice and now they speak in many voices: cynical, sentimental, fantastic, realistic, existential, traditional, arch-conservative, arch-liberal, patri-
otic, nihilistic. It is certainly healthier, with no single authoritarian voice
predominating, but it can be confusing."

Champlin is a founder of the Los Angeles Film Critics Association and
has written many books, including *George Lucas: The Creative Impulse—
Lucasfilm's First Twenty Years; Hollywood's Revolutionary Decade;* and *A Life
in Writing: The Story of an American Journalist.* In 1999 he lost his eyesight
and wrote *My Friend, You are Legally Blind: A Writer's Struggle with Macular
Degeneration.*

CHARLES CHAMPLIN

———

February 18, 1976*

Any relationship a filmmaker has with a critic is apt to be conducted gingerly, depending on what he said about your last film. If he panned it, you think he's an idiot completely bereft of any taste or integrity. If he spoke well of it, you think he is a man of remarkable perception and one of the most cogent observers of the current film scene. I think one of the great characteristics Mr. Champlin has as a critic is a balance and moderation in what he says. I have disagreed with him and I have agreed with him, but I have never felt that he wrote with less than discernment and intelligence. Perhaps what's most important of all is that he cares very much about film.

Thank you. Something else about being a film critic, perhaps here in this town more than anywhere else, where you are in the presence of the filmmakers and the performers and the writers and the directors, is that there is really so little dialogue on film with the critic, and one of the things that has pleased me about my acquaintance with Chuck Heston, which now goes back many years, is that he is secure enough—and I think that's what it amounts to—to argue. We've had a marvelous exchange of letters, which goes back almost ten years. I just wish there were more people in this town who would take me or any other critic to task and point out, not that we are congenital idiots, but that there is another way to look at the film in question. I have never claimed infallibility, only honesty.

I've always felt that it's not fair to argue with a critic about his opinion of your work, because obviously one is prejudiced about one's own work, and one's opin-

*Charlton Heston moderated this seminar. The transcript also contains segments from a seminar Charles Champlin gave at the American Film Institute on October 31, 1979.

ion could surely be described as less than totally objective. I'm happy to say you've given me some good notices but you've given me some bad ones too, and I've never come back at you on those. I think there should be a ground rule that a critic should be protected from somebody coming up and beating at him because he didn't like what they wrote.

I can think of times when that wouldn't be too bad an idea. I think there's a kind of etiquette around town that you don't say anything to critics one way or the other. If he praises you, you don't acknowledge that. If he savages you, you don't acknowledge that, either. I suppose there's a certain kind of self-preservation involved, the feeling that you're going to come up against the critic again and maybe he'll take umbrage at the challenge.

Tell us how you became a film critic.

I come from a small town in upstate New York. It's a resort town, in the sense that people would resort to almost anything to get away from it. That's a tired joke. Actually it's a very pleasant little town where they make champagne. My family had been in the wine business and I discovered quite early that wasn't for me. I always wanted to be a writer, going back to about the time I discovered I could play neither cornet nor shortstop. I didn't necessarily want to be a film critic. Interestingly enough, a lot of the people who are into film—the French critics who became filmmakers and Bogdanovich and some of the people around here—either saw film writing and criticism as the entrée to or the next-to-last step before becoming filmmakers. I thought of writing in a more general way, although I was turned on to movies early at the Park Theater in Hammondsport, now long gone. It had about seventy splintery seats and a kind of Ichabod Crane of a projectionist named Frankie Walters. The films we got in Hammondsport had been spliced so many times that I was really at an advanced age before I knew you could get through a whole feature without the film breaking at least once. We used to sit there in a small un-air-conditioned theater listening to Frankie up in the booth, screaming and throwing film cans around because of the condition of the prints. When I was about eight he let me open the curtain, which was my introduction to show business. I never saw any Metro films, because under the block booking situation at the time you couldn't get MGM films in Hammondsport, so I had to ride a bike about eight miles to the next town where they did show Metro films.

I went to high school in upstate New York and then went to Harvard, where I majored in English. I started college before the war and went back and finished up afterwards. Then I went to work as a trainee at *Life,* sorting pictures for about six months, and then was a *Life* correspondent in Chicago and Denver. I went back to New York and wrote about politics and other disasters from 1954 to 1959. I did political-convention stories in 1956, general assignment writing and reporting, but nothing yet in the arts. I decided I just couldn't take living in New York, so I asked the magazine to send me out here. I arrived in 1959, and then as always Hollywood was in a crisis. Fox was teetering on the edge of bankruptcy and I think they had a skeleton staff of about a hundred and fifty running the studio. There was a strike and everything was shut down in late 1959 and early 1960.

I did long interviews while I was here with Aldous Huxley and Christopher Isherwood, and I think the editors of *Time* decided that maybe I could talk to English people, so I was sent to the London bureau and covered all the arts over there from 1962 to 1965, a wonderful time to be in England. I did stories on Julie Christie, Tom Courtenay, John Schlesinger, Tony Richardson and David Lean, who was just finishing up *Lawrence of Arabia.* I met Peter O'Toole just as he came back from all those months on a camel. He was on his way down to Kent to a place that specialized in high colonics, to try to get his insides back in shape. There was a lot going on. David Hockney was beginning to emerge as a painter, and there were five symphony orchestras.

It was while I was in London in 1965 that Otis Chandler had begun to make changes at the *Los Angeles Times.* Those of you who are from Los Angeles will remember how different the *Times* has become since 1960. It was always fat and gray and prosperous, but until Otis Chandler became publisher it resembled the right wing of the Republican Party. There's a wonderful story about Los Angeles television that I think is also true of the *Times* in those days. The typical story would say, "Last night on Mount Sinai Moses handed down the Ten Commandments. The three of particular interest to the West are . . ." The *Times* was fairly provincial until Otis opened foreign bureaus. But they never even had an entertainment editor. I had lived here and was known a little bit, so they took me on as entertainment editor. For the first couple of years I was not reviewing films, I was just writing a column a few times a week.

I didn't have a particular desire to be a film critic and at one point even asked Arthur Knight if he would become the critic of the newspaper. He was working for the *Saturday Review* and teaching at USC and just didn't feel he wanted to make that change. It suddenly occurred to me that I had perhaps, without consciously realizing it, been spending a lot of time getting ready to become a film critic. I'd been doing a lot of general-assignment reporting dealing with the real world. I'd been working professionally as a writer for about twenty years and had been increasingly involved with the film process, so it seemed to me that maybe I should just have a go at it. It's curious because there's no body of dogma that tells you how to become a film critic, though there are collections of writing that are probably the only things worth reading by way of getting into film criticism. I took off on a sort of unescorted trip to try to figure out how you went about being a film critic for a daily newspaper, which I think is a little bit different from being a critic for a weekly or a monthly magazine, or for a trade paper.

The policy of the *Los Angeles Times* is to review everything that opens for business. The exceptions are the lecture films and a few of the hardcore films, about which there isn't really a lot you can say. But everything else we review, so you can imagine what the process involves. You're doing a Disney film one day and *Seven Beauties* the next, and then something with John Wayne and then *Jaws*. The point is that sheer personal choice or preference obviously would not get you very far. "I like" or "I don't like" will not suffice, because you're going to have to be able to report with some kind of fairness and discernment about films which you obviously do not pay to see. I don't know anybody whose taste or gluttonous appetite for films can embrace at a "like" or "don't like" level the whole range of films that a reviewer is called upon to see. You have to have some mechanism that allows you to be fair to a wide range of films, some of which you might not dislike but that are not really your cup of tea. It seems to me that this is a very important critical quality of the film reviewer. I suppose what sets the critic apart from the audience that's going to lay down the four bucks for an evening is that the critic is bound to ask what the intentions of the creative forces behind the film were, and what kind of audience the movie seems to have been made for. I think that the measure of a poor critic, and the fault you often find in young critics particularly, is an arrogant attitude that if they don't like it, that's it. Well, that's not really enough. I think that the measure of a good critic is how well he can justify his position in terms of citing the evidence in favor of a film or the evidence that seems to weaken it. Even if I make clear at the start of a review that I think a film doesn't work, I try to give the reader some sense of what the experience of watching that film will be so that he can decide whether to go see the film himself and then place his judgment against the critic's.

There was nothing in film going on at college when I was there. I tried to catch up with everything but confess that when I hosted a show on public television and introduced *Potemkin* and *M* and all those classic films, I was seeing the majority of them for the first time. You're going to have a new generation of film critics that will have come out of the universities, possibly out of graduate studies. I have certain apprehensions about that, because having squeezed the vital juices out of Shakespeare, the academics might also be able to do it to film. I don't think film can be defeated by academia, but I'm just not sure. Whatever else is true, people in college now, whether film majors or not, have the option almost everywhere to take film history and analysis courses. They can see *Birth of a Nation* and *Potemkin* and get some sense of the film past.

In general the way I think you proceed as a critic is simply to try, first of all, to accurately isolate the intentions of the film. Whether you like the film or not, you've got to try to figure out what that the filmmaker seemed to be trying to do, because you're going to have to try to state those intentions. That's part of your obligation to the creative side of the audience. Once you've discerned the intentions of the film, you've got some sort of a measure on it, because all intentions are not created equal, and whatever it was that Bergman was trying to do in *Scenes from a Marriage* and *Cries and Whispers* was obviously different from the intentions of, say, *Jaws*. I'm not going to say that the intentions behind one film are necessarily less honorable than those behind another, but the levels of intention are many and varied. So then the question is: how well have those intentions been brought off?

It's there that you get into all the elements that go into filmmaking. It seems to me that, particularly over the last decade, when the possibilities of film have really opened up, there is virtually nothing that motion pictures cannot show or deal with. The spectrum of film is so much wider now than it used to be. Under the Hays Code, and until the dawn of television, all movies were in effect G-rated and aimed, theoretically at least, at the whole family. Some were less appropriate for children, but theoretically there was nothing in a movie that was threatening to the least sophisticated or the youngest member of the audience. Now that old monolithic mass audience no longer exists, so the film critic is placed in a rather different position in society. It seems to me that more and more he's under a heavy obligation to describe as sympathetically and as openly as he can the experience of that film. There are all kinds of audiences out there now, and part of the critic's function is to introduce the film to the audience that may want to see it. I'm not suggesting that his powers of judgment have been diminished or are less important, but I do think the critic has to be of service to the audience in a lot of different ways.

I've often cited *Sunday Bloody Sunday* as an example. The critics described that film as being about a ménage à trois, a bisexual one, in contemporary London. Once you have said that about the film, a certain part of the readership says, "No way. Thank you very much. I wouldn't go near that film for any amount of money." Fair enough. Another part of the readership, for various reasons of clinical interest, personal identification or whatever, says, "I don't care whether it's good or bad. I'm going to go see that film." Fair enough. Then maybe there is some part of the readership that feels the critic has some credibility, and if you say that film is a classic, a masterpiece, the greatest film since last week, maybe those people will want to go see it. These people have no opinions one way or another about the material, but if it's described to them as a superior piece of filmmaking, they'll go see it. What's important is that you've served different segments of the readership with the same piece of copy. The audience that now exists for motion pictures is probably more attuned to the critics than film audiences have ever been. I think that's just the nature of the demographic shift of the audience that still goes to movies. The famous postwar baby boom has come of age, and they are well-educated people. It means that the critic no longer finds himself in the position that the critics of forty years ago were in. When James Agee and Dwight Macdonald were writing thoughtful criticism, they were fighting upstream against a torrent of mass taste and perhaps felt very lonely. But today you have a different movie audience out there, and I think you find that a lot of the films that do very well at the box office will also have done well in top-ten lists across the country. I don't think that means the critics have sold out to popular taste. Rather, I think that popular tastes and critical tastes are far closer together than many people think. The critics haven't gone soft; it's because the audience is very different from that automatic-habit-formed audience of the past. Today's audiences want something more than they get on television.

Of course we're all fallible, and there were those of us who didn't like *Jaws* and so on, but I think that an audience really pays heed to the critics. Again, it may not be whether the critic likes or dislikes the film but the way the critic sets up and describes the film. The critic—or reviewer, if you prefer a less pretentious term, I don't have any preference—has a kind of double responsibility. On the one hand he's responsible to the creative community. He really does have an obligation to the people who make films. On the other hand, his primary responsibility is to his readership. Conflicting obligations? Not at all. I think you fulfill your obligation to the creative community by trying to understand and state, as sympathetically as you can, what the intentions of the film were. I remember after a review I did of a film called *Secret Ceremony* several years ago, which I didn't think was successful, I received a note from Joseph Losey, the director, who I'd had occasion to interview when I lived in London. He wrote to me and explained some of the problems he'd had with the film, including interference on the financial side. I don't think he felt the film was as unsuccessful as I thought it was, but he said, "At least you tried to see it as a movie and not as a crime against civilization." That is a phrase that has stuck with me.

Do you find yourself taking more pains with important films than with Walt Disney films?

In all candor I would have to say yes. I think you go to see some films with a greater degree of expectation than you do others. You go to see a Disney film and you know pretty much what you're going to get. Disney films are hard to review, because by now they can only be compared to each other. Every critic has some kind of private Walt Disney spectrum. "It's better than *The Gnome-Mobile* but not quite up to *The Parent Trap*." I think there's an irony in your question, because the more a film aspires to do, perhaps the more severe the test that the critic puts to it. Such a film invites being taken as seriously as you can, so the complaints you would bring to *Cries and Whispers* will be things you might forgive any ordinary picture for. About those films you say, "Who cares? It's a formulaic picture." One really is as thoughtful about films as they demand.

One of the hardest parts of your job is reviewing the work of a filmmaker you consider to be just terrible, yet somehow you have to separate the film from the fact that you don't personally march to his or her drum.

I think every reviewer ought to put these words over his desk: "There is a bad film in every good filmmaker and a good film in every bad filmmaker." The world is really full of surprises, and as much as you might admire *A Woman Under the Influence*, you will then confront *The Killing* *of a Chinese Bookie.** As much as you might admire *The Four Hundred Blows* and *Bed and Board* and *Day for Night*, you then come up against *The Story of Adèle H.*,† which I find to be a piece of cotton candy, a very disappointing film from Truffaut. There are others who feel differently. There are people you come to recognize as competent craftsmen, who bring their films in on budget without any particular personal signature except a kind of nice, well-lit competence, but given an interesting piece of material can rise to it and come away with a film which is interesting and has a kind of roundness that maybe some of the other work didn't have. I can think of people whose work I've gone to see without any real expectations and have been really delighted to find that because of a kind of maverick script, they've produced a maverick film.

In a larger sense what worries me about being a critic is the danger of getting closed off, getting too professional, seeing too many films, running the risk of losing a certain kind of openness to a film which is not what you expect, which violates some of the canons of filmmaking, and being so rushed or tired or jaded that you don't see it. That really is scary. I remember when I worked in London there was a young art critic for the London *Times*. He was then thirty-four years old. It was a time of ferment, and the people who were coming out of the Royal Academy were really full of vital juices. He resigned his job because he said that he was no longer absolutely sure he understood what the artists who were ten years younger than him were doing. Of course they replaced him with a guy who was fifty, so his honorable gesture came to nothing.

I don't know how long a critic should review films. You can read some reviews and say, "Well, maybe they've seen too many films." I think Bosley Crowther‡ today has a diminished reputation. It's too bad, because he did great and noble service for many years when there weren't a lot of people writing about foreign films. He was very sympathetic to these strange, harsh and abrasive films, but then when *Bonnie and Clyde* arrived he not only didn't like it the first time, he kept going back to it and still didn't like it. He was unceremoniously eased off *The New York Times*. He was, as somebody said, Bonnie and Clyde's last victim. Maybe the point was that he was by then a little too sure of what he thought movies ought to be and do. I may have to be reminded of that condition in myself later on, but I hope not for a while yet. I think it's just a problem of being

---

*Both films were directed by John Cassavetes.
†Three films directed by François Truffaut.
‡Bosley Crowther (1905–1981), longtime film reviewer for *The New York Times*.

open, of not being certain that a particular director is going to always make good films or that there's no hope in somebody else. When the critic's transcendent love of the medium begins to erode, as it sometimes can in the continuing presence of mediocrity, then it's time for the critic to worry. Maybe he should shift his ground a bit and go into landscape gardening. Some people have been in the chair too long and are unable to be uplifted by anything. I look at my tongue in the mirror every morning just to see if there are any telltale signs of fatigue.

Do you feel that critics should ever address themselves to how worthwhile a director's intention is?

A critic has the right to be angry sometimes. I think it's more than permissible for a critic to be angry about the intentions of *Death Wish,* for example, which is the liveliest example I can think of at the moment. I think it's right to be baffled as to what the intentions of Cassavetes' *Chinese Bookie* are. I think what you see a lot of in film criticism—and you read it perhaps even more in book reviews—is really abuse of the creator for not doing what he obviously never had any intention of doing. You can't condemn Walt Disney for not making Jean-Luc Godard films. I think the critic also has the responsibility to step back occasionally and see whether Hollywood films in general are doing everything they should, or whether there are certain kinds of films that are having trouble getting financed, and point out that there is danger in the assumption that you can buy a hit simply through the lavish expenditure of money. There's a danger of jumping on bandwagons that turn out to have lost their wheels.

How do you feel when you give a film a bad review?

I find that the longer I review, the more hesitant I am in the matter of assigning credit and blame, because the more you know about the filmmaking process, the more you realize that it's a collaborative medium. For example, it's an easy critical shorthand to credit the actor with everything the actor does. A lot of people think that Robert Montgomery invented all those wonderfully urbane lines he used to say in those comedies of the thirties. But you quickly realize that there are a lot of people involved in a performance: the actor, the writer, the director, the editor, and maybe the casting, which goes back to the producer. I'm less concerned about praise that's handed out erroneously than I am about blame that's handed out inaccurately. You have to be as precise as you can. Sometimes you see an actor in a number of performances for a number of directors and you have no problem in ascertaining that he or she is a very good actor and a strong personality. Maybe with newcomers you might think it was the skill of a sympathetic director who helped evoke that particular sensitivity out of the performer. One just doesn't know. As I read criticism, I would have to say that the actor gets all kinds of credit that he may or may not deserve. I think it's one of the few consolations for the slings and arrows that actors come up against.

I think by and large actors are treated sympathetically in films. An actor is seldom singled out as a target as the director can be. One thinks of Pauline Kael and the arrogance of her convictions. She fails to recognize how little she knows about how films are made, and the degree to which filmmaking is a collaborative process.

I would say that of the critics working in this country, Pauline is highly idiosyncratic, but I do find that more often than anyone else she will look at a film in a way I find interesting. Whether I agree with it or not, it seems to me that her approach to that particular film is interesting and challenging. When she did a piece in *The New Yorker* talking against the studio system, about which I think a great many negative things can be said, I did feel that she wasn't in touch with that system as it really operates. She chose as her example the way that Warner Bros. had handled *Mean Streets* for Martin Scorsese. Her argument was that they had abandoned this marvelous film which otherwise would have presumably become a big hit. Well, I admire *Mean Streets,* and my own impression is that Warners tried very hard to market a film which is really extremely hard to watch. It's a very demanding film that I think really never had any real prospect of finding a mass audience. I think it will be seen in revival houses for as long as anybody watches anything, but the hope of it being a mass-audience picture was doomed from the beginning. You can't accuse Warner Bros. of failing to market a film that is not susceptible to marketing. Obviously there are some films that you can't keep audiences away from. Whatever you think about *Jaws,* you look at it and know it's going to make a fortune, just as you know that a film like *Badlands,* which is an austere and immaculately made film, is never going to find a mass audience.

If you don't make a film that will draw enough people to pay for the cost of making it, they won't let you make more than one or two more.

The critic is theoretically concerned only with the merits of a film, or lack of them. Knowing how much a film cost doesn't affect your aesthetic judgment, but unless he's insane, a critic cannot help but be aware of the economics of the industry. When you think of all the commercially viable and interesting films that could have been made for a fraction of what some Hollywood films cost, I think it's almost impossible not to be appalled by the conspicuous waste represented by some films. When the big films fail, they simply absorb all the risk capital that could have gone into any number of much more personal films. I've been really depressed lately about the industry, because I think too many studio executives lack real confidence and judgment.

Have you any opinion as to why fewer and fewer films make money?

I think it relates to the condition of the world. For a time, when the movies had this new freedom, they began to get into hard-edged things and social realism, exploiting the new freedom of the screen in a positive way rather than a negative way. But as Vietnam wore on, as the economy continued to fall apart, there was this continual erosion of confidence in the processes of government. I think people found it harder and harder to go out and experience yet more psychic pain in the movie theaters, this despondent view of the human condition. You might ask, "How can you explain disaster films? Aren't they a kind of psychic pain?" I think not. I have a theory about why they have succeeded. I think people turned back to the movies, as they always have done, for escape or diversion from all of the really pressing, urgent problems we find in society. Films like *Earthquake* and *The Towering Inferno* are a dramatic demonstration of pain and suffering, but also certain positive human values, like heroism and self-sacrifice. Audiences came away with a certain kind of reassurance from those films. One of the dangers that exists in a studio, particularly where you have a succession of managers who are not essentially creators but who are agents and lawyers and comptrollers, is that they really don't know how to analyze films except on balance sheets. I think they're often inexact in pulling out the reasons for the success of a film.

Many avid moviegoers I know say they have stopped reading reviews before they go to films because they're synopsized so thoroughly that you know the outcome of the film before you go. How much of a synopsis do you think you need to include in a review?

Any critic who points out that the butler did it should be hung by the thumbs. It becomes a terrible problem sometimes, because to comment meaningfully on the film you've almost got to say where it ends up, and you don't want to do that. I don't know any critic who is eager to give away too much of the movie. I find myself writing reviews which are oblique enough so that people, having seen the film, can come back to the review and understand it better, because they'll understand what I was alluding to. It's a tough problem not to write a review that says, "This is what happens from start to finish." I've written a review for *Taxi Driver,* the new Scorsese film. I don't know how many of you have seen it, but it's about the making of a psychotic killer and is a brilliantly made film. At the end is this bloodbath, and then suddenly a coda. The audience had reason to believe that he's been killed when he hasn't been, and in fact is now sort of an ironic hero. He's back driving his taxi and seems to be purged and happy. It's part of this mischievous notion that violence is good for you, which is popular among a certain generation of young film writers and which I felt I had to deal with in my review. You don't find out from me who gets killed or what the circumstances are, but I think it's impossible to deal with that film philosophically without writing about this coda. I really think it has to be talked about in terms of its attitude toward violence.

Do you find there are general places where filmmakers seem to fail in their intentions?

I would say inadequacies of the script compromise the intentions of the film more often than any other single thing. Perhaps it's also the casting, when the wrong person is hired for whatever reasons. I do think that very personal and private films often seem to be made almost as confessional acts, like diaries meant to be locked away from prying human eyes. Such self-indulgent films never achieve universality or touch other people's experiences. I think a film should have some larger relevance.

Do you walk into every movie hoping to be entertained?

I walk in as open as I can be. I don't read the production notes ahead of time. This is a town where there are constantly rumors about movies. You hear that the editor of this film tried to kill himself by jumping off his stool, or they couldn't work out how to put that film together. As a critic you try not to hear those kinds of things. You watch with a bifurcated mind, in which you're letting it happen to you. If it's going to move you, it moves you. But on the other hand you're analyzing the film and thinking about the process and seeing if it works, and if it doesn't work, then why doesn't it work? I don't think you can look at film without being aware of craft. You're aware of editing, of cinematography, and camera angles and movement. By the time the film is over you have a fair idea of what you think about it.

The only times I see films either by myself or with a very small group are independent or foreign films. Oftentimes the print doesn't come in until just before they open and you've got to have a quick screening someplace. I happen not to think that it makes any difference whether you see a film by yourself or with an audience. If it's a comedy, obviously I'd much rather see it with an audience, because laughter is infectious. But generally I don't think it makes any difference. I remember seeing *Man of La Mancha* at the first press screening with probably two thousand people. It was just a disaster, really painful. Peter O'Toole finished singing "The Impossible Dream" and there was this echoing silence because the soundtrack had been designed to allow for applause. On the other hand, the screening of *The Odd Couple* was one of the most pleasurable I've been to. I started making little marks clocking the laughs, and I got up to more than two hundred individual laughs. It was just a wonderful experience to be there. I remember the first screening at the Directors Guild of *Bonnie and Clyde.* It was absolutely electric. You knew you were in the presence of a very special film.

Do you feel that your lack of knowledge of film history hinders you as a critic?

I don't come out of that film history background, but on the other hand I've been around as a journalist looking at the world a lot, and I find that very helpful. When it comes to films where critical judgments matter, I'm content-oriented, not form-oriented. For example, when it comes to a film like *Carnal Knowledge,* you've got to talk about what Jules Feiffer and Mike Nichols seemed to be saying. You've got to say, "Does their indictment of the relationships between men and women in middle-class America hold up?" A critic has to identify it as an indictment. This film is very much about something. It has a point of view toward a slice of history. Of course the performances are good, but it's more important to talk about the sexual mores that the film addresses. Film history doesn't offer you an awful lot of clues, except to say that Howard Hawks once told it another way.

On the other hand, the critic has several functions, and one of them is to know the kind of vocabulary films had in the past so I can understand whether a new film is simply a re-enactment of something that's been done a million times before, or whether it really is moving into new ground. It's my feeling that of all the major art forms, film is the one that hasn't yet found out where it's going. Its boundaries are still open. When I think about art, it seems to me to be folding back in on itself. Sculpture or painting, for example, are perhaps finding new materials to work with, but there are no new explosions. Music, particularly classical music, seems to have folded in on itself. I remember going to a John Cage concert in which a necklace was dropped into an amplified tin can. To me that represented a certain kind of sterility in music. But movies are still finding new things to do. Look at *Cries and Whispers*. Maybe there aren't any new places for film to go in terms of spectacle, but in terms of their internalizing of the human condition and states of consciousness, there are lots of places for the movies yet to go.

Have you ever thought it would be necessary to try to make your own film, in order to understand more of the filmmaking process?

While a number of filmmakers have used criticism as a station toward becoming filmmakers, I don't think it's necessary. I think the critic is basically a writer, not a filmmaker or a musician or anything else. The man who's going to review serious music certainly has to be a musicologist, but he doesn't necessarily have to be a pianist or a cellist. If he's a bad writer and a good cellist, I don't think he's going to be a good critic. James Agee, of course, did both. I think Agee, given his druthers, would probably have given his whole life to writing movies, but in his particular time and place it didn't seem to work out for him. He had to earn a living and the living presented itself as reviewing movies for *Time,* although he certainly had enough feeling for the form to be able to write movies, and his scripts include *The African Queen.*

Your word as a critic can have a tremendous impact in terms of pure dollars. I wonder if you have ever felt compromised?

Obviously everybody hopes that you're in great comfort as you watch a movie. One rather dashing producer called me up for one of his films and said, "The press screening is on such-and-such a night, but if that's not convenient for you, Chuck, let me know. We will screen it in your bedroom if it would be more convenient for you." You get that kind of offer of creature comfort. But I know that ultimately I'm going to say what I think about that film.

How would you characterize your own private taste in films, rather than your professional taste?

Ultimately film reviewing, like all other forms of writing, is extremely autobiographical. We try to create the impression that we have Plato whispering in one ear and Aristotle prompting us in the other, with Demosthenes waiting for us in the lobby. Of course it's not true. Everything a good critic writes is personal. But if you set out in the first instance to try and describe to yourself and to the reader whatever it is you think the creator set out to do, you're well on your way. Presumably I reveal a great deal about myself every time I write a review. I suppose we're all captives of where we've been. Small-town Middle America, I guess. Failed Catholic by origin, I get accused occasionally of being somewhat of a moralist. I certainly define myself as a humanist. I hope I don't come at films dogmatically, but I am certainly more taken with films that speak to and are aware of the human condition, even though the story and characters might depart from such an awareness. On the other hand I'm certainly not a devotee of the happy ending, and what I like about the best films in recent times is their openness. Over the last twenty-five years films have lost the automatic audience they had for so long. But having lost that steady audience, a marvelous historical irony is that they have come of age as a medium. Today they have complete freedom of expression, and perhaps this happened when the mass audience moved over to television. People always say, "Why don't they make films the way they used to?" Well, you couldn't, because they don't make the world the way they used to. We cherish films of the thirties and forties because they take us back into a simpler world. But I don't think you can retrieve that world today. You can see *Casablanca* and weep, yet I can't imagine making an equivalent of that film today.

Do you ever read the scripts of the films you review?

Never. It can be dangerous. Occasionally I'm curious and read them afterwards. People are always trying to get me to read scripts of films that they're trying to peddle, but I find it important not to comment on them because a script is really only a blueprint.

What it comes down to, I think, is that the critic either has credibility or doesn't. That doesn't happen after any one review. Over a period of time, anyone who reads a particular critic finds that he is reliable or not. People come up to me and say, "If you tell me I'm going to like a film, I know I'll like it, because you haven't been wrong so far." While a reviewer might work from models—Pauline Kael, James Agee, Otis Ferguson, Vernon Young—each critic finally comes to understand his or her job through a process of trial and error, guided by one's own sensibilities and approach to thinking about movies. Everyone has to discover it for themselves. When people ask me how to become a critic, I say, "You have to write first and foremost, because the critic is first, last and always a writer. Then you have to know something about the medium, and love it too."

There seem to be so many critics in an adversarial relationship to what they see on the screen. People say to me, "You're very kind to films." Well, I don't feel in an adversarial relationship to films. Every critic goes to every film not as an adversary, and hopefully not as a pessimist, but as an optimist. What keeps me going is that constant hope of resurrection. You have to hope that the next one you see is the one that's going to knock you into the aisle and make you come alive and restore your faith in the medium, because otherwise you say, "What the hell am I doing with my life?"

Books by Charles Champlin

1982 *The Movies Grow Up: 1940–1980*

1992 *George Lucas: The Creative Impulse—Lucasfilm's First Twenty Years*

1995 *John Frankenheimer: A Conversation with Charles Champlin*

1998 *Hollywood's Revolutionary Decade—Charles Champlin Reviews the Movies of the 1970s*

1999 *Back There Where the Past Was: A Small-Town Boyhood*

2001 *My Friend, You Are Legally Blind—A Writer's Struggle With Macular Degeneration*

2006 *A Life in Writing: The Story of an American Journalist*

The fact is that "experimental" is often used as a bad word. It doesn't have any real meaning except to differentiate experimental filmmakers from other filmmakers. Basically it means that Shirley Clarke is not a Hollywood filmmaker.

SHIRLEY CLARKE
(Born in New York City, 1919—Died 1997)

Shirley Clarke was a contentious pioneer of independent filmmaking who once proclaimed, "I have an enormous need to find a barricade to die on." Her visit to AFI in 1975 demonstrated the conservatory's commitment to expose its fellows to a wide spectrum of cinematic creativity.

Clarke was a rare breed in the fifties and sixties, a woman making her way through the challenging territory of directing and producing feature films with controversial subjects, and finding ways to get those films before an audience. Her first feature, *The Connection,* based on Jack Gelber's Off-Broadway play, filmed in black and white, partly in her kitchen, and released in 1962, portrayed a group of heroin-addicted jazz musicians living the beat culture of the period. Its earthy language caused it to be banned in New York, where it became a test case of censorship issues. Two years later she shot *The Cool World* in Harlem on a shoestring budget, and then shocked audiences with *Portrait of Jason,* a full-length documentary about a gay black alcoholic hustler whom she described as both a genius and a bore.

"Clarke was quick, domineering, short-tempered but with a sense of humor," wrote Andrew Gurian, a protégé and videographer. "She could spend several days behind her closed door, sulking and speaking to no one, or she could behave like a cannonball and flatten everything in her path." Yet this street-smart woman was raised on Park Avenue, the daughter of a wealthy manufacturer. She attended seven different colleges without graduating. Her far-flung educational journey may have stemmed from the fact that her father was tough on his two daughters. Shirley's sister, the novelist Elaine Dundy, said that coming home from school was like returning to prison.

Her father objected when Shirley pursued a career as a dancer with Martha Graham. She presented her first work as a choreographer at seventeen

Shirley Clarke speaks to the AFI fellows
at Greystone, January 8, 1975.

and became president of the National Dance Association at twenty-one. She acquired a Bolex camera as a wedding gift and began exploring the intersection of dance and film, and before long was committed to filmmaking. She first achieved success in 1960 collaborating with Willard Van Dyke on *Skyscraper,* a portrait of New York City centered on the construction of 666 Fifth Avenue. The twenty-minute film was nominated for an Academy Award and won prizes at Venice and Edinburgh.

In 1961 she signed the manifesto "Statement for a New American Cinema," and in 1962 co-founded with curator and filmmaker Jonas Mekas the Film-Makers' Cooperative and the Film-Makers' Distribution Center. Both were designed to provide a rallying point for the growing number of New York filmmakers who were grappling with the challenges of producing and distributing their work. Clarke confronted what she considered serious discrimination against women artists. "I happen to have chosen a field where I have to be out there, to be in charge of vast amounts of money, equipment and people—and that is not particularly a woman's role in our society." Roger Corman saw *The Cool World* and tried to hire her for one of his low-budget productions. "What Roger wanted was for me to be twenty-two years old and shoot his script, each scene in wide, medium and close-up so that later he could edit it," Shirley remembered. "For me to make a cheapie film I didn't respect with a script I didn't like, without the right to at least do it the way I want—for God's sakes that's insane."

Clarke lived for many years in New York's legendary Chelsea Hotel, where she filmed many of her projects and held court, maintaining a bohemian salon with notable figures such as Andy Warhol, Agnès Varda, Susan Sontag and Arthur C. Clarke. For all her gritty combativeness, she remained stylish and elegant, with a cigarette between her lips and carefully chosen outfits showing off her dancer's body.

In 1975, frustrated by her inability to find financing for her projects, Clarke moved to California and became a professor of film and video at UCLA, where she continued to champion the idea of independent film until 1983.

The Cool World was screened before Clarke's seminar. She combined professional actors and kids from Harlem's street gangs to make the fictional story look like stark reality. It was Frederick Wiseman's first credit as a producer and featured a jazz score by Dizzy Gillespie and Yusef Lateef, with a cameo appearance by Gillespie.

SHIRLEY CLARKE

January 8, 1975*

How did you conceive the idea for The Cool World?

After I had done *The Connection* it was a marvelous period for me. It hadn't yet opened because we were trying to get the word "shit" into the film and so were involved in a court case. But I was still sort of hot stuff, and one of the men who had put up about $3,000 for *The Connection* was a lawyer who wanted to make films. He came to me saying he could raise some money and asked if there was something I wanted to do. I had read Warren Miller's novel *The Cool World* but hadn't seen the play, which hadn't gone over all that well. One of the things that attracted me to the story was that it took place in Harlem, so this would be an opportunity to make a film there. *The Connection* had been done on a set and I felt there were certain aesthetic problems with that because although it purported to be real, it really wasn't. It was a made-up pad. So working on *The Cool World* there was real excitement and the possibility of working like the neorealists in Italy. Every once in a while Carl Lee—who co-wrote the script—and I had seen shots in Hollywood films that had been made for real on New York streets and they were always so alive and exciting. So here was a chance to go in and to do something that hadn't really been tried in the United States, which was to shoot a 35mm film feature on a real location.

We thought the subject was not only relevant but extraordinarily timely and very important. It was released in December 1963 and the first of the riots began about two or three months after that. We thought we

*James Powers moderated this seminar.

could alert people that there was a situation going on right under their noses that they were choosing to ignore. They could drive past Harlem in their cars and choose not to see it. Harlem didn't exist. All the Harlems of the world didn't exist. We wanted to say that, quite to the contrary, they not only existed but were tinderboxes getting ready to explode. When the film played at the Venice Festival in 1963 a lot of the early reviews claimed that the film was dishonest, that it was not the truth, that it was a fantasy made up by somebody named Shirley Clarke. Of course that wasn't true. The script was based on the novel and was translated to film by myself and Carl Lee, who is a black actor who had grown up in Harlem. I never would have attempted to make the film had I not been able to work with Carl. There would have been no way of my knowing whether Warren Miller was right or whether what I was seeing on the street was right or whether I was being put on or not.

Carl spent four months getting involved with the actual street gangs and casting the kids. We went to the schools and they would always bring forward these bright young kids. We'd get them to read the script and it was just disastrous. But when we got the actual gang kids it didn't matter whether they could read or not because we would do improvisational things with them that were similar to things in the film, and suddenly the script came back to us the way we had written it. We realized that we should just stay with the kids and let them lead us. The story had a plot that we had to follow and there were certain things in each scene that the actors had to accomplish and there were lines that had to be learned, but they had permission to say whatever they wanted and change anything they felt didn't sit right. What usually happened, though, was that they found security in the original script. In the editing I cut out an awful lot of extra "mans." They couldn't say anything without the word "man" on the end of it. There's a great line in the film where one kid says, "You're a great man, man." It's great but it's ridiculous.

All the street scenes were shot by a black cameraman named Leroy McLucas, who is now a director. I knew an all-white crew couldn't go up to Harlem and get away with shooting on the streets. We based the style of the film on the way the documentary footage was going to look. In other words, I gave Leroy lists of shots I wanted. I would say, "Okay, I want lonely dogs early in the morning in the Harlem streets," or "I want little children playing dangerously near the curb with cars too near them. Swish pan onto something, stay with it, and then swish off so that later I can cut at any point during the shot and also be able to change the sequences around." Leroy went out with all these endless lists and, of course, shot more than my list. He has a fantastic eye. Baird Bryant was the cameraman for all the dialogue scenes, the interiors and the exteriors. We wanted to match the quality and look of what had been done on the street, so we used the same kind of film stock and exposure that Leroy had used for the other scenes. Practically the entire film was 35mm hand-held.

Then there are certain action scenes that were filmed on the streets where we had to go with our mostly white crew. At that time there weren't all that many black people interested in being behind the camera. They all wanted to be actors in front of the camera. Many of the black people who were on the crew are actually now working as directors and sound people, some of them out here in Hollywood. So we had this motley mixed crew. There were a number of scenes where someone would come down the street and say, "What's that white bitch doing exploiting you?" The minute anything happened the police would of course walk away from us. It was the cast that literally saved the situation each time. They would turn to the people and say, "Look, we're working. This is what we want to do, so cool it." My assistant spent a great deal of the time alerting the people to what we were doing, telling them what the film was about. Even so, there had been some bad advance publicity that a film was going to be made that was going to exploit the Harlem kids, and there were a few times where we went running down the street with our cameras clutched to our breasts.

The most extraordinary and gratifying aspect was the kids, all forty of them, who were finally chosen to be in the film. You all know how tough it is to make films and how you spend most of the time sitting around waiting for the lights to get moved or something. The discipline of these kids was beyond anything I had ever seen in my life. Though we were told by everyone we talked to not to use them, that we wouldn't be able to handle them, it simply wasn't true. I think one reason was due to the work that Carl did. I remember one day—and this was way before the advent of theater games, empathy sessions and so forth—I saw him in this empty room running around with all the kids screaming, "I am me!" He was giving these kids not only a release of their energies but a sense of themselves. I remember hearing him say, "Look, guys, when this film comes out, you're gonna be able to walk down the street. Everybody's really gonna recognize you and be proud of what you've done!" They had an enormous sense of pride, and an even bigger sense of the twenty dollars a day they were being paid. An unfortunate thing that happened in most cases was that their parents took their money. When the kids were being cast we used to give them a dollar and a half for lunch and carfare to come down to Forty-second Street, but once they were in the film they were getting twenty dollars a day, only it was Mommy and Daddy who were actually getting the money, so every now and then we'd slip them a dollar or two.

How long did it take to shoot?

It was probably a six-month shooting period, though we shot for maybe thirty or forty days, which was still heavy. *The Connection* was shot in twelve days. Little did I realize or understand the difference between the set and a city and how much you could get accomplished in a single day. The ratio of footage on the dramatic scene was between four and five to one. I'd get hooked into wanting the camera to move slowly around someone, move down to someone sitting, then slowly pull out, move over to another guy and zoom in. There were times where we were doing eleven takes. It was driving me insane. For the scene when the kids are walking down the stairs talking, you wouldn't believe it but I insisted that we move the lights down from floor to floor. It never occurred to me just to paint over the background and keep the camera in the same place and not move the lights. I did some really batty things.

The main problems with the film, those things about it I don't like, are due to my inability at that time just to let go. I insisted that everyone breathe at the moment I wanted them to breathe, that every movement of the camera went exactly as I intended. In totally uncontrollable situations I wanted full control but also wanted it to look open and free as if it had just been picked up on the run. Some of the camera movement really bugs me because it's ever so artfully snaking around the place. Also we were working with a nonunion crew, and an awful lot of the people on the crew were friends, which isn't the easiest or most professional way to shoot a film. It was a small crew of only six people. People had to alternate because even that was too many people in some of the rooms we were filming in. With big crews it's hard for everybody to know what's going on in everyone else's head, and they do only the job they've been given. With big crews people don't get a chance to contribute what they might very well be able to contribute, because if they step out of that line, they mess up the whole orchestration of a forty-member crew. We never had that problem.

I agreed to start shooting without all the money, and a couple of months into the shoot there wasn't any money left and the weather was bad, so we spent a couple of months doing the interiors. The city gave us a couple of tenement houses they were about to tear down which we furnished and decorated. It took a year to edit the film. We started shooting in August 1962 and the film came out in December 1963.

But the beauty of it is that for those of us who don't know how it was shot, it feels like you're just walking around the room with those kids.

I think that's helped by the decision we made to take a subjective camera view. The whole film is from the point of view of one or another of the characters. The film was purposely shot in black and white, and is a little grubby, all to make you believe it's a newsreel. I got enormous flack about the sound. People said they couldn't understand the words. I kept telling them it wasn't a sound problem, but that they just weren't listening to the black kids' voices. Nobody seems to have any problem hearing it now. A great deal of the film was radio-miked, a certain amount of it is post-synched and the rest was picked up in a room without the acoustical advantages of even this room. It was shot in the middle of New York with all the interferences you get, which is partly what fools you into believing it's real, because we're used to hearing background sounds in newsreels. I even added airplanes to the soundtrack.

Was the music score written specifically for the piece?

What do you think?

I got the impression that it was.

Inch by inch, frame by frame. It was the most extraordinary job. I began as a dance filmmaker, and all my films, no matter what else they are, are very choreographed. I think film tends to be choreographic in its basic nature. In my dance films the music was specially written. If you have two cuts that don't match, let the sound carry over and it will fool the eye into thinking that the two shots go together. One of the best ways to get unity from disparate images is to make sure the soundtrack has a strong throughline. A lot of the sequences hold together because the music takes us from one shot to the next.

We were told that you were an experimental filmmaker. What does that mean?

It means I've experimented in learning how to make films. It's a funny word for which we don't have a real definition. For instance, if you refer to me as an independent filmmaker, out here that would be understood to mean a producer who produces independently for a major studio. If you come from New York or San Francisco and you make features, they are generally independently produced. If they're experimental that tends to mean they aren't showcases to get to Hollywood, they're films made for the intrinsic value of the film itself. You wouldn't call the work of the neo-realist Italians experimental, but when you do that kind of work in America, it's experimental. The fact is that "experimental" is often used as a bad word. It doesn't have any real meaning except to differentiate experimental filmmakers from other filmmakers. Basically it means that Shirley Clarke is not a Hollywood filmmaker. It's not that I don't want to be; I just don't happen to be. Certainly my films are done in a manner much closer to the way the Italian and French filmmakers work. The world of experimental cinema has had a very patchy history over the past twenty-five years. Every year or so a new independent feature will get made, usually with a great deal of artistic acclaim, and rarely will that filmmaker ever get the chance to make another film.

I started by making my own little films. They didn't go anywhere, as they were the equivalent of student films, but by making a number of short dance films and then experimental shorts, and then longer shorts, I ended up doing everything myself. I did the camera and sound and editing, but because I was such a rotten cameraman I tried to cover it up by editing, and in the course of editing learned what was missing so that the next time I went out I found I was learning about directing. I also had the advantage of having been a dancer and a choreographer, so I had some sense of the beginning, middle and end of things. But being a total filmmaker is a great advantage, and it's something that's not as appreciated in Hollywood as it is both in Europe and within the independent film movement, where it's not unusual that people do everything themselves and are expected to know everything about filmmaking.

The first thing I learned when I worked in so-called commercial cinema is that people are always saying, "That's not the way we do it." But if I was vehement enough about the way I wanted to do it and stuck to it, that's the way it was finally done. The crew even got excited about it. Most of the time they're fairly bored, so if you come along with new ideas, they're happy to go along with experiments and explore with you. They just want to know that you really mean it and that you know what you're talking about, so if someone says, "You really can't do that," I can say, "Well, I've done it that way in the past."

Do you find it difficult to get your films seen?

What happens is that you raise the money to make the film, but nobody realizes it costs twice as much to sell it. They never realize that after they've made the film they're going to have to peddle it. As for independent distribution, just forget it. You'll never see a nickel. There's no way to make quick money and be called a commercial success. And if you're not a commercial success it's hard to find backers ready to go one more time, because no matter what the backers say—and I would never take money from anybody that couldn't easily afford it—deep down they hope it'll be a big hit. My backers had to be satisfied with sponsoring artistic successes, because they never saw their money again. I've never seen any money even though I own something like twenty-five percent of almost every film I've made. There's never anything called profit with work like this. If you own a piece of the gross, you're fine, but forget about owning a piece of the profit. Films like this never make any profit.

There seem to be some people who are getting bold enough to move past distributors and take their films directly to exhibitors.

We tried it for three years with the Film-makers' Distribution Center but we didn't have sufficient funds. With *Portrait of Jason,* a film I knew no distributor would take, I paid for it myself. I took that film around the country to universities and I made $20,000 that year, but it was the most horrible experience I've ever had. Lonely and desperate, going from one town to the other, meeting hordes of people but not getting to know anyone. I felt like a record, playing back on myself, and I got to hate the film. If you look into film history you see that Robert Flaherty did the same thing with *Nanook of the North,* and it's how Maya Deren* sustained herself in the early days of experimental filmmaking. Every year she went on a three-month tour of what was called the university circuit, which she really established, and made enough so she could exist the rest of the year. But for me it was terribly tough to do and it's very hard to agree to do again. The solution was to try to get a number of us independent filmmakers together, so we formed the Film-Makers' Distribu-

*Maya Deren (1917–1961), Ukrainian-born American experimental filmmaker.

tion Center. We had a good opening success with Andy Warhol's *Chelsea Girls* and then worked with a couple of other films, including one of Bob Downey's.* But we still had to have somebody to travel around the country selling the film, theater by theater, or do it by phone or mail, and it was never done well enough. The other thing was that the theater screening the film has to advertise it properly to bring in the audience, and unless you put up that money yourself, the theater isn't going to spend enough. The theater will only pay for one tiny blurb each week. When you see big ads, they're paid for by the producers or the distributors, not the exhibitors. Maybe in the long run this form of distribution might be a solution, and if there are enough films getting produced this way and the filmmakers gather together to distribute together, maybe another United Artists can be formed. In other words, perhaps they can form some kind of producing distribution company where independent people can come in with their own projects, bring in their own money, and have the advantage of the group energy and everybody working together for themselves and each other.

What's happened to The Cool World? *Is it being shown?*

I had a marvelous experience not too long ago. Miloš Forman told me that his cameraman was in awe of me. I said, "Why?" He said, "Because he studied you in school." I said, "They really study American film that thoroughly?" And he said, "No, only three directors: Lionel Rogosin, Shirley Clarke and John Cassavetes." Apparently at some point somebody had gone through Czechoslovakia with copies of films known as New American Cinema under their arm and left copies at various archives. *The Cool World* played through France, Sweden and Germany. It even did well in Japan. In the United States it played at what were called the art houses and the black theaters. I have rarely met any black filmmaker who has not seen *The Cool World.* Even today I would say that, at any one time, in some three-bit art-house theater, one of my films is playing. They fit into that category of American classics, which means that nobody really makes much money, but they do get shown in schools, universities and small theaters. *The Cool World* was my most successful film. What was fantastic was that it didn't just play art houses, but also a theater on Forty-second Street, where it was held over for two weeks thus confirming my belief that *The Cool World* is really a neighborhood film. I believe it was incor-

*Robert Downey (b. 1937), American underground filmmaker.

rectly distributed from the beginning. It never should have opened in an art house.

The film was sneak-previewed at the Paris Theatre in New York, which is sort of the Radio City of art houses. The people who went that night were expecting to see a French comedy, and when the film was over there were six people remaining in the audience—me and my five friends. Everyone else had left or asked for their money back. The next night it was to play on 148th Street in Harlem but I didn't go because I was really depressed by this experience. The phone rang and someone said, "Get up here quick, you won't believe it! It's fabulous!" The audience was just screaming with joy at the actors, screaming at Littleman to knife his father, "Get him, get him, go get him!" The audience was roaring with laughter. They got the humor. Then it opened at Cinema Two and it was playing what is known as mixed houses. Half the audience was sitting there in tears with their hearts breaking and the other half was laughing uproariously at "black" humor. All my daughter's white friends would say to her, "Why are all these black people laughing?" It took years to get these two groups together. It was as if there were two different movies, depending on which audience was watching.

This film makes it clear, no matter how experimental you are, that you really are a dramatist.

There are a lot of actors who become directors. Their films have a problem that the work of someone who was, for example, an editor and becomes a director, doesn't have. Actors tend not to have a complete overview. They want each scene played to the hilt, but never understand its relationship to the next scene. They don't understand that a scene is part of an overall structure that has a beginning, middle and end. Whether it's an abstract film or a dramatic narrative story, you tend to know if the film was made by an actor-turned-director. Now, a writer-turned-director, or an editor-turned-director, has that ability to see the entire thing and understands that you throw away something in return for something that's going to happen later. You let a scene lay there or you let a scene not get all its points for brilliant acting, in return for the effect it will have later on. The director's job is not only to cast well, but also to know that this kind of casting will pay off because A plays well against B, that it's not that each actor is individually brilliant, but that they're going to play well with each other. "It's beautiful, but we don't need this much now. Hold it for later." That's what a director does in a film. The director is the one person who has to see the entire film. We know the end of the story while we're shooting—it's not being made up as we go along. This is the difference between a dramatically created film and a cinéma-vérité film which doesn't know precisely where it's going and is shooting up a storm to get enough material to eventually make a film.

At the same time I was doing *The Cool World*, Pennebaker* and Leacock† were doing a similar cinéma-vérité film in East Harlem, and they ended up having to use a narrator on the soundtrack because they were constantly losing their cast to the police. They often didn't get the scenes they needed. I was having endless arguments with Ricky and Penny about the legitimacy of what I was doing, because I think deep down they didn't agree with me, and I didn't really agree with them. I thought it was perfectly okay to re-create reality, but they felt that unless you could shoot what was happening as it was actually happening, then it wasn't real. But the truth is that with a dramatic film you've got control of the entirety of the film, so you can maintain a constant outlook. You can't order life the way you want, but you can sure order your script. Then it becomes the job of the director to see that it has constant organic growth and development.

I've enjoyed seeing your films for the last two days, but I wonder why you haven't carried this particular style into your video work.

A very simple reason: video is totally unsuitable for it.

Why?

None of these things could have been made as videos, and that even goes for *Jason*. Films are meant to be seen by an audience in a darkened room, on a large screen. They are carefully planned to be seen that way. They're edited, they're made in pieces and put together, and that's just diametrically opposed to the nature of the electronic medium of video.

In presentation?

No, in reality. In absolute basic reality. The fact that a video camera can seemingly do what a film camera does, doesn't mean that's what it actually

*D. A. Pennebaker (b. 1925), American documentary filmmaker.
†Richard Leacock (1921–2011), British-born American documentary filmmaker.

does. Things that work in film are not things that work in video, and vice versa. To me, electronic media is another kind of communication, a much more crystalline and direct, person-to-person kind of communication. Video can be everything from a Proustian novel to the kind of interaction things that I do. To take a medium and use it in a way that doesn't get you the kind of image you want is not very satisfying. The fact that something isn't running at 24 frames a second but at 30 cycles really changes the movement within the image. It changes the dimensionality and even the sound. There are just so many hundreds of things that get changed. Now, the truth is that some of the young people today have grown up with the video Portapak* and with the possibility of how much cheaper video is. They use it as if it were film, and there's nothing wrong with that, but just make sure you realize there's a difference between film and video. I've seen *The Cool World* on television. It cuts every fifteen minutes rather nicely for the commercials. I once saw it on television where it wasn't cut into much and it was rather boring. But it sure wasn't meant to be seen the way video is watched, with insular, small groups of people or at home in a spatially different space. To me, video is the Watergate hearings and all the implications of that experience.

I've had people come along with forty hours of tape of an event they attended. They're going to take those forty hours and edit it down to a half-hour? They're going to go out of their fucking minds trying to do that. They can't sit and find what that half-hour is and shoot that, instead they let that load of tape go clumping through the recorder? To me it suggests that they aren't willing to learn about the reality of the situation. Let's say we were going to videotape this session here today. Five or ten minutes would have been plenty for us to know what took place. We don't need all of an hour and a half to do it. We could argue this forever and probably we'll all be doing just that because we're in at the birth of a new art form. There must have been enormous arguments in the early days of filmmaking as to whether it was really theater or documentary or magic or a passing fad. It will take thousands of films to define video as a medium.

Where do you get the money to make your films?

I haven't made a film since 1969. I hate to point out that my sex could be the reason. If you've seen *The Cool World* and you're a Hollywood pro-

*Early, portable video camera, first introduced in 1967.

ducer, are you rushing out to hire me? Not that you doubt my talent or my competence, but the average Hollywood producer tends to be afraid of me. I'm not really on the side of money. It's not my first priority. I'm on the side of film, and I would ask a producer for a lot of things, such as having the final say, in order to remain on the side of the film. In 1969 I came out to Hollywood to be in a film called *Lions Love* by Agnès Varda. In fact, I came to the American Film Institute for help and they turned me down in a very evil, vicious way by asking whether I thought they should back failures. Failures! I was furious and vowed never to return to this mansion again. I walked out—only to return six years later. It shows you what a weak person I am. I'm still bitter about it, but it wasn't only with AFI that I had problems in Hollywood. Shelley Winters was trying to have me direct her in a film she had written and she had a whole setup here, but it just didn't work out, and then I blew a job in New York and went into a deep depression. I'd still be there if video hadn't come along and pulled me out of it. It was just a fluke that I discovered it. And anyway, I'm an eternal optimist. If I keep busy I'm okay but if I'm not busy I get really sick, and with video I found the perfect thing to keep me busy. I have a video troupe we're touring. We're doing interesting things, and my daughter is doing some fantastic things, so I'm beginning to think that maybe Mommy should see if she can swing one last film. I'm here on

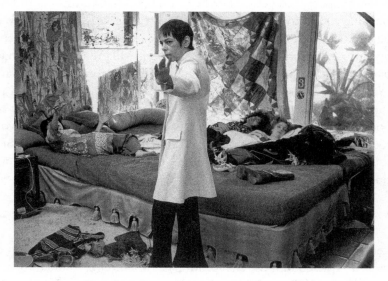

Clarke played a fictionalized version of herself seeking studio financing
for a film in Agnès Varda's *Lions Love* (1969).

vacation but also casing the place. I'm not too sure that the situation is at all different than it was when I said goodbye in 1969, but I still believe that anybody here in this room who really wants to make their first film will make it. I don't know how we're going to solve the problem of making films because the distribution problem hasn't been solved. Maybe you're going to solve it. I'm ready to join you.

Can you tell us what projects you want to do now?

I don't usually talk about new things. I'm superstitious. But I do have two films. One I describe as a film about two girls, a combination Marx Brothers–Hitchcock. I don't know why people don't want to immediately give me $400,000 when I say that. What more do they want to know? I resent that they want a script or anything else. The other thing I want to do is a video drama for Barbara Schultz, who has a program called *Visions* funded through a Rockefeller or Ford grant. They're doing dramatic television projects. It'll give me a chance to try out an idea I've had in my head for a couple of years.

How do you hope to overcome this obstacle you have in getting money in Hollywood?

I never expected to get money here. I hoped that all this damn tongue-wagging about how women should be directing films was a reality, not a fantasy, and that when I arrived and they heard I was here the phone would start ringing. But it hasn't. Maybe it will. Who's to say what will happen? I'm not as tough as I used to be. I'll compromise. I don't have too many years left, so maybe I should give it a try. Maybe I should go on someone else's trip, and maybe out of that will come my own. If somebody had a picture that I liked I'd be happy to give it a try. Maybe I'm fooling myself in thinking that if I pull that off, they'll think I'm safe and then hire me. After all, I did a short that got an Academy Award nomination. How much safer can you be?

How do you maintain artistic integrity?

Let me tell you a story about Luis Buñuel. When he was sixty, a producer in Spain offered him the chance to make whatever he wanted to, and his remark was, "Why wasn't I asked that when I was forty?" Between the ages of forty to sixty he was in Mexico not really doing what he wanted. He feels that he was putting in survival time. Many of those films are astounding, but they weren't the films he really wanted to make. Obviously he accepted the producer's offer. The point is that it looks kind of rosy when you describe certain people's careers, but look at Robert Bresson, look at Carl Dreyer. They made five or six films in their whole life. That was it.

I think women are really going to come up now and show us how to do it.

We're ready. There are some really good women around and they've already done some work, but I haven't seen any jobs open to women making feature films. I haven't seen any women directors hired by the studios, and there aren't many more women making features than when I was doing it ten years ago. It may be coming, but it hasn't started yet. It's getting late.

You have an appointment?

I'm going to my yoga seminar. Getting ready for higher experiences. But I've enjoyed talking with you and if any of you can find a way that I can borrow two damn video monitors from this place it would make me very happy. I've come here free and offered my film and my goodwill to the students. I seriously wouldn't have come except that I wanted to see all of you, because here I am angry with the American Film Institute. When we called and asked if we could borrow two monitors for Tuesday night to do a video demonstration, because we don't have the money to rent them at fifty-five dollars apiece, we were told no, that they were being used.

We don't have two. People think that we have a lot of equipment here, but we don't.

That aside, it's a pleasure for me to see that you all really appreciated the film. That makes me feel very good. Looking back over my career isn't always easy. A retrospective tends to be kind of a downer—you feel half-dead; but to see that young people are looking at your films as if they're still relevant is a good feeling.

Films as Director

1953 *Dance in the Sun*
1954 *In Paris Parks* (also producer and editor)
1955 *Bullfight* (also producer and editor)
1956 *Moment in Love* (also producer, editor and production designer)
1957 *Brussels Loops* (also producer and editor)
1958 *Bridges-Go-Round* (also producer and cinematographer)
      Skyscraper (also producer and editor)
1962 *The Connection* (also producer and editor)

1963 *Robert Frost: A Lover's Quarrel with the World*
1964 *The Cool World* (also screenplay and editor)
1967 *Portrait of Jason* (also producer and editor)
1978 *Trans*
      One-2–3
1980 *A Visual Diary*
1981 *Savage/Love*
1982 *Tongues*
      Performance
1983 *The Box*
1985 *Ornette: Made in America* (also editor)

An editor is a storyteller. It really is the most important thing. I suspect you're either born with an aptitude to tell stories or you're not.

ANNE COATES
(Born in Reigate, Surrey, England, 1925)

In his biography of David Lean, historian Kevin Brownlow tells of Anne Coates struggling through *Wuthering Heights* and other novels in school. She had a young girl's passion for horses and dreamed of being a racehorse trainer when she was taken to see Lean's *Great Expectations* on a school outing. She told Brownlow, "Suddenly the whole thing came alive to me. These extremely boring books which I was plowing my way through were suddenly up there on the screen and I was carried away. I thought, 'What a marvelous thing to be able to do.'"

Coates, a niece of the British film mogul J. Arthur Rank, worked as a nurse in a plastic-surgery hospital before she decided to pursue a career as a film director. She got a job for a company that made religious films and then was hired at Pinewood Studios. "I went straight into editing," she remembers. "At that time in England there weren't many things women could do. There was script girl, secretary and editing." She was an uncredited assistant working on Powell and Pressburger's *The Red Shoes* before becoming an editor in her own right. One of her first important credits was *Tunes of Glory,* starring Alec Guinness, for director Ronald Neame in 1960.

Two years later Coates was hired to cut together elaborate tests that Lean shot of Albert Finney for *Lawrence of Arabia.* She was anxious when the time came to show her cut to the great director and his team. "I never saw a frame go by—I was so frightened." The lights came up, Lean stood and said to the group, "That's the first time I've ever seen a piece of mine cut exactly as I would have done it." Finney turned down the role of T. E. Lawrence, opening the door for Peter O'Toole, and a door opened as well for Anne Coates.

Lean hired her to cut *Lawrence,* thus providing a creative challenge and

Anne Coates at her Moviola with actor Anthony Steele, who starred with
Alec Guinness and Jack Hawkins in *Operation Malta* (1953).

learning opportunity. "David said things like, 'It's what you take out which
makes the movie, not necessarily what you leave in.' He taught me to be
brave." Recalling the four-minute scene of the Arab column departing for
Aqaba with Lawrence looking on in delight, she said she wouldn't have dared
let it run so long. "David said, 'If you really believe in a scene, hang on to it,
hold it until the bitter end. When we get the music and sound effects on it, it
will be perfect.' And of course it was."

Coates recalls that in the early days of film, women were hired to splice
film and cut negative because they were thought to be more patient and careful. "When men realized how creative editing could be, they elbowed women
out of the way and kind of took over. But I've never looked at myself as a
woman in the business. I've just looked at myself as an editor. I'm sure I've
been turned down because I'm a woman, then other times I've been used
because they want a woman editor."

Coates has been nominated five times for the Academy Award for film
editing: for *Lawrence of Arabia, Becket, The Elephant Man, In the Line of
Fire* and *Out of Sight*. She won the Oscar for *Lawrence*. In 1995 she was
honored with the American Cinema Editors Career Achievement Award.

David Puttnam presents Coates with the Academy Fellowship Award at the 2007 BAFTA Awards.

In a career spanning sixty years she has worked with Sidney Lumet, Miloš Forman, Lawrence Kasdan, Richard Attenborough, Steven Soderbergh and David Lynch. At age eighty-three she declared she would retire only when the phone stopped ringing and she stopped enjoying her work.

ANNE COATES

—◆—

March 1, 2000*

How do you feel when talking about such an intuitive job as film editing?

Some of the best editors I know are absolutely unable to talk about how they work. To be honest, I find that I can't talk about editing at all. I make an effort, because people are always asking me to talk about the films I've worked on over the years, some of which are important. I remember doing an interview once with Walter Murch. We were talking about how we edited and it worked beautifully, because he could theorize about everything and all I talked about was how intuitive I find the process, and I threw in some anecdotes, which I suspect I'll do here today with you. The thing that is so important is that an editor is a storyteller. I suspect you're either born with an aptitude to tell stories or you're not. I don't think it's something you learn.

How did you start working as an editor?

Actually I wanted to be a racehorse trainer, and before that a ballet dancer. I was very talented when I was eight or nine and the Sadler's Wells Ballet was interested in me. I can't honestly remember why I chose not to go, but I then became fascinated by horses and would ride all the time. Then when I was at boarding school they used to take us to the movies. That's when I really became interested in film and started going all the time. I thought always of being a director. That was my ambition, but I

*Philip Linson moderated this seminar. The transcript also contains segments from an interview conducted in spring 2009.

found out that the only really interesting job a woman could do at that time was be an editor. I certainly didn't want to be a hairdresser or a script girl. When I found out that David Lean and Charlie Frend* and Charlie Crichton† had been editors I was even more interested, so I started trying to get into the industry. Of course you couldn't get into the union unless you had experience and you couldn't get experience unless you were in the union, so I wrote to all the laboratories and everyone else. One of the companies I contacted made religious films based on Bible stories, short ten-minute dramatizations that they would send out to churches. That's where I learned to handle film. I did all the odd jobs and got to know the people working next door in educational films. I would sit and watch one of the editors working. Eventually I joined the union and got a job at Pinewood Studios. I remember at the interview they asked me if I could do this and that, a long list of things, and I said yes to everything. I hadn't heard of most of it but I told them I could do it all. The first morning I had to use this huge splicing machine. Before that I'd worked on a tiny little splicer and really didn't know what to do, but there were two of these things in the room, so I sat down at the first one and someone else came in and sat down at the second one. I just watched what he did and copied him, and no one ever found me out.

Are you often involved in a film from the very start or are you brought on only in the postproduction stage?

It depends on the director. I like to watch the director working on the floor with the actors and crew because it helps me assimilate the film. I find that useful because often the director will come up and chat to me about a particular problem. Some directors rely on their editors enormously. I like to know what he wants from a scene and help him to achieve that. If I see him working on the floor—I don't even necessarily need to hear him working with the actors—and see how the performances are changing a little bit here and there, it helps me a great deal. I know some editors don't want to go anywhere near the set during filming, but that's not how I work. I find talking to the actors, and also the cameraman and sound crew, very useful. Much better to engage with them at the start of a shoot than come down from the editing room later on only to complain about things. On one film I was asked by the producers to be

*Charles Frend (1909–1977), British director.
†Charles Crichton (1910–1999), British director.

on the floor all the time with the director and help him block the scenes, but you wouldn't do that with a really first-class director. He might call you down occasionally about a problem and you've got to be ready for that, to be able to go down and contribute an idea. Always have an idea. Never say you don't know what's happening. Very unwise. The way I like it is for me is to be there from the very first rehearsal, although this doesn't happen very often. On *I Love You to Death* Larry Kasdan had the cameraman and me and the production designer there from the very first rehearsals with the actors, asking for ideas. It also happened many years ago with *Tunes of Glory,* one of my favorite films, with John Mills and Alec Guinness. Ronny Neame had me in right from the beginning so that we all lived like it was in an officers' mess. We all ate together and got to know each other.

I like to watch dailies with the crew, because if the director has a problem he can say so there and then. It's very useful to hear him say, "I like how that take played. Did you see how the actor inflected that line? Perhaps think about using that take." It's also important for me to start editing while the shooting is still going on, so you can tell the director that he might be missing a shot, and also get a feeling for what the director is looking for. A little pinpointing in the direction I might go is something I appreciate. Some directors like to have that kind of control, while others will leave me alone the entire time and come in only once I have a cut ready to show them. I like it best if a director comes in every two or three weeks and just sees what I've been working on, and lets me know what he thinks. On the movie I just finished, *Erin Brockovich,* Steven Soderbergh didn't see a single cut sequence before I'd finished the film. On *Out of Sight* we did work a little bit together during the shooting, because it was the first film I'd done with him.

Some directors don't really get that involved in the cutting. John Sturges wasn't in England very much when I was cutting *The Eagle Has Landed,* and came back to see the fine cut. Then he went away and came back only to do the music. I never saw him again. I had worked for two months with John Ford on *Young Cassidy* before he was taken ill. He said, "I never choose dailies. I'll always leave that up to you. I may never come to see the film after you cut it." I was somewhat shocked. Every director is different, from David Lean to David Lynch, and everyone in between.

Do you have discussions with the director about character and theme? Is that useful to you?

I find it very useful, but some directors aren't communicative so you just hope that what you see in the material is also what the director wants. Usually I know the script and cut it the way I feel it. Now that we're digital you can do all sorts of different versions, but I don't. I have a point of view, and cut just one version and then run it for him. Essentially my job is to try and enhance what I feel he's trying to get out of the story. I think cutting is very personal, very instinctive, and if you start cutting a film and really aren't doing it the way the director wants, it's best to just call it a day and leave.

Have you ever argued with a director?

There was a sequence in *Out of Sight* which for some reason Steven wanted out and the studio wanted out, but I thought the scene was important, so I fought for it. If a film has to be cut, I would rather do it myself, so at least I know it's being done right. But who has the final say? When there has been a fight between the director and the producer, I've always tried to do what I think is best for the movie. I may not be right, but you've got to have an opinion.

It's obvious how a writer and director can impose a style on a film, and to a lesser extent a cinematographer. But can an editor also impose her style on a film?

I think they can. At the same time I think what an editor can most usefully do is try and bring something different to each film. I'm sure that there is a certain style—or more probably a sensibility or feeling—that editors bring to their work that shines through, at least to the more analytic viewers. Years ago my daughter was taking an editing class and the teacher started talking about the "Anne Coates style." I didn't even know I had a style! If there's one thing I try to bring to every job it's a sense of clarity. Some directors have a tendency to overcut. By that I mean they cut out important little things that add that little bit of clarification the audience needs. Directors obviously know their films very well and some have trouble looking objectively at them. One mistake directors can make is assume that the audience knows what they know. It's sometimes only a line or two that helps bring things into focus, but during the paring down of a film when you make sure there isn't any fat left on it, it's possible to throw the baby out with the bathwater.

How do you know when a scene or a film is working?

Films have their own kind of rhythm, and a scene will suddenly come together because you start to understand the rhythm of a picture as a whole. As I keep saying, I find editing not something I can really talk about. It's really just a feeling from the heart. When I start a new film I usually cut one or two scenes and think, "My God, they're awful! I've lost my touch. I'm going to give up." Then you cut a scene and suddenly it works and you get so excited and it's just great and you're off. You get a feeling for the film.

Are there any kinds of rules you can give us about when a cut needs to be made?

Generally I don't think there are any rules when it comes to cutting. That said, I was always taught that with a well-shot scene and good acting, don't cut in until you really feel the need to see a close-up. One of the things I've done on more than one occasion when I've been brought in late, to try and save a film, is take out some of the cuts and simplify everything. I'm a great believer in letting shots breathe. Sometimes you can find the essence of the performances—and even the story—when you slow the whole thing down. The people who hire me for jobs like that often think I'm going to make things faster, but sometimes you can slow things down and still make the film shorter. The more engaged the audience is with the characters, the quicker the story moves.

The old-timers would give the editor wonderfully well-blocked master shots, but that doesn't happen very often these days. I think a master shot is also terribly important for the actors because they play the whole scene and can interact with each other. Running the entire scene in one go means the actors can really feel the emotions at play. Often performances in master shots are very different to those in close-ups. Many actors will tell you they save their best work for the close-ups. Actors are a canny bunch, hoping that you'll use the close shots rather than the master.

Can you say when the tradition of shooting master shots seemed to fall away?

It was probably around the time when music videos and commercials, with their very snappy cutting, came in. The thing I learned at the beginning of my career, particularly from David Lean and people like that, is to have the courage of your convictions. Lean taught me to hold a shot for foot after foot, which I would never have dared to do on my own. I was brought up with the idea that you shouldn't cut until you really need to.

If a scene is playing well, why cut? Today that idea is perhaps trouble-some, because these days directors shoot much more in bits and pieces, and don't shoot master shots as often as they used to.

Can a film sometimes develop during editing into something different from perhaps what the director originally envisaged?

I've worked closely with directors on rewriting scenes to make them work. One film I did was so bad that we reshot the whole of the ending, and the people who died in the original version were still alive in the new version. In a way the editor is more involved in the smaller films than the bigger ones, which have lots of writers and producers. In fact I went out and shot the ending on that picture myself. I used to shoot a lot of second units, but on the really big pictures there is always a second-unit director, so you don't get the opportunity. I used to lay my own tracks and cut my own music and do all sorts of things. Now all those things are taken over by specialists and it's not as much fun as it used to be.

You've been called an "actor's editor." What do people mean by that?

My editing is always guided by the actors and their performances. After reading the script, my thoughts might change completely after seeing the performances. Sometimes that even happens during rehearsals, before anything has been filmed. Certainly one of the editor's most important jobs is cleaning up a weak performance.

What are your thoughts about the fact that you now work with so many special effects, and that the postproduction process is digital?

I would rather work on films that are about people and human situations, but it's quite fun working on special effects. With one film I did we had a tie-in with Coca-Cola, but only after finishing the film did we realize that we'd cut every shot with a Coca-Cola can out of the film, so we digitized a can and stuck it in. Another time we were working on a scene where the whole point of these people staying in a hotel for the night was the fact that their car had broken down and had been left in the garage. God knows who made this mistake, but there was a car parked outside the hotel in one of the shots, so we just digitized it out. It was cheaper to do that than go back and reshoot. But at the same time I think it's possible to perfect things in a sterile way.

One of the other dangers of cutting digitally is the loss of what we call "thinking time." An editor needs time to think. Certain things strike you only after a period of time. There is often no way you can think of certain things under pressure. An editor often needs that space. Of course now with things digital the studios think you can do it all very quickly. I have never learned to be absolutely magical with my fingers because I want to have the time to think that I used to have when I was hanging up film and rewinding on a flatbed editing machine.

Can you talk about your experience cutting Lawrence of Arabia *in 1962 and then revisiting it years later for the restoration?*

When I first worked on the film we worked seven days a week until two or three in the morning for four months, to get the picture ready. These days nobody gets a picture ready in sixteen weeks, but we did. It was pretty remarkable.

I hadn't seen *Lawrence* for fifteen years when they approached me. As soon as they said they were going to put the film back together, I said, "Oh, thank God! We'll put those goggles back." I don't know whether any of you remember, but at the beginning with the motorbike accident there

Opportunity came for Coates when she cut a screen test for David Lean
and he chose her to be his editor on *Lawrence of Arabia* (1960).

is now a shot of his goggles hanging on the bush. I thought it was such an important shot. It was just so sad, the death of this young guy. David Lean felt the same way, but somehow it was taken out. When I rang David, the first thing he said was, "We'll be able to put those goggles back." In 1962 we had to cut the film down by fifteen minutes after the release, and then seven years later took out another twenty minutes for television. But it was more complicated than it sounds, because we didn't just cut out chunks. We changed things around each time. We put in close-ups, maybe, to bridge across from one piece to another, or used another take. So to put the film back together was a lot more complicated than it sounds.

Can you talk about the scene where Omar Sharif comes riding in? Whose decision was it to hold that shot for so long?

I'm sure it was David Lean's idea. I actually had most of the picture cut together before David finished shooting, and there were certain scenes which needed a lot of work and some that didn't. When it came to the mirage sequence with Lawrence and Ali, I had thousands of feet of film to work with. David had shot it with three cameras about three or four times with him coming closer and closer from a distance. I think the most interesting thing was what John Box, the production designer, did. He put little black marks out in the desert so that your eye goes to them. You're not really conscious of it, but if you ever see the film again on a big screen—you can't see them on a little television screen—you'll see that there are these stones lying there, subtly leading your eye to a certain point on the screen. We cut the scene many different ways. I was pretty young when I did that and was rather inclined to cut things off too quick. David said, "No, get the rhythm. Let it flow."

How do you decide to take on a project? Do you read the script and then talk with the director? Do you visualize the shots?

I never go see a director without reading the script to see if it's something that interests me. I try to work with interesting directors. But I don't visualize the cutting as such. For me it's really just deciding whether it's an interesting story that I feel I can bring something to and will be exciting to work on. I might choose to work with someone like Steven Soderbergh because I think he might shoot in an interesting way for me to cut, but what's more important is being able to visualize a story and see how it's going to turn out as a whole rather than start thinking about the more technical side of the job.

Do you find storyboards useful on action scenes?

I think they're sometimes quite useful, particularly if you've got a second-unit director and crew, but for ordinary scenes I don't think it's necessary or helpful. Having to follow storyboards is very restricting. I think an editor needs to have much more freedom to move within a film.

Can you talk about the seduction scene in Soderbergh's Out of Sight? *Where did you get the idea to cross-cut those two scenes?*

In the script it was basically the bar scene followed by the bedroom scene. Originally, it was a much simpler structure. I cut the bar as one scene and it played very well, and then I cut the bedroom as a silent sequence. Then we started experimenting and getting a little more adventurous, and we start cutting the two scenes together and trying things. The idea was to mold them together, because what they were doing and what they were talking about were sort of in opposition to each other. Cutting them together made it just more sexual. We evolved the scene very slowly, matching things together, like his hand on the glass which cuts to his hand on her knee. Things like that just sort of floated together, but we didn't have any great ideas when we started.

Do you always try to show the director a first version of the film precisely as it is in the written script, or do you feel it's your job to start cutting things down from the start?

I don't generally take dialogue out before I show it to the director. At the same time I don't use all the cover shots I might have at my disposal. Sometimes directors give you cover but they don't want to see it up on the screen. It's a safety thing, because a cover shot can be very useful if you need to cut lines out or compress things. But I don't generally cut lines out unless they seem really awful. I think it's my job to show the director the complete film as written. Of course, later on the director might say, "See if we can take some lines out of that scene."

How did you find working with David Lynch?

They sent me the script of *The Elephant Man* and I said to myself, "My God, I couldn't cut this, having to look at this monstrous face every day on the Steenbeck." By page thirty I was in tears, and by the end of the script I knew I had to cut the film. I went to the interview and was sitting in the outer office and this young boy came out. I was about to say, "Tea with milk and sugar, please," when he introduced himself as David Lynch. He literally looked eighteen. He was a very unusual character, but I liked him a lot. I loved his determination. We did argue, because I didn't always understand the way he wanted to do things. At the time I had young children and I remember him suggesting I take them to the Royal Hospital Museum, which is where the real Elephant Man was. They have all sorts of monstrosities there, like babies with two heads. He said, "Take the children there for a treat. While you're there have some sandwiches." This totally typifies David. The idea of taking children there and eating lunch was hilarious, but he was totally serious. He was pretty way out and very opinionated about the way he wanted things done. He's very imaginative and has marvelous ideas on sound and music, and the way he wants those things to interact with each other.

What do you feel are the differences between working with first-time directors and producers and more established ones?

On the whole I like working with young directors. I've found it disappointing a couple of times working with older directors whose work I've admired, because they are so set in their ways. Young directors have such wonderful enthusiasm and excitement, and they're much more willing to experiment. They love it when I'm able to contribute ideas. Everyone thinks that the directors get all the glory, but in the old days the producers were so creative. What we're short of today are really creative, imaginative producers. If we could get more young people to come out of film schools and work as teams, as directors and producers, it would be very important. When I look back even on people like Sam Spiegel and Hal Wallis, I see now how creative and helpful they were and what wonderful films they made. So some of you, please: go out there and produce!

Films as Editor

1952 The Pickwick Papers	1980 The Elephant Man
1953 Grand National Night	1981 Ragtime
1954 Forbidden Cargo	1983 The Pirates of Penzance
1955 To Paris with Love	1984 Greystoke: The Legend of Tarzan,
1956 Lost	Lord of the Apes
1957 The Truth about Women	1986 Lady Jane
1958 The Horse's Mouth	Raw Deal
1960 Tunes of Glory	1987 Masters of the Universe
1961 Don't Bother to Knock	1989 Farewell to the King
1962 Lawrence of Arabia	Listen to Me
1964 Becket	1990 I Love You to Death
1965 Young Cassidy	1991 What About Bob?
Those Magnificent Men in Their	1992 Chaplin
Flying Machines, or How I	1993 In the Line of Fire
Flew from London to Paris in	1994 Pontiac Moon
25 hours 11 minutes	1995 Congo
1966 Hotel Paradiso	1996 Striptease
1968 Great Catherine	1997 Out to Sea
The Bofors Gun	1998 Out of Sight
1970 The Adventurers	2000 Passion of Mind
1971 Friends	Erin Brockovich
1972 The Public Eye	2001 Sweet November
A War of Children	2002 Unfaithful
1973 A Bequest to the Nation	2004 Taking Lives
1974 11 Harrowhouse	2007 Catch and Release
Murder on the Orient Express	The Golden Compass
1975 Man Friday	2010 Extraordinary Measures
1976 Aces High	
The Eagle Has Landed	
1978 The Legacy	

There's no point in fighting the fact that you've got three weeks to make a picture and there's no point in spending half of three weeks moaning that you've only got three weeks. You simply go out and do your best in the time you've got.

ROGER CORMAN
(Born in Detroit, Michigan, 1926)

Roger Corman came to the AFI for his first seminar with more screen credits than any other visitor before or since. His credits as producer, executive producer and director number in the four hundreds. He earned his stripes as the producer and sometimes director of extremely low-budget exploitation films in the fifties, his first requiring only $12,000. Their titles reveal more than a hint of their content: *Teenage Doll, Naked Paradise, The Cry Baby Killer, A Bucket of Blood, Attack of the Crab Monsters, The Saga of the Viking Women and Their Voyage to the Waters of the Great Sea Serpent* and *The She Gods of Shark Reef.*

One might be surprised to meet the man himself and find a tall, genial, buttoned-up gentleman in a suit and tie, who might be mistaken for a United States senator, a congressman or even the director of the FBI, all roles he has played in his occasional acting stints.

Corman's family moved from Detroit to Beverly Hills, and after high school Roger went north to Stanford, where he earned an engineering degree before returning to Hollywood hoping to break into the movie business. He worked as a messenger at 20th Century–Fox and spent time in the story department. Whether the demands of the story department were so challenging, or simply because he was naturally curious, he went to England to study literature at Balliol College, Oxford. Upon his return, he became a literary agent before embarking on a producing career. His engineering background gave him a knack for organizing efficient production schedules with no frills. He delivered films for a price to American International Pictures, which played them in drive-ins and on the second spot on double bills. Television had crippled the movie business, but these films appealed to teenagers who wanted to get out of the house. Samuel Z. Arkoff, the cigar-chomping head

Director Roger Corman tests a machine gun during production
of *Bloody Mama* (1970).

of AIP, would look at Corman's dailies and call him to complain, "Roger, for
chrissakes, hire a couple more extras and put a little more furniture on the
set."

Perhaps the most significant Corman legacy is the cadre of filmmakers
who got their start with him. He provided opportunity to would-be directors in exchange for working cheap. Among the debut films made under the
Corman banner were Francis Coppola's *Dementia 13*, Jonathan Demme's
Caged Heat, Peter Bogdanovich's *Targets*, Martin Scorsese's *Boxcar Bertha*,
Joe Dante's *Piranha* and Ron Howard's *Grand Theft Auto*. Howard observed
that you can't help getting weary working for Corman. At one point Corman told him, "If you continue to do a good job for me on this picture, I
can promise you, you'll never have to work for me again." Another who
went through the Corman school was Jack Nicholson, who appeared in *The
Cry Baby Killer, The Shooting, Ride in the Whirldwind* and *The Little Shop of
Horrors*.

In 1960 Corman broke away from black and white to make *House of Usher*
in color and Cinemascope. It was his first critical success and led to a series of
Edgar Allan Poe adaptations. Corman's films all made money except in 1962
when he decided to make a serious film about school desegregation based on
Charles Beaumont's novel *The Intruder*. Although he received some of the
best reviews of his career, it was his first loser at the box office.

To this day Corman—who wrote an autobiography in 1990 titled *How I Made a Hundred Movies in Hollywood and Never Lost a Dime,* and in 2010 was awarded an honorary Academy Award—believes that the combination of being conservative fiscally and outrageous conceptually was the reason for his success.

ROGER CORMAN

—

March 11, 1970*

I think almost everybody here is interested in how to make films with moderately scaled budgets. How did you originally get into filmmaking?

I started as a writer and sold a screenplay for Writers Guild minimum, which I think was $3,000 at the time. I tried to get more from the producer, so we compromised and he agreed to give me an associate-producer credit and another $3,000. On the basis that I had $6,000 in my hand and I was an official associate producer, I raised $5,000 more, which made $11,000. I felt if I could get a total of $15,000, I'd make the film. A fellow came in to direct it because I wasn't directing at that time. This was around 1954. He asked me how much I would pay him and I said, "If you can raise $4,000 more, you can direct this picture." He did, and we made the picture for $15,000 in cash and a series of deferments. We shot it in six days, all on natural locations, including Malibu. If you look closely you can see trucks moving down the Pacific Coast Highway as the voice-over says, "Deep in the uncharted jungle of South America . . ." It was a science-fiction film that I called *It Stopped the Ocean Floor*. We made a deal with Robert Lippert, who had a small distribution company at the time. He felt that was too arty a title and said, "You're going for the high-class market, kid, and *It Stopped the Ocean Floor* won't do it." So he changed the title to *Monster from the Ocean Floor*. He said, "You've got to tell them what the picture is about." He may well have been right, because the picture did reasonably well and we went from

*James R. Silke moderated this seminar. The transcript also contains segments from seminars Roger Corman gave at the American Film Institute on October 16, 1970, and January 18, 1995.

there. Then it was simply a matter of taking profits from that one and putting them into another picture.

Is it possible to get distribution on a nonunion film?

That was a union film. On the films that I've personally directed I've always used an IATSE* crew, until the very last picture I did, when I used a NABET† crew. On the films I've financed we'll sometimes go IA, sometimes NABET, but generally we haven't gone for a seal of any kind. The way the seal works is that the major studios have contracts that state that every film they make must have a union seal on it. What we've done is just buy the seal once the film is finished by putting a few thousand dollars into the IA pension fund. If it's a new filmmaker, somebody making his first picture, generally they'll give us the seal. However, if you're not distributing through the established majors—Metro, Fox, Paramount or whatever—you don't need a seal. I've sent a number of pictures through Walter Reade, AIP and the newer distribution companies. The business is changing rapidly. It's moving away from the majors faster than the majors themselves are really aware. I think this is extremely healthy. I would say the majority of films in the art houses in New York City are probably not handled by the majors.

So you can get your films screened in theaters?

Yes. It's a myth that the projectionists in the theaters won't screen a picture that doesn't have a union seal. As you know, the projectionists don't even look at the films—they're out of focus and misframed. They have no way of knowing if there's a seal on them. A friend told me that when they ran up against this problem they simply duped a seal off another film and stuck it on their own.

In what areas do you feel you are able to cut the cost of your films?

I cut costs right at the beginning with the director. With directors like Bruce Clark, Monte Hellman and Irvin Kershner, their deal was to write, direct and cut. So I had, as it were, three elements right there and, frankly,

*International Alliance of Theatrical Stage Employees, Moving Picture Technicians, Artists and Allied Crafts of the United States, Its Territories and Canada.
†National Association of Broadcast Employees and Technicians.

they did not get a great deal of money for doing this. I was giving them an opportunity to make their first film, which hopefully I would make a profit from, and hopefully their career would take off. In each of these cases it did. A couple of people have said to me I should take options on the directors I back. I've never done that on the basis that it's an even trade on the first film. He gets a small amount of money and makes his film, I get the profit and he gets the opportunity to start his career. If I were to take options on him for his second film, I'd be starting to exploit him. As far as cutting costs, it's really just a matter of cutting out the frills. Generally, shooting on natural locations is cheaper than shooting in a studio. On *Targets* Peter Bogdanovich shot a good part of the picture in a little rental studio on Santa Monica Boulevard.

What's the smallest union crew you've worked with?

Probably twelve or thirteen. Three men on camera, three men on sound, a couple of grips, possibly an electrician, and a prop man. At one time they required four men on sound and there was a minimum of one man on props. When the bulky sound equipment became condensed the number of sound men dropped down to three, but just about that time the prop local decided you had to have a minimum of two prop men. So you gained on one end and lost on the other. IA has just come up with what appear, on paper, to be good concessions. They've cut the number of men on their crew for pictures costing a million dollars or under. I assume that anybody who's planning to make a picture for under three million dollars is going to be able to make certain cuts and then go with that minimum crew.

What kind of ratios do you shoot with?

I used to shoot on a very low ratio. If I had a finished film of seven thousand feet, I would shoot maybe thirty thousand feet, but these days I'm up to maybe a hundred thousand feet or more just to get the same thing. It's one of the luxuries as you move up.

What sort of controls do you have when you finance a student filmmaker?

I don't think anybody other than the director can have a great deal of control during shooting unless they just come in and completely take over. I exercise most of my control before the shooting and afterwards. I'll check out the script very carefully, the production staff, the casting, and then I'll have some sort of control over the cutting. During the actual shooting I never even go to the set. I really feel it's best that I say, "Okay, I'll back this man as a director. He should have the opportunity to simply go and direct his film." The only time I'll step in is if he falls behind schedule, or when I see something in the rushes that really causes me to jump out of my chair. I may have words with him about that. But if the work looks even somewhere near what I would consider to be commercial and acceptable standards and he's near his schedule and budget, I prefer, frankly, not even to talk to him. I just let him make the film. On a film that goes smoothly I'll generally look at his second or third cut in the projection room and tell him my thoughts on it. On others I'll go into the cutting room with him when I think there are problems. I've never been to the set of the majority of the films that I've backed.

Is a four-week shooting schedule the norm?

A four-week shooting schedule is a little bit long for this type of picture. Monte Hellman shot his two westerns and his science-fiction picture while working on two-week schedules. On *Naked Angels* Bruce Clark went a little bit beyond that. We had some words and he finished the picture fairly quickly after that. We haven't done one in two weeks for some time now. With the second-feature market gone, we're moving up to three- and four-week schedules and aiming for the top of the bill.

How many setups do you do in a day?

It varies according to whether you're shooting interior or exterior on location. On location exterior you should be able to get thirty or forty setups a day, maybe more.

How about location interior?

Location interior will slow you down heavily, because lighting anywhere is slower than shooting with the sun. Lighting on natural locations is also slower than lighting in a studio. If you're getting forty setups a day on exteriors, that might drop to twenty-five with interiors. On this last picture I backed with these guys from UCLA I found that they were working much slower than I'd ever been accustomed to, and yet they were conscientious. I attributed this to the fact that they were used to working at

Shelley Winters starred as Ma Barker in *Bloody Mama* (1970). Corman
(center) directing Winters and Clint Kimbrough.

school and the idea of making sure they got a certain number of setups a
day was not particularly important to them. When I backed Francis Coppola he had been my assistant for something like eight or ten months and
already learned what was necessary.

How long do you spend in preproduction?

A long time. Several months. I believe the only way to make a film efficiently on a low budget is with a tremendous amount of preparation.

What does that consist of? Location scouting? Storyboarding?

I don't do storyboards, but I do scout the locations very thoroughly. I have
every location picked in advance. I know pretty much how I'm going to
shoot. It's a myth that I design all my shots before I start the picture, but
sometimes I have up to seventy percent of the shots worked out in
advance. I'll have a kind of a plan with certain symbols that I've invented
for myself. I have an engineering degree, so this way of working probably
goes back to how I was trained. Knowing exactly what you're going to do
in advance is one of the greatest advantages to shooting a low-budget film.
On the other hand, after having planned that much in preproduction you
must stay flexible enough so that if it doesn't work, you throw it out.

You're there on the set and you're working with the actors and it doesn't work, so you've got to say, "Okay, I'm going to throw out the couple of weeks' work and do it another way." There are big differences between me and Alfred Hitchcock, who designs every shot and sticks to that very closely. I read an interview with him and he said, very logically, that he thought better in his office than he did on the set. He figures out his pictures in advance. There are also big differences between me and somebody like Francis Coppola, who, on *The Rain People,* didn't know where his locations were going to be. It was part of his method of shooting. He started off from New York with a crew and some of the cast who were friends of his, on the basis that it was going to be a tour of the United States, shooting as they went, hoping this would give him a certain amount of spontaneity. I don't think Francis will be quite so spontaneous in the future. On the other hand you don't have to lock yourself in quite as much as Hitchcock does.

I remember a picture called *War of the Satellites.* When the Russians sent *Sputnik* up, we got the news one morning. I was having lunch with a special-effects guy and we started talking. I said, "How fast could you give me some special effects on this stuff?" He said, "I could have it ready in a couple of weeks." So I called Allied Artists, with whom I'd made a couple of films, and said, "Give me seven to eight weeks and I can ship the negative to the lab for printing." We started that day. The script was written in ten days, but while it was being written we were building the sets and casting. That's an extreme example.

Do you rehearse?

I talk extensively with the actors before the picture is shot, about the characters, about what I think of them and so forth. If there's time I do improvisations, which I have great faith in because I think it helps establish relationships between the characters. There are problems with the Screen Actors Guild when it comes to rehearsal time. A little bit of rehearsal can really help, but you end up paying your actors so much money that you might as well be shooting with them.

Did you ever study acting?

Like many others I went to Jeff Corey's class, where I met Bob Towne and Jack Nicholson.

Could you make most any script in your own particular way, or is there a certain kind of script with a certain type of story that lends itself to the type of work you're doing?

I feel that any script can be made for any budget. You can make *Doctor Zhivago* in six days for $50,000, but it's going to look different than David Lean's version. The first picture I directed was called *Five Guns West* and it had five people in it, five men who rode north from Texas. They met an old man and his daughter at a deserted stagecoach depot. The crucial thing was that it was deserted. That was the entire cast. I feel that you'd better not try to make a spectacle on a low budget. I think you dissipate a great deal of your efforts, and everyone else's, if you try to make something small look big rather than taking something small and making it look good.

Do you always have an assistant director and a production manager?

When I came out of college I tried to get into the Directors Guild and they kept me out for seven years. When I said I was going to become a director, within a day I got a call from them saying, "You must join the Directors Guild." As a member of the Directors Guild I must, whenever I work in the United States, use a first assistant director and a second assistant director. Sometimes I have a production manager, but that's very rare, and when I back a film myself I've never carried all three. I have certain first assistants who are also production managers. The production managers break down the script and get a shooting schedule and lock in specific things such as the crew, the locations, rental of equipment, and so forth. I never really believe that the picture is going to be done right until I see the script broken down and a shooting schedule and a list of locations. Once I have that I can visualize the whole thing. I try to do as much of the advance planning myself and put the production manager/assistant director combination on the job probably about three weeks before I shoot. When I was making very low-budget films I used to put them on a week before I shot.

Who does the cost estimates?

I'll generally do that myself. I'm not a believer in accurate budgets, on the basis that we work in such an intangible medium. A couple of pictures I did for the majors had the budgets broken down to the penny, which is ridiculous. There's really no point to it. Possibly because of my engineering training I know that no set of figures is accurate beyond the loosest item in it. There's no point in figuring out to the penny how much a film is going to cost you. I'll never break down a picture closer than to the nearest thousand dollars. Even then, you're best off going to the nearest ten thousand. I take a certain pride in the fact that I don't figure my budgets that accurately, because despite that I really believe that I've been closer to our budgets than just about anybody else.

Do you arrange for financing from sources outside the industry?

I used to when I first started. In the last few years, on the bigger pictures, I've gotten my financing totally from the distribution company. On a lower-budget film I'll finance it totally myself.

What kind of inducements to nonaffiliated backers can you offer on a low-budget picture?

The inducement I offered them when I started, when I needed outside financing, was based on the formula that putting up the money bought them fifty percent of the picture. The filmmakers got half and the moneymen got half. That was predicated on the basis that the filmmakers got very little money up front. We got just a few thousand dollars' salary and then went in for fifty percent of the profits, and on that basis this was generally a fair split. I never had trouble getting financing on that basis.

Where did you find outside backing?

Initially from fellows I'd known in college who had saved a few thousand dollars. A person could come in for five hundred dollars or a thousand. The two things that always bring in investors are, first, the opportunity for profit and, second, the glamour of being associated with making films.

Could you go into the problem of deferments? I can see how you can defer salaries and certain things, but how do you defer lab costs?

The lab cost is the biggest individual deferment on a production. Most labs will give you credit and do the work for nothing, providing you have a contract with them that states they get the first money returned, on the basis that any film, if it's at least reasonable, has got to get back the twenty thousand dollars it costs to do lab work. After all, that's what a television sale will give you. Most labs will give you credit on the basis that developing doesn't really cost them a great deal because they've got the machines turning at night anyway, and whether they throw an extra amount of film through isn't important to them. As a matter of fact, the money they make processing your film is not important. They get their money if you have a successful film and they make a couple of hundred release prints for you. That's what they're gambling for.

The other deferments are whatever you can negotiate at the time. I used to give percentages of profits, although these days I prefer to give a flat amount of money. The reason is that the first film I ever made is fourteen years old and I'm still sending out percentages of profits every six months. It's a tremendous headache. It cost maybe twenty thousand dollars and we're sending out checks to some guys for ten bucks. It's ridiculous. Another way to do it is to give a percentage of the profits but limit it to a certain number of years. On that basis you have a percentage of the profits of all the money made over the first seven years, after which the profits are going to be so small we're not going to bother. At the beginning I gave a percentage of the profits rather than fixed amounts of money because most people were willing to gamble for profit percentages on the basis that if you have a real winner, they can make an astronomical amount of money.

What percentage went into the crew?

I always paid the crew. I never gave percentages to the crew, except sometimes the head cameraman. Once or twice I would sometimes give a little percentage to people who did more than just work on the crew, like bringing equipment. I prefer to save the percentage of the profits for people who are contributing more than, say, five hundred dollars of their wages. Most of the good actors are in the Actors Guild, and when you're making a very low-budget film with beginning actors, all they're really going to be asking for is Guild minimum, so you're just better off paying it and nothing else.

What effect did the failure of The Intruder *have on you?*

Up until that time I'd made sixteen or seventeen films and every one had been a success. I'd never had a failure. It got to the point where I could go to AIP and just tell them an idea and they would back it. I bought this novel and developed the script about the integration of schools in the American South, and to my complete amazement everyone turned me down. So I backed the film myself. It starred a new young actor called Bill Shatner. It got tremendous reviews and won a number of festivals but was the first film I made that lost money. We just couldn't get the seventy thousand back. It really changed my thinking. I thought that despite all the reviews I'd done something wrong. I'd taken a subject that was very unpopular and controversial. I believed in it and still do, but there were enough people in the country and in the world who were against it. I was clearly making a message film, and after that I decided I would make films that on the surface were entertainments but that below the surface would have real meaning for me. Audiences could come and be entertained, but those who were looking a little more intently would see that there was something else moving below the surface.

Can you talk about how Targets *was distributed?*

Targets went through Paramount, but I now believe that if you have a little picture you're better off not to be with the majors. It costs them so much to distribute that they're not interested in the little pictures. I was a little shaky on *Targets* myself. I wasn't convinced that we had a commercial success, so Paramount gave me a part advance and part guarantee that was slightly in excess of the negative cost. I said, "Okay, I got my costs back. Now let's see what Paramount can do." They did nothing. They opened it up in New York and got sensational reviews but didn't do any business. They opened it in an art house in Los Angeles and the same thing happened, so they just pulled it because they didn't want to spend the money on prints. A company like AIP would have pushed that picture on the basis that if they even picked up twenty thousand dollars it was worth their while. To Paramount it wasn't worth screwing around with the film, so they just said, "We'll sell it to television and get our money back later on." It's an example of how you can be worse off with the big distributors.

Do you make the distribution deal once the film is finished?

There are certain rules of thumb. One of them is get your distribution deal before you make the picture, because if you make a bad picture and you don't have distribution, you're in real trouble.

How do you get distribution before you make a picture?

You simply show the script to the distribution companies and say, "Here's the script, here's our director, here's our budget, here's our cast."

Will the small distributors do that?

If they like your project they'll guarantee your distribution, but they won't generally guarantee you money back.

Don't they insist on seeing the picture before they come to any final decision?

If they give you a distribution contract before your picture is made and say, "This is dependent upon seeing the picture," you have no distribution contract. If any of those things are left open in your distribution contract, you have a worthless distribution contract.

How do you specify how ambitious a distribution effort they will make?

It's difficult. When I was negotiating with Paramount on *Targets* I said I wanted a guarantee. They said, "You're not with AIP now." I said, "That's why I want the guarantee from you guys." It's like I said, a small company will probably try harder. With a major you're better to get it written into the contract that they'll open it in a certain number of houses and spend a minimum amount of money on advertising. They'll slough it off if you don't have that in writing. Paramount lived up exactly to their minimums and never spent a penny more. We had it written that they had to open the film once in New York and once in Los Angeles, and that's all they ever opened. One house in New York, one house in Los Angeles. They did strike a few prints and sold it off as a second feature with one of their bigger pictures, but they knew there was no money in the second-feature market, because the cost of your color prints is roughly equal to what your rental is going to be. So they were just playing games at that point.

Could you tell us about sanctions you try to build into the contract so you can police what the distributor is earning from your film and so you make sure you get your cut? You seem to be very conscientious in paying ten-dollar royalty payments.

I'll tell you what happened with Paramount on another picture. They had given me an advance of quite a bit of money and were going to charge interest on that sum. The advance is almost completely paid off and I was looking over a statement and saw that they were still charging me interest on the entire sum. Of course the idea is that the interest is only on the unpaid balance. In addition, the picture had played on television six months before and there was no money indicating that. I got a letter saying these recalculations would be made in the next report. There was nothing as to why such an error had taken place, no admission of guilt, no apology or anything, simply that I was right and the interest would be recalculated and the television money would be put on the report and sent to me. That's the way the game goes.

In your experience, are distributors fairly reputable?

Not particularly. Surprisingly the smaller ones have been more honest. I had a tremendous thing with a major studio once where I protested bitterly, and finally we signed a contract in which they gave me several hundred thousand dollars more than their distribution agreement said I was due, and I, in turn, signed a paper saying I accepted the distribution report as true and accurate, on the basis that they couldn't go on record as stating that there was anything wrong with their distribution report. I remember talking to a veteran producer who had made those Randolph Scott pictures in the forties and fifties that were very successful, and then made a fortune in the early days of television. He owned something like fifteen of these films that were making money hand over fist, but he was getting no reports that anything had been sold to television. He went into the Columbia offices in New York and said, "I know you guys are making a fortune off my westerns. Where's the money?" They said, "There's a little bookkeeping problem. You'll have the money." He said he got a check for $700,000. Like I said, that's the way the game goes.

When did you first become aware that you were the object of considerable curiosity and discussion in France?

Somebody sent me an issue of *Cahiers du Cinéma.* They gave what I thought was a rather incredible review of a picture I'd shot in ten days. I had no objection. I thought it was great.

How long does it usually take from the time you get the script until you get a release print?

I'd rather put it another way, because you might very well be still rewriting your script the day before you start shooting. On *Wild Angels* and *The Trip* we were rewriting while we were shooting, but on the last picture, *Gas,* we're still rewriting and the picture has already been shot. Obviously the longer you have between the time your script is finished and the time you start shooting, the better it is, because you can plan more carefully. With a film like *War of the Satellites,* where we were trying to grab the headlines, we went from starting shooting to an answer print in something like five weeks. Of course that's extreme, and needless to say the film isn't particularly good. On most of our low-budget films I'd say we used to run anywhere from ten to fourteen weeks.

There's a myth that you made The Little Shop of Horrors *in a single weekend.*

I shot it in two days and then we had a night of pickups, shooting the exteriors. I really did it more as a gag than anything else. The picture was made because I was having lunch with the head of a small rental studio and he told me there were some sets still standing. I told him, "Don't tear them down. Let me see what I can do for a couple of days." We worked out the whole storyline in one night and the script was written in ten days. We spent three days rehearsing on the set and then shot it. I remember the first day of shooting we started at seven in the morning, and less than an hour later the assistant director said, "Roger, we're already hopelessly behind schedule." When it was over my friend Robert Towne said to me, "You should remember that making films isn't a track meet. It's not about how fast you go." I said, "You're right. I will never shoot a two-day film again." I think after *Little Shop* we did start getting a little more serious, and our budgets increased. I'm not certain that the quality of films increased, but we started making different types of films.

Was Little Shop *successful?*

Moderately successful. We got amazingly good reviews and it went to film festivals and commercially it got its money back and made a little profit.

How many setups were there in the film?

I'd say we got about fifty setups a day. It was made for about thirty thousand dollars. As a matter of fact we doubled the number of setups, because I was working with two cameras, which I don't normally like to do. It's easier to do now when you're working in color, because, as you know, everybody's bouncing the light off ceilings and off umbrellas, and you get uniform lighting. When we were shooting in black and white, you didn't want to use much bounce light, because the whole essence of the tradition of great cameramen was that they would use lighting to create depth in black and white. There was a tremendous difference between good and bad photography in black and white, and it showed when you used two cameras.

Could you comment on building sets on location?

When I shoot on location I want to use what's there. I think you defeat your own purpose if you build a set on location. On the other hand you may need an interior that might not be readily available, and you generally will want a cover set in case it rains three days in a row. You want to be able to move inside. For conditions like that it might be worthwhile to build a set, but normally I don't do it.

Corman with Bruce Dern (center) and Peter Fonda on the set of his biker film, *Wild Angels* (1966), which preceded *Easy Rider* by three years.

Did you set out to make a series of bike movies?

No. What happened is that the first bike picture, and the first Edgar Allan Poe picture, *House of Usher,* were done for American International, and their policy is always when you have a winner come right back immediately. I think there were seven Edgar Allan Poe pictures done, at which point I said, "That's enough. I can't do any more," and they laid off for a couple of years. I just simply wanted to do *House of Usher.* With the bike thing I just wanted to make what was eventually called *The Wild Angels.* I didn't want to get into the same trap as I had on the Poe pictures, so I said I'd be executive producer—whatever that means—on another bike picture, which was called *Devil's Angels.* It did well and all these other ones came along and I figured, "Okay, I've started the damn cycle, maybe I'll end it," so I backed Bruce Clark with *Naked Angels,* which was also successful. I began to think they'd go on forever. I believe now that they're the new western. The concept of the individual riding freely on his motorcycle in an open setting represents to people just what the horse and cowboy did. That is, the guy who works nine to five can identify with them.

Do you have a dream to make at least one supremely good film?

I would hope to do that, but until now haven't worked on that basis. I've really gone on the basis of doing what seems right at any given time and just doing the best job I can, no matter how commercial the subject matter may be, just giving it my best shot each time. Of course I'd like to have unlimited time and an unlimited budget, but it hasn't worked out that way. There's no point in fighting the fact that you've got three weeks to make a picture and there's no point in spending half of three weeks moaning that you've only got three weeks. You simply go out and do your best in the time you've got.

You mentioned the Edgar Allan Poe films. I was wondering if there was a reason why you deviated so far from the original story of The Pit and the Pendulum.

The Pit and the Pendulum as written by Poe is really just a fragment, so what Dick Matheson and I did was use the story as the third act and invent our own first and second acts. Basically we invented our own story, hoping it was something vaguely in the spirit of Poe.

*I wonder, with the repercussions from the conspiracy trial in Chicago, if films should maybe start moving in that political direction?**

I agree totally with you. We should be making pictures oriented towards the youth market and the current protest feeling or whatever the hell you want to call it. I'm working on a picture based not on the trial in Chicago but on a police raid on the Black Panthers in Chicago, where the police said there had been a tremendous gunfight, and later information seemed to indicate that the police went in and shot up the place.

Is there any particular type of project that you're interested in now?

As a director, I want to do pictures that I'm personally interested in. As a producer, it's important to function efficiently in what is essentially a businesslike manner. I don't want to corrupt this gathering, but with the new distribution company we will be backing some young filmmakers. They'll be youth-orientated pictures budgeted around a hundred thousand dollars. We'll probably go for another motorcycle film, as there seems to be no reason to step away from it. I'd also like to get back into science fiction and horror. We'll start backing people on the same basis as before. It'll be short money for the writer-director, on the basis that he gets his first chance to make a film.

With a percentage?

Not anymore, although what's interesting is that the guys who got percentages came in closer on budget than the guys who didn't get percentages, so we may give a little percentage on that basis.

When you're looking for these writer-directors, to what extent do you want them to come in with some kind of treatment and to what extent do you give them a theme and have them develop something?

Generally I'll pick the subject matter. I'll say, "Okay, we'll go with the bike picture," or "I think we need a contemporary horror story." Then I'll turn

---

*The interviewer is referring to the "Chicago Seven" conspiracy trial that started in September 1969. On February 18, 1970, a little more than a month before Corman spoke at the AFI, all seven defendants were found not guilty of conspiracy.

it over to the guy to see what he can come up with. A lot of these things are just talk at the start. You just throw ideas back and forth.

So you're not on the prowl for properties, as it were.

If somebody has written a screenplay and it's a good screenplay, it'll be offered to the majors before it'll be offered to me, in the hope that somebody will give the writer a lot of money. I assume that if somebody brings me a screenplay it's because it has already been turned down by the majors, and since I don't have that high a regard for what the majors are doing I wonder why I should take what they've already passed on. I'd rather start from scratch and have something designed specifically for the type of movies I'm interested in.

Let me finish by saying that the fact that you're young and starting out gives you a tremendous advantage. I was still claiming to be a student filmmaker ten years after I started making films. Don't fall into the trap of saying, "If I pretend to be from Metro, then I'll be more accepted." Go the other way and say, "I've got a little amount of money and I'm trying to get started." In general, people will be glad to help you.

Films as Director

1955 *Swamp Women*
Five Guns West (also producer)
Apache Woman (also producer)
1956 *The Day the World Ended* (also producer)
The Oklahoma Woman (also producer)
Gunslinger (also producer)
It Conquered the World (also producer)
1957 *Naked Paradise* (also producer)
Carnival Rock (also producer)
Not of This Earth (also producer)
Attack of the Crab Monsters (also producer)
The Undead (also executive producer)

Rock All Night (also producer)
Teenage Doll (also producer)
Sorority Girl (also producer)
The Saga of the Viking Women and Their Voyage to the Waters of the Great Sea Serpent (aka *Viking Women and the Sea Serpent*) (also producer)
1958 *I Mobster* (also co-producer)
War of the Satellites (also producer)
Machine Gun Kelly (also producer)
Teenage Caveman (also producer)
She Gods of Shark Reef
1959 *A Bucket of Blood* (also producer)

The Wasp Woman (also
producer)
1960 *Ski Troop Attack* (also producer)
House of Usher (also producer)
The Little Shop of Horrors (also
producer)
Last Woman on Earth (also
producer)
1961 *Atlas* (also producer)
Creature from the Haunted Sea
(also producer)
The Pit and the Pendulum (also
producer)
1962 *Premature Burial* (also
producer)
The Intruder (also producer)
Tales of Terror (also producer)
Tower of London
1963 *The Young Racers* (also
producer)
The Raven (also producer)
The Terror (also producer)
The Haunted Palace (also
producer)

X: The Man with the X-Ray Eyes
(also producer)
1964 *The Masque of the Red Death*
(also producer)
The Secret Invasion
The Tomb of Ligeia
1966 *The Wild Angels* (also producer)
1967 *The St. Valentine's Day Massacre*
(also producer)
A Time for Killing
The Trip (also producer)
1968 *The Wild Racers*
1969 *Target: Harry*
De Sade
1970 *Bloody Mama* (also producer)
1971 *Gas!—Or—It Became Necessary
to Destroy the World in Order
to Save It* (also producer)
Von Richtofen and Brown
1978 *Deathsport* (also producer)
1980 *Battle Beyond the Stars* (also
executive producer)
1990 *Frankenstein Unbound* (also
producer)

Corman is credited as producer on more than three hundred films in addition to those he directed, including *The Cry Baby Killer*, 1958; *Boxcar Bertha*, 1972; *Capone*, 1975; *Piranha*, 1978; *Masque of the Red Death*, 1989; *Baby Face Nelson*, 1995; and *Dinoshark*, 2010. He appeared as an actor in *Naked Paradise*, 1957; *Atlas*, 1961; *The Godfather: Part II*, 1974; *The Silence of the Lambs*, 1991; and *Apollo 13*, 1995.

Those people who don't enjoy my kinds of films have not permitted themselves to enjoy them. If a film doesn't fit within a preconceived box that those people have constructed, they say it doesn't work. They have cut themselves off.

ED EMSHWILLER
(Born in East Lansing, Michigan, 1925—Died 1990)

Ed Emshwiller enjoyed a successful career as a graphic artist and painter before turning to motion pictures. He stamped experimental films with his own individuality in the sixties and expanded the horizons of American avant-garde filmmaking. Emshwiller's work received acclaim and honors from critics and cinema scholars, but the mass audience rarely saw his films, which were most often shown in museums and at festivals.

Emshwiller studied art at the University of Michigan, the École Nationale Supérieure des Beaux-Arts in Paris and the Art Students League in New York. His work as an abstract expressionist painter led to his hyperrealistic cover illustrations for science-fiction magazines with striking images of fantastic worlds, imaginary planets and surreal characters. These works, which he signed "Emsh," earned him five Hugo Awards.

By the late fifties, Emshwiller had obtained a movie camera to document his work, and soon it opened his eyes to the medium's potential. His interest in dance led to *Dance Chromatic* in 1959, in which animation of his paintings is superimposed upon a dancer. There followed a series of collaborations with choreographer Alwin Nikolais. *Thanatopsis, Totem* and *Film with Three Dancers* all pushed at the boundaries of illusion and reality and received recognition at festivals in Venice, Cannes, Oberhausen, Berlin and Edinburgh. *Relativity,* from 1966, "meditates on the place of man in the cosmos" by using photographic effects to show vast interstellar distances in parallel to restlessly moving close-ups of the human body.

When I became head of the motion-picture service of the United States Information Agency under Edward R. Murrow in 1962, I screened the work of young filmmakers from around the country in search of men and women

Filmmaker Ed Emshwiller was trained as a painter.
He served on the AFI board of trustees from 1969 to 1975.

who could bring fresh vision to USIA documentaries. I saw one of Ed's films
and invited him to Washington to explore whether his abstract style could be
channeled to USIA's objective of "telling America's story abroad." Ed agreed
to make two twenty-minute documentaries: *Art Scene U.S.A.,* exploring the
many avenues of creativity in our country, and *Faces of America,* an impres-
sionistic portrait of America's diversity. The concept of telling a story on film
under a contract with the U.S. government was a radical departure for an
artist with Ed's backgroud, as it was for USIA, but the foreign-service officers
and civil servants gradually warmed to the tall man with the ponytail and
sandals. Murrow liked the idea that his agency would engage an experimental
artist, and Emshwiller's work proved effective and was well received by audiences overseas.

Some years later, when we launched the American Film Institute, I
invited Ed to join AFI's board and enjoyed watching him collaborate with

Gregory Peck, Jack Valenti, Francis Coppola and others from the mainstream of American film. His advocacy of independent filmmakers was a valuable asset in AFI's early days.

Emshwiller taught at Yale, the University of California at Berkeley and the State University of New York in Buffalo, and in 1979 he joined the California Institute of the Arts as video artist and dean of the School of Film/Video. He used video synthesizers and computer systems in ways that enlarged his range of expression, and became respected as an architect of the medium's electronic vocabulary. His later work included *Sunstone,* an experiment in 3-D computer animation, and *Skin Matrix,* in which he modified live-action images with a computer. In 1986 he received AFI's Maya Deren Award for his career achievement.

When I first read the transcript of Emshwiller's 1971 seminar while writing this book, I was disturbed by the confrontational tone of some of the questions addressed to him. But I'm pleased that Ed responded to the provocation by articulating with clarity the unique nature of his work. He makes a persuasive case for the artist who sees film as a means of personal expression.

ED EMSHWILLER

December 8, 1971*

*I must say right away that my prejudices are for narrative films and that I find
your kind of films uninteresting and uninformative in subject, and unimpressive
and unpleasant in treatment. Please take it as an academic statement and not as
a personal attack.*

This is a matter of taste, and you have established your territory. My turf is
different. Narrative film is of secondary interest to me. I'm not denying the
narrative form, it's just that I'm not emphasizing it. I'm de-emphasizing it,
you could say. I was originally a painter and an illustrator. I'm not a writer.
I came to film from graphics and visuals and am slowly discovering the
word. To my mind, most movies are illustrated stories where the real creative work has been done by the writer. It's his concept and the director is
simply an illustrator. Now, I've been an illustrator and it's a fun job. I enjoy
stories and I've enjoyed visualizing stories that other people have written.
But I think there should be something else. There should be cinematic
poets. This is the area of filmmaking I am most concerned with. When seeing my films, the person who doesn't care for poetry, who prefers prose,
says, "What's this poetry jazz all about? It's nonlinear. It doesn't add up in
the same fashion that perhaps a novel does." For me, the meanings that
come from poetry don't lend themselves well to translation into words, so
the kind of movies I'm involved with cannot be dealt with as easily as literary forms. It's very difficult to translate music or a painting into words.
Even poetry is very difficult to translate from one language into another.

*The moderator for this seminar is not recorded. The transcript also contains segments from a
seminar Ed Emshwiller gave at the American Film Institute on September 24, 1969.

Could you trace for us the development of your thinking?

I believe my early films were largely structured in very simple terms, thematically speaking, with a beginning, a middle and an end. I've been involved in a lot of different kinds of films and every film is somewhat different, but with all of them I'm dealing with things thematically—in formal, almost musical and choreographic, terms. With all the films I have an idea of the structure, the kind of material I'd like to work together into the body of the film and a kind of general feeling that I'd like to wrap it up in. I don't have a shooting script but I do have images that are important to me. I define certain kinds of ideas I want to explore within a certain framework. Very often I'll make little sketches on three-by-five cards. These are perhaps like a novelist's notes that he uses to find the form for his writing. I use these things but, unlike the novelist who then creates it all out of his head, I go and gather material that is meaningful to me in some way and that relates to the general theme that interests me. To this extent my films are not preconceived. I don't just go out and wave a camera and shoot everything and wonder what I'm going to do with it. I have certain themes, certain visions and images that fascinate me and that I want to explore thematically.

When I think in terms of the theme of the film, I might have something that I want to start with. Then, through the mechanics of filmmaking, I start to engage those themes directly by seeking out the images or by creating them. When I've got a certain number of these they start to inform me. When shooting I'm conscious of the ways in which a shot might fit into a sequence, and maybe I'll shoot it a couple of different ways because perhaps I can use it to generate some new part of the film. I'm constantly exploring all the possibilities, even though some of them are blind alleys that are locked off. Whole blocks will be dropped because they don't seem to have developed or led further into the film. But often those blocks intrigue me and lead to other films. So I'm constantly threading a path through an ever-expanding series of branches.

Images, it seems to me, have all kinds of reverberations. It's that whole varied indefinable spectrum of reverberations that play against one another in an almost sensual or nonspecific way that appeals to me. I feel that I'm subject to all kinds of pressures—historical, personal, psychological, social, intellectual—that press upon me from all sorts of directions and shape my seeing and my responses. When I'm dealing with whatever thematic imagery or concepts that interest me at a given time, I respond out of all of these multidimensional pressures. If I add these together, I

Emshwiller, behind the camera, directed and photographed his films,
creating distinctive images.

can create some kind of a gestalt. I will see a shot and think, "This plus
that might be something." For one film I recorded sounds for months
with no picture, discovering relationships in the material. The sound
made me want to stick things together, one block of material next to
another. Words are another color on the palette that I'm trying to mix in.
I like to throw down a big heavy block that is shaped and formed in one
way and say, "Look at this." Then I completely switch and throw in
another block right next to it. At first perhaps these two seem not to be
about the same thing, but because they have been placed next to one
another they become like a lot of our experiences in life which seem to be
completely unrelated, but then suddenly seem connected in a way that
neither one alone could have conveyed. Suddenly you see and understand
something that neither of these experiences would have told you by themselves. That's the kind of thing I like to deal with. It means I shift styles,
because style is often a way of saying something, a way of seeing and viewing. By looking at something through several different styles or several
different ways, I feel I'm dealing more fully and, for me, more completely
and more satisfyingly than if I did it all from one consistent standpoint.
That's a device I find useful in structuring my films.

A film becomes structured when I work out how to put the blocks
together. I like to shoot, look at what I have and see what it tells me, and
then shoot some more and put it together, moving forward step by step.

Obviously this is inefficient from a commercial standpoint. You can't make movies in Hollywood on that basis because it's incredibly time-consuming. What's going on is a search. It means alternating from shooting and editing and trying things. There is no deadline. A lot of my films could be structured in several different ways. I wind up doing it by trying to find the way in which those various factors fit together so they seem to me the most effective way of using the material. The final structure is the most satisfactory solution. When I'm shooting out in the field I am, to a certain extent, editing as I shoot. I think how a specific shot might correspond to the rhythm and feeling of the film as a whole. The actual form of the film is discovered in the editing room. I'm up there in my little attic laughing my head off because of all kinds of weird relationships I find in things. My wife hears me and says, "Oh, there he goes again." I'm thinking of these relationships I found fascinating that I want to share. "Look at this. Look at what I found. Have some of this."

The accidents of the process also teach me things, so that it all becomes a process of organic growth. A life experience is what it really is. I find film a fantastically rich and sensual medium to work with, and I make film a living experience for myself. What I like to do is caress and penetrate the world. I like the adventure of going through things, into things, after things. When I'm using a camera I feel I'm dancing with the environment. I try to be responsive to it and the rhythm of what I'm encountering. As a painter I would sit in a very internalized world in my attic and go round and round in my head, and then these things would come out through my hand. Today I split my time between my attic and the real world. I make films in a very physical way, which is how I like it. I find filmmaking to be an encounter art. In other words, the world is very intractable and I am engaged in a form of conflict in order to achieve the making of the film. I have to deal with other people who have their own moments which I either have to oppose or find some way in which it coincides with my own needs. I think film is a sensual medium, done from the gut. You move through all this cerebral business. That kind of stuff you can't shake. You can't get rid of it even if you want. But what I want to do, what I feel about film, is to be out there, gliding around trying to catch something, really dancing in the universe. You're trying to accommodate something out there that isn't under your control. Making films is like playing a game. You're right in there. I want to see if I can deal with certain kinds of things that have been eating at me. Ideas have been bubbling up inside and I want to see if I can find a form for them which I can share with other people. Through the process I also hope to learn more about these ideas and in the process have an adventure.

You know, I hate to verbalize and intellectualize things. I don't theorize. I respond out of my own experience. We all have to fight this kind of thing again and again. We use language, which is the most flexible means of communication, but obviously you can't neatly translate one medium into another. There is a lot lost in the translation. There is much that is cut off by defining it. The whole idea of paraphrasing a picture is, to me, a very painful thing. Very painful, because I always feel that there is so much being cut off when we define such things, even though I know it's got to be done.

Do you have any kind of feeling of responsibility to the people who are watching your films?

Absolutely. Those who are attuned to film poetry of the sort I'm interested in like the films. Those that aren't, don't. You don't like them, but there are lots of people who do. At the same time I can't say that I want to make a film that is going to strike a happy medium for a broad audience.

How do you define satisfaction in your work?

Very simply: those things that seem meaningful and those things that give me pleasure. That's all there is to it. I consider myself the audience. I figure that if it works for me, it will probably work for somebody else. When people come talk about Art with a capital A, it gets pretty pretentious. I really think that most of the people making films are out making what feels good to them. Some of them are very heavy, serious people and some have fun and some, like most of us, have a mixture of pain and fun.

I'm just trying to make a link between you and your audiences in terms of satisfaction.

I believe that anyone who talks to another person, or gives a painting or a piece of music or a piece of film to others, is sharing something. That's what human beings are all about. They share things with others. I am simply sharing my vision with other people. Some people will accept it and some people will reject it. That's all there is to it. I'm saying, "Look, there are other ways to see." There is a spectrum of filmmaking and there

are many different ways in which people can see these things. I think
about some of the innocuous kinds of films I made in the early days.
What astounded me was that some people were offended by them. But
things change, and the type of information that people accept today visually is very different from what they accepted ten years ago, simply
because of television ads. It's a different world today, literally a different
world. People have different visual experiences today than they used to.
I'm really interested in my vision and know I'm not unique. I'm part of
the human community. There are others who have the same feelings, tensions and interests that I have, and all I'm doing is saying, "For those of
you who respond, look at what I'm doing. This is what I feel and see."

*But my complaint is that you're saying, "I'm preaching to my converts, the whole
time. This is me. Here I stand. Thank you very much. This is what I believe in. If
you don't like it, go away. I'm making no attempt to make you see my point of
view. Here it is. If you like it, good. If not, too bad."*

I would like more people to see the work. Let's use an analogy. I have a
neighbor, for instance, who doesn't like fiction. The only thing he cares
for is what you call fact. So in essence, this man probably wouldn't like
what you'd call a regular, narrative film. All he would like is a good, solid
documentary. That's all he wants to look at. To me he's cutting himself off.
He's really truncating his possibilities. What I'm saying is that the area of
film poetry, which is something I champion, is being neglected. I would
like more converts, if you want to put it in those terms, and I would like
more people to see my work. It's like any art form or language. You learn
it when you're a baby. We are exposed to language and pick it up by osmosis more than anything else. Well, I would like to see more film poems, so
that people are exposed to them and accept them as a valid form.

Sometimes I've been asked about teaching film. I think the best way,
from my standpoint, is an arrogant stance, but I believe it. The best way I
can teach films is by making a better film than the one before. Then people can analyze them, they can criticize them, they can say, "He's too far
out, let's do something halfway." Actually that has happened to the so-
called experimentalists, the underground filmmakers. A lot of the things
they investigated in tentative ways have been taken by others and put into
the mainstream. It happens constantly. It's kind of frustrating to the people in this area because they don't get money for it, while the people who
find a way of bringing it to the audience—in some cases by diluting it,

and in some cases really bastardizing it and other cases doing an excellent job—do make money.

Could you say something about the economics of your filmmaking?

I really do feel that good films need not cost millions of dollars and require large crews. I think it's fine to have big production values, but good films can be done as a private vision with very modest means. I do all my editing on a little synchronizer and a Moviscop, which is a 16mm viewer. I do all my transfers on a Siemens projector and all my mixes on my own tape recorders. I do everything myself in my attic except laboratory processing of the film and the soundtrack. I take a certain satisfaction in trying to make what I think are good films—others can challenge that—with a minimum of means. On average these films take about five years to cover the out-of-pocket costs. Nobody makes anything on them. It's akin to writing poetry. Very few poets make a living as poets. By now I've been working in this field for a dozen years and have made quite a few films. The rental income and the occasional sale of prints is enough now so that I could almost feed my family, but not also make new films. I just use them to keep my family and me at subsistence level. I used to finance my films by cranking out magazine and paperback covers very rapidly and creating the films on minimal budgets. Then I received a grant and several commissions to make documentary films. I'm fortunate in that I get a lot of requests either as cameraman or as a producer, so I can earn money to do my own films. I like to work with other people as a cameraman because it exposes me to their thinking and gets me out of myself. It teaches me other ways of seeing and doing and working. I enjoy that. When I'm working as a cameraman for someone I try, to the best of my ability, to create that vision which I understand him to have. I also do a lot of lecturing at colleges. I have a very fragmented life.

What poets of the written word do you read? Could you elaborate more on the distinction between film poetry and poetry that uses the written word?

I'm not a real student of poetry, although my wife is a writer and she's my prime source for writing more than anyone else. I honestly don't pay that much attention to that kind of thing. It's a damning confession, but it's true. I just don't read much poetry. I don't go to movies, either, for that matter. I'm pretty much off in my own dream world.

You're almost saying that you have a direct link to your subconscious, to your intellect, to your emotions, that you go out with your camera and shoot things directly out of that stimulus and then you sit down at a Moviola and it just pours forth. At what point do you start imposing conventional narrative structure on your images, which is what you've got to do?

I don't understand. You mean I have to change my ways?

There is a point where you impose on your material, out of your subconscious, a narrative structure. What is that structure, and where does it evolve from? After all, you are a man with a past, with a history, and it's a narrative past.

Right. But it's a past that has exposed me to a number of different means of communicating, and not all of them are narrative. Some of them are musical, some of them are dance, some are spatial. Some are the juxtaposition of images which, in a poetic sense, strike up associations.

You keep using the word "poetry." I don't know what you mean by that word.

I tried to explain that I'm not very good with words, and that's one of the problems here.

But it keeps coming up in your discussion, and I think it would help to know what it means.

I'm not the kind of person who can define words. I have to use words here and in a certain kind of way that's a trap. In other words, in this discussion I'm not dancing for you and I'm not playing music. If I were a poet and a student of poetry, maybe I could reply in poetry. As it is, I'm trying to wrestle with words, but I'm not clever in those terms. To me, poetry is about making an idea more powerful by not speaking about it directly.

Your films are the first nonnarrative traditional films that we've seen here in months, and it struck me how conditioned I've become being here. It's like going to a live football game for the first time in years instead of watching it on television.

I'm glad you brought that up, because it's something I've always felt. Even in the early days when I was working in pure, absolutely nonnarrative filmmaking, I was very conscious of the fact that a plot makes it very easy to maintain interest over a period of time. Plot is a series of obstacles for someone to identify with. What I'm interested in is how long can interest be maintained, and what are the forms of film that can be created that don't rely on plot? People will look at the Ice Capades and sports for an hour and a half. Of course these games have the built-in interest of the competition and score. But ask the same people to watch a ballet or modern dance or perhaps listen to a concert, which is no more abstract than a football game, and they won't. It's strange to me. It would be nice if people would allow themselves to enjoy a wide spectrum of experience instead of cutting things off and saying, "I won't do this or that." There are so many ways in which our preconceived notions, which are largely culturally determined, cut us off from enjoyment. The hurdle is overcoming what people are culturally conditioned to look at, which is predominantly conventional, narrative films. It's difficult to break out of that. Those people who don't enjoy my kinds of films have not permitted themselves to enjoy them. If a film doesn't fit within a preconceived box that those people have constructed, they say it doesn't work. They have cut themselves off.

I remember being very intimidated when I was at art school. I felt that I didn't know the proper way to look at a painting, that I would have to learn a lot more. Then I realized that I didn't have to know anything more, that I could just sit there and not think that I had to be trained in order to understand it all.

That's very good. I remember going once with my mother to a dance concert and she was sitting in front of me, and halfway through there was an intermission. She turned around to me, absolutely livid. She was furious. She didn't understand what it was all about. You could tell that she felt she was being abused. All it really amounted to was that it wasn't the kind of dance she was used to. She felt that someone was either putting a fast one over on her or they were talking in a lingo that was so special that she didn't know all the little cues to it. Unfortunately she did just what you were saying, and what a lot of people do, which is not let herself be open to it and let it happen on a level that she could respond to. This particular dance was a highly visual, almost psychedelic experience, but she wasn't ready to accept that. She wanted, in this case, a narrative, Martha Graham–style dance.

Imagine you are a painter who has been taught to look for the illustration of a concept, but then you come across the work of someone who is not at all interested in the idea of illustrating a concept. What he's interested in is the relationship of colors on the canvas and the textures and the emotional impact of the dynamics of the line and form. When you look at his painting you are so desperately looking for that kind of relationship between concept and image that you tend to not enjoy the fact that you are responding, on some level, to the color and lines. For me, that kind of imagery, whether it's culturally or genetically transmitted, is something we all share, just as we share words. It's that kind of thing that I think I'm trying to share. All I'm saying is, let's open up the door to another room.

So why doesn't it work for some people?

They are accustomed to a certain kind of diet. You've all tasted something different today. You can reject it, or spit it out, or come back for a second helping. Again, it really comes down to the degree of exposure you have. When you encounter an abstract expressionist painting, you have very little to go on to make any kind of judgment except all the other illustrations you've been looking at. At that point you say, "Boy, that guy sure doesn't know how to draw." But after you've had a certain amount of exposure to other kinds of work, you get into the various value systems that are at play within abstract expressionism, which means you can make comparative judgments. You're judging, for example, how effective one thing is compared to another, and the only way to do this is by exposure to a number of different examples. I think one of the difficulties with the avant-garde or experimental films is that there are so many different kinds. People have different goals and objectives. You have constructivist films, minimalist films, surrealist films, political considerations. You have all kinds of values operating. Saying "Judge these, one against the other," is a little bit like judging apples and oranges. They're simply different animals.

<hr>

Films as Director

1959 *Transformation* (also editor and cinematographer)

Dance Chromatic (also cinematographer)

1960 *Lifelines*

1962 *The Streets of Greenwood* (also screenplay, editor and cinematographer)

Thanatopsis (also cinematographer)

1963 *Totem*

1964 *Scrambles* (also cinematographer)

1965 *George Dumpson's Place*

1966 *Relativity*

1970 *Image, Flesh and Voice*

Carol (also editor and
   cinematographer)
Branches
1971 *Film with Three Dancers* (also
   screenplay)
1972 *Scape-Mates* (also screenplay
   and cinematographer)
1976 *Family Focus* (also editor and
   cinematographer)

1977 *Sur Faces* (also editor and
   cinematographer)
1978 *Dubs* (also screenplay, editor
   and cinematographer)
1979 *Sunstone* (also screenplay)
   Eclipse (also cinematographer)
1987 *Hungers*

The horrible reality is that the movie market is dominated by teenage boys who have been conditioned to see things ten and fifteen times, and if you can get them with something like *Jurassic Park,* you are looking at so much money. But it's harder and harder to make a movie that's about a woman, and that's just a grim reality of the marketplace for those of us who want to make movies about women.

NORA EPHRON
(Born in New York City, 1941)

The female writers of the golden age I met in Hollywood were invariably strong-minded and witty—elements of a survival mechanism, I expect. Today, Nora Ephron demonstrates those qualities in her screenplays, books and essays—and in her life. She is one of America's most successful woman directors, as well as a screenwriter with three Academy Award nominations.

Nora Ephron made the transition from journalist-screenwriter to director with *This Is My Life* (1992).

She was born in New York, but when she was four her playwright parents moved to Hollywood, where they raised Nora and her three sisters. Phoebe and Henry Ephron were writers of popular films like *Carousel, Daddy Long Legs, Desk Set* and *What Price Glory.* Nora started writing because of her mother's mantra: "Everything is copy." She remembers storing up ideas and funny stories from the life of her family in Beverly Hills. Later her parents suffered depression and alcoholism. A 2009 *New Yorker* profile observed that Nora has succeeded in "molding her parents' instability into a world of entertaining wackiness," often in collaboration with her sister and frequent collaborator, Delia.

After graduating from Wellesley College she lived in New York, making her name as a journalist before marrying Carl Bernstein of Watergate fame. Together they decided to rewrite William Goldman's script for the film of Woodward and Bernstein's Watergate chronicle, *All the President's Men.* Their rewrite wasn't used, but a producer who read the script offered her a job writing a television movie, and then she was hired to write *Silkwood* for Mike Nichols. Roger Ebert praised *Silkwood* as the story of an ordinary woman who was "hard-working and passionate, funny and screwed-up, who made people mad simply because she told the truth as she saw it." Ephron and Alice Arlen were nominated for an Academy Award for best adapted screenplay.

Her marriage to Bernstein ended bitterly when she was seven months pregnant with their second child. Ephron—who is inclined more toward action than self-pity, and for whom everything is indeed copy—turned the painful experience into a barbed and witty best-selling novel, *Heartburn,* which Nichols made into a film starring Meryl Streep and Jack Nicholson. "I think what I learned from my mother was a basic lesson of humor," Ephron told a reporter. "If you slip on a banana peel, people will laugh at you; but if you tell people you slipped, it's your story—you are in fact the heroine of slipping on the banana peel."

Her first big success came with her screenplay for *When Harry Met Sally,* which starred Billy Crystal and Meg Ryan and was directed by Rob Reiner. This led to her first directing assignment, *This Is My Life,* about the struggles of a single mother working as a standup comic. The film wasn't a success, but led to her next opportunity as a writer-director, *Sleepless in Seattle.* Ephron made the most of it, crafting a widely praised box-office hit starring Tom Hanks and Meg Ryan. Peter Travers wrote of Ephron in *Rolling Stone*: "She's a major talent with a wicked gift for tickling the funny bone, exposing hidden truths and then, just when you're not looking, slamming you in the solar plexus."

Her writing and directing career continued with hits and flops; among the latter were *Mixed Nuts, Lucky Numbers, Michael* and *Bewitched.* However, disappointments that might sidetrack someone else's career seemed to provoke Ephron to come back with her best work: *You've Got Mail,* again with Hanks and Ryan, and *Julie and Julia,* her 2009 hit that brought Streep her sixteenth Oscar nomination.

In 2002 she wrote *Imaginary Friends,* a play about the turbulent rivalry between the writers Mary McCarthy and Lillian Hellman, which played briefly on Broadway, and she continues to write books and commentary. Joan Didion, Ephron's friend and fellow novelist, screenwriter, and playwright, commented on Ephron's resiliency: "I'll tell you one thing about Nora—she really knows how to pick herself up and turn herself around and start over."

Sleepless in Seattle was screened for the fellows the day before Nora Ephron came to the AFI.

NORA EPHRON

September 30, 1993*

I read an article that said Lynda Obst and Dawn Steel were looking for something for you to direct. That struck me as being unusual and I'm wondering how it happened.

After *When Harry Met Sally* was a hit I was in a position to try to direct something. It had nothing to do with its being good or bad, it just made a lot of money. As Tom Hanks says, "You have a hit, every day is Christmas. You have a flop, every day is Vietnam." I knew *When Harry Met Sally* was the kind of script that would work for someone to direct as their first movie because it was basically a two-character piece and a fairly simple movie. But after Rob Reiner made it so much better than I ever could have, I thought, "Well, I don't really have to direct." But then Dawn Steel, whom I had gotten to know when *Heartburn* was at Paramount, became the head of production at Columbia and decided I should direct something. She was looking for creative filmmakers and was seeing a lot of people who were, let's say, about as good as I was and giving them a chance, so she thought why not? And, of course, she was a woman and I'm a woman. So Dawn said to Lynda Obst, "Let's find something for Nora to direct." They found this Meg Wolitzer novel called *This Is Your Life* and sent it to me and I immediately wanted to make it into a movie. I also knew I wanted to do it with my sister Delia, who is also a writer. I very much wanted to have a collaborator, because there's a certain moment when you have to start directing, and it's very hard to continue writing when you're shooting. If a scene isn't working I

* Lynn Roth moderated this siminar.

like to change it, through improvisation or writing, and I thought, I can't direct and not have a writer close by. I thought it would be great to work with Delia because the material was very much our meat. We had grown up with parents who were screenwriters where everything that happened in the house ended up in a screenplay. *This Is My Life* is partly about using your life as material in your work. It's also about the problem of combining motherhood with having kids, and that's something Delia and I lived through both as mothers and as daughters. So it was a delicious thing for us to collaborate on.

About that time I had a movie made, *My Blue Heaven,* which really didn't come out as we had hoped. I realized that if you make movies with Rob Reiner and they're big hits, you don't necessarily want to direct, but when a script of yours that you liked is just destroyed in your opinion—of course, it's always your opinion—the writer always thinks he or she had nothing to do with it. I looked at *My Blue Heaven* and thought, "Well, I could have screwed that up just as badly as Herbert Ross did and he got paid two and a half million dollars, so I might as well think about directing." Meanwhile, of course, I was writing this movie about women. And one of the real nightmares, if you write a movie about women, is who are you going to get to direct it? Men don't want to direct movies about women. A director wants to direct something he connects to. It takes a year of his life. I use that pronoun because most of them are guys. One of the things you have to do when you're a screenwriter is to make the director want to direct your movie—to invest the director in the script. So when the director says to you, "You know, this scene reminds me of something that happened when my second wife and I were breaking up," you would be a complete idiot not to stick it right into the movie. That's what it means to invest the director in the movie. When you develop a script with a director, part of what you're doing is putting enough of the director's ideas in so that he will feel he wrote it.

So I wanted to do this movie of *This Is Your Life*—which became *This Is My Life.* Was I going to get to direct it? I mean, it's my life already—I'm the right person to direct this. So suddenly I went from being someone who didn't much care whether I directed to someone who had this script that she was passionately in love with and determined to make into a movie. By that time Dawn Steel had been thrown out of Columbia, so we spent a horrible year in turnaround trying to get a studio to commit to it. Eventually Joe Roth, who made a lot of people's first movies in his brief time running Fox, said he would make it for nine million dollars. Of course it didn't make a nickel, but I got my second movie from it.

How did you become involved in Sleepless in Seattle.

I was the fourth writer. It already had a director. Kim Basinger was kind of interested in doing it, if you can believe it, and they wanted a three-week rewrite and sent it to me. I had done *This Is My Life* for Directors Guild scale and it wasn't enough to keep me going for a year, so I was looking for a fast killing and I took on this rewrite. I'd made a horrible financial error years earlier when I refused to do the production rewrite on *Fatal Attraction* because I thought it was a disgusting, sexist movie. Then I saw it and realized that I was completely wrong, that it was basically a male nightmare and was quite a brilliant movie in its own disgusting, sexist, but brilliant way. I could surely have put my children through college with the deal I could have made on that. So along came this other Adrian Lyne thing and I thought, "Well, I'll do this. I'm dying to work with this guy. He's so weird and he's so serious—he's so hilariously serious." I wanted to do it, but he was in a really grouchy mood about the project and didn't hire me. He hired Bill Goldman, so I still didn't have anything to do.

Then they sent me *Sleepless in Seattle*. I looked at it and it was a very gloopy script. It was nothing like the movie that you saw—nothing like it. It was not a comedy at all. There were about two little jokes in it—the kid had the jokes. One of them was "Jed's got cable," which gets a laugh, you know. I hadn't read the original Jeff Arch screenplay, which I eventually read after we finished shooting, which is interesting if anyone wants to look at the progress of the story, just for fun. In the original version the father made the phone call to the radio shrink. He not only made one phone call, he made six phone calls, and they went like this: "I'm so sad and droopy. My wife died and I don't know what to do." Clunk! It was an unmakeable movie because no male actor would ever have played a wuss like this. Ever. By the time I got to the movie, David Ward, who's a very good screenwriter, had done a couple of rewrites and made the fundamental change that made it all possible—he had the kid make the phone call.

Sometimes the studio will say to you that it just needs "character" when the truth is that all it is is a character piece, so the main thing it's missing is the thing that it is. Neither of the characters existed in any way. They weren't likable people, but there was this sort of fabulous dirt that you could grow wonderful grass in if you just knew how to do it. There was the idea of destiny, the idea of the global village—which wasn't remotely fleshed in. You could see that you could have enormous fun doing things called "Everybody in America tells the same jokes, reads the same books, has the same statistics, knows that it's easier to be killed by a terrorist than to find a husband after the age forty." The idea of the little boy who wants his father to find a wife and who wants a new mother was all there. They just hadn't been done. The idea of *An Affair to Remember* was in there, it just wasn't funny. And even though the screenplay wasn't particularly good, the last scene, on the Empire State Building, was great. It was powerful. So I thought, "I know how to make these people into people and how to give the thing some drive." I did a three-week rewrite and put in my favorite character—Jessica, who's the most autobiographical character in it—just a completely hopeless, bossy human being.

I turned this screenplay in and what happened then was really kind of funny, because I'd never been through it in my life and I never will again. It was like a teeny-weeny explosion. In forty-eight hours, every agent, every actor in Hollywood wanted to be in this movie—except for Kim Basinger. And the original director didn't want anything to do with it, because I think he knew it had become a comedy and I don't think he thought it should be a comedy. So off he went, and when the dust settled they offered it to me to direct. I said, "You know, this is not ready to go. This needs a huge amount more work. This doesn't begin to have the kind of texture that I like in a movie."

I have this fanatical thing about having every single character in a movie have a moment. Even the guy who delivers the mail has a little scene. He doesn't just give the mail, he's got this dopey conversation about hiccup cures. I want every actor who comes into a movie to have a reason for being there. I want to get good actors to come because they'll know that even if they only have one scene, it'll be a good scene. If they say to someone, "I was Meg Ryan's brother," they'll say, "Oh yes, I remember that scene." I want that, not just because I want good actors, but because it *makes* a thin movie. This is a thin, character-driven movie, and because you don't have suspense, you don't have car crashes, you don't have guns, all you want is delicious character things. You know the scene where Rita Wilson tells the story about *An Affair to Remember* and starts to cry? There's no reason for it. It doesn't move the plot along. But you just can't imagine the movie without it, because that's what the movie is. All the little themes of this movie come together in that scene—about women and men and how different they are.

You've been on the set as a screenwriter and as a director. What's the difference?

One of the differences is that a scene like that Rita Wilson scene is one that, I swear to you, any director in the world would have said, "What's this doing here?" I love long scenes and I've always had this horrible time with directors. They're always saying, "This scene is too long." And I'm always saying, "Trust me. Try it." But the truth is, if they don't want it, they don't want it, and there's very little you can do about it. They're going to cut it down eventually, or cut it out. On *Heartburn,* it was one of the really heartbreaking moments. I had this hysterically funny scene that Mike Nichols just didn't get. He kept saying, "It's too long," but that was his way of saying, "Couldn't we just throw it out?" Eventually he shot it in such a way that he couldn't use it. He shot it in one master, so it was a four- or five-minute scene with no coverage and people standing still. Well, you can't do that—you can't. One of the things I learned on my second movie that I didn't know on my first movie is keep everybody moving, so that even if you have a long scene, like that scene with Rita at the table, everyone keeps moving—the kid gets up and moves over, Rita gets up and goes to get the Kleenex, her husband gets up and goes to get the wine—so that you can have a scene that plays at four minutes without the audience getting bored.

We should probably mention Sven Nykvist.

Yes, we should mention Sven. One of the reasons why my second movie is better than my first, besides that I had twenty-five million dollars to spend compared to nine, is that I was able to hire the world's greatest cinematographer. It was my second movie and I think it was his one hundred and second. Very few cinematographers can do what Sven can do. He loves working with long scenes, because all Ingmar Bergman did was long scenes. They would shoot ten-minute scenes and then cut because the film ran out. Sven always says, "Faces and teacups"—his career has been faces and teacups. He's not like Michael Ballhaus, who's a great cinematographer but is always wanting to move the camera around the table, whether it matters or not. I'm never going to have a camera moving around a table in a movie because what is this about? It's just about the camera moving around the table. And Sven can light in two seconds, because he didn't have any lights when he was working with Bergman. *Fanny and Alexander* was shot with candles. And that scene where Tom Hanks goes out on a date, when he goes over and says, "The ipecac is in the cabinet, in case either of you drinks poison," you can't see Tom because he's in the part of the kitchen where there is no light. I cannot tell you how many cinematographers would have wasted ninety minutes putting a key light there so Tom would not be in the dark. Sven doesn't care about that. Some people are in the dark and some people are in the light. Everything is so gorgeous. Meg's skin—he's fantastic about skin and he's always screaming at the makeup people about not having much makeup so that people will look as if they're alive. Sven is the greatest person.

Have you ever had the situation where your sister thought something was funny and you didn't?

Oh, sure. And then I get my way because I'm the director. I'm always going to be a director who cares more about words than pictures. I'm making written movies rather than visual movies. Whatever tradition that is, I'm in that tradition. So it isn't that I saw things in a certain way as a writer and now I want to be able to see them in the way I saw them. It's really that I want to hear them the way I wanted to hear them. Although seeing is important too. I remember when Alice Arlen and I wrote *Silkwood*. It's July, it's Oklahoma, Karen Silkwood works in a plutonium factory, she has to wear a jumpsuit. She left for work every morning at 7:30 when it was already about ninety-three degrees. We knew she would get out of bed and put on a pair of shorts and a T-shirt and then go to the plant, take off her clothes and put on a jumpsuit. So it seemed to us she would put on a minimum of clothing. The first night we were in Dallas shooting the movie, Alice and I went to see the costumes and Meryl Streep was sitting on a couch in this dark wig that she had decided she wanted because she wanted to look like Karen, and she was wearing a kind of leather skirt and cowboy boots and tights. I said to Alice later that it was like the *QE2* had set sail and we're in this little dinghy going, "Wait! Wait! This isn't what we meant." But Meryl had found Karen, and Meryl didn't like how she looked in shorts. So our little visual image of Karen had just gone away that instant.

It's like if you're going to a party and you're a little nervous about it and you imagine what the room is going to look like and who's going to be there, and then you walk in and the room doesn't look like that and the people you thought were going to be there aren't there. In that moment the image of what it is replaces the image of what you had, so it's like a hologram, this little ghost that flies away. You forget what you used to think it ought to look like. And that's what it is being a screenwriter. You're always having your image replaced by what it becomes. When you get to direct, you can actually draw the floor plan that you had in mind when you wrote the scene. You can make that happen for yourself.

Ephron directs Tom Hanks in *You've Got Mail* (1998), following their
earlier success with *Sleepless in Seattle* (1993).

*When an actor comes to you and says, "I don't think this character would say this,"
or when Meryl Streep would say, "I don't think Karen Silkwood would wear this,"
how much room do you give the actor?*

It's a collaboration. Sometimes you try to find one thing that you can start
with. Let's say you're talking about costumes. Meg and I spent days going
through clothes until we found two or three things we absolutely agreed
on. The word I was obsessed with on *Sleepless* was "timeless." I was determined to make a movie that if you looked at it in twenty years you
wouldn't necessarily know when it was made. You wouldn't say, "Oh, god,
look at her pants, this has to be 1993." Meg had started out with all sorts
of things that I wasn't crazy about, but when we began to find the one or
two things that were touchstones, then we could say, "No, this doesn't
work, it's too stylish." You can see that the skirt lengths are all different.
From that starting point certain things became obvious, like Christmas
dinner. It was obvious that Meg would wear red velvet because we were
trying to do timeless. It was obvious the mother should, in some way,
look like Meg was dressing like her. So the mother was in a very deep-
green velvet. I had this taffeta plaid blouse that I always used to wear at
Christmas dinner and that became the inspiration for the taffeta blouse. I
thought she should have an add A Pearl necklace—it was a little American
classic. I don't know if any of you grew up with add A Pearl necklaces but
you get a pearl every birthday. That's the thing about movies. You make

all of these decisions as if they are absolutely earth-shattering, but what makes a movie work is something so much bigger than those little teeny decisions. One of the great paradoxes of filmmaking is that every little decision has to be approached as if it's earth-shattering, and yet none of them really matter.

The only thing that really matters in *Sleepless in Seattle*, once you have Meg and Tom and a script that's pretty good, is that you get the phone call to work. You're home free if that phone call works. Tom shot his side of that phone call way before Meg shot her side. We looked at it and we knew—we didn't know we had the hit that we were going to have—but we absolutely knew that we had done the thing that you had to do to get the movie to work, which was that he was great in that sequence. Now Tom is a person who is always saying, "I don't think he would say that." We worked with him for weeks before we started shooting. He would improvise and we would rewrite with him. Tom hates to play only one thing at a time. You may remember when he walks in the door and gets on the phone, he's grieving, he's pissed, he's angry, he's sarcastic, yet he's unbelievably tender towards his child while doing all four of those other things, and he makes a joke. That's six off the top of my head—six things he's playing simultaneously. And then, of course, when he sits down on the bench and talks about his wife, one of the things that makes it so great is that he's still holding back. It's an amazing four minutes of performance. And we knew Meg's end of it would work because Meg can walk in and sit down and cry, just like that. She always says she had such an early start in soap operas because she could just walk in and cry.

I asked someone, "What is Nora like on the set?" He said, "Details. Details." Do you want to tell the avocado story?

The avocado story from *Heartburn*? Well, I do have this thing about details. I really do think that if you have guacamole on the table, it should be good guacamole, and of course I drove the prop guys crazy sending them out for Hass avocados. And of course it didn't make any difference—the movie didn't work. It's striking a balance between caring about details and knowing that on some level they don't matter. When I read the script of *Sleepless*, two things happened. One was that it was a script with a beginning, middle and an end, which is always nice. The other is that I went to bed thinking about it and sat bolt upright, turned on the lights, woke up my husband and said, "Look at this." [*Draws an outline sketch of the U.S.A.*] This is a movie about the United States of America. That's where the little map came in and all the jokes about nobody knowing where anything is. You're always just looking for one thing that makes you go, "Yes! Yes, I have an idea!"

You spoke of the scene with Rita Wilson with all that action and movement. Was that written in the script?

No. I almost never write that in. I do some blocking in the storyboards, but when you rehearse the actors you try to find new things. One of the scenes I'm proud of in *Sleepless* is the scene where Tom goes out on a date. That was a scene we had rehearsed very carefully and hung the mirror for. He just never stops moving in that scene—he comes downstairs, he goes over to the mirror, he comes back, he goes to the map, he goes out the door—all that stuff. We found a lot of it in rehearsal, but some of it— pulling the map, for example—was in the script. So some of it you write, some of it you have in your head, some of it you do when you storyboard, some of it you put in in rehearsal and some of it happens the very day you shoot.

I love improvising, but I almost never let anybody improvise within the scene once we get to shooting it, unless the scene isn't working. I have this fanatical thing that you can fool around with all kinds of things as long as you know what the scene is about. The individual lines aren't very important as long as you never lose whatever the scene is about. And the scene with Rob and Tom was completely written until the end when I said to Rob, "Why don't you suggest that he take out Victoria?" And Rob said, "Okay, what does she look like?" And I said, "She's got this little snub nose." And Rob said, "Pert, pert, pert." And they started that improvisation that led into the Cary Grant thing. I'm a fanatic about writing improvisations. I said, "This works, this doesn't work. Leave this in, throw that out, try it again." And they did it again. I always try to shape it so that it works for the scene. You always want to tell your actor what the end of the scene is. You always want to tell them what the middle of the scene is. Most actors are not writers and they need your help. So you have to be careful that when an improvisation happens you're on top of it, you're shaping it, you're throwing out stuff that is maybe over the line. Also, actors sometimes do a very naughty thing, which is they steal a line from their own character that's coming seven scenes later. Cher used to do this in *Silkwood,* and it would drive me out of my mind. She'd have this wonderful idea and it would turn out that it was coming up in a later scene. You have to be on top of that stuff.

What was your motivation for picking out those pieces of music?

Just as I had this timeless thing about the clothes and the furniture, I had it about the music. I started out knowing that I wanted "When I Fall in Love" at the end of the movie, although I wanted Nat King Cole to sing it. That's almost the only thing the studio wouldn't let me have my way on. Before we started shooting we had this Joe Cocker "Bye Bye Blackbird." The Joe Cocker thing became a touchstone for me, because it was a classic done in an unusual way. It became this little rule—could we find songs that you hadn't heard in that exact way? So of course when we found the Jimmy Durante version of "As Time Goes By," it was a sign. We couldn't believe it because it was not only this unbelievably romantic song, done by this great performer in a version that no one had heard, but it's a song that is probably more associated with love in the movies than any song ever written. So it was "Do you dare use this song?" "Yes, we do! We have found a way to use this song and you didn't believe we could put this in the movie after *Casablanca.* Well, we're going to." So that's what I kept looking for. You almost never hear a woman singing "In the Wee Small Hours of the Morning." It's a guy's song. We found that.

The music in this movie has to be, in some weird way, something that you believe they share when they're so far apart, so that when they're both out on that pier and "Bye Bye Blackbird" is playing, you almost want to believe that it could be going through both of their brains. Some of the guys who do scores are like amazing mathematicians. You say, "I need a music cue that's forty-two feet long," and they can write it. But I'd rather take existing music and try and make it work, than an original score. Nick Meyers, my music editor in New York, is really a mad genius. He had this idea to use the original score from *An Affair to Remember* at the end of the movie. And many of you, I'm sure, don't know that when she runs toward the Empire State Building and they lay eyes on each other, you're hearing the original score recorded by the 20th Century–Fox Orchestra in 1955, which Nick found in a film can in a warehouse at Fox. We recorded it with our own orchestra and played the two next to one another, and there's no comparison with what they used to do in the old days—they used to have two hundred violins. We couldn't afford two hundred violins, so that was a kind of wonderful little extra overlay.

You mentioned that when you got the Sleepless *script you could see right away what it needed. Have you found some sort of method that lets you do that with your own material?*

I hope you understand that I've only made two movies, so many of you know as much as I do, but I had this amazing experience of working with two great directors who let me stand on the set and watch them work: Mike Nichols and Rob Reiner. I went from being this person who thought, "Why are you changing my screenplay?" on *Silkwood* to working with Rob on *When Harry Met Sally.* Rob comes out of television and he rewrites constantly. He just works it as if it's a television script and there are a whole bunch of people in the room and you're all arguing and yelling. I learned from Rob that you have to be ruthless about a scene. You absolutely have to be ruthless. You listen very carefully when you start reading actors, and if a good actor can't make a scene work, you better fix it or you're not going to get away with it. One of the hardest lessons I learned, but I learned it really fast, was if the scene isn't working when you're shooting it, change it. If it doesn't work after you've seen it, ask for a reshoot. And don't send the film in to the studio if you possibly can help it, because you don't want them to see that you screwed up. Be tough on yourself. If it doesn't work in dailies, it's not going to work when it's cut.

When you write an original you're so deeply involved that it's hard to know what it is. That's one reason I often send my scripts to a whole bunch of people and say, "Give me notes. Tell me what isn't working. When did it slow down for you?" Then, when I cut the movie, I have a group of friends who are *really* my friends, and I ask, "What didn't work? What did you hate? What did you think of this song?" I ask them about anything my editor and I are concerned about. It was very hard for me to understand that was what you had to do—rather than being afraid of criticism, you have to almost masochistically seek it. "Tell me what's wrong—please, please. I can fix it now." At the same time, you should never take a note from someone who doesn't like your script. Only someone who likes it can help you. Now, if everyone hates it, you're in trouble, obviously. But there are things that some people like and other people don't respond to, and the ones who don't respond to it are not going to be helpful because they aren't buying your premise. Now they may say to you, "I don't understand your premise," and if seventeen people say that, you'd better think hard about what isn't working. There are people that I didn't invite to early screenings of *Sleepless* because I knew they don't like movies like this and I didn't want to hear a note from somebody who would go, "Oh god, this is too schmaltzy for words." You have to hear from someone who's going to want to see a romantic movie. You can't invite your cold-hearted friends to see romantic movies.

Obviously there's a distinction made between so-called men's films and women's films. Are you comfortable that this distinction exists in Hollywood, or are you try-ing to break it down?

Well, *Sleepless* is not a women's movie. No movie that makes a hundred and twenty-five million dollars is a women's movie. A women's picture—I'll name one I love, *Fried Green Tomatoes*—is a movie where your audi-ence is going to be between seventy and eighty percent women. *Sleepless* is a date movie, a married-couple movie, a "I want to be in love" movie. It's funny enough to overcome the fact that it's sentimental. It's definitely not one of those movies I call Guys Chasing Guys, which is what we mostly see in our local theaters. But it's not *An Affair to Remember*, it's not *Ran-dom Harvest*, it's not *Fried Green Tomatoes*, it's not a movie about a woman's dilemma—which I think is at the heart of the classic women's picture. *This Is My Life* was definitely a women's picture, and it's very hard for a women's movie to make money. The reality is that women do not drive the movie marketplace. Women drive the television marketplace. Women watch a lot of television, and that's why *Roseanne* is on the air and *Murphy Brown* is on the air. Women get all these good roles on television now, all those things that great actresses like Barbara Stanwyck and Claudette Colbert and Jean Arthur used to do. The horrible reality is that the movie market is dominated by teenage boys who have been condi-tioned to see things ten and fifteen times, and if you can get them with something like *Jurassic Park*, you are looking at so much money. But it's harder and harder to make a movie that's about a woman, and that's just a grim reality of the marketplace for those of us who want to make movies about women.

You talked about naming your scenes. What do you use in order to communicate it to the actors and your crew?

I almost always know what the sections of the movies are called too. There's a section in this movie where Tom starts to think about going out with girls. It's a clear little section, and every scene that he's in is pretty much about that, starting with the scene with Rob, followed by the little boy having a girlfriend, followed by the phone call to the date, followed by going out on the date. So when I work with Delia, we're rigorous about saying, "What is this section of the movie called?" We're structural fanatics. For the scene with Rita crying over the movie, I said to the actors, "This is a scene called Boys Against Girls." It's exactly what I said to the actors in its companion scene, which is Rosie and Meg in the newspaper newsroom. Once you know what the scene is about, you know many things. You know there's going to be a two-shot of the girls and a two-shot of the boys, but there's never going to be a two-shot of a boy and a girl. In the case of the scene when Rita really starts crying, you know, not just for blocking purposes, but for purposes of math and logic, that the little boy should go over and stand with the men, because it's about boys and girls.

Could you talk about letting go of the writing and changing your view or approach to the material now that you're the director?

I don't think you ever let go as a writer when you're the director. You're so obsessed with performance and you're smart enough to know that something isn't working, but you're not necessarily smart enough to know how to fix it. I could never conceive of directing without a writer, partly because I always thought I was so fabulously helpful to the directors I worked for, who probably wanted to throw me off the set. Somebody's got to be taking care of the words, and when you're directing, you're *looking*. I'm the kind of person who really gets rattled if it's the wrong flavor ice cream on the table and it doesn't go with the pie. I want someone who is sitting there thinking, "No, no, no, that line isn't right. No, no, no, they aren't saying that the way they should." I'm very willing to give it up to Delia because we really are some sort of great, fabulous blob. We're these sisters who do these movies. I don't know how it would be with another writer.

Rob Reiner has mentioned that When Harry Met Sally *is autobiographical.*

He's never said that, though the character of Harry is completely modeled on Rob. Rob had this idea to do a movie about two people who become friends and make a decision not to have sex because it will ruin the relationship, and then they have sex and it ruins the relationship. That was the idea and that's what we started with. I interviewed Rob and his producer, Andy Scheinman, for about three days about their lives as single men. When I got through, I knew I had a character, because Rob is a comic character. He is the all-time gloom-and-doom guy, but he's funny.

Now, not all gloom-and-doom guys are funny. Woody Allen is a gloom-and-doom guy who's not funny in real life. Rob loves his depression and is wildly funny about how depressed he is. He was just this delicious character, and of course I knew if I modeled the character on him there would be a good chance he would make the movie, which, as I told you, is part of your job as the screenwriter. So now, obviously, math applies here. If he's gloomy, she must be cheerful, right? I mean, you're already halfway somewhere. So if he's kind of a mess, it makes her kind of neat. This is a romantic comedy where certain rules—that probably began in *The Taming of the Shrew*—apply. All of the guys I know, including Rob, have slept with a friend that they shouldn't have slept with and pretty much ruined the friendship, and the women I know have done the same thing. So we had that operating. In some sense what you're hoping for is that it's everybody's autobiography.

Can you compare Rob Reiner's style with Mike Nichols?

Some scenes in *Sleepless* are little love letters to Mike, scenes called, "I would not have known how to stage this if I hadn't watched you." The difference between Mike and Rob is that Mike came from the theater and Rob came from television. Both are in the school of filmmaking that I hope I am at the very lower reaches of called, "It's probably more about words than pictures," as opposed to the Scorsese people. If you had to divide them into two groups, the camera people and the word people, Mike comes from the theater, so he's much more from the writer's point of view, the kind of person who, when you get the script, it's pretty much locked and you trust the material and you work with the actors as you do in a play to find your way into the material. Rob comes from "Let's change it if we don't get it right away because we have to shoot this baby and get it on the air." That's a big difference. Mike talks to actors in this amazing way. I learned from him something I would never have known if I hadn't watched him casting.

   I just love actors. There are a lot of directors who don't love actors, who think that they are needy—and, by the way, some of them are. Some of them are just pains in the ass. But when six actors have failed and the right actor comes in and makes a scene work, you want to cry. It's so amazing. In *Silkwood,* the first time she's contaminated and the machine goes off, Meryl puts her hands up and she sinks to the floor. You just can't believe what this actor has done with this thing you hoped would be half of what it is and it becomes twice as good as what you thought it could ever be. Mike is the kind of director who works in this metaphorical way, so he says to actors, "You know, it's like when you were in high school and you thought nobody was ever, ever, ever going to go out with you." He will try to find some way of expressing it. He won't say, "Be more insecure." It's like a three-cushion shot. He'll let the actor find a way into it.

Rob will give readings. He'll say, "Do it faster," "Do it slower." He'll do anything to get the reading. Rob is such an amazing actor that he can give actors readings. I just don't do that, and every so often an actor will say something in a way that if you'd given them a reading you would've never gotten this loopy way that they read it. My favorite example in *Sleepless* is when Meg says, "I've become obsessed with this man I heard on the radio who lives in Seattle," and her brother says, "It rains nine months of the year in Seattle," and she says, "I do *not* want to move to Seattle." I mean, I never heard it that way. It was such a weird, insane, fabulous reading. That's why you just fall in love with actors.

Films as Director

1992 *This Is My Life* (also screenplay)

1993 *Sleepless in Seattle* (also screenplay)

1994 *Mixed Nuts* (also screenplay)

1996 *Michael* (also producer and screenplay)

1998 *You've Got Mail* (also producer and screenplay)

2000 *Lucky Numbers* (also producer)

2005 *Bewitched* (also producer and screenplay)

2009 *Julie and Julia* (also producer and screenplay)

Before becoming a director, Ephron wrote the screenplays for *Silkwood*, 1983; *Heartburn*, 1986; *Cookie*, 1989; *When Harry Met Sally*, 1989; and *My Blue Heaven*, 1991.

I come to the set knowing my lines and knowing what I'm supposed to do. I don't bump into the furniture and I don't trip over the cables. So if we have to do it more than three times I need you to tell me what's wrong.

MORGAN FREEMAN
(Born in Memphis, Tennessee, 1937)

Morgan Freeman traveled a long road to his station as one of America's most admired screen actors, gaining his first validation at the age of forty-nine for an attention-getting performance in *Street Smart*. He grew up in the hill country of Mississippi where his father was a barber and his mother a housekeeper. He wanted to fly and joined the Air Force, but had to settle for a job as a mechanic. The assignment in California led him to explore acting in Los Angeles when his military service ended. He moved on to New York where he had small parts Off-Broadway, dancing at the 1964 World's Fair behind Chita Rivera, and minor roles on Broadway. From 1971 to 1977 he had a long run as Easy Reader and Vincent the Vegetable Vampire on *The Electric Company* on PBS.

Once Freeman was discovered by Hollywood, the roles came one after another, enabling him to make more than fifty films following his breakthrough role in 1987 as Fast Black in *Street Smart*—the performance that prompted Pauline Kael to ask, "Is Morgan Freeman the greatest actor in America today?" She said he gave the role a scary, sordid magnetism, and that his success in sustaining the character's authenticity was like "sustaining King Lear inside *Gidget Goes Hawaiian*." The playwright Alfred Uhry approved Freeman to play Hoke in the Off-Broadway production of his *Driving Miss Daisy*. Only later did he see *Street Smart*, thinking, "This loathsome swine is going to play my beloved Hoke?" At the first rehearsal Uhry was floored at Freeman's reading. "His eyes which had been so icy in the film were warm and wise and wary at the same time. He was absolutely my Hoke come to life—every facet realized."

Freeman went on from his triumph in *Miss Daisy* on the stage to play Hoke in the film and earn his second Oscar nomination. Through the years

Morgan Freeman as Eddie "Scrap-Iron" Dupris, his Oscar-winning role in *Million Dollar Baby*, 2004, with his co-star and director, Clint Eastwood.

he has brought wisdom, humor and gravity to the screen, delighting audiences with his performances in *Glory, Lean on Me, The Shawshank Redemption, The Power of One, Unforgiven, Amistad, Bruce Almighty, Batman Begins, The Bucket List, The Dark Knight, Invictus* and his Best Supporting Actor win in *Million Dollar Baby*.

When asked who had the greatest influence on him as an actor, Freeman will say Sidney Poitier: "That diversity didn't exist before Sidney ascended to stardom, and the fact that he got there was enough for me to believe I could get there. I told him one time that he was the star that guided my ship of life."

Freeman came to the AFI after being selected to receive the 2011 AFI Life Achievement Award. The fellows and faculty screened *Glory*, and AFI graduate Ed Zwick, the film's director, moderated the seminar.

MORGAN FREEMAN

— ◆ —

April 6, 2011*

There are very few actors who somehow manage to make every director's best film. When you look at David Fincher's best work, Frank Darabont's best work, Chris Nolan's best work, it's just remarkable that Morgan Freeman keeps turning up. Clint Eastwood said, "He seems to be the only person who manages to do as little as I do, and gets away with it." Morgan changed my life as a director. I had done one very small romantic comedy and I was setting out to do this large movie called Glory *on a small budget. I wanted him to be in the movie and asked if he would come in, but I knew I had nothing important I could offer him by way of salary. Morgan walked into the room, sat down and said, "Okay, you got me."*

What Morgan did was bring that generosity and humor and goodwill that enabled the whole enterprise to take place, because his moral authority communicated itself to the entire set.

Can I just bust in right here? Ed's sort of putting himself down as a director, but you've heard the term "big ears"? That means a director who listens. I think that's the reason *Glory* worked as well as it did.

I want to ask you what makes a good director and what makes a bad director?

A good director? This is something I heard from Mike Nichols: "A good director is a good casting agent." Once you've cast a part, that's it. Now you're directing the movie—you're not directing actors. A bad director thinks he knows every part and knows how it should work. The only

*Ed Zwick moderated this seminar.

good director I know who can do that is Fincher. But most good directors—Clint Eastwood is a good case in point—they have nothing to say to actors except, "This is where you're gonna start. You have your marks and the camera will be here. Acting is *your* job."

And a bad director?

Bad directors know everything. They listen to nobody—not to the DP, not to the actors. They know exactly what they want and they'll shoot until they get what they think they want. That may be seventeen, eighteen, nineteen takes. Once you do more than three or four takes, trust me, you begin to shake the actor's confidence. I come to the set knowing my lines and knowing what I'm supposed to do. I don't bump into the furniture and I don't trip over the cables. So if we have to do it more than three times I need you to tell me what's wrong. And don't say, "You looked to your left on that line when you should have looked to your right." I like the fast directors who stay out of the way. But that's personal; some actors like a lot of takes. They want five, six, up to seventeen, eighteen, takes. I've worked with actors like that and I don't care. They ask for another take, fine, I can go with it.

What about the development of a character once you first have the script?

I'm a quick study. Character is on the page. A lot of writers write minutiae—exactly why he wants you to say certain things. They'll put "beat" in the script so you got a clear direction right there, but once you're getting ready to do it, I don't want these directions, because I can see where the writer wants to go with it. I read the script and I got it. And if I don't get it, I just say, "I don't think I'm the one you want for this."

What do you do when you find yourself with problems in a scene and it's not working?

I don't have problems. I've not experienced a problem with getting the scene across. If I have, I think it's because I took a job for money and didn't know what I was doing in the beginning.

Do you try to think about investing some part of yourself in each character? Or is it just intuitive?

I try to get as far away from me as I can. I used to marvel at De Niro, who was just a total chameleon. He would walk down the street and you wouldn't know who he was. That's what I want. I want to be able to walk down the street and have nobody notice. Once I was in a play Off-Broadway in New York playing a wino, and in order to get to the stage I had to go through the lobby. On opening night I got my costume and my makeup on, I'm already in character, and I walk into the lobby and they wouldn't let me in. That's what you want.

I think the more the designer or the DP or the writer understands what an actor goes through to create a character, the better they're going to be able to create that for that actor. Then all the actor is obliged to do is to be—is to act.

I like "be," better than "act." The costumer comes and says, "Well, these are the clothes that I'm thinking of for the character. What do you like out of these things?" Your total involvement there is dressing yourself. I had a great time in *Street Smart.* I auditioned for the part and I got the job and the costume designer—I think it was Jo Ynocencio—she said, "What do you want for clothes?" And I said, "I don't want anything that's crushed, I don't want no platform shoes." She said, "Armani?" And that was my costume. She spent the entire budget putting me in proper clothes. I'd met a pimp in Chicago who, as you know, is a procurer. "I can get you what you want. That's the kind of pimp I wanted to play. Dressed really nice, but still a pimp. Still a bad boy.

When you walk on the set, how do you find your way?

I think as an actor you have to be accommodating to the limitations of the director and his camera. If they say we have a choice of this or that, then you have that choice. "Well, why don't I sit over here, or can I stand over there?" But you always realize that they have limitations, so you work with it, and that's where we become partners. In the rehearsal, do what you want to do. Most of the time the director is watching where you go and figuring out how he's going to accommodate you, but sometimes he can't because of the way the lights are set up. "Hold on, move that." That's what makes moviemaking so much fun.

What was your first experience on a movie set?

I was hired in 1969 by Jack Klugman, who was doing this little movie about kids who were trying to save this pony from the glue factory, so they were keeping it in their parents' apartments, and it would change apartments every day or so. This was back when we were all Afroed out, and they rewrote my character three times because they liked what I was doing. That was my first on-camera experience, and I was good at it. It's like you do something and you have all the power. That's what it feels like when you step on the stage or you step in front of the camera. I feel more power in front of the camera than I do on the stage.

Good things didn't happen for you right away in your career.

No, they did not. It took a while.

Between 1971 and 1977 you were on The Electric Company *on PBS.*

It was still running until 1983, but I had no more work after 1976. I worked Off-Broadway and a little on Broadway, but not much. It didn't start for me until '86.

How old were you then?

I was 49 when I did *Street Smart.*

That's interesting, because it feels like you've had a full career, having made fifty movies since you were fifty.

I always say it didn't have to happen at all. I'm very lucky and very grateful that I had a career. I see people walking the streets of Los Angeles and I think, been there, done that. If you just keep tap-dancing, something good will happen. Don't sit down and say "I can't."

Many of the fellows here feel the burden of thinking it's all got to happen right away.

If it happens right away, it's going to stop right away. That's a foregone conclusion. It's just like weather. I'm a sailor. At sea we have a saying, "Weather that's short foretold is soon past. Long foretold, long last." So take your time. Learn what you're doing. Keep moving forward and just keep plugging, because this isn't easy work.

What do you look for as you read through scripts, trying to decide what roles you want to play?

It's like reading a book. If you read a script and it's a page turner—all right now, you've got a good story. In any good story you're going to follow one character, and that's pretty much how you do it. When I read *The Shawshank Redemption,* they didn't say who they wanted me to play. I called my agent and said, "Any part." He said, "Well, they want you to play Red." Yes! I would have done anything. I would have played any one of those parts. It was that good a story.

What do you do when you have a script and there's not as much on the page as you need to build a character?

I once got a job in Boston in a play by Bertolt Brecht called *In the Jungle of Cities.* It was just a series of long monologues. Michael Moriarty was in it, and I played the character who was a pimp. I had to sit on stage during these long monologues and still be alive. So I went out and bought myself these little packs of tobacco and a thing of rolling papers, and I sat and taught myself how to roll a joint on stage. We don't want to be caught acting. If you're caught acting, you're pretty much shooting yourself in the foot. Sometimes paying the rent demands that you do certain stuff, but the craft is all about those parts you can lose yourself in.

Most actors, when you say "Action," their blood pressure goes up. But the actor you want to work with is the actor whose blood pressure goes down and who relaxes into being of that moment.

I never thought about that. But the minute you said it I could feel it. That's what happens. Clint never says "Action." He just says "Any time, man."

Do you ever work with directors who ask you to improvise?

I've worked with Nicholson and with Chris Rock, and both of them are inveterate improvisers. I don't have any problem at all with actors improvising. Sometimes you'll get into an improvisational thing and a director will just sit back and let it go until it peters out. It can be fun, but I generally don't improvise.

Is there any story you'd like to tell as an actor?

As an actor, no. I'm too old to tell the stories I want to tell now, because I can't do the things I need to do to tell these stories. I wanted to tell the story of the Buffalo Soldiers, the story of Bass Reeves, who was a deputy United States marshal who worked for Isaac Parker in cleaning out the Oklahoma territories from the bad guys back when Parker had the mandate to make the territory safe for settlement. We had given it back to the Indians and then changed our minds. These are the stories that I've always wanted to tell, so now I'll have to tell them as a producer or maybe as a director. Or I can be executive producer and just sit down and let somebody else do all the work.

You talked about losing yourself in a character, so what made you say yes to playing God?

Things were marching along in the latter stages of my career, and I keep hearing "gravitas, gravitas, gravitas." I knew that somebody was going to come to me with a God part. I remembered George Burns' God, so I knew it's doable. I was just waiting for the right one, and *Bruce Almighty* was it. People ask me, "What kind of research did you do?" I don't need to do any research. I know God. Simple.

Freeman with Jihmi Kennedy and Denzel Washington in *Glory,* 1989.

What do you look for in producers?

I think the best producers are good at blowing smoke up your butt. They're telling you how good the dailies look, how great the picture's going to be, how it couldn't have happened without you.

What's your favorite film?

One of my favorite films is Baz Luhrmann's *Moulin Rouge.* I'm particularly enamored of *The Last Samurai. The Outlaw Josie Wales*—Clint Eastwood. *High Noon*—Fred Zinnemann. I can just keep on going.

You've played so many roles that were based on historic men of color. What are your thoughts on personal responsibility to bring these characters alive?

I think your responsibility in terms of any character—living, dead or future—is to be as true to that character as you possibly can. If he's a bad guy, he's a bad guy. If he's a sleazeball, he's a sleazeball. If he's a good guy, he's a good guy. If he's sanctimonious, he's sanctimonious. Whatever he is, that's what your responsibility is. Truth is the default position for all of us.

Films as Actor

1971 *Who Says I Can't Ride a Rainbow!*	1991 *Robin Hood: Prince of Thieves*
1973 *Blade*	1992 *The Power of One*
1980 *Brubaker*	*Unforgiven*
1981 *Eyewitness*	1994 *The Shawshank Redemption*
1984 *Harry & Son*	1995 *Outbreak*
Teachers	*Se7en*
1985 *Marie*	1996 *Moll Flanders*
That Was Then . . . This Is Now	*Chain Reaction*
1987 *Street Smart*	1997 *Kiss the Girls*
1988 *Clean and Sober*	*Amistad*
1989 *Lean on Me*	1998 *Hard Rain*
Johnny Handsome	*Deep Impact*
Driving Miss Daisy	2000 *Under Suspicion* (also executive producer)
Glory	*Nurse Betty*
1990 *The Bonfire of the Vanities*	

2001 *Along Came a Spider* (also
     executive producer)
2002 *High Crimes*
     The Sum of All Fears
2003 *Levity* (also executive producer)
     Dreamcatcher
     Bruce Almighty
     Guilty by Association
2004 *The Big Bounce*
     Million Dollar Baby
2005 *Unleashed*
     Batman Begins
     War of the Worlds
     An Unfinished Life
     Edison
2006 *Lucky Number Slevin*
     10 Items or Less (also executive
     producer)
     The Contract

2007 *Evan Almighty*
     Gone Baby Gone
     Feast of Love
     The Bucket List
2008 *Wanted*
     The Dark Knight
2009 *Thick as Thieves*
     The Maiden Heist (also
     producer)
     Invictus (also executive
     producer)
2010 *Red*
2011 *Born to Be Wild*
     Dolphin Tale

Freeman appeared on television early in his career including *The Electric Company,* 1971–77; *Out to Lunch,* 1974; *Roll of Thunder, Hear My Cry,* 1978; *Attica,* 1980; *Death of a Prophet,* 1981; *Ryan's Hope,* 1981; *Another World,* 1982–84; and *The Atlanta Child Murders,* 1985. He directed *Bopha!,* 1993.

Usually if people are talking about what something means in a movie, it means you've got a movie people want to see. It's like the obelisk in *2001*. People went around for years sitting in McDonald's and Bel Air cocktail parties saying, "What the hell does that obelisk mean?"

WILLIAM FRIEDKIN
(Born in Chicago, Illinois, 1935)

Billy Friedkin got a job in the mail room at WGN-TV in Chicago right after high school and within a few years was directing documentaries and live television shows—some two thousand, according to his count. He was aggressive and energetic and soon had offers in Hollywood, where between 1967 and 1970 he made four distinctly different attention-getting films: *Good Times,* starring Sonny and Cher, *The Birthday Party,* based on the Harold Pinter play, *The Night They Raided Minsky's* and *The Boys in the Band.*

William Friedkin lining up a shot for *The Exorcist* (1973). It became the highest-grossing picture of all time, until it was surpassed by *Jaws* a year later.

Although these pictures established him as a director, they were not big at the box office and Friedkin was concerned about his prospects. One night he had dinner with Howard Hawks. Hawks talked and Friedkin listened: "Every time I made a film with a lotta good guys against bad guys, it had a lotta success."

Friedkin was given the directorial reins on a hard-edged New York drug-smuggling story, *The French Connection,* based on the novel by Robin Moore. Gene Hackman played a good guy coping with bad guys. No one anticipated that Friedkin would turn it into a major critical and financial hit, filming a brilliantly executed chase between a car and an elevated train that reflected his confident command of the tools of his trade. He earned an Oscar for Best Director, and *The French Connection* became the first R-rated film to be recognized by the Academy as Best Picture. Friedkin was reported to be, at age thirty-two, the youngest person to win the directing Oscar. Later it was discovered that he was in fact thirty-six, so the record for youngest recipient returned to Norman Taurog, who was thirty-three when he won for the 1931 film *Skippy.*

Friedkin next turned his hand to *The Exorcist,* William Peter Blatty's best seller about the demonic possession of a young girl. It had been turned down by Mike Nichols, Arthur Penn, Peter Bogdanovich and John Boorman, who saw it as a difficult story to put on the screen, but Friedkin rose to the occasion and gave Warner Bros. a blockbuster. No other director had scored two consecutive box-office successes of this magnitude, and Friedkin found himself financially comfortable and on the top rung of the Hollywood ladder. He and Francis Coppola and Peter Bogdanovich, three of the most successful directors to come along in some time, formed a production company with Paramount that would give them full creative control over their pictures as well as participation in gross revenues. But the Directors Company never jelled, with Bogdanovich's *Paper Moon* and *Daisy Miller* being the only two pictures the company made. Friedkin had second thoughts about the deal and decided to make pictures elsewhere, and before long the directors disbanded and went their separate ways.

In the thirty-eight years since *The Exorcist,* Friedkin has directed a dozen films, including *The Sorcerer, The Brink's Job, Cruising, Deal of the Century, To Live and Die in L.A., Rampage, Jade, Rules of Engagement, The Hunted* and *Bug,* none rising to the success of his 1970s hits. More recently he directed two television episodes of *CSI: Crime Scene Investigation* and, with the encouragement of his friend the conductor Zubin Mehta, has directed several operas.

WILLIAM FRIEDKIN

—◆—

January 9, 1974*

I graduated high school when I was sixteen, and not because I was smart. They used to skip guys regularly in grammar school that they didn't want anymore. I started in the mail room of a television station in Chicago. They all thought I'd take over the mail room one day because I was one of the best mail-room guys they ever had. Live TV was just happening, and there were all kinds of dramatic and musical and variety shows, and I thought I could probably make a career out of live television. Within six months I'd become a floor manager, which is like an assistant director in films. By the time I was seventeen, I was directing live television. I did about two thousand live TV shows in eight years, and I would probably still be in live TV if I hadn't been fired from every station I worked for. I used to get in trouble because I would try a lot of things. Sometimes after sign-off a couple of the cameramen and I used to go to the sound stage and experiment. The chief engineer would see us playing with his cameras and his equipment and I got fired. I figured I had to do something, so I came out to Hollywood and became a movie director.

I made a documentary in Chicago called *The People vs. Paul Crump*. It was about a black man who was on death row for years at the Cook County Jail. A friend of mine was the chaplain at the jail and said, "You have to meet this guy. He's a fantastic, incredible guy. He's been totally rehabilitated in prison and may have been railroaded here in the first place." In those days in Chicago if they were looking for a black man to

*James Powers moderated this seminar. This transcript also contains segments from seminars William Friedkin gave at the American Film Institute on September 5, 1990, September 2, 1992, March 15, 1994, March 12, 2003, and January 16, 2008.

go down on some charge, they'd just literally pick one off the street and beat a confession out of him. The chaplain told me the facts of his story, which interested me, though it took me a long time to get up the nerve to go down to the jail and meet the guy. When I finally met him he shook my hand and stared right into my eyes. People seldom do that. I looked into his eyes and something about this guy just nailed me. Crump held my hand very tight and I felt a great sense of connection. I just thought, "I don't know what he did, but this is a human being and I don't want to see this guy die." I listened to his story for three or four weeks and decided I had to make a film to save his life. The money was put up by the local ABC station in Chicago, who didn't really want to make the film, but I really did, so I went and did a big selling job on it. They said, "Can you make it for five hundred dollars?" I said, "Absolutely." Well, it cost about seven thousand and they went crazy and I got fired.

The film ended up being instrumental in commuting his sentence to life imprisonment. It was the first film I ever made. I knew nothing about how to make a film. I went into an equipment-rental house in Chicago and said, "I want to make a movie and if you'll teach me how to use the camera and get sync sound we'll rent your equipment." Fortunately for me the Arriflex 16 camera and the Nagra had just come in. They taught me how to load film into a camera and focus the thing, and I set out to make this movie with another guy who worked at the TV station. That half-hour lesson was the only one I ever had in filmmaking. We just went out and shot things we thought would be good. We had to make stuff up and improvise. I decided not only to re-create the circumstances of the crime, but also show the techniques that the Chicago police used to exact a confession from him. I knew police in Chicago and they showed me how they would beat a confession out of somebody.

I decided that if I was going to continue making documentaries, they were all going to be biased. I'm not interested in anything that gives equal time to both sides. I have strong opinions. Of course that's frowned upon. The documentary filmmaker is meant to say, "I'm just showing things as I find them." But of course that's not true. Where you decide to put the camera is a choice, how you edit the film is a choice, and those choices represent how you feel about the material. With *The French Connection* I realized I could create my own fictional reality using documentary techniques. The style of that film is based on the idea of going somewhere to make a documentary with a camera and not knowing exactly what you're going to shoot. You have to be flexible in order to arrive in a place and record what's happening.

Anyway, the film got complicated, because Crump named the police officers who beat a confession out of him, and ABC bleeped them out and then decided to ban the film anyway. But the power of the story transcended our lack of technique and the film won an award at the San Francisco Film Festival. The governor of Illinois saw the film and voted to pardon Paul Crump from the electric chair. Then the producer Dave Wolper saw it and hired me, and that's how I came out here. The first movie I did in Hollywood was called *Good Times* with Sonny and Cher. It was 1966 and I think it was seen by eleven people in Topanga Canyon. It had a happy but short life. I'd like to have the rights to it now, though.

How did you become interested in suspense?

I used to make up stories and scare the little girls in my neighborhood. I have vivid memories of making up these outlandish stories that would drive them to tears, and the more response I got, the scarier those fantasies would be. I guess the pictures that had the most effect on me were suspense films like *The Wages of Fear,* or *Les Diaboliques* by the same director, Henri-Georges Clouzot. Then I went to work for Hitchcock. As a matter of fact I did the last *Alfred Hitchcock Hour* ever made. My contact with Hitchcock consisted of him coming on the set on my first day of shooting to film his introduction. I was really terrified because he was this great director. He came up to me and stared. He said, "Mr. Friedkin, you're not wearing a tie. Usually our directors wear ties." I thought he was putting me on, but he was absolutely straight. That's all he ever said to me.

I went to school on *Psycho,* I've seen it thirty times. I figured, because of *Psycho,* I could get away with a lot in *The Exorcist.* I figured he had about forty-five minutes in *Psycho* where absolutely nothing happened. It's a dull sort of story but the audience is so expectant. The audience knows that they're coming in to see this horrific suspense film but they don't get it immediately. They're getting edgy, and then suddenly Hitchcock whacks them with it and he's got them in his back pocket. I said, "What I'm going to try and do is make this *Exorcist* go on for about an hour with nothing happening and see how long I can pull the string." I'd been wanting to make a film where I could do that for some time. I had this book which I knew scared a lot of people, so I figured that was going to be the one.

How did you find working with the old studio crews during your television days?

I had good and bad experiences. On that *Alfred Hitchcock Hour* I was working with a cameraman who was there every week called Jack Warren. I was this kid who'd never done anything before. Warren was a great old guy, but a bullshit artist, like most old-timers in the business. He used to call me Chief. "Well, Chief, what are you going to do today?" The guy who produced the show said to me, "No matter what you do, make sure the first shot you do is easy, and get it in one take. The crew has to have confidence that you know what you're doing. If you're out there banging away at take seventeen the first time out, you're going to be history here before lunch." When I hear things like that, I fight against it. So I set up the first shot as some complicated thing, the kind of shot you never see on television. Jack Warren freaks out. "Holy shit! It'll take hours to light!" I said, "That's the shot. That's what we're going to do," and I walk away. Never argue with these guys. "I'll see you later." So he goes out and lights the shot. I managed to get three or four pages done in that one single shot. Jack said, "They aren't going to like it. Where's the coverage?" So the rushes come out and the executives see them, and the next day I'm standing on the set and overhear the producer of the show and Jack talking. The producer said, "That opening shot was great. Incredible. We've never had anything like that on the show before." Jack said, "You liked that? It was my idea." That has been my experience with the old-timers. They have one way of working, and if you go against that, you're in trouble. For the most part they want things simple, so they can get the hell out of there and go home. If you find yourself working with someone like that, you have to work on igniting them, like you would work with an actor. You have to show them that if he does the shot, he's likely to win an Academy Award. You have to motivate him.

When I made *The French Connection* I called a friend in New York and said, "Do you know a good young cameraman? I don't want to work with any of these warhorses. I want to work with someone fresh and new who's up for anything." He said, "There is a guy. He's never done a feature but he's done some commercials." It was Owen Roizman, and when I told him I wanted to shoot in the street without lights, in real police stations, only bounce lighting, no key lights, no big equipment trucks, he said, "I'd love to shoot that way." I hired Owen without even seeing his reel, and he was nominated for an Academy Award for the film.

Did you know you were going to do The Exorcist *when you read it?*

Yes. Absolutely. I read it and thought, "This is pretty powerful and scary stuff here. It would make a good movie." Blake Edwards had asked me to direct the film version of *Peter Gunn,* which was a television series. Word was out that *Good Times* was a hot picture. It turned out to be a dog, but Blake heard it was a good picture and he wanted a young whatever, and I was a young whatever, to direct *Peter Gunn.* So he gave me the script, which I read and really hated. I didn't know what to say to Blake, because I wanted to do a picture, but not *that* picture. So I went back to see him and said, "I really hate this script. As a matter of fact, I think it's the worst piece of shit I ever read in my life." Blake was a little stunned and said, "Really? Is that your comment?" I said, "Yeah." He said, "Well, I'd like you to tell it to the fellow who wrote the script. He's sitting in the other office." In comes Bill Blatty, a nervous kind of guy with a facial tic. He came in and sat down, and Blake said, "Bill Blatty, this is Bill Friedkin. He's read the script. Bill, why don't you tell him what you think of it?" After I told him what I thought, Bill Blatty broke into hysterical laughter and said, "You know, you're absolutely right. It really is a rotten script and nobody around here has the guts to say so." That finished him. He was off the picture too, and Blake went on and made the film.

Bill and I kept in touch over the years. I was in postproduction on *The French Connection* when I started reading *The Exorcist,* and it really wiped me out. I called him up and said, "This would make a great picture. I'd love to do it." He said, "That's terrific. Warner Bros. just paid me $640,000 for the rights. I'll tell them you're interested." The studio wanted either Arthur Penn, Stanley Kubrick or Mike Nichols, but Bill said, "I have director approval, and if you want to do it, I'm going to hold out for you." We threw out the script, which was full of a lot of flashbacks and flash-forwards, and started from scratch. I just wanted to tell a straight-ahead story from beginning to end with no craperoo. I literally just marked up the book, gave it to Bill and said, "This is the script." He rewrote it from that. From day to day we would get new ideas and bring new stuff in. I went out and saw an actual arteriogram and a pneumoencephalogram being performed. I wrote down what they did, gave it to Bill, and he put it into script form. It was a very collaborative process, but I'm not going to say I wrote a line of it. It's his screenplay and he deserves whatever accolades he gets.

Did you have any interest in demons or exorcism before you made the film?

No, but I did a lot of research and came up with quite a few startling facts. The thing that turned the tables for me was when I discovered that the

story was based on an actual case. Blatty put me in touch with some people who were involved in the case and I made some cassette tapes with
them and learned that a lot of the stuff in the book isn't half as farfetched
as the stuff these people were claiming happened in 1949 to a fourteen-
year-old boy in Silver Spring, Maryland. *The Washington Post* did a number of stories on it. The exorcism took place over a three-month period
and was performed in St. Louis, in front of doctors and nurses and relatives of the boy. All the manifestations in the book and the film are classic
symptoms of possession. There was recently an exorcism that lasted three
months in San Francisco that was performed by a Jesuit priest. There was
also one in 1972 in West Germany on a thirty-three-year-old woman that
was widely publicized in the German magazine *Stern*. These cases don't
get wide publicity, which I suspect is a good idea, because I see some of
the reactions to the movie. I think if you reprinted *The Washington Post*
stories on the 1949 case, just the bare facts of what was going on in this
household, it would drive people up the wall.

Did they claim it was a demon or the devil?

Churchmen are split on the whole question. Less than a year ago, Pope
Paul issued a statement where he claimed that he and the Catholic
Church still accept the idea of a personified devil. Not just an abstract,
metaphysical, evil force, but a personified devil who is capable of taking
over the souls of mankind. You find a lot of highly placed churchmen who
call that poppycock. Bill Blatty takes great pains in the book to state that
this girl is possessed by a demon and not the devil.

Could you talk about the problems you had with the special effects in The
Exorcist?

In the old days when they wanted breath to show in a room they used to
build a stage in the Glendale Ice House. Well, the Glendale Ice House
doesn't exist anymore. In order to show breath on a set consistently you
have to refrigerate the room. In other words, you have to build the set literally inside a refrigerated cocoon, which is what we did. We shot it in
New York in Hell's Kitchen, on Fifty-fourth Street. On one stage I built
the interior of the entire house: two stories and a staircase and all kinds of
rooms on the first floor, two bedrooms on the top floor, and a trap door
leading to the attic. Then we had a second stage on which we built a
refrigerated cocoon with a duplicate of the little girl's bedroom. On the

second stage we also built a duplicate of the hallway, which wasn't refrigerated, because I wanted shots of people coming down the hall, and you'd see no breath coming from them, but then they open the door to the bedroom and suddenly you see their breath. The entire bedroom set—four walls with a removable ceiling—was built inside a cocoon which was able to take the cold down to ten below zero. At the end of each day's shooting we had to turn on the air conditioning to build it up for the next day's shooting, because we'd arrive in the morning and once we'd been shooting for four or five hours with the lights turned on, the temperature would go up and there'd be no more breath in the room. We had to stop shooting, turn off the lights and build the cold up. The entire set was balanced on a bowling ball—literally, a bowling ball—which permitted us to rock it back and forth. There were different beds which did different things. One bounced up and down, another just went sailing up into the air. There were three different sorts of weight devices for the various effects on the bed, but that was largely a question of trial and error. We also had to have the curtains in the bedroom blowing, even though the windows are shut. We did that by building little invisible traps in the windowsill with powerful fans underneath the set and pumping air up through them.

How did you do the levitation?

There are a few things I don't want to discuss. One is the levitation and the other is how the head turns around, only because I know these very wonderful seminars get reprinted and sent around the country, and some guy at a news desk in Miami will read it and put it in the paper and it will limit people's enjoyment.

How did you work out the problems with the little girl speaking with those voices?

She mouthed everything, but we also recorded her own voice as a guide track and for a while I thought we might use that recording. When I started the picture I thought, "I'm just going to get a good, ballsy, masculine voice to do this thing." But it occurred to me that it would be much more believable if I could get a female voice that had some masculinity to it. Most of her voice is replaced by Mercedes McCambridge's, but some of the voice is her own. The stuff that was most effective was recorded in sync to her own dialogue, line for line. All Linda Blair did was mouth the words as best she could. Mercedes McCambridge, who smokes heavily, was able to speak in that emphysemic voice and get that wonderful wheezy sound. We would experiment. She would swallow three raw eggs and drink some Jack Daniel's and then we had her tightly tied to a chair. It sounds like she has three or four different screaming animals in her throat. We recorded that very close up and then made a loop out of it. After we had dubbed the girl's voice I felt there was something wrong. It occurred to me that I had to keep the demonic presence alive, even when it wasn't talking, and that's when we decided to put the looped wheeze in.

How did Linda Blair handle playing that role?

The media makes up shit that you can't believe. They said after making *The Exorcist* Linda Blair was in a mental hospital or something. She was a delightful little twelve-year-old girl, and every time we'd do a take of the most monstrous things imaginable the prop man would hand her a milk-shake. I made every scene a game with her.

I knew that the only way I could make this movie was if I had a child who was able somehow to grasp and deal with this horrible stuff that had to be performed. I really thought I might never find such a person. We had casting directors look at thousands of women across the country, starting at age twelve. Then we started looking for sixteen-year-old young women who looked younger. We couldn't find anyone, and I seriously thought it wouldn't be possible to make the film. Then in comes this eleven-year-old girl with her mother. I ask her the same questions I asked the others. I said, "Do you know what this story is about?" She said, "Yes, I read the book. It's about a little girl who's possessed by the devil and she does a lot of bad things." I said, "Like what? What sort of bad things?" She said, "Well, she pushes a man out of a window and she hits her mother in the face and she masturbates with a crucifix." I said, "What?" I'd never heard that from an eleven-year-old. I said, "What does that mean?" She said, "What?" I said, "What does 'masturbate' mean?" She said, "It's like jerking off, isn't it?" I said "Uh-huh." Then I said, "Have you ever jerked off?" and she said, "Sure. Haven't you?" I said, "You're hired."

Can you talk about how you cast your films?

What a director does is communicate, and he does it largely through actors. I try to envision the kind of person I want, or don't want, in any given role. For example, I didn't want a known actor in the part of Father Karras in *The Exorcist*. I wanted a man to come on wearing that collar who had never been arrested on a morals charge or had his picture in the paper for being at a party with Henry Kissinger's ex-wife. I remember in *The Sandpiper*, when Richard Burton came out wearing a collar, the whole audience burst out laughing. So I wanted somebody who was going to be believable as a Jesuit priest. The first quality I look for is intelligence, because that's what I think makes a good performance. In the case of Father Karras I wasn't going to hire an actor who hadn't had a Catholic education. I came up with Jason Miller, who had never done a film before. He was a milkman in Yonkers and had written a play called *That Championship Season* in New York, which ended up winning a Pulitzer. He'd acted in a few Off-Broadway shows and regional-theater, but had never done anything that might be called "major." He fulfilled all the requirements. He was trained to be a Jesuit at Catholic University and studied for the priesthood for three years before dropping out. He was extremely intelligent and I thought he had an inherent sensitivity that I could photograph.

Why does someone become an actor and why does someone become a director? An actor wants to be controlled; the director wants to control. It's that simple. If you're working with a real actor, you'll find that they want the director to have a point of view. When an actor is dealing with his or her own insecurities, "maybe" is the worst word the director can use. Of course, you don't want to give orders. You want to make the actors feel as if they're coming out with their own ideas, but that you, the director, know precisely what the right ideas are. You want to do this by suggesting things. When I'm on a set with an actor, I've got to communicate effectively with that person, and one way to do that is to create an atmosphere of play. In other words, "This movie isn't the end of the world. It's a lot of fun. I love what I'm doing and I know you love what you're doing. Now, let's talk about your character in this scene." Constantly compliment the actors. They really are children. Even Robert Redford wants to be told what to do. He's scared to death that you won't know how to use him best. If he thinks you do know how best to use him, it's going to fly. The only way you can free up actors is if you know exactly what you want. Often you'll find that the actor has a better way of doing things, and of course you have to be open to that, but at the same time you need to have the whole movie worked out in your head.

On *The Exorcist* I was having terrible trouble with a scene. It was the most frightening experience I'd had as a filmmaker. There I was working with the greatest living actor, Max von Sydow. He's really astounding. But for this one scene he had to say, "I cast you out, unclean spirit," or some-

Friedkin with Ellen Burstyn on the streets of Georgetown,
where he shot *The Exorcist.*

thing like that. He just couldn't do it. It was horrible, pathetic. I asked
him to do it again. We spent all day on it and didn't get a usable take.
Well, that happens. So the next day we try it again and still he can't get it
right. It's even more problematic because the line is coordinated with the
ceiling cracking above him. I've got guys up there cracking the ceiling, so
by this point we've gone through about twenty ceilings. Three days go by
and I still don't have a usable take. I'm going crazy and sit down with
Max. I say, "Max, what can I do? I'm lost. I'll bring Ingmar Bergman in to
direct this scene." I told him we were going to rewrite the scene and cut
the line out, and have him just die of a heart attack. He said, "The problem is that I just don't believe it. I'm not a Christian. I don't believe in
Christ." I said, "Max, you played Jesus in *The Greatest Story Ever Told.*
What are you telling me?" He said, "Yes, but I didn't play him as a Christian. I played him as a man, a carpenter. I just don't believe the words." So
we had to find a shortcut. We came up with another approach to the
material which meant that he wouldn't have to feel and believe what he
was saying, which is how he normally approaches a scene. Every good
actor has their own approach to their art, and the first job of the director
is to find out what that approach is and make the atmosphere on the set
comfortable enough for them to perform. Directing is about communicating—first with the actors and then to the audience.

Did you have any kind of personal or religious experience during the filming of
The Exorcist? Was there a sense of spiritual community?

During the filming we were a very close-knit, and I guess you could say
spiritual, community. Everyone who worked on that picture really had
strong feelings about the subject matter. The crew was as handpicked as
the cast. Before the picture started Bill Blatty and I went down to the
UCLA parapsychology lab run by Dr. Thelma Moss. It was part of the
research I did into ESP, parapsychology, the occult and actual cases of possession, all of which I felt applied in some way to this film. We participated in a number of experiments, like Kirlian photography. Are you
familiar with Kirlian photography? It was invented by a Russian in the
thirties. He was an electrician, not a physician or a camera guy, who discovered a process by which you could photograph the aura of something
directly onto a piece of negative, without a camera, by running electric
current through it. Every animate object has an aura. For example, a
freshly cut leaf is placed on a piece of film and current is shot into it. You
can literally photograph the energy flowing out of the stem of that leaf.

I had three pictures taken of my index finger, one second apart, but at
each second I had a different thought. For the first photograph of my finger I was thinking about something that gave me a lot of pleasure. For the
second photograph I thought about a person I hated. For the third picture
I thought of something I was looking forward to, an event in the future.
Each picture taken one second apart on the same piece of film had a totally
different aura and different colors. The shot where I thought about this
person who angers me had a glowing red aura. There was a red ball flowing
right out of this white spermatozoic substance. The one where I was thinking about someone I had a great deal of affection for was beautiful. It
looked like one of those sunflowers. The healthy aura is white with a yel-
lowish tinge around the edges. You can read about Kirlian photographs in
the book *Psychic Discoveries Behind the Iron Curtain*. Bill Blatty had his
imprints taken and the operator said to him, "Have you been sick lately?"
The fact is he had been bedridden for the last two weeks. His aura through
all three pictures was pale and listless. Mine was sort of healthy and
vibrant. I was in good health, he was not, and it showed in his aura.

One of the people at the UCLA lab is a mesmerist. I've been mesmer-
ized, and it's a far-out trip, I have to tell you. It largely consists of someone
who stands over you in a dark room and passes his hands over your aura
for about two hours. He doesn't touch you. He literally affects your aura.

Bill Blatty and I each brought in an object. Bill had brought a religious medal that had belonged to his dead mother. The mesmerist guy didn't know anything about Bill or his mother, alive or dead. He held the medal and sat there with it for about twenty minutes not saying a word. He was in intense concentration and then the first thing he said was, "I feel hot and cold. Hot and cold." Later it occurred to us that it had to do with the fact that the medal once belonged to someone who was dead, but was in the possession of someone who is living. What then happened for the next hour was absolutely incredible. The guy started to describe the whole history of Bill Blatty and his mother. He said, "I see a woman," and he described a photograph. I turned and looked at Blatty, who was going ashen-faced, and knew the guy was hitting close to home. In the middle of this recital he said, "Someone's on a motorcycle and the motorcycle crashed." About two months before that Blatty had been in a motorcycle accident and couldn't walk.

I kept all this in the back of my mind when I made the movie. It was an example of an experience that convinced me there was more on heaven and earth than I had ever dreamed of.

Working with the supernatural for two years and thinking about it, are your own nerves now jumpier or calmer?

I don't go too much into the supernatural, mainly because there are too many freaky cats involved with it. If Karl Menninger* regularly lit a candle to Satan I'd be up there saying, "Yes, there must be something to this," but I don't see too many people I respect getting into the supernatural. That said, I've read enough to have the feeling that anything is possible. We accept a lot of things on faith. I've never seen Australia, but believe it's out there. Either the girl in *The Exorcist* was possessed and exorcised or she wasn't. There aren't too many in-betweens. If she wasn't, then perhaps she had a disease for which there's no name and therefore no cure. Fifty years ago we had no cure for schizophrenia, so it was madness. Now you can treat schizophrenia with drugs, electricity and psychosurgery. But fifty years ago if you manifested the symptoms of what we now feel comfortable in describing as split personality, you went into the nuthouse and that was it. Maybe the 1949 case would have been diagnosed differently if they had arteriography and pneumoencephalography and psychosurgery

*Karl Menninger (1893–1990), American psychiatrist.

and more sophisticated methods of X-raying and operating on the brain. But they didn't, so they called it demonic possession.

You haven't had any complaints from the American Medical Association?

One of the really big hospitals has a sign up: "Don't See *The Exorcist.*" I guess the doctors think they come off badly. I went to Dr. Norman Chase at NYU Medical Center, a brilliant guy, and said, "What would you do if you were confronted with these symptoms, like the 1949 case?" He said, "I would go through this whole number with pneumoencephalography and arteriography," which is the most sophisticated way of X-raying the brain. None of that is in Blatty's book, but we put it in the film. I asked Chase, "What if after all that you didn't find a problem with a lesion of the temporal lobe?" He said, "I would have to remand the patient for further observation." I said, "What if you remanded the patient for a year or two years?" He said, "I'd be at the end of my rope. Then it goes to psychiatry. The ball is in psychiatry's court."

Was the actual exorcism scene shorter than originally planned in the script?

It might have been five or six minutes longer. The actual Roman ritual of exorcism is about thirty pages, but it's very repetitive and involves a lot of common prayer, so I sort of edited it for the highlights. An exorcism generally lasts weeks or months, and I didn't flatter myself that I could get people to come back next week to see the rest of the exorcism, so it runs about seven or eight minutes in the picture. A lot of people have told me they think the film is too slow. That bothers me, because I love speed on the screen. I shot three and a half hours of usable film of street life in Iraq, but I got it back to the cutting room and said, "I can't use it. It'll really mess up this story if I do an essay on Iraq." Having said that, there are three or four shots in the film that shouldn't be in there but that I couldn't pull out because they're just so beautiful. There was a shot of Max von Sydow walking through a bazaar where they're making shoes. We did it without any light. The sun is pouring through these holes in this cave. It was just so beautiful, but it didn't belong in the movie, so I got it out of there and the scene played a lot better. Later I said to the editor, "Put those damn shots back in." He said, "Why? They fuck up the scene." I said, "They're gorgeous. If they believe any of the rest of the stuff in this film then they'll believe this shot." So we stuck it back in. It doesn't belong in the picture, but I just love it. The sound is so nice with all these guys making shoes. It's my favorite moment in the picture, but it has nothing to do with the story.

What is the meaning of the sequence in Iraq?

The entire Iraq sequence is about a premonition of death, the future encounter with the demon that Father Merrin has.

I was aware that we always saw the demon with those short flashes throughout the film. It seems as if there were new faces all the time, never the same one.

That's right. My theory is that if any one of us were captured by the Frankenstein monster or the Loch Ness monster, at the end of three days we'd be playing chess with him because familiarity breeds a certain relaxed quality. I didn't want the audience to feel they had too strong a handle on what that demon looked like. I wanted to hit the audience with something new every time, like a new weird way she's talking, or vomit or a levitation shot. Nothing too long. The more you stare at a face, the more comfortable you're going to become with it. The whole idea of always showing a different face each time is to put you off guard and make you uncomfortable. The thing we're most uncomfortable with is whatever is behind you. It's what you can't see. Every sound you hear on that darkened street, every twig that bends under your feet, every leaf, every footstep makes you afraid. Expectancy is what an audience brings to a Hitchcock film and to *The Exorcist*. It's why in *The Exorcist* there are so many shots of people turning around. As a filmmaker you play on the knowledge that fear is whatever is behind you. It's like a cold chill on the back of your neck.

Are there any principles you adhere to when editing?

The only principle I use is one I took from Michelangelo Antonioni, even though his work, which I admire tremendously, is totally different from mine. What I perceived from him is the sense of not repeating a shot. You can look at an Antonioni film and they'll be a hundred different shots without a repeat, as opposed to what people are used to after being conditioned by television, where you see all these predictable patterns. The best piece of advice I can give you about editing comes from Diaghilev and his advice to Cocteau: "Étonne-moi." Astonish me.

I saw The Exorcist *in Westwood. The sound was very loud. Was it meant to be that way?*

Yes. It took me three months to get the soundtrack right. As a matter of fact, I set the sound and light levels in each of the twenty-four theaters where the film opened. One of the most interesting things about film-making is seeing what happens to your picture, because no matter what you hear, the projectionist has final cut. You've got to set the sound and light levels, and take a hard-line policy and make sure you get what you want. The standard setting for how much light you're supposed to have on the screen is fifteen and a half lamberts. Most of the theaters in the country run anywhere from three up to twelve, so it's almost impossible to have your picture seen the way you actually shot it, even in some of the best theaters in the country. We would show up in all the theaters before the picture opened and set the sound and light levels. In some theaters we replaced the screen. The guy who we sent out to Minnesota said, "There are potholes in the screen." So I called up the head of distribution and said, "Well, we'll have twenty-three prints, please, not twenty-four. That theater in Minnesota isn't getting a print." He said, "Why not?" I said, "Potholes in the screen." He said, "They put up a hundred thousand dollars for the picture." I said, "Fine. They can put up another five thousand and replace the screen." So we replaced the screen and billed them for it. We replaced the lenses on the projector at one of the New York theaters. At the end of the run they can either buy the lenses or go back to the crap they've been using. I want people to see the picture in focus. After all, I shot it in focus. My editorial crew and I checked every print that went out from the MGM lab, and rejected about a third of what they initially ran off for us. Unless you really care, and give it time and raise hell, you ain't gonna get what you shot into the theaters.

How did you come to make The French Connection?

Phil D'Antoni, the producer, who also produced *Bullitt,* wanted to do a picture with me, so we looked for a story. One day he said, "There's a book here about these two crazy guys called Eddie 'Popeye' Egan and Sonny 'Cloudy' Grosso. They're after a guy called Frog One and they chase him around New York. He's got $32 million worth of heroin that he smuggled into the country in the panel of a 1965 Buick." I said, "Say no more. Let's do it." Even the names Egan and Grosso turned me on. So Phil gave me the book. I took it home, opened it, read about eight pages,

Friedkin working with Gene Hackman (center) as Popeye Doyle and
Fernando Rey (right) as Alain Charnier in the Academy Award–winning
The French Connection (1971).

fell asleep. Couldn't read it, never finished it. I came back the next day
and said, "Phil, this is really dynamite. Let's make it." That's the truth.
Popeye and Cloudy and Frog One. To this day I've never read the book.

Phil and I spent months writing a script, but every studio in town
turned the film down, and a lot of them turned it down twice. D'Antoni
was financing the script out of his own pocket and there were three different versions. Finally we got a guy called Ernest Tidyman, a crime reporter
for *The New York Times,* who we used more or less in a secretarial fashion.
We dictated the script to him. He had never written a screenplay but we
had the galleys of the first *Shaft* novel he'd written, which we thought had
a nice feel to it. To this day he's never met Egan or Grosso or any of the
people involved. Eventually Dick Zanuck from Fox called and said, "I'm
going to get fired from here in a couple of months. I always liked that
crazy story you guys had. I've got a million and a half dollars hidden in a
drawer. Can you make it for that?"

How responsible did you feel to the true events of the case?

When you make a fiction film, there's no such thing as a true story. The
French Connection case took place over an eighteen-month period. There
were maybe sixty or sixty-five law enforcement people involved. As you

can see in this story, it's boiled down to the largely fictional essence of what three or four law-enforcement people did and what, perhaps, three or four of the bad guys did. What we gave you, at best, is an impression. At worst it's a distorted impression of events. "Based on a true story" is just jive. Everything is based on a true story. *The Creature from the Black Lagoon* is as much of a true story as *The French Connection*.

What I try to do is immerse myself totally in as many peripheral or tangential phases of that subject, so I'm literally swimming in it before I expose a frame of film. On *The French Connection* I spent the better part of a year—three or four nights a week—just traveling with those two policemen. There was no script to that picture. Until *The French Connection* I hadn't been able to bring my documentary training into a fiction film. I set about to make this film as believable as possible by using a hand-held camera, to get the feeling we had just dropped in on the events. It occurred to me after a lot of hand-held stuff that it wasn't looking too good. It was kind of phony. Then I thought of a way to make it really feel like a documentary. I would stage the scenes with the actors but wouldn't tell the cameraman what was going to happen. All I would tell him was that three guys are going to come in this room and that it was up to him to find the shot. Have him fish around for the scene. Very often I would shoot on the second camera and induce even more this sense of the camera not knowing what was happening. On the average movie set you can't pan the camera 360 degrees because you'll see the crew and the lights and guys standing around eating donuts. For the sake of reality I thought, "Let's get the crew the hell outta here. The camera is going to go anywhere." I wanted to achieve some kind of cinematic cubism. You're familiar with the cubist painters, who wanted to give the illusion of a three-dimensional image inside the flat canvas? Even when we go into a police station, it's a real police station, not a set. We didn't set up big lights, we just put little lights on stands and bounced them off the ceiling and went with natural light as much as possible. I wanted to open it up to the possibility of the fourth wall being photographed.

The whole film was ad-libbed dialogue from my experiences, and later from the experiences of Hackman and Scheider with the actual cops. They spent a month with Eddie and Sonny and knew how they talked and reacted, and that's what we got on film. They would come to me with a lot of stuff and we'd put it in the picture. The bar scene where they go into an all-black bar and bust it is taken verbatim from what I saw the cops do over and over again. A lot of the people in that scene are from the actual bar, and Eddie and Sonny were on a first-name basis with everybody. For the sequence at the start of the film I just let Hackman and Scheider and this guy just wail on. I used two cameras and chose the best moments from the single take we did. That's how we got that wonderful tagline from Hackman. I forget exactly what he said, something like, "Not only am I going to bust you for those two bags back there, I'm going to run you in for picking your feet in Poughkeepsie." Very Pinteresque. Eddie Egan used that line all the time.

The Egan-Grosso interrogation technique is very simple. There are questions that we all have the answers to, like "What's your name?" and "What's your address?" and "What are you doing here?" And then there are some questions for which we don't have answers. Their interrogation technique was having one guy come in with the question that the guy had to have the answers to, and the other guy would hit him with some far-out questions that he couldn't even understand. One would say, "What were you doing in that bar back there?" and the other one would say, "Have you ever been in Poughkeepsie?" The guy is sitting there asking, "How come this guy wants to know if I've ever been in Poughkeepsie?" I was once in an interrogation room where Egan was questioning a transvestite who had a few bags on him. Egan said, "You got a lawyer?" And the guy says, "No—yes—no—yes." "Well," Egan says, "is it yes or no? Have you got a lawyer or not?" "Yes, I think I have a lawyer." He says, "Have you ever been circumcised?" The guy said, "What?" Egan says, "Take off your pants and I'll tell you." The guy stood up in the squad room and took down his drawers, and Egan said, "No, you've never been circumcised. You're going to need a circumcised lawyer." He picked up the phone and said, "Hello? Let me have the circumcision division." He's got the guy going absolutely crazy. It's an absolute sidesplitter. Egan is really an insane man, a lunatic, but that's the shtick he used for years, and I tried to get a little bit of it into the picture.

Was recording the sound a problem?

I really believe in soundtracks and give them as much attention as the picture. In many cases I finish the picture and then start thinking about the sound. Sometimes the sound will match the imagery and sometimes it will be a counterpoint to the imagery. I grew up on radio in the forties with the greatest dramatic shows imaginable, full of sound effects. They were scarier than any movies I've ever seen.

Was Gene Hackman your first choice?

He was my last choice. He bored the shit out of me, but there wasn't anybody else, so we used him. I had a very antagonistic relationship with Hackman on *The French Connection*. Gene really didn't want to go into himself and find that character, so I was purposely provocative with him. One time Egan was on set and watched Hackman play a scene, after which he turned to me and said, "He's more me than me." Hackman just hated that and would fight it. Eddie Egan used to imitate Gene Hackman's imitation of him. He wanted Paul Newman to play him. At the 82nd Precinct, where he worked, in Bedford-Stuyvesant, they used to have casting lists on the wall, and he would invite all these cops to put down who they thought should play him. It was always these handsome movie stars. Frankly I saw this guy as a fat drunken bum. Originally I had a guy to play him who wasn't even an actor, a newspaperman in New York called Jimmy Breslin, a heavyset, heavy-drinking guy, a dark Irishman with a great sense of humor but a foul temper. That was my impression of Eddie Egan. He was a fearsome character, a kind of a monster, but with a contrasting humorous side. I rehearsed with Jimmy for three weeks, running around New York. We would rehearse and improvise a scene on a Monday, and Breslin was terrific. But by the next day he'd forgotten what he'd done the day before. By Wednesday he'd forget his name. He just couldn't sustain a performance. I still was going to go with Breslin until one day he said to me, "I got a confession to make to you. When my mother died on her deathbed I promised her I'd never drive a car and I still don't know how to drive a car." I figured for this picture you have to drive a car, so I just decided to broom him and go with an actor.

Phil D'Antoni and I were sitting around, and he asked me who I wanted to play the French guy. I said, "What about that guy who was in *Belle de Jour*?" We didn't know his name, so I said to the casting director, "Hey, you know that guy who was in *Belle de Jour* and works with Buñuel all the time? Let's see if we can get him." So the casting director goes out and says, "Okay, we got the guy. His name is Fernando Rey. He's available and he's going to cost this much." Great, so we hire him. I go out to the airport to meet the guy. I'm looking around and I don't see him, and suddenly I get paged. I go up to the booth and there's this guy standing there. It's Fernando Rey, but he's not the guy I was talking about! It turns out I was talking about Francisco Rabal. Rey is slick-looking, with a goatee. I'm driving him to his hotel and thinking, "Holy shit." I always saw the character as being more rough, so I suggest he shave his goatee. He says, "Oh, I can't shave my goatee. I have scars all over my chin." This guy is effete compared to the guy I want. Then he says, "And another thing. A lot of this dialogue is in French. I don't speak French. I'm Spanish." I get him back to the hotel and head to the office and grab the casting director by the neck. We call Rabal's agent and it turns out Rabal doesn't speak a word of English and was unavailable. So we had to make the film with Fernando Rey. And of course he was terrific.

Was the subway scene when he gets away from Doyle made up, or did it really happen?

That's from the original case. That's how the guy gave the slip to fifty cops. They were probably all paid off. The original guy, Jean Jehan, was six-foot-six with a shock of white hair. No way in the world you could miss this guy in a crowd. He got through fifty narcotics cops in New York and escaped out of the country. He was discovered later in France and the narcs tried to get extradition on him through the French government, but it turned out Jehan was the head of the Union Corse, the Corsican Mafia, during World War II, and had cooperated closely with the French Resistance. As thanks for that his buddy Charles de Gaulle did him a favor and vetoed the extradition.

You say the film was improvised. Did that include the car chase?

There was nothing scripted on the chase. When the chase scene was edited, a secretary wrote down all the shots and that became the official screenplay. I had been building Bill Hickman, the stunt driver, up to this for weeks. I looked at him and said, "Hickman, you have no guts. You're chicken shit. You need a couple of drinks to drive good." I kept getting his goat. Finally he said, "I'll tell you what. I'll show you some driving if you get in the car with me." So I got in that car and he went at ninety miles an hour for twenty blocks, with just the siren on top of the car. We broke every stop light. We went through everything, including people on the street. We went in and out of lanes. There was no control at all. The whole thing was shot at speed with both cameras. One was on the front bumper, and I operated the second one from inside the car over Bill's shoulder. Most of the point-of-view shots from the car are from that run. The crashes that happened weren't planned. But if you'd seen the dailies of the chase, it wouldn't have been impressive. What makes it work is the combination of the shots and the sound. The moment with the woman and the baby carriage is a shot of her crossing the street, which was done with a zoom lens. We then cut to a shot of Gene Hackman, who at that moment is actually sitting stationary in a car. We're making things reflect in the windscreen, but he's not even moving. Then add a reaction shot of her, cut all those shots together and boom!—it looks like he's driving at her. If you can somehow involve the audience in the idea of what's going on, you can get away with a lot. I used to go hear Slavko Vorkapich lecture. He was a theorist who used to do montages for MGM films. He used to talk about "deep immersion." When the audience is deeply immersed in a scene, you can break every rule in the book and it'll appear seamless.

You mean you broke the law?

In New York City they don't pay too much attention if you drive like that. The film *Bullitt* had come out a few years before, and I wanted to create a chase scene that topped *Bullitt*. If you look at the chase in that film, it's two cars flying through the streets of San Francisco with no people around. They cleared the streets and filmed. I wanted to do a chase with people around. Then I realized I didn't want two cars chasing each other, because that's still *Bullitt*. Phil and I sat down and talked about the chase but we weren't getting anywhere, so I said, "Let's just start walking from my apartment and let's not stop until we come up with a good chase scene." We walked about fifty blocks in one direction, throwing ideas around. I see the elevated track and wonder how fast a train travels. We started developing this idea of a car chasing a train and found out that the top speed of a train is about fifty miles an hour. Then we had to go back and figure out how one guy gets on a train and the other gets in a car. It had to be done realistically. We had to make it logical and still get one guy in a car and another in a train.

Was there anything that didn't make the final cut of the film?

The original version of the film was much more character-driven. Now it's plot-driven. The original concept was about the thin line between the policeman and the criminal, and how that line is very often crossed. The criminal is often a decent guy. He dresses well and knows how to order wine. He's nice to the woman he's with, he's a gentleman, he's a gourmet, he has manners, he never raises his voice—and he's a drug dealer. I've had occasion to meet some of the members of organized crime in this country and there isn't one of them that you wouldn't want as your uncle or father. But the cop is a loudmouthed scumbag. The guy with the badge is a brutalizer of women. He has no life and doesn't care about people's lives on the street. I was trying to make a film about the thin line between the policeman and the criminal, and how those lines constantly overlap.

Do you plan anything before you shoot?

Sometimes I see an entire picture in my head before I do it and then, like a novelist, set out and write a visualization instead of prose narration and dialogue. I make sketches, and from those sketches write out in longhand a complete verbal description of every single shot in every sequence. I have those notes mimeographed and duplicated by the assistant director for everybody working on the scene.

Sometimes, a year or two later, when I'm in the shower, an idea about a shot or a scene comes to me. I suddenly realize how I should have done it. Ideas in the shower are always better than how I actually did the scene. For example, I had a whole different idea for the ending of *The French Connection* which I think is better than the one I have, and I would give almost anything to go back and reshoot it.

What is it?

I thought what a great ending it would have been to see two junkies sitting on the East River at seven o'clock in the morning on a wintry day, nodding off, and a barge is moving downriver dumping all this heroin, which is what they did with all the confiscated stuff. Whenever a court case on this junk was closed, they would take it out and dump the bags in the East River. Of course, as we all know, a lot of bags didn't get dumped. They got sold back onto the market. But I had an image of these two guys watching $32 million worth of heroin floating by as they sat there. It reminded me of *The Treasure of the Sierra Madre.* I'd shoot it tomorrow if I could. There would be a lot of prints to correct.

Endings are tough to come up with. The truth was that the Egan character and the guy from the Federal Bureau of Narcotics were constantly feuding, and Egan even told me once that if he had the chance he would have killed that sonofabitch. So I thought, "That's the ending. He kills the guy." I thought this would be very dramatic, because by the end of the film it seemed to me that the fictional Egan character I'd created had flipped out. He was no longer dealing with anything rational. In fact there was a sequence I shot where he's down in that room at the end of the film. He sees the French guy coming at him from everywhere and starts shooting, and pretty soon he's shooting at shadows. I even had Gene Hackman running at himself in the Santa Claus suit he wears in the first scene. In the end I thought it was all too esoteric, so I just had him run down the hall. That's when I got the idea for that single off-screen gunshot that ends the film. In every town or college I went to, people would ask me what that gunshot meant. It wasn't in the script. I did it in the dubbing room the day before I left as a kind of a joke. I said, "Let's put a gunshot in off-screen." The mixer said, "Why?" I said, "So we can end this thing with a bang." So we stuck it in there and just let it go. A number of the studio executives said, "What the hell is that gunshot?" I gave them all kinds of explanations. I said, "It's possible that Doyle has become so crazed that he's firing at shadows. Another possibility is that his partner put a bullet in the dead cop to take the onus off Doyle for having shot the guy." I ad-libbed about three or four possible explanations, none of which were in my mind when I put the gunshot in. I just thought it would be nice to have this thing go bang and end up on a black screen. That was it.

In a way the whole idea behind that ending is for the audience to draw their own conclusions. I found that people who saw the film were split right up the middle. I had as many people tell me that it was a putdown of cops as told me that it was the most accurate realistic story of the life of a cop. I got citations from police organizations. I also had the head of the American Civil Liberties Union in Connecticut telling me it was the greatest example of police procedure he's ever seen. In Rome I was accused of being a fascist by the Italian press. All I tried to do with *The French Connection* was make the picture and tell the story straight as I saw it. If you do that, people inevitably put their own handle on it. Usually if people are talking about what something means in a movie, it means you've got a movie people want to see. It's like the obelisk in *2001*. People went around for years sitting in McDonald's and Bel Air cocktail parties saying, "What the hell does that obelisk mean?"

Did you work closely with Harold Pinter when you directed The Birthday Party?

I decided to rehearse the film for three weeks and then give two complete performances of the play for Pinter. The entire movie, in other words, was rehearsed as if it were a play to be performed on the Friday of the third week to an audience of one person. Two performances, one before lunch and one after lunch. At the end of these performances we were all wondering what his reaction was going to be. He stood up, took off his glasses and said, "Well, certainly some very interesting work is going on here. Of course, you're not doing my play." Then he read from his notes and explained that there were six words that were wrong throughout this two-hour-and-fifteen-minute play. He cited the words and what they were to be, and we laughed. "Is that all, Harold?" He said, "Yes, that's all, but they have to be right. If you want to do my stuff, that's it. It's got to be verbatim." Of course we understood that.

During shooting we came to the celebrated interrogation scene where these two guys—an Irishman and a Jew—browbeat this other guy. It's kind of an elaborate tease or interrogation about things for which there are no answers. Some of it is very Kafkaesque. Among the questions they ask this guy that he can't answer is "Why did the chicken cross the road?" There were two lines that Patrick Magee, who's in the film, remembered from when Pinter first wrote the play back in 1960. The Lord Chamberlain was the censor of the British theater and you couldn't make any reference to either the Queen of England or the Crucifixion, so there were two lines in the play that were deleted. One of the questions was "Who hammered the nails?" The other line was "Who drove the screws?" Both referred to the Crucifixion. So Magee told me about those lines right in the middle of shooting. I said, "Jesus, where the hell are these lines in the scene? They're great." They weren't in the film script. So I called Harold in London, woke him up, and said, "Magee told me about those lines you had to cut in 1960." He said, "What are you talking about?" I gave him the lines and he said, "I've never heard those lines before." I said, "Oh, come on," and told him that they were in the original version. He said, "Wait a minute, let me find it." Fifteen minutes later he came back and he said, "I've got the damn scene here and those lines aren't in it." Then he said, "Wait a minute. Do you think those lines work?" I said, "Work? They're fantastic. They're the best lines in the scene." He said, "Keep them."

When you shot The Boys in the Band, *how did you go about adapting it from a play to the stage?*

I just shot the play. I'll never do another play on film ever again. I loved *The Boys in the Band* as a play but don't feel it worked well as a piece of cinema, because it works so well as a play, and the two media just don't go together. A good play like *The Boys in the Band* relies for its effect on, essentially, good dialogue, verbal effects and the interplay between characters. Compare this to my concept of a good film, which clearly needs to be more visual. *The French Connection* had twelve reels, six of which have no dialogue at all. It works a lot better for me because it's a story told in pictures. I'm told that in Thailand, when they run American films, often they can't afford to subtitle the film, so they stop the film every few minutes and someone explains to the audience what just happened. I want to make films that you don't have to stop every ten minutes. Anyone with average intelligence should be able just to look at them and figure out what's going on. As a director you want to work essentially with visual elements. You want to emphasize things that you wouldn't find in any other medium.

Which filmmakers have most influenced your work?

There's a scene in *Day for Night,* a wonderful Truffaut picture, where you see this little kid sneak into a theater and steal the still photographs from *Citizen Kane* from a movie display. Like most youngsters of my generation, I was influenced by *Citizen Kane.* I've seen that picture maybe fifty times. I've studied it on the Moviola. It's a veritable quarry for filmmakers, just as Joyce's *Ulysses* is a quarry for writers. The films I admire the most, just off the top of my head, are *Citizen Kane, Paths of Glory, All About Eve, 8½, The Magnificent Ambersons, Night of the Hunter, Rififi, L'Avventura, La Notte, 2001* and what might be my favorite picture, Raoul Walsh's *White Heat.* The director whose work I'm most interested in is Kubrick. Then of course I've got to see whatever Antonioni is doing. When I called up Max von Sydow and offered him the part in *The Exorcist,* I said, "Max, I'm going to give you a chance now to work with a first-rate professional filmmaker. I think you've done a lot of good work in Sweden with those amateurs. It's about time you had a chance to work with the heavyweights here in Hollywood." Obviously anyone who's interested in movies has to see early Bergman, *The Seventh Seal* up through *Persona.* But if you want to know what has influenced me more than anything, it's the fact that I'm just a guy from Chicago who never got past high school. My old man never made more than fifty bucks a week. I remember stories in Chicago that haunt me. I used to see cops shoot guys in the stomach and holster their guns, and you'd never see it in the newspaper. I saw a man die in the electric chair. I photographed an autopsy and the birth of triplets. Every piece of film I've ever exposed is both an adventure and an education. That was the world I knew and saw. My curiosities went beyond that, but my influences were right there in the streets of Chicago on the west side.

What do you think of the so-called personal film?

I'm not interested in them. I'm interested in films for audiences. If you've ever really been involved in filmmaking, you know that there are too many people who contribute to the success of a picture. It's true that one intelligence can and does generally inform a project, but the fulfillment of that vision requires a great many talents. To deny this is a joke. It's usually film critics not competent to judge a goddamn thing who deny it. Long after most of the film criticism in this country finds its natural habitat— wrapped around garbage—the great movies of this country will go on entertaining generations. These are movies that had contributions from cameramen like Gregg Toland and Stanley Cortez and Freddie Young and Owen Roizman and Geoffrey Unsworth and Ozzie Morris, guys who generally don't get their names in the paper but who very often say, "Wouldn't it be great if we did the shot from here?" And it turns out to be the greatest shot in the picture. Or a sound man or editor who contributed to the success of that picture. Of course the director usually gets the most attention, and I'm happy about that because I'm a director. If an editor got more credit for movies, then I'd be an editor. I'm on an ego trip, like everyone else. I enjoy the fruits of success, the money and the ability to order my own existence. But you can't erase the essential point that this is a collaborative medium.

I believe that the major reasons to make a film are to move people emotionally, either to laughter, tears or fear. There are other reasons to make movies, like to educate audiences. I've done that and would do it again. But if you're working for Warner Bros. or Paramount, all these guys who are putting up a lot of bread hope to get their investment back. You're working for them, and also for an audience which has to stand in line with three dollars in their hand. I don't know anybody who ever said, "Jesus, go see this picture, because it's got a wonderful philosophy in it!" People want to see movies because they want to be moved viscerally. I'm interested in having an entire audience in the palm of my hand.

Don't you think you can have a visceral reaction from a quote-unquote "cerebral" movie?

Those films don't make a quarter and nobody in this country is going to finance them. Of course that's no reason for not making them, and if you can convince someone to finance you in that in good faith, God bless you.

But American cinema is story-oriented, just like American literature. Scott Fitzgerald, who is probably one of the greatest writers that this country produced, had a piece of paper stuck on his wall that said, "Action Is Character." That's what I think is best about American cinema. Characterization is best fulfilled through the action of the film. American cinema is based on the action line, but European cinema isn't necessarily. I can knock out a better action film than any of those cats, but if I tried to make an Eric Rohmer film, I'm out of it. There's a kind of muscular, visceral, storytelling sense to the American cinema that I feel is best embodied in the work of Raoul Walsh, D. W. Griffith, John Ford, Hawks, Wellman. That's what people all over the world expect from American cinema. Actually there are some interesting ideas going on in *White Heat*, but if the film was the ideas first and then the action, to hell with it. Nobody wants to stand in line in the rain for that.

Kubrick feels that they do.

I can't see Stanley starting a picture without a story. His films are great stories and his genius is the great style he uses to tell them. I'm not negating style, but if you have only style no one is going to be interested. I really believe that when people have colonized the moon they'll be watching John Ford pictures. I think that the young filmmakers of my generation who had a chance in the early sixties to break into the Hollywood tradition of storytelling really blew it. What we all did was copy Godard and Truffaut and Fellini. We ripped them off and made a lot of chicken shit that isn't worth the celluloid it's printed on. Audiences stayed away from movies for a long time and the American film industry went right over a cliff, until a few guys got it back on track, people like Bogdanovich and one or two others, who made pictures that told stories again.

If I switch off the tape recorder, will you explain how you did those effects in The Exorcist?

If everyone promises not to repeat it.

We promise.

Is there anyone who doesn't promise? Seriously now—don't hustle me. You've got my back against the wall now.

How many head turns didn't work?

We discovered things as we went. It was all experimentation, and what we arrived at was ultimately at the end of a long period of trial and error. We got together in a room, six guys, and wondered how we were going to make the neck bulge and get the vomit to project and how to get her up in the air without strings and make her head turn around 360 degrees. We got that thing working so well we could have done anything we wanted. We had effects you wouldn't believe that I actually chickened out on. I just didn't think people would dig it. I'm only interested in whether it worked or not. That's the only question a filmmaker needs to ask the audience.

Herbie Gardner, who wrote *A Thousand Clowns,* told me a story about Alfred Hitchcock. Herb was flattered to have been invited by Hitchcock to come out to Hollywood and write a film for him. He gets out here and finds that Hitchcock has drawn out the whole picture. All he wants Gardner to do is write the dialogue, or in effect the captions for these cartoons. Herb explained that he couldn't do it, but he was so intrigued and honored to be invited by Hitchcock that he said, "I'm not going to do it, but I'd love to see what these boards are." Looking at these boards, he sees in one frame a shot of a guy being pushed off the Verrazano-Narrows Bridge. Two frames later, that same guy is sitting in a café on Fifth Avenue. Herb couldn't make sense out of this and asked Hitchcock, "How do we get from the guy being pushed off the bridge to him on Fifth Avenue? How do we take the audience from there to there?" Hitchcock said, "Mr. Gardner, the audience will go wherever I take them, and they'll be very glad to be there, I assure you." If I have a philosophy in a nutshell about what I'm trying to do as a filmmaker, that would be it.

You're a big superstar director now. How much control do you really have over your life and career?

I can do whatever picture I want, any way I want. I bought a Mercedes this year. It's a good car. But I don't own much. I'm trying to start a post-production facility. I have some dough in the bank. I made a million dollars on *The French Connection.* I have a lot of money to play with, but I'm the same guy I was. I was a sonofabitch when I was broke, arrogant and quick-tempered, and I'm a sonofabitch now. I haven't changed. These are the clothes I had fifteen years ago. I like them. I'm not out to impress anyone or fake it. I just like it. It's a good gig. Directing is a good job. If they changed all the rules and they said, "You have to stand in line to pay money to do this work," I'd be the first guy in line. It's problematical. It's often disappointing. It's frustrating as hell. It's extremely demanding and totally satisfying work. There are guys out there really working for a living, cleaning streets or coal mining, or teaching. Directing is playing. I live in a mad, unreal world. It's a constant struggle to maintain a sense of balance and sanity, which is why I go to movies and sit in theaters and eat in McDonald's. The hamburgers are lousy but you can overhear conversations. I ride the subways in New York. The best thing I can wish all of you is pretty simple. If you're really sincere about wanting to make films, then go with it, because it's a gas of a life. It takes you places and puts you into things that you didn't even know were happening. Film is such a great medium with so much possibility. None of the guys whose work I love have even scratched the surface.

There is so much to be accomplished by people your age. Your generation is so into film. There is such a hunger for it. But most of the stuff we're producing is shit. It's not saying anything new or different. Just go and do it, but in doing it remember what you're doing it for. You're doing it for the audience.

The life expectancy of a director is probably less than that of a professional football player. A director has seven or eight years where he's really giving the public what they want. It isn't easy. One of the reasons it isn't easy is because you do a successful picture, make a lot of money and buy a house in Beverly Hills. The only people you ever see are your butler and cook and the guy who drives you to the studio. You leave an air-conditioned house and get into an air-conditioned car to go into an air-conditioned office from which you go to an air-conditioned screening room. You never touch a dog on the street or talk to a guy in a bar or on a subway, or know what the hell he wants. That's why a lot of guys don't know who their audience is.

Always remember what a gift you have, which is the chance to serve the audience and not look down on them. When I look at that line outside the theater in Westwood, I see everybody. We're all in the line. I don't see the Three Stooges and a couple of rabbis from Cleveland, and nobody else. Everybody is there, and that gratifies me. That's why I made the pictures I did. I don't know anyone, including Alain Resnais who makes heavy-headed pictures, who doesn't want long lines outside the theaters. He might want it on his own terms. I want it on my terms. His standards may in fact be higher than mine. Yours might also be. All I'm saying is, don't let your standards get so lofty that you put yourself above the audience. The luckiest thing I know of is the gift given to every filmmaker: he is permitted to serve the audience. Never forget that.

———◆———

Films as Director

1967	*Good Times*	1987	*Rampage* (also producer and screenplay)
1968	*The Birthday Party*		
	The Night They Raided Minsky's	1990	*The Guardian* (also screenplay)
1970	*The Boys in the Band*		
1971	*The French Connection*	1994	*Blue Chips*
1973	*The Exorcist*	1995	*Jade*
1977	*Sorcerer* (also producer)	2000	*Rules of Engagement*
1978	*The Brink's Job*	2003	*The Hunted*
1980	*Cruising* (also screenplay)	2006	*Bug*
1983	*Deal of the Century*	2011	*Killer Joe*
1985	*To Live and Die in L.A.* (also screenplay)		

Friedkin also directed documentaries including *The Bold Men,* 1965; *The People vs. Paul Crump,* 1965; and *Pro-Football: Mayhem on a Sunday Afternoon,* 1965; and movies for television and episodes of television series including *The Alfred Hitchcock Hour,* 1965; *The Thin Blue Line,* 1966; *The Twilight Zone,* 1985; *Tales from the Crypt,* 1992; *12 Angry Men,* 1997; and *CSI: Crime Scene Investigation,* 2007–09.

> Television is an industry. It is really big, big, big business. The heart-breaking thing about it is expecting CBS or the other two networks to turn out art, any more than you'd expect General Motors to turn out a wonderful car. They're not really interested in that. They're really interested in the famous bottom line. It was William Paley who called television "the best cigarette-vending machine that was ever invented."

LARRY GELBART
(Born in Chicago, Illinois, 1928—Died 2009)

Larry Gelbart was one of America's great humorists and comedy writers. Mel Brooks, who started out with Gelbart on Sid Caesar's *Your Show of Shows,* called him "the fastest of the fast—the wittiest man in the business." His humor was often barbed. When he and Dustin Hoffman were at odds during the filming of Gelbart's screenplay *Tootsie,* he said, "Never work with an Oscar winner who is shorter than the statue."

Gelbart wrote for movies, television, radio and Broadway, gathering Tonys, Emmys and Oscar nominations. He started out in his early twenties writing for Bob Hope, Jack Paar and Danny Thomas. His first major success was on Broadway with one of the biggest musical hits of the sixties, *A Funny Thing Happened on the Way to the Forum,* a Tony-winning collaboration with Burt Shevelove and Stephen Sondheim. Twenty-eight years later he won his second Tony for *City of Angels.* His screenplays include the Oscar-nominated *Tootsie, Oh, God!, The Notorious Landlady* and *Movie Movie.*

He was the creator, writer and sometimes director of one of the most successful television series in history, *M*A*S*H,* and the creator of one of the least successful television series in history, *United States.* The title of the latter was a double entendre intended to suggest united—as in a married couple. "I was too clever by half with that title," he admitted. "People thought it was something from the *National Geographic.*"

United States premiered on NBC in March 1980 and ran for just seven weeks. Nevertheless, Gelbart described it as "some of the best work I've done." The premise, he said, was to examine "the one marriage in two that

Woody Allen said Larry Gelbart was the best comedy
writer he ever knew. Gelbart developed *M*A*S*H*
for television, co-wrote the book for *A Funny Thing
Happened on the Way to the Forum* on Broadway,
and co-wrote the screenplay for *Tootsie* (1982).

doesn't end in divorce, because the partners have found a way to get through
the ups and downs of that most intimate relationship." Beau Bridges and
Helen Shaver starred as the couple, and there was no laugh track. NBC president Fred Silverman called it "revolutionary," and many shows since have
reflected the innovations of *United States*.

The fellows screened several episodes of *United States* before Gelbart came
to talk about the challenges of dealing with networks. He spoke about
M*A*S*H and *United States*, which at the time of the seminar was on life support at NBC. It is often said that you learn more from your failures than from
your successes—which is evident by the grace and humor with which Gelbart
explored his dilemma.

LARRY GELBART

———◆———

April 16, 1980*

Would you like to make an opening statement, or should we just start with questions?

Let's start with questions. I'll finish with an opening statement.

Why don't we start with United States. *Did NBC come to you, or was it your idea?*

No. I went to them. It seemed like a good idea to go to NBC because, obviously, they're the hungriest of the networks, and I went to see Mr. [Fred] Silverman in December of 1978 and described the show very simply in one or two lines, saying, "It would just be a very different series." They hear the word different so often that they figure it's going to be more of the same. They're not quite sure what you mean when you say different. I think I threw them a curve in a sense because it *is* different. The main selling point was not the show or the content of the show, but rather the idea that I was asking for as much time as would be necessary to have all twenty-two scripts written before we went into production. The big kicker was for them to buy that idea. The critical reaction to the series has been marvelous. We've had almost uniformly good press and the mail is about fifteen to one in favor of the program. But the ratings are rather dismal. We've been down near the bottom for weeks and weeks and weeks. This week we have the dubious distinction, since we had two half-hour episodes back-to-back, of finishing sixty-eighth and sixty-ninth—last and next-to-last—for the week. No one's ever managed to do that before.

---

*The moderator for this interview is unknown.

I don't think it's simply a matter of the show's difference that's causing these great numbers of people not to watch. I think it has to do with promotion, or lack of it, or improper promotion, as well as a disastrous time slot. But obviously there's some part of the program, too, which doesn't appeal to some people. But I'd like to think that NBC should explain why it's not doing as well as it's doing.

For M*A*S*H, *you used film, so why this decision on* United States *to shoot on video and to work without a laugh track?*

To do the show on film would cost twice as much. I had nothing to do with the economics of *M*A*S*H*—it was a Fox package. I had everything to do with *United States*—it was an independent production. We used tape, but I tried to use a lot of film technique. Most of it is shot with one camera. We have four-wall sets. We light from the floor. There's none of the usual three-camera setup, moving from set to set to set. So while we did use the one medium, we borrowed from the other's techniques.

Why do twenty-two episodes of United States? *Is there some growth within the characters that you wanted to accomplish within that span? Or is it just glimpses?*

Just glimpses—they're just bits of the mosaic. And twenty-two because we do twenty-two to a season in this country. In England, writers usually write all of the series in advance, but they only do six. They're a little more sensible than we are.

Last night's episode was a series of interviews done as a documentary. What is your rationale in always using the medium close-up from one camera angle on each character?

Well, the cinematic aspect of last night's episode was the least of it. I just wanted people to hear what the characters had to say about themselves and each other and how they relate to each other. They were being questioned by a team of researchers for a book, so the camera was really dropping in and listening to them and watching them answer questions for a printed medium rather than the film medium.

You had a lot of characters.

And a complaint from an editor who said he hated all the jump cuts. He said he thought it was a terrible slur on his trade. I guess I was more interested in the words than the pictures.

Would you care to tell us what exactly you had to do to adapt M*A*S*H *the movie to* M*A*S*H *the TV series?**

Mostly it was a matter of miniaturization. All the characters were there. In fact, there were more people than we needed and we dropped one character. There were three doctors in the film and we dropped the one played by Tom Skerritt. Adapting for the pilot was really a matter of making a twenty-five-minute movie instead of one that ran for two hours. Our work was made terribly easy by the definition the characters had from the novel and the film. Our big task was to come up with what we thought would be a fresh storyline, borrowing nothing from the picture except the characters and the mood and spirit of it. That's not the hard part, really. The hard part comes when a network says, "Okay, we buy the pilot." Then you say, "My god, now what do we do? We have to keep turning them out."

Could you say how you develop a script for a half-hour TV comedy show?

Invariably I do some kind of research, whether it's reading or talking with people about the background for the particular show. That went on endlessly with *M*A*S*H*—conversations with doctors and nurses and chopper pilots and an actual visit to the MASH unit in Korea. With *United States* there was a lot of reading and a lot of remembering from my own marriage, areas that seemed to lend themselves to dramatization. A TV series is a collaborative effort. You rarely find yourself in a room alone thinking of an idea. Most shows on *M*A*S*H* started with conversations with the director Gene Reynolds. We would kick things back and forth, and pretty soon we would have what we thought was the basis for an idea. We more or less created a formula that was helpful, if only as something to ignore, as the basis for a structure of each show. We generally thought in terms of two acts, with five scenes per act, and then a little tag. We would do step outlines, detailing for the writer what was expected to be

---

**Gelbart wrote the pilot for the TV series *M*A*S*H,* based on the 20th Century–Fox film *M*A*S*H* (1970), which was written by Ring Lardner, Jr., and wrote, co-produced and/or directed its first ninety-six episodes.

accomplished in each scene, which characters would be involved and so forth. *M*A*S*H* was a terribly well-planned program from the writer's point of view because, whether I wrote the script or someone else did, the writer went to work knowing just what had to be contained within each of those scenes. After that, it's just a matter of sitting down and having what's called sitzfleisch. That means that the meat on your behind stays in the chair and you do the pages.

How do you produce a comedy series on television? Are step outlines given to a writer? Is it filling in the blanks?

M*A*S*H was unique in one way: writers were given very complete outlines. That's not to say some writers didn't come in with ideas of their own, but it wasn't a question of filling in blanks. It was a question of writing the whole show to an agreed outline. They were responsible for fade-in, fade-out and everything in between. The next time we met would be after they had done a first draft, and we'd go over it almost line for line and say where we felt it could be improved. Generally, after that I would take it and do whatever adjustments were necessary for whatever reasons. Different shows work differently. There are many shows where so many hands go over a script that by the time it gets on the air, the writer has very little that he can call his own. The window of entry into the writing of episodes is also very small, because most shows have writing staffs and those staffs have a certain number of episodes which they're promised as part of their deal. So the outside writer, the itinerant writer, is probably the least satisfied cog in the operation, because most shows employ an awful lot of people to work on other people's scripts.

The process of having someone else changing every line doesn't seem very rewarding for the writer who wants to create his own characters.

No, it's not a very rewarding experience, it really isn't. The best thing that can happen to you if you want to do a comedy is for it to be *your* series and for *you* to dictate what it's going to sound like and look like. There's some satisfaction in that. But if you're somebody outside a series, and if you're doing one show for MTM this week and one show for Tandem next week and one show for Fox and one show for whoever, you can't get as involved and close to the work. You're giving them what they want much more often than what *you* want. The answer is just get your own series.

Do you think the viewing public is ready for what we might call some serious drama?

I don't really know. I thought they were. I hoped they were. My wife and I wouldn't have spent a year of our lives on *United States* if I didn't think there was some hunger out there for something challenging.

You can prepare the roast, but if folks aren't at the dinner table at the right time to eat it, it goes unappreciated.

Or they have seventeen hot dogs on the way to the house. I think they're so full of fast-food comedy and drama that they have no appetite for gourmet cooking.

Isn't it in the networks' interest to deliver the best audience they can to the appropriate sponsors?

They love noncontroversial material because clearly you don't want to upset a Preparation H user. They don't like to make waves. If you're not going to make waves, then you're not going to have what they call "downers." I'm beginning to read that NBC affiliates consider *United States* a downer. That's the first thing. So you look for material which won't depress anybody or make them unhappy. What's better than a blue light going around and cars coming around corners? Something else that's really sad is that in the same way an audience can be dulled and blunted in their appreciation, so can a whole bunch of people trying to make a living. I don't think you can work for Hallmark and then sit down and write a lot of wonderful sonnets. I think a lot of people in TV have worked too long at the wrong things.

How can you get United States *out of the 10:30 p.m. slot on Tuesdays?*

I can't. NBC put it on at 10:30 and I went along with all of the rationalizations that they put forward as to why it would be wonderful there. I quickly saw, when my wife and I had a tough time staying up to watch the first episode, that we were in trouble. They have since been moving it on a moment's notice—from one night to another, from one hour to another hour—with the result that we lost listings in *TV Guide* and the daily newspapers. It's just been impossible for an audience to guess where we're going to be. We've been preempted all of the month of May, which is a little bit like the Godfather giving you a kiss on the cheek. I don't know where we'll come back, if we come back.

Do you think there's any rationale to this switching around of schedules so quickly?

It's hard to see how. They are third. I mean, NBC can't come in laster than last. There is, in this business, such a desperate need to succeed immediately that despite a year of calm and civilized talk about "This show's going to have to find an audience. We're going to be patient. We're going to nurture it"—wham! The first week the ratings are low and right away it's, "What happened? Where can we put it? Where can we stick it?" "God, we're in trouble!" I forgot the question. I got carried away on my own sound effects.

If you had to do it over again, would you still go ahead and write all the episodes in advance?

Yes. It's all been shot and I would do it the same way. Any other way and I can imagine what the meetings would be like. "Maybe they should buy a dog," "Maybe she should die and he should marry a black woman," "Maybe three marines move in." They would go nuts. This would be comedy development to the rescue. No, I would fail all over again the same way, I really would.

I assume that this is autobiographical in that pieces were drawn from your marriage. Did you ever feel embarrassed or say, "I can't tell that"?

When my wife and I saw it, we were both surprised that I'd been as extroverted as I have without any embarrassment. There's just not that much different about our marriage from other people's, really. That was liberating. It was better than analysis. I got paid instead of the other way around.

I think it's courageous, that's why I said that.

In retrospect, it seems courageous, though it didn't feel that way at the time. I think it helps to get old.

Do you ever think about another full-length project for the Broadway stage?

Yes, I do. But you're sitting around in a cold theater in Baltimore, you say, "God, it would be nice to have a series and be in the sun." I'm afraid there is no ideal condition, but the theater is the most satisfying. It's just wonderful. It's like this experience talking here with you, only I'm sitting in the back of the theater and seeing the effect, or lack of effect, that my words are having. There's such collaboration between the writer and an audience, it's marvelous. And unlike film or TV, it's not trapped. Theater is very plastic. It's such a luxury to take a show that's been running for five years and make it something else and improve it from a Monday to a Tuesday, if you're that insane. I sit at home and watch *M*A*S*H* and constantly rewrite it, but nobody hears those gerbil-like thoughts in my head. But with the theater, you can still play with your work.

My feelings about United States *were that it was interesting, but to me it wasn't television. I'd rather be in the theater to watch the two people and their relationship, to see it all happen right in front of me. Do you have those doubts?*

Yes, I do. But then I rationalize. The show is static and I'm sorry that it's not satisfying. It's pretty boring to depict boredom so convincingly that you bore your audience. There's an attempt here to capture in twenty-four minutes what it's like in a relationship where the only action is emotional. I'm not sure whether it's difficult just because it's inherently difficult for an audience, or if it's difficult because it's in the medium I've chosen for it—because it's on television and preceded by something which has a good deal more action. I'm not sure whether it's the medium or the message. I really don't know.

Is there such a thing as development money for a Broadway play?

There are advances, but they're minimal next to Hollywood money, which you know is unreal. It's all speculative. That's why the writer has the kind of respect he has in New York. Writers are treated in a callous way in this city, with a kind of contempt, because they're all working for somebody.

Do you think television audiences may want more personal involvement?"

I've heard that before, that people feel embarrassed at sharing the characters' physical intimacy or even a kind of negative intimacy. I know it's foreign to the box, and I don't know whether it can work there, truly. I've begun to think that this is kind of a bridge show. There was nothing between what has been and what I tried, no transitional period. Perhaps this will be a transitional show for a show that can take something good from this, and maybe another form will emerge.

Is there anything you try to accomplish in the first act of every episode that's different from a feature-length story form?

I said we had a formula on *M*A*S*H,* but I kept trying to make it unpredictable. I've tried that with *United States,* too. Most shows have what they call the bible. It's a big list of do's and don'ts that helps you get in a certain rut. When I did *M*A*S*H,* I would get unsolicited scripts from people who wanted to write for television. The hardest ones to read were the ones that were written for other series as well as for *M*A*S*H,* because no one's individuality came through. The writers would be using the characters' stock expressions and running jokes which made it difficult to determine whether that writer had his or her own sense of humor or style. You could always tell much more quickly what someone had to say or how they had to say it if they sent you something totally original.

I was wondering if you could tell us how writers relate to television as an artistic medium.

[Sighs.] The sigh is because of the expression "artistic medium." Television is an industry. It is really big, big, big business. The heartbreaking thing about it is expecting CBS or the other two networks to turn out art, any more than you'd expect General Motors to turn out a wonderful car. They're not really interested in that. They're really interested in the famous bottom line. It was William Paley who called television "the best cigarette-vending machine that was ever invented." There are the Neanderthals, the radio writers. I'm part of that group—people who worked in radio for the comedians and knew how to turn out the same stuff every week. They were either trained for or aspired to the stage or film or literature, or all three. The younger crop of electronic babies know most of what they know about comedy from television. I think my group was from a harder school. In radio you really did have to win the approval of a live audience sitting there in a studio. There was no help, there was no sweetening.* I think a lot of people make lots of money these days writing stuff that's not terribly funny, but by the time it goes through the process it appears to be funny. I don't think there's a great sense of the audience

---

*The practice of enhancing applause and laughter in postproduction.

among the television comedy writers. I think there's a great sense of personal survival and personal ambition and competition and envy and all those good things. I don't think there's a lot of thinking that goes on because you've got to keep turning the stuff out. That's one of the reasons for the twenty-two scripts—to be able to think about it a little more.

It sounds like a very depressing trend.

Well, it *is* depressing. I think most commercial television is depressing. There's no drama on television. There's a lot of B-movie stuff. Most of it is meant to divert and to please. One year it's cop shows, the next year it's westerns, the next year it's doctor shows, the next year it's back to westerns. I think the audience is the last group that anybody thinks about in this city. It's what will work, what worked before. The best word you can use in a story conference is "another." "This is another *M*A*S*H.*" "This is another *Mary.*" "This is another *Shirley.*" "This is another *Mork.*"* They love that. If writers think that way, they're not thinking, "What does the audience think?" They're thinking, "What does this executive think? What can I sell him? What will he buy?" It is depressing. I'm depressed.

What comedy on television do you think is good quality?

It's hard for a comedy writer to watch other comedy. You're either rewriting it, anticipating it or judging it. Comedy is largely a matter of surprise, and after doing it for a lot of years, it becomes harder and harder to be surprised. I like to watch things that are happening. The worst thing that ever happened to television, I think, was tape. The live quality was always marvelous.

Is it easier to write comedy with somebody else than by yourself?

I think it depends on, first, obviously, who you are. Some people can't be funny in front of other people. It's a little like going to the bathroom; it's very personal, very private. I've written in a room with twelve or thirteen people, I've written with one other person and I've written alone. Working with other people, when it's cooking, is wonderful. It's like a jam session, and a lot of good things have gotten done that way. But right now, I'd rather work alone.

---

* The Mary Tyler Moore Show, Laverne and Shirley and Mork and Mindy.

Gelbart joined Sid Caesar's writing staff at age twenty-five. Gelbart (second from left) in the writer's room with Sheldon Keller, Mel Tolkin, Selma Diamond, Mike Stewart, Gary Belkin, Mel Brooks and Caesar. Gelbart left Bob Hope to work with Caesar, and Hope told Caesar, "I'll trade you two oil wells for one Gelbart."

If I were to get out of here and try to get work as a writer, where would I get the most practice writing?

At home. You can't knock on a door and say, "I'd like to write here." I'm not being facetious. An actor can say, "Here's my picture. I've done this stuff, and if you want I can give you a reading of the soliloquy." But the only thing a writer can do is say, "Please read this."

Would you say there are a lot of dissatisfied writers who are trying to write motion-picture scripts who end up working in television?

Writers bitch as much as they write. We're a very disgruntled group. If you didn't know that before today, you certainly know that now. There are statistics which are a little scary about the number of scripts in development as against the number produced, so obviously, most people's work doesn't reach the screen. It's a big comedown for people to expect to have their work seen on the very big screen in a long form and to have to settle for doing this little miniature work. I think there are over four thousand members of the Writers Guild, but only a small, depressing number make their living in features or television. I don't know what the rest do to make a living.

Is there a snobbish attitude from those who write feature films?

Yes, I think so, and yet I feel that criticizing television is like shooting ducks in a barrel. There are as many good hours of television as there are film in a year, and theater too. A lot of good stuff gets done. The thing that studio executives know the least about is comedy. I think it scares the hell out of them. They read it and quickly pass it on to somebody else to say, "What did you think?" That person, of course, passes it on to somebody else. They'll trust the people who have proven that they know how to make people laugh—Mel Brooks, of course, and Woody Allen, people like that. But I think it's because they basically mistrust their own judgment that they don't make as many comedies as this town used to, and they used to make wonderful comedies. I think, too, television has blunted the audience's appreciation of what's funny, or given them another idea of what's funny. So film comedy has suffered. They don't have laugh tracks to go by in a movie house. Anyway, that's six other thoughts.

What comedians have you been influenced by?

Going all the way back, the Marx Brothers, of course, though I didn't realize how much until *M*A*S*H* and there was a real-life person who sounded just like Groucho doing my lines. I also love the Ritz Brothers— Harry Ritz. The nearest thing to him in our times is Sid Caesar—that kind of dynamic, slightly insane comedy. Fred Allen too, and a man named Ed Gardner, who was the star of a radio program called *Duffy's Tavern,* which was the first show I worked on. He was a tremendous influence. I've been influenced by a lot of comedy writers that nobody knows, because I was around them when I was very young and a lot of it rubbed off. I once told Groucho Marx I liked the Ritz Brothers and he was furious. He thought that was like comparing a sidewalk hoofer with Fred Astaire. And there's Laurel and Hardy, and W. C. Fields—all the easy ones. But I guess at a certain point you stop being influenced.

Do you want to direct?

No, not really. I wouldn't direct anybody else's material. I just don't know what it would be to pick up somebody else's work and interpret it. I have too much respect for the word. I have trouble rewriting myself because I think, "How can I touch that? Somebody wrote that."

Did this year's Academy Awards make any big mistakes?

No, they were as dull as I expected them to be. Awards get on my nerves after a while. We're so busy awarding ourselves awards. I once did a special, a long time ago, for David Susskind. I'd love to see it again. It was called *The Best of Anything.* It was an hour show that dealt with the American need to hand out plaques and cups and prizes. We opened with Art Carney, who was the star, as he said, "Good evening, ladies and gentlemen," and immediately someone gave him an award for his having said, "Good evening, ladies and gentlemen" in the best way that hour.

<hr/>

Films and Television as Writer

1950–54 *Your Show of Shows* (television)

1954–57 *Caesar's Hour* (television)

1962 *The Notorious Landlady*

1963 *The Thrill of It All*
The Danny Kaye Show (television)

1966 *The Wrong Box* (also co-producer)
Not With My Wife, You Don't!

1971 *Eddie* (television)

1971–72 *The Marty Feldman Comedy Machine* (television—also producer)

1972–83 *M*A*S*H* (television—also producer)

1973 *Roll Out!* (television—also producer)

1974 *I Love You, Am I Trapped Forever?* (television—also producer)

1977 *Oh, God!*

1978 *Movie Movie*

1980 *United States* (television—also producer)
Rough Cut

1981 *Neighbors*

1982 *Tootsie*

1984 *Blame It on Rio* (also executive producer)

1983–84 *After MASH* (television)

1992 *Mastergate* (television)

1993 *Barbarians at the Gate* (television)

1996 *The Nutty Professor*

1997 *Weapons of Mass Destruction* (television)

2000 *C-Scam*
Bedazzled

2003 *And Starring Pancho Villa as Himself* (television—also executive producer)

I try to do a play every other year on the theory that the stage is the actor's country and you have to go back to get your passport stamped every so often or they'll take away your citizenship.

CHARLTON HESTON

(Born in Evanston, Illinois, 1923—Died 2008)

Charlton Heston learned he had Alzheimer's disease in 2002 and made a brave public announcement reporting his condition and declaring, "I'm neither giving up nor giving in." I called him to commiserate and he told me of a letter he had just received from a studio electrician, who wrote, "Just my luck. The only movie star who ever remembered my name has Alzheimer's."

Chuck, as he was widely known, and I were colleagues and friends in the early years of AFI, when he was its chairman and I its director, and later when

Charlton Heston won the Academy Award for Best Actor for his portrayal of Judah Ben Hur in William Wyler's *Ben-Hur* (1959).

we were co-chairmen of the board. We were kindred spirits until his emphatic views on gun ownership took him down a path that led to the presidency of the National Rifle Association, and distanced him to a certain extent from good friends. I continued to admire him because he had proven time and again his willingness to stand up for what he believed in, and for a long time that was the American Film Institute.

When you are in charge of an organization like AFI, you find many people who offer to be helpful and wish to be associated in one way or another. There are some who offer their help and then deliver beyond your wildest expectations. Chuck Heston was one of those. He often flew to Washington to testify before Congress on AFI's behalf. He would make his own plane reservations and buy his own ticket on the red-eye flight from Los Angeles, landing at dawn in Baltimore. He would ask only that we find a young person with a station wagon with a mattress in the back to pick him up so he could get an hour's sleep on the way to the Capitol.

Heston studied drama at Northwestern before heading for New York, where he worked in the theater and live television. He came to Hollywood in 1950, making his debut in *Dark City* for Hal Wallis. Two years later Cecil B. DeMille cast him as the hard-driving circus boss in *The Greatest Show on Earth,* which led to his role as Moses in DeMille's *Ten Commandments.* He loved history and many of the characters he played reflected that interest: General "Chinese" Gordon in *Khartoum;* a Marine officer in *55 Days at Peking;* Andrew Jackson, twice, in *The President's Lady* and *The Buccaneer;* Michelangelo in *The Agony and the Ecstasy;* John the Baptist in *The Greatest Story Ever Told;* and his Oscar-winning role of a prince in ancient Jerusalem in *Ben-Hur.* He played a wide range of other parts, and was probably most proud of his role in Orson Welles' *Touch of Evil.*

Chuck worked with many great directors and published diaries about his learning experiences on the sets of Welles, Wyler, Vidor, Stevens, Peckinpah and Carol Reed. One day on location for *The Big Country,* he approached Wyler with what he was convinced was a valuable idea. He picked up Wyler's script to explain it and noticed in small letters on the flyleaf of the leather binder the names of Wyler's previous films: *Dead End, The Heiress, Dodsworth, The Little Foxes, Jezebel, The Westerner, The Best Years of Our Lives, Roman Holiday.* Heston recalled closing the binder, turning to Wyler and saying, "Let's do it your way."

He was a thorough and patient actor but conscious of the distance between aspiration and achievement, observing, "You never get it right. Never once was it the way I imagined it lying awake at four o'clock in the morning." His goal remained "to get it right one time."

CHARLTON HESTON

—◆—

November 14, 1979*

When did you start acting?

I started training to be an actor when I was quite young. There is an element of luck in that. By pure chance a geographical accident moved me
from the remote north woods in Michigan, where I had been raised, to a
community on the north shore of Chicago that was served by what was
supposed to be the best public high school in America. It included a fantastic basic training in theater which I took advantage of, not really being
equipped for any of the other activities in the school. I won an acting
scholarship to Northwestern University which has always been a fertile
training ground for actors. I was there at the same time as half a dozen
people whose faces you would recognize, if not the names, and twenty
others who were bloody good actors. I went to New York where I just
about starved to death as a juvenile. I was too tall and had a heavy voice,
so I was unemployable.

Can you talk about how you got your first acting job?

My wife and I lived in Hell's Kitchen after World War II. That was when
you could be both broke and happy in New York. There was an organization called Theater Incorporated that announced they would give an
audition to any combat veteran. I'd had a very easy war but still qualified

*James Powers moderated this seminar. This transcript also contains segments from seminars
Charlton Heston gave at the American Film Institute on October 28, 1970, March 14, 1975, January 20, 1976, July 27, 1977, November 6, 1991, and March 5, 1997.

Heston talking to the AFI fellows in 1979, on one of his many visits to Greystone. Heston served as chairman of AFI from 1972 to 1982.

under those terms, so I took the audition, and they said, "We're planning to do a production of Middleton's *The Changeling* and you might be good for it. Stick around." They put it off, so I went down South and took a job directing in Ashville, North Carolina. I went back to New York and Theater Incorporated had gone out of business, so I went home very depressed and said, "That's the end of that, damn it. Now what?" My wife said, "Go out and do the rounds. Didn't you read that Katharine Cornell was casting *Antony and Cleopatra?*" So I went to their offices. If anyone is ever really casting something, the offices are jammed by people who probably have genuine appointments, and maybe had actually met Miss Cornell or worked with her, or at least worked in a professional theater on Broadway. None of these applied to me. Of course the hall was crammed with people. The girl inside the office came out and ushered in someone who actually had an appointment, and I slipped into that empty seat. They worked through eight or nine people until I was the only one there, and she said, "I don't think we have your name?" I said, "Charlton Heston. Maynard Morris of MCA sent me up." I'd never been inside MCA and never met Maynard Morris. She said, "Well, we're a little ahead, I guess we can see you." That's two pieces of luck already. The third was that I happened to have studied Granville Barker's preface to *Antony and Cleopatra,* so I was able to talk about it, and the speech I was asked to read happened to be one I knew a little bit. With that I got my first job on Broadway. Don't ever say luck doesn't count.

In a way, the world of live television in the fifties was a film school for you.

Absolutely. It was a fantastic opportunity the likes of which has not occurred since. I worked with people like Johnny Frankenheimer and Frank Schaffner. The first acting I really did for a camera was live television in New York. They had four cameras and there would be marks I had to hit. I did Rochester in *Jane Eyre*. I would stand there saying, "I will come back to you!" and then while the camera holds on her, I would go off and change my clothes. They'd be pulling up my pants while I was doing the close-up. There's a special technique to all of that, so I came to film with something of a reputation from live TV, which was a great advantage for me and Jimmy Dean and Walter Matthau and George C. Scott and Jack Lemmon and all those guys.

When live television started in the late forties, the contract system still dominated at the studios. Paul Newman, for example, was under exclusive contract to Warner Bros., so he couldn't work in television. No one in movies could work in television, not the directors, the actors, the writers or the producers. People of any reputation in the theater wouldn't work in it because it didn't pay anything to speak of and was considered kind of tacky. So that left this whole medium that nobody knew anything about to a bunch of unemployed twenty-four-year-olds. I remember they came to Frank Schaffner and me and said, "Could you guys do a ninety-minute version of *Macbeth*?" When you're twenty-three you can do anything, because you don't know it's supposed to be hard. Over a fifteen-month period, as an actor with very little Broadway experience and no reputation, I got to play in *Jane Eyre, Taming of the Shrew,* Bernard Shaw's *Cashel Byron's Profession,* some Turgenev, Henry James' *Wings of the Dove, Macbeth, Wuthering Heights* and *Of Human Bondage*. The actor doesn't draw breath that isn't going to be good in one of those parts.

I recently saw your Macbeth *on stage and wonder what the differences are between stage and film acting.*

If you want me to tell you all about acting, you missed a golden opportunity, because the time when I could tell you all about that was when I was studying it at Northwestern. Since then I have discovered there is more and more about which I know less and less. Film acting on the one hand is an art and thus highly subjective and personal, insoluble by pragmatic solutions, and on the other hand is both a craft and a profession. Since the practice of that craft involves the expenditure of the highest-priced raw materials and man-hours of any of the arts, an examination of acting as a craft may be useful. A lot of the problems actors encounter stem from the fact that we have responsibilities as workers in a highly expensive industry, and you cannot gainsay that fact. Art occasionally results from this process, but art is always rare in the best of circumstances. When your raw materials cost something like $35,000 a day, if you fail to practice your art successfully, you don't get any more electric trains to play with. That counts whether you're a director or an actor.

The differences between stage and film acting aren't as profound as you might imagine. The differences, in my judgment, are primarily technical and pragmatic. Obviously there are different rules, like a sonnet is different from an epic poem or free verse. I began on the stage, where, no matter how much the director gives you, the curtain goes up and the thing belongs to you. On stage, the actor is the medium. The play can only come through me. Film is another matter. On the screen it comes through the camera. On stage you have to speak loudly enough so they can hear you. On film you have to hit your marks so you stay in focus, and if you're doing a scene where we're talking and I'm mixing a drink I have to be careful not to put the glass down on my line or on yours. The fact is I have never found film acting that different from stage acting. A lot of people would argue with that, but I suspect that such arguments come from those who have done only one and not the other.

There are actors who are enormously effective on the stage whom somehow the camera does not love, and I use that phrase advisedly. The camera is a very mysterious instrument. Nobody in the world can tell what the camera will think of somebody—but it is absolutely necessary that the camera loves you, and this has nothing to do with the way you look or the way you sound or how smart you are or how well you can act. It just has to do with what happens when the camera starts rolling. Nobody knows until they take the film out of the bath and put it up on the screen.

I have no quarrel with actors who come into films without much stage experience, but if you've had stage training and you don't do plays, you're crazy. You not only must do plays, you must do Shakespeare. I ran into Robert De Niro in a restaurant last year. I think he is one of the best American film actors, and I had the temerity to go up to him and introduce myself. I said, "An actor as good as you are has to do Shakespeare.

You will never reach your full potential if you don't try those roles." He said, "Everybody keeps telling me that." But it's true—those are the parts. You must never pass up a chance to waltz with the old gentleman.

I try to do a play every other year on the theory that the stage is the actor's country and you have to go back to get your passport stamped every so often or they'll take away your citizenship. I have never been away from the stage for more than maybe two and a half years at any one time.

Do you have a general technique when it comes to acting?

My technique as an actor is catholic. That's with a small *c*. It's not so much a question of dogma as about what works for you. When you're studying acting, it's very much like being an apprentice in a religious institution, an acolyte serving the high altar. You feel the only truth is your truth. You become deeply skeptical and contemptuous of anybody who does it a different way. Those people are, in fact, agents of the Antichrist. The longer you work, the more ridiculously clear this becomes. Finally one comes to realize—at least I have come to believe strongly—that all that matters when it comes to acting is that it works. It doesn't matter how you studied or whom you studied with or what method you use to achieve whatever meager legerdemain you manage to bring off for the audience. The only thing is that it works.

When I was studying acting, I was trained in what was then called the Stanislavsky theory. It's now called the Method, with a capital *M*. You do improvisations. The center of it is that you can best persuade an audience if you can persuade yourself. That's fair enough. It can work just fine. But I like to get at a character from the outside. I have heard actors say it's marvelous to work from the inside, and that sounds fun, but how the hell do you find the inside if you haven't found the outside? At least I can't. I have to know what kind of clothes he wears and what kind of pen he uses and what sort of a watch and things like that.

What kind of working relationships have you had with directors?

I've had the great good fortune of working for a remarkable number of, dare I say, world-class directors, ranging all the way from King Vidor and Cecil B. DeMille to Sam Peckinpah, with George Stevens, William Wyler, Laurence Olivier and Frank Schaffner in between. It's clear to me that the medium really does belong to the director.

Heston, Stephen Boyd and William Wyler in Rome during the filming
of the classic chariot race in *Ben-Hur.*

The actor-director relationship is something you have to know about.
It's one of the most important jobs a director has. Let's explore that a little, from my point of view. I have very strong Puritan-work-ethic convictions about the actor's responsibilities to the director, particularly in film.
On the stage, no matter how talented your director is, no matter how
much he may give you, on opening night he goes across the street and gets
smashed while you're up there by yourself. Film is different. What happens on the shooting floor often has very little relation to the finished picture. One of the first lessons you learn as an actor is that the work you
think is your best might never make it into the finished film. In the case
of a director like Wyler, for example, or Stevens, he may not even print
what you think is your best performance. Often he doesn't need your best
performance from start to finish of the scene, because he will take the

opening few seconds from one take and cut it together with the middle of another, and finish with a third.

I'm often now in the position of being involved in a project before any of the other creative contributors. Now, you can have talked about the project, you can have approved the choice of the writer of the first screenplay and the director and been deeply involved in all the conferences that led to the decision that you needed a new screenwriter and all that, but once you start shooting only the director knows the picture he has in mind. A film only exists in a director's skull, that lonely little projection room he runs it in every night alone, at two in the morning, lying in bed.

I often find these days that the director has made fewer pictures than I have, but even though I may have had the approval on his employment, once I have approved it I have to surrender a large part of the control to him. All control, in fact. I call directors "sir" even though I'm now at a point where at least half of them are younger than I am and make a hell of a lot less money. This doesn't mean he doesn't accept suggestions. If an actor says, "This feels very uncomfortable to me," you have to examine it. What I say to directors now, to those with whom I haven't worked before, is, "Look, I have a loud voice and very strong opinions. I've been involved with this project a long time and I'll tell you what I think. But if you can't persuade me of what you think, and you still want to do it that way, just say, 'Chuck, do it that way because that's the way I want to do it.' " Cross my heart, I truly think that's what I'm paid to do. I'm a professional actor. I'm supposed to be able to do it not only my way but his way too, and if he's the director his way has to be *the* way.

I really urge you to abandon the democratic method. We live in a time when we're highly sensitive to the democratic approach to every problem. But the democratic approach doesn't work in making a movie. I promise you it doesn't. It's a lovely idea to say, "We're all making the movie together and I'm willing to get ideas from everybody, from the cameraman to the prop man." But directing only works as a dictatorship.

Have you noticed that the better the actor, the more willing he is to give in to the director?

I'm flattered to agree with you. Actors who are anxious about surrendering their concept are often insecure. I know some of my colleagues would not agree with this. That's one of the reasons why a director has to be something of a father figure. I realize that's a very unfashionable phrase these days, but the paternal relationship between director and actor is a very valuable one. I have known and worked with a number of very gifted directors whose careers were thwarted, or indeed completely aborted, because they were not good captains. The closest analogy to a film company I know of is a military operation. I'm not talking about everyone having his shoes shined and lining up in formation. I'm talking about preoccupation with logistics, the importance of weather, food, fatigue, transport, supplies, communication, morale and authority. Good command is vital. I spent a good while in the army, and that's why it's not an idly chosen phrase. The director who doesn't have any authority, along with talent, self-discipline, intelligence and physical endurance, is going to be in trouble. A man who cannot somehow earn the respectful and admiring obedience of a company is going to have problems. The men who are good captains have a good leg up. I don't pretend that there are no good directors who are not good captains, but it is a big help. You know, it's fashionable, and perhaps accurate, to describe actors as children. Some of us are somewhat unpredictable, unstable and perhaps childish, and there is a great deal of insecurity, anxiety and uncertainty. It is an insecure profession, after all. That's why a director needs to be a captain. I choose that word carefully, because it has a masculine connotation. I do think it's harder for a woman to be a director, because she, too, must somehow be a captain. Not a mother, a captain. The kind of captaincy I'm talking about doesn't depend on appearance or shouting but on a real ability to command, in the true sense. It's not about demanding obedience and discipline but eliciting it.

Something else needs to be said, which is that actors need to be praised. Actors need to be told when they've done a good job. But there's another side to that coin, which is: don't be too unstinting of your praise. I've worked for directors who after every take say, "Jesus, that's marvelous! Just great, baby! Could you just do one more and maybe just a little . . ." And you say, "Faster?" "Yes, yes. Faster, faster." After every take they say how marvelous it is. It makes me wary and suspicious. You start to play defensively. "If this guy is going to take whatever I give him and say it's marvelous, that's no good. I better do it safely." You have to fall somewhere between the Wyler school of never praising the actor and the other school of pouring praise over him like a bucket of warm chocolate.

I'm sure you tire of speaking of Ben-Hur *after all these years, but it's such an amazing film, because it can be seen both as a grand spectacle and as a very small film of people in conflict.*

Heston took pride in working with many of the finest film directors.
Here he talks with Sam Peckinpah on the set of *Major Dundee* (1965).

Wyler refused to surrender to the incredible, physical assets available to him. *Ben-Hur,* as you said, is finally a story of people. The chariot race had enormous, quite incredible, physical potential. Yet Wyler, with that set full of screaming extras and nine four-horse chariots, chose to use only three long-shot cuts of the full set, amounting to something like forty-five seconds of film in the entire sequence. He resisted. As he cut it, the race is not a spectacle, it's a conflict between two men. A surprising proportion of the race is in close-up. If you're making a picture like that, I think the main responsibility of the director is to refuse to be seduced by all the stuff that's there for him. Willy was one of not many who could do that.

Technology has given us so much more opportunity to do unusual things that you couldn't do with a camera before. The equipment is lighter, more portable; the film is faster, the lenses are faster. Everything is more readily available to you, and directors sometimes tend to get caught up in exclaiming how wonderful a shot is. But what is it about? How does it serve the story? I remember something Wyler taught me. I had come back from seeing some film and was saying how well directed I thought it was, and he said, "You have to be careful with that. If everybody says, 'Isn't that well directed?' it means they weren't paying attention to the story." The direction should not call attention to itself. Neither should the acting or the writing.

Do you like to improvise?

I've worked with directors who like to improvise. I love to improvise. It's great fun. Actors are enchanted by it. It's a great game and can produce fascinating results, but at the same time can be haphazard. Something is sacrificed for the gains. Let me also say something here. I try to exercise creative controls very circumspectly and with as much responsibility and wisdom as I can muster. As an actor you have to recognize the integrity of the writer's contribution. At the same time, the writer has to recognize that film is a collaborative undertaking. Now we get to a highly controversial point, and next time you have a writer in here, quote me and hear how mad it makes him. The fact is that you can't write a film script totally in the typewriter. There are things that are true about a script that you aren't going to find out sitting in front of a typewriter. You've got to be there on the ground. The economics of film, particularly television, deny the writer the opportunity to collaborate at that stage. He's long gone and been paid off and his phone number's been taken out of the Rolodex. Of course his work has been absolutely vital, but I also feel an actor should be able to make a contribution. An actor should be able to make up lines that are honest and real. If the writer can't make up better lines than that, then he probably isn't as good a writer as he should be. This by no means is meant to denigrate the writer or diminish his role, and I do think the ideal situation is if the writer can be on the set. I've worked in just a couple of pictures where the writer was there throughout the shooting, including Christopher Fry on the set of *Ben-Hur,* and it was an immensely satisfactory arrangement. But the economics generally mitigate against it.

Your career is identified with characters like Moses, Michelangelo and General Gordon. How do you tackle that type of role?

I've been very fortunate in having had the experience throughout some fifty films of playing so many extraordinary men. I believe in the extraordinary man. I think they are more valuable than you and I, and the chance I've had to scrape around inside the skulls of men like Michelangelo and Gordon and Mark Antony and Cardinal Richelieu and Henry VIII and Macbeth is terribly important to me. For one thing, it's been educational, because I'm afraid about the only serious reading I do is biographical and historical research, and to explore even superficially one or two biographies of a man like Richelieu or Michelangelo is enriching. To play them is of course another problem, particularly in the context of the couple of decades I've been making films, because we live in a time that tends to reject the concept of the extraordinary man. We're fond of saying that we live in the century of the common man. Ours is the century of the victim. Our attention is oriented towards the individual as victim and towards people as survivors. The phrase that's tossed around often—I really think it's lost all currency and most of its meaning—is the "antihero.' I really don't know what the hell it means apart from someone who obviously is not a hero. The whole idea of a hero is out of favor, and you find the phrase "great man" put in quotes more often than not. I reject that. I believe the significant work of the world has been done not by us but by the extraordinary individuals that this species produces every so often. Along with the opposable thumb and the enlarged cortex, I think it's probably one of the characteristics that marks *Homo sapiens* off from the other mammals and has given him control of the planet, and that is the capacity of the species to produce a truly extraordinary individual who is more competent, more able than his fellows. The men we're talking about fall within that category. I remember when I was researching Thomas Jefferson, I heard a remark that I like because it somehow spoke to me as an actor. Thomas Jefferson was described by a contemporary as "a man able to write a sonnet, break a horse, dance a minuet, run a surveying line and tie an artery." I submit to you that none of us probably knows any one individual who can do all of those things.

General Gordon was an odd, thorny, difficult, interior person, perhaps a bit mad but quite extraordinary. Actors tend to deal in fragments. A word or a color will be meaningful because you feel you can use it, or it just speaks to you. I was reading a contemporary account of Gordon, which quoted one of the Sudanese who had been around him a great deal who said, "When Gordon looks at you, you feel that you cannot lie." I tried to use that with my performance.

Heston with Orson Welles and actor Mort Mills
on the set of *Touch of Evil* (1958). Heston described
Welles as the most talented man he ever met.

What was it like to work with Orson Welles on Touch of Evil?

With Orson it was fun. I don't think I've ever worked with a director who communicated better with actors. He could somehow persuade you that every setup just happened to be the most important setup in the picture, and then he would tell you why. Even if it was just walking down the stairs and getting into a car, he could explain why this just happened to be the most crucial shot in the whole film and why you must concentrate on getting it right. This all made for a very stimulating time.

Orson is the most talented man I've ever met, which doesn't mean that I think he was the best director or the best writer or the best actor, because I don't. Whatever talent is, that subjective, immeasurable quality we call talent, Orson has it. Indeed, he may have it in too large a measure. So many things are so easy for Orson. He can think of a solution to a scene or a new idea or a fresh approach so readily that perhaps he has never developed the qualities of creative discipline that motivate a George Stevens or a William Wyler or a Frank Schaffner, and this possibly has hampered his career. Certainly the paucity of films we've had from Orson

Welles is a rebuke to us and to Orson. He is marvelous with casts and
crews, and he can charm the birds out of the bloody trees. Crews would
waive meal penalties and actors would waive twelve-hour turnarounds for
him, but he not only failed to try and charm studio executives, he seemed
deliberately to alienate and antagonize them. This is, I think, some kind
of a tragic flaw. He's an extremely complicated, utterly charming but at
the same time unpredictable and in some respects, I'm afraid I'd have to
say, unreliable man. It's all very well to say that he should be allowed to
make a film a year in any way he wanted, but film is unique among the
artistic media in that the raw materials cost a great deal of money. The
"paper and pencils" are very expensive and the artist cannot afford to buy
them for himself. Therefore they are bought by an entrepreneur who both
expects and deserves to get his money back, and if he doesn't, he won't
buy you any more paper and pencils. No matter how uncomfortable that
makes you, it is fair. But Orson, along with many other filmmakers, really
doesn't think it's fair. He can be terribly difficult and opaque with those
fellows, and naturally they don't like it. But this is simply a reality of the
economics of the industry, and if you are unable to recognize and respond
to it, then you won't get to make very many films.

Touch of Evil is not a great movie, as Cahiers du Cinéma wrote many
years ago. They said it was undoubtedly the best B picture ever made. I
cannot resist boasting about how it came to pass that I was in Touch of
Evil, because it may be, in the last analysis, one of my most significant
contributions to the medium. Universal sent me a copy of the script when
I was up in Michigan during Christmas of 1956. It was a police story and
kind of interesting, but I wondered, how different could this be from all
the others? It would really depend on the director. So I called them and
said, "This isn't bad. Who's going to direct it?" They said, "We don't
know, but we have Orson Welles to play the heavy." I said, "Well, he's a
pretty good director. Why don't you have him direct it?" This seemed to
strike them as the most radical suggestion I could have made, as though I
had said, "How about if my mother directed this picture?" They said,
"We'll get back to you on that," which they did, and said, "Yes, that's a
pretty good idea." In fact it terrified them, because Orson enjoys the reputation of being an enfant terrible, even though he's actually a very fast
and efficient director. He should not have been penalized by this entirely
spurious reputation he has as being profligate.

Recently I was planning a picture and it looked like the shooting
schedule was going to be forty days. That seemed quite brisk to me, so I

said, "I don't think forty days is enough. I've never made a picture in forty days, but I'm not going to argue with you if that's what you say, so let's shake hands and be friends." I felt quite virtuous about it, until not too long ago I checked my notebooks of the time—which I was looking at to assist Peter Bogdanovich, who is writing a book about Orson—and saw that we made *Touch of Evil* in thirty-nine days.

Did you improvise any of the film?

One night we were shooting in this seedy old hotel and there were very limited amenities available, so Orson and I both went down to the basement, this just filthy-looking place in the hotel, at three in the morning. We were peeing into an open toilet they had in the corner, one of those situations where the muse strikes. Orson stood there and he said, "This is a fascinating basement, isn't it? You know, we ought to do that scene down here where you talk to Joe Calleia," who played the policeman. "As a matter of fact we ought to do it tonight. If we get Joe out of bed he'll be all upset and uncertain, and that'll be good because that's the way he should be in the scene." Within fifteen minutes Orson was talking to the production manager, who said, "Orson, we already built a set for that scene. We're going to be shooting it next week." Orson says, "We can shoot it tonight." The guy says, "What about the rest of the scene we were planning to shoot tonight?" Orson says, "I don't need that. We can do one shot after dusk tomorrow and cover it. On top of which we'll be shooting inside and we don't have to quit when the sun comes up. Get Calleia down here quick." So they got poor Joe Calleia out of bed, and he comes down rubbing the sleep out of his eyes. He was supposed to be disturbed and upset in the scene anyway. It's one of the best scenes he had in the picture. I don't know if I can offhand think of another director, in my experience, who improvises to that degree.

Why do you think the film was not such a success?

Nobody ever has the answers to that question. Orson shot the picture very efficiently and with great creativity. It got to a point where you couldn't get seats in the dailies in the studio screening room. When Orson finished shooting and began to cut it, I sat in the cutting room with him. It's the longest time I've sat in a cutting room except on a picture I directed myself. This was, of course, a very valuable learning experience for me. I'm not quite certain exactly what then happened, because I went off to do *The Big Country* for Wyler and was gone on location all summer. When I came back I saw a rough cut of *Touch of Evil* that wasn't quite finished. Apparently Orson was unavailable for some shots that the studio wanted to do. Now, Orson has a phone phobia. He hates to talk on the phone and, in the classic phrase, does not bear fools lightly. At a certain point the studio was unable to reach him and finally said, "The hell with it. We really don't need much more. We'll do it ourselves." The upshot of this was that they shot about a day and a half of purely geographical shots and maybe a line or two, intending to clarify the somewhat ambiguous story line. I was in almost all the shots, so I know what they were. The picture was cut, dubbed and scored, but when he eventually saw what they had done, Orson became convinced that his film had been mutilated. Of course it's since become something of a minor classic.

You have to remember that this was long before *Last Year at Marienbad,* and audiences were uneasy at not knowing what was going on. These days they couldn't care less. For example, you never even really know which side of the border you're on. That was Orson's choice. It was this ambiguity that the Universal retakes were designed to clarify, although it still is somewhat ambiguous. They said, "We want to straighten some of these things out." I think the only basic creative mistake Orson made with the film was that he felt impelled to maintain the fiction that I was playing the leading role, which of course is not true. He felt constrained to attempt to disguise that fact from me by putting in one or two scenes and handling a couple of other scenes to advance the idea that Vargas, my role, is the central part. I remember we were shooting down in Venice, California, which at the time looked incredibly like a Mexican border town. We'd been shooting Quinlan's death scene for several nights and finally finished at six in the morning and went to have scrambled eggs at some coffee shop. I said, "Orson, I must tell you one thing. There are two or three scenes in this picture that you put in because you knew I was supposed to have the leading role. But the story is really about the fall of Captain Quinlan. You didn't need to put those other scenes in." *Touch of Evil* is the story of the decline and fall of Captain Quinlan, and Vargas is a witness to that, a catalyst, a narrator with a certain passive quality—nonetheless the picture is about Quinlan, and one of its virtues is Orson's performance. It would have been a better film, in my opinion, if Vargas had merely been reflective and reactive to this character of Quinlan.

Could you say what you learned about acting from Welles?

Orson insists he hates acting but of course is a very good actor and is really able to communicate with actors. It's not too often that you learn about acting from directors, because that isn't what they do. They sometimes make you act better, but to really understand the process is another thing. Orson really understood the process. I remember we were looking at dailies one day and he leaned over and said, "You know, Chuck, you have to work on your tenor range. Those of us with great bass voices love to rumble along in them. The tenor range is a knife edge, the bass is a velvet hammer. You have to use them both." That was very useful. I'd never thought of it before. He also taught me that looping dialogue in the studio after shooting didn't have to be a necessary evil. Looping involves rerecording dialogue for scenes where the original production track isn't clean. As an actor, I always felt I could never match what I had done on set. After working with Orson, I regard the looping process as another chance to achieve something of quality.

What was it like filming the opening shot of the movie?

It took us all night and went very well except we had a bit player playing one of the customs men and he couldn't remember his line. I can understand this, because he would see this whole vast complex of filmmaking bearing down on him from about a quarter of a mile away and just froze up when we got to him. Finally Orson said, "Look, I don't care what you say. Just move your lips. But please don't say, 'Oh, God, I'm sorry, Mr. Welles.' " Finally at about five in the morning, just before first light, we got a printable take.

I think an equally interesting shot is the scene when Quinlan comes into the apartment of the suspect and plants the dynamite. The scene ran something like twelve or thirteen pages, and in a normal A-picture schedule that's three days' work. Orson rehearsed meticulously on what soon became evident was a master shot that would encompass the whole scene. They had to pull doors out and all kinds of stuff. The camera was on a dolly and microphones had to be planted on the set. The scene, aside from being long, had four or five speaking roles, with a couple of extras coming in with coffee, and it had an insert of the dynamite, as well as action in three rooms. It was really very tricky, with perhaps thirty moves by the actors throughout the shot. It was an unusual scene to consider doing in one continuous shot, but Orson was determined. We rehearsed all morning, and as you probably know, on every movie set part of the production procedure is to report to the production office when you start rehearsing, when you start doing takes, and when you make a print on the first shot. We went through the whole morning and never turned a camera. Inevitably after lunch the executives began to arrive on the set, though they were not bold enough to approach Orson directly. He can be a somewhat formidable figure. They huddled about in uneasy little groups in the back, talking to one another and shaking their heads, and we went on rehearsing. We never turned a camera until nearly half past five in the afternoon. Then we started doing takes, and of course it was difficult and things went wrong. Finally we got a print at about a quarter past six and Orson said, "Fine. That's a wrap. We're two days ahead of schedule." He shot no coverage on the scene. That shot was the whole scene, and it works. Of course Orson's purpose was a larger one. He wanted to demonstrate to the studio how fast he could work, and the studio, of course, was delighted. The shocked executives went from being practically prostrate with gloom, from the depths of depression to heights of euphoria and visions of a ten-day schedule. Of course Orson never did it again in the whole picture, but they always thought he might.

One final Orson story. Many years later he was sitting in a restaurant having lunch, and a young man came up very politely and obviously very nervous. He said, "Mr. Welles, I must tell you that *Citizen Kane* is the greatest movie ever made. I wanted you to know that." Orson said, "Thank you, my boy." The young man said, "There's just one question I've always had about it. At the end, when Kane is lying in bed and he says 'Rosebud' and drops the ball and then dies, there's no one in the room with him. So how do we know those are his last words?" Orson just looked at him and said, "My boy, you must never repeat that to a living soul."

Do you like watching dailies?

I always watch dailies. I think the actor who says that he never watches dailies is either a liar or an idiot. I watch them because I learn from them. I always take notes and put them in my journal and refer back to them later to see how my impression of the scene when I saw it in dailies compares with my impression in rough cut, and then how it works in the finished film.

If an actor asks you if he can come to dailies—and I think he *should* ask you, as it's part of the courtesy an actor owes a director—there is no reason not to allow him to, unless he seems to be terribly insecure and uncertain. Inexperienced players can get preoccupied with the way they look or the way they sound. The theory I have heard from directors is that an actor can look at his dailies and become so preoccupied about making changes that it will screw him up. Or, conceivably, you might have gotten him into a situation where he's doing something you want, of which he is entirely unaware, and then he wants to change it after seeing the dailies. The fact is, very few people know how to look at dailies intelligently. The arguments against having actors watch the dailies are that sometimes the director likes to talk to the editor and the producer about how lousy everything is, and if the actors are sitting there, that tends to discourage them. You can avoid that by having them watch at a different time.

I'm interested in how much you think a director can help an actor with his part and which of your roles you feel a director helped you the most with. Conversely, if you wish to say it, which director do you think you got the least help from?

Obviously I would be disinclined to answer the second half of that question, though I do have some candidates. I think in performance terms I was probably directed better by Wyler than anyone else. Yet Wyler is not good at communicating. He is somewhat arbitrary and even irritable in his approach, but he has an incredible capacity for knowing when something is right. It's not true he does twenty takes on every shot, but he does do seven or eight on an average, and I promise you that's a high average. I think the most I ever did was twenty-three.

It seems to me that part of what I'm paid for is to adjust to the way different directors want to work. Wyler prepares extensively and pores over the script and glooms through the night thinking about it all. But I'm convinced that he doesn't do the really creative work until he gets on the set. He shows up every morning as though he's never been there before and doesn't quite know what he wants, even though I'm positive that he has worked through in his own head all the possible ways of shooting the scene. He just wants to explore them with the actors. One time in ten he might see something new and say, "Actually, let's have the camera over here instead of over there."

The hard thing about doing a scene for Willy is that the actor gets the precarious feeling of building a tower of toothpicks on a milk bottle. You get very irritable, because Willy's manner is irritable when he's directing. It's as though he were a watchmaker, trying to fit all the pieces together but the watch isn't keeping time. If the actors would just do what he tells them to do, it would be okay, but they don't, and he gets somewhat testy. I don't mean he screams and rants, but his manner is just testy. He'll say,

"Why did you do that thing at the beginning, Chuck?" I'll say, "What thing at the beginning?" And he'll say, "That frown. That's awfully phony. Don't do that phony stuff, Chuck. Just talk to her." I'll say, "Okay, fine." Then finally he'll say, "Yes, okay. That's pretty good. But it's not very spontaneous." "Jesus, Willy, I'm trying to remember all that stuff. of course it's not spontaneous. We've been putting stuff in and taking stuff out for two hours. How can it be spontaneous?" Then he'll say, "I don't know, but it has to be." So he keeps fiddling and poking and twisting until he thinks, that's it, that's the best he can do. I'm sure it's very seldom as good as what Willy is hoping for, but when as a director you're satisfied that your actors are doing the best they can, then you've got to call a halt and move on.

Wyler is seldom complimentary. When he finishes a setup he just walks away and tells the script clerk which takes he wants printed. The first time this happened was after we had worked an hour and a half on a setup on *The Big Country,* and I said, "Willy, let's not quit now. I can get it. Let's stay with it." He said, "Chuck, if I don't say anything, that means it's good." That was the policy that prevailed through five months of shooting on *The Big Country* and nearly nine months on *Ben-Hur.* On *Ben-Hur* I worked every day of six-day weeks and some seven-day weeks. It was raining and cold and I was tired because he would shoot a very long day. About the seventh month I was waiting outside the sound stage in the rain for my limousine at the end of the day, and he was waiting for his. I said, "Well, good night, Willy. I'll see you tomorrow." He turned to me and said, "Good night, Chuck. You were very good today." I said, "What?" He said, "The scene, you were good." I said, "Oh, thank you." That was the only time. Doing a picture for Wyler is like getting the works in a Turkish bath. You damn near drown but come out smelling like a rose.

The only way as an actor you can bear Willy's method is knowing that he's just as hard on himself. When I worked with him he had absolutely no ego about saying that what he'd been doing was terrible. He could work three, seven, nine, eleven takes on a scene, pushing you in one direction, saying, "Why are you being so harsh?" I'd say, "Willy, you told me I was supposed to get angry at her." He'd say, "That was a terrible idea. I shouldn't have told you that." If he didn't feel it was a good idea anymore, he would abandon his previous choice like an orphan in the storm and go on to a fresh one. That's a marvelous ability, and it takes great security to do that. With Willy you mustn't come in having done elaborate preparation. Or, at least, you mustn't come in with evidence of that preparation.

On *Ben-Hur,* I decided it was important to sketch out the boyhood of Judah Ben-Hur and his past life and family relationships, and so on. This is the kind of exercise that most actors are taught in school. It's great fun and very good training, and I guess it's also useful. I wrote three or four pages of this stuff, which was not bad, and showed it to Willy, and I got in terrible trouble with him. He regarded it all with extreme suspicion. He thought this was just show-off and too actory. It's one of the reasons he doesn't really like working with actors. He thinks they're frivolous and irresponsible people with no brains.

Do you read film critics and reviewers?

When they say nice things I'm struck by their perception and insight, and when they say lousy things I think what idiots they are. I think in reality there have been a few first-class film critics. James Agee. Perhaps Bosley Crowther. I think Chuck Champlin here in Los Angeles is remarkably good. A critic, being a writer, is likely to know something about writing and to make trenchant and reasonably accurate observations about a script, at least as it strikes him. But the thing they are least likely to be able to observe with any technical accuracy is acting. I remember the first play I was ever in, Godfrey Tearle, a brilliant, now-dead actor, said to me, "You know, I've been acting for more than fifty years, and I have yet to see the critic who knew the difference between a good performance in a good part and a bad performance in a bad part." I think he was correct.

What are your views on the effects of violence on young viewers?

Film is the art form of the twentieth century, and filmmakers naturally think of themselves as artists. The artist likes to feel that he has no responsibility other than to his own artistic integrity, but I think the filmmaker has to assume a certain social responsibility as well. I know that some of my colleagues would disagree, but I feel quite strongly about it. I've turned down a number of pictures in the last few years I might otherwise have taken because I think you have to be on the side of society. It's all very well to say, "I want to make an anti-establishment statement," but film is a terribly powerful tool. It's not like a painting or a poem or a novel or a newspaper article. Film crosses national boundaries and language barriers. It can even speak to people who can't read, to people of diminished mental capacity, and it really makes me nervous to see pictures that are too strongly aimed against society.

When you read the script of Planet of the Apes, *did you look on it as something that would be fun to do? Did you realize it was going to be such a success?*

The producer kept peddling the idea around the studios. All we had was the rights to the book and sketches, and he would take them to the studio heads and they'd say, "Talking monkeys? Rocket ships? You guys are kidding. Get outta here." Finally we went to Fox at a time when Dick Zanuck had just taken over. Dick said, "You know, this is all fine, but what if the makeup doesn't work? Supposing they laugh at it? It might just look like actors with rubber noses." He said, "I'll tell you what. I'll put up $50,000 to develop the makeup. We'll do a test and if it looks good, then we'll go with it." It wasn't easy. The makeup took three hours to put on and almost an hour to take off. Most makeup you can just tear off, but you couldn't with this. So we did a full-scale screen test, and Dick said, "Go."

We were all confident of the commercial success of the film because it was clearly so different and radical. I think *Planet of the Apes* is significant because it was the first of the space operas. It kind of revivified a genre that had existed in the thirties and forties as Saturday-matinee stuff, and of course the picture was so successful that Zanuck said, "We've got to do a sequel." I said, "Well, there's only one story and you've done it. The rest is just adventures with the monkeys." Dick said, "Chuck, we can't do a sequel if you're not in it." I said, "Well, I'm very grateful to you for doing the first film. I'll tell you what. I'll be in it if you kill me right away." He said, "Okay, that's fair enough." Then he phoned back and said, "Look, do you mind if you disappear right away, and then we kill you in the end. You come back in the end and we kill you so they keep thinking they're going to see you." I said, "That's fair enough." I just really didn't want to be in the film, even though one of the best performances I ever did in my life was to persuade the director that it would be a great idea to blow up the whole world. I figured they couldn't do any more sequels after that, but of course they were smarter than I was. They went backwards and started from before the first film. I think they finally did three or four more of them. In Dick Zanuck's place I would have done exactly the same thing, because each picture cost a little less as they were amortizing the sets and wardrobe and makeup from the first one.

Are you still looking for those roles that are the antithesis of what people think Charlton Heston is about? Do you ever think you need to do something against the grain?

Every public actor has to deal with the fact that as his career continues, he is followed by the lengthening shadow of all the roles the audience remembers him in. Of course the audience's perception of those roles colors how they see him in other parts. I've been more fortunate than some of my colleagues in getting some elbow room there, because I've done a somewhat wider range of parts than some actors. To take one of my contemporaries, it would be too late now for Paul Newman, good actor though he is, to put on doublet and hose and play Lorenzo de' Medici. He has established himself as the quintessential twentieth-century urban American male, just as Humphrey Bogart had before him, and he's created some marvelous performances. But there comes a time when he is denied the chance to move outside that. Fortunately for me, very early in my career, I began to put on false noses and white wigs and funny clothes and write with feathers, and by now a French audience will accept me as a sixteenth-century French cardinal, a Mexican audience will accept me as a twentieth-century Mexican lawyer and an English audience will accept me as a Tudor king. If you want to broaden your range, you've got to fight for it.

Do you have any final advice for beginning directors, writers and actors?

I suppose it all could be boiled down to one sentence, which is the best observation on film acting I ever heard. It was made by I think the best American film actor that ever lived, Spencer Tracy. He said, "It's simple. You come to work on time, know your lines and don't bump into the furniture."

Look, you don't need me to tell you that it's an incredibly difficult way to make a living. It would be better if you could say, as you could to a talented athlete, "If you're good enough, you'll make it." But that's not necessarily true of a writer or a director or an actor. So much depends on chance and timing. Many years ago I came out here to make a film for Hal Wallis, and I met Cecil DeMille, who was always very courteous to people. One day I was driving off the lot in an open convertible and he was standing on the steps of his building with a group of his staff around him talking about whatever they were talking about. As I drove by I waved at him and he nodded back. I was told later that he turned to his secretary and said, "Who was that?" She looked through her book and she said, "Charlton Heston. He's a New York stage actor. He just did a picture for Hal Wallis called *Dark City.* You ran it two weeks ago. You didn't like it." And he said, "I liked the way he waved just now. We'd better have him in to see about the circus picture [*The Greatest Show on Earth*]." I got the part. So my advice to you all is simple: wave nicely to people.

Films as Actor

1941 *Peer Gynt*

1950 *The Clock*
      Julius Caesar
      Dark City

1952 *The Greatest Show on Earth*
      Curtain Call
      The Savage
      Ruby Gentry

1953 *Three Lives*
      The President's Lady
      Pony Express
      Arrowhead

1954 *Bad for Each Other*
      The Naked Jungle
      Secret of the Incas

1955 *The Far Horizons*
      The Private War of Major
         Benson
      Lucy Gallant

1956 *The Ten Commandments*
      Three Violent People

1958 *Touch of Evil*
      The Big Country
      The Buccaneer

1959 *The Wreck of the Mary Deare*
      Ben-Hur

1961 *El Cid*

1962 *The Pigeon That Took Rome*
      Diamond Head

1963 *55 Days at Peking*

1965 *The Greatest Story Ever Told*
      Major Dundee
      The Agony and the Ecstasy
      The War Lord

1966 *Khartoum*

1967 *Counterpoint*

1968 *Planet of the Apes*
      Will Penny

1969 *Number One*

1970 *Beneath the Planet of the Apes*
      Julius Caesar
      Antony and Cleopatra (also
         director and screenplay)
      The Hawaiians

1971 *The Omega Man*

1972 *Skyjacked*
      Call of the Wild

1973 *Soylent Green*
      The Three Musketeers

1974 *Earthquake*

1975 *Airport 1975*
      The Four Musketeers
      The Fun of Your Life

1976 *The Last Hard Men*
      Midway
      Two-Minute Warning

1977 *Crossed Swords*

1978 *Gray Lady Down*

1980 *The Mountain Men*
      The Awakening

1982 *Mother Lode* (also director)

1984 *Nairobi Affair* (television)

1987 *Proud Men* (television)
      The Two Ronnies (television)
      *Christmas Night with the Two
         Ronnies* (television)

1988 *A Man for All Seasons*
         (television—also director)

1989 *Original Sin* (television)

1990 *Almost an Angel*

Treasure Island (television)
Solar Crisis
The Little Kidnappers
    (television)
1991 *The Crucifer of Blood*
    (television)
1992 *Genghis Khan*
    Crash Landing: The Rescue of
    Flight 232 (television)
1993 *Wayne's World 2*
    Tombstone

1994 *True Lies*
1995 *In the Mouth of Madness*
    The Avenging Angel (television)
1996 *Alaska*
    Hamlet
1999 *Gideon*
    Any Given Sunday
2001 *Town & Country*
    The Order
2003 *Rua Alguem 5555: My Father*

Heston appeared on television early in his career including *The Clock*, 1950; *Suspense*, 1949–51; *Lux Video Theater*, 1951; *Studio One*, 1949–52; *Robert Montgomery Presents*, 1952–55; and *Playhouse 90*, 1956–58.

Cinematography allows you to tell the world who you are. You are working with light and with composition, and all that comes from learning, but it also comes from inside. If you want to know something about me, watch my movies, because they are reflections of who I am.

JANUSZ KAMINSKI
(Born in Ziebice, Poland, 1959)

Janusz Kaminski left his native Poland when martial law was declared in 1981 and made his way to the United States. He studied for five years at Columbia College in Chicago, learning English and developing a fascination with movies, then came to the AFI Conservatory as a cinematography fellow. Like so many aspiring filmmakers, he found opportunity with Roger Corman, photographing several films and catching the eye of Steven Spielberg, who hired him to film a Civil War television pilot. Spielberg liked what he saw and chose Kaminski to be the cinematographer for *Schindler's List*.

Schindler's List was filmed in black and white in Kaminski's native Poland and was marked by innovative techniques that give a realistic feeling to the story of concentration-camp life in Germany during World War II. Kaminski's first major feature earned him an Oscar and gave him immediate status as one of the world's leading cinematographers. He photographed *The Adventures of Huck Finn, Little Giants, Tall Tale, How to Make an American Quilt* and *Jerry Maguire* before Spielberg enlisted him to photograph nine consecutive projects between 1997 and 2005.

They continue to enjoy one of the most fruitful collaborations between director and cinematographer in cinema history, turning out *The Lost World: Jurassic Park, Amistad, Saving Private Ryan, A.I. Artificial Intelligence, Minority Report, Catch Me If You Can, The Terminal, War of the Worlds* and *Munich*. In 2000, Kaminski directed a supernatural thriller, *Lost Souls,* starring Winona Ryder and Ben Chaplin; and he was acclaimed for his photography of Julian Schnabel's *The Diving Bell and the Butterfly* in 2007, which earned him the Technical Grand Prize at the Cannes Film Festival. He rejoined Spielberg for *Indiana Jones and the Kingdom of the Crystal Skull* and *War Horse*.

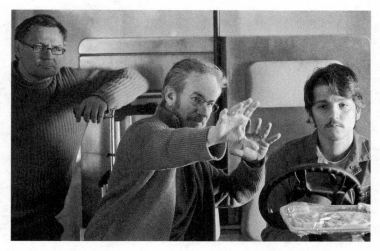

AFI graduate Janusz Kaminski with Steven Spielberg on the set of
The Terminal (2004). Kaminski has photographed eleven films for Spielberg.

Kaminski believes that part of his responsibility is to invest his work with his own life experience. "Those who think cinematography is simply the mechanical act of capturing an image on film have never spoken with a cinematographer," he says. "Or more precisely, a cinematographer with heart."

His return to speak at AFI as a former fellow reminded me of a comment of Barack Obama's during his presidential campaign. When asked if he had contemplated the problems in America's inner-city schools, Obama said, "When I am president, I intend to go to those schools and those children will see themselves in me." I expect when two-time Oscar winner Kaminski came to AFI and sat down with the AFI fellows, they saw themselves in the master technician and storyteller.

JANUSZ KAMINSKI

January 20, 2006*

You're originally from Poland?

Yes. I came to America in 1981 with about two pounds of luggage, not
speaking English, really naive and stupid. I was always fascinated by
America, so the first chance I had to get out of Poland, I never went back.
I went to Vienna and asked for political asylum, and after six or seven
months I was sent to New York. The first three days in New York I found
it just too overwhelming, so I went to Chicago. I knew I did not want to
live in a little Polish enclave in the suburbs, get a car, get a color TV, get
construction work and be one of those people, so I went to a very extensive English program for several months and then to Columbia College in
Chicago. I said, "Me must study film." The chairman said, "But you
speak no English." I ended up taking part-time film classes and working
part-time, and studying English part-time. In the film class we were
divided into groups, with four in each group: cinematographer, director,
producer and actor. I drew the straw for the camera. There was a teacher
there who told me, "You're good at it. You've got talent. Stick with it."
This was the first time anybody told me I was good at anything. I worked
really hard at school. I would shoot anything there was to shoot. Everyone
wants to be a director, nobody wants to be a cinematographer, so there
was a lot of work to be done. By the time I finished Columbia College I
had shot about thirty short films, most in black and white. It was a great
experience, because I could experiment. I would put on the filter and pan

*Frederic Goodich moderated this seminar. This interview also contains segments from semi-
nars given by Janusz Kaminski on January 7, 1994, September 4, 2002, and February 11, 2004.

left and right, and then realize why that might not be a good idea. You realize that a shot out of focus can actually be really good. You learn all the mistakes at school, because if you make mistakes when you're being paid, they'll just replace your ass.

I was really scared of Los Angeles. Living in Chicago we never really knew much about Hollywood other than it's the Mecca of filmmaking and that it's a very intimidating, mean place. I decided to come to AFI but perhaps was overqualified. I had already shot so many short films that when I arrived here I wasn't interested in becoming a camera assistant or loading film or putting the lens on the camera. Becoming a cinematographer is not about learning how to thread the film through the gate, it's about knowing how to tell the story through lighting, through camera blocking, through shadows. You have lights, the director, actors, a production designer. Whether you are doing it with video camera or with 70mm, you are a cinematographer telling a story in nonverbal language. You give the director the possibility to use the medium, which is the camera and lighting and grain and film emulsion, to enhance the story.

After the AFI you went to work for Roger Corman?

Through AFI I met a guy who was shooting a movie for Roger Corman. I asked him if he needed a gaffer and he said, "No, not right now. I need a key grip." So I became a key grip. Meantime the gaffer got another job, so I became the gaffer and called my friend from Chicago who came to work as a key grip. We did something like twelve movies in one year. We all worked as the grips, electricians and gaffers. We would do movies in fourteen days, working eighteen hours a day. Everything was shot around Venice Beach, because that's where Roger's studio was located. Sometimes I would shoot second unit, sometimes I would shoot B camera, and eventually I ended up shooting three movies for Roger as a full-fledged cinematographer. They were exploitation movies, naked girls running around with axes. Working for Corman was great because I learned how to work really fast, which will always impress certain directors who might give you a job. What I really learned from working with Roger was to rely on my instinct, and certain tricks that would work for me in a time-constrained environment. You learn that certain angles work, certain lighting setups work, but mainly you learn that your instincts are really important. You learn that only by doing.

The Polish cinematographers are always so good. Is it genetic?

Cinematography allows people from other countries to work and participate without really being able to communicate clearly in English. It's a
profession that attracts people from all over the world. If there's a country,
there's a cinematographer.

A few years ago you directed the film Lost Souls. *What compelled you to move
from cinematography to directing?*

I wanted the challenge. I think working in a nonverbal language is amazing, and cinematography is something I'll do professionally until I can no
longer stand and hold a light meter. But directing is just another form of
expression, another challenge. I felt ready, because I knew English well
enough to venture into the verbal world. That's not to say I was bored
with cinematography. It is my first love. But I wanted to see what it feels
like to be in the editing room, what it feels like to work with a composer,
and primarily what it feels like to work with actors. Directing is totally
different from being a cinematographer. Cinematography will not prepare you for being a director. Cinematography will prepare you to know
how to color the scene, but not how to direct the actors. It's a totally different animal. I found directing very rewarding and challenging and disappointing. My biggest concern was whether I would be able to
communicate with the actor, and I'm not talking about my accent. I'm
talking about how one phrase can trigger an emotional response. You can
intellectualize about performance for hours, but you use one single word
when talking to an actor and that might set something off in them. Basically, after the first week of me directing, the cinematographer, Mauro
Fiore, who is a good friend of mine, was on his own. For the first week I
was still trying to find out my reason for being on the set. I would go
behind the camera but then realize that wasn't my position. I said to
myself, "Let Mauro do his work and let me talk to the actors."

Do you feel that being a cinematographer allows you to express yourself?

Cinematography allows you to tell the world who you are. You are working with light and with composition, and all that comes from learning,
but it also comes from inside. If you want to know something about me,
watch my movies, because they truly are reflections of who I am. I'm
happy, I'm dark, I'm careless, I'm serious, I'm stupid. That's all in the
work. I'm just trying to put a little bit of my story into what's already been
written. You can get five cinematographers, five directors, same story,

same actors, and all of it will be different, simply because you bring your own perspective. Each person creates a totally different story because they bring the emotions they have experienced throughout their lives. With some movies I'm there because it's a job, and of course it's fun that I get to light this huge set and all that. But occasionally you have a chance to express yourself through really great storytelling, and then it's a little bit different. With those films I have very strong ideas in terms of where the camera should go. I remember when Ivan Passer* came to the AFI and explained he was going to make a movie and the studio was asking him, "What's the movie about?" Ivan said, "Well, I have a really hard time telling you what the movie is about, because if I knew what the movie was about, why would I want to make it?" I discover what the movie's about as I'm making it, even if I do have a general concept. There is mystery to the thing. There aren't clear answers when you're making a movie.

If you think of the two movies Steven Spielberg and I did recently, I happen to like *A.I.* more than *Minority Report*. I think *Minority Report* is just a great summer blockbuster, whereas *A.I.* had real personal resonance in my life. I appreciate stories about people who are not loved and who would like to be loved. I think that's a theme that prevails in Steven's life, and one I am also very aware of and responsive to. Perhaps we have such a strong collaborative relationship because we have the same pains and desires.

Are there certain methods the director can use to convey what he wants to the cinematographer?

Get a magazine and you'll find all the inspiration you need in there, as well as the ability to communicate very clearly. You can say, "I like the way she's lit here in this photo and how he's standing here." There are many ways of expressing yourself without verbalizing it: references from other movies, photographs, paintings, art books. You think, "That looks really great. Can we do that for this movie?" The references are all around you.

Do you ever have the urge to operate the camera during shooting?

Occasionally I'll go behind the lens when I'm really scared, when I'm right there on the edge, when it's either too bright or too dark, so I want to see what's happening. But other than that you want to be right next to the

*Writer and director of the Czech New Wave who immigrated to the United States.

director. It's really between takes when the ideas are floating around, and as the cinematographer you really want to be a part of that. I have no desire to go behind the camera. I can operate and do so with commercials all the time, but the key is your collaboration with the director. You don't have to be his friend, you don't have to love him, but you do have to be on the same page as him. If you're not watching the scene while standing next to the director, if you're watching the scene through the lens, you might not see some of the magical things that are happening.

What kind of conversations with Spielberg do you have before you start shooting? How specific are they?

It's a really simple relationship: he directs the movie, I photograph it. Intellectualizing about making movies doesn't really count for much in America, because the director is responsible for such a huge industrial machine. Filmmaking isn't an industry that encourages risk taking. There isn't much of an auteur sensibility any longer, because you're shooting the movies with extensive coverage, all these amazing creative shots with unnecessary close-ups or over-the-shoulders. It becomes a very safe medium. All the intellectual conversations you might have with the director are usually quite interesting but ultimately a waste of time. You talk about ideas for three weeks before you start shooting and very quickly realize that none of those ideas apply, simply because the director is suddenly paralyzed in the face of having to direct this huge hundred-million-dollar movie and tell a hundred people where to stand and what to do. With Steven, we just don't waste time on intellectual conversations. Very seldom do we talk about what the movie will look like. We might say, "Okay, it would be interesting if it wasn't as slick as *A.I.*" We did *Minority Report* right after *A.I.*, so we wanted it not to look as slick and elegant, which meant we said, "Let's make this movie kind of dirty." That's as much conversation as we had. For *Minority Report* we looked at one movie, *The Ipcress File*, which I find to be an amazing piece of cinema. We looked at it because of the really interesting angles, but for *A.I.* we didn't have any conversations. I think the beauty of our relationship comes from the lack of desire to discuss all those things. When he sees talent, he hires it and lets that person do the work they were hired to do. He's got a tremendous amount of filmmaking to offer to me, and I've got a tremendous amount of filmmaking to offer to him.

How has that changed over time?

It hasn't changed. Steven does his work, I do my work, and we mutually respect our decisions. I like to be left alone. Just let me do my work. Our first conversation before we started *Schindler's List* was: "I'm making this movie in black and white. Do you want to do it?" "Sure, I want to do it." There were no long conversations about concept. I went to Poland for three months and he arrived on the set three days before we started shooting. Nothing was very precise. There were no storyboards. A lot of the ideas just happened as we were shooting. It was very instinctual. With *Saving Private Ryan* he got to the set two days before. There are very few conversations, because he hires people he can fully rely on. You have to understand that Spielberg is a huge operation. He's a producer, he runs a studio, he's got a wife, he's got seven kids, and on top of all that he's very much involved in charitable organizations. He doesn't have time to waste on useless conversations in terms of what this movie will be about. It's like the Ivan Passer story. Steven discovers what the movie is about as he's making it, which is perhaps different to the way he used to make films, when he would work everything out in advance. He has become much more poetic and free and adventurous in terms of wanting to discover what the movie's about as he's going into it.

Can you talk about filming in black and white?

I didn't really know black and white, even though I did shoot black and white in film school. With the tests for *Schindler's List,* Steven wanted to shoot black-and-white negative, but the studio insisted we provide them with comparison tests between color negative and black-and-white negative. Black and white is really no big deal. Anything you shoot in black and white is gorgeous. Color is much harder.

How much input does Spielberg have in camera placement?

That's the director's job. You put the camera where you think it should go. That's what he's getting paid for. It's another story as to how much collaboration there is on the set, because some directors are not interested at all in placing the camera, while others enjoy it tremendously. Usually at the end of a day of shooting, Steven and I will talk about the setups for the following day. He'll give me the angle and we'll block the scene with stand-ins. By the time we arrive on set the next day we more or less know what the shot is about. I drive straight from the lab, where I've been looking at the material from the previous day. I'm fighting the traffic, so

Steven usually gets there maybe half an hour earlier, because he's still trying to figure out what the hell he's doing. He drives to the set because that
gives him an hour and a half of thinking time, when he can fully focus on
what the day's work will be, which is a luxury in his life.

How do you see digital postproduction affecting the role of the cinematographer?

It gives you another tool to work with. It allows you to use your creativity,
because even if we shoot digitally, where everything is being controlled in
postproduction, it's still the cinematographer's aesthetics that are being
controlled. You sit at a computer and change things, making it lighter or
darker, adding things, taking things out. If I know that later on I can
change things digitally, I spend a little less time fixing certain things as I'm
shooting the movie. And that can be really useful. In terms of color cor-
rection, for example, you have full control. With the new technology you
can take a digital shot, put it on your laptop, make changes, and send it to
the lab saying, "Make the shot look like this." I don't actually do this
myself, because I have no idea how to use a computer. A colleague shows
me his work, and if I don't like it he does it again. Then, when it's as good
as I want it to be I send it back to the lab.

What would you say is the riskiest thing you did in Schindler's List?

There were many scenes that were risky, like flaring the light right into the
lens or going really dark. I remember I was very nervous about shots I felt
were way too dark. I told Steven and he just said, "Don't worry about it.
If it's too dark we'll reshoot it," which is amazing confirmation from the
director. "You can take as many chances as you want." There is only one
Steadicam shot in the whole film. Often we would lay the dolly track and
the operator would then sit on the dolly and hand-hold the camera. We
wanted that jerkiness, that urgent feeling that suggested we weren't staging the action but rather stealing the shots.

On *Saving Private Ryan* the hand-held camera concerned me. I would
look at the dailies before Steven did. For the scene of Tom Hanks on the
beach, I couldn't even see Tom. I just saw soldiers running, because the
camera was moving so much. I think that was riskier than *Schindler's List*
because if it's too dark you can always print it up, but if it's shaky you can't
fix it. It was funny, because after the first two days of dailies Steven's assistant comes in and says, "Steven wants to talk to you." I think, "I'm going
to get fired." I walk to the production trailer where he was cutting and he

was very excited. "How did you do that? How did you get this stuff? Can we do more?"

Could you talk about your collaboration with production designers?

The collaboration with the production designer is as extensive as you can imagine, because everything that comes out of him goes in front of my lens. Even if directors don't want to talk about the visual style of a film, a production designer like Rick Carter, who is a real artist and worked on *A.I.*, is someone you really want to share all your ideas with. I'm not just talking visual metaphors and the significance of certain colors and locations and costumes. I may have an idea and he says, "That's a silly idea. Why would there be a red wall?" "Well, I'm going to put a tiny bit of light on the wall so it will become a motif of the assassination that's going to happen." Or I'll say, "Rick, paint this wall with full matte, don't give me any sheen. And on this one, give me a little sheen, because I'm going to put the light through a window." Subtle things like that. Rick is fantastic because he'll manage to find a location that really works, not just for the story but also for the logistics of the movie. You can't just have one location here and then the next one a three-hour drive away. You'll never get the movie finished.

Your movies seem to have very particular color motifs.

It comes from a very clichéd approach: when people are sad you go blue, and when people are happy you go warm. It really does work like that. It's even more important when it comes to light. In *Schindler's List* we didn't want to photograph Ralph Fiennes in a menacing light, because his character is already evil. You don't have to add anything with the lighting. But Liam Neeson's character is a much more confused guy, so he has this half-light and these really dramatic angles. He's got a light for the eyes and strong backlight, because that's his character. The quality of light is much more complicated than color. Color really is very simple. You put a guy in the warm light, you feel one way. You put a guy in the blue light, you feel another way. Blue for sad, warm for happy. Do that and you'll succeed. Ultimately what we're trying to do is to trigger an emotional response. For *Schindler's List* Steven and I looked at films like *In Cold Blood*, which was shot by Conrad Hall, and films shot by Gregg Toland, but the biggest inspiration for me was the book by the photographer Roman Vishniac called *A Vanished World*. He took pictures of Jewish settlements in Eastern

Europe between 1920 and 1930, including shots of the Krakow ghetto. His pictures had such a timeless quality. I thought that if he could get such beautiful work by just pointing the camera and with natural light, I could do even better with modern technology and lights.

When I read the script for the first time, I begin to see certain things. Often I write little notes for myself about the characters in terms of where they travel emotionally and what their visual environment might be. What might the light look like? Then I let it sit for a few days and read it again, this time marking certain things in terms of the colors. Colors aren't written into the script but they are extremely important, because clearly color is a form of storytelling. Occasionally you'll read, "A beautiful orange sunset" or "It's a rainy blue day." Other than that, colors aren't detailed on the page. But in a way actually they are, because the storytelling gives you a color palette. You read the story and learn about the characters and start to see them in certain light and color. Sometimes it will be very conventional: a sad scene is blue, a happy scene is orange. That's a good starting point. It doesn't say in the script that Schindler should have dramatic lighting, but it does say this character is confused, so how do you convey the confusion? What technique can you employ to show this guy as someone who isn't sure of what he's doing? During the second read of a script I start coming up with visual ideas. Maybe I draw the storyboards. I also start pulling reference materials from newspapers and magazines. Then, three or four weeks before the movie, I start dreaming the scenes. And when I start dreaming the lighting, I'm ready.

◆

Films as Cinematographer

1990 *Grim Prairie Tales: Hit the Trail . . . to Terror*
The Rain Killer
1991 *Killer Instinct*
The Terror Within II
Pyrates
Cool as Ice
Crackdown
Wildflower (television)
1992 *All the Love in the World*
Mad Dog Coll

1993 *Trouble Bound*
The Adventures of Huck Finn
Class of '61 (television)
Schindler's List
1994 *Little Giants*
1995 *Tall Tale: The Unbelievable Adventures of Pecos Bill*
How to Make an American Quilt
1996 *Jerry Maguire*
1997 *The Lost World: Jurassic Park*

Amistad

1998 *Saving Private Ryan*

2001 *A.I. Artificial Intelligence*

2002 *Minority Report*

    Catch Me If You Can

2004 *The Terminal*

2005 *War of the Worlds*

    Munich

2007 *Mission Zero*

The Diving Bell and the

    Butterfly

    Hania (also director)

2008 *Indiana Jones and the Kingdom*

    of the Crystal Skull

2009 *Funny People*

2010 *How Do You Know*

2011 *The Adventures of Tintin*

    War Horse

> Very often an actor doesn't really know what's happening and is led
> down the garden path. It's only the director who knows. As an actor
> I resent this to a certain extent, but at the same time it's not wrong.
> It's not necessarily a process of deception. The actor doesn't need to
> know everything. He's more of a tool.

JACK LEMMON
(Born in Newton, Massachusetts, 1925—Died 2001)

In 1971, an enterprising AFI fellow named Steve Carver was making his thesis film and wanted Jack Lemmon to play a role. The actor was already an Oscar winner and world famous for *Some Like It Hot* and *The Apartment,* but I asked him if he would meet with Carver. He replied in Lemmon speak, "You got it, kid." He agreed to play the lead in Carver's thirty-minute film, which involved a significant commitment of time and a week of night shooting with a young AFI crew. Jack would regale friends for many years with his story of driving a car in a scene and being arrested by the Los Angeles police. His willingness to jump on board and help a young filmmaker reflected his innate generosity.

Jack enjoyed a privileged youth in Massachusetts, where his father was president of the Doughnut Corporation of America; he attended Exeter and Harvard, where he discovered his love of acting. After studying in New York with Uta Hagen and working on the stage and in live television, in 1954 he was cast by George Cukor opposite Judy Holliday in *It Should Happen to You.* On the set Cukor kept urging, "A little less, Jack—a little less." At one point the frustrated young actor snapped back, "I'm doing so little now, I'm hardly acting." "Dear boy," Cukor whispered, "you're beginning to understand." Lemmon said it was the best piece of direction he ever received.

His early films included *Mister Roberts,* for which he won an Oscar, *My Sister Eileen, Bell Book and Candle* and *Some Like It Hot,* films that made him a star and put him squarely on track to be a light-comedy leading man. But he expanded his range when he combined the comic and the serious in *The Apartment.* Jack thought he had still more to offer and took on complex and challenging dramatic roles that allowed his humanity to shine through in *Days of Wine and Roses, The China Syndrome, Missing, Glengarry Glen Ross*

Jack Lemmon talking with AFI fellows at Greystone in 1988.

and *Save the Tiger,* which brought him a second Academy Award in 1973. As for *Glengarry Glen Ross,* Jack always insisted on calling it *Gene Barry, Glenn Close* "because it was easier."

In his later years he moved easily between film, stage and television. He made eleven pictures with his favorite co-star, Walter Matthau, including his memorable role as Felix Unger in *The Odd Couple.* Jack once told me about inviting Matthau to a sneak preview of a comedy in Long Beach. They sat together and there were very few laughs and people were walking out. When it was over and the lights went up Jack turned to his friend. "What do you think, Walter?" Matthau replied, "Get out of it."

Lemmon continued his association with Billy Wilder, racking up seven films with him. Jack was a risk taker, ready to put his star reputation on the line to make it possible for filmmakers to get financing for difficult subjects. He would go out on the high wire and create unique moments, trusting directors to make choices that would protect him from excess. He once said, "I am particularly susceptible to the parts I play. If my character was having a nervous breakdown, *I* started to have one." He developed a habit that became his signature on movie sets. Just after the camera started rolling, he would murmur, "Magic time."

Jack became a dear friend and came to the premiere at the Academy of Motion Picture Arts and Sciences of *George Stevens: A Filmmaker's Journey,* the film I made about my father. Seated behind me, he leaned forward with moist eyes during the applause at the end and whispered, "My father made doughnuts. Can we make a ten-minute film about him?"

JACK LEMMON

March 17, 1971*

What has been the response to The Out-of-Towners?

The head of the entertainment department of a major magazine was incensed by the entire film. She said, "This is ridiculous. The writer is taking too much of a liberty." Which he was. Neil Simon took the liberty of making a kaleidoscope of everything that might or could happen. It is rather unbelievable, having it all happen to show the horrors of living in a major city. He picked New York, I think, only because that's his city and he knows it well. It could have been any other major city. One lady, the critic of a magazine, got up ten minutes before the film was over and left. There were several people from Paramount's publicity and promotion department, and as she left they asked, "What's the matter? Don't you like it?" She said, "It's preposterous, as if these things could ever happen!" She was mugged in the lobby going out. Literally. Took her bag, knocked her down. She never got out of the theater. We got a lousy review.

Do you feel there is a specific kind of character that you play?

I don't, but some people do. I'll explain what I mean. A thing began to happen to me after a number of film roles, and I know why it happened, but it was never intentional. I think it emerged, unwittingly, because of an approach I took to acting a long time ago. After I was through with my education, through with college and everything, I went down to New

*This transcript also contains segments from seminars Jack Lemmon gave at the American Film Institute on March 29, 1982, January 4, 1983, and March 7, 1988.

Lemmon with Sandy Dennis on location in Central Park for
The Out-of-Towners (1970), an original screenplay by Neil Simon,
directed by Arthur Hiller.

York, and in about 1948 I started to get work. But the parts were terrible. I worked in soap operas in the early days of television when there were just kinescopes, no film, no tape. Then I began to work with a group under a man named David Alexander. They were professional actors and we did scene-study classes. It wasn't about trying to learn how to act, it was just scene studies. We would do scenes and then we would have a group discussion about them. It was a very good class for me because one of the main reasons for the class was finding out what you do when, as an actor, the material you're working with is absolutely godawful. And ninety percent of the time it *is* awful. What do you do legitimately as an actor to make it more exciting?

David suggested we work with obstacles. What that does is frustrate the character, and the more you frustrate the character within a scene, the more the audience empathizes and the higher the level of dramatic conflict becomes. As a result of working that way, after a while, I think people began to empathize with me. I would do everything to frustrate the characters I was playing because I think it's more interesting, more understandable, more human. For instance, I remember doing a terrible live show, years and years ago, in which I was a nineteen- or twenty-year-old just smitten with a young leading lady in the theater. This was the plot, you see. She was several years older than I was and gorgeous and all of that. The scene, which was the worst I have ever read in my life, involved me going back to her dressing room. I got an idea which the director liked and we used. Not that it was so great, but it does explain what I mean about obstacles. Instead of her sitting there at her mirror, as was indicated in the script—where she's taking off her makeup and being condescending to me, as I'm trying to get through to her saying, "I love you, won't you marry me?"—at a propitious moment, the director had her just say, "Excuse me." She goes into the bathroom and closes the door. Now, the lines are still there, but it meant that I had to declare my love through a closed door. It was an obstacle, and it gave the whole thing a sense of frustration. I love working that way, and I think it gives rise to what you're saying about people feeling that there is a particular character I play. When it gets tough I love being able to frustrate a character, because all of a sudden he comes alive. You find that in the better scripts this kind of thing is built in. In *The Apartment,* that cold I had when I call all those executives and tell them they can't use my apartment is an example. Instead of a routine conversation the cold takes the whole thing to another comedic level.

You were a child star, weren't you?

I was no star, I'll tell you. I wanted to act as far back as I can remember. For what neurotic reason, I have no idea.

Your biography says that you were on the stage with your father.

That's true. It was actually in a semiprofessional production, *Gold in Them Thar Hills* or something like that. It did kind of whet my appetite. What happened was that I blew my lines and the audience laughed, and I heard the laughter and liked it. There was a response of some kind, and maybe that was what I needed. I've often thought about what drives someone to be an actor. If you're dedicated to want to be an actor enough to go through the dreck of fighting against the odds for an entire career, then you really need it. You don't just want it, you need it, and I guess I did. I was an only child. I don't know if that has anything to do with it or not. God knows I was loved.

You once played John Wilkes Booth on television.

Yes, and I loved it. I really got very involved in that, especially when I jumped out of the box in Ford's Theater after having shot Lincoln hollering, "Sic semper tyrannis!" It was about a ten-foot drop and I was wearing spurs, which were authentic, because the horse was waiting outside. And exactly like Booth they caught on the flag and I pulled all my tendons. I had to drag myself off the stage. Everybody said, "Gee, that was terrific!" I was dying, absolutely dying.

People say that being a serious actor, even being a Shakespearean actor, isn't as tough as being a comic. What kind of comic actors have you liked?

There's a body of work in Chaplin, there's a body of work in Keaton, there's a body of work in W. C. Fields. But there are also various performances you can find where a guy hit it just right at one particular time.

I agree that comedy is more difficult on every level—in the writing, in the directing, and especially in the cutting. Timing in film is always complex, but especially in comedy. A pause in a dramatic scene can vary more than it can in comedy, but a comedic punch line has to be timed just right. You can actually louse up a beautiful comic scene if you don't cut it correctly, because what you're doing is presuming that you know what the timing of the scene should be, which might be different from the timing of the actor delivering his lines. And of course it all depends on who's watching the film, and where and when. The problem with thinking you know precisely how to cut a comic scene is that you aren't there in front of the audience when it's being screened. The audience changes all the time. I could play a scene on stage one night in Philadelphia one way and it might lie there, so the next night I can play it differently. But I can't do that in a film. You just have to play comedy on film as if there aren't going to be any laughs. That's my theory, anyway. Never try to allow for the laughs when it comes to cutting the film. Even if they laugh for twenty nights in a row, one night they won't. The fact is that people don't laugh when the house is one-third full like they do when it's entirely full. You may enjoy it just as much, but you just don't laugh.

I would love to suffer from that marvelous disease called They Couldn't Hear the Lines for three pictures in a row. I could retire. In *Some Like It Hot* the theaters reported back to United Artists that it was the biggest repeat business they'd had on any film in ten years. The same customers came back for a second time because they couldn't hear a lot of the lines thanks to the laughing. A case in point is the scene where I walk into the hotel room and say, "I'm engaged." I announce that I'm going to marry Joe E. Brown. But Billy Wilder hands me two maracas and says, "After every line you've got, do a little dance with these." I thought he was crazy. But on the set I start with these maracas and slowly it begins to dawn on me what he's doing. It was one of the most marvelous directorial inventions. If we had done the scene without the maracas, you wouldn't have heard another word of dialogue for a full page after "I'm engaged." The audience was laughing too much. But the maracas gave us a legitimate device to take long beats in between the laughs.

What is your definition of a good director?

A good director brings with him a sense of leadership that you trust. The most important thing is trusting the director, so you don't feel you have to protect yourself from him. Someone open to suggestions and change is also important. A director who comes onto the set knowing exactly what he wants is an insecure director. Those kinds of people have tunnel vision. He walks down Main Street but never wanders down the little alleys. He thinks he's in total control but really isn't. The good directors are open to all suggestions. They don't impose their views on the actor but rather allow the actors to try any crazy thing they want. One time I came to the set and said to Billy Wilder, "I've got a great idea." He said, "Don't tell me." I said, "Don't tell you? You won't even listen to it?" He said, "Just do it. Don't tell me, because I might misunderstand you. I might say no before I understand what you really want." I once saw Wilder take suggestions from a prop man and use them.

What about a definition of acting?

George Burns put it beautifully. He said, "The most important thing about acting is honesty. If you can fake that, you've got it made." That's the whole thing in a nutshell.

Now that you've directed your first film, has your attitude toward the relationship between the actor and the director changed?

After *Kotch* it's only been strengthened. The key thing is that as a director you must allow an actor to bring every possible thing he can to the role. I don't care how long it takes and I don't care how much it costs. Screw the front office. You must create an atmosphere in which actors have ideas and can contribute. The director has to be the captain of the ship who sits back objectively and says yea or nay. He has to allow them to try every conceivable thing that could come into their minds. If an actor has one good idea out of fifty, that's a hell of a high percentage. The moment the actor says, "I've got an idea," panic sets in for some directors. "Oh, my God, it's not my idea! It deviates from what I was going to do." Obviously directors should have worked things out and know how to shoot the scene four different ways, but you shouldn't be locked in. You should be secure enough to be open to any suggestions from anybody whom you trust and respect.

If you're an actor who decides to direct, be careful not to try out any of the parts in front of the actors who have been cast in the roles. There is a great tendency to say, "Wait a minute, try it this way." Just say "Roll" and "Cut." Don't interrupt when that spark gets going. Don't refine, don't hone, don't do anything. Just shut up.

Is there always a temptation, on the part of the actor, to direct?

Many actors seem to have the desire to direct. Directing is basically more creative and less interpretive. I've had big arguments about this. I think that acting is essentially interpretive. It becomes creative only for actors who are genuinely creative. Creation comes from the writer and from the director. Even the director is interpretive compared to the writer. Once the director has all the creative bricks at his disposal, he builds the house. He shapes the actors, he makes the selections. Very often an actor doesn't really know what's happening and is led down the garden path. It's only the director who knows. As an actor I resent this to a certain extent, but at the same time it's not wrong. It's not necessarily a process of deception. The actor doesn't need to know everything. He's more of a tool.

Do you enjoy directing more than acting?

It took us almost two years to get *Kotch* done, and it may yet stink. I enjoyed the experience more than any other single thing I've done in my professional life. I've failed in a lot of things and I may fail in this one, but if it is successful I would like very much to direct again. I've never worked harder in my life. It's an unbelievably difficult thing. Maybe it was because it was my first attempt at directing. As an actor I always find that I'm thinking twenty-four hours a day, but as a director it has to be forty-eight hours a day, because everything ultimately comes down to you. You really have to make all the decisions.

How much of the script are you given ahead of time?

It's rare you won't have a complete script. Most of the time the studio is petrified and they want to make sure they have a script that's finished and fully budgeted before production starts. It's really done for budget reasons. I don't think they give a damn about the actors. The only writer I know who doesn't give you a full script, never has and never will, is Billy Wilder. He writes like a playwright, usually in three acts, and very often his scenarios will say "Act One," "Act Two," "Act Three." Billy feels that not having written the complete script keeps his energy up, because he feels that ninety percent of the work is done when the script is done. He knows where the plot is going to go but hasn't actually written it. It's a strategy that works for him. I've done four or five films with him and you can't wait to get those pages, because you don't know where it's going to go.

Do you ever feel the desire to change a script as you're rehearsing?

I find that whenever I do anything written by Neil Simon or Billy, I never have the desire to change a single word. It's very seldom an actor will go through an entire script and not find something uncomfortable. I can hardly remember any times, out of the six or seven different things I've done with Neil and Billy, where I've ever wanted to change a word. With those two, if you do take out even a single syllable, the meter is gone. It's like editing Shakespeare. You just can't do it.

How do you go about choosing a role?

Usually I look for something I haven't done before. If a film is a hit, producers want to do the same thing again, and assume the actors do too. Above all I have to be taken with the writing. One thing I'm always drawn to is growth. Does the character go somewhere or just stay in the same place? It's amazing in how many scripts the characters are the same at the end as they were at the beginning. If you can find a script where the character grows and progresses, you really have a chance to excite yourself and the audience. If I'm taken with the script and the character but don't have the foggiest idea how to play the part, then often I'm interested in it. If I read a script and know immediately how to play the part, then either I've played that role already or the writing is only skin deep and there isn't that much to the part. It's exciting when you just keep peeling away layer after

Billy Wilder and Lemmon on the set of *The Apartment,* 1960,
the second of their seven pictures together. "Happiness,"
said Wilder, "is working with Jack Lemmon."

layer and there seems to be so much between each line. You discard one interpretation after another and they all seem to be legitimate. In a strange way, the better the writing, the more difficult it is to play the part well. There are only so many ways to play a role that's lousily written.

The other thing I look for is a script that's hard to label. For example I don't call *The Apartment* a comedy. I felt at that moment Billy Wilder was at the height of his powers. It's a brilliant use of comedy and drama. It was daring in its directness, with a leading character who's an inch short of being a pimp, and yet by injecting a love story, Billy made you care about this man. Nine out of ten people watching the film don't realize they're getting a message about the lack of morals and ethics in the world of business, and in society in general. It's rare that you can touch people dramatically and comedically with the same story. I don't know another writer alive who has the guts to have Shirley MacLaine in one room of this guy's apartment who is committing suicide, and in the other is a hooker he's picked up. It was daring as hell.

Who have you found most comfortable to act with in comedy?

Walter Matthau. He's probably the best actor I've ever worked with who does everything he can not to achieve his potential. I'm serious about that. He's probably the very best there is, so unbelievably bright and tal-

Lemmon with close friend and frequent co-star Walter Matthau in
The Odd Couple, 1967, based on Neil Simon's Broadway hit.

ented. He can do so many things he doesn't even bother to do because he's
more concerned about who's ahead in the third race that afternoon. In the
meantime, he's doing Hamlet's soliloquy. He is also unbelievably naive
about understanding where a scene is going and what's really happening,
which is great. You can push him around a little. As brilliant and as bright
as he is, he's also a square. He can sit and look at a scene and come up with
the most obtuse, marvelous approach and yet, at the same time, not realize where the scene is really going. It's unbelievable. It'll drive you crazy.

Do actors need to be intelligent to act well?

I've never known a really outstanding actor who was dumb, who only had
instinct. Maybe I'm just being protective, but I think the sensitivity it
takes being an actor goes hand-in-hand with an intelligence that's above
and beyond the norm. Good actors are able to perceive more than the
average person does, to feel it, digest it and then be able to put it back out
there. That's the function of the actor, and I think that when they're very
good, they're also very bright. They may be an emotional mess. They may
be a two-year-old idiot. They may be neurotic or psychotic, but that
doesn't mean they aren't bright.

Could you talk about working with Marilyn Monroe?

She was fascinating, but she had her devils. She might have covered it up, but she was tormented and very unhappy. I got along with her well and loved her very much as a person, but at the same time was totally thrown by her. I could no more get close to her than fly to the moon. In a way she really wouldn't expose herself, although at that point in her life she had every reason to act that way after what she had been through. I still can't figure out her talent. I think she was absolutely brilliant, but I still don't know whether she knew how to act. She had a self-barometer, some built-in mechanism that knew when a scene was right for her. She only knew one way to work. I've never seen anything like it. She would just stop. She would never wait for the director to say, "Cut." She would just say, "Well . . ." and walk off, and we'd start again. You'd get trapped if you were saving yourself for a last-minute spurt, because there wasn't going to be any last-minute spurt. She just knew when it was going right for her. At times she acted at you instead of with you. It was selfish, but it was the only way she knew how to do it, and the scenes worked, there's no question of that.

There were two parts of her mind working. One was focused on the part she was playing, the other was looking on at the performance. All actors have that to an extent. There's always that little spark back there which means you know when you've got the audience and when you don't, because otherwise the part takes you over, which is something I really don't believe in. I think that literally "becoming the part" is a lot of baloney.

One of your most famous roles was in a film in which another director took over halfway through.

It was on *Mister Roberts,* and we were petrified when that happened. It was about halfway through when all of a sudden I came to work and everybody was just sitting, pale white, with long faces. Pappy Ford—John Ford—had gotten sick about one or two in the morning and they rushed him to a hospital for surgery. Mervyn LeRoy was going to take over and finish the film. I'd only done a couple of films and was filled with panic. So was everybody else. But Mervyn did a very smart thing. He looked at all the uncut rushes and whatever had been loosely pieced together, and came on the set and said, "In no way am I going to attempt to make a movie that's mine. I want to do my damnedest to try to shoot it somewhat the way I think Ford would have shot it." And he did a hell of a job. To this day it would take a true aficionado to work out which scenes were done by Mervyn and which were done by Ford.

Let me tell you a story about Ford and how I got the job in *Mister Roberts*. It was a terribly lucky thing, because it made a vast difference in my career. When I first came to Hollywood I tested for a part, which I got, in a picture with Judy Holliday called *It Should Happen to You*. George Cukor directed. It was a marvelous experience and I adored working with Judy. At around the same time I tested for the lead in a picture called *The Long Gray Line*, a part that Tyrone Power eventually played, directed by Ford. The character ages from twenty to eighty years old, so for a couple of days I sat up in makeup. They took all of these plaster casts and rubber molds and everything else. I had straws up my nose so I could breathe. It was murder. I had never experienced claustrophobia until then. I thought I was going to die. I thought they were trying to kill me. They resented New York actors, that's all I can tell you. Anyway, they got me back to a sound stage and we shot a test of me as an eighty-year-old Irishman, and Ford, whom I had never met, kept saying, to Harry Cohn, "I'm not going to look at any kid, for chrissake. I want Tyrone Power to play this part." He never looked at the test and went ahead and made *The Long Gray Line*. Then towards the end of the shooting, when Ford was done with location shooting and was back at Columbia, a friend of mine who was an editorial assistant at the studio threw on the screen test at the end of some rushes that Ford was looking at. Ford said, "What's this? Who the hell is that?" My friend said, "I don't know, it must have been in with the other stuff." So on comes me as this eighty-year-old guy, and afterwards, when the lights go up, Ford turns and says, "He makes a lousy old man but he'd make a very good Pulver," and walks out. Remember that Pulver is twenty-one years old. Not only that, he didn't even know what I looked like without all that makeup.

Later I was walking on the set of *The Long Gray Line* and this old guy with a hat and a patch over one eye, clawing on a handkerchief, wearing a tattered old coat and sneakers, looks at me and says, "Hey, are you Lemmon?" I say, "Yes." He says, "You're all right. You'd make a good Pulver." I say, "Well, spread the word, will you?" He asks, "Do you want to play it?" I said, "Of course I want to play it, are you kidding?" I figure this guy is a grip or something. He says, "Spit in your hand." I say, "What?" Again he tells me to spit in my hand, and he spits in his hand and sticks it out. He says, "Come on, aren't you Irish?" I don't know why but I say, "Yes." He says, "Then spit in your hand." There was something about him, so I spit in my hand and shake his hand, and he says, "I am Ford and you are Pulver." And he just walks away.

▬◆▬

Films as Actor

1954 *It Should Happen to You*
    Phffft
1955 *Three for the Show*
    Mister Roberts
    My Sister Eileen
1956 *You Can't Run Away from It*
1957 *Fire Down Below*
    Operation Mad Ball
1958 *Cowboy*
    Bell Book and Candle
1959 *Some Like It Hot*
    It Happened to Jane
1960 *The Apartment*
    The Wackiest Ship in the Army
1962 *The Notorious Landlady*
    Days of Wine and Roses
1963 *Irma la Douce*
    Under the Yum Yum Tree
1964 *Good Neighbor Sam*
1965 *How to Murder Your Wife*
    The Great Race
1966 *The Fortune Cookie*
1967 *Luv*
1968 *There Comes a Day*
    The Odd Couple
1969 *The April Fools*
1970 *The Out-of-Towners*
1971 *Kotch*
1972 *The War Between Men and
        Women*
    Avanti!
1973 *Save the Tiger*
    Get Happy (television)
1974 *Wednesday* (AFI student film)
    The Front Page
1975 *The Prisoner of Second Avenue*
1976 *The Entertainer* (television)

    Alex and the Gypsy
1977 *Airport '77*
1979 *The China Syndrome*
1980 *Tribute*
1981 *Musical Comedy Tonight II*
        (television)
    Buddy Buddy
1982 *Missing*
1984 *Mass Appeal*
1985 *Macaroni*
1986 *That's Life!*
1987 *Long Day's Journey Into Night*
        (television)
    The Murder of Mary Phagan
        (television)
1989 *Dad*
1991 *JFK*
1992 *For Richer, For Poorer* (television)
    Glengarry Glen Ross
1993 *Short Cuts*
    A Life in the Theater (television)
    Grumpy Old Men
1995 *The Grass Harp*
    Grumpier Old Men
1996 *Getting Away with Murder*
    A Weekend in the Country
        (television)
    My Fellow Americans
    Hamlet
1997 *Out to Sea*
    12 Angry Men (television)
1998 *The Long Way Home* (television)
    Puppies for Sale
    The Odd Couple II
1999 *Inherit the Wind* (television)
    Tuesdays with Morrie
        (television)

Lemmon appeared on television early in his career including *The Philco Television Playhouse*, 1949; *Suspense*, 1949; *Studio One*, 1949–50; *Danger TV*, 1951; *Kraft Television Theater*, 1957; and *Alcoa Theater*, 1957–58. He directed *Kotch*, 1971.

Most of the executives at the studios aren't trained filmmakers. They make the decisions but don't really know about how film works. They're afraid of the people who come up with the magic, yet still end up telling the filmmakers what they think the movie should be and whether it works or not. My feeling has always been that the fundamental starting point must be the director's interpretation of the story.

GEORGE LUCAS
(Born in Modesto, California, 1944)

For three-quarters of the first century of motion-picture making, the brightest talents were richly rewarded, but it wasn't until the release of *Star Wars* in 1977 that a filmmaker was on track to become a billionaire. George Lucas was just thirty-three when his imaginative foray into outer space changed an industry that would soon become dominated by distribution concepts like "franchises" and "tentpoles."

Lucas was raised in northern California and his interest in film developed in San Francisco in the sixties, where a new breed of experimental filmmakers was showing its wares. He studied film at USC and met Francis Coppola on an internship at Warner Bros., where he was assigned to observe Coppola on *Finian's Rainbow.* Lucas then joined forces with Coppola in founding American Zoetrope in the Bay Area as an independent environment for young filmmakers. "The grand lesson we had in those days was that the artist rules," Lucas said later. "That's why we ended up in San Francisco." There he expanded a short film he had made at USC into his first feature, *THX 1138.*

Lucas next made *American Graffiti* with Coppola and Universal. He cast newcomers who would later become major players, including Richard Dreyfuss, Ron Howard and Harrison Ford, in a modestly budgeted film that reflected the small-town experiences of his youth. *American Graffiti* struck a chord with young audiences and earned the thirty-year-old Lucas Academy Award nominations for screenplay and direction, as well as best-picture recognition from the New York Film Critics and the National Society of Film Critics.

Coppola's long preoccupation with *Apocalypse Now* led to the end of Zoetrope, so Lucas started Lucasfilm and a visual-effects studio, Industrial Light and Magic, which enabled him to pursue his ambitious vision for *Star*

George Lucas with Mark Hamill, who played Luke Skywalker in *Star Wars* (1977).

Wars, an intergalactic tale of good versus evil. The stunning success of the film surprised everyone except Lucas, and positioned him for a grandly remunerative decade with the next two episodes of *Star Wars* and his collaboration with Steven Spielberg on *Raiders of the Lost Ark* and *Indiana Jones and the Temple of Doom.*

In 1985 Lucas built his Skywalker Ranch near San Francisco, which was designed to address his own production needs and provide pioneering developments in editing, sound and visual effects to other filmmakers. His companies operate today under the umbrella of Lucasfilm Ltd. and continue to be leaders in production, animation, technical services, video games and the licensing of related products.

Along with his successes, Lucas had some failures—*Willow, Radioland Murders, Howard the Duck*—but his innovation and entrepreneurial skills enabled him to build and maintain a thriving enterprise. His first three films established him as a director, but he told *Rolling Stone* in 1980, "I hate directing. It's like fighting a fifteen-round heavyweight bout with a new opponent every day." So more often than not, he functioned as writer and producer on his films. However, in 1999, when he finally tackled the long-awaited first chapter of the *Star Wars* saga, *The Phantom Menace,* he was back in the director's chair for the first time in more than twenty years. The first major live-action film to be projected digitally, it was the top box-office hit of 1999.

Attack of the Clones continued the *Star Wars* franchise in 2002, followed by *Revenge of the Sith* in 2005, both of which Lucas directed.

Lucas prides himself in celebrating the potential of the individual to overcome any limitations and follow his dreams. "Dreams are extremely important," he says. "You can't do it unless you imagine it."

The day before Lucas received his Life Achievement Award in 2005, he gave a seminar for the fellows.

GEORGE LUCAS

—◆—

February 26, 2005*

How did your interest in film come about?

It was basically a fluke. I grew up in Modesto, a farming community in
central California. It was very Norman Rockwell–esque. I lived in a small
suburban neighborhood with lots of kids. I spent a lot of time raking
leaves and mowing lawns. I grew up in the forties and into the fifties, with
the birth of rock 'n' roll and then the hippies and the Vietnam War. There
wasn't any television and we had only two movie theaters in town. I
would mostly go to the movies as a teenager to chase girls. We got a television when I was about ten, but the problem was that there wasn't much
to watch on television. I do remember reading a lot. I loved reading history books, everything from Alexander the Great to the Civil War to
World War II. The only other entertainment was comic books, although
I did have an electric train that took up most of my bedroom and I was
always building things in my little workshop—chessboards and doll-
houses, that sort of thing.

When I was about fourteen we moved to a walnut ranch outside of
town and I got my first car. After that, the main thing we did for fun was
drag the main street of town. We would just cruise up and down. I wasted
a lot of time there over the years. I'd race around the orchard and spin out
and smash it up, and started going to a foreign-car service to fix my car
up. I got a job working there and eventually got involved with amateur,
and, later, professional, sports-car racing. I wasn't paying much attention

*Jon Avnet moderated this seminar. This transcript also contains segments from an interview
George Lucas gave to AFI on March 3, 2005, and from an interview conducted in 2009.

at high school. I found it all pretty boring and spent all my free time working on my car. I had a hard time with math and science. I was much more interested in the humanities, things like anthropology and history.

A week before I was to graduate I was driving home and was about to turn into our driveway when another kid from my school, driving along in his lowered Impala with chrome wheels and showing off to a girl, rushed past at nearly a hundred miles an hour. He broadsided me and my car flipped seven times. I had a racing seatbelt and a roll bar, but for some mysterious reason this huge aircraft seatbelt broke and I was thrown free of the car before it wrapped itself around a tree and became a piece of twisted metal. I was very fortunate somehow to escape death. When I was in the hospital recovering, I spent a lot of time thinking about what I should do, because it didn't seem like car racing was going to play a big part in my future. I decided to go to junior college to study things I was really interested in. After that, I truly felt that every day was a gift.

At Modesto Junior College I was finally able to take classes I couldn't take in high school. A whole range of human experience opened up, and I just fell in love with it. I studied sociology, anthropology, psychology and generally had a great time immersing myself in the social sciences. I became excited by ideas and learning. I wanted to go to art school in Los Angeles and become an illustrator, but my father wanted me to take over the stationery store he ran. I remember telling him, "I'll never work a job where I have to do the same thing day after day." My father was devastated. He'd worked very hard to give me the store and thought I'd end up a starving artist in a garret somewhere. He was convinced that artists didn't make any money. So, since he would be the one paying for school, and knowing I was basically a lazy underachiever, he said, "Do whatever you want, but I'm not paying to send you to an art school, because artists don't make money." I said, "Okay, I'll go to San Francisco State and become an anthropology major." My best friend was going to USC to become a business major and wanted me to go with him and take the entrance tests, and by some kind of miracle I actually passed and was accepted. So I asked my friend, "Do they have an anthropology department?" He said, "I don't think so, but they've got this cinematography school and I think they teach photography." So I went there, and lo and behold it was a school where you could learn to make movies. I couldn't even imagine such a crazy thing! At that time nobody wanted to be a film student. Once I arrived, the first thing I took was an animation class.

Why animation?

It was the only production class I could get into. Since I hadn't taken any
film classes, I had to take Arthur Knight's film-history class and also a
class where we did still photography. But animation was an upper graduate class, and I was allowed to take it. They gave me one minute of 16mm
film to test the animation camera and a little list of exercises. I had to go
up and down, and pan across, and do this and that, so I turned it into a
one-minute movie and then added a soundtrack. It ended up getting into
film festivals and winning awards all over the place. I just said, "Hey, I
know how to do this, and I don't even have to think about it. It's great." I
fell in love with filmmaking immediately. It's one of those wonderful
things when you find your passion. You find what you're talented at and
suddenly it all clicks. I ended up spending days and nights eating candy
bars and working in the editing rooms. That's where I was really happy.

I loved all the practical exercises we had to do in class. They gave us a
series of pieces of film and said, "Cut these together. Tell a story." The
shots were of a couple of guys getting into a fight, but they were full of
bad screen direction and other film-grammar problems. The exercise was
fundamentally about storytelling. Like a puzzle, we had to sort it out and
make it coherent. It was a way of forcing us to ask ourselves, "Why am I
confused here? Ah! It's because both people are looking in the same direction but they're talking to each other." It would be like giving someone a
whole bunch of sentences without any caps or punctuation and being
told, "Turn this into a paragraph." The easiest thing was just to edit the
shots into what it actually was, the story of a guy who bumps someone
else's car and gets into a fight. But some students were very creative and
turned it into something completely different.

In each class it became clear that most students never finished their
films. But I was determined to make a completed movie with a mixed
soundtrack. There were a bunch of us there, maybe a couple dozen out of
the two hundred, who were really ambitious and talented. We migrated
towards each other and caused a lot of trouble for everybody else. This
was in the sixties, a time of "We should all help each other." The school
sometimes gave someone a break if his work wasn't really good enough. If
a guy was a real idiot and wanted to make a film, we all had to help him,
even if he didn't know what he was doing. Our little group didn't believe
in that. We ended up kicking one director off a film and taking it over.
That's how I ended up making *1:42:08,* a short we filmed up at Willow

Springs Raceway. We did it in color, which was unheard of at the time, and strictly against the rules. None of us wanted to wait around for other students to learn how to direct. We just wanted to get our work done. In our senior class we were given five weeks to make a complete movie and another ten to make a second.

I was something of a troublemaker at film school. Later, when I went back to graduate school for a semester I decided to make a film in color, in widescreen, with a cast and crew of about twenty-five people. It was a project that had to be conceived, shot and finished in five days. I was inspired by an e. e. cummings poem and called the film *anyone lived in a pretty (how) town*. We shot it all over the city even though the rules specified we weren't allowed to shoot further than a hundred yards from the USC Cinema Department. We did that one in color, too. The teachers said, "You can't do it. You'll have to take it to the lab and it'll take a week just to have it developed. You don't have the time and it'll cost too much." We worked well together and knew what we were doing, so we ended up finishing it in only four weeks, and spent a whole week cutting a trailer and making posters which we put up all over campus. That infuriated the faculty even more. What happened then was the school wouldn't screen it. I said, "Why not?" They said, "Well, yours is the only film that's finished. It would embarrass the other students." That's when John Milius punched the guy out. But that was the way things worked in film school. I started out as a street filmmaker with a wild imagination. That forces you into situations where you're always working under the constraint of available resources. Essentially that's what film school was for us.

Did everyone at film school want to work in the business once they graduated?

The truth is that nobody really expected to get a job in the film business. That's why it was so hard for USC to get the number of students it needed. We expected to work for Lockheed making industrial films or at Disneyland as a ticket taker. The idea that we were going to somehow make movies—and certainly in any way radically change the nature of the film business—didn't occur to anybody, apart from Francis Coppola.

One of the things we stress here at AFI is collaboration.

Film is an interesting medium, because it's really a benign dictatorship. No matter how you do it, that's the way it works. When I was at American Zoetrope, later on in the sixties, there was a group of diehard Communists who finally revolted from the company and started their own company called Cinema Manifesto. Their idea was that everybody on the crew was equal and everybody would have their input on the script and with the actors. What happened was that you had everybody on the crew telling everybody what to do. It was hopelessly naive and ridiculous. Let's face it, film is a medium where you have one dictator who has his little staff, half a dozen people, and between them they pretty much determine everything that happens. Then you have to have a devoted crew that is willing to follow that group anywhere, under any conditions. The whole idea is to achieve and maintain loyalty and get everyone to contribute, but to keep them in line so they don't feel they're making their own movie.

Basically the director is putting forth his vision and everybody is helping him realize it. It's very hard to achieve this when there are a lot of people at the top trying to make decisions about what the movie should be. That's what happens with studios. Most of the executives at the studios aren't trained filmmakers. They make the decisions but don't really know about how film works. They're afraid of the people who come up with the magic, yet still end up telling the filmmakers what they think the movie should be and whether it works or not. My feeling has always been that the fundamental starting point must be the director's interpretation of the story. Regardless of whether it works or not, everyone should follow what the director thinks is the right thing to do.

Steven Spielberg and I used to have contests to see who could shoot

Kate Capshaw, Steven Spielberg and Harrison Ford with Lucas
on the set of *Indiana Jones and the Temple of Doom* (1984).

Lucas and Francis Coppola (center), executive producers of
Kagemusha (1980), visit director Akira Kurosawa in Japan.

most in the fewest number of days. The movies don't suffer. It's like running a race. Find someone you want to compete against. The whole point
is to beat them, but in a friendly way. It's a lot more fun running with
someone than by yourself. If your friend is running around the track and
falls down, you stop and pick him up, just as he would pick you up if you
fell. That's why so many people ended up with us at Zoetrope. There was
a bunch of really talented and great guys around, and we wanted to help
each other. Even today we're all pals, because we were standing outside the
gates of the film industry together trying to get in, boosting each other up
to get him over the fence. When one guy got up, he reached down and
pulled the other guys up.

*When you started at USC, were you seeing a lot of films in class as well as going to
the art-house theaters?*

We would go around to the various art houses. It was the dark ages. There
was no DVD or home video, so if you wanted to see *Citizen Kane* you literally had to wait for it. You had to check the paper every day or see what
Arthur Knight or the UCLA professors were playing in their classes. Of
course two hundred other students were doing the same thing, so as soon
as something would show up everybody would say, "You've got to go over
there, they're going to show *Gone With the Wind*. It'll be the last time

you'll ever get to see it." Or, "They're showing *Seven Samurai*." We would talk about *Yojimbo* and I think it was two years before we actually got to see it. I was seeing ten or fifteen movies a week during that period. Film students work twenty-four hours a day, living on chocolate bars and coffee. That was my life at the time.

This was the time of an incredible array of great European films being distributed in the United States. As film students in the sixties, many of us were centered on that kind of work. I was a huge fan of Godard because I was an editor and experimental filmmaker, and he was pushing the boundaries. When it came to how to tell a story, Fellini was everything to me, as was Kurosawa. With him especially, an American audience was being made to explore a radically new but fascinating foreign culture. What did any of us know about the history of medieval Japan? We were really being dumped into an alien environment. I loved being thrown into the middle of something with no explanation. I assume it's the same for someone who grew up in a village in China. They would look at a western and say, "What is going on here? What is this place?" I find that fascinating, and have used the technique of not explaining where I am, but rather just focus on the emotional center of the characters. I'll drag the audience through the cultural landscape and they'll pick up everything they need to know indirectly. So those three—Godard, Fellini and Kurosawa—had a profound effect on me, and I watched every film of

Lucas and Steven Spielberg present Akira Kurosawa
with an Honorary Academy Award in 1989.

theirs I could. Antonioni I liked, but you had to like him intellectually, and I preferred the emotional directors, like Truffaut. I liked films that grabbed you, drew you in emotionally and shook you up.

Modesto is right next to San Francisco, and I would drive to the city on the weekends when I was still at high school and see underground stuff, the Stan Brakhage, Bruce Conner, James Broughton and Canyon Cinema kind of movies, in the beatnik coffeehouses and café backrooms. I was infatuated with all these weird little 16mm movies. As somebody who liked visual communication, I responded to that kind of imagery. At USC we also watched a lot of films from the National Film Board of Canada, abstract films by people like Norman McLaren. I had never seen anything like that, and for a time it was the kind of work I wanted to do. I also liked documentary filmmaking, so when I actually got to school I said, "What I'm going to do is become a documentary cameraman and editor, and make experimental movies on the side." I was extremely interested in non-story, noncharacter movies. To me that kind of work was pure cinema.

What do you mean by pure cinema?

One of the key ideas of nonnarrative, experimental movies is picture and sound playing against each other, the juxtaposition of music with the images. That's where the real art is, pushing that as far as it can go. I was fascinated with the mechanics of it, just like I was with automobiles.

Maybe more than any other art form, film is a combination of all the senses. The unique thing about cinema is that it's about what happens when you create motion and cut from one image to another. Whether or not you have a soundtrack, just the juxtaposition of those images can create emotions in the audience. That's really what was being taught at USC, because Lester Novros* was there, and the head of the department was Slavko Vorkapich,† who had worked with Eisenstein. When we were in school, the first thing they threw down on the table were Eisenstein's books *Film Form* and *Film Sense,* so we were very montage-oriented and focused on silent movies. At the time I was focused on the notion that there was a certain vocabulary and grammar of images that had been developed during the silent era that got lost when actors started talking.

Film works psychologically differently from the written word. A book

---

*Lester Novros (1909–2000), American animator (*Snow White and the Seven Dwarfs*) and special-effects pioneer (*2001: A Space Odyssey*).
†Slavko Vorkapich (1894–1976), Serbian-born film director and editor, former dean of USC Film School.

is not a movie. If you've got a brilliant piece of literature, it probably won't translate into a movie. If you've got a bad piece of literature, it might. In the same way, if you have a great cinematic event, there's no way to articulate it in words. It's one of those things you have to experience. What you're doing when reading or listening to a story is using a part of your brain that takes language and converts it into meaning. It's an intellectual process. With a film you're not doing that. Film is very direct, like life. You're sitting there and it attacks you. With movies you use your ears and eyes in combination. I could never adapt a book into a movie. I think truly cinematic stories have to be rooted in the moving image, not literature.

So the building blocks of the stories we told at film school were strictly cinematic. That might sound obvious, but what I mean is we weren't adapting plays or writing scripts based on our favorite novels. The fundamental question was: how does this medium actually function? What's actually going on here, practically and emotionally and psychologically? I became fascinated by that idea. All you're really doing as a filmmaker is playing psychological tricks on the audience. You have to understand psychology and neurology to know how those tricks work. The more you know about it, the more effectively you'll be able to manipulate it and the better you'll be able to trick the audience into believing. In many ways *Star Wars* was designed to be a silent movie. Though it's probably not quite as extreme as *American Graffiti,* it's really all music. It's rooted in the fundamental structures of cinema.

The group of yours that came out of USC is a fascinating one. You as director, Walter Murch as the arch-technician, Caleb Deschanel as the cinematographer, John Milius as the writer.

Yes, but at the same time we were all directors and writers and cameramen. We specialized and were better at one thing than another, but we could all do all of it. John Milius and Walter and Caleb ended up directing, and I ended up writing.

Why did you establish yourself in San Francisco rather than Los Angeles?

It turned out I had mild diabetes, so wasn't eligible for the draft. It meant I'd never have to go to Vietnam and fight. After I graduated from USC in 1966 I spent the summer working as a cameraman shooting second unit for people like Saul Bass. I worked on a lot of industrial films for him and learned a lot, because he really understood about the language of graphic art. Then I was an editor on some USIA* films with Verna Fields, which are kind of government propaganda films for the rest of the world. In the fall of 1966 I was asked to come back to school to help my old camera instructor Gene Peterson and teach a cinematography class. It was the middle of the Vietnam War and the Navy was sending military personnel to USC to train them, these Marine sergeants who had been in the service for ten years. There was a very real disconnect there. This was the middle of the sixties and there was a huge conflict between the hippie students and these hardened Marine sergeants with their crew cuts. Nobody wanted to go near them. They weren't really assimilated into the department, and I got handed the class. The one advantage was that the Navy had five Arriflex cameras with all the lenses, and color film too, whereas the rest of the department had only two little Kodaks and an Eyemo. Most students would do anything to get hold of cameras and film, so I agreed to help with the class, which essentially was about how to shoot with available light. How do you tell the story with only a small amount of equipment? I split the class in half. Half of these soldiers went off on their own and did a movie—they were happy to work by themselves—and I took the other half and ended up making the first version of *THX 1138,* which was written by some friends of mine. We'd all been at a party talking about our ideas, and they wrote down the basic story of *THX.* Then they decided not to make it, so I said, "I still like this idea. I'll make it into something."

THX won some awards and as a result I was offered two scholarships, one to work at Columbia Pictures for producer Carl Foreman, to do a little behind-the-scenes documentary on *MacKenna's Gold,* and the other to work at Warner Bros. It was what they call the Samuel Goldwyn Memorial Scholarship. I got to work in a department of my choosing at Warners for six months at eighty dollars a week. I figured, "I'll do them both, what the heck." It was interesting because I figured I should see what theatrical filmmaking, which we weren't exposed to at film school, was all about. The Columbia job was great, because there were two guys from USC and two guys from UCLA, and we had two Land Rovers, cameras and film. One guy made a film about the producer, one made a film about the director and another made a film about one of the horse wranglers. All these films were supposed to promote *MacKenna's Gold,* but I decided to make an abstract film about the desert. Foreman went through the roof and wouldn't approve mine. He said, "This isn't going to do us any good. You have to do something that will sell on television." I could be a very

*United States Information Agency.

difficult person in those days. If I wanted to do something, that's what I was going to do, and I wasn't going to bow to anybody, not even Carl Foreman. Finally I beat him down, because we were running out of time, and I made my film. I spent six or seven weeks wandering out there on the set of *MacKenna's Gold* filming landscapes, sunsets, moving clouds and grazing sheep. It barely touched on the making of the feature film. As it turned out, my finished film, which I called *6-18-67*—the day I finished the film—won a bunch of awards and even ended up on television. If I didn't want to make theatrical films before that, I certainly didn't want to make them after, because watching Foreman and the crew make *MacKenna's Gold* was the most boring, stupidest thing I had ever seen in my life. I found it frustrating that there was so much sitting around doing nothing, which to my mind was a real waste of time and money.

Then I went to Warner Bros. Unfortunately the studio had just been sold to Seven Arts and the day I arrived was the day Jack Warner left. It really was a ghost town. It was the sixtieth anniversary of the film business, and all the old entrepreneurs who had started Hollywood were nodding off and selling the studios. In the sixties and seventies the studios were being sold to huge corporations which were buying what they considered valuable assets and then saying, "Okay, now what do we do?" They needed new people to run the places and make films for them, and they turned to the film schools. *Easy Rider* and a lot of these films aimed toward the youth market had, by making money, created great opportunities. The studio said, "Young people! We need young people!"

I latched on to the crew who were making *Finian's Rainbow,* directed by Francis Coppola. I had actually met Francis before at a function at USC. We had a dinner and he had come and pontificated, as we were all wont to do. He was only twenty-five but we all looked up to him because he was the only film student who had made it into the industry. He had actually written a screenplay and directed a film, and he was like the student-film god. He said, "You can be an observer on this picture." I sat there for about a week watching this insane ritual they were going through, and got really bored and went back to the production department. I said, "Look, can I get off this thing?" I'd just done the same thing for six weeks out in the desert, which convinced me that I had no interest in Hollywood movies. I had learned everything I could about that kind of filmmaking and knew I didn't want to do it. I wanted to make documentaries. So I asked if I could be reassigned to the animation department, where I knew there were all these cameras sitting around and lots of short ends of film. I said, "I'm going to go over there and make a movie."

At that point Francis heard I wanted to leave. I was twenty-three and he was twenty-eight and we both had beards, and everybody else on the picture was over sixty. He said, "What do you mean, it's boring?" I told him I wanted to make my own movie. He said, "Stick around and come up with one good idea every day." So that's what I did. I had a Polaroid and would go around and get angles for him, because as it turned out Francis' real expertise is, first, working with actors and, second, as a screen-writer. Those are the two things I really don't like doing. All I cared about was editing and photography. So I started picking angles and working in the editing room, and he realized I knew what I was doing. We meshed very well. It was sort of two halves to a whole, and it turned out to be a very good experience. He said, "If you're ever going to direct movies, you're going to have to learn how to write." He forced me to become a writer and work with actors and do all that theatrical stuff I really didn't have any interest in.

Francis and I are very different in that Francis is very bold and I'm very conservative as a person. Not politically, but if there's a five-hundred-foot drop I would have no interest in jumping off. But Francis would do it. He'd say, "Come on, let's go." I would just be there saying, "You can't do that, you're going to get killed!" He would jump off and land on his feet, and I'd say, "That is the damnedest thing I've ever seen." He would say, "You've got to learn how to do this, George!" I'd be thinking, "Someday you're going to get killed." He managed to persuade Warner Bros. to bankroll his film *The Rain People*. He said, "I'm going to make the film with only fifteen people. You can be the assistant art director, the assistant director, the assistant camera, and the assistant everything. We're just going to travel around the country and film." He convinced me to come along because he said he could get money from Warner Bros. for the feature-length script of *THX*, and that I should write a draft of the screen-play and also make a documentary about the shooting of *The Rain People*. That turned out to be *filmmaker,* which was more a diary film than any-thing else. We ended up in Ogallala, Nebraska, in a warehouse, editing for five weeks. I looked around at this place and said, "You know, we don't have to make movies in Hollywood. You can make movies anywhere in the world. We're here in Nebraska, for godsakes." So I went back to San Francisco, where I met John Korty, a local filmmaker. He had a little stu-dio in Stinson Beach, just north of the city. It was a garage with a projec-tion room and editing equipment, where he made these soulful independent movies. I immediately called up Francis and said, "You've got to come and see this place. It's fantastic, just what we want." We both

Lucas and Francis Coppola with R2D2.

thought it was paradise and that we could create something similar, but bigger, right there. I said, "We'll have a little screening room and an editing room. We'll make our movies on the road." We went back to Los Angeles, got our clothes, headed back to San Francisco, found places to live and set up in a little warehouse full of editing and mixing equipment which Francis had bought, and we've been in San Francisco ever since.

How did you come to make the feature version of THX 1138?

I was working on another film with John Milius, something we had started in school, called *Apocalypse Now,* and Francis was working on *The Conversation.* Francis and I also brought other directors in from film school. Walter Murch, Matt Robbins, Hal Barwood and Carroll Ballard all came up from Los Angeles and we cranked out scripts. We were doing all these movies for absolutely nothing. I was trying to get what became *THX 1138* down on paper. I said, "Francis, I'm a terrible writer. I don't know how to do it." He said, "Listen, if you're going to direct, you're going to have to learn how to write." So I wrote the script and showed it to him and he said, "You're right. You can't write. We'll go up to Arrowhead and sit for a few weeks in my cabin and write a script." Francis was very good at cranking out scripts. I had a very personal idea of what I wanted the movie to be. I didn't want it to be a regular theatrical movie. Every time Francis had an idea, I said, "No, I don't want to do that." He was thinking in a very traditional sense and I was thinking in a very abstract sense. Eventually he said, "All right, I give up. We'll hire a writer." So we hired a playwright from New York, who wrote a screenplay, but it just wasn't at all what I wanted. I wanted to make a movie that basically had no dialogue, but here was a playwright who basically only knew how to write dialogue. I had already more or less written the story, and he was trying to develop character where I didn't really want character. Walter Murch and I were very much in synch, so I said, "Let's see if we can sit down and write a movie that we feel works." We rewrote the screenplay and Francis didn't quite understand it, but he said, "Come on, we'll get this thing made."

Of course Warner Bros. didn't like the script, which was supposed to be the first film from Zoetrope, but in 1969 Seven Arts–Warner Bros. was sold to the Kinney Corporation. Immediately Francis said, "We're going to tell them we have the new *Easy Rider* and this exciting new youth-oriented production company. We'll make youth films really cheaply, like American International Pictures. The first day the new studio heads arrive, we're going to hit them with all our projects, including *THX*." Of course he wasn't going to mention that the script had already been rejected. He just told me to start casting the film. I had an art director who was going around figuring out locations, and I also had a casting director. I had no idea what we were doing, but Francis spoke to the new studio executives the first day they arrived. He said, "We're in the middle of production here. We don't know what's going on with you guys down there, but it seems very confused to us. Put up the money now. Either shape up or ship out." I remember Francis coming back to San Francisco from Los Angeles saying, "Your movie is a go! And I also made a deal for six other pictures."

We ended up making *THX 1138* with a crew of literally sixteen people down in the BART subway system, which was being built at the time. I wanted to film some scenes in Japan and even went over there to check locations. I'd never been out of the country before. I was going to see if I could film around nuclear reactors and visited these hyper-modern giant energy facilities. In the end I realized we would never get permission to film in the places that interested me, so I junked the idea. I was the second assistant director and the second art director and the second cameraman, and I was also writing the script in the morning. I knew it was a one-shot deal, that I would probably never get a chance to do a movie like this again. When we showed the film to Warner Bros. they were dumbfounded. They had absolutely no idea what the film was about, so they cancelled the entire Zoetrope deal and told us to get out of town. I'm not sure if they actually ever read the script, and because we were up in San Francisco, way off their radar, they couldn't be bothered to come up and check on us. In the end they hated the finished film and were furious with Francis for not taking a stronger hand and making *THX* a more commercial film. They never wanted to see us again, except as a goodbye they said to Francis, "And by the way, you owe us three hundred thousand dollars." It was a very disheartening and destructive moment, and is the reason why Francis went and made *The Godfather*. He was in debt, and didn't really have much of a choice.

I find the exposition of THX *very impressive. It's all done so actively. No one ever stops to explain things.*

It's constructed on this idea I learned from Kurosawa, that you can submerge audiences into a strange environment and let them struggle to figure everything out themselves. "How does all this fit together?" The plot is simple enough that you don't need a lot of complicated exposition thrown out to the audience. The idea of the film is that some people are living in a prison in their own mind and all they have to do to get out of that situation is decide that's what they want to do. *THX* really is kind of a power-of-positive-thinking movie. In 1970, people were moving away from emotions. We were living in a society that was becoming increasingly commercial and consumer-oriented. The film is about leaving behind the dilemma of your life and getting into a place where you can be more of a human being. It's certainly a hopeful film. At least, that's how I always saw it.

At the time I really was still very much into abstract filmmaking, and in a way the film is a kind of futuristic work of cinéma vérité. I wanted to take people into worlds but not really explain anything about them. The film is actually broken into three pieces. Each piece is a story unto itself, although the same fundamental story is told in three different ways. *THX* is constructed on an experiment that Walter Murch and I were playing with at the time, the cubist idea of having everything be seen from different angles, but none of it is actually connected. It's a prismatic view of a future. The soundtrack isn't connected to the visuals and the visuals aren't connected to the story and the people aren't really connected to the environment. Because Walter is so clever with sound, the sound is detached from the picture. We were working independently of each other, so I would adjust the image after listening to the sounds he gave me. Everything in the film is operating separately and simultaneously, rather than as a unit. It's just this kind of bizarre cubist painting where you're looking at all sides at once and trying to put it into some kind of reality. At the age of twenty-two we thought that was a great idea.

American Graffiti kind of followed that same kind of idea. From one point of view it's a swirling Wurlitzer of a movie where you're listening to all this music and watching all these characters, but everything is disconnected from everything else. In terms of people not stopping to explain things, with *Star Wars* I wanted to throw the audience right into the middle of everything at the start and feed them certain things as the story was moving along. The opening scene of the first *Star Wars* movie comes literally halfway through the story.

Did the idea for American Graffiti *come from your experiences growing up in Modesto?*

Absolutely. After the studio deal fell apart, my idea for *Apocalypse Now* collapsed. I had been offered a lot of money to direct a studio film, but felt I had to focus on my own projects. At that point Francis challenged me to make a comedy. Thanks to his influence, I was definitely moving toward character-based narrative storytelling and away from abstract expression. He said, "Do a real movie. Do something that's warm and human, not some weird, arty science-fiction film. I'll bet you can't do it." I decided I wanted to make a film that was, in some way, optimistic. Part of that came from wanting to make something completely different from what I had been doing before. That's when I started the treatment of *American Graffiti* with Bill and Gloria Huyck, who I had gone to school with. We ended up with an eighteen-page treatment that laid out the story, all the intercutting of the four characters. They said, "Call us when you get some money and we'll write the script." By this time Francis had gone to make *The Godfather*, so I went off and tried to get my movie off the ground. I tried for two years. I went to every single studio and everybody said no. Luckily *THX 1138* had been invited to Cannes. They had just started Directors' Fortnight, for the work of first-time directors. They showed films off a little back alley for all these young, angry filmmakers. Of course Warners wouldn't pay for us to get there, but Walter's wife was from England and I said, "The movie's not going anywhere, so let's just take the last money we have"—which was about three thousand bucks— "and just tour Europe with backpacks on bicycles and rail passes." I decided to stop at United Artists in New York. The head of the studio, David Picker, was in New York and I said, "If I could just get to him, maybe I could pitch this and they can make it happen." I went and visited Francis on the set of *The Godfather* and slept on his couch—his wife was pregnant at the time—and went to Picker and pitched *American Graffiti.* He said, "Let me think about it. Call me when you get to Cannes."

So I got on a plane and flew to Cannes. I was a student and had no access to anything. They wouldn't even let us have tickets to our own movie. They were showing *THX 1138* and we had to sneak in the back door. Finally Picker said, "Okay, I like your idea. Go ahead and do the film." I called Bill and Gloria from Cannes and they said, "We're in the middle of a movie. We can't do it now." I was sitting there in Cannes and it was going to be a while before I could get back. I wanted to get the script done, so I called another friend of mine who was also from USC and asked him to come in and help me write it. I ended up back home with a completely worthless screenplay about drag racing that was basically *Hot Rods to Hell.* It was completely different than the original treatment. This scriptwriter had grown up in New York and had no idea about what cruising was really all about. My intense desire to get a writer had backfired on me, and I ended up without a usable script and no money, because I'd spent it all on hiring this guy. So I ended up writing the script in about three weeks. I took it to United Artists and they canceled the deal. They said, "This isn't a movie. This is a montage with a lot of music and no characters. You can't tell a story by intercutting four different stories going on simultaneously. You should tell one kid's story and then tell the next and then the next. It's nothing more than a musical montage." The kind of structure I had presented them just wasn't done in those days. I was telling the stories of four different characters—separate stories that didn't really inform each other. The only connections were right at the start and at the end of the film. But it was all too innovative for the studio to stomach, and they said, "If you have four stories, tell them one at a time."

I went to every single studio in town and nobody wanted anything to do with it. Eventually Universal picked it up, thanks to the very last vestige of one of those studio offshoots that had sprung up in the sixties after *Easy Rider.* Universal had one that made *Two Lane Blacktop* but they'd decided not to make any more of those kinds of films. Dennis Hopper had just made *The Last Movie* in the Andes and pretty much killed off the whole thing he'd started with *Easy Rider,* but I managed to squeeze *American Graffiti* in at the very last minute, before they closed that operation down. They said, "We'll do it, but you've got to get a big star." I said, "It's a movie about teenagers. There's no role in it for a star." They said, "We'll take a big-name producer instead." Francis had just finished *The Godfather* and was the hottest thing in Hollywood, so he said, "Sure, I'll put my name on it." That's how I got *American Graffiti* made. Today so much television is done the way *American Graffiti* was done in terms of intercutting, with completely separate stories going on simultaneously. The other major problem I had to overcome at the studio was resistance to my idea of using existing music and have it run all the way through the film—to have a hundred-minute movie with a hundred minutes of music. It was going to cost a lot to get the rights to all those songs. I had structured each scene around a specific piece of music. It was my concept from the start, even though everyone thought it was a crazy idea. In the end, of course, it worked out well, and today every other film does the same thing. Of course after the film was a hit, things became easier for me. I went from being a starving filmmaker to incredibly successful in a period of only a couple of years.

What were the themes you were working with when you made American Graffiti?

The thing I had noticed in the seventies was that the world of hippies and free love, that world of the mating ritual with cars—which existed only in the United States, really—was completely disappearing. I said, "Since I devoted so much of my life to it, I ought to be documenting it. Everyone should know what kinds of lives we were living back then." It really all started in the late thirties and went all the way up until the sixties. So in a way my prime motivation to do *American Graffiti* came out of my interest in anthropology. I began to realize that cruising around in the way we did in our cars never happened anywhere else in the world. In the early seventies, when the film came out, you had to get stoned and fall into bed with somebody. After *American Graffiti* was a success, kids kept coming up to me saying, "So that's what it's about! I feel that way inside, but I never felt able to express myself that way." Kids had no idea they were allowed to be nervous about girls, which is the way it was when I was young. I got so much feedback on how it changed people's lives. The film was full of the kind of drama a teenager should go through but that wasn't considered cool at that moment in time.

I think *American Graffiti* is ultimately about change, and resistance to change. Characters are put in situations where they have to make decisions about their lives. These are characters who are fearful of leaving town, of getting out of their cells, even though the door is wide open, because it means they have to experience something new. In this respect the film is thematically similar to *THX* and to a short I made at USC called *Freiheit*. It's also at the heart of *Star Wars*. When a major change needs to be made in life, when you need to leave a safe environment, the question becomes: are we brave enough to venture into the unknown? The major conflict in the film is whether Curt will leave town or stay. Will he go out into the big world and leave his "cell"? It's not about freedom in the political sense, though obviously I believe in that. It's about being free enough to escape the cage and shackles of your own mind. It's about going beyond the idea of being in a physical prison to the next, more important step, which is one I'm confronted with all the time when I meet people. It's something I was fortunate enough to break away from when I was eighteen or nineteen. It's about stepping out of your own mind and keeping your brain open to new ideas and thoughts, and not just jumping to conclusions like "That's not possible" and "I can't do that."

In terms of my own personal philosophy, that's how I got to things like *Star Wars*. People say, "You must have been on drugs." But no, I just let my imagination run rampant. I just let my mind go free and wander around. I just take down the box around my mind. The great thing with cinema and fiction is that anything you can come up with can become real.

Though you say working with actors is not your forte, the ensemble playing in American Graffiti *is spectacular.*

I was lucky enough to cast the film with Fred Roos. Normally a casting director will go and pick out the few people he thinks the director should see. The director then picks from among the select group and you're done. But I said, "No, I want to see everybody." I saw literally thousands of people. I had readings to see who could act and then Haskell Wexler and I shot screen tests on 16mm to see how they looked on film. I did screen tests in ensembles and would mix the actors up not just to see how good they were but how they played off each other. I shot the film very much like a documentary, with two cameras fairly far from the actors. I used long lenses, and the actors would play the scenes against each other and not so much to the camera. They never knew who was on camera, so they had to play the scenes more like a theatrical play. I've been accused of not talking a lot to actors as a director. I can't deny that, but with *American Graffiti* I trusted my instincts in hiring the right people for the roles and putting them in the right situations. Casting really is one of the most important processes when it comes to film directing.

My first exposure to acting was at USC. As a film student, I was required to take several classes in the theater department, including acting and theater directing, which involved being up on stage actually doing a performance. It wasn't easy, getting up there in front of everyone. In fact, when I graduated high school I vowed I would never give another public speech again. Of course, that's all I do now. I have one at least every other week, and have done for years. If you're going to direct actors, it's important to know what actors go through every day. The things I learned in those classes really helped me years later when I was confronted with crew members who would belittle actors because they think actors just sit in their trailer, get dressed up, speak a couple of lines, then go back to their trailer. Crew members have a tendency to look down on actors and think they have especially cushy lives. Sometimes what I've done, while we're setting up a shot, is take a page out of my USC schoolbook and say, "Okay, we're going to start by taking a short scene and have all you crew guys play it out in front of the camera. Just read the dialogue in front of us all." Some of them were so scared they couldn't do it, and as a result really understood that the actors are doing a real job that involves exposing themselves to the judgment of others. I'd say, "What they do involves a lot more than you think." And of course without actors, no one else would have a job to do on the film set.

The key is establishing trust between the actor and the director. The actor doesn't want to be made a fool of or look stupid, and it's the director's job to make sure that doesn't happen. The director has to enhance the actor's performance in any way he can, and get the absolute best from him. At a certain point, that's what lies at the heart of the director's job. Again, the only way to know how to do that effectively is if you've been through the process yourself, so having some experience of acting is crucial for any director.

Didn't Haskell Wexler shoot American Graffiti *at night while also doing something else during the day?*

What happened was that we lost our permit to shoot in San Rafael. We had negotiated these permits, but on the second day they said, "Sorry, deal's off. You can't shoot here anymore." I said, "Why?" "One of the bartenders said you were blocking traffic in the middle of the night and it's hurting his business." We said, "But we've got a contract." "I'm sorry, the city council met this afternoon and voided it." Immediately we went out to Petaluma and looked around, and I said, "Okay, we'll shoot it in Petaluma." Now, what I'd done on *THX 1138* was hire two cameramen who were also operators, with the idea that I would basically do all the lighting and photography for the film myself. It worked out pretty well, and Haskell was always there if I needed to ask him questions. On *American Graffiti,* I planned on doing the same thing. I would have two cameras and two cameramen, and shoot documentary-style, using available light—but this time with a huge cast and a twenty-eight-day schedule.

Of course, because almost the entire film takes place at night, the entire shoot was a night schedule. Actually, they were short nights, because it was July, so we couldn't start shooting until nine o'clock in the evening and had to quit at five the following morning, when the sun would come up. I shot the first week and it was a nightmare. The cameramen were struggling, even though they were using fast Nikon lenses and Éclair cameras. There was literally a quarter-inch depth of field, and they couldn't keep anything in focus because of the low light levels. By the end of the first day we were half a day behind. We tried to catch up, but then a building on the street where we were shooting caught fire at two in the morning, and the entire street was shut down.

That weekend I was moaning to Haskell, "I've got a problem." He said, "Look, I'm shooting commercials during the day, but I'll come up on Monday." For five weeks he came up after shooting commercials all day in Los Angeles and lit the picture. I gave him a "visual consultant" credit.

I read that you did that newspaper montage in The Godfather. *Is that true?*

Caleb Deschanel and I shot that. Everybody was working on *The Godfather*. At Zoetrope everyone worked on everything, helping each other out. Francis would say, "Hey, I need a couple days, can you go out and shoot this for me?" Sticking together, helping and supporting each other, is a great secret of surviving. Being mean or competitive just isn't a healthy way to try to get through your life.

When did you get interested in the work of Joseph Campbell?*

When I was in college I had read his book *The Hero with a Thousand Faces,* which really intrigued me. I realized at some point down the road that if I had gone to San Francisco State I would have gotten my degree in anthropology and would have probably ended up in New Guinea making films for National Geographic. If I had gone to art school in Los Angeles and studied to be an illustrator, I would probably have gotten into animation. So I looked at the situation and said, "You know, no matter what route you take, if you follow the things that you really enjoy doing you're going to end up pretty much in the same place." It's the same thing with Luke Skywalker, who can't escape his destiny no matter what he does. There is a calling he has to answer. It wasn't until I started working on *Star Wars* that I said, "Hey, I can use mythology as a basis for what I'm doing." That's when I really immersed myself in Campbell's books and did a lot of other research. Much later, Joe recorded interviews with Bill Moyers for *The Power of Myth* at Skywalker Ranch, where he talked about connections between *Star Wars* and his work. I learned a great deal from him, and in a way he was my Yoda. In fact, it was Joe who said that these days, it's the artists who communicate myth to society. He called it "creative mythology."

So the concept of Star Wars *came before your close reading of Campbell?*

I knew the basics of it, the rigors and consistency of the hero's journey. Once *American Graffiti* was done, I sat down and worked on two projects, both Saturday-matinee serials. One used mythological motifs, the other a supernatural MacGuffin. In the end I decided to go first with the Flash Gordon one that I thought would appeal to younger people, because I wanted to make a space-opera movie, an old-fashioned Errol Flynn movie for twelve-year-olds. I said to myself, "I'll do one big Hollywood movie,

---

*Joseph Campbell (1904–1987), American writer on comparative mythology and religion.

the way Hollywood used to make movies, and I'll do it as a children's film using the basic mythological motifs, all those things I studied in anthropology. I'll distill them down into a traditional ritualistic coming-of-age story, put it in the context of a Saturday-matinee serial, and set it in outer space. I'll pitch it to the studio, and if it doesn't work I'll go back to doing documentaries. At least I'll have taken this as far as I can."

So I started rereading Joe Campbell and Bruno Bettelheim. I wanted to know all I could about the classic mythic structures that went back thousands of years, and researched for two years while I was writing various drafts of the script. I wondered if the psychological underpinnings of these three-thousand-year-old motifs were still valid. I wanted to go back ten thousand years and figure out what worked for audiences around the campfire, and which of those structures still matter. It's just my anthropological bent. Could I really use them in a modern science-fiction film? What are the motifs that cross all cultural boundaries? What are those common threads? It's things like our relationship with our parents, the need for friendships and community, compassion and heroism, the idea of God. Are the emotions and ideas that are rooted in age-old psychologies and stories the same fundamental emotions and ideas of today? I think they are. In some ways we haven't come very far. I also wanted to create an old-style traditional cause-and-effect narrative with a beginning, a middle and an end, something I had purposely avoided with *THX* and *American Graffiti*. I think westerns used to fulfill all these mythic storytelling needs, but no one was making them anymore. In short, I just wanted to make a modern-day fairy tale for adolescents.

I had a whole bunch of historical, political and spiritual themes running through the story. I wanted to come up with something that was universal, and always ended up with this reluctant hero, either a prince or a farm boy. I chose the farm boy who goes through a series of trials and confronts things intuitively. He trusts his feelings. In the traditional motifs, the hero usually deals with a feminine figure. The original story started with her. Of course *Star Wars* still starts with her, but originally the whole thing was more directly focused on her. Princess Leia is the one actually out to save the universe. These other clowns come along for the ride, but she's the driving force. I spent three years writing four different versions of the script. The emphasis shifted as I went through drafts to where I spent more time with the guys trying to rescue her than her locked up in the Death Star. Of course there needed to be a sidekick, and that ended up being the droids. I added the touch—which I took from Kurosawa's *The Hidden Fortress*—where the story is told from the point of

Lucas enlisted Alec Guinness to play Obi-Wan Kenobi in *Star Wars* with an
offer of two percent of the gross profits, leading Guinness to observe, "I can live
for the rest of my life in the reasonably modest way that I am now used to."

view of the two lowliest characters. Then we move to the hero of the tale,
Luke Skywalker, and finally the rogue antihero, Han Solo. Obi-Wan
Kenobi is the sage who brings wisdom into the story. Then, of course,
there's the villain who has to be vanquished at the end. We go through a
series of trials, which in this particular case turns out to be the Death Star,
and then the hero returns and is rewarded. He's a changed person because
of his experience.

I was playing with the idea of accepting responsibility and trying to
make the world a better place. Even though he wants to get away from the
farm, when it really comes down to it and he's confronted with the fact
that he needs to go off and help save this princess, Luke says to Ben, "I
can't. I have my work to do. I've got my obligations to my uncle." He can't
escape his destiny. Luke has a calling, and absolutely has to respond to
that. It's not so much a self-propelling situation, more one where fate
takes over. If you let things pass you by, it's inevitable that the situation
will deteriorate to the point where you no longer have a choice. You can
avoid things as much as you want, but eventually you'll be forced to act.
At a certain point—and here I'm talking about real lives—it becomes
unnatural if you choose not to make certain changes in your life.

For someone who doesn't like writing, you certainly seem to do a lot of it.

My real strength is conceptualizing a story. The irony of ironies is that mostly what I do now is write. I truly am somebody who dislikes writing and having to develop character. I hate writing dialogue, yet I've been nominated for two Academy Awards as Best Writer. Go figure. Just be careful what you don't like. You'll end up doing it for the rest of your life.

Presumably your desire to make a Saturday-matinee serial with a supernatural MacGuffin became Raiders of the Lost Ark?

Raiders was something that emerged while I was developing *Star Wars*. I came up with this idea of an archaeologist adventurer who goes after supernatural artifacts, but after *Star Wars* I didn't have the energy to make it myself, so I tried to talk various friends into doing it. Phil Kaufman came up with the idea of the ark, this supernatural artifact, as a MacGuffin that drives the story. One day I was sitting on a beach in Hawaii with Steven, who was just finishing *Close Encounters of the Third Kind*. We were building sand castles and he was musing about how what he really wanted to do was a James Bond film. He'd gone to the producers and asked them if he could do it, and said he would only do it if he could bring Sean Connery back. They didn't want to do that, so Steve backed off. I turned to him and said, "I have the perfect film for you. It's basically James Bond." I told him the story and immediately we hired Larry Kasdan to write it, as he'd been doing such a good job on the script of *Empire Strikes Back*.

Were the studios interested in Star Wars *when you first approached them?*

I had to take it to United Artists first and they turned it down immediately. I took it to Universal and they turned it down immediately. Then Alan Ladd, Jr., who had seen a screening of *American Graffiti* and liked it, said, "Look, I don't understand the story. I don't understand what you're pitching, but I think you're a talented guy. I'm not going to bet on this movie because it's too weird. But I am going to bet on you." That's how I got it. I found somebody who was interested in me, not in the project itself. That said, I had only $10 million to make the film. For what we were trying to put on screen, it really was a low-budget production.

What was it like writing the three new Star Wars *films? Unlike a film with a traditional three-act structure, where there is a resolution at the end, the new films chart the downward spiral of a single character.*

You have to remember that I started with one story, which for various reasons was then split into several separate films. The original arc followed this one man who you see become a monster, but by the end you feel sorry for him. If you look at the first *Star Wars,* it's about the rebirth of hope. We have this awful monster, and the hope is that somebody— Luke—is going to combat that monster. For the original release I wanted to call it *A New Hope.* That title got pushed to the wayside, as did the idea that the first film, released in 1977, was actually episode four, because we didn't want to confuse anyone. But when you think about it, "a new hope" is what *Star Wars* is really all about. Luke is the new hope. The second film, *Empire,* is a real downer, and I was nervous about doing it. It's the middle act of a larger arc, but as a stand-alone movie I was extremely concerned with the fact that the hero gets his hand cut off by his father, which is emotionally and symbolically wrenching. I wondered if I could do this to the audience. Of course I did end up doing it, but I certainly didn't do it cavalierly. I thought long and hard about whether I could take the story in that direction. And then, of course, *Return of the Jedi* brings us back up again and ends on a positive note.

Years later, when I went back and started to tell the back story of Anakin Skywalker, it immediately became clear to me that the material is far richer if you have seen the first three films, and understand just how far this man falls and what his story is. Most people who saw *The Phantom Menace* and the other two new films know how the whole series ends, so in a way the new films are like a flashback. Even though the trajectory of *The Phantom Menace, Attack of the Clones* and *Revenge of the Sith* is straight down, we all know that in the end there is a positive resolution to the entire six-part story. That's what allowed me to go the distance and write those scripts. I realized very early on I would be writing a part of the story that ends very badly. I certainly don't think I could have sat and written those new scripts first, with the story that starts with a ten-year-old boy, before I had been emboldened by the success of the first three films.

What did you know that no one else knew when you negotiated the merchandising rights on Star Wars?

I had gone through two movies which had been tampered with, and finally both had been dumped. They forced me to cut *THX,* and eventually released it into the least number of theaters they could. They put resources behind *American Graffiti* only once it became a hit. The studio actually hated the film, and again I had to make cuts. It was only about five minutes, and I always felt they forced me to cut things just because they could. They were flexing their muscles. Finally, after some screenings with real audiences, not these dried-up old studio people, they figured they might have something on their hands. But even then it took a while for the film to really make an impact, and there certainly wasn't any ad campaign behind it in the lead-up to the release. Fortunately *American Graffiti* overcame being dumped, whereas *THX* never did.

When Fox decided to go with *Star Wars* I negotiated with them. I wrote a little deal memo that was two or three pages about how much money I was going to get, how we would split the profits, all that stuff. They ended up just handing over their boilerplate contract, which I never signed, because it took me a year to come up with my first draft of the script. During that time we were working on the contract, trying to make a deal. Then *American Graffiti* came out. It was a giant hit, but my feeling was that I'd just been really lucky and it wouldn't happen again. In the meantime I had ended up with a screenplay for *Star Wars* that was nearly two hundred pages long, so I said, "Okay, I can't film two hundred pages so what I'm going to do is take the first act of the script and make the movie from that." I knew I wanted to make the other two movies at some point and didn't want the studio to be able to stand in my way.

My assumption was that the first film wouldn't do very well and the studio would bury it, just like the other two, and I'd never be able to continue working on the story because they would end up owning the rights. Once *Graffiti* was a hit I said, "I'm not going to change the deal. I'll leave it all exactly the same. The money's the same, everything is the same. But the one thing I want in the contract is the sequel rights." They were looking at it from a very pragmatic point of view—which corporations do—and said to themselves, "We can pay this kid a million dollars now and take the sequel rights, or we can give him the $50,000 he's asking for plus the sequel rights to a movie that may not be worth anything. Since most movies aren't worth anything, let's just not worry about it." So they signed away the sequel rights. It was the same thing with the merchandise-licensing rights. Actually, they didn't give me those outright. I had complete control over merchandising, but split the revenue with them for a period of time. Of course the merchandising of the film became huge. I had no idea that absolutely everyone would want to buy shirts and pillowcases and toys. Why I was so interested in pushing the toys speaks to one of the basic ideas behind the film, the imagination of adolescents. Have a good time, open up your mind, don't be so locked down to the way things are. When the toys came along I thought it really connected to this idea of play. It's about seeing *Star Wars* in the theater and then coming home and playing with these characters, using your imagination to make up new stories and create new adventures. It was about alternative realities. I wanted to help kids dream of heroes and exotic creatures in faraway lands.

What is it like knowing you have created such a profound cultural phenomenon?

It's like being in the eye of a hurricane. I don't feel it as profoundly as I know other people have. It's quieter where I am. Lots of things are swirling around outside, but I'll never have the experience of going to a theater and discovering the movie for the first time. We struggled to make it and didn't know whether it was any good or not. During editing I remember being convinced I'd made a lot of big mistakes. Then I went through what the first editor had done and decided we needed someone else on the job, so I started working on it myself. Today, when I watch the film, I can see all the flaws, and was very unhappy because I didn't get to do a lot of the things I had originally wanted. For a long time I even considered it half-finished and was very disappointed in the film.

Can you tell us what your original conception was of Apocalypse Now?

At the time Carroll Ballard was working on an adaptation of the Joseph Conrad story *Heart of Darkness*. At the same time John Milius and I were working on a story that was based on stories and incidents John had from Vietnam veterans he'd been interviewing, guys who had come back from the war. That's where the surfing on the beach and the Playboy Bunnies idea came from. We sat down and I said, "We have to find a way of connecting all this. Why don't we have him go on a journey to solve a problem?" So John made him a Special Ops guy who has to undertake a mission and kill a rogue officer. We thought putting him in a helicopter would be too easy, so we put him on a boat going upriver. Obviously it's a symbolic and mythic trip up the River Styx. Carroll's version then fell apart, and Francis suggested we incorporate things from Conrad into our story. The only major difference between our version and the film that Francis eventually made is that at the end of our script there's a huge battle with the Viet Cong and they wipe everyone out except Willard and four or five other Americans. Then HQ sends a helicopter to get Willard out of there and he shoots the helicopter down. Francis' film ends on a much more existential note.

I loved the whole idea of cinéma vérité and went to see all those films, so I thought about making *Apocalypse Now* in the same kind of way that Haskell had made *Medium Cool.* I loved *Dr. Strangelove* and the Richard Lester Beatles films and wanted to make a very acerbic black comedy, but also thought Peter Watkins' *The War Game* and *Punishment Park,* which in a way were influenced by cinéma vérité, were extraordinary films. So I was going to shoot *Apocalypse Now* as a documentary in the Philippines and here in the Central Valley. It was going to be a big-budget picture, a black comedy of how insane it was over there, a modern-day *Dr. Strangelove.*

Do you ever care about critics and what they say?

I think when you're young you have a tendency to make the mistake of reading the critics and getting upset and annoyed. If you're going to put things out into the world that other people are going to judge, you have to have a thick skin. Nobody likes to have people who aren't involved in the process make statements about your work, and also about you personally. It didn't take me long to realize that if you don't read them, they don't exist. Filmmakers always say, "We don't notice the critics," but in my experience most do actually listen. All that happens is they get their feelings hurt, which affects their ability to do their work. At the end of the day I'm not sure that there's anything positive about critics. Basically, being as self-critical as I am means that apart from my friends, I don't listen to what people say about me.

Education is important to you, isn't it?

Yes, I'm very involved in education. The fact is that anyone who makes motion pictures is a teacher. I established an educational foundation and have a Web site called Edutopia, which is all about trying to find the best practices for people to learn, and supplying that information to legislators, school boards, people who work at schools, students or parents. It's about conveying to as many as possible what we consider to be the best ways for a child to learn. I think education is the single most important thing the human race can spend its time on. Perhaps this comes because my own time at school was so miserable and there were few teachers who inspired me. I believe our only chance of survival on this planet is using our brains and working with the next generation.

I'm a great lover of film, but when I was in school, film was considered as some kind of unimportant distraction. Only in film school were people taking it seriously. Even today the academy, with its ivory-tower mentality, doesn't think of film as a legitimate discipline. One of the things that greatly interests me is the notion of communication, something that led me to establish the Institute for Multimedia Literacy at USC. I want to expand the narrow view of communication from only the written and spoken word to include what are now considered "the arts." At school, words are considered much more important than images. But thousands of years ago they had equal status. In fact, in the beginning was the image, not the word. Today music and film, if taught at all at school, are considered relatively unimportant or "artistic." But that's not how I see them. Kids today certainly know how important images are. Kids who can't even talk intuitively understand musical forms and—because so many of them spend so much time in front of the television—visual communication and film grammar. They know a lot of the rules without learning them in a formal setting. We learn about grammar and spelling at school, but not about screen direction and perspective and what diagonal lines and perspective mean, and how using blue here means something different than using red, or filming from this angle tells a different story and conveys a different emotion than from this angle. In music, learning the basics of theory—about why certain chords affect you emotionally and make you sad while others make you happy—is the same thing. Ultimately, playing an instrument or designing a poster or making a film is all about communicating with people, and each form of communication brings with it a unique set of grammar and skills that have to be understood and taught.

In this day and age, the power of multimedia is all around us, every minute of the day. Of course kids should learn how to write, but they should also be taught film and music and graphics. If you want to be a great painter, you should go to art school, just as someone who wants to be a composer should go to music school, but the fundamentals of both should be taught to young kids. When I grew up, we were still feeling the fallout of Nazi Germany and those vast and complex propaganda campaigns. It was the time of the Cold War, which brought with it fears of the power of Soviet propaganda. We had the growing power of Madison Avenue, where they were beginning to take those techniques and apply them to the commercial world. There was a whole raft of books at the time about this, like Vance Packard's *The Hidden Persuaders,* full of ideas that were integral to the educational structures of the time.

What we're trying to do through Edutopia is build critical minds that don't accept anything at face value. Students should be able to look at something and say, "Just because I see it on television or read it in a book, that doesn't necessarily make it the truth. I'm going to figure out myself what's true and what isn't." A good education system will give you the tools and procedures and knowledge of how to find information quickly, and then analyze it and determine how accurate it is. Children really do learn best when learning comes directly out of their curiosity. It's all about teaching kids how to find and assess information, and then have them use it in a creative endeavor.

What was the concept of the Skywalker Ranch?

The concept was originally that Francis and I didn't want to work at a studio. That's why we moved to San Francisco. Back in the late sixties, just before we set up Zoetrope, Francis had visited a studio in Denmark which was in an old mansion near Copenhagen. That's where we got the idea that we should buy a big old house and set up everything for ourselves there. That was the original idea behind Zoetrope. But even though we had offices in the city, I always had a bug about having an artistic retreat—not a big glass building in an industrial park, but a big old house in the middle of nowhere. After *Star Wars* I built a place in the woods. Mostly what creative people do is think, and I realized we needed a place to do that. It's not a race-around-and-do-things kind of house. I wanted a place full of the most advanced technology where we could sit, see the trees and think about things. Skywalker Ranch, if anything, is devoted to giving people a chance to work in a beautiful environment and then go out and sit on a stoop for a few minutes and watch the birds fly by. Another reason for the ranch is my interest in architecture. It speaks directly to my love of building things.

You said earlier that with film, up to a point, anything is possible and can become real. Is turning your imagination into cinema a question of technology?

With something like *Star Wars,* yes. Part of my problem is that over the years I've dreamt up things that couldn't be put on screen unless I moved the state of the art and technology forward. Science fiction is great on paper, but it's much harder when it comes to cinema, because for at least a brief moment you have to make it appear to be real. It's really determined by available technology, and for many years those hurdles were impossible to overcome. The connection here is actually that all art is technology, whether it's picking up a charred stick and drawing pictures on a wall or creating the Death Star. You don't see gorillas painting pictures, but when you think about our ability to pick up something and draw a picture on a wall or to beat a drum, and have those things convey an emotional message, that's a huge leap from being a monkey.

We're always limited by the technology we have. Every artist, especially those working generations ago, is both a creative person communicating emotions and—in most situations—at the same time an engineer and a scientist trying to move the medium forward. They use their talent to figure out not only how to build a house or put something as beautiful as possible onto a canvas, but also how to construct something that will actually stay standing or develop oil paints that will last the ages and that you can paint over what you had already done. You could study something and put it on your canvas. If it didn't look right, you could scrape it off or paint right over it and do something else. That technology changed painting forever. It's the same thing with digital technology. Storytelling on film is now more malleable than it's ever been. Like a painting, you can say, "Oh, I didn't mean that. Forget that I did that. Erase that character. Add this color." When I'm editing, I spend a lot of time manipulating things, trying to fix the director's mistakes. These days I'm used to getting my film out of the mess that I created myself. The move from celluloid and the photochemical process to the digital process has pulled the cinematic arts in a new and very exciting direction. Artistic revolutions have always gone hand-in-hand with technological ones. Artists aren't doing their jobs properly if they aren't banging up against the technological ceiling. They want to go where no one has gone before. With new inventions come new ways of conveying emotions. If I can tell you a story or draw something on a wall or put something onto a cinema screen that makes you feel a certain way, that's art. This is why I've spent so much time developing technology. For me it has always been about storytelling.

I made *Star Wars* the same way I made my student films. It was about saying, "Okay, I've got this amount of limited resources, but I'm going to do four times as much as the other guy." The script was carefully written in terms of what could be done with special effects at the time. In the mid-seventies, just panning the camera around a spaceship was tough enough. Fantasy films had fallen out of favor in the fifties, because everybody wanted to get very psychological with their deep Freudian masterpieces. People forgot about special effects and the studios even shut down their special-effects departments.

With *Empire* it was a case of creating a two-foot-high green creature with big ears and a walking stick and making him seem alive. Believe me, that was really pushing the technology at the time. I knew I couldn't go to Coruscant or have Yoda fight with a light saber and all the other things about Jedis and pod racing I had written into the back story. I didn't even consider that at the time. The first thing I wanted was to be able to edit digitally on a computer. This was back in 1980. I spent some time and capital on the computer division of the company to develop educational software, and then came up with the idea of using revenue from video games to finance an educational-software company. Eventually we spun the computer division off and sold it to Steve Jobs. The goal was to create a digital character that looked like an actual character. There were testing grounds for the special effects we were working on, like *The Young Indiana Jones Chronicles,* and eventually we arrived at the stage where we said, "Why don't we try to do a digital dinosaur?" We had thought about doing *Jurassic Park* with puppet animation, but when the tests came back we nearly had tears in our eyes. We were looking at the screen and saw this *Tyrannosaurus rex* running. It was the Holy Grail of digital animation. You might compare it to the invention of the light bulb or the first telephone call. For me, it really was that momentous. We had created a realistic digital dinosaur that we could do anything with and that would work seamlessly in a movie. Finally I could put on screen everything I'd always wanted to do. For decades I'd had the overwhelming drive to get the images in my head out into the screen. It had always been easier to write fantasy than to film it. Now Yoda could jump and fight. I could go back and tell the back story of *Star Wars* if I wanted to and even fix the original films. Technology had finally caught up with my ideas, and I was faced with a real decision. Should I go off and do my personal films that I'd always told myself I was going to make, or should I make three more *Star Wars* films? Now I could show pod races and go to Coruscant. We didn't have to be stuck on Tatooine or some snow planet.

Will you eventually make chapters seven, eight and nine of Star Wars?

Never. There never were plans for chapters seven, eight and nine. After *Return of the Jedi* my feeling was, that was the end of it. Those first three episodes—which actually were numbers four, five and six—were all I ever intended to make. Originally the three films were going to be one single film, this one episode of some bigger thing you would never get to see. I had written a detailed back story and knew who everybody was, where they came from, and what the story was, but I did that only as a character study and to help me with the exposition of those first three films. What precisely is this world? What are the politics of it? Who are these people to each other? Ultimately the reason I decided to make episodes one, two and three is because the arc of the entire story was so compelling to me.

Based on what you were saying earlier about myth and Joseph Campbell, what exactly is a story?

The idea of art is to connect with someone emotionally. Something is artistic if it speaks to you emotionally. One way is through a story. A tool was needed to create a sense of community in preliterate societies. It was storytelling and metaphor. The thing about a story, which usually comes out in the form of a metaphor, is that you can structure it and use it to talk about things that aren't necessarily immediately logical and that are emotional, yet deal with these things in such a way that people will accept and learn from them. For most of human history we didn't communicate intellectually. Rationality as we know it today was nowhere to be seen. We communicated emotionally. Look at the cave paintings in France. They're not literal images of antelope. They look like spiritual beings. It's the same thing with the ceiling of the Sistine Chapel. Those aren't merely literal interpretations of people. If you sat down and analyzed those images through the lens of art history or academia, you would miss something. Storytelling is the same thing. A story is infused with spirituality and morality that explains the values of a society. It's designed to teach people and create a common bond between members of a community. Story-telling is history as distorted through the lens of social engineering. You can write the Ten Commandments and put them on a post in the center of the town square and most people aren't going to pay attention to them. But if you tell people a mystical story that goes beyond logic and speaks to basic emotions, it really makes an impression. Stories existed back then— and today too—to teach us things about ourselves. They are mnemonics, because by definition mnemonics are easier to remember.

If you watch kids and understand how they work psychologically, you'll understand how everyone works. Kids don't like listening to instructions, so over many, many generations we have developed a series of stories to help kids move from childhood into adulthood. If you want a kid to remember something, to really act on it, you have to tell them some kind of story. If you say, "Your uncle went through this experience and learned this lesson: don't lie," they understand immediately. Or, "If you do that, the gods will strike you dead." But if you try to give them a lecture and say, "I don't want you to lie. It's a bad thing to do," they don't get it. Story is a way of communicating family and community history in a sufficiently oblique and creative way that it's not rejected by those you're talking to. It's exactly why I said earlier that I made *Star Wars* for adolescents. A good story is infused with what you and your society believe to be true in terms of values and belief and spirit and economic systems. That's how you transfer information from one generation to the next. Whether you're drawing pictures on a cave wall or telling stories around the campfire or writing novels or composing concertos or dancing or making a film, it's all the same thing. Every good story has those elements buried in there. After all, you have to attract people and hold their attention. No one wants to be preached at.

For me, it's all about maintaining human civilization. Thousands of years ago tribal society was just the family. Outsiders married in, and soon the tribe was more than just one single family. It was made up of several families. Usually the father would lay down the law by telling stories about his father and his grandfather and the rituals of things they used to do. This is how things were passed down. Soon the tribe, which was by now lots of families living together, outgrew that dynamic. What was needed was a practical mechanism by which it would be clearly stated that going after your brother's wife or killing somebody is not acceptable. What needed to be made clear to everyone was those things that society will not tolerate and those things that are believed in.

How do you use these ideas to create stories?

In order for it to really connect with people, a story has to be constructed on tested and classic arcs of human tragedy or human desire. These structures really do work. Storytelling was originally an oral medium. You, the storyteller, would be paid to sit with an audience. If you weren't good at it, you didn't eat that night. The storyteller went from town to town, sitting around the fire telling stories. If the audience liked you, they'd give you a great dinner. If they didn't, they kicked you out in the rain. You would watch the audience carefully and when it started reacting in a certain way, you'd say, "Well, that works. But with this part here they're falling asleep, so I'm going to cut that part out." The storyteller discovers what audiences like and respond to, and leaves out everything else. That's why we all respond to certain motifs and narrative archetypes. They've been tested on audiences. It's stone-age marketing.

As far as the story itself goes, in the first act you introduce all the characters. In the second act you introduce the problem. In the third act you solve the problem. Of course you can maneuver things differently. What I've always liked doing is throwing out the first act and starting with the second. It's about telling the audience, "If you look carefully, you'll be able to tell who these people are and what they want." A good storyteller can move the building blocks around. One thing I did with *Empire Strikes Back* was put the physical climax of the movie in the middle and the emotional climax at the end.

Do you make films for yourself or for audiences?

I make films for both. First of all, I'm making films for myself. Second, part of myself has a desire to entertain a group of people, to give them the wondrous experience I have when I watch a film. I'm saying, "I love this. This excites me. I think this is a fun story and here is an inspiring character. This makes me cry, therefore I'm hoping you will too." It's all about emotion. That doesn't mean I can't put intellectual elements into it, but first and foremost I construct the thing on the emotional fundamentals of the story.

For years now you have been at the head of a huge empire. How do you balance the demands of the industry with your personal life?

I wouldn't be alive if I couldn't make movies. I don't know how to do anything else. When I was young, before I had my kids, I basically had no life. Once I got bitten and fell in love with film, nothing else existed for me. Fortunately, when my kids arrived, they saved me from the marginal life I was living. They made me into a human being, or at least a half a human being. After I finished *Return of the Jedi* I went through a divorce and determined at that point that raising my daughter was the most important thing in my life. I figured I could produce a few films with some friends just to help them out, but my main focus was really raising my kids. I ended up adopting a second daughter and then a son, and I knew I couldn't direct and raise these kids at the same time. A director goes to work at six in the morning and doesn't get home until ten at night. He isn't free to go to parent-teacher conferences. So I said, "Well, I'll be a producer. I can take days off when I need them, and basically focus on raising my kids."

If my kids hadn't come along I would have no idea what being a human being was all about. They've taught me more and enriched my life beyond anything imaginable. For years I was trying to make my way in the industry, and that's all I had time for. You know what they say about men, that there isn't a second in the day that goes by that they don't think about sex? Well, when it comes to filmmakers, there isn't a second in the day that goes by when they don't think about film. That's the way it works, especially if you're a writer/director. If you're a director, you might have some kind of excuse: "Well, I've got to wait for the scripts to come in. I've got to wait for my agent to get me a good deal." But if you're a writer, there's absolutely no excuse. If you don't do the work yourself, you're just moving backwards. If you're not directing your scripts, you should be turning out five or six scripts a year.

If you want to make noncommercial art films—like I wanted to make underground films—you need to understand before you start that your film probably isn't going to make money. If you want to make films that are artistic in nature and aren't going to appeal to the mainstream, you can scrape together money from a few dentists and friends of your parents and spend it on your film. Once you've finished and the money is spent, then you move on to the doctors and scrounge more money for your next film. Whoever puts money into your film is going to lose it. I just couldn't work like that. The only way I figured I could do it was to make a lot of money, and then waste it by making movies that nobody wanted to see. In doing this, I discovered I knew how to make popular movies, and more importantly I enjoyed it. Even with all the problems, I enjoyed making *Star Wars*. I enjoyed the experimentation. I never cared how critics classified me or what awards I won. I simply wanted to make the films I wanted to make. So the question was a simple one: how do I get enough money to pay for that independence? I was always stubborn and wanted complete run of my imagination. Because of my time at film school, at an early age I came to understand the power of the medium and how good films really can be. I had to become self-sufficient. I had to build an empire simply to make the movies the way that I wanted to make them. I wanted to make my own future and not have to have to beg, borrow and steal to get the money to make my movies. I didn't want to have to listen to the studios and make films on their terms, and, fortunately, *Star Wars* gave me an opportunity to become independent of the studio system. I also decided to step back from being a director and put my company together. I worked on the scripts of the next *Star Wars* films, talked endlessly with writers doing the rewrites, cast the movie, oversaw all the art direction, the special effects and the editing. I figured I would find people I was compatible with, who shared my vision and who I could trust, and who could do the on-set work with the actors and crew the way I thought it should be done.

The thing is that if you really can't stop thinking about film, then you're going to make it. The people who come in wanting to be famous and make money are misguided, because this is a bad job. It's terrible. Really it is. There are many easier ways to make money and become famous. When you make a film you're dealing with the largest group of psychotic, neurotic, difficult people you could ever imagine. And I don't even have to work with the studios! Those people who come in and just say "I need to make films" are the ones I'm interested in. It's a very unfriendly environment for creative people because the corporate mentality is very risk-averse. Making movies is basically gambling. You're all professional gamblers. That's what you're going to do for a living, and you have to get good at it, because every time you make a film you're rolling the dice. If you want to make money, I suggest you go into the stock market. Only one in ten movies ever breaks even. This is not a good thing to do if you actually want to earn a living. I got lucky, but I'm one in a million.

The most difficult thing in the world is finding out what you want to spend your time doing. You just have to figure out where your talent is. Usually you do this by going to your sweet spot, or—as Joe Campbell would have called it—your bliss. My feeling is that you should chase whatever you're talented at. If you've found your talent and your passion, the money will come. You will survive and live a happy life. At your age you've got to focus on your work. Some days you'll wonder why on earth you're subjecting yourself to such pain and hardship. It takes strength to stick with things that society—and your parents—consider a waste of time. But when the films start being made, and you really feel that you're expressing yourself and learning something new every day, you'll know why you're doing it. None of this will be easy, but if you're sufficiently obsessed or crazy about it, and refuse to give up, in a few years you'll have a job. You'll start cursing the corporations that are telling you to do incredibly stupid things. You'll realize you don't need them, that you can do it on your own, that you can beat them at their own game. Then you'll go back to Kansas or wherever it is, you'll get together with your friends, you'll work hard and see things through to the end, you'll master your craft, and end up with a bunch of really great films.

Films as Director

1971 *THX 1138* (also screenplay)

1973 *American Graffiti* (also screenplay)

1977 *Star Wars IV: A New Hope* (also producer and screenplay)

1999 *Star Wars: Episode I—The Phantom Menace* (also producer and screenplay)

2002 *Star Wars: Episode II—Attack of the Clones* (also producer and screenplay)

2005 *Star Wars: Episode III—Revenge of the Sith* (also producer and screenplay)

Lucas is credited as producer on many films and television projects including *Star Wars: Episode V—The Empire Strikes Back*, 1980; *Raiders of the Lost Ark*, 1981; *Body Heat*, 1981; *Star Wars: Episode VI—Return of the Jedi*, 1983; *Indiana Jones and the Temple of Doom*, 1984; *Labyrinth*, 1986; *Willow*, 1988; *Tucker: The Man and His Dream*, 1988; *Indiana Jones and the Last Crusade*, 1989; *The Young Indiana Jones Chronicles*, 1992–93; *Indiana Jones and the Kingdom of the Crystal Skull*, 2008; and *Star Wars: The Clone Wars*, 2008. Lucas also directed several short films including *Look at Life*, 1965; *Herbie*, 1966; *Freiheit*, 1966; *1:42:08: A Man and His Car*, 1966; and *Electric Labyrinth THX 1138 4EB*, 1967.

> The ideas come in fragments. I don't know where anything is going.
> When a few fragments start hooking themselves together and they
> marry to a fragment that you didn't think was going to relate at all,
> it's a big surprise.

DAVID LYNCH
(Born in Missoula, Montana, 1946)

I was in Washington in 1968 planning AFI's Center for Advanced Film Studies
when a student from the Pennsylvania Academy of Fine Arts applied for one of
our student-filmmaker grants. He sent along samples of his work that were distinctive and impressive. We awarded David Lynch a $5,000 grant to make *The
Grandmother,* the story of a neglected boy who "grows" a grandmother from a
seed. It occurred to me then that David was precisely the kind of person that
the film institute we were building should be designed to help. He was an artist
with a vision so unique and so far from the mainstream that no studio executive
would give him a second glance. Could AFI provide a pathway for people like
Lynch to master their craft and find an audience for their work?

In 1970 David applied to the AFI Conservatory and was accepted. He
remembers walking up Sunset Boulevard to Greystone: "I thought for sure
I'd died and gone to heaven," he said. "At AFI all day the greatest cinema
played in the Great Hall. And we listened to filmmakers—foreign voices
along with powerful American voices." It was in the stables of the Greystone
mansion that he spent several years making *Eraserhead,* his feature-length AFI
thesis film. I remember David coming to my office one day. He was normally
optimistic and cheerful—a contrast to the darkness of his work—but this day
he was intense and insistent. He wanted me to call Sid Solow, who ran Con-
solidated Film Industries, and ask that he provide $5,000 worth of film pro-
cessing for *Eraserhead* and defer payment. I remember this moment forty
years later because somehow David's vulnerability poignantly expressed the
innate frustration of filmmakers. The materials they require to bring their
ideas to the screen have always been disproportionately costly.

Mel Brooks saw *Eraserhead* when it was released in 1977 and hired
David—whom he described as "Jimmy Stewart from Mars"—to direct *The*

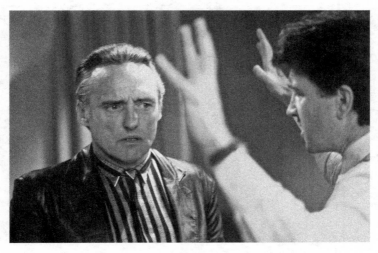

David Lynch directs Dennis Hopper in *Blue Velvet* (1986).

Elephant Man, the true story of a grotesquely deformed Victorian-era man, thus introducing a young man who was regarded as an eccentric visionary into the world of commercial filmmaking. The film earned eight Academy Award nominations, including Best Director and Best Adapted Screenplay for Lynch, and put him in play as an internationally known filmmaker.

David's distinctive vision has defined his storytelling. An unsuccessful liaison with Dino De Laurentiis on *Dune* was followed by success and another Best Director nomination with *Blue Velvet,* followed by his bold 1990 television series *Twin Peaks,* which told the story of a small town full of dark secrets. With these projects, Lynch let his audience feel that he trusted their intuition—that not everything in a film has to be *understood.* His abiding hope has been that people will come out of his films "with a strange, fantastic feeling that opens some little door that's magical."

Through the years Lynch has surrounded himself with trusted collaborators on his feature films—*Wild at Heart, The Straight Story, Mulholland Dr., Inland Empire.* He has also produced comic strips, short films, musical compositions and online series and explored coffee making and transcendental meditation. His personal Web site offers short videos, including a daily weather report for Los Angeles, and in 2005 he established the David Lynch Foundation for Consciousness-Based Education and World Peace.

David's wide-ranging work has an unsettling mix of violence and comedy, the surreal and the beautiful, and a view of the world that is very much his own. We can only wonder where this Eagle Scout from Missoula, Montana, found such a distinctive voice.

DAVID LYNCH

✦

November 8, 2006*

You made Eraserhead *while you were still a fellow at the American Film Institute?*

I was writing a script. That was a good experience, because I learned a lot about writing and the structure of a feature film from Frank Daniel, who was dean of the school at that moment. But the screenplay turned out to be not so hot, and I got upset about something on the first day of the second year and stormed up to Frank's office and said, "I quit." I stormed out with my buddy and we went down to the Hamburger Hamlet and when I got home my wife said, "The phone's been ringing off the wall." They wanted me to come back and said I could do anything I wanted to do. They said, "What do you want to do?" I said "*Eraserhead.*" They said "Good. You'll do *Eraserhead,* then. Go for it. How long a film is it? How long is the script?" I thought this was a funny question. I remember wondering why they wanted to know that. I said "Twenty-two pages." And they said, "Okay, then, it's a twenty-two-minute picture." I said, "Well, I think it's going to be a hair longer than twenty-two minutes. A hair." Then they decided that it would be forty-five minutes. So that's how it got started. It doesn't make a lot of sense. Not to me, anyway. But that's how it goes.

Thanks to AFI I had an unbelievable setup for four years. The AFI let me film there even though I wasn't technically supposed to be there that

---

*Gill Dennis moderated this seminar. This transcript also contains segments from seminars David Lynch gave at the American Film Institute on October 14, 1981, April 15, 1992, September 8, 1999, and October 10, 2001.

long. It was such a gift. We went to school in the Doheny Mansion in Beverly Hills, and down below they had horse stables, a giant garage for firewood for the mansion up the hill, a set of greenhouses, maids' quarters, car garages and more quarters above that. Also a hayloft above the horse stalls. Hay. So I had a place down there to build sets. I had a camera room, an editing room, a permanent set, garages filled with stuff. All the lights. I had two 35mm cameras and a black-and-white half-inch tape video camera. I had cabling, lenses. Unbelievable. I was living in the best part of Beverly Hills with this setup. It was such a gift and a blessing. We shot solidly for one year and then ran out of money. Then it was piecemeal for the next four years. Shooting for three years and then postproduction for another year. AFI really backed me. They helped me see it through. They made a deal with the lab where at least I could get things developed and then when I got money I could get stuff printed. Before I even got there I got a phone call from George Stevens, Jr., and Tony Vellani that completely changed my life. I won an AFI independent-filmmaker grant at a point in my life when I thought things were over. I mean, it was dark. But the AFI really did help me. I cannot think what things would be without that.

Eraserhead *is one of the strangest movies I have ever seen. I just cannot figure it out and I was wondering if you could . . .*

Help you out? Well, I can't, because there are so many ways to interpret an abstraction, and each person interprets it for himself. Every interpretation is fine and valid. Really. Go wild with it. If I say what the film means, it becomes limiting to everyone else. I had a very specific thing in mind, and yet it was very far underneath the surface. I could no more have written out that thing than fly to the moon. It was too deep inside to bring up into the screen. The things in *Eraserhead* would be extremely hard to get into a Hollywood film. That's the downside to Hollywood, because people have to explain things with words, and that is a completely limiting way of doing cinema. If you have to sit and explain to a man in a suit what the film is, it becomes a one-thing film. Everybody and his little brother has to understand every single part of it, and mystery and strange abstractions that mean volumes to some people fly right out the window. I see them go. I watch them. I know what *Eraserhead* means for me and want you to work it out for yourself.

The beautiful thing about film is it can tell abstractions as well as specific things. Film is a language where intuition can come into play. Intuition, they say, is the heart and the mind working together to create an inner knowing. When we see things in life that are abstractions or think about things that are abstractions, sometimes our intuition creates an inner knowing—a personal understanding of the thing. That's all there can ever be. We bring ourselves to everything. You can never not trust that personal understanding. It's not analysis. It's quite different. Like dreams, sometimes it's hard to tell your friends what you know inside. Words just don't quite do it. But with a film you can respond and explain. Learn to trust your intuition. Standing in front of an abstract painting— it's a circle and colors—the painting is talking and the viewer is taking part. It's a dialogue. Something is building in the viewer that is going to be different for the next person who comes and stands in front of that painting. Different interpretations, but always valid and interesting. It's a beautiful thing.

Is that your goal when you start making films? Do you want to visualize abstractions?

It's falling in love with ideas and then the beautiful process of translating those ideas to film. That's what it's all about. It's also about going into another world and experiencing that world. That's what it's like going into a theater. It's best not to know anything about the film. The lights go down, the curtains open and you enter another world. It's so beautiful.

So that's your goal, to take the audience into another world?

Yes. That, and tell the story and express the ideas.

Can you talk about the development process? I'm trying to imagine what it's like with an executive sitting in the room with you while you're trying to tell them your idea.

Executives have a lot of problems of their own, because they have to make money, and that's the scary part. When they listen to things they can't get a handle on they become afraid. They usually say no to an idea that's too far off the main path, so I haven't had a lot of success with the studios. But I have had good lunches with these people.

Eraserhead is a film that is abstract and subtle and personal. How much will you let the cinematographer come inside your head?

Lynch's first film after graduating from AFI was *The Elephant Man* (1980), produced by Mel Brooks and starring John Hurt.

Well, let's see. Two people shot *Eraserhead*. A guy named Herb Cardwell started out. He shot for nine months, and then Fred Elmes* came in and he shot for about two and a half years. Over the course of time you develop a dialogue. It's action and reaction. You shoot something and then see it and start talking about it. That leads to something new. The camera people may not know what you know or vice versa, but there is a meeting point where the work is done. All the things come together if one person is in charge of all the different elements.

Can you talk about when you feel violence works and doesn't work in a film?

It goes by feeling. All the things that have to do with life should somehow be in film.

What attracted you to the script for The Elephant Man?

I was at Nibblers restaurant at Gale Drive and Wilshire Boulevard having lunch with Stuart Cornfeld. He'd called me months before, after he had seen *Eraserhead,* and I liked the name Cornfeld. I went around the house

---

*Fred Elmes met David Lynch at AFI and was director of photography on Lynch's *Blue Velvet,* 1986.

saying "Stuart Cornfeld" after he called. I asked Stuart if he had any ideas for me, something to direct, and he mentioned *The Elephant Man.* As soon as I heard the name *The Elephant Man* a little bomb went off in my head and I knew that I was going to do it. It was a long road from that lunch, but I didn't ever veer off until it was finished.

Can you talk a little bit about Dune?

I'd rather not. What would you like me to talk about?

How did you come to make the film?

I don't know why Dino De Laurentiis thought of me, but he signed me up with a contract that said if *Dune* is a success I would be obligated to do follow-up pictures. At one point I was starting to write the second one, but the first one didn't do well enough to get the second one finished. It was a mixed blessing, that whole experience. I learned a tremendous amount making the film, but half the film was cut out, and it needed much more of a story than it ended up having, and there was a real failure inside me for a long time afterwards.

Do you want to talk a little bit about where stories come from?

Not really. The idea is the most magical thing and where they come from and how they happen is one of the great mysteries of life. Some kind of combination triggers pretty much the whole thing and it goes into the conscious mind. Good ideas are something we all hope for. Ideas are ideas and the whole thing is to translate them into film. Certain ideas lend themselves to cinema. They make a magical thing that can only be said with picture and sound, and those are the ones that I really love if they're on the foundation of a good story. I don't know where ideas come from, but to me they remind me of fish. You have to sit quietly with your pole and your bait. The bait is just the desire for an idea. If you sit quietly, one will swim close and you might catch it. The big ideas are swimming very deep, so you have to be able to go down there and get them.

How do you know when to throw back the fish?

You can tell when you bring up a bad fish. There's an honesty that happens when a lot of people get together and hook into your film. It's a horribly painful thing to do, but by sitting with an audience you can learn an awful lot. You don't have to give them pencils and have them fill out cards or anything. You can just feel everything.

The idea is like a seed and you really know the seed and it's talking to you, but you don't really know about the oak tree. You don't know how it will turn out. You just know about the acorn, but it's growing out and if you're really true to it you'll get this tree. Many people study trees from various angles and they paint them and they study the bugs that grow on them and stuff like this, but if you've done a good tree it may have harmonics that you don't even understand. That is the wonder of the thing, of the process. I know that people see these things from different angles and write many things, but I think it all kind of holds together if you're true to the idea.

Where do the characters fit in?

Not all ideas come complete. Often ideas come in fragments. It's a very important fragment that sparks enough in your mind so you know it's important. It's like fishing. That becomes the bait and you just sit quietly in a chair and concentrate on this and others will swim in and hook themselves to it eventually.

How many hook themselves on while you're shooting?

Nothing is finished until it's finished. I hear stories about Hitchcock knowing every single thing that's going to happen. I don't see how that's possible, and I think that would be pretty boring. You need to have a script and a story and the ideas, but as you go in you start seeing the three-dimensional thing in front of you. Things keep talking to you as you're rehearsing and building and it becomes more and more complete; or something isn't working and you realize why and you adjust it. It's an ongoing process all the way through to the very end, and hopefully at the very end all the parts unite and the whole is greater than the sum of the parts. But it's never finished until it's finished.

Could you tell the story about the man in the mirror in Twin Peaks?

The man in the mirror? Oh, yeah. Well, strange things happen. We were shooting in the bedroom of Laura Palmer, and Frank . . . I can't remember his name . . . that's too bad. Anyway, Frank was the set dresser, and he was moving a dresser in front of the door, rearranging furniture, and someone on set said, "Frank! Don't lock yourself in that room." I pictured Frank in that room, locked in there, and I went running in and I said, "Frank, are you an actor?" And he said, "Well, actually I am." "You're going to be in this movie," I said. So I did a scene with a panning shot across the room and I put Frank down low, hiding, frozen behind the bars of the tailboard of the bed, and the camera pans around and holds on him. I didn't know where I was going to fit it in or what it meant. Then we went downstairs to do the last setup, where Mrs. Palmer is on the couch and she's really sad and overwhelmed with grief and things are passing through her mind and she remembers something and she bolts upright with a scream, so the operator has to crank up with the low gears to keep her in the shot, and he did it beautifully. It was perfect and I said, "That's perfect!" and he said, "No, it's not perfect. Someone's reflected in the mirror." I said, "Who was reflected in the mirror?" He said, "Frank was." Then I knew I was on to something. By the way, thank you for letting me smoke.

I was wondering if you wanted to talk about endings?

What I learned is that a feature film has a beginning, a middle and an end. It's a beautiful thing and you can do so much within that form, but at the same time we've seen so many films that are like verses and choruses. You know what's coming up and you can feel it go from the beginning to the middle and you can feel the ending coming. Television is so appealing because you can have a continuing story that will lead you here and lead you there. Something could come up and could relate to something from way back long ago. I love detective novels, but at the end you know the answer and it's really pretty depressing to me, because it always seems a little too simple. I think the film *Chinatown* has one of the most beautiful endings. It gives you so much room to dream.

I watched Blue Velvet *for my feminist-theory class, for my psychoanalytic-theory class, for my linguistic-theory class. Every time they approached it using a different theory. How aware are you of theory?*

I'm not aware of theory. If I'm aware of theory at all, it's about staying true to the ideas.

You've created a lot of action through soundscapes and music.

Film is picture and sound working together. Dialogue has its own way of working and it can be like music. But then there are room tones and presences and things that we realize are seeping into our ordinary lives, and we have control over all those. Those are sound effects, but they can become close to music. Then there are sounds that give a mood and aren't quite music, but they support that scene and those ideas. It's a tricky business finding music that will support the emotion or mood. And there's dialogue, which is a kind of information but has to be a certain way. It's like music. It has a pace, it has some curves to it. Then there are sound effects like a door opening, and those sound effects can be wrong or right as well. You maybe have ten or twenty door sounds to pick from but only one of them is right, or maybe you know a few of them might be right but you've got to get it to sit in the picture in a particular place and be correct. But it's just a sound effect. Then there are other sound effects that are more abstract, like music. There are many times when several pieces of music are going. So it's not just a case of throwing in a bunch of stuff. It's an experiment of action and reaction, and testing it until the sounds marry with the scene and elevate the scene. It's a subjective thing and it's arrived at through a lot of experimentation. These days we've got so many pieces of equipment that we can go fairly fast, but the danger is that we can get lost because there are so many choices. When it starts marrying you can clean it and perfect it and move on to the next thing.

Could you talk about editing?

Well, editing is very depressing in a way, because at that point it is what it is. You cut stuff together and you look at it and if there were loaded guns around you might kill yourself. It's a process that is sometimes very painful, but by acting and reacting and trying to hold your objectivity, you can eventually get there. It's an experiment. You lose scenes you thought you would never lose and you take on a little bit of a scene that you thought was a throwaway. But those combinations make it happen. The film seems to want to be a certain way and an editor can help you get it that way. You need an editor who is anxious not only to make it work but to take some strange chances. Experiment. And a lot of times through experimentation you get to some beautiful places. A lot of times you go down a wrong road and you get in trouble. But you have to be willing and you have to be with people who want to take the chance and experiment.

You take bizarre characters out of context and establish their world for us. I won-
der if that's a conscious decision.

Strangely, not too much of what I do is conscious. It's all done on a feeling. I can tell when something isn't right, and I have enough of a dialogue
with people to express what to do to change it. It's all happening under
the surface. That's why it's hard to talk about. It just happens in a strange,
abstract way. A lot of times I don't think about what the film even means
until the film is completely finished and I see it again and see more closely
what it means.

Before you start shooting do you think about the overall visual conception of the
film?

No, it's action and reaction, mostly on the day. And then other ideas come
in. Even though you've been feeling the original ideas for a long time, on
the day itself other things just jump up. It's just more real. You go with
what you feel.

What was it like taking Wild at Heart *to Cannes?*

That was pretty much of a thrill because I'd never been there and in my
mind it's the number-one film festival in the world. I didn't expect to win
anything, and then on the steps going up to pick up the Palme d'Or the
two people running the festival leaned forward and said, "It is something.
It is definitely not nothing." So I knew that it wasn't nothing.
     Let me tell you about my other Cannes experience. We had an oppor-
tunity with *Eraserhead.* Some people came and looked at it and said it
would be great for this Directors' Fortnight. The deal was for us to finish
the film up as much as we could and get it to New York City. I didn't have
a single nickel and I was sick with a cold on the day I was supposed to go.
I had these twelve rolls of sound and twelve rolls of picture because we
didn't have a composite print, and I got on this redeye and got to New
York early in the morning. New York scared me tremendously in those
days. I got down to the screening room and it wasn't even open when I got
there, and then when they opened it up I saw four cans of film in front of
me and the projectionist said, "Yes, they're ahead of you and we'll get to
you when we can." I kept drinking coffee and having donuts at this fantastic little place down the street and then about four in the afternoon the
guy started running *Eraserhead.* They finished up. I packed up my film

Mulholland Dr. (2001), was an aborted ABC television series which Lynch
made into a feature film starring Naomi Watts (left).

and said, "Well, what's the deal?" They said, "They'll let you know." I
went back to LA and two or three days went by and I finally contacted
someone and they told me that they had gone back to France two days
before I even went to New York and there was no one even in the theater
seeing any of those films that whole day.

Where did the story of Mulholland Dr. *come from?*

I don't know where. In this case it came from ideas from the ether. They
sometimes come in the form of a book and sometimes in the form of a
screenplay, but before a book and before a screenplay the ideas come
from somewhere, and that's the trick: where these ideas come from and
how they come to us and how we can get them and what we do with
them once they have come to us. It seems as if they come from outside of
us, and for me they come in fragments. It would be beautiful if they
came all at once and it was one big thing and it was possible to pick it up
and you were off and running. The first fragment in this case was the
words "Mulholland Dr." married with a certain knowledge of that road,
and then it went to night and then the sign at night with the wind
and headlights just gently illuminating that sign. That was the beginning
of it.

When did a character first appear?

I can't remember how it unfolded, but there was always going to be a girl coming to Hollywood. How it got to where it is now was a pretty long journey. Sometimes when I get enough things together I dictate the script, because I don't know how to type. I think that the dictating is, for me, really very good and useful, because there is someone in the room and that person has to be a certain type of person so you don't feel a fool for saying things or going down a wrong road. I was dictating and I began to speak about the cowboy and just like that he walked right in and began to speak. And that's how that happened. The ideas come in fragments. I don't know where anything is going. When a few fragments start hooking themselves together and they marry to a fragment that you didn't think was going to relate at all, it's a big surprise. It's such a huge, long process and some ideas come while you're shooting and then more ideas come toward the end. It's ongoing and never finished until it's finished.

So where did the story of Inland Empire *come from?*

I started experimenting with the Sony PD150. I looked at this camera as a toy, but then the more I used it, I just fell in love with it and the freedom I had with it. I started getting ideas for a scene here and a scene there and started shooting them. I didn't know how one scene would relate to another, but I committed to this camera and kept going, and then a thing happened where I saw how these things could relate and more was born out of that and now it is what it is.

That's a nonanswer.

It's a damn good answer.

Which sequences did you see connection between?

When you write a script there are a whole bunch of things going on that if you were to talk about would really muddy the waters. The script-making process involves getting ideas, writing them out and moving things about. Then you get another idea and start seeing things emerge. Hopefully. With the shooting, you get a scene and shoot it. Get another scene, shoot that scene. Then you wonder how they relate.

What about the tales that the Polish woman tells? Where did they come from?

They came from where ideas come from. This is the most magical thing about the world, that once in a while, when we're really lucky, we catch an idea. They just pop up. The idea tells us everything. Every single thing. So you get an idea and it just pops up like that. Sometimes you'll get a little jolt of happiness and inspiration and energy with it, and if you start writing it down you realize there is so much there in that moment because you keep writing one sentence after another to flesh out that idea and you realize that idea carries an awful lot with it, all the moods and sometimes the characters. The whole thing is there if you start writing it out.

So he's leaving the house and sees his reflection?

Yes.

And evil is born?

Yes.

Tell us about evil, David.

In my mind, we live in what they say is the field of relativity, but now modern science says it has discovered and verified the existence of the unified field and that this is at the base of all matter and mind. Unity of all the particles, all the forces of creation. A pure positive ocean. And they say it's bliss consciousness, here, there and everywhere, but hiding at the base of everything. It starts to emerge, forming everything that is a thing, and as it emerges, that's when things get kind of weird. Over trillions and trillions of years. Negativity, or evil or whatever, is really just the absence of that powerful unity. So it's kind of borne out and they say a few different things about how it's borne out, but it's a real, great playground for us, built out of consciousness. And here we are.

I know you're involved in transcendental meditation, which is concerned with bliss and beauty and love. But your movies are often very focused on the darker side of humanity.

I've been asked that, as you might imagine, a couple times before. My answer is that stories, all through time and into the future, have conflict. Light and dark. Love and pain. Struggle. All kinds of things. It's so beautiful. They're always going to have that. But the storyteller doesn't have to suffer in order to show suffering. Having a lot of energy and tremendous focusing power and leaping up out of bed is beautiful. Feeling strongly about something is beautiful. Negativity, anger, sorrow, depression, stress, hate and fear—all these things constrict the flow of creativity, the flow of ideas. Anger is a constricting thing. Real depression—you can hardly get out of bed. The ideas don't flow. I want anything that can blow such negativity away. I want to rid lives of such thoughts. I want to be able to expand understanding and awareness. I want to get at those ideas at a deeper level and get more energy and more happiness in the doing—and still have an edge. That's why I meditate. You don't become laid back or lose all interest. It's the reverse. So that's the ticket. And then you tell the stories that are inside you. Each person has these stories that come along. Just stay true to those ideas and enjoy the doing of it. If you don't enjoy the doing, there goes that part of your life. You suffer in the doing? That's not good. It can all be so beautiful. And then if you have done that and you don't have any success, at least you gave it your best shot and you enjoyed the doing.

You can't control what's going to happen after a film is over. You just can't. I promise you that. Along the way, that's what you can control. That's what you should be focused on. Every single element. Try to get all the elements to feel correct. If they do feel correct, and as you enjoy the doing of the thing, then you get a chance for the whole thing to hold together.

How do you collaborate with your producers?

Producers are there to help facilitate the making of a film. They have a whole set of problems and I don't want to know about their problems.

Do you plan on going back to film or are you happy with digital?

Digital from now on.

Is there a particular way that you work with actors?

You look at them in the eye and you're close to them and you see the way they react to this word and that word and you start talking to them. You have to feel free to say what pops up. There are no rules. Why are you talking to them? Because what they just did didn't quite feel correct to you. So you need to talk to them. You explain what you meant by that word there that they misinterpreted, and you talk like friends. And you talk and talk and talk and they say, "I got it this time." And they go again. And maybe there are one or two little tweaks and then you go again. Actors have to make it real from a deep place. My job is to get a feeling on the set that's safe, so they can let go of the personality they are born with and take on this other one and make it real. They have to get in there and catch it.

How much information do you give the actors?

When you talk to the actor in one scene, you're defining a character that you hope is going to continue on and work in some unknown scene that you're hoping to catch later. It's a tricky way to work. In a normal way of working you have a script and there are some scenes where you say, "This is a good scene to start talking about, because it defines the character so much that if we work on this scene, the rest will come like that." Common sense. That's the way to do it.

What about in rehearsals?

You rehearse before you start shooting and you pick a scene that helps you define the character. The first rehearsal could be a million miles away, but by rehearsing and then talking, rehearsing and talking, it gets closer and closer and closer. Along the way a thing happens and they catch the character, so now the two of us are going down the same road and the actor brings all he has to that character. If there are changes I will re-rehearse before we start shooting.

Do you believe in time?

I love time. Time is the weirdest thing. A lot of people got real interested in time when Einstein started saying it's different for places, you know, different observers. A lot of people got hip to the fact that time can go fast or it can go slow and you can slip in time backwards or forwards. The beautiful thing about cinema is this flow in time, like music. The sequences are like those movements in big pieces of music and they flow one into another in time. The way time moves is so critical. But then again, that's based on the idea you have. The feel of the idea tells you how fast or slow to go. The words are in the script. You can't really write out the pace. One Sunday afternoon when I was shooting *The Elephant Man,*

I was lying on the couch and I heard Samuel Barber's Adagio for Strings. I went nuts because the whole end of the film suddenly comes to the front of my head. I call up Jonathan Sanger, the producer, and say, "Jonathan, I've got to get this music and put it in the film." He went to the store and got nine versions. I listened to all of them and none of them were the thing I heard, so they went out and got more and finally there it was, André Previn's version. But just the pace of it—this went a little harder and this went a little softer—the way it flowed was the ticket. The same exact notes. It makes a difference. Time is so beautiful.

That television set at the beginning of Inland Empire, *is that in Poland?*

Yes. In Poland. There's a film festival, the Camerimage film festival, in Łódz, Poland. Łódz is a town sort of in the center of Poland, and these guys have been putting on this festival that celebrates the director of photography for about thirteen years. They asked me and Fred Elmes to go over. They were going to give us an award for *Blue Velvet* and basically Fred took the award, but I said I'd love to come over because I heard in Eastern Europe there are many, many factories. I said, "If you guys could help me get into some factories to photograph some nude women . . ." And they said, "No problem." So I went over there and made friends with the gang and then I kept going back there and I got an idea for a scene there. That was one of the things that started pulling the fragments together. The whole Polish connection.

Which was the scene?

I don't want to say but there were many there. Everything is there in the film, and that's the strangest part about it, because I like telling stories, but so many people do a film and then people will ask them to talk about it and I think that's sort of absurd in a way—you know, talking about the particulars of the film. No?

So we won't do that anymore.

Because you work real hard to get a thing to feel correct for you, and then it's finished and you want it to go clean and pure into the world. They started making behind-the-scenes films. Sometimes they are interesting, but telling us how they did the effects is like magicians telling how they did a magic act. It's a delicate thing. The magic goes away.

I've heard recently that there is a formula floating and that if you could zero in on that formula you've got a hit film. That could be true on the surface, but if you go down in there, I don't see how they could write out a thing for that. There are certain things a human being loves and you could kind of get a handle on those, but if you see films from the thirties that are emotional, they don't seem so emotional now. It was for that time. There's just another layer or patina that is always working. It's something beneath the surface, something you can't write a book about. It's delicate. It's abstract. It's the thing that cinema can do, but you've got to catch it with all the elements working together.

Do you think that the changes in technology and in audience viewing trends will affect storytelling in the future?

I thought things were going to change more than they have, but it turns out that, like painting and theater, film doesn't really change. The structure for telling a story hasn't really changed.

Is there a truth out there somewhere?

Yes, there's a truth for me, but the truth is like a mountain: people see it differently as they walk around it.

What filmmakers or films influenced your work?

I wasn't a film buff when I was growing up. There are filmmakers that I like and I don't know how they've influenced me. I like Billy Wilder, Hitchcock and Fellini, Bergman and Jacques Tati. Painters influenced me. I like factories and smoke and diners. Those are my favorite places. I wouldn't want to live in those places, but I like to work with them. I like Formica. Actually, my greatest influence is the city of Philadelphia. I lived there and suffered in that town for five years. I was picking up on so many things around where I lived, and I think the window for picking up things is open for a certain part of our life, and I think that part when it was most open for me was Philadelphia. But sometimes you have to close the window a little bit to protect yourself. In Hollywood, once you're on a roll, you don't get out amongst the people so much and you get your ideas secondhand. And that's a danger.

How long have you been smoking?

I was smoking when I was at the AFI, but then I quit for twenty-two years. My generation's the last one that can really say we didn't know about it when we first started. I just love tobacco, but in the back of my mind, like every smoker, I'm thinking about when it will be the correct time to stop, and that's usually tomorrow. Or the day after.

Do you go to see many movies?

Not so many. I don't have the time. It frightens me to go to the movies, because as I'm sitting there waiting for the curtain to open I'm filled with a fear for the director and I feel that it's my film there and it seems as if these people around become so hostile to me. I have great empathy for those directors.

───────◆───────

Films as Director

1977 *Eraserhead* (also producer, screenplay and editor)

1980 *The Elephant Man* (also screenplay)

1984 *Dune* (also screenplay)

1986 *Blue Velvet* (also screenplay)

1990 *Wild at Heart* (also screenplay)

1992 *Twin Peaks: Fire Walk With Me* (also producer and screenplay)

1997 *Lost Highway* (also screenplay)

1999 *The Straight Story*

2002 *Mulholland Dr.* (also producer and screenplay)

Rabbits (also screenplay)

2006 *Inland Empire* (also producer, screenplay and editor)

Lynch made short films including *Six Figures Getting Sick*, 1966; *The Alphabet*, 1968; *The Grandmother*, 1970; *The Amputee*, 1974; *Does That Hurt You?*, 2002; *Darkened Room*, 2002; and *Lady Blue Shanghai*, 2010. Lynch also directed for television including *Twin Peaks*, 1990–91; *Mulholland Dr.*, 2001; and *Dumbland*, 2002.

There are reasons why they've been doing it this way since the Greeks. There are things that hold our attention and there are things that don't—and there are reasons why. There are a lot of interesting ways to go, but not all of them will suspend your disbelief, hold your attention, keep you emotionally involved and move you.

JAMES MANGOLD
(Born in New York City, 1963)

The precocious James Mangold started making films as a child with his artist father's Super 8 camera in New York's Hudson Valley, and at the age of seventeen arrived at the California Institute of the Arts to study with British-American director Alexander Mackendrick. It was at CalArts that Mangold learned the fundamentals of directing and screenwriting. He was just twenty-one when he was hired at Disney, which turned out to be a sobering experience. After writing *Oliver & Company,* a reasonably successful animated feature about a kitten taken in by a pack of pickpocket dogs, he found himself in the cross-currents of big studio politics and was dismissed. He moved to New York to study film at Columbia University under the guidance of Miloš Forman, who helped him develop *Heavy,* a story inspired by an overweight friend in the upstate New York town where Mangold grew up. He wanted to make a film about a large man who is invisible, and he cast Pruitt Taylor Vince as the pizza chef and Liv Tyler as the young waitress he longs for. *Heavy,* his first feature as a writer-director, earned him the best-directing prize at the 1995 Sundance Film Festival.

Mangold then cast Robert De Niro, Harvey Keitel, Ray Liotta and, against type, Sylvester Stallone in his modern-day western, *Cop Land,* which was well received by critics. Angelina Jolie won an Academy Award for her performance as an engaging sociopath in Mangold's next film, *Girl, Interrupted,* which he followed with the lighthearted *Kate and Leopold,* starring Meg Ryan and Hugh Jackman. His 2003 thriller *Identity* featured John Cusack, Ray Liotta and Amanda Peet and was a box-office hit. In 2005 he collaborated with his CalArts mentor Gill Dennis on the screenplay for *Walk the Line,* the story of Johnny Cash and June Carter Cash. Under Mangold's direction Reese Witherspoon won the Oscar for Best Actress and Joaquin

James Mangold studied at CalArts with Alexander
Mackendrick and received the best directing prize
at Sundance for his first film, *Heavy* (1995).

Phoenix was nominated for Best Actor. In 2007 he remade a film he had first
seen in Mackendrick's class, *3:10 to Yuma,* with Christian Bale and Russell
Crowe, and in 2010 he directed Tom Cruise and Cameron Diaz in *Knight and
Day.*

From his early days as a low-budget Sundance independent, to his current
status as an A-list Hollywood director, Mangold has consistently demonstrated his love, appreciation and understanding of cinema. All of his films,
from the genre-bending *Cop Land* to the biopic *Walk the Line,* come from a
skilled storyteller who is able to produce sophisticated mainstream fare while
exploiting the power of what Mackendrick called "preverbal cinema."
"Toward the end of my time at Columbia," Mangold explained in a 1997
interview, "I was teaching undergraduate writing and directing, and I was
always telling my students to write as if they were describing a movie to a
blind person."

Mangold's experience as a film student at CalArts, his understanding of
the frustration and the blind spots of students who are learning screen storytelling, and his capacity to explain film grammar and dramatic construction,
made him an especially valuable speaker at AFI. The seminar was moderated
by his colleague and former teacher Gill Dennis.

JAMES MANGOLD

———◆———

September 9, 2005*

You had quite an auspicious start in the film business.

I've been making movies since I was about ten or eleven years old. I grew up in upstate New York, where I was a Super 8 movie freak, and at the age of seventeen decided to go to the California Institute of the Arts just north of Los Angeles, where I spent four great years. In my final year I made a movie that, in retrospect, was very much designed to get me hired. I had read in *Newsweek* about this new television series called *Amazing Stories* that Spielberg was working on, so I made a short film—solely to get a job—that was based on another short film I had already made. I was terrified because my time at school was ending, and it seemed I could either go back to New York and work in a camera shop or stay in LA and somehow find a way to become a filmmaker. So I made the film with the help of Gill Dennis and Alexander "Sandy" Mackendrick, who were both teaching there and who both opened up to me the power and joy of writing and directing.

On graduation day I passed the film off to three CalArts trustees who happened to be at the ceremony. One was Jeff Berg, the chairman of ICM. One was Barry Diller, the head of 20th Century–Fox. The third was Michael Eisner, head of Disney. I gave them all tapes, went back and sat with my parents at the graduation ceremony, and said, "You won't believe who I just met and gave my tapes to!" This was Friday, and on

*Gill Dennis moderated this seminar. This transcript also contains segments from seminars James Mangold gave at the American Film Institute on January 5, 2000, and March 26, 2003, and from an interview conducted in summer 2009.

Monday I had to get out of my dorm room. Over the weekend I was packing when the phone rings. It's Michael Eisner calling from his car. He said he watched the film three times and that I was the kind of person he wanted to be in business with. He said, "Do you have an agent?" I said, "No." He said, "Just talk to Jeff Berg. He'd like to represent you. You should call him. I'll talk to you later." He hangs up. I'm sitting there stunned, surrounded by all these boxes. The phone rings again and it's Barry Diller calling from a plane. I can barely hear him, but I think he tells me to ring Jeff Berg. Then the phone rings again and it's Jeff Berg. He says, "Do you have an agent?" I say, "No." He says, "Well, I'm a pretty good one. Why don't you come down and we'll talk." I'll always remember what he said to me when we met in his office. I was twenty-one. He said, "Are you ready for this?" He tells me to go home and in a month he'll have a deal set up at either Fox or Disney.

To jump rapidly forward from that little fairy tale, I ended up in a very strange position at Disney. Let me say that the up side to this kind of adventure is that in some ways it validates your apparent talent and the money you have spent on your education and your own movies. But there is a dark side to getting into the business early. You understand so little of the political nature of a movie studio. It can be a very frightening place. I entered Disney not understanding that I was caught between the moving tectonic plates of the rivalry between Michael Eisner and Jeff Katzenberg. Jeff had his own young filmmaker who was his protégé, and I was Michael's favorite. You imagine that when you arrive these people want to make your movies, because they've seen your previous films—and they did, after all, bring you into the fold. But they really don't. They want you there because you seem to show some facility for the technical side of making a film, and what they really want is that you make the pictures they want made.

What happened is that I was fired from a TV movie because it was too dark. I had hired all these inner-city children for some kind of animal story, this "A Deer Lost in Manhattan" tale set on some low-income housing project. It all looked much too gritty and miserable to the executives, so they closed us down, and I ended up working off what I owed them by writing *Oliver & Company*. One day I was summoned to Jeff's office and he said, "You're not explosive enough to want your deal. It's over." I left, went downstairs, took my box from my office, walked out and really didn't go back for a long time. I had been so lifted up but was then dropped from such a height. I doubted if I wanted to be a filmmaker anymore. What I had witnessed in the hallways and offices of this studio had shattered my idea of filmmakers as artists in control of their ideas and movies. I just didn't know if I wanted to do it anymore, so I went back to school.

What kind of a teacher was Mackendrick?

Seeing as this is a film school and you're all film students, it's worth me talking about what I learned from Sandy, because I learned an awful lot. He's a really good starting point for many of the things I think about when I'm writing and directing.

For a man of incredible charisma and ego, Sandy had tremendous personal power. He wasn't shy about his opinions or his knowledge or experiences, but he was very effacing about his own work, which included extraordinary films like *Sweet Smell of Success*. When you would rave on about one of his films, Sandy would roll his eyes. He looked at his own work with the kind of severity and dissatisfaction with which he would look at student films. The amount of energy he committed to the effort was always probably greater than any of us deserved. You'd work through the night typing the seven-page script of your short film and you'd hand it in on Wednesday, which was mentoring day. You'd come in Thursday and Sandy would have written—in the most beautiful longhand—seven pages in which your crappy little short was undone and unwound and analyzed in a way that it never deserved. He was teaching by example, how hard we were going to have to work. He was leading by example of industriousness. You knew that there was no way he didn't take home your script, think about it, write on it, mull over the themes of it, make connections with other existing elements and threads in literature, and when he came back to you, there was a kind of respect given to the work, as well as an annihilation. Sandy was giving us a sense of the kind of commitment you had to make in order to create something decent. The notes he wrote to us and handed out in class—which I still have—are the best-written articulations of filmmaking I've ever read.

I think Sandy felt he was responsible for just the basics, getting us up to speed on the fundamentals. Sandy felt that all too often, at least in film school, people wanted to jump right in and immediately be Kubrick and Antonioni, but he was insistent that personal expression could come later. Sandy had a way of supplying people who arrived without any clue with a framework on which to build; and to students who arrived with a lot of steam, he tempered you. Of course he was met with the resistance of young artists feeling he wasn't getting their personal vision. I think some of the lessons that Sandy had to offer could only be absorbed with time. Some of them are the most basic and perhaps boring lessons about drama: this is a piston, this is a cylinder, this needs to go in this. There are reasons why they've been doing it this way since the Greeks. There are things that hold our attention and there are things that don't—and there are reasons why. There are a lot of interesting ways to go, but not all of them will suspend your disbelief, hold your attention, keep you emotionally involved and move you. Some of those reductive and conservative lessons aren't necessarily the lessons you want to accept when you're eighteen years old. But what Sandy gave me—and every student who spent time with him— was a set of tools that to this day I use when writing and directing.

Sandy was talking about how to use the basic building blocks of visual communication, the same way we use verbal structures to communicate. No matter how creative you are, everyone from Stephen King to Sartre has to use subjects and predicates, verbs and nouns. It's just that simple, and Sandy was saying that experimenting without really grasping the basics was taking on too much. He was happy for us to challenge the fundamental structures of dramatic construction, but only once we truly understood them. Film is a layering process. Before you learn how to play the trumpet, you have to understand the basics of a musical scale. He was trying to get us to answer the most basic questions, like, what is a story? Before deciding where you're going to put your camera, let's first make sure you *have* a story.

Many teachers stress the idea of visual storytelling. Do you think about that when you conceive of your films?

One of the questions I've always asked myself when reading a script or working with ideas for films is, why is this a movie? The bread that the movie is built on, the starch which holds it together, should be a series of images. The thing should not work for blind people. Essentially it's a false medium if it's a medium that works just fine when you're not paying attention with your eyes. The way I think about it is that there are filmed plays, and then there are movies. What really interests me is something that could only be a film. This idea couldn't be turned into a play or novel or anything else. You want to concentrate on creating something that is uniquely cinematic. When I made my first film, *Heavy,* we were all on the heels of movies like Tarantino's *Pulp Fiction.* It was the most verbal, tongue-in-cheek, aggressive, high-octane, rock-and-roll moment in independent filmmaking, and in a way what I was doing was running completely counter to it. I can't help but think that the kind of conservative streak I have in me wasn't in part shaped by Mackendrick's ideas. He tried to teach us how to make films that were very entertaining, but also that were not susceptible to fashion in some way. He asked us, "What were you after? What were you trying to make here? What part of moviemaking are you playing with?"

Sandy urged us to build our films with images first, to make sure everything was comprehensible visually—and only then add dialogue. His own work taught us many lessons about what he called the preverbal language of cinema. *Sweet Smell of Success,* for example, is no less a visual film than *The Ladykillers*—even while Clifford Odets' dialogue is flying at you endlessly. While it's a film brimming with rapid-fire dialogue, it is completely decipherable as a silent film. Turn the sound down and see if you can't understand who is doing what to whom. Even though critics are always raving about the dialogue—and sure, it *is* good dialogue—most of what's being said is actually just details of exposition you don't really need to know. And I think for a lot of people the words sail right over their heads as they watch the film. The words are an enhancement or an added color, but the thing really does dance and sing and tell a story on a preverbal level first.

Can you talk about studying acting at CalArts?

More often than not, when I get out of my car and walk onto the set of the movie, what faces me is not a problem that can be solved with a lens or a filter or a light. I have the best technicians around me. If I can articulate what I see in my mind, they'll probably be able to realize it. But that task of making a moment seem real on the screen, one that involves character and emotion and actors, is much more difficult, and probably ultimately much more fulfilling.

One of the reasons Sandy was fascinated with getting us—and sending me in particular—to an acting school was that I think he felt film students were becoming glorified technicians. Knowledge of film stock and lenses were becoming our basics. And we were watching and mimicking movies we admired, so we were becoming experts in being faux Kubricks or faux Spielbergs or faux Ken Russells or whatever it was at that moment. But this meant our ability to express ourselves was limited because, while we were learning to use lenses and microphones, the most primal tool—the making of a performance with a human body in front of a lens—was a skill and a world completely unexplored.

The start of it for me was Mackendrick saying, "I'm not going to speak to you next year." I still remember being in his office and him saying, "You've drained me. There's nothing left I can give you. I have nothing left to offer. You've taken all my classes twice and you've been my teaching assistant. I think you should go to the acting school next year." I don't know whether he thought he would meet some resistance, but it seemed absolutely thrilling to me. I was probably a good experiment for him, because I was a complete technocrat and I was frightened of public speaking. The idea of being with actors in a studio doing plays all year seemed positively exhilarating.

Still today on film sets I'm startled by how much of the crew around me have an innate hostility or resentment toward the actors, that the actors are perceived to be babies. "Why are they different than us?" But these people who express these opinions have never seen themselves blown up in a close-up the size of a building. They've never woken up having had a fight with their loved one knowing they have to play this very happy scene today, and that whatever they succeed or fail at doing will then be ripped apart in fifty national magazines. We filmmakers exist behind the lens with this incredible sense of anonymity, but our failures and successes are borne by the actors. So having some sense of what the actor has to go through on a daily level has served me very well as a director.

When we were shooting *Heavy* there was a moment when the DP was getting frustrated because Liv Tyler was doing a very emotional scene and she kept wandering out of this single source of light he had in this very dark tavern for her to land in. He kept going up to her after takes to say, "Can you please remember to stand here and not here?" I could see she was getting very frustrated, because she was trying to maintain an emotional state between takes. Suddenly I asked the DP to step back, took one of the bar stools and moved it to where he didn't want her, and said, "That's all we need." It was reminding me of Sandy saying, "Stand in the actors' shoes. Walk in their shoes. If there's something awkward, walk it. Is it ridiculous? Inhabit these moves and understand them." Of course Liv hit the mark on the next take, and it's the one in the film.

The whole basis of the actor-director relationship comes from their confidence that you're looking out for their best interests. They smell and taste you during rehearsals, but it's during the first couple of days of production when the actor really gets to answer a simple question: "Am I going home feeling worse about the work than when I arrived this morning?" If so, then there's a problem. If I can make a scene better, the actor

Mangold chose Joaquin Phoenix to play the hard-living singer Johnny Cash
in *Walk the Line* (2005). Reese Witherspoon won an Oscar for her
performance as June Carter Cash.

will come to realize that you, the director, are concerned about their performance and that you'll do anything you can to help them give a better
performance. I always remember when that moment of trust with an
actor occurs. There have been only a few instances when it didn't happen,
which makes a shoot very difficult indeed.

How did you come to make Girl, Interrupted?

When we were making *Cop Land* there was something I was always talking to my wife and producer, Cathy Konrad, about, some vague idea I
had about a movie about depression. But I wanted to do it as a horror
movie. I figured depression was the worst kind of uncontrollable, dark
and invisible evil. It was also this strange moment of Prozac mania when
everyone was talking about mental illness. It turned out that Winona
Ryder had seen and loved *Heavy* and wanted to talk to me about making
a film of the book *Girl, Interrupted.* I was very touched that anyone had
even seen *Heavy,* but wasn't too sure about the script that had been sent to
me. But then I read the book, and two days after we wrapped *Cop Land*
we met with Winona. I confessed to her that I had no idea how to take
this book, which was extremely elliptical, full of brilliant philosophy and
snapshots from life, and try to make a movie out of it. Yet I found the
whole thing really curious, not least because it seems this particular actress

was trying to reach for something greater than she had previously been reaching for. When you make movies with stars, the first thing that's important is seeing if they're really hungry for the role. It was clear Winona wasn't glazing over when we talked about it, and she wasn't interested in it just for the check. She was clearly focused and interested, and could even act out scenes from *Heavy* in front of me. As a director—and an opportunist—it all seemed very exciting. Cathy and I talked about it for a while, and decided to take on the challenge. I realized I'd have to run in very different directions from the book—which really has no story whatsoever—so I just did it. I had a draft of the script four months after I sat down to start writing. Basically I had to throw up on screen as moments of drama and conflict things that the book deals with in a meditative fashion. I had to make them into scenes with people actually doing things to each other.

Did you do any research?

Not really. I had books strewn over my desk, but the key influences were *The Wizard of Oz, Slaughterhouse-Five, Black Narcissus* and Jack Clayton's *The Innocents. The Wizard of Oz,* to me, is about depression. Dorothy is living in this black-and-white world of adolescence where everyone is scolding her. She's clearly upset about more than her dog at the start of the story. There's clearly something nagging at her beyond her dog when she sings "Somewhere Over the Rainbow." The whole journey in that film— going into this magical universe where trouble melts like lemon drops, meeting these characters who she befriends, each of whom is missing some part of their personality or psyche, and then never really discovering what she's searching for, and even more than that being told she could have gone home any time she wanted—all of these fable-like aspects were more important than research I might have done. In the book *Girl, Interrupted* there wasn't some key or secret to this girl's problems. It wasn't as if her daddy burned her with cigarettes or her brother died in a boating accident and it was all her fault. That just wasn't there. It's about her discovering, quite simply, that she has to pull it together herself.

You talked earlier about visual storytelling. How do you actually put those images down on paper?

I rarely write camera direction in a script. I really find it a turn-off because it pulls me out of the story. And anyway, there are much more creative ways of getting a director to shoot something the way you—the writer—see it in your head. Instead of literally issuing orders to him, like "Close-up: Katherine," why not describe the color of Katherine's eyes, that they're red, and that there's a tear welling, or that the lids are trembling, or her bangs are blowing in the wind? All those things tell me I'm not in a wide shot.

The job of the screenplay is to get the movie made. A producer with money in his pocket needs to say, "I want to make this movie." An actor needs to read this script and say, "I want to be in this movie." If the script doesn't read well and excite these people, it'll never become a movie. So don't write, "Katherine walks from left to right." Who cares if she's walking left to right? What's important is that you see the screen door slamming and feel the wind blowing her skirt. So write it! It won't be a head-and-shoulders shot of that actress crossing the porch if the way her dress blows is something that seems truly evocative and relevant to the story. I rarely refer to a lens or a tracking shot in my scripts, I just write what I want the audience to see. If I was describing something to my grandmother and she couldn't see, I wouldn't say, "It's a 27mm lens tracking low." That means nothing! I'd say, "He's walking down the hall, he looks really powerful." To me, that's obviously a low tracking shot. It's also a much more enticing invitation for an actor and director.

At CalArts there were clear reasons why—as Mackendrick kept on reminding us—we wanted to write shooting scripts when we should be writing screenplays. Most people at school were coming from a kind of technical mania more than any kind of storytelling tradition. We weren't products of theater groups, but of lonely childhoods spent in an attic with a film projector. The movies that inspired us throughout the seventies were highly technical. The new development was how incredibly well mixed and well shot and controlled these movies were, and how modern in their sense of sound and image. Every young filmmaker wanted to make sure their script pages guaranteed that whoever was reading them understood how I, the director, was going to be using a sound effect of the drop of a faucet here or helicopters there, like Coppola did in *Apocalypse Now.* We were really going out of our way to sell that, and if anything was getting short shrift, it was the story. Sure, the images were all in place, but what the hell is going on here? What is this scene about?

Sandy had a unique challenge with all of us young and impatient film artists. We were terrified of becoming what we saw as hacks, not being able to tell our stories in some stylish or definitive way, which at that moment in film culture our heroes—Scorsese, Coppola, Lucas and

Kubrick, the king of them all—were doing. For a nineteen-year-old, it was all about asserting style over story. We were writing scripts with sharp elbows, making sure you saw what auteurs we were going to become. Sandy's point was that before any of that would come into play, we needed to do the work of actually telling a story and justifying the rolling of all this film. He was both a welcome and unwelcome voice that way. I don't think it's any different from a young actor immediately grabbing a pipe and growing a mustache and starting to research how people in the military in the forties handled their revolvers, all before they know what their character actually wants. Being pushed by Mackendrick to see the story first wasn't the kind of message we wanted to hear. It's like being told to make your bed. Before you go running outside, you better make sure all your stuff is put away in the right place. But as savvy young students trying to redefine cinema and take short cuts, and skipping the stale old narrative dogma, the thing that you're most liable to do. So focus on it. Work out your story. Create your characters. Decide who is doing what, with which and to whom. And only then bring in the cameras.

———

Films as Director

1995 *Heavy* (also screenplay)
1997 *Cop Land* (also screenplay)
1999 *Girl, Interrupted* (also
    screenplay)
2001 *Kate & Leopold* (also
    screenplay)

2003 *Identity*
2005 *Walk the Line* (also screenplay)
2007 *3:10 to Yuma* (also producer)
2010 *Knight and Day*

Often if I want to change an actor's performance I won't talk to them at all. Instead I'll talk to the other performers in the scene and push them in different directions, and if the actor is good, he or she will respond differently.

ALAN PAKULA
(Born in New York City, 1928—Died 1998)

Alan Pakula thrived first as a producer, then as a director-producer and occasional screenwriter. He was a tall, dignified man with a carefully trimmed beard who in another life might have been a professor or a psychiatrist, innate skills he used in his widely appreciated work with actors.

He studied drama at Yale and explored Broadway before making his way to Hollywood and a job in the executive offices at the Paramount studio, where he had the opportunity to learn the business of moviemaking and observe the work of his favorite directors, Alfred Hitchcock, George Stevens

Alan Pakula collaborated with cinematographer Gordon Willis on six films, from *Klute* (1971) to *The Devil's Own* (1997). Here he confers with Willis on the set of *All the President's Men* (1976).

and William Wyler. He formed a producing partnership with a successful director of live television dramas, Robert Mulligan, and they made a stylish feature-film debut in 1957 with *Fear Strikes Out,* the story of the mental illness of baseball player Jim Piersall, portrayed by Tony Perkins. They hit the bull's eye with their second picture, *To Kill a Mockingbird,* for which Pakula and Mulligan received a Best Picture nomination as producers, and Gregory Peck won an Oscar for his first non-leading-man role as Atticus Finch, a widowed lawyer in a southern town who takes a stand for racial justice.

Pakula's success as a producer was his passport to directing. *The Sterile Cuckoo* is a story of young love in which he cast Liza Minnelli in her first acting role and guided her to her first Oscar nomination, proving that he had a gift for leading actors through challenging roles.

Klute took him into darker territory, with Jane Fonda playing a New York call girl in a role that earned her the 1971 Oscar for Best Actress. *The Parallax View* starred Warren Beatty and explored the political paranoia of the seventies. Pakula's greatest success followed with *All the President's Men,* the Woodward-and-Bernstein account of the Watergate scandal that brought down Richard Nixon. The director's grasp of human psychology, screen craftsmanship, stylistic restraint and sensitivity with actors made the detective story come alive, with compelling performances by Dustin Hoffman, Robert Redford and Jason Robards, Jr. The picture received eight Oscar nominations, including Pakula's only nomination for Best Director.

Presumed Innocent and *Sophie's Choice* were other high points in a career that included occasional failures, when he boldly but unsurely plunged into a very personal story with *I'll See You in the Morning* or dream psychology and repression in *Dream Lover.*

Pakula became expert at shepherding actors through roles of psychological complexity, guiding Meryl Streep and Robards as well as Fonda to Oscars. Harrison Ford, who starred in *Presumed Innocent* and *The Devil's Own,* said that Pakula created an atmosphere that enabled actors to do their best work: "Alan understood what the costs were for actors in terms of being vulnerable—not only in portraying vulnerability, but the vulnerability that's at the core of nearly every actor."

In 1998 Alan Pakula died a tragic death in a traffic mishap on the Long Island Expressway. At the time he was working on an adaptation of Doris Kearns Goodwin's biography of Franklin and Eleanor Roosevelt, *No Ordinary Time.* He often described himself as an admirer of the directors of the Golden Age and placed Jean Renoir at the top of his list, but he never set out to imitate or model his films on the work of others. His friends knew him as a man of high purpose and integrity who created a distinctive film legacy.

ALAN PAKULA

———◆———

July 11, 1978*

Did you always want to be a film director?

I toyed with the idea of being a psychoanalyst. The resemblances between being a director working with a group of actors and being a psychoanalyst are obvious enough. Acting is an emotional tool, and you have to have some sense of the person who's doing it and what they have to contribute to their character in order to get the performance you want out of them.

I decided to become a director when I was seventeen and directed my first film as I hit forty. That should be encouraging to all of you not to give up hope. My first experience as a director was when I was at Yale, where I directed a one-act farce by Chekhov. I was in love with the theater and what attracted me to the theater was working with actors. I'll never forget after the first day of rehearsal, going back to my dormitory, sailing along the street with great, goatlike leaps, thinking I had discovered fulfillment. I felt that I had become some kind of catalyst for these actors, that they were finding things in themselves and the characters that they wouldn't have found without me, and for better or worse doing things that they wouldn't have done without me. This was overpowering. I felt I had found my vocation. I remember bounding through campus feeling like someone out of a Thomas Wolfe novel who had just discovered the ecstasy of life. As for film, I loved it from a childlike point of view. A Saturday without a film was no Saturday at all. But initially I was interested

*This transcript contains segments from seminars Alan Pakula gave at the American Film Institute on November 20, 1974, May 27, 1976, and September 12, 1984.

only in theater. I was afraid of all things technical and felt I should just stay with the stage.

I came out here because my father, a middle-class businessman, was rather disturbed by his eccentric son who wanted to work in the world of theater, and it was easier for me to come to California rather than fight with my family. The first thing I did was work for three months at Warner Bros. on their cartoons. I knew somebody there, and he said, "Come on in." They paid me almost nothing and all I did was just clean the place up. I was a not-so-glorified gofer. Then I started at a little theater in Hollywood called the Circle Theater, which was run by Sydney Chaplin, Charlie's son. Charlie would come down and direct a couple of plays, which was wonderful to watch. It was right before he was exiled to Switzerland. He was a superb actor but one of the worst acting coaches I've ever seen. There was a production of Camus' *Caligula* that Sydney was in, and in the final week Charlie came in to direct. One of these young California actors was struggling with Camus' text. I'll never forget Chaplin at the end of the first act, staring into an imaginary mirror and playing this mad emperor. This joyous, hideous Pan character that he created in front of your eyes was overwhelming. It was stunning. The awful thing was that the young actor then had to get up and do the same thing. That's why he wasn't a good acting coach. The actors were paralyzed. He used to say to Sydney, "Relax, Sydney, relax," and you'd see Sydney become more and more tense.

I directed a play there, a production of Anouilh's *Antigone,* and met Dore Schary, who was head of production at Metro, and also Don Hartman, a producer-director-writer who had done some of the *Road* pictures with Bob Hope and Bing Crosby, and some of the early Danny Kaye pictures for Goldwyn. I soon became an apprentice to Don. It turned out to be the end of an era, and I witnessed the last great gasp of the studio system. Within a few years it had all changed. I touched it and it crumbled. Six months later Don became head of production at Paramount and asked me to go along with him. So suddenly at the age of twenty-two I found myself as assistant head of production at Paramount. It was a fantasy training ground for me. I learned by watching dailies. I watched Billy Wilder's dailies. They were making *Shane* at the time and I watched George Stevens' work every day. It was fascinating, because I had long memoranda on every film that was made, which taught me a great deal. I read so many scripts and—quite outrageously—wrote notes on them. I would see a film I was certain would never be a success become a huge hit. I read the script for *Rear Window* and thought it wasn't so great, but then saw the dailies and could see Hitchcock's visual mind at work. I learned there are certain movie scripts that sell quickly because they read very well but don't play well on the screen, and there are other scripts that are written simply to be filmed and absolutely not read. Most front offices can still be fooled by something that reads in a tour-de-force kind of way, something that works on a literary level.

I kept saying, "I want to direct," and Don Hartman said, "Why don't you become an Irving Thalberg and work as head of a studio?" I said, "I want to direct." He said, "You're a producer, not a director. If enough people tell you you're drunk, for God's sake lie down." I became a producer and spent five or six years in the front office, working with writers and sitting in meetings. I saw Audrey Hepburn's original screen test for *Roman Holiday* and was in on the meetings in which the major decision to be made by six or seven grown men was about whether Audrey Hepburn's teeth needed to be straightened. Nobody thought I could work with actors because they had never seen me work with actors, which was the reason I had come to Hollywood in the first place.

Then I met Bob Mulligan and produced my first film, *Fear Strikes Out*. I think working with Bob set me back in directing several years, because I so enjoyed working with him. What happened was that even though I had been in the front office for six years, working with writers and producers and directors, following pictures from the time the story was purchased through to the release, and then successfully producing all these films for Bob, I felt that time was running out. I was in my late thirties and thought if I didn't start directing then, I never would. Eventually I took an option on a book called *The Sterile Cuckoo*. I was going to hire a young director instead of Bob for that film, but suddenly thought to myself, "Why don't you use a man who's not quite so young, but certainly is a marvelous director: me?" I did, and suddenly life came into focus. I was forty years old.

Do you plan everything in advance when shooting?

I'm somewhere in the middle. On the one hand is Hitchcock. I don't plan everything in advance and say, "That's the way it's going to be." I've learned a great deal from Hitchcock, even though I think my sensibilities are utterly different. At the same time I'm not John Cassavetes, either. I try to do a lot of planning, but once the planning is done I throw an awful lot of it away while I work. I generally keep one primary concept in my head, backed up by months of preparation, but then try to use all the accidents that happen on the set and when I'm working with the actors. I look for surprises and what other people can give me. Once I start shooting a scene, I don't necessarily use what I did in rehearsal. Let's say we're about to film a new scene, one we haven't blocked since the rehearsal a few weeks before. I throw the crew off the set, everybody except the script supervisor and the actors and myself, and maybe an assistant director at the door to keep everybody out. There are a lot of poker games on my pictures. Somebody at Paramount once said to me, "Your technicians go wandering around the lot in the middle of the workday." Well, I don't want the actors to be afraid of exposing themselves or making fools of themselves when we're rehearsing.

I try to guide the actors to the conception of the scene I already have—and one that I might have already spoken to the cameraman about—without them realizing. I say, "Read the scene. Let's get it on its feet." I see where their instincts lead them and right away find out where their problems are with the scene. They might fall into the pattern I wanted or they might come up with something better. Then I call in the cameraman and run the scene for him, and tell him what my rough visual conception is. He'll say, "That's fine," or "I don't think that works." Sometimes there are scenes that are so carefully designed visually that I'll have to say to the actor, "Look, you have to do this for the camera."

If you shoot a scene six weeks after you rehearse it, you can't lock yourself into what you did during rehearsal, because six weeks later you're a different person. For me it's terribly important I keep myself loose, working with what's happening on the set that day. I know that if I planned everything to such an extent that there was nothing left to do on the set, I'd go to sleep in the middle of the picture and it would be a disaster. I love rehearsing. My rehearsing is kind of strangely disordered. I do a certain amount of blocking, but that's not why I rehearse. I really rehearse to get into character, to improvise, to explore, to see what the actors' problems are in terms of their characters, where they might be going wrong. But even more important is to find what the actors can bring to their characters, because rehearsal is where the final rewrite comes. It comes from the actors. The creation of a character is an integration of the actor with the character. Some critics don't seem to understand that. When *Klute* came out, Roger Greenspun, who was the second-string critic of *The New York Times,* wrote that Jane Fonda was just playing herself. Of course that was ludicrous. Jane wasn't playing herself. Yes, she was using things from inside herself to create this character, but what was she supposed to use, things from inside Barbra Streisand? It just shows that reviewers have no comprehension of what acting is.

We got to the end of the third week of rehearsals on *Klute*—this was on a Thursday, and we were going to start shooting on Monday—and Jane came to me and said, "I can't do it. I don't understand it and I'm all wrong for it. You've got to replace me. I'll do anything to get out of it." I said, "I'm not going to let you out. You'll be fine." She said, "I'm not going to be fine. I'm going to be terrible." It was genuine panic. Jane is one of the most gifted people I've ever met, and I think she probably has a greater potential range than any American actor of her generation, but when she said she was wrong for the part she was genuinely scared. When we were shooting *The Sterile Cuckoo* on location, it rained the first day, and instead of doing some easy little transition we wound up doing the only thing we had any cover set for, which was Liza Minnelli's scene where she breaks down in the phone booth, which is the most bravura scene in the film. It was a mistake to ask her to do that scene on the first day. On *Klute* the first thing we rehearsed was a major scene, the first confrontation between Donald Sutherland and Jane, where he comes up to her apartment and there's a man on the roof. When I saw Jane absolutely terrified, I realized that there was no way I could shoot the really important scenes first, so I went to the production manager and said, "I'm throwing out the whole shooting schedule. We're going to go on location on the streets of New York instead of starting at the studio this week." He turned pale and said, "Do you know what that means, Alan? We're supposed to go on location on the streets the third week. We'll have to get new permits." I said, "We can't do it any other way because I realize now that Jane has to be led very gently into this."

Do you work differently with each actor, depending on the kind of person they are?

I have no one way of working with actors. If there's a rapport between an actor and a director, communication is not necessarily verbal. When I start with an actor, I'll say, "I will talk and discuss the character, but if at any moment it bores or confuses or cuts you off creatively and starts to stifle you, just tell me to stop. My feelings will never be hurt." You, as a director, might be saying things that are very meaningful to you, but sometimes it doesn't help the actor. And if it doesn't help the actor, then you have to do something else. Often if I want to change an actor's performance I won't talk to them at all. Instead I'll talk to the other perform-ers in the scene and push them in different directions, and if the actor is good, he or she will respond differently. There's a scene in *All the President's Men* where Dustin is talking to the bookkeeper, played by Jane Alexander. He's trying to get her to talk. I wanted an intense concentra-tion from him, which comes from his fear that she's going to stop talking. Hoffman needs her to tell him everything she knows. All I did was tell Jane, "Whisper. Make it hard for him to hear you. Every take, just lower your voice a notch." Dustin knew he couldn't break into what she was saying because her character would just withdraw.

I think the essence of working with actors is melding their innermost qualities and ideas with the character that's written in the script. You have to ensure that the actors feel free enough to open themselves up and try things. You also need to be strong enough to know what fits into your concept and what doesn't. That's one of the reasons I like the rehearsal period, because I like to see what does and what doesn't work for the actors. I learned that long ago. When I worked with Liza Minnelli there was a thing I would do that worked for her. Halfway through the film we were in a very difficult scene and she was having trouble, and she sud-denly said, "Alan, could you just tell me the story of this film?" Now, she knew the screenplay backwards, but I took her to my trailer and said, "Once upon a time . . ." I told it as you'd talk to a nine-year-old child, in the most simplistic terms, and that helped her at that moment. But if I sat down with Jane Fonda and said, "Once upon a time . . ." she'd think I was out of my mind.

What do you make of the idea of the director as the "author" of a film?

If you don't have anything to say, don't make a film. You must have a con-cept, some specific reason why you want to tell that particular story, some passion that is driving you. Once you have that concept, it's incumbent upon you to communicate it to the people you are working with, because even if you are what they call an auteur, you are, for better or worse, dependent on the collaboration of other people. For some strange reason I always look the most talented when I'm working with the most talented people.

Was there a particular visual you were aiming for with Klute?

I wanted to get a sense of a very claustrophobic world. The fascinating thing when the first draft screenplay was sent to me was the sense of people caught in compulsions over which they have no control. When I was running around New York looking for locations, I would look through the camera and everything would be vertical. You get a sense of what urban living is like. You really are locked in. It's claustrophobic. I wanted to get that sense of compression, so Gordon Willis took the Panavision screen and wiped out all the horizontals and over-the-shoulder shots. There's a kind of inhuman scale to the film with people feeling trivial and claustrophobic at the end of tunnels, having lost a sense of their identity, which, to my mind, is the essence of the psychology of prostitution. There's no sense of your own importance.

Jane Fonda's apartment in *Klute* was originally three separate little rooms, based on a real call girl's apartment, but we turned it into this long, unfinished tunnel, this big, endless, disturbing, subterranean studio room. I wanted a sense of being trapped in space, of being caught. It drove me crazy when I saw the film on television, because there's a shot which really reveals the room and how trapped she is in this space. The camera slowly dollies back and keeps moving until she's this tiny little figure trapped at the end of a long tunnel. It's a nightmare image. On television they cut out the whole move back.

The environment in the film is a world without sunlight. The opening sequence is one of the few times you see sunlight, and it's the only time you see a family. I wanted to start the film at Thanksgiving with a family celebration in sunlight and people who belong together, because then we move to an alienated world of people who don't belong anywhere. They all live separately. There's no sense of family. If you notice, in the first scene with Donald and Jane, his back takes up two-thirds of the screen and all we see is her little face. Again: compression. She's always being squeezed or isolated.

The film is called Klute, *yet the film is really about Bree Daniels.*

The screenplay was submitted to me by Andy Lewis and it was called *Klute.* I had a meeting with Andy and said, "It's really about the girl, but we can't call it *Bree* because some critic is going to say it's a hunk of cheese." The reason I did *Klute* was the character of Bree Daniels. It's the story of a girl who is destroyed by her own compulsions. It's a melodrama in which the girl's tragic flaw nearly destroys her. If she didn't have this obsessive need to seduce men, she wouldn't have gotten herself into this situation, and that fascinated me. If she were an accidental victim I don't think I would have been so interested. But the fact that she's a prostitute with an obsessive compulsion pushed me to make the film. I'm fascinated by compulsions, by bright, rational people who behave in ways they can't control. She has a compulsion to seduce men. She feels impotent and the only way she feels any sense of power is when she is sexually in control. This is the compulsion that almost destroys her.

I wouldn't have done the film without Jane. I met her just a couple of weeks before I was sent the screenplay. Her agent had sent me a script that I wasn't interested in, but I said I would meet with Jane anyway. We talked for hours about a lot of things: women in our society today, compulsive behavior, sexuality. It was just a wonderful, freewheeling discussion, and I came out of it thinking, "I don't want to do this script, but I'd love to work with that woman." About two weeks later *Klute* was sent to me. She was in New York for the opening of *They Shoot Horses, Don't They?* and I called her immediately. The script had a kind of tabloid quality, which threw her off when she read it. She said, "I don't know what I feel about it." We talked for half an hour and she said, "Look, do you really want to do it?" I said, "Yes." She said, "Okay, I'll do it." Out of such little statements, films get made.

I worked on the script with the writer, and during that time Jane changed considerably. At the time I first met with her to talk about *Klute* she was living with Roger Vadim and was not yet a political figure. She came to the set with this great passion. I was concerned that her mind was not going to be on the film because she was involved in so many causes. She has this extraordinary kind of concentration. She can spend the entire time somebody is lighting a scene on the phone making endless calls, raising money, whatever it is, and seem totally disinterested in the film. But when you say, "We're ready for you, Jane," she says, "All right, give me a few minutes." She stands quietly for three minutes and concentrates, and she's completely in the film and nothing else exists for her. When the scene is done she goes right back to the phone. It's a gift that a lot of good actors have, and she has it to an extraordinary degree.

When I was doing *Klute* I thought, "I couldn't be telling a story that's more different from my first film." While *The Sterile Cuckoo* is about the loss of innocence, *Klute* is hardly an innocent film. The styles of the two films are so different, but I realized there were similarities, primarily that they both deal with middle-class, controlled, repressed males. One is a boy and one is a man, both falling in love with self-destructive, very alive, witty, vibrant, spontaneous, surprising, delightful ladies who almost destroy them, and in the process they destroy themselves. That same theme is in both films and I'm sure unconsciously that must have been what attracted me to them. I was fascinated in exploring what it is in John Klute that attracts him to that kind of girl, because to get involved with a hooker—I don't care if it's Jane Fonda or whoever is playing it, no matter how attractive—involves a certain amount of self-destructiveness.

I was also interested in the theme of the middle-class American, the square man who has lived his life by simple, almost Victorian rules. Klute is righteous, a man of very strong will who has led a life of total decency. He has controlled his baser emotions and his hostilities, and has no use for people who have compulsive behavior. He's a Frank Capra, Mr. Smith kind of character, living with solid, small-town American virtues, believing in free will and that we are all completely responsible for our own actions. He feels that self-destructive people should be able to control themselves, that they are wiping out themselves and an awful lot of the world. He is thrown into discovering what happened to his friend, which puts him into this world of total compulsive behavior where he falls in love with a girl whose behavior is uncontrollable. He falls in love with somebody who is everything he despises, and it breaks open his whole comprehension of human experience. He realizes it's much more complicated than his rigid, simplistic, nineteenth-century ways. He has to learn compassion for the complexity of the human condition, and he gains some realization about his own complexities. It breaks him out of the silent majority and starts to turn him into a more compassionate and emotionally alive human being. In his own way Donald Sutherland, as John Klute, was doing a male version of Bree Daniels. Donald is a complicated, fascinating man, mercurial and full of moods, and with his own complications, because emotionally he was going through a very difficult time in his own life. He was breaking up with his wife and had just come from *Alex in Wonderland*, which is an exhausting tour de force of a film.

Did Jane Fonda research the role by talking to call girls?

Yes, I had a call girl sit down with us and tell Jane everything. The first thing she explained is that you get your money first, because once it's over you're not going to get as much. Two, you make sure that the man thinks he's different from all the other johns, that he really is special, that he turns you on, and the only reason you're doing it is because you need the money even though you would really rather do it for free. She said, "They all believe you. I've lost all respect for men, because psychiatrists, judges, doctors, politicians all believe they're different, every one who comes along." The other thing is to get him excited as fast as possible because time is money. The call girl gave Jane all those things, and Jane came in the next day ready to play the scene with the john. Of course she was wonderful. She came up with things I never would've thought of, like when she whispered in his ear and said, "What do you want? Come on, tell me what you want." He whispers something in her ear and she says, "Oh, I like your mind." That came out of Jane being in character and having a simple action, which was to turn on this man as much as possible, to make him think he was exciting to her. Once she was really in character, she couldn't do much that was wrong.

Were the scenes with the psychiatrist in the original script?

I went into those scenes with great trepidation. They seemed inhuman to me, scenes where no real human interaction could take place. They were too full of explicit characterization and exposition, and because of that I felt the only chance for them to succeed was if you really felt this girl breaking down before your eyes, if you really felt this emotion, this recognition of her tragic flaw. The only chance for that was with improvisation. I said to Gordon Willis, "I want the simplest lighting and no camera movement. I want the camera on Jane's face." We improvised all day. I just kept feeding film into the camera, reel after reel. I would talk to each actor separately. Jane would come out to the anteroom after each take and I'd talk to her there, and I'd talk to Vivian Nathan, who played the psychiatrist, in the office.

There were things that were interesting to me but would have been boring to the audience. It got to be around four in the afternoon and I had nothing I could use. It was interesting stuff in that Jane was totally in character, but being totally in character she was very hard to get through to. We'd been shooting for about five hours and she'd never actually said, for example, that she was a prostitute. I kept saying, "Why don't you tell her you're a prostitute?" and Jane said, "I keep trying to tell her and every time I try to tell her, she changes the subject. She doesn't want to know." And Vivian said, "Every time I try to get her to tell me she changes the subject." That was fascinating, because I'm sure that's how analysts and patients function in reality. I didn't want to say to Jane, "You've got to say it," because then I figured we might as well have just stuck to the script. We were running out of time, and I said to Vivian, "Okay, really give it to her. You've been very kind and compassionate until now, but this time really give it to her. Be hostile. Don't be so patient and kind." I thought that would really start breaking Jane down. So Vivian did what she was supposed to do. She said, "You tell me all these things, but you're inconsistent and self-righteous," and so on and so forth. But the angrier she got with her, the more controlled Jane became. Relaxed, kind of happy, the exact opposite of what I'd been reaching for. We ran out of film and I said, "Jane, what happened? Didn't that get you angry?" She said, "Alan, for Bree Daniels hostility is the easiest thing in the world to deal with. When she's gotten an emotional reaction from someone, she knows exactly where she's at. She can be angry back, or she can control it. She's made the other person vulnerable. She's gotten to them." Of course she was right. For a girl who said "I'm all wrong for this," she really knew that character.

Do you look for that flexibility in actors so they can deal with your directing style?

Certainly I look for something in their unconscious, because actors can't bring you something that's not inside them. I look for surprises that are right for the character or, if not the character as written, things that may be better for the story. There are different kinds of actors. There are very bright, intelligent actors who work very hard at home memorizing everything. They come to the set totally prepared. They are so prepared that if an earthquake should happen, if all the other actors in the scene fell into a pit and died, they would carry on with their prepared line reading. With such people, real life will never have a chance to emerge, because they know exactly what they want out of the scene and they know precisely what their character should do. I don't like working with that kind of actor. I would rather go with really gifted people or amateurs, rather than a professional with that competence but without any intuition.

The curse of bad directing or writing is overformalizing. When I went to Yale as an undergraduate I majored in drama. I remember a book called *Fundamentals of Play Directing*, which was full of inductive reasoning where you figured everything out. Upstage left was the mystic area for mystical characters, and down center was the stable, solid area for your stable, solid characters. We were taught exactly how to direct, how to get your concept, how to execute it. The whole method was laid out. The trick, I believe, is to learn all the rules, agree with the ones you agree with and disagree with the ones you disagree with, then head out on your own. You each have to find your own method. The very nature of being a creative person is being, in some way, eccentric. You shouldn't imitate anybody. You can suck up certain techniques that you can use for your own ends, but when you're examining other people's work, never forget that you do it only to get a greater sense of self and to find out what is best for you and how best you should work.

When you look at a script, how do you decide that you want to turn it into a film?

I give myself good reasons why I want to make a film. I write down endless notes which I almost never look at again, because it makes me feel better. I take these little kids' notebooks and endlessly free-associate. I couldn't start a film without writing things down. It's when everything locks in.

Since so much of your work is based on dealing with images, how do you begin to introduce these images to your actors in the rehearsal stage?

I don't tell them anything about it. Often when the actors come into rehearsals there are designs of the set around, so they have a sense of the world they're getting into. If the locations are nearby I'll take the actors to see them and, if I can, rehearse there in order to give the actors a sense of the world they'll be living in. Talking to the actors about the visuals can make them want to play some kind of abstract result, when what they should be doing is trying to find out who the character is, not the style in which that character should be played. It's important that Jane Fonda has a sense of the claustrophobia of the world she's living in as Bree Daniels, but it's not important that she know how Gordon and I will achieve it visually. If you start lecturing actors about abstracts, if you say, "I'm reaching for kind of an absurd romantic quality," the actor says, "I'm supposed to play an absurd romantic? How am I supposed to do that? I'm supposed to play American baroque? What the hell is that?" Knowing that the style of the film is baroque helps me. It may also help the art director. But actors need specifics.

What stage of the filmmaking process do you most enjoy?

The worst thing about making a film is that there are just so damn many people. The essential lack of privacy. You're like a comet with this huge tail. Every time you move, they're all there in back of you, all with questions, waiting for you to give an answer. That's why when you get in the editing room it's all so wonderful. Suddenly there's a kind of medieval cell, this monastery where you can work in peace on your film. I just love being in the editing room, and it's very hard to get me out. The most difficult thing is working without that privacy on the set. It's the opposite from doing a novel or a painting. It's the most public creative act that I can think of.

But of course it's also a challenge. If you're going to work with that many people and have that lack of privacy and have to deal with all those egos, you might as well use those collective talents and in some way make your work a synthesis of all of those minds. There are two sets of egos that you have to preserve: one is the ego of the people you're working with, and the other is your own. Sometimes they seem quite incompatible as goals, but it depends on the kind of work you want from people. Of course the director needs to go into this with a very specific conception of what he wants, otherwise you'll end up with a totally bastardized picture full of everybody's "good ideas." I pride myself on having specific conceptions when I decide to do a film and a specific vision of what I want that film to be. But, unlike an author or composer, I'm dependent on other people. I work with a writer, with actors, with a set designer, with the cameramen, with endless numbers of people. There are some directors who believe there is one concept for the film and everybody else is a puppet who lives only to work toward that concept. I believe in surrounding myself with people who are gifted in what they do.

I love surprises on the set. Things happen that you never would have thought of. I don't want to work with puppets. I don't want to work with anybody who I don't feel has something to give, has some idea I might not have thought of without them, in whatever department, whether it's costume, sound, production design, anything. I communicate my conception to them and use their creativity and gifts to help carry it out. The first thing is to make everyone know that all ideas are welcome. I'm not making one-man pictures. The environment has to be one where everyone has the fearlessness to be outrageous in some way and know they're not going to get punished for it, that even if the ideas are lousy it won't take away their sense of themselves. The great danger is that people will do safe work. They'll never do anything that might make a fool of them. They have to know that I'll make it clear that my own ideas are lousy too. I'll make fun of myself. I try to keep a very loose atmosphere.

In the end, if the film is successful, it's a synthesis of so many people that it's impossible to remember who did what and when. One of the things that amuses me about reading critics is they'll say, "So-and-so did this and so-and-so did that," but I can't remember a week after I shot the film who did what. I believe the making of a film is a life process, and no matter what the conception is to begin with, you'll always see changes emerge. Things come alive in spontaneous and surprising ways. One of my favorite examples is from *All the President's Men.* Jason Robards, who played Ben Bradlee, editor of *The Washington Post,* came up to me after he saw the film and said, "You know, the moment of mine I really like is when I walk out of the office and I do that thing with the desk." It's a scene when he gently taps a desk as he walks by, to show how happy he is. He said, "That was all you." I said, "That was all *you.*" He said, "No, it was all *you.*" We never resolved it. I know it was all Jason because I remember being so thrilled when he did it. At that moment he owned the world. The thing that *was* my idea in that scene was to have him play it in

Robert Redford enlisted Pakula to direct *All the President's Men.*
"*All The President's Men* would have been made without me,
but it would not have been made without Bob Redford.
His passion for seeing that film made was awesome."

a dinner jacket. That one thing dramatizes so much: he's the captain of the ship that is the office of the newspaper, but he also has a whole other life. Bradlee's character is crucial. He is the star personality in that newsroom, not Woodward and Bernstein. If he doesn't seem to have the power, if he can't threaten them, if he's intimidated by them, then the film is over. Jason did it brilliantly. He's one of the great American actors.

How did you come to direct All the President's Men?

All the President's Men would have been made without me, but it would not have been made without Bob Redford. His passion for seeing that film made was awesome. Bob approached me about doing the film months before I said I could do it. I had read the book, so I reread it and then read the screenplay, which worked at the level of entertainment. I was concerned that it was really "Butch Woodward and Sundance Bernstein." I didn't want to make that film—two big stars loving and laughing as they bring down the president of the United States. My other concern was the casting of Bob. Now, I'm a great admirer of Bob as an actor. I saw him when he was twenty-one years old in a small part on the stage and was incredibly impressed. I was concerned because I felt the extraordinary quality of that story, as a piece of American folklore, was that it was the story of two young unknown men without reputation, both struggling to keep their jobs at *The Washington Post*. My concern was that Bob as a movie star was more famous than Richard Nixon and wondered if he would be able to sublimate himself and his personality to this story. Woodward and Bernstein were learning as they were going along, and I felt that Bob had this incredible sense of competence on the screen. As it turned out, Bob was in total agreement and had the same concerns I had.

I didn't want to editorialize. *All the President's Men* was not a picture out to get anybody. A lot of people don't believe me on this, especially a few Republicans I know. Investigative reporting is about exposing things about people in power, whatever side they're on. This is not a story of good against evil or anything like that. It's about reporters getting a story because they are obsessed with getting the story. The question the film answers, in the simplest terms, is: what was it like to have been these two young men who broke through this cover-up and discovered these facts that eventually led to the destruction of some of the most powerful people on earth? There really isn't a moral viewpoint to the film. What fascinated me was the power of the pen and the typewriter, of words to triumph over the most powerful people on earth. I thought if I could dramatize that idea, it would be extraordinary. That's how I came up with the idea of the typewriter at the start of the film. That wasn't stuck on after the film was done. The typewriter—and the sound of typewriters—is a theme through the whole film. You see it right at the end with the teletype machine, which is a relentless sequence. You see how the work of these two men turns into type. Words become a weapon. The sound of the typewriter at the start is like a gunshot.

Another thread through the film is the tedium of the work Woodward and Bernstein did. How do you deal with the passing of time in a film? Extending time and compressing time is one of the essential techniques of directing, but how to give a sense of that without going through some old-fashioned montage of calendar pages floating off or newspapers moving across the screen as days pass? Think of Bob Woodward on the telephone, and think of the shot in the Library of Congress with the camera moving up and up as they work through all the library slips. It demonstrates this concept of little objects, paper index cards, bringing down the most incredibly powerful people. Those pieces of paper are the key to this whole detective story. That shot dramatizes this whole sense of the needle in the haystack. It's about this endless search by these two men who are dwarfed by this huge building. *All the President's Men* is a story about work. The film isn't about these guys' private lives. The details of their personal lives are trivial compared to what they did as reporters. I felt that if there wasn't a relentless rhythm to the film, then it would fall apart. If you stop the story to show some kind of happy romantic life—or an unhappy romantic life—then you'll pop the tension and never get it back. The truth of these people is that at that point in their lives the most important thing was the work.

On the other hand there is one other very different way they obtain information: Deep Throat.

When I first met Bob Woodward I said to him, "My biggest concern is how to blend Deep Throat into the style of the film." Everything in the book rang true to me, but I got to Deep Throat and thought it really was too much of a gift to a movie director. Of course Deep Throat was what everybody remembered about the book. I said to Woodward, "Look, I don't want to know who Deep Throat is," which is a lie, but I knew he wasn't going to tell me, so what are you going to do? I said, "Was he an amalgamation of several people? It's very important for the film, because if it gets out afterwards that there's no Deep Throat, it's going to make the film look ridiculous." He said, "It was definitely one person." I said, "Did you definitely meet in garages at night? Three in the morning? Did you really take all those cabs and do all those things?" He said, "I definitely did those things."

The bottom line is that I trust Bob Woodward. I got to know him fairly well and he's obsessed with truth. There's a lot he won't tell you, but I don't think he lies. I still had trouble with him, though. I went up to his apartment and said, "So where did you put the pot with the flag?" That's how he made contact with Deep Throat when he wanted to talk. He said, "Right on the terrace, right here." I looked around. Now, the terrace at Bob Woodward's apartment at that time faced the back courtyard. It didn't face the street, so unless Deep Throat lived or worked in one of those buildings, he would've had to walk into that courtyard every day to see if the flag was out, which I would think would be fairly foolish of him. But Bob said it was true. I said, "Before we cast that part, if you're not going to tell me who it is—and I don't expect you to—at least give me some hint, so if I cast Golda Meir in the part it won't be so embarrassing." I told him I had cast Hal Holbrook and he said, "Fine."

Bob Redford said to me, "You know, one of the big reasons I wanted you for this film is because you can scare people." I never thought of myself that way. I always make kindly films, I thought, by and large. Then suddenly I did *Klute* and I was perverse and scary. Woodward and Bernstein said they genuinely feared for their lives at one point, and that Deep Throat actually said to Bob, "Your lives are in danger." The whole thing of not speaking inside Bradlee's house and making him go out on the lawn was true. Ben corroborated it. The Deep Throat scenes were also an opportunity to put Bob Redford into vulnerable situations, to conquer that problem of him looking overconfident.

Let me tell you something about Bob Woodward. He's from a very religious town in Illinois called Wheaton. The most famous person to come out of there was Billy Graham. His father remarried a woman who had three children. At Christmas they opened up the toys his stepmother had got them all and Bob knew that the toys she had bought her children were better and more expensive than she had gotten him. He just knew, looking at them. He went to every toy shop and department store in the area and priced all the gifts. He went down to his father's office with a comparative cost list and said, "This is unfair." And his father gave him the money, the difference between what his toy cost and what the other toys cost. Out of that way of looking at the world, Richard Nixon fell.

The newsroom in the film looks very realistic.

The first thing I said to Bob Redford was, "I can't do this film unless I can spend time at *The Washington Post,* because otherwise you're going to get all my childhood memories of all the old newspaper pictures, and Ben Bradlee will sound like Rosalind Russell."

Bob said, "Maybe we can get the *Post* to allow us to shoot in there at night?" This wouldn't have been practical, because there are only four or five hours a day when it was comparatively empty, and by the time you had your lights set up you'd have to be out of there. When we were preparing, the *Post* was very generous in letting me be in the newsroom. Ben Bradlee said, "I'm letting you hang out here because, what the hell, if you're going to make the film anyway, you might as well know what the truth is," which I thought was fairly enlightened on his part. But they were worried about the film. I think they were more worried than Nixon or Colson or anyone else. Bradlee said, "You're going to go on to make other films. Redford will be riding off into the sunset in his next film. But as far as the American public is concerned, I'm going to be stuck for life as being whoever is going to play me in the film." Katharine Graham, whom I admire a great deal, had real concerns that it had all gone too far already. The *Post* had already seemed to take too much glory. I think she felt there was a neurosis that hits any institution that has been so successful, and that it could bog the place down and destroy its future. How many times in a generation is that kind of story going to take place? She just wanted to say, "All right, let's concentrate on the work. Let's get back to reality." Like the rest of us, I think she was also worried that the whole thing would be Hollywoodized and they would look foolish. She was very nervous, and said to me, "You could change the name of the paper." I said, "If that's the case, there's no way we can make the film."

George Jenkins, the production designer, did an incredible job of re-creating things. For example, when you see Hugh Sloan's little room, the floor plan was the floor of Sloan's real apartment. I walked on the set after it had been dressed, and the set dresser had done this very fancy job with the whole thing. I said, "It should be like Grandma's furniture. I want that sense of an Ivy League Virginia squire." I wanted Sloan to sit in a wing chair to capture that sense of remoteness, his sense of dignity. When Woodward and Bernstein leave the house, they're standing in the hallway. I said to George, "Can you get any Federalist wallpaper? Eighteenth-century stuff?" Nobody sees it, but it made me feel terrific.

The *Post* newsroom, which is a ninety-percent-accurate duplicate of the real one, is a world with that ruthless white fluorescent light without shadows, and bright blue and red desks. It's a world where nothing is hidden, a world with truth. Everything there is examined under this merciless glare. This helped represent the basic notions of investigative reporting, the idea of trying to expose the truth, and is a wonderful symbol of that world as compared to people hiding out in Washington. I wanted to talk to Gordy about that, because he isn't known for very bright cinematography. He's actually known for his great dark photography, to the extent where after seeing *The Godfather II,* one critic called him "the Prince of Darkness." When I talked with Gordon about doing the film, I said, "It's important for me that the core of this film is overlit. It's a world without shadows. The lighting is hard and white with that fluorescent lighting." There's a whole concept about light and sunlight in the film. Usually when you do melodramas and detective stories and who murdered whom or who took what money or who stole what, you create these worlds where people live off the underbelly of our society. Their lives are in disarray. They live in dark, dreary places. They are drug addicts or nymphomaniacs or alcoholics, and it's all rather moody. But the world that our detective-reporters walk through in *All the President's Men* is a world of sunlight, where the grass is mown, houses are clean and bright and cheerful and orderly looking. In the midst of all this middle-class bourgeois cleanliness and brightness and cheerfulness, Disneyland happiness, is decay and all these crumbling things. I wanted that counterpoint.

Were there any problems with the fact that everyone in the film is portraying a real person?

Our one obsession was to stay true to the reality of the situation. I would often make notes and tape recordings with Bob and Carl. We spent several days in my hotel room where they just reminisced about what happened in terms of all the personal things they remembered that aren't in the book. When there was any question about a scene, Bob Redford would go to his dressing room and call Bob Woodward, and Dustin would go to his dressing room and call Carl Bernstein. While I had to free Bob Redford to become Bob Woodward, and Dustin Hoffman to become Carl Bernstein, I didn't want them to imitate them. I thought that would be total disaster. Yes, there would have been certain basic constants that Bob and Dustin would have to play to create their characters, but that had to be melded with their own inner lives. At one point Carl Bernstein wanted to come out to the set in Burbank. One of the things that makes Carl a good reporter is that he gets absolutely wide-eyed about new worlds. He found it all fascinating. But I said, "I'd rather you not be around at certain times. I don't care once we're close to being finished, once we're cutting, but I can't have Dustin suddenly look up and see the real Carl Bernstein. We're let's-pretend people. You being there would be very inhibiting."

I had actors who interviewed for *All the President's Men* coming in and saying, "I'm going to give the performance of my life." But I didn't want them to give the performance of their lives when they're playing some- body who worked for the Committee to Re-elect. The key to the story is that none of these people in reality knew it was an important story. They just know that there are a couple of dumb reporters at the door bothering them, making them nervous. They don't know these reporters are going to bring down the president. One of the things that makes the film work is that the audience knows how important this story is long before the characters on screen do, so little things hold them that wouldn't have if they didn't know how important they will turn out to be. I find that audi- ences delight in feeling they know more than the characters on the screen do. Hitchcock uses that a lot. He'll reveal something to the audience that the characters don't know, and then you say, "Wait until that character finds out. If he only knew what I know—oh, boy!" It's the child in you that makes you feel superior, because you know a secret.

Redford produced the film. How was it working with him as an actor?

The minute we got into production and he started acting we started fight- ing like mad, but eventually came out of it good friends. He cared desper- ately about this film, and I think his worry was that it wouldn't work. As far as the character Bob played, the problem was that this is a repressed character. It's the toughest part in the film. The essence of Bob Woodward is how much he cared about the story. He's full of compressed energy that is always there but never really exposed. We had to show how all this was going on inside Bob. I couldn't tell him to externalize it, because if you start externalizing, giving those certain colors, it's all out the window. Basically, the role of Bob Woodward is not the kind of obvious part Red- ford would play. It's not the flash of a smile in *The Sting*. There's nothing to hold on to. Dustin has all the color. I said to Bob, "If you start playing the same kind of surface colors that Bernstein has in real life, there's going to be no contrast between the two of you, and the controlled energy that propels this film to its finale won't be there. You're not going to like me for this, but you've got to concentrate and you've got to think, and the audience has got to be able to see you think and they've got to feel your concentration. This story has to mean as much to the audience as it means to Bob Woodward. It's thankless work, because Dustin is out interviewing people but you're in the office playing with a telephone. You can't even see the character you're playing to. But that's what it's about. That's what this kind of reporting is about." I got obsessed with keeping his energy contained. Bob felt there wasn't even a part there for him to grab on to. Just to make sure I drove him crazy, when he would be walking in a scene I kept saying, "Bob, get your hands out of your pockets." I didn't want him to appear jaunty—and there is a jaunty quality about Bob Redford—because there's something contained about Woodward. There's something about him that always seems ready and mobilized to jump into action. It's held in, reserved, controlled.

There's a scene which I think is stunningly acted, and yet it's not bravura acting. It's a five- or six-minute take, all in one shot, when Bob is making those phone calls about Ken Dahlberg. I wanted to show how one phone call leads to another phone call which leads to another, all nonstop, so I didn't want to cut from a long shot to a medium to a close-up, because it breaks the flow. I wanted a relentless kind of energy. At the same time I didn't want it to be one static thing. I wanted to be able to build the intensity but didn't want it to be so obvious, so what happens is that the camera never stops moving in that shot. It's really imperceptible, but as he makes those phone calls he becomes more and more concentrated, the story builds, the rest of the world wipes out and he just gets bigger and bigger. There's nothing by the end of that scene except him. I tried to give him some freedom, but he was locked in because of the way we were shooting, and because Gordon was using a diopter. A diopter is two lenses ground into one, so there's double focus. In the shot we have Bob on the phone in the foreground and there are things happening in the background on the left-hand side of the screen, people watching television. Both foreground and background are in focus. Bob couldn't put his hand beyond a certain point, less than a foot, because if he did he would go out of focus and kill the shot. Bob was wonderful in that sequence. He was just battered by it. It's one shot where by the end he has aged ten years.

I talked with Gordon at length about all the shots of people locked in at their desks on the telephone. With a moving camera, the kind of audience concentration I wanted to create would have been broken. This is where Hitchcock is the master. He never does anything that isn't germane. His camera doesn't move or cut unless there's a reason. Bob Redford was surprised when I told him that the camera would be in the same place for all the shots of him on the phone. He said, "We're only about fifteen minutes into the film. You want me just to sit there while I make these phone calls? You're going to have inserts of him scratching into his scratchpad, right?" I said, "Yes." He said, "Well, all right, if that's what you feel." I said, "If we start moving the camera now, we'll use up movement we will need later on, when it's important." It's like people using exclamation points. You move the camera now and it won't mean anything when you do need it to mean something. There are very few moves in the first part of that film, so that even something like the camera moving in that close to Bob when he's making the Dahlberg call seems like a big move. At the risk of boring people, I want the audience to know what it means to be locked in that office. They've got to know what that concentration is like, what hard work it is. This really is a story about people working hard. The moves start getting bigger and more manic as the story builds. They start getting more exciting when they start getting faster. The first really big move is when Bernstein finds the girl who knows about Ken Clawson. It was about half the length of the room. We gradually prepare the audience with these moves. Finally we get to the big move in the newsroom, which was designed from the beginning, across the whole diagonal of the newsroom, after Bernstein makes the phone call corroborating the Haldeman story and they run to catch Ben Bradlee in the elevator. The shot represents their manic triumph, but if I'd had moves like that earlier it wouldn't have meant anything.

By the way, the inserts during Bob's phone conversations were of his own doodles. Fortunately Bob once wanted to be an architect and painter, and can draw.

The film ends when they discover that Haldeman was involved, but the book ends with Nixon's resignation. I was wondering how that decision was made.

We stopped about two-thirds of the way through the book. The audience leaves with the third act dangling. Its impact depends, unlike any other film I've ever dealt with, on you knowing how the story is going to end, on you knowing more than the characters know about what's going to happen once the film is over.

Curiously enough, in terms of storytelling, ironically we stop on their biggest defeat, the moment when they are most discredited, this moment when their story seems to have been proven wrong. That was in Bill Gold-man's original screenplay. What was marvelous about this was that even though they're defeated at that moment, when they get back to their type-writers they know that they've been right all along. What worked for the film was the very thing everybody said would make the film uninteresting to audiences and be the reason that nobody would want to see it, which was that everyone knew the ending. The audience is far more aware of how important the story is than the characters on screen, but that worked to our advantage. The film ends with Nixon on television at the height of his power taking his oath and with our men just typing away. But we know how powerful their work is going to be, that this man at the height of his power is going to be destroyed by what's coming from those type-writers. It made the story a lot more interesting for the audience to see how close Woodward and Bernstein came to giving up, how close we came to never having discovered the story. Those narrow escapes became the suspense, the Hitchcock elements of the film: "My God, they almost didn't make it!" We stopped the story at that point because from that point on in the book a lot of other people took over. The ball was in motion. The Senate committee and the television networks and other newspapers became more important. We were trying to tell that part of the story when they were out there alone, the two of them and *The Washington Post* more or less against the world. When I first met with Bob Red-ford, I said, "One of the dangers of you in this film is that you seem so competent to audiences, but in reality these two guys fumbled their way onto the story. They were learning as they went along." It's certainly not "Butch Woodward and Sundance Bernstein," but in its own simple way it is a heroic story.

The characterization of Woodward and Bernstein suggests there was just a touch of blind ambition.

Bob Woodward and Carl Bernstein themselves were quite insistent in encouraging us to get that side in. They were afraid that if they came out as these cornball Warner Bros. World War II heroes, like Errol Flynn, then they would be the laughingstock of all their journalist friends. They were terrified about that.

Can you talk a little bit about how you manage to achieve such a heightened sense of tension in your films?

Supposedly that's the reason Bob hired me for *All the President's Men*. He felt a tension in *Klute* that he hadn't felt when he read the script. He felt there was a strange, threatening quality in some of my work. But I was a little concerned about this, because the terror in *All the President's Men* is kind of unknown. I said to him, "It builds and builds, but it mustn't get too specific." I had a very difficult problem in characterizing the antagonists because, of course, you don't see them. We do see Nixon three times in the film but only on television, something that for me actually made him even more unreachable. There's something about not seeing a character in person but only seeing him secondhand in the media which makes him above you, beyond you, untouchable.

The other way the heavies of the story are characterized is through buildings. One visual theme is Washington itself. I wanted those huge stone monolithic buildings to look fascist. I wanted to start out with pretty, picture-postcard views of Washington, like ancient neo-Greece temples with cherry blossoms. It's all on a human scale, bright and peaceful and romantic and shiny and open. They make you feel good and human and proud to be American. Then as the film goes on, the buildings start to get bigger and grayer, and the people get smaller. The buildings suddenly start to become threatening. They represent the hidden power. You become more and more aware of the power behind those stone walls and closed doors.

Those picture postcards have long since died. There's a sense at the end of the film that suggests something like this could happen again, that a certain kind of watchfulness and vigilance is always going to be required. It's a continuing possibility. The books are never closed on those threats to our system, or to ourselves.

Films as Director

1969 *The Sterile Cuckoo* (also producer)	1979 *Starting Over* (also producer)
1971 *Klute* (also producer)	1981 *Rollover*
1973 *Love and Pain and the Whole Damn Thing* (also producer)	1982 *Sophie's Choice* (also producer and screenplay)
1974 *The Parallax View* (also producer)	1986 *Dream Lover* (also producer)
	1987 *Orphans* (also producer)
1976 *All the President's Men*	1989 *See You in the Morning* (also
1978 *Comes a Horseman*	producer and screenplay)

1990 *Presumed Innocent* (also
    screenplay)
1992 *Consenting Adults* (also
    producer)

1993 *The Pelican Brief* (also producer
    and screenplay)
1997 *The Devil's Own*

Pakula produced films he did not direct including *Fear Strikes Out*, 1957; *To Kill a Mockingbird*, 1962; *Love With a Proper Stranger*, 1963; *Baby the Rain Must Fall*, 1965; *Inside Daisy Clover*, 1965; *Up the Down Staircase*, 1967; and *The Stalking Moon*, 1968.

Someone once said the actor is the salesman of the story. Another said he's the director's ambassador. If you want to get the best out of your actors, let them know that you like them and trust them personally as men and women—that you're not merely a technician, using them as you would use a camera or the scenery.

GREGORY PECK
(Born in La Jolla, California, 1916—Died 2003)

Gregory Peck came to meet with the fellows on the eve of receiving the AFI Life Achievement Award in 1989. It was a homecoming of sorts, because he had been the first chairman of AFI's board when the Institute was founded. I have a fond memory of sitting with Greg in my Georgetown garden on a Sunday afternoon in 1967 writing the description and goals of the new organization that we would announce at a press conference in Washington the following day.

By then Greg was one of the most respected figures in motion pictures, and his stature contributed to the credibility of the fledgling AFI. Born Eldred Gregory Peck, he was raised in La Jolla on the California coast and attended St. John's Military Academy in Los Angeles before going to the University of California at Berkeley, where courses in theater lured him away from his premedical studies. He discarded "Eldred" and headed for New York as Gregory Peck. At the Neighborhood Playhouse Sanford Meisner became a mentor and helped him with small parts on Broadway until Hollywood called. His first role was in an undistinguished film called *Days of Glory*, in which he played a Russian partisan in World War II. When Peck became an advocate of the importance of preserving films at AFI, he noted that it would be fine with him if they didn't bother with *Days of Glory*.

His next performance, as a Scottish missionary in *The Keys to the Kingdom*, brought him his first Oscar nomination for Best Actor, and soon he was sought by leading directors, including Alfred Hitchcock for *Spellbound*, King Vidor for *Duel in the Sun* and Elia Kazan for *Gentleman's Agreement*. He climbed to the top of the ladder of leading men, playing the commanding officer of a bombing squadron in *Twelve O'Clock High*, the gunslinger Johnny Ringo in *The Gunfighter*, the reporter who falls in love with Audrey Hepburn

Atticus Finch was Gregory Peck's favorite role. Mary Badham played
his daughter, Scout, in *To Kill a Mockingbird* (1962).

in *Roman Holiday* and the conflicted public-relations executive in *The Man
in the Gray Flannel Suit.*

Peck took an interest in producing and developed a partnership with John
Huston for the making of *Moby Dick,* but the picture encountered difficulties
during production, and Peck was disappointed with his performance, once
saying that he was not "mad enough, not crazy enough, not obsessive
enough" in his portrayal of Melville's Captain Ahab.

To Kill a Mockingbird, the adaptation of Harper Lee's novel, was the film
closest to his heart. He received his fifth Best Actor nomination and was
awarded the Oscar for his performance as Atticus Finch in the film, which
was produced by Alan Pakula and directed by Robert Mulligan. Peck's capac-

ity to express dignity, honesty and decency gave dimension to the role; he captured the spirit of the lawyer in a small town that reminded him of his own youth.

In 1963, when I was running the motion-picture division of the United States Information Agency under Edward R. Murrow, I asked Greg to narrate two films after the assassination of President Kennedy. The first was called *The President,* a short film produced to introduce Lyndon Johnson to the world, and the second was the feature-length *John F. Kennedy: Years of Lightning, Day of Drums. The President* led to a friendship with Johnson, who appointed Peck one of the founding members of the National Council on the Arts in 1965. My father was also appointed, and the two of them became the members concerned with how the new National Endowment for the Arts would address film. My father believed that the true measure of a motion picture was the way it would be regarded in the future—it was from him that I learned to believe in the test of time. It would not be long before the National Endowment provided funding to establish the American Film Institute, to preserve the important films of the past and educate the filmmakers of the future, with Gregory Peck as its chairman and me as its founding director.

Peck went on to be president of the Academy of Motion Picture Arts and Sciences. The Academy honored him with its Jean Hersholt Humanitarian Award, and Johnson presented him the Presidential Medal of Freedom in 1969, calling him "a humanitarian to whom Americans are deeply indebted."

Greg was consistent in encouraging the motion-picture industry to raise its sights and recognize the responsibility that went with the opportunity to make films. In accepting AFI's Life Achievement Award before an audience filled with Hollywood leaders, he referred to the heads of Hollywood studios, saying, "I would like to suggest that they stop and think about this: making millions is not the whole ball game, fellows. Pride of workmanship is worth more. Artistry is worth more."

GREGORY PECK

———✦———

March 6, 1989*

Gregory Peck is being honored by the American Film Institute with its seventeenth Life Achievement Award. The award is presented to an individual whose work has stood the test of time. Greg Peck's films do indeed stand that test. His contribution to the world around him goes beyond his work. As the founding chairman of the American Film Institute he spoke of the urgent need to save America's film heritage and expressed concern over the excessive commercialism that has become so identified with American film. He also called for the creation of an advanced study center where young filmmakers could master their craft. That would be you, sitting here today. Does someone want to start?

I can start. You've just seen *To Kill a Mockingbird.* We went down to Alabama to the hometown of the author, Harper Lee, to see if we couldn't shoot the film there. But the story took place in 1931, and by 1962 the town had just changed too much, with television aerials and paved streets, so we reconstructed it on the Universal backlot. Harper won the Pulitzer Prize for this autobiographical novel. She was Scout and I played Scout's father. She came to the set on the first day of shooting and watched the scene when Atticus comes home from the courthouse. It was usual for the kids to run down to the corner and walk down the street talking with their father until they got home. As we were doing that little scene, I glanced across the street and behind the camera saw Harper. Her cheeks were glistening and I thought, "Wow. We're just tearing her up. We're breaking her heart." Bob Mulligan, the director, did it in one take. Afterwards I walked over to Harper and said, "I think I saw some tears on your

*George Stevens, Jr., moderated this siminar.

cheeks when we were playing that scene." She said, "Oh, Gregory, you've got a little pot belly just like my daddy." So we got off to a good start.

Could you talk about how the screen character of Atticus Finch evolved.

It seemed to fall into place very easily. Bob Mulligan and Alan Pakula sent me the novel, and I sat up one night and read it. I called them the next morning and said, "If you want me, I'll be there." They developed a screenplay, and brought me in from time to time as a kind of consultant. The character was one I understood from the moment I read the book. I had a small-town upbringing. I was a kid who climbed trees and rode around curled up in a rubber tire. My father wasn't the town lawyer, but he was the town druggist, so it all fell into place. It was like swimming downstream the whole time. It was a kind of gift, beginning with Harper Lee and with Mulligan and Pakula. I've had more plaques and statues and certificates for that one than from any other picture, but looking back on it I think it was the easiest picture to make of any I can recall. We identified emotionally with everything that happened—with the family life, with the father and children, with the problem of defending the black man who was falsely accused. Our emotions were involved, and we played on these emotions. The only difficult thing was to keep them under control. Brock Peters, the actor playing the man falsely accused and found guilty, was telling his side of the story. He was overcome with very genuine, deep feelings, and he wept. He didn't lose control, but the tears were genuine. I stood on the floor questioning him as his defense lawyer, asking, "What happened next? What did she do?" Brock's face was streaming with tears and I couldn't look at him because I began to choke up. I thought, "This would be a helluva thing if the lawyer and the accused man are both up there weeping." We seemed to be on a track, and as long as we stayed on that track and played on our feelings, we really couldn't go wrong. Once in a while that happens, and when it happens the acting is easy.

Can you comment on the value of rehearsal?

People work in different ways. I've watched Cary Grant stand offstage on the set with the camera going and Bob Mitchum and Deborah Kerr already performing in front of the camera. He'd look at the last few pages of a script, put it down and walk on in the middle of the scene and be Cary Grant. I enjoy preparation and study. What counts really is the final result and what's up on the screen. I like as much rehearsal as I can get, and it seems that the directors I felt most comfortable with, and with whom I've been able to do my best work, do too. It can be two or three hours or half a day or twenty minutes, depending on what's needed to get the key to unlock the scene. I certainly want enough time so I feel I have a grip on it. William Wyler would rehearse for an indefinite period of time until he felt the scene was ready. Others work more quickly. Jack Benny once said his best ad libs were the ones he'd rehearsed the most.

Could you talk about the qualities of the directors who help you do your best work?

Mulligan's a perfect example. He's what actors call an actor's director. He has a very special understanding of what the actor has to go through to get to the center of a character and deliver a truthful, sensitive performance. He started in college theatricals and moved on to television and finally film. What actors appreciate is having a friend they can trust sitting right

Robert Mulligan (right) chose the Universal backlot
for *To Kill a Mockingbird,* after failing to find
suitable locations in Alabama.

there by the camera. You really play only to him. It's not true that you play to the electricians and the grip and the dozens of crew members standing around. They have their own jobs. You're playing to the director. You're going to do your best if he likes you and you like him and there's a genuine rapport and friendship. If there is abrasiveness or friction between the two personalities, you're not going to quite trust yourself to go all-out and play on your feelings. That's what directors who get the most from the actors contribute. If the director has provided me a comfortable, warm atmosphere and he takes what I bring in and adjusts it, or does whatever he wants with it, then we're home free. After all, the actor's there to tell the story. Someone once said the actor is the salesman of the story. Another said he's the director's ambassador. If you want to get the best out of your actors, let them know that you like them and trust them personally as men and women, that you're not merely a technician using them as you would a camera or the scenery.

You've spoken about your early days living in New York and spending nights sleeping in Central Park. Did you consider giving up and going home and getting a real job?

Sure. I thought about it all the time. When it wasn't on my mind, my father was writing to me reminding me that I was off on a fool's errand and that I should go to medical school or law school. At one time I thought of going on to take a master's and a Ph.D. and becoming an English professor. All those things seemed eminently more respectable to my dad, and to offer more promise of a future for his son than what I did, which was to run off to New York as soon as I got out of school and arrive there knowing no one. But to me it was an exciting adventure. I think I had $195 when I arrived. I found a six-dollars-a-week room and a job at the 1939 World's Fair. Then I got a job guiding tourists in Rockefeller Center and was awarded a scholarship at the Neighborhood Playhouse by Rita Morgenthau and Irene Lewisohn, two great New York ladies. My teachers were Sanford Meisner and Martha Graham. Sometimes I would go up to these wonderful ladies and hit them for a ten or twenty. Someone had given me a Ronson black enamel cigarette case with the lighter built in. At the corner of Forty-sixth Street and Sixth Avenue there was a hock shop. I guess I pawned that case twenty times. When he saw me walking in he'd get out the six dollars and I'd hand it over, and he'd give me the six dollars and I'd sign and take the pawn ticket, and later I'd come back and get it. But it was all an adventure. You could go to the automat and get spaghetti for a nickel and broccoli for a nickel, sweet potatoes for a nickel, and an orange drink. You could get a whole meal for twenty cents. It's true that I slept in Central Park, but those were, relatively speaking, crime-free days. A lot of people were sleeping in Central Park in the good weather. I put my stuff in a locker at Grand Central until I could afford another rented room. Gradually my living standards went up, and I had a terrific room for twelve dollars. But everybody I knew was short of money. Life was great down in the Village. It was at the end of the Depression during the FDR days, there was a lot of idealism around, a lot of liberal politics being discussed, and most young people I knew believed in the New Deal and social programs and a better society. So life was good.

Why didn't you ever try directing?

I never had any ambition to do it. Probably something in my makeup. I don't know that I particularly care to analyze it. I just never wanted that job. I've enjoyed being behind the scenes, producing several times. I enjoyed the preparation of the script, the casting, giving the director all

Peck as Captain Ahab in John Huston's production
of Melville's *Moby Dick* (1956).

the help I could give him, taking part in the editing and then in the marketing. It may come as a surprise to you, but not everyone wants to be a director.

There was a tremendous amount of talent on Moby Dick, *from the original book to the screenplay by Ray Bradbury and John Huston. Do you feel that the film was as good as it could have been?*

I've always felt it fell short of being a classic for a variety of reasons. It had been made twice before and I think ours was the best of the three, but it's a most difficult book to translate into film. Certainly everybody set out to make a great film, but there were a lot of physical hazards and a lot went wrong. We shot for twelve weeks in the Irish Sea between Wales and Ireland, scenes that were supposed to be in the South Seas, with the rubber whale. Sometimes we went for days without turning a camera because the weather was blustery, cold and rainy. We obviously were in the wrong part of the world. But at that time John was in love with Ireland and was riding to the hounds and wearing his red coat and everything was Irish, so he decided to shoot it there. A real mistake. I wouldn't think we got more than fifteen minutes of usable film during those twelve weeks on the Irish Sea. We eventually went down to the Canary Islands off the coast of Morocco. At the end a lot had to be done in the studio, where tons and tons of water were dumped, mostly on me, from tanks that were attached to beams overhead. There were times when the whale looked very much like a rubber whale. Special effects have certainly improved a great deal since then. So it was a star-crossed production with a lot of unforeseen mishaps. We were supposed to have finished in fourteen weeks, but it took twenty-seven. It went over budget to a fantastic degree. Warner Bros. was extremely worried. Maybe somebody else will make a fourth *Moby Dick* and pull it off, and we'll have the film classic that the novel deserves.

What made Melville's novel so difficult to adapt?

The book has scores of pages of his philosophy. Melville digresses at great length into the science, technique and business of whaling. You could make a documentary of whaling in the nineteenth century out of just a couple of chapters. But in films we have the obligation to present a story. I suspect one of the tried-and-true formulas is that your central character must face a series of crises, and eventually one great climax from which he emerges radically changed, usually for the better. You get your principal character up in a tree in the first act, you shake the tree in the second act, and in the third act you get him down. This is linear storytelling. I don't say it's the only way to make films, and some of my favorite films have not been linear, but we didn't seem to find that in *Moby Dick*. John and Ray Bradbury were fond of what you might call Melville's malevolent philosophy, that if there is a God he is a malevolent God. He is a God who will allow suffering, agony, disease, war and pestilence. Is he toying with us? Where are we in relation to whatever kind of God there is? Melville seemed to come to the conclusion that God wasn't a very nice person, and the whale, as I see it, became the symbol of that malevolent God. He proceeded to declare to the death that he wasn't really a pawn in the cosmic game.

You played Horatio Hornblower, one of my all-time favorite fictional characters.

That was great fun because of Raoul Walsh, and if you remember, George, I brought Raoul to the AFI about twelve years ago. One of the saltiest, funniest, toughest old men I ever met. His type hardly exists anymore. He was really a nineteenth-century kind of fellow. Crusty, a curmudgeon, very funny, ribald, death on the ladies in his younger days, and he had a great gusto for making films. What he made best were adventure films that always had an edge of comedy. I made a picture for him with Tony Quinn called *The World in His Arms*. I watched it recently and saw the hand of Raoul Walsh in every scene. It moved. It had vitality. It was fun. The story was a little hackneyed—not a landmark in the art of the cinema, but it had Raoul Walsh written all over it. He didn't have much patience for long speeches and didn't really listen to them very carefully. He had only one eye and sometimes seemed to be reading a newspaper while you were playing the scene. Then he would say, "All right, print." You'd say, "But Raoul, I forgot a line," or "I garbled a word or two," and he'd say, "Did you, kid—what was that?" If he thought it didn't matter, that the audience's attention would be somewhere else, he'd say, "Kid, it's fine. Let's go. Let's keep moving." He had directed and been an actor in the silents. When I brought him to AFI he just killed. He was so amusing and so knowledgeable. I don't think any of the students had met a man like that. I remember one young fellow said, "Mr. Walsh, we understand that you were an actor before you were a director." "Well, my boy," he said, "I played John Wilkes Booth, the man who shot Lincoln, in *The Birth of a Nation*." They stood up and applauded on that.

Peck, Ingrid Bergman and Alfred Hitchcock on the set of *Spellbound* (1945).

What was Alfred Hitchcock like as a director?

He was a fascinating man to work with. His preparation was legendary. You sensed that he could roll the entire film in his head while you were working. He knew long before you came on the set—maybe even before you were cast in the part—where he wanted you to be standing at a given moment and when he wanted you to move and what expression he wanted to see on your face. Of course, this has its advantages and disadvantages. I think Cary Grant had a kind of facility that made him the perfect Hitchcock actor. What Hitchcock did was to play tricks on the audience. It was a clever kind of con game he and the audience were playing together. His stories were designed to entertain and keep you in suspense. I came from the Sanford Meisner school of acting and the Method, and I don't think Hitchcock had too much patience for that. It took me time to arrive at the exterior that he had visualized, and sometimes he would say, "Now at this moment, Greg, let your face drain of all expression." Well, I didn't quite know how to handle that. I didn't have the technical facility to give him exactly what he wanted in the externals, and though we were friends for years I don't feel I was the perfect Hitchcock actor. I wish I'd been able to work with him twenty years later when I had more self-confidence, more poise and more facility. But I value the experience of knowing him. I learned from him.

Ever since you made Gentleman's Agreement, *I know you've been supportive of Jewish causes. How did it feel to put on Josef Mengele's clothes when you played him in* The Boys from Brazil?

I thought I was helping to make a very powerful case against that kind of a man, that kind of a political philosophy, that kind of inhuman era in history, by playing, so to speak, the devil's advocate instead of the good guy. I was just wearing the other hat. How did I feel playing him? Well, I really couldn't identify with him very closely. I could find very little in my past experience that was useful in playing Mengele, so what I did was use technique. I put on a miserable little mustache that seemed to grow right up my nose. I shaved my hairline and dyed my hair black. I studied the German accent. It was all those externals that I used to try to make that character believable and acceptable. It was certainly a stretch for me. Pauline Kael didn't think much of it. But, on the other hand, Laurence Olivier liked it.

Did you debate whether to try and humanize him in some way?

Peck evaluates his makeup for the role of SS
officer Josef Mengele in *The Boys from Brazil* (1978).

I did humanize him in two scenes. There was a ballroom scene with the Nazi head honcho in Uruguay where I spotted a girl, and I played it so I became subtly obsessed with this girl's bosom. I whipped her off to dance. But the director Frank Schaffner cut it out of the picture. He didn't want me to have that little quirk. There was another time, near the end, when I came to the Pennsylvania farmhouse where one of my little cloned Hitlers lived. Left alone, I looked at a photo album with all these pictures of this child whom I regarded as my own, because I had cloned him from a bit of tissue from Hitler's arm. I allowed my character to get a little soft and loving while flipping the pages of the album. I loved it, but Schaffner cut that out, too, so we had a character who was evil and nasty from start to finish.

Another character who didn't have a lot of appeal as a personality was General MacArthur, yet you made him into an interesting character with a wonderful humanity.

After my research and reading and viewing of thousands and thousands of feet of film of MacArthur, I concluded that he wasn't a monomaniac, that he didn't have a strong desire to be the president of the United States, and that his military records in World War I, World War II and in the administration of Japan were great ones. His fault in the conduct of the Korean War was that of overweening pride and hubris. He tried to override President Truman concerning the taking of the north of Korea. MacArthur was convinced he could do it, that it would be good for the free world. He was convinced that Truman was being overly influenced by the liberals and the British, and he went too far. He spoke out over the president's head to his friends in Congress and to the press. I never questioned that Truman was right to fire him, but if you study MacArthur you find that ninety percent of the man was a true patriot and a genuine American hero. Unfortunately his imperiousness and his mannerisms annoyed people. His downfall was great pride in his knowledge of the military and the Far East, and his capacity for leadership. I ended up liking the man, but not without recognizing that his overwhelming self-confidence and belief in his own abilities eventually brought about his downfall. Those were the feet of clay on General MacArthur.

Do you find yourself affected by the roles you play?

I think you're affected while you're doing it, as I described in *Mockingbird.* The purpose is for the audience to feel those emotions. They're the ones you want to cry, to laugh, to get a lump in the throat, to be in suspense about how this is all going to turn out. You and the director are serving it up to them. It's good if you get your feelings involved so long as you're in control. The head has to control the heart.

Could you comment on the relationship between film acting and stage acting?

I think it's a wonderful idea to go back and forth, and I wish I had done more of that after I came out here. It just didn't seem to be the fashion in those days. You were either a picture actor or a stage actor, though today some of the best actors are doing both. The direct communication between someone on the stage and hundreds of people sitting out front is a wonderful thing, and at its best is an experience that can't be duplicated in a film theater. It has an immediacy. You're sharing an experience, going from A to B to C together. The actor and the audience are partners. It gives the actor poise, authority and command, because if you're not in command up on the stage, not many minutes go by before they begin to sneeze and cough and rustle in their seats, at which point you've got to get them back. You have to reach out and get their attention. It's a challenge that strengthens the actor, so I think the best kind of career is one where the actor doesn't stay away from the stage for too long.

How different is it making pictures today than earlier in your career?

When I came out here and started working I just went from one film to another, and made about three a year. I knew a couple of films ahead of time what I'd be doing. There were five thousand people working on the lot, and you'd see people in the commissary in cowboy costumes and cho-rus girls and monsters—people working on five or six different feature films. It was a factory. Fox was turning out a feature film every week. Hol-lywood must have been turning out close to four hundred films a year. What is it today? About a quarter of that. The economics have changed. I made a couple of very big films early in my career. *Duel in the Sun* cost something like $4 million. They spend that today on the appetizer. A film I made recently is of a comparable size and scope in the number of people involved, in the locations, in the stunts and the spectacle, and it cost $28 million. As a result studios are much more careful about deciding to make a picture. A picture like that is a big gamble for those executives who are going to be held responsible by the big boys upstairs, looking at the sheet at the end of the year and saying, "This isn't good enough. We'll get another fellow." So they're more cautious, and imitate each other more. They climb on somebody else's bandwagon more readily. And coupled to the rising costs of production is the change in the number of people going to the cinemas. I think it was eighty million people a week before television caught on. I would guess today it's about fifteen million a week. They're staying home for most of their entertainment. We had people like Darryl Zanuck and Jack Warner and Harry Cohn and L. B. Mayer who ran their own shop, who decided what books to buy, what plays to buy, what originals to commission. They had directors and cinematographers and art directors and actors under contract. They pushed a series of buttons and you had a team and a starting date. It was a whole different way of working.

Willy Wyler made about seventy pictures. He had a lot of batting practice rather than waiting two or three years to get the pieces together to make the next one.

He even made some two-reel westerns when he was a young man in the 1920s. I'm sure all you young directors would like to know that the fellows who directed silents, who lasted through the years, had a special gift for telling the story with the camera and minimizing the need for excessive talk. You asked about Wyler. Henry King was another. Raoul Walsh was another. There was a great fellow named Henry Hathaway who had been a prop man and later became a director of silents. We called him Terrible-Tempered Henry. He was just death on wheels on the set. He yelled and screamed and foamed at the mouth and chewed cigars all day long. He cursed and turned the air blue. But there was something about his knowledge of how to tell a story with pictures that made his films work, including *True Grit.* His use of the camera, his sense of where people ought to move, where they should stand, his visual sense, his kinetic sense—everything just worked. Everything dovetailed. I was lucky to work with a number of those fellows who had their training in silent films. You learn a lot from them.

Making *Roman Holiday* with Wyler was the six most joyous months I can remember making films. He was an actor's dream. He always knew when it was right and would never accept anything but your best. That's a great comfort when you're out in front of the camera. I never tired of his endless takes. Never got bored with it. Never felt put upon, not once. I had done a scene in a very early picture, *The Yearling,* a three-page scene with Jane Wyman, the little boy and a young deer. Seventy-two takes over

Peck and Audrey Hepburn relax on the set of *Roman Holiday* (1953). Peck's contract called for solo star billing, but during the production he urged William Wyler to provide newcomer Hepburn equal billing above the title. She won the Oscar for Best Actress.

a period of almost three days. We got it toward the end of the third day. Clarence Brown, who had directed most of Garbo's pictures, was the director. He was stubborn. He had been an engineer and wanted the scene in a master take. The problem was we had slow Technicolor film and a lot of brutal lights. It was 120 degrees in there and the deer didn't want any part of that. While we were talking about playing the scene the deer would trot off to the cooler shadows. We'd be maybe a page into it and we'd hear clop, clop, clop. Clarence would say, "Do it again." We had to be good seventy-two times. Everything depended on whether or not the deer would stay in there and let us talk about him.

So when it came to Wyler it was easy. Thirty takes was a breeze. The one experience I recall, which says a lot about why he shot so many takes, was a scene in *The Big Country*. Charlie Bickford is showing me his vast cattle spread in a shot that had two and a half pages of talk. We did it over and over and over again. Wyler scratched his head and didn't say anything other than "Let's do it again." Now, Bickford was a solid character performer. Once he had a performance in hand he would do it exactly the same every time. You couldn't detect any variation, and it became obvious to me after about ten takes that Willy was looking for some variation. When it got up to fifteen, eighteen, twenty, Bickford—who was a hot-headed, red-haired Irishman, and pretty good bottle man on top of it—began to steam. He got red as a lobster and said to me, "What the hell does the guy want?" I said, "Just keep doing it, Charlie, he'll know when it's right." He got hotter and hotter under the collar, and after twenty-seven takes he blew sky high. He turned the air purple for miles around and said, "What the goddamn hell do you want me to do with it, Willy?" And Willy said, very calmly, "Well, I want you to do it better, Charlie." So Charlie stomped off the set and went to his dressing room. Willy sat very calmly by the camera, and after a while said to the assistant director, "When's Charlie coming back?" The assistant said, "Well, Mr. Wyler, I don't think he's coming back. He's in his trailer and all hell is breaking loose in there. I looked through the door and I think he's downing a bot-tle of Jack Daniel's." Willy said, "Well, you go and tell him we haven't got-ten the scene yet and if he doesn't come out soon we'll call his agent and the Screen Actors Guild and see what can be done about this." Eventually, Charlie did come back and we did it about five more times exactly the same. Willy finally said, "All right, that's it." The script clerk had nota-tions on every take, and Willy said, "Let's print 27, 24, 21, 18, 12, 9. And there's something good in 6." He printed nine takes and used bits of all nine to get pretty close to what he wanted, although I don't think he was ever really completely satisfied. That was Willy Wyler. Bickford didn't take to it, but I always liked it. I liked the idea of trying to reach further and further, and maybe hooking that golden ring—getting it as good as you can before driving home that night—feeling like you did a good day's work.

Can you characterize what makes a good script or a good role?

When you're given a good script, it's like the apple fell out of the tree and hit you on the head. All you have to do is live up to it. This becomes the challenge for you and your director, to give a hundred percent to what the writers have given us. It doesn't happen all that often. Most often there's work to be done. There are sequences that don't move forward. The writ-ing is discursive or beside the point. As time went on I formed my own company, produced some pictures and most of the time was accepted as a kind of an associate collaborator with the director and the producer. Usu-ally I would turn in memos suggesting how I thought the script could be improved. Sometimes they were accepted and sometimes not, but I had the privilege of having my say. What it comes down to is we all stand or fall on what's on the page. I've worked with very great directors, and when the script was flawed there wasn't too much they could do about it.

You've talked about seeing films on cable and cassette, and I was wondering how you felt about that in terms of film history.

The fact that people are able to see films from ten, twenty, thirty years ago more readily has to be good. Many of them are still fresh and extremely watchable and entertaining, and they provide a look back at what we were doing then, what we were like as a people, what made us laugh and what touched us. The studios were the last to realize the value of their film libraries. Now that they know there's money in it they're all out for film preservation, but before that it was left to the AFI, Eastman House and the Library of Congress.

Do you feel that you've had to change your acting technique with the years?

The greatest virtue of film is that the camera can peer into your mind. The art of film acting is really the art of conveying your thoughts and feelings with a minimum of demonstration. It takes enormous concentration, but if you get it, then you have what appears to be totally realistic behavior on the screen, people living the roles. Nowadays the masters of the art of acting, like De Niro and Pacino and Richard Dreyfuss and Bill Hurt, all act in a realistic manner that I admire very much. They all do a variation on the Stanislavsky method by finding the inner truth and hooking on to that. Sanford Meisner put it this way: the emotions are the river that's going downstream. The actor is the canoe that rides the stream. If the stream is calm, the canoe floats calmly on the surface. If the stream is turbulent, the canoe is tossed about and may even turn over and sink.

Are there any films of the past few years that you feel have the same qualities of great films like To Kill a Mockingbird?

The Killing Fields and *Chariots of Fire,* two of David Puttnam's films. I took away something of value from them. And I like some of the comedies that have been made recently. I liked *Midnight Run* with De Niro and Charles Grodin. I loved watching *Lawrence of Arabia* again—it's great, great filmmaking. These days I want to see comedies more than drama. I tend to shun too much mayhem and bloodshed. I don't like to see people blown to bits with automatic rifles and bazookas. I don't like to see gasoline trucks go up in flames when I know people are inside. The kind of red meat that a lot of young directors, or for that matter middle-aged directors, toss to the audience offends me.

Are there any special roles from the stage or history you'd like to play?

I wish I could give you a nice answer that could strike a chord, but it's just great writing that I long for. If I do any more pictures, which I may not, it will be because the writing is superb. I'm at the time of life where I don't want to work unless there's a chance of making a picture that will stand what George Stevens referred to at the beginning of this seminar as the test of time.

———◆———

Films as Actor

1944 *Days of Glory*	1956 *The Man in the Gray Flannel*
The Keys of the Kingdom	*Suit*
1945 *The Valley of Decision*	*Moby Dick*
Spellbound	1957 *Designing Woman*
1946 *The Yearling*	1958 *The Bravados*
Duel in the Sun	*The Big Country* (also
1947 *The Macomber Affair*	producer)
Gentleman's Agreement	1959 *Pork Chop Hill*
The Paradine Case	*Beloved Infidel*
1948 *Yellow Sky*	*On the Beach*
1949 *The Great Sinner*	1961 *The Guns of Navarone*
Twelve O'Clock High	1962 *Cape Fear*
1950 *The Gunfighter*	*How the West Was Won*
1951 *Captain Horatio Hornblower*	*To Kill a Mockingbird*
R.N.	1963 *Captain Newman, M.D.*
Only the Valiant	1964 *Behold a Pale Horse*
David and Bathsheba	1965 *Mirage*
1952 *The World in His Arms*	1966 *Arabesque*
The Snows of Kilimanjaro	1968 *The Stalking Moon*
1953 *Roman Holiday*	1969 *Mackenna's Gold*
1954 *Man with a Million*	*The Chairman*
Night People	*Marooned*
The Purple Plain	1970 *I Walk the Line*

1971 *Shoot Out*
1974 *Billy Two Hats*
1976 *The Omen*
1977 *MacArthur*
1978 *The Boys from Brazil*
1980 *The Sea Wolves*
1982 *The Blue and the Gray*
    (television)
1983 *The Scarlet and the Black*
    (television)

1987 *Amazing Grace and Chuck*
1989 *Old Gringo*
1991 *Other People's Money*
    Cape Fear
1993 *The Portrait* (television—also
    executive producer)
1998 *Moby Dick* (television)

You have to give the audience more than they expect, something of such kinetic explosiveness that they say, "I can't really be seeing that. This is an unfamiliar image to me, and I can't stand it."

ARTHUR PENN
(Born in Philadelphia, Pennsylvania, 1922—Died 2010)

Arthur Penn made his mark as a director in three spheres: theater, motion pictures and television. In 1953, at the dawn of live broadcasts from New York, he directed two dramas by Horton Foote, *The Death of the Old Man* and *The Tears of My Sister,* the latter starring Kim Stanley. He was soon at the center of television's Golden Age, directing for *The Philco Television Playhouse* and *Playhouse 90,* and his storytelling skills opened doors for him on Broadway and in Hollywood.

Penn had five consecutive hits on the New York stage between 1958 and 1960: *Two for the Seesaw, The Miracle Worker, Toys in the Attic, An Evening with Mike Nichols and Elaine May* and *All the Way Home.* His first film, *The Left Handed Gun* with Paul Newman in 1958, was not well received, and he learned the discouraging lesson that studio executives would not hesitate to reshape the final result of a film against the director's wishes. But he scored with *The Miracle Worker* in 1962, which won Oscars for Anne Bancroft and Patty Duke, and garnered him a nomination for Best Director.

Penn saw himself in the mold of Elia Kazan, a theater director who brought his skill with actors to Hollywood and mastered the new medium. Penn had a special ability to dramatize emotional moments, and his films in the sixties ranged from bold experiments like *Mickey One* to *Bonnie and Clyde,* a triumph that connected with the antiestablishment sentiments of young audiences and changed the way Hollywood looked at movies. Paul Schrader credits Penn with paving the way for the new generation of American directors who came out of film schools.

Penn's career was marked by a continuing struggle between his storytelling instincts and the power of the studios, resulting in just fourteen films

Arthur Penn's success as a director ranged through
television, theater and motion pictures.

over a forty-year span, including *The Chase, Alice's Restaurant, Little Big Man,
Night Moves* and *The Missouri Breaks.* The struggle to gain sufficient control
to make films that match one's own standards is something many ambitious
directors have faced, and it was especially difficult for Penn, a man of considerable dignity. "I was out of fashion," he said in an interview. "My time was
over, unless I was willing to live out in Hollywood and keep trying to generate projects and keep trying to stay in the public eye. None of which I was
willing to do."

So he continued to live in New York, and took it upon himself to revital-
ize the Actors Studio, while still working in television and making the occasional film. His legacy includes a host of memorable films and a strong
connection to his audience. As Tom Luddy and David Thomson wrote,
"Time and again, Arthur Penn told a gripping story and let us know that the
movies were a way of uncovering our deepest feelings about our world."

In 2006, when the Directors Guild honored Penn, he admitted that he
wished he had been bolder during his career. "Too often I censored myself."
He concluded his remarks with a plea to his fellow directors: "Let us see your
human secret. It's your gold: share it."

ARTHUR PENN

January 30, 1970*

Most of the industry spokesmen who have come to speak here have been very encouraging in principle but rather discouraging in fact. They assure us that the industry is changing, but what they really mean is that the market is changing and different kinds of films need to be produced. But there hasn't been much they can point to that might be seen as an opening for young filmmakers.

I think that's absolutely accurate. Anybody who characterizes making motion pictures as an industry is the kind of person who'll suggest that you undertake some apprenticeship to the point where the powers that be develop sufficient confidence in your submissiveness and willingness to be a part of the structure. At that point they'll finally take a chance and put some money down on your head. I think the audiences that go to films today frighten the studios considerably. What they want is that you bring your youth—your membership in that mystical generation—to the job. But don't bring so much that you invade their sensibilities. This is essentially the line you'll constantly be confronted with—one of individual conscience—that all of us face in varying degrees.

The question is, how much of the so-called film industry is, to borrow a phrase, genuinely the only game in town? Does one definitely have to work within the system? Is the establishment the only way to go? My sense is that increasingly it's not the way to go. Without copping a plea, before this moment there really was no other way. For want of individual boldness on the part of the guys who made the films, and because making

*Jim Silke moderated this seminar. This transcript also contains segments from a seminar Arthur Penn gave at the American Film Institute on October 7, 1970.

films is so expensive, one found oneself necessarily going to the studios. This has been the state of play up to now. But it would be my warmest contention that each of us—me included—would do well to search our own conscience and discover whether or not membership in this relatively elite society, one that has built into it a considerable amount of wealth and technical well-being, is necessarily the way films should be made. It is my most earnest belief that it isn't the way they should be made. One does not have to go through the studios. Each day we're seeing increasing evidence of the self-destruction of those institutions to the point where they're beginning to disappear, not because of any external forces but through a series of internal decisions. They have invalidated themselves. The studio system is a kind of self-consuming beast.

Could you give us examples of the problems you've encountered at the studios?

Well, to begin with it's a loaded deck. You come in with either a script or an idea to which they respond. At that point they say to you, "How much will it cost?" You're then expected to provide something of a budget. Now, I don't know how to make up a budget for a film. I can't provide one because budgets vary enormously depending on which studio you make the picture for and what their overheads are. The question is: how much of their obese presence will you allow to be laid onto you?

So what you do instead is enter into their game by saying, "I can't tell you how much the film will cost, but I think I can tell you the number of days it'll take to make." They then say, "Okay, so how many days?" You break it down and say, "Ninety days," which is how long it took to shoot *Little Big Man.* They then take those ninety days and through some mystical process begin to break it down into dollars. They come up with a sizable amount, but one that doesn't contain any margin for error. One of the things about the art of filmmaking—if we can call it an art—is that because money is such a vital component of the process, at least as it's practiced in Hollywood, if you get to the set and have a bad idea and execute something poorly, you don't have the opportunity within that ninety-day schedule to do it again. So what I do is, instead of choosing a single particular way of doing a given scene, I work on it from a multiplicity of viewpoints. Consequently I end up with a considerable amount of film with varying angles and degrees of closeness, which means I can alter its rhythm when it finally finds its place in the film. Since the ninety-day schedule doesn't allow a real margin of error, inevitably that figure is really only a guess, a statement of intent rather than anything to be held to. But once the studio says yes and the wheels of production start to grind, the onus of guilt and all the responsibility shifts onto the filmmaking unit. The crew is all unionized, so what may originally have been conceived of as ninety days with a six-man crew becomes something else again with a 170-man crew.

Some producers characterize the director as someone who says one thing but delivers another. Of course this isn't wholly accurate. In fact it's wholly inaccurate. What might be much closer to the truth is that you enter into a mutual contract where you put up with each other's inadequacies. And never forget that the inadequacies of the studio are very considerable indeed. With the demise of so many studios, one is confronted by an incontrovertible fact: the studio executives have what would most properly be characterized as a "negative identity." They don't make the films. In fact, they genuinely exist to stand in the way of films. They police them and oppose them by coming out to Montana and saying, "Why are you shooting so much film?"

Does this affect the ownership-point system?

Do people here understand how that works? What often happens is a director will reduce his salary so as to participate in ownership of the film. But this ownership is predicated on the original ninety-day budget, which you know on day one you won't be able to hold to. So you're essentially giving up ownership in your film. I think for each $10,000 you go over budget you lose one percentage point and, very quickly, your ownership of your film. This myth that the so-called creative people in Hollywood are in partnership with the studios is, to a large degree, inaccurate.

What is the nature of interference from the studios?

It's not so much interference, more a genuine kind of malaise and melancholy in the hearts of the executives. After the screening of one film of mine, you could cut the air with a knife. One of the executives said, "We had no idea it was going to be so personal." Another guy rather wittily said, "I wish I'd known it was going to be that kind of film—I would have brought my kid to tell me what it's about!" Essentially this was the level of dialogue that afternoon. So with a light heart I skipped out of there with the print under my arm and jumped off a bridge.

In my experience it's been like this with almost every film. When we finished *Bonnie and Clyde,* the film was characterized rather elegantly by one of the leading Warner executives as a piece of shit. It went downhill from there. It wasn't until the picture had an identity and a life of its own that they acknowledged it was a legitimate child of the Warner Bros. operation. A few days after finishing *The Left Handed Gun,* I was invited to see an assembly. I was then uninvited to ever attend such a thing again. That was my total contact with the material after I'd shot it. Later, United Artists was very anxious that Elizabeth Taylor play the lead in *The Miracle Worker* because she'd expressed considerable interest in the role. Fred Coe, Anne Bancroft, Bill Gibson and I had all worked together on Broadway on *Two for the Seesaw,* which had then been purchased from under us and made into a very bad film, so we decided we weren't going to let that happen again. We wanted Anne to do the film of *The Miracle Worker.* We greeted United Artists with this fact after they'd purchased the rights to the play and they were deeply chagrined. After months of negotiation we hadn't given in, but consequently the project was regarded as a risky film by the studio and the cash given to us very tight. When indeed we did exceed this modest budget—$1,300,000, with $200,000 of that to purchase the play in the first place—by even a slight margin, the excess came out of our salaries. We all ended up with half a salary. Now, the salaries weren't bad to begin with, but we ended up with $37,500 each. This is a film that one would think has been a successful and money-making picture. But it's only in the past few months that we've gotten back the remainder of our salaries. So I would say these are clearly rather stringent conditions under which to work.

The man is hanging over your shoulder, and if you want to get this or that shot then you're going to pay for it yourself. It gets to hurt when you realize you can get a better shot but you're going to have to lay out all the bread for it yourself.

How does the relationship between the people with the money and the creative people work?

If the man who is putting up the money for your film is putting up money only for your film, it's a very different relationship than to a corporation that's putting up money for twenty pictures. There's an interdependency among all the films a studio makes, which means they're hedging their bets. The prime consequence of this is a kind of middle-think where the acceptable tone of everything they choose to finance is gray. The sense of something anomalous, revolutionary, unusual, perverted or out-of-hand just isn't built into the self-censoring structure, which tends to take out the highs and lows.

I suggest that the best way to make films would be for the investor to participate—to a degree—in the filmmaking process. This will make it his film as much as it is the director's. Having someone who says "If this picture bombs, then I can always lay it off on another picture or make a deal with the distributor later on" has generated a lack of genuine paternalism on the part of the producing organizations. They are not the true fathers of their films.

How would you distribute films under this kind of structure?

I don't know. This is only a guess, but I think the whole business is going to change. Perhaps the studios will become solely financing and distributing organizations. The less studio infrastructure there is to maintain, the less burdensome they are to the film itself. Although you won't get the one-to-one relationship that I fantasize about, at least you won't have the daily anxiety of these enormous studios imposing such large overheads onto your film. When that happens, the film inevitably has to accommodate itself to a broad spectrum of taste, and by so doing, anything that might offend people, or that might individuate or particularize it, is removed.

On the other hand I think that what's going to happen is that theater owners will wake up to the fact that with the demise of so many studios there will be a scarcity of films, and to some extent they're going to move into the position of financing films themselves. One of the choices available to those directors who are able to achieve that sublime state of being, those able to make a film for two or three hundred thousand dollars, is to have the distributor invest in the film. It may be one of the more burdensome things you have to put up with, but it's not nearly as burdensome as working with a major studio. And if the distributors don't like the finished film, they won't distribute it.

How would you propose that the studios be run?

I don't believe studios have a genuine function and see no reason for them to exist today. In the old days the idea was that the studios were turning out quality product every year, fifty or sixty films every year at a given studio. They had their own means of distribution and were completely self-contained units. That's no longer the case for any studio here in town. So what we're seeing is that the studios are ceasing to have a genuine function. If they weren't so well placed in terms of real estate, they would have been consumed a long time ago. Century City is what really saved 20th Century–Fox.

There have not been many top-quality directors working on small-budget films for small audiences.

Yet there's no question this is the way to go. The key is to make films for less money—much less money. Up until recently it's been extremely difficult, if not impossible, for directors who enjoy any kind of reputation to work on small-budget films. The point is that what is considered a minimum crew depends on who is making the film. It's perfectly possible to make a film independent of any of the unions, but for a director with a reputation—for those of us tempted to move in this direction—the fear that confronts us is that our films won't be projected by the union projectionists. The consequence is that one might invest several hundred thousand dollars in a film and have no way of distributing it. This issue has actually become considerably disarmed as a possible fate, because in recent years union support has been purchased for a fixed sum after production has finished.

Could you see yourself working like this?

Yes. I would like to persuade myself that I'm going to try and confront these kinds of alternatives as a way of making films, though I'm not sure I have the guts to do it. I think what the studios are interested in is your individuality and anomalous character, and they will pay lip service—including to some small degree subsidizing the American Film Institute—in order to try and bring you into their structure. But I would counsel that you resist this as hard as you can. Explore the ways to make films that don't involve the majors. I believe that we are at a time of massive change in filmmaking, and it lies with you—and those of my generation who have the guts—to bust it open. I think Francis Ford Coppola is trying it, I think a few guys back east are trying it. Those winds of change are more important than those who are entrenched in real estate out here.

What I also believe is that the criteria for verisimilitude which is obtained in American films—not least of which is pride in the high degree of technology—are essentially an inhibiting factor. When one looks at so many of the European films at the same level, they don't com-pare. I'm not saying favorably or unfavorably, but they just aren't compa-rable. They have a different character, a rougher human character to them.

For example?

I would say almost all the work of the Nouvelle Vague. Certainly what Godard has done—though not so much Truffaut, who is more of a metic-ulous technician—and Chabrol, Bertolucci, even some of Bergman's films. To pass with merely an acceptable level of technique and craft is almost unheard of on a Hollywood soundstage. There are simply too many men with too many functions whose existence depends on their ability to have an effect on a given shot. You cannot phase them out. I know it sounds absurd, and as the director you should be able to tell them to stop, but it's almost impossible for them not to put up a light, and before you know it there are six people involved in the light that you didn't even want in the first place. But they show up on the set in the morning and are very earnest about being there. Consequently you have to feed and transport them and, if the film is on location, house them. What happened in Calgary where we were shooting *Little Big Man* was that we ended up with something like forty-three drivers to transport a crew of two hundred. This meant that lunch hour was a sight not to be believed. We fed our teamsters and the crew, and it was not uncommon that during our bigger battle sequences we had a thousand people for lunch.

Mickey One *was heralded as a landmark of New American Cinema. Could you tell us how the film came about?*

I made an arrangement with Columbia Pictures because at the time I was "hot." The deal was that I would make two films, whatever I wanted, and they would give me a million dollars per film. *Mickey One* was the first of those. They didn't have the right to refuse anything, and I even had the right to deny them the privilege of reading the script, although that was fundamentally impossible, because one of the clauses in my contract said they had to be able to evaluate the script and determine if it was possible to make the film for a million dollars. In other words, I couldn't start a film that would end up with them spending five or six million dollars.

They read the script of *Mickey One* and they hated it, but they went ahead with it anyway.

It's an extremely meaningful film to me, even though it suffers from an unfortunate obscurity. I thought it was all crystal clear for audiences, but some of the things I thought I was saying with the film apparently weren't there, which was distressing after the fact. I went into a deep tailspin as a result of what was apparently a befuddling experience for most of the people who saw *Mickey One*. What's interesting is that the clarity of the film is there, because it seems to have increasing meaning for a new generation of filmmakers and viewers. It seems that what I did was somehow assume these future generations were already there. Now, I don't want to suggest that I really anticipated anything or was ahead of my time. After all, there was a considerable amount of ineptitude involved too. I wasn't fully aware of what I was doing and wasn't always working totally consciously. I blew it in a couple of places where I think I could have made the whole thing more lucid without altering its central structure—its cyclical form—and themes. The end result was that by mutual agreement Columbia and I didn't make the second picture under that agreement. We made *The Chase,* which cost $8 million, but not another $1 million picture.

Penn directing Marlon Brando, who starred with Robert Redford and
Jane Fonda, in the Sam Spiegel production *The Chase* (1965).

Is there a particular way you work with actors?

I'm of the American Method school of acting and directing. What I search for are controlled accidents. We set up the scene quite clearly but then try to introduce qualities that might throw the actors off and catch them in an unguarded moment. This might cause them to make what might be regarded as a mistake, but what I consider to be quite illuminating. It's all about getting inside the well-prepared actor.

Alice's Restaurant is full of this, because Arlo Guthrie really can't act. I would set up the situation and tell him how to play it, and he'd tell me he couldn't play it that way. So I'd say, "Well, do what you do." And it would often be very different from what I would have in mind, but it would be invested with his personality and would often disarm the other actors. It produced a kind of electric response from Pat Quinn and Jimmy Broderick. The other actors were wonderful stimulants to Arlo, and pretty soon he found himself able to believe in these make-believe situations. Another example is the woman who plays Bonnie's mother in *Bonnie and Clyde*. She's not an actress, she's a local schoolteacher who was watching us shoot one day. We were struck by her resemblance to Faye, so we asked if she would play the part. She was so uninvolved that it threw Warren into the task of trying to engage her so he could elicit some kind of unprepared response from her.

Dustin Hoffman does this kind of thing constantly. One of the social activities at CBS Films is to go to the dailies of *Little Big Man* to study the close-ups on the actors and listen to what Dusty is saying off-camera. He does this constantly. He's always asking other actors to do it to him, not to play the scene but to try and break him up, unseat him. He wants to be caught unaware.

How do you respond to what critics write about your work, particularly Pauline Kael's piece on Bonnie and Clyde?

I was outraged by it. It was one of the worst pieces of reportage inside a great piece of criticism I've ever read. She suggested that whoever made this film was pretty good but that I was not very good. Now, I don't know who else made this film. She adored it, she thought it a first-rate piece of work, but she had the sense that the script had sprung full-blown from nowhere and that we had somehow gotten it onto the screen through the marvelous presence of Warren Beatty and Faye Dunaway and a terrific cameraman. Well, that's a lot of crap. And it's also irresponsible. She called my office to check out certain things and there were many things she could have informed herself about had she been disposed to doing so.

It seems to me there was some genuine underlying condition that caused her to write that way. I've never met the lady and I do think she is clearly one of the leading analytic minds about film. But when *Mickey One* was screened at the New York Film Festival, I had a rather heated encounter with [*New York Times* critic] Bosley Crowther. As a result of having heard something derogatory Pauline Kael had said about *Mickey One,* I said she seemed to be a lady on the make. She had come to New York and was going to try and make her name. That probably got back to

Penn with Faye Dunaway and Warren Beatty on the Texas location of *Bonnie and Clyde* (1967).

her. What also happened was that Kael called up from San Francisco right after we finished *The Chase* and asked, "How is the film going? I thought *The Left Handed Gun* was a first-rate piece of work and I liked *The Miracle Worker* a lot. I hope this is going to be good, but I must say I've been disappointed by so many people." She talked about Tony Richardson, who made *Tom Jones,* which she thought was just terrific, and then made *The Loved One,* which she thought was a piece of crap. So I said, "I just don't know." When that piece about *Bonnie and Clyde* came out in *The New Yorker,* I must confess that one of my first thoughts was that it smacked of a lady spurned. I had somehow failed her. One of the things that Pauline Kael's reviews have as a strong undertone is a kind of female sexuality. Calling her book *I Lost It at the Movies* suggests something to me.

The opening shots beautifully set up Bonnie's relationship with Clyde. We learn what she sees in Clyde and what she wants from him. But I'm not sure I know as precisely what Clyde sees in Bonnie.

The next scene explains this, where he sees her as a completely sympathetic partner, a nondemanding partner who has similar aspirations to the romantic as he does. The scene after that is where he starts to divine her fantasy life. When they're walking down the street together, before Clyde robs the bank, Bonnie's sixth sense tells her there is romance, escape, excitement around this guy. It just wasn't within my capabilities to get all of that into the first location. The nervousness was intentional. I really wanted them both to be so high-strung and high-pitched that they would do anything.

When she says, "Stay there, I'll be right down," he stays there instead of running, even though he's been caught breaking into the automobile.

No, he hasn't. He's been caught looking at an automobile. He hasn't broken into it, he hasn't touched it really. He's intrigued when he sees her standing naked in the window. He feels there's a purity there, and I was trying to suggest that even before he appears, Bonnie is a girl with a real hunger. She wants to be a movie star and have her name in the paper. A girl who would stand up in the window like that is a girl willing to do a lot to become famous. And there's a big part of Clyde which we discover a little more subtly—it's not quite so narcissistic as it is in Bonnie—

concerning this drive he has to become a public personage. It's something alive in both of them.

Did you have a fix on the characters before you started shooting? You have described a process where you keep yourself open, where you're never caught in an idea or a concept you can't change, depending on the situation. How much improvisation do you allow?

A good deal of it is intuition. During discussions with the actors I'm able to explain my understanding of the character, what the intention of the character is in a given scene and what the line of intention might be in the Stanislavsky sense. It's important to suggest to an actor that they are operating within a structured situation, but at the same time that they can turn loose anything which occurs to them, so long as I—the director— make the final decision about what is appropriate.

With *Bonnie and Clyde* there were many things that happened between Warren and Faye that I wasn't anticipating—for example, the business with the match just before he robs the bank. When it happened, I said, "Gee, that's beautiful. Let's get that on film." When those kinds of things happen, they become extremely meaningful. In that scene Clyde's line of action might be to make everyone think he's somebody more than just a boy walking along the street with a newspaper under his arm. As the scene unravels he becomes more and more involved in this, until finally she says to him, "Prove it." There is actually a lot of dialogue missing there. When he takes out the pistol she says, "You've got one all right, but you don't know how to use it." Well, on paper lines like that seem good. Actually, when you play the scene they seem good, but when you finally see it up there sixty feet wide it's really corny. So we cut a few lines but left the action and behavior.

What about when they introduce themselves to each other? Was that in the script?

It was a tough dramatic problem. I thought of a lot of ways of doing it and none of them really suited me. I thought it was a terrific piece of writing on the page but behaviorally it was kind of a cheat, so I thought about withholding it until the worst, most inappropriate moment. I thought it should interrupt the most complicated and important piece of action and that Clyde should introduce himself before he's aware of what he's really doing. In the original script it was in the same place, but it said something like, "He comes out. They look around for an automobile, and she says, 'I'm Bonnie Parker,' and he says, 'I'm Clyde Barrow,' and they jump into the nearest car." So the lines were meant to come somewhere between the time when he's gone in to rob the grocery store and when he comes out with the money in his hand and they drive off.

How closely did you work on the Benton and Newman screenplay?

Pretty closely. The script was in good shape when I first read it. What they had down cold was the behavior, the kind of southern interaction between Blanche and Buck, between Buck and Bonnie. A lot of that is intact in the film. But I restructured the interior section of the film considerably. The family reunion occurred quite a bit earlier than it does in the finished film. The kidnapping of Velma and Eugene also occurred at a different time. The issue was about the sense of escalation of the foreshadowing of death in the story, that somehow this desirable public life they're enjoying is also bringing them closer to death. We altered the sequence of scenes to escalate upward from that chatty little kidnapping scene, which ends with him telling them he's an undertaker, to the scene with Bonnie's mother.

In the reunion scene Warren was concerned that he didn't have enough to play. I thought he had enough to work with, but a writer named Robert Towne—who is a close friend of Warren and was with us in Texas—came up with what I thought was a superb turn. Bonnie's mother turns to her and says, "You try to live three miles from me and you won't live long." It was meant to convey the puritanical Baptist idea of "You danced a lot and now you've got to pay the piper." Clyde is trying to charm the pants off her, and she says, "That's not gonna work." It was Robert's line and it helped enormously. It helped Warren play the scene, and it certainly helped Faye and the mother.

What was the point of that scene? You play with jump cuts, and slow motion, too.

I went for a grainy look and some shots in slow motion to suggest that Bonnie is trying to grab hold of the past, but it's slipping through her fingers—it's just not possible to recapture any longer. She and Clyde have reached the point of no return. In a matter of hours this scene is going to drift out of her life and into her memory, so I decided to use the film as a representation of that emotion. The location was chosen because of the sand and the rusty color. It's the only time in the film we ever get away from the green and slightly urban look of the small towns. We shot it through gauze on location but optically balanced some shots afterwards.

How did you plan the coverage needed to create the feeling of violence? How do you divide up all the pieces of action in the scenes—for example, the one where the police surround the house just after the brother and his wife join them for the first time? It's made up of so many different shots. How do you put them together in your own mind and decide what's necessary to create the scene?

I see it all together in my mind to begin with when we get to where we're going to shoot. In this case it was at the end of a driveway with a garage. The actors were upstairs in the house, which meant they would have to get downstairs, into the garage and out that driveway. What happens then—and this may be a better answer to your question—is that I take the whole thing apart.

One concern in breaking it down like this is that you want the energy of the basic concept to remain. On cutting from shot to shot, energy has a tendency to dissipate, and all you're really doing is drawing attention to the changes of angle. By cutting, there's nothing added except a greater sense of geography, which means one can now see here where previously one could only see there. Of course there are certain things one wants to be close to. When they explode out of the garage with the car, that has a real kinetic force to it. If you're too far back you lose that sense of explosion. We wanted the experience to be one of just rocking you back in your seat as much as the police must have been rocked back by this thing hurtling out of the house.

Of course there is also a human element in every scene. What do we want to know about the people, particularly the principal people, in terms of that event and how they react to it? For example, a very decisive moment takes place in that scene when we see Blanche. Up until then she's been a pain in the ass, but here she becomes an absolute raw hysteric. And the problem of how you deal with a hysteric when you're part of a criminal gang becomes an organic element of the story thereafter.

Let me say something about coverage. I shoot an awful lot of film. I like to do the master shot, then cover it from all angles. Shooting over-the-shoulder, individuals, medium close-ups gives me an awful lot of material to work with. All you have to deal with is the lab bill. We were shooting a scene and I realized there was a moment where the dramatic tension was going soft. I felt that if I didn't get some kind of coverage I wouldn't be able to control the speed and rhythm of the scene, so I shot it with an individual of Warren, an individual of Faye, and a tight close-up on each. This gave me the opportunity to alter the tempo. It's always important to have a safety valve, something that can get you out of a situation. On a given day you arrive on the set with a certain rhythm in mind, one you feel is right for the first scene of the film. But you rarely shoot in sequence, and if you don't provide yourself with material that enables you to expand or condense time and change the rhythm, you'll be obligated to cut the film to the rhythm you felt that particular day. The point is that the atmosphere on the set on a particular day might not necessarily be right for the scene once it's placed in continuity in the finished film. Of course the other reason why I shoot a lot of film is that I like actors. I enjoy pushing them as far as they can go.

Are you conscious that you're maintaining the geography of the scene in our minds at all times?

Yes, particularly in a scene like this, otherwise you're going to have Bonnie and Clyde and the cops all moving in the same direction. These are not fixed rules by any means, but they can be useful, believe me. I'm making a film at the moment where we're shooting Custer's Last Stand. Before Custer and his men are surrounded, he's chasing some Indians up a hill. He gets all the way to the top of this hill and then here come six thousand more Indians, and he's caught in this enormous pincer movement. It's a hard thing to show. I wanted that one moment when Custer, as it says in the script, gets to the top of the hill and sees every Indian in the world. We only had four hundred extras, so we kept moving them around. They chased him, then they were ahead of him, then they were behind him, then they went around him. So screen direction becomes extremely important.

You didn't storyboard that?

No, I don't storyboard. I don't know why. I guess it dates back to my days in live television, where there was no possibility of storyboarding and everything was shot right on the spot—on the air, as we say—at the moment we were transmitting. I prefer to be open to what the actors do, how they interact to a given situation. So many surprising things happen on set, and I have the feeling that storyboarding might tend to close your mind to the accidental.

Most of the tracking shots in Bonnie and Clyde *are in the first section of the film. Did the script call for this?*

The script didn't specifically call for tracking shots. I just decided we would use lateral and horizontal moves for a while and then, as the film goes along, start moving more nervously and abruptly as the jump cuts become more conspicuous.

When Clyde robs the bank you cut to a long shot of the town. Is that for geographical reasons?

There is a multiplicity of reasons. First of all there's the question of what the street is like before the robbery and what it's going to be like afterwards. It's a relatively empty street in an empty town. It's the first long shot we've seen of the town, with only one person standing on a corner. It adds an ingredient of drama, the question of "Is that guy going to stop them? Is he going to catch Bonnie and Clyde?"

The original script ends with Bonnie and Clyde dying, but we never actually see them killed. It's only hinted at. I was wondering why you changed it.

The way the film originally ended was with the deputies gathered in the bushes waiting for them. We cut between Bonnie and Clyde, who are getting closer, and the deputies waiting. There was kind of raw comic dialogue, things like "Man, it's cold. I wish I was home with my wife." "I wish I was home with your wife, too"—that kind of country talk. Then Bonnie and Clyde arrive and at the moment the shooting starts comes a blackout.

Now, these are people I'd read about in the newspaper in the early thirties, practically the first identifiable personalities I remember as a kid. I felt we couldn't end the story like that. I thought we had to turn them into legends, move from reality into a new degree of experience. In a certain sense it's the same reason why we didn't do it in black and white. It was to say that this is not a document of what happened. It leaps forward in time and brings it up to the present, which is where the idea of changing rhythms in the final scene came from. I wanted the scene to say "We're moving out of this kind of time and this kind of place into another experience." The ending was so clear to me when I read that script. In fact it was the only thing that was clear.

How many cameras did you use for the last scene?

We shot as a gang of four cameras running at different speeds, and shot a master, then a shot each of Warren and Faye. Later on we got them into a two-shot. One of the cameras was moving at an enormously high speed, so it ran out of film very quickly. The actors were wired. Every one of those bullet hits is a squib. We didn't have to rehearse because you can feel them go off. They're in a metal dish and have a little powder and blood in them. It took us half a day to prepare the actors. We got one shot in the morning and one shot in the afternoon.

What did you tell the actors to do in the final scene, just before they are shot?

As I remember, I gave Warren something very simple. I took for a fact that Clyde is a country boy who did a certain amount of hunting, and when you see a bunch of birds like that, something has caused them to spook. To me he's saying to himself, "It's not kosher here. Whatever is going on in those bushes isn't right."

Was the Judas scene, that strange shot tracking through the town, conceived by you or the writers?

Originally it was a two- or three-page sequence where Sheriff Hammer and C.W.'s father meet in the ice-cream parlor. There was dialogue of them preparing the situation, but you really don't need it. I remember I lifted the dialogue out of the scene before we shot it. It's almost abstract, a classic betrayal scene. I evolved it as a straight pan shot. Actually it would be a nifty thing for us to study someday, because there are something like five cuts in that pan. They're hard to see, and I didn't believe it when Dede Allen told me she'd done it. She made the whole thing shorter, which helped the shot enormously.

The details are there. The father walks out with ice cream and that night you see C.W. eating it. The next day we're back in the town. You shoot from the backseat of the car through the front window and there is the ice-cream parlor again.

That was all intentional, because we wanted to make it clear it was the same town. We wanted you to say, "Oh my god, it's going to happen on the street!" And then you have the shot of C.W. looking at them from across the street with an almost sort of they-can-walk-on-water look on his face. He's thinking, "They did it! They got away. They proved my faith in them!"

Are there any particular ways to direct violent scenes?

I think you have to make the decision before the fact whether or not you're really going to play the violence, or whether you're going to do a ritualized version of the violence. You see the ritualized versions in Japanese Kabuki theater, or Kurosawa's films. If you really want a kind of verisimilitude, I think you have to go beyond the objective into the subjective. You have to explode into the unconscious of the people watching, and to do that I think you have to blow the frame apart with the most significant cuts. You have to give the audience more than they expect, something of such kinetic explosiveness that they say, "I can't really be seeing that. This is an unfamiliar image to me, and I can't stand it." This goes back to Eisenstein, the scene on the steps in *Battleship Potemkin.* When he finally cuts to the woman with her glasses and the blood on her face, it's so unbearable. It's a spectacular piece of montage. There's a dead steal from it in a certain sense in *Bonnie and Clyde* with the guy on the running board. I wanted audiences to believe they'd just seen a man shot in the face through a window.

Is there a way of setting up violent scenes?

If anything, the thing here is to divert the audience, to lure it away from the possibility of violence. I think it's more effective this way.

The moment when they look at each other, just before the machine guns start, is one of total recognition of what is about to happen. How did you get us to the point that we actually care about these two pretty awful people?

I think a balance is struck somewhere early on in the film and they cease to be awful people. I wouldn't stand by this, historically, for a minute, but dramatically speaking it's right to say there is a certain validity to whatever it is they're doing. They certainly start out as a couple of punks, but slowly we begin to endow them with characteristics. They watch a man return to his home which has been foreclosed by the bank and, with the mindlessness of that act weighing upon him, without premeditation, Clyde finds himself telling this man, "We rob banks." He's saying they have found an identity for themselves, which is to be on this farmer's side rather than on the bank's. What slowly happens is that their story takes on mythic proportions, and pretty soon they find themselves faintly heroic figures. I think audiences resist this for a while, but then begin to fall in with them. Somehow beyond all the reality of what we've been confronted with comes this escalation into a kind of fairy tale, into a kind of fable upon which we begin to hope for certain things. Once you start doing that, we've got you. You're hooked.

I was wondering if you encourage your actors to watch the daily rushes.

Yes. Everybody connected with the picture can come to the dailies. Watching dailies is a depressing experience, because there's no way in which you're not learning to deal with the fragmentation of the film shoot, and fragmentation kills. I find that when you don't allow the actors to see the dailies, a kind of anxiety seems to develop around them. They start asking people who did see them how they look and what they did wrong. If an actor is going to be depressed about his performance, let him watch the dailies himself. Let it be self-generated. But of course it can also be useful. The actor can discover repetitive mannerisms that he may not be conscious of and may want to steer away from. You can make things quite clear to an actor from their having seen dailies which would not otherwise be clear. What you do see every once in a while is an actor just take off and do something golden, and then everybody comes out of the dailies licking their chops.

How was it working with Warren Beatty?

Warren isn't the easiest guy to work with. He's a very insistent and extremely intelligent guy who'll make you defend what you say until either you make it very clear to him or completely abandon your position. In the case of *Mickey One* we were working on a fairly obscure piece of material and I got to the point of saying, "Warren, shut up and do it my way. I can't discuss it with you anymore." What that did was deprive us of a certain kind of interchange, something we enjoyed enormously on *Bonnie and Clyde,* where Warren would say to me, "I'm going to question you and quarrel with you any time I want to. And you can tell me to shut up or quarrel back with me. But you always finally have the right to say, 'Look, I said everything I have to say about it. I'm directing the picture and you're acting in it, so do it my way.' But I want to be able to talk to you about it." So that was the way we worked and it worked just fine. We had some very raw exchanges and often the crew would think we were fighting, but in point of fact we were really just engaging and trying to kind of irritate each other. It was, "No, goddammit! I don't want to see that cold, dead, handsome face show up on the screen one more damn time. I'm sick of it. It's not enough just to deliver that good-looking body. Go to work!" A lot of Warren's best acting comes out of that state of mind.

Did you have a rehearsal period?

No, we rehearsed it as they were preparing the dolly track. For the first scene, for example, I let Faye go upstairs and left Warren downstairs. They just started to play the scene with each other, and the movement along the sidewalk developed. I had the idea to do a long tracking shot, but I wasn't absolutely fixed on it and would have done something else if it had occurred to me and I liked it. Essentially they could either stand in front of her house and talk, which seemed to me not very interesting, or walk along the street. I kept pointing out the nuances in the scene, like the waitress thing, which was very important to me. Warren was right on it. Faye, I think, had an even campier idea of how to play Bonnie at this point, and she wanted to turn it on even more when he said, "I'll bet you're a movie star."

The day we got to the town to shoot, it turned out they were ginning cotton. All the cotton in the area had ended up in this town to be ginned, so you hear that sort of *chooka, chooka, chooka.* That had to be incorporated somehow into the awareness of the actors and it accounts for a certain kind of disconnectedness which they have when they talk to each other. What Faye is looking at offscreen is that ginning operation.

Did you even have a script reading before shooting?

Yes, but it was highly informal and it was in my motel room. There's no money for script readings on most pictures. We would sit around and talk, but often we got our best rehearsal in the motel the night before we shot a given scene.

Do you give the actors explicit instructions?

No, I watch what they do and then suggest it might be more interesting this or that way and tell them not to overlook this or that fact. But I try not to tell them how to do it, ever. Very occasionally I'll give the actor a line reading, but I prefer setting a problem in motion which will result in what I want, rather than telling them how to achieve the final result.

In the past you've spoken about why you feel The Miracle Worker *is not such a good film.*

Yes. I overarticulated and overdramatized—and consequently decinematized—a large portion of that film. When we did it on stage we had to use dialogue to establish the basic dilemma confronting Annie Sullivan, which is that here is a child who cannot be reached. Of course this is visible to everybody from the moment the curtain goes up, just as it's visible to anybody when the film starts. It was important that we had scenes where it's clear Annie was not just addressing herself to this physically handicapped child, but also to the reverberations of that physically handicapped child as they were experienced by the child's parents, most particularly by the father. There were major scenes between Annie and Captain Keller in which they argue it out nose-to-nose. Finally he'd say, "All right, you can take her to the carriage house. But two weeks only, Miss Sullivan. Two weeks, and then she comes back to us." Well, "two weeks" is a theatrical device. It's something which says to the audience, "You're not going to be in this theater all night." Two weeks means time will run out on Annie Sullivan and Helen in that carriage house. I realize now that in the film this scene could have been done much more effectively if I'd just let the camera sit on Helen, then on Annie, then on Helen, then on Annie, cut to the Captain, cut to Annie. We could have gotten rid of vast amounts of dialogue just by confronting the sheer enormity of what lay ahead of Annie Sullivan in terms of her work with Helen. But I didn't. I was comfortable with what I'd done on the stage and it had worked for me there, so I did it in the film. And in that regard I was hoisted by my own petard.

Are you able to choose your cameramen?

I fantasize about the kinds of relationships European directors and cinematographers have. You hear about some of these great love affairs. I had only one experience like this, on *Mickey One,* with French cameraman Ghislain Cloquet. It was just marvelous. He really understood the script and could envision images which supported the story. He was fast; there was no nonsense, no posturing. You have to recognize that in Europe it's a very different kind of relationship. There the cinematographer and the director work together. Here a director is part of the management and the cinematographer is head of the crew, the chief technician. If a technician has something to say, he goes to the cinematographer and asks him to ask me something, so one doesn't get the feeling of working with real colleagues. There's a sense of, "The director wants this. How do we retain our standards and still give him what he wants?"

Why were you fired from The Train?

The script had been around for two years or so. It had gone to every studio, and I was looking for a really strong action picture. William Morris sent me a whole bunch of scripts and I chose *The Train,* because I saw that I could impose an interesting story onto it. They asked me who I wanted and I said, "It should be one of the big butch Hollywood stars." So we put a call in to Burt Lancaster, right then and there. He asked me, "Is this a script you really like?" I said, "Yes." "Okay, send it to me." A week later he called me and said, "You've got a deal." So that was it. We went to United Artists and put a package together. Now, even at this point there were a lot of things I didn't know. I didn't know that Burt owed United Artists a million and a half dollars from his production company Hecht-Hill-Lancaster which was going to be written off on this picture. In other words, he was going to close out his debt to the studio in the amount of a million and a half dollars. This was in addition to receiving a quite considerable salary.

It's worth looking at Lancaster's career at this point. This is my interpretation, and he's got every right in the world to deny this and say I'm full of crap. He had gone off and done *The Leopard,* which is a film I hadn't seen at that point, but it was a book I admired and it was something I think Burt was very proud of. It was enormously well received in Europe, it had opened at the Cannes Festival where it won a prize and Burt won great accolades. I had only met with him once in Hollywood, before I went to Paris to prepare *The Train.* The next time we met was in Paris and he was really ebullient. Everything was gold. It couldn't have been nicer. Then *The Leopard* opened in this country and got blasted. I think Burt linked me in his mind with that group of arty European directors like Visconti, at least more than he did with those kind of solid, reliable action directors like Frankenheimer. When that moment of panic hit, it hit pretty badly. I didn't know it at the time. It actually hit him before he came to France, where I already had started shooting. Then Burt showed up and we went to work. First day we had a very amiable lunch, then worked on a scene. I remember we were working on a scene in the cab of an engine with Michel Simon, who doesn't speak any English. I was shooting rather a lot, and I heard Burt saying, "Oh, Christ, not another angle, come on!" And I'd say, "Yes, one more." And then I remember saying something to him like, "Look, this next take, I don't want to know what you're doing or what you're thinking, but I wish you'd have a private thought, something you wouldn't like to tell me. I don't care what it is." And there's kind of a very fishy look from Burt. Anyway, we wrapped for the day and I saw some dailies and went home and this friend of mine who was writing the picture called up and said, "Hey, I just left Lancaster, and you're off the movie." And I said, "That's impossible. I created this movie, I can't be off. I made it happen." I was stunned. Then the head of United Artists came to Paris and said, "Any discussion is academic." That was the end of that.

Did you ever see the finished film?

I saw it only recently on TV and I thought it was okay, though it missed the point entirely. Frankenheimer threw out our script, which had a very different emphasis to it. He made an action movie and we wanted to make a movie about the commerce of war. That was really the center of it. There was an art dealer, played by Claude Dauphin, who was the major character of the whole piece and who was completely written out of the Frankenheimer version.

Something that's very important for you guys to bear in mind is that when you make a deal with actors, you're not making a deal with them to be in your film, you're making a deal with them to be in United Artists' film or Warner Bros.' film or Columbia's film. In the not-too-distant past the contract used to read "Warner Bros., who hereinafter shall be known as the author . . . " I'd gotten Jeanne Moreau and Paul Scofield to come be in this nonsense action film because I kept telling them, "Look, I know it's just this now but I'm going to do that with it." They signed on as friends, anxious to work on a picture with this kind of complexity, and when that was no longer true they were trapped in a rather awful situation. Both tried to get out but couldn't. It taught us all a lesson.

Do you worry about success?

Yes. It's a constant dilemma, one you can't really avoid, I suppose. But there comes a moment—it happens overnight—when you find yourself living in a manner not only to which you're not accustomed but which you don't deserve. I don't mean to be moralistic or socialistic about it, but it just seems improper. I don't have the mechanism just to go out and give everything away, even if something inside tells me I should probably do just that.

What's your next project after Little Big Man?

I don't have one.

Do you like the security of knowing there is another thing in the pipeline?

I used to, but now not so much. I used to do work compulsively. There was a time when I would go nuts in the theater. I had five shows running at once on Broadway. They couldn't stop me. I would finish one, it would open and we'd start the next one. I got that way a little bit in the movies.

Do you have your own production company?

Tatira-Hiller. Tatira is Warren and Hiller is me. Having your own production company is one of the greatest myths in the world. It's one of the things that the studios discovered they can give you without actually giving you anything. You have the sense of being autonomous and your own boss, yet in reality you have none of that. When it gets down to the nitty-gritty, if somebody puts up the bread for something, it's their project.

Let me finish by telling you a story about the scene in *Bonnie and Clyde* when they ride out of town to their deaths. It goes back to what we were talking about at the start of our discussion. Back in the day, you went to work at the studios as a director. You were called the director and your job was to shoot the movie and tell the actors what to do. But in point of fact the movie was really in the hands of the technicians. They were the fifty-two-weeks-a-year men who turned out films for the studio. The point is that there are procedures and standards and norms which have been solidified. If a cloud goes over a shot—as it did in that scene in *Bonnie and Clyde*—then it's not going to cut with the next shot. I said "Let's go" and one of the guys said "Cloud coming!" I said, "Well, for Christ's sake, let's shoot with the cloud coming." And he looks around and says, "Right, he wants to shoot with the cloud coming . . ." I remember I was about to buckle, but Warren screamed, "Shoot it, shoot it— now!" We started to roll and he took off in his car after Faye on the other side of the street. It was Warren who gave me that last kick in the ass to get over wanting to be a nice guy with the technicians. The amount of resistance! This "We've never done it like this before" way of working. Directors in America have to deal with this notion of "We have thirty years experience of doing it. We do it better than anybody in the world." And, in one sense, that's absolutely true. But they also do it more impersonally than anybody in the world. The amount of negativism on set when I say I want to do a particular kind of tracking shot! "You can't do that! Absolutely no way!"

By the time we did *Bonnie and Clyde,* it had become more common to use more than one camera. But on my first picture there were a couple of times where it seemed absolutely logical to me to use more than one camera. We would do a big action sequence and then go back in to cover it. So one time I said, "Here's the main camera, the A-camera. Let's put another camera over here." The cameraman said, "I can't do it. I'm lighting for this camera." And I said, "Well, okay, you're lighting for this camera, but look, stocks are a lot faster now and the cameras and lenses are really good. Why don't we put a second camera here?" He said no. So finally I said, "Look, you've got to do it." So he said, "Okay, I'll do it." But he made up a slate which read, "Not responsible for this camera." He knew it was going to be seen in the projection room and he was certain that an executive was going to have a sufficiently discriminating eye to be able to detect whether or not this was the camera he'd lit for, which was absolutely not the case at all. As a matter of fact the stuff was a lot better on that camera than it was on the one he'd lit for.

This all goes back to the studio heads, who are for the most part quite ignorant. They watch the dailies, even though they don't really know what the dailies relate to. They barely remember the script they originally read, because they made the deal a year ago. They're sitting in this screening room at Warner Bros. and three minutes of film comes on from this picture and three minutes of film comes on from that picture. What happens, of course, is that some executive jumps up and says, "Aha! A cloud! Who's the cameraman on that picture? Get him out of here!" This is all because in his mind, it's an anomaly. It didn't happen yesterday and it hasn't happened for the last three weeks, and none of the other shots have clouds in them, so it must not be any good.

I know I'm laboring the point and I'm doing it in comic-book terms, but there's an important idea behind this: trying to break the rules in Hollywood is an important goal. Your mission should be to put your personal stamp on the film.

Films as Director

1958 *The Left Handed Gun*

1962 *The Miracle Worker*

1965 *Mickey One* (also producer)

1966 *The Chase*

1967 *Bonnie and Clyde*

1969 *Alice's Restaurant* (also
         screenplay)

1970 *Little Big Man*

1975 *Night Moves*

1976 *The Missouri Breaks*

1981 *Four Friends* (also producer)

1985 *Target*

1987 *Dead of Winter*

1989 *Penn and Teller Get Killed* (also
         producer)

1993 *The Portrait* (television)

1997 *Inside* (television)

Penn directed many television programs early in his career including episodes of *The Gulf Playhouse*, 1953; *Goodyear Playhouse*, 1953–55; *The Philco-Goodyear Television Playhouse*, 1953–55; *Playwrights '56*, 1955–56 and *Playhouse '90*, 1957–58; and *Flesh and Blood*, 1968. He is credited as executive producer of *Law & Order*, 2000–01.

I have never met a producer who was not interested in my particular concept of the "blackness" of a script. I sought to present as forceful an image as I could in order to counter the prevalent one.

SIDNEY POITIER
(Born in Miami, Florida, 1927)

Sidney Poitier is one of the most accomplished and elegant actors in motion picture history. His path to that high station is in many ways more remarkable than the achievement itself. He was raised in the Bahamas on Cat Island, where his father was a potato farmer and there were no stores, telephones or paved roads. At age fifteen, Sidney was sent to live with his brother in Miami, and two years later he hopped a freight train to New York, a young man without an education who spoke with a Caribbean accent. He found work as a dishwasher, then responded to an ad at the American Negro Theater where he was escorted out the door with the question, "How do you think you can be an actor with that accent?" After working with a Jewish waiter who took it upon himself to help the young dishwasher with his English, Sidney returned to the Negro Theater and offered to be their janitor in exchange for acting lessons. In time he was playing small roles on the stage, eventually gaining recognition in a supporting role in a Broadway production of *Lysistrata*.

Darryl Zanuck brought Poitier to Hollywood in 1950 for a role in *No Way Out,* directed by Joseph Mankiewicz, in which he portrayed a black doctor tormented by a wounded racist played by Richard Widmark. Even as a young actor trying to break in, Sidney committed himself, out of respect for his father, never to accept a role that lacked dignity. "From the first part, from the first day, I always said to myself, 'This must reflect well on his name.' "

He received increasingly prominent roles throughout the early fifties, in *Cry, the Beloved Country, Red Ball Express* and *Go, Man, Go!,* until his breakthrough performance in *Blackboard Jungle*. In 1958, Stanley Kramer cast him as a prison escapee manacled to a racist, played by Tony Curtis, in *The Defiant Ones*. Poitier received an Academy Award nomination, the first time in

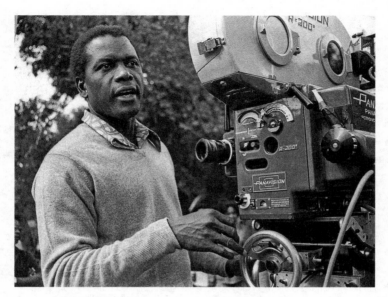

Sidney Poitier's career spanned more than half a century in front of and behind the camera. He directed *Uptown Saturday Night* in 1974.

the Academy's thirty-year history that a nonwhite had been nominated for Best Actor.

In 1965 I headed the American delegation to the Moscow Film Festival while serving as head of motion pictures at the United States Information Agency for Edward R. Murrow. I persuaded the State Department to let us take *The Defiant Ones,* despite their concern that it might show America in a bad light, and with assurances that we would only show it to small groups of Russian filmmakers. The Soviet festival chairman saw an opportunity and announced a Sunday-night public screening in the seven-thousand-seat Kremlin Palace of Congresses. I decided that Poitier's presence would save the day. I reached him by phone in London and he agreed to fly to Moscow on Saturday. When the Russians got word that Poitier was coming, they canceled the Sunday-night Kremlin Palace screening, rescheduling it at the Sports Arena twenty miles outside of town on Sunday morning. I had to explain the disappointing change to Sidney when he arrived from London. Early Sunday, Sidney, Stanley Kramer and I got in a van, arriving at the Sports Arena at 9:30, and were shocked to see a line circling the building. Seventeen thousand people watched *The Defiant Ones* and cheered at the climax when Poitier pulled Tony Curtis up onto the moving train. Afterward they swarmed below the box where Sidney sat, applauding and cheering with

moist eyes. It was a demonstration of the value of free expression and the
compelling screen personality of Sidney Poitier.

In 1959, Sidney made a triumphant return to Broadway in Lorraine Hans-
berry's *Raisin in the Sun,* and two years later he repeated the role on the
screen. In 1964 his performance in *Lilies of the Field* made him the first
African-American to receive the Oscar for Best Actor. *To Sir, with Love, In the
Heat of the Night* and *Guess Who's Coming to Dinner* secured his place as one
of Hollywood's most prominent leading men.

Starring together in *Buck and the Preacher* in 1972, Poitier and his friend
Harry Belafonte had a falling out with the director, and Poitier was asked to

Poitier accepted an Honorary Academy Award in 2008 in
"the name of all the African-American actors and actresses who
went before me in the difficult years—on whose shoulders
I was privileged to stand to see where I might go."

take over. This started a directing career that included *Uptown Saturday Night, Let's Do It Again, A Piece of the Action,* in which he starred alongside Bill Cosby, and *Stir Crazy,* a successful comedy with Richard Pryor and Gene Wilder.

Poitier writes books, is active in civil rights, was a founding trustee of the American Film Institute, serves as the ambassador to Japan for the Bahamas, and has received the AFI Life Achievement Award and the Kennedy Center Honors.

On August 12, 2009, in the East Room of the White House, I witnessed an event that no one could have imagined when the teenage boy from Cat Island jumped on that freight train to New York. The first African-American president presented the United States' highest civilian honor, the Medal of Freedom, to the nation's first African-American film star. "In front of black and white audiences struggling to right the nation's moral compass," the citation read, "Sidney Poitier brought us the common tragedy of racism, the inspiring possibility of reconciliation, and the simple joys of everyday life."

During the ceremony I noticed a senior White House advisor, a young black lawyer, watching intently as the president presented the medal. He told me afterward that when he got his first job after law school at a New York firm, he rented videotapes of Sidney Poitier movies to figure out how he should dress.

Sidney Poitier is a major figure in the history of motion pictures, and an artist who has had profound influence on American life.

SIDNEY POITIER

———◆———

January 28, 1976*

When you first moved from acting to directing, what were your biggest problems?

I have been acting for many years, so there are certain mechanical responses I have to any kind of an acting situation. I have had occasion to explore in my work most of the emotions an actor might come in contact with throughout the course of a day, so I don't have to dig too deep to find how to re-create it. After so many years, much of it is second nature. But with directing I'm dealing with a new area—so much of my attention on a very specific level is devoted to that. My greatest difficulty came on the very first day, when the self-doubt that must be faced by any director hit me. How to use the camera as an instrument of your own creative process was new to me. I had very sympathetic actors to work with but felt the panic building up in me when I shot my first setup. I was scared. Then I began to watch the actors unfold in the frame that I had structured and it began to make sense. They seemed to be real as they began to move and to talk to each other. I was in the scene myself and at one point said, "Hey, it's nice. It's working. I like what they're saying." What they were doing had some kinship to my view of reality and I began to relax.

You're in a scene with three or four other actors and you can't hear whether it's working. But you can feel it and at the same time you can hear yourself. You're feeding them lines, you're responding to lines from them. I think it takes a touch of schizophrenia to be able to act and direct at the same time.

*James Powers moderated this siminar. This transcript also contains segments from seminars Sidney Poitier gave at the American Film Institute on May 29, 1991, and May 4, 1994.

We're starting out as directors. What can you tell us that would help us talk better to the actor?

It depends upon the individual personality. Actors are very sensitive instruments. In order for them to do their work, actors have to expose areas of themselves that are terribly personal. Even the act of playing a part that doesn't require obvious exposure is tough for most actors. Their ego is forever exposed. So when they do open up for you, you have to keep them open, like a flower, because once you have jarred them, you've lost them for the moment. You will, at some time or another, work with an actor who, by his or her particular nature, is a nervous individual. The nervous energy, the adrenaline, the juices that are rolling when they're in a work situation, are such that you have to husband it very carefully, because it can go traumatic on you very quickly. If the actor is not secure, his automatic response is to withdraw. He will put some kind of protective screen between you and him. He will listen to you, but his tools won't function.

I will never give an actor instructions that other actors can hear, unless it's a general instruction. This may be my neurosis as an actor but I find that if I'm given a specific instruction on the floor that everybody else can hear, all those people become arbiters as to whether I did or did not fulfill that instruction. Obviously this can inhibit an actor. It puts an unnecessary and unintended pressure on him. What I do is move the actor a step away from the other actors. I'll talk in his ear and tell him what I need. If there are two actors involved, I get them to work in concert, without telling one what the other guy's instructions are. In doing this I find that my actors are completely confident. They will try anything, because apart from themselves the only judge of what they are doing is me.

What are your views on white people writing roles for black actors?

I suppose that you would characterize my career as a fairly successful and substantive one, if you were to look at all forty-two films I have made. The fact is that most of the scripts I did were written by whites, which is to say that to require you to write only for whites makes no sense. To require me or this gentleman to write only for blacks also makes no sense. A writer has a point of view on something and with his script speaks to that point of view. If he isn't going to speak to that point of view then he will be speaking exclusively to the point of view of the people who put up the money, and that's not the job of an artist. The artist must bring his views and ideas to his work. So write what you want to write. Throw it out there and it's going to be subject to all kinds of critical response, fairly and unfairly. But that's the nature of life.

Is Hollywood as conscientious today as when Guess Who's Coming to Dinner *and* Lilies of the Field *were made?*

Hollywood never really had much of a conscience. You could count on both hands the guys responsible for that energy of which you speak. They are men like Stanley Kramer. They are men like Walter Mirisch, Joe Mankiewicz and Ralph Nelson, who bucked the system and said, "I want to make this picture!" *Lilies of the Field* cost two hundred and forty thousand dollars. The studio that produced the film made Ralph Nelson, the director, put up his house as a completion bond. The social conscience that you're talking about was always only a handful of men. This town never was infected by that kind of goodness.

I recently watched In the Heat of the Night *and was amazed by how many scenes were carried by your eyes and your silences. Could you talk about your technique?*

I had two great teachers, Paul Mann and Lloyd Richards, who has just retired from Yale and who taught me that there is nothing new in a character that I had not already experienced myself as a thirty-five-year-old. Nothing. The actor need not go outside himself to create a character. By the very maturation process of life, we are exposed to all of the emotional complexities that any actor will need in any situation. By our late twenties or mid-thirties we have had all kinds of experiences—feelings of embarrassment, fear, shame, joy, anger, panic, courage. We have felt every conceivable emotion, and for actors that is the storehouse we go to. I always dipped into my own life. When I read a script, I respond to how close the writer comes to the reality that I understand. I look for that seamlessness between art and reality. When I can find those scenes, when the dialogue is the speech of real people, when what the dialogue conveys is crystal clear to me, then they've really got me.

Did you study acting in high school or college?

No. I didn't study in high school. I never got that far. I was a very peculiar child in that I came from a very large family, but it was not what we would call a closely knit family. I grew up on an island with no automobiles. We lived very near an ocean and before I could walk I was taught how to swim. Once I could swim nobody paid me any attention anymore, because there was nothing you could do to get into trouble. If you fell in the water you could climb out. So I grew up alone. I grew up before I was prepared for it, and had the captainship of my life. I got into being my own best company and did an awful lot of daydreaming. As I grew up, the habit pattern of daydreaming—something that has been, I suspect, very helpful to me—armed me with an ability to slip in and out of characters. When I was about twelve we moved to a part of the world where I could see movies, and I would relate to other people what I had seen. I enjoyed doing that more than actually watching the movies themselves.

I started studying acting in New York. Originally I had no intentions of becoming an actor. I had just come out of the army and was looking for things to do. I was equipped to do nothing but work with my hands. Washing dishes was very cool because I got two meals a day, which is dynamite when you live by yourself. So I was a transient dishwasher,

Poitier starred in Sydney Pollack's first feature film,
The Slender Thread, 1966, which also featured Anne Bancroft.

meaning that I would work one restaurant one day and would go back to the employment office and they'd send me to another. I was a relief dishwasher. One day I decided to get a steady dishwashing job. In order to do that I bought a black newspaper in New York called the *Amsterdam News*. I opened it up and they had a marvelous collection of jobs for unskilled workers, but opposite the want-ad page there was an ad that said "Actors Wanted." Over here it said "Dishwashers Wanted" and over here it said "Actors Wanted." So I went to this place, 135th Street and Lenox Avenue. I walked in and there was a man there, a big, strapping guy, and he said, "May I help you?" I said, "I came to see about the job." He said, "What job?" I said, "In the newspaper." He said, "Are you an actor?" I said, "Of course," and he gave me a script. I had never seen a script in my life, so I took this thing and he said, "Go up on the stage." I went up on this little stage and he's sitting out there and he said, "Turn to page twenty-eight." I turned to page twenty-eight and he said, "You read John and I'll read the other part. Start when you're ready." So I started to read. Now let me just tell you that I quit school when I was twelve and a half. I didn't start until I was eleven, so I'd had a year and a half of school. By the time I got to New York I could barely read, and now I've got a script in my hand, so I start: "So . . . you . . . are . . . going . . . tomorrow . . . with . . . me . . ." The guy came up on the stage and snatched the script away from me. I wasn't a very big kid then. He said, "Did you have to come in here and waste my time like this?" This is while he's got me by the scruff of the neck, leading me towards the door. He opened the door and said, "Get out of here, boy. Stop wasting people's time. Why don't you go out and get yourself a job as a dishwasher or something?" That's a true story.

So I'm walking down the street, back to catch the bus to go downtown to see about my dishwashing job. I said, "How the hell did he know? How could he look at me and tell that I was a dishwasher?" I suppose there was something about my ambience. Now, I didn't mind that he had thrown me out. I had taken a chance. But inherent in what he had said was a challenge for me to rise to, so I decided I was going to become an actor, not because I wanted to become an actor but to prove to me and to him that I could do it. I decided to audition again. I didn't know that you could go to a drama bookshop and buy little books with plays, so I bought a copy of *True Confessions* and memorized two paragraphs. I went over there and sat with all the other people waiting to audition. They call me up to the stage. I'm dressed to kill, in my pretty suit, and I read from the magazine. There was a deathly silence. Then a woman named Osceola Archer, the artistic director of the school, said, "Would you do an improvisation?" I said, "Yes!" I had never heard the word before. I was hoping that she would say something that would clue me in, which she did. She said, "All right. Make out that you are in the jungle and are surrounded by the enemy. All your compatriots have been killed or captured. You know there is no way out. What you are going to do is go out in a blaze of glory. Let's see what you do." So I got out there and with the help of my imagination from when I was a kid conjured up the jungle and everything. I started reading lines and saying, "Come and get me!" I'm shooting up at the trees and then I get hit. "Oh! I'm hit!" I started to fall, and then I remembered about my suit. I had to fall so that I wouldn't dirty my suit. There I was, lying dead, making sure my suit wasn't dirty, and they said, "Okay. Thank you. We'll let you know." Well, I got in that time. The reason was that there was an exceptionally high percentage of female actors auditioning and the small percentage of male actors were, as a group, pretty poor. They selected something like eighteen girls, but there were only three or four guys who showed any promise, so they had to pad the male side. Absolutely true. I mean, the pickings were so lean that they took me! They said it was only on a trial basis and that after three months, if the teacher thought that I was not improving, they would have to ask me to leave. Well, at the end of three months they asked me to leave. True story. But of course I wasn't ready to leave, because that would destroy my whole plan. There was a man named Abe Hill who was the administrator of the school, and I said, "Mr. Hill, you don't have a janitor for the school after hours. I'll be the janitor. I'll take care of the stage and the stairway and the floor of the auditorium if you let me stay for another three months." He snapped me up! He said, "It's a deal!" So I began doing the janitor work right after classes, but at least I was able to stay in class.

After a year I got a job on Broadway. Osceola Archer had decided to do a student production of *Days of Our Youth* and there was a dynamite part in it for a young actor. She didn't think I was ready for any of that stuff, so she hired a young actor by the name of Harry Belafonte. Harry's father was a janitor in Harlem and Harry used to help his dad on certain evenings, and he happened to be helping his dad one evening when he was supposed to be at rehearsal. On that particular evening a producer/director by the name of James Light came up to see what Osceola was doing with *Days of Our Youth,* and everybody was getting restless while we were waiting for Harry to show up. Finally they said to me, "Why don't you read Harry's part until he gets here?" After we ran through it this guy said to me, "Why don't you come down to my office next week and we'll have a talk?" He was about to produce a black version of Gilbert Seldes' version of *Lysistrata* and hired me to play Probulos. I had twelve lines in the whole show. It's opening night and backstage there was great frenzy. The curtain goes up and I'm in the first scene. I walked out on the stage and some magnet drew my eyes right dead into the audience of two thousand people, and all twelve of my lines flew out of my head. The other actor throws me his line and instead of answering him with my first line, I give him my ninth line. I can see his eyes rolling in his head. He's going to try and recover, try to put me back on track, so he shoots me the prompt for my second line and I give him line number eight. Now I'm really flustered. I'm standing there speaking lines and they make no sense and the audience thinks it's really a part of the play and they think it's hilarious. I give three or four more lines and the audience is just laughing in the aisles, so I walk off the stage, because I can't stand being made fun of like that. They start applauding and I think they're glad to get rid of me. I go upstairs and get out of costume, knowing that I'm finished with theater. This is the end of my theatrical career. Back to dishwashing. I go walking the streets. The reviews came out and killed the play. They destroyed it. New York in those days had something like ten daily newspapers, and every one of them said, "Who was that kid who came out there in the first act? He was funny, he was so terrific, he was just delightful!" So somebody was smiling on me up there. From there I went to Paul Mann and Lloyd Richards, who really taught me how to work.

You were one of the first successful black movie actors. What was your relationship with the writers and the directors, as far as your character and the story were concerned?

When I started the only leverage I had was to refuse to work on a particular script if it had objectionable portions, or certain comments that were antiblack or antihuman or just against my own sense of integrity, my sense of my being as a human entity. You know, my father was a very interesting man. He was the poorest man in the village in the Caribbean where I grew up. My mother used to go to the grocer and buy empty flour sacks and use them to make clothes for me and my brothers and sisters. It was the cheapest cloth she could find. But my father was never a man of self-pity. He always had a wonderful sense of himself, and every time I took a part, from the first part I played, from the first day, I always said to myself, "This must reflect well on his name."

Sometimes I would say, "Thank you, but I cannot work on this project." That was always a last resort. Since I had no real weight short of quitting, I would raise my objections as seductively as I could. I have never met a producer who was not interested in my particular concept of the "blackness" of a script. I sought to present as forceful an image as I could in order to counter the prevalent one. The prevalent image in those days was that Negroes were lazy and shiftless. So in my pictures I was cool and hard-working. If you look at the films you'll see that I tried to present that which was most lacking: a guy with a job other than the usual menial ones. I played doctors and lawyers. I played a psychiatrist for Stanley Kramer. Of course some of those films are heavily dated today, but I believe in the historical evolution of things. You and I are in this room partly because of that history. I had certain job opportunities partly because there were black actors before me who died and never had a shot. I am here partly because of the dues they paid, people like Frank Wilson, Canada Lee, Rex Ingram, Hattie McDaniel, Louise Beavers. They endured and paid all sorts of heavy dues, and my little stint was not unrelated to theirs, as yours will certainly not be unrelated to mine.

The films you have directed have been very successful commercially. Do you have any projects you know won't make any money but that you want to do anyway?

No. I don't have any comments to make that are intended specifically for very few people. If I have something to say in my films, I want to say it to everyone, or to as many people as I can. If I find a dynamite piece of material which is apolitical, I'll zap my own politics in it here and there. I'll have a sequence rewritten or add a comment that dovetails with my political philosophy, with my social philosophy, and with my general philosophy of life. I'll steer the point of view toward something I can live with. I'm not beyond writing a scene and putting it smack in the middle of the movie if that will tilt the point of view ever so slightly towards what I think is important.

Did you ever have difficulties making certain films because of your race?

I've had difficulties making certain films but really never had any difficulties because of race. That's not to say I haven't had an enormously long-running relationship with racism. I've had that, but I'll spare you the details, because it isn't germane to my being here today. I will say only that my attitude toward it is simple: I concluded when I was young that my race was a fact of my life, and simply decided not to let it stop me.

What turned you on to directing? Was it something of an extension of your acting career?

It was a practicality in terms of career management. I knew that as a principal player my days were numbered, and I thought I would either segue into being a character actor or find myself sitting around bowling or something. I didn't go into directing because I had an overwhelming desire to displace Truffaut or any of the other guys. I went into it to add some longevity to my career. I decided early on that the only way to stay close to the creativity I really love is to be sufficiently diversified, so every time I worked with a director I started asking technical questions about the camera and the things related to how I could involve myself in this business when I was no longer a viable product as an actor. I kept trying to expand my horizons. I wound up writing five movies with a professional writer and directed eight or nine of them. I've been at this business for many years. I've known for a long time that you can be hot for three years and then you're gone. Things change in the business, and it has nothing to do with how good you are. It has to do with a lot of other things, not the least of which is luck. So I chose to spread my bets and cover as much ground as I could by learning to do as many things as I could.

My first day on the set as a director was in Mexico. Harry Belafonte and I were acting in a picture called *Buck and the Preacher*. We had hired a director, a man named Joe Sargent, who happens to be a very good director. So we go to Mexico and started shooting, and Joe's view of the material turned out to be somewhat different from Harry's and mine. We were producing, Harry and I, and there was a conflict of points of view, so we asked Joe to withdraw. I called Columbia Pictures and said, "We would appreciate it if you would send us down another director as quickly as you can, because Mr. Sargent, as good as he is, doesn't see the material as we do." They said, "Okay, we'll look for someone." I said, "In order to not shut down, I will direct for the next two days until someone arrives." So two days became three and three became four, and after about ten days they still couldn't find anyone to send down that they were happy with. Meanwhile my stuff is being sent back to them to look at. Finally they

Poitier first turned to directing in 1977 with *Buck and the Preacher*. His most
successful effort was *Stir Crazy* (1980), with Richard Pryor.

called and said, "Why don't you just continue shooting?" That's how I
started directing. I was just thrown into it.

A lot of your directing choices have been comedies. Why is that?

That wasn't by design, it was necessity. Serious films about black life in
America were harder to mount than comedies.

*You talk about using your own emotional history. Was there ever a role where you
had to delve into yourself but were resistant to do so?*

As an actor I was always fearful of *Othello* and stayed away from it. I would
do it in scenes in class and many times was offered the role with quite substantive actors playing Iago, but I never felt comfortable about jealousy as
an emotion for me to play. I could play it but was never comfortable with
it. I don't know why, and you're looking at a guy who was in psychoanaly-
sis for eleven years. It was a block for me. I suspected once that somewhere
early in life I got this thing about jealousy being an unworthy emotion.

*A lot of directors and producers and writers and actors have come through the AFI
and expressed dissatisfaction about the attitude of the studios and the lack of flex-*

ibility in making intelligent films. I wonder why the collective will of such a powerful group of creative people is unable to affect what goes on in Hollywood.

There are component elements to the inability to effectuate the kind of cohesion you're talking about in the creative community. There are three elements to Hollywood. There are the studios, there are the actors and there are agents, and all three are important. Actors do what their agents say, not in terms of what parts they will play, but how they behave in terms of their fees, their remunerations. To give you an example: I was in a group called the First Artists Corporation with Steve McQueen, Paul Newman and Barbra Streisand. Dustin Hoffman came in later. I thought we had a perfect union. Each of us would get a hundred and fifty thousand dollars fee as an actor. We would get ten percent of the gross as a part of our fee. We would own fifty percent of the profits of the film. I did four films for First Artists. Newman made three, Barbra made three, Steve made three, Dustin made a couple. We made twenty-eight movies. Agents and the studios destroyed that union, because McQueen's agents knew they could get five million dollars up front instead of working on a picture for our group. Barbra was being offered huge sums, Paul was being offered huge sums. So between the offers from the studios and the agents who are maneuvering on behalf of the actors, the studios and the agents won, and the First Artists Corporation never got beyond twenty-eight films. It's not easy to pinpoint the bad guys, because everyone has a right to look out for their best interests.

With rare exceptions Hollywood is not a place that is really interested in art. The artists don't control the business. The business is controlled by the men who handle the money. It's a business, and unless you have really committed and passionate artists who want to articulate something about themselves or about their lives or about their time, you're not going to get very much from Hollywood. Look around you. The very best actors in this business constantly work beneath their talent. We haven't yet had a meaningful film on some of the most pressing problems and situations and conditions in America. Take abortion, the pros and the cons of it. Take racism, the truth of it. We stay away from religion, we stay away from all kinds of things. It's a tough game you're playing, but I envy you because you're on the threshold of the future. You will be participants in shaping that future. I don't have that kind of time, nor will I have that kind of strength, but you should know that by depending on your own efforts you can be more creative than you realize. Things are going to change, and the business will be in need of people like you with new ideas and strong commitments and a vision. So carve out a niche for yourself.

A lot of us here hope to be directors. I tend to be a little pessimistic about my chances when I look at Hollywood and see that you are the only black director who is consistently working.

I would like to remind you of how fortunate you and I are. We have twenty-six or twenty-seven million people who have arrived at a point in their self-awareness that they want to see themselves on film. There was a time when the forerunners of those people—when they were perhaps ten million—were not necessarily satisfied, but they were happy enough going to see other people in movies. There was never a time before now when there was a conscious, individual effort to say, "I want to see myself—in all of my dimensions—on film." That is the best gift you could have, twenty-six million people who can deliver a seven-million-dollar gross for you, even if nobody else went to see the picture. Black or white people don't care how much money you spend on a movie. If that movie touches them, they'll tell their friends to see it. All those people turning on their television sets across the country. It isn't by chance that *Sanford and Son* and *The Jeffersons* are successful television shows. You really have something to work with. Unfortunately you've also got to deal with the hierarchy of the economic structure in this town. So deal with it. Learn to be entrepreneurs. I don't care how good a director you are, you've got to know how to put deals together. You've got to make it attractive to the guys you're going to get the money from.

You doubt the future, but it's going to be dynamite! We black people have a hell of a long way to go, but over the last fifteen years we've come a hell of a long way. When I first walked on the 20th Century–Fox lot, the only other black person there was the shoeshine boy. I worked at Columbia Pictures when there wasn't another black person to be seen. Today it's different. I'm a believer in history, and where you are sitting now would have been paradise for those who went before us. In the early days there was a man named Oscar Micheaux, a black moviemaker at a time when it's impossible to conceive of there having been a black moviemaker. He did not ask permission for what to make. He did not get a collective democratic point of view on what he should do. He made his pictures and you know what he did? He put them in the back of a car and traveled the country. If there's anything useful that I can tell you guys today as young filmmakers, it's that story. That's what you have to do. Not necessarily put your films in the back of your car, but you have to be true to your own vision and make those pictures that you want to make. So all I can say is, "Buck up and go get 'em!"

━━◆━━

Films as Actor

1950 *No Way Out*	1969 *The Lost Man*
1951 *Cry, the Beloved Country*	1970 *They Call Me MISTER Tibbs!*
1952 *Red Ball Express*	1971 *Brother John*
1954 *Go, Man, Go!*	*The Organization*
1955 *Blackboard Jungle*	1972 *Buck and the Preacher* (also
1956 *Good-bye, My Lady*	director)
1957 *Edge of the City*	1973 *A Warm December* (also
Something of Value	director)
Band of Angels	1974 *Uptown Saturday Night* (also
The Mark of the Hawk	director)
1958 *Virgin Island*	1975 *The Wilby Conspiracy*
The Defiant Ones	*Let's Do It Again* (also director)
1959 *Porgy and Bess*	1977 *A Piece of the Action* (also
1960 *All the Young Men*	director)
1961 *A Raisin in the Sun*	1988 *Shoot to Kill*
Paris Blues	*Little Nikita*
1962 *Pressure Point*	1991 *Separate But Equal* (television)
1963 *Lilies of the Field*	1992 *Sneakers*
1964 *The Long Ships*	1995 *Children of the Dust*
1965 *The Bedford Incident*	1996 *To Sir, with Love II* (television)
The Greatest Story Ever Told	1997 *Mandela and de Klerk*
A Patch of Blue	(television)
The Slender Thread	*The Jackal*
1966 *Duel at Diablo*	1998 *David and Lisa* (television)
1967 *To Sir, with Love*	1999 *Free of Eden* (television)
In the Heat of the Night	*The Simple Life of Noah*
Guess Who's Coming to Dinner	*Dearborn* (television)
1968 *For Love of Ivy* (also original	2001 *The Last Brickmaker in America*
story)	(television)

Poitier appeared on television early in his career including *Kraft Television Theater,* 1952; and *The Philco Television Playhouse,* 1952–55. Poitier directed but did not appear in *Stir Crazy,* 1980; *Hanky Panky,* 1982; *Fast Forward,* 1985; and *Ghost Dad,* 1990.

I think the single most helpful thing for working on a screenplay is learning something about acting. What is required at every moment of a script is the ability to generate truthful behavior within imaginary circumstances. When you start work as a screenwriter, one of the key principles to remember is, at any given moment, who wants what and why.

SYDNEY POLLACK
(Born in Lafayette, Indiana, 1934—Died 2008)

Sydney Pollack transformed a youthful fascination with the actor's craft into a prolific career as a director and producer of motion pictures. His parents were first-generation Russian-Americans who raised their two sons in Indiana. After high school, Sydney headed for New York. "As soon as I got off the train, I knew I had made the right choice," he recalled. "As soon as I walked down the street, I felt that I was at the center of something." He studied with Sanford Meisner at the Neighborhood Playhouse, later becoming Meisner's assistant. He worked as an actor on stage and in television, leading John Frankenheimer to take him to Hollywood in 1960 as dialogue director for the child actors on *The Young Savages*. "I taught acting for years," he said, "without knowing that it was the thing that started bending me toward directing."

Pollack had a role in *War Hunt,* a 1962 low-budget Korean War film, where he became friends with fellow cast member Robert Redford. He directed episodes of *The Defenders, Naked City, The Fugitive, Alfred Hitchcock Presents* and *Ben Casey,* using these opportunities to master the director's craft. In 1965 he was given a chance to direct his first feature, *The Slender Thread,* starring Sidney Poitier and Anne Bancroft. This began his lifelong practice of placing important stars at the center of his films. He earned his first Oscar nomination in 1969 for *They Shoot Horses, Don't They?* with Jane Fonda. Three pictures with Redford, *This Property Is Condemned, Jeremiah Johnson* and *The Way We Were,* showed his ability to tell stories in different genres, as did *Three Days of the Condor* and *Absence of Malice.*

His most ambitious film also starred Redford. *Out of Africa* was an epic romance based on the life of Isak Dinesen, played by Meryl Streep, set in colonial East Africa, and in 1986 it brought him Oscars for producer and

Sydney Pollack directed Dustin Hoffman in *Tootsie* (1982),
and played the role of his agent.

director. Pollack saw himself as a traditionalist and enjoyed the challenge of
working within "the strict parameters of a given genre and striving to find
some new voice within it." He never set out to establish a personal style. "I
think that my films are conventional in form, but not necessarily in point of
view."

Pollack had left acting behind for nearly twenty years when he started
shooting *Tootsie* in 1981. The production was fraught with conflict and published speculation that it would be a catastrophe. Dustin Hoffman became
insistent that Sydney cast himself to play the agent for Hoffman's character.
He finally agreed and his portrayal is a highlight of what became one of his
biggest successes, causing many to observe that Pollack's impatience with
Hoffman showed through on the screen. After that he often acted in other
directors' films, including *The Player* for Robert Altman, *Husbands and Wives*
for Woody Allen and *Eyes Wide Shut* for Stanley Kubrick.

Pollack discovered that there were many scripts he would love to see on
the screen. "That's two hours of my life, but directing a film is two years," he
explained. So he decided to produce, at one point forming a partnership with
fellow director Anthony Minghella. He produced *The Fabulous Baker Boys,
The Talented Mr. Ripley, Cold Mountain* and *The Reader,* and both produced
and starred in, alongside George Clooney, *Michael Clayton,* for which he
received his sixth Best Picture nomination from the Academy.

Pollack directed his first feature in 1965, about the time that Golden Age directors and industry leaders like Fred Zinnemann, William Wyler, John Ford and John Huston were ending their careers. He worked to extend their legacy by being a statesman in the film community, known among directors as a supportive colleague who took strong stands for the integrity of films and the rights of artists. He was always a realist, prepared for the ups and downs of Hollywood. When his big-budget film *Havana* opened to negative reviews and small audiences, his response to a critic was straightforward and very much in character: "To tell you the truth, if I knew what was wrong I would have fixed it."

SYDNEY POLLACK

—◆—

April 7, 1983*

Did you always know you were going to be a success in this business?

I've heard both answers to that question from other people, and I'm always amazed when somebody says they did know. When I was growing up I wouldn't have believed that I'd have the opportunity to make films for a living. For me it started as a fantasy. I said to myself, "I think I'd like to be an actor," but that seemed like a very far-fetched idea. I was born and raised in the Midwest, in South Bend, Indiana, which is not a paragon of culture, not by a long shot. It was a factory town, as far away from New York and California as can be, where you either had to play football or basketball or die. You didn't want to tell anybody you wanted to be an actor. Deep down, I don't think I ever believed I would make an honest living as an actor. I'm sure luck comes into it. I'm sure hard work comes into it. I'm sure natural skill or talent, all of those things, are part of it.

How did you get your first directing break?

I studied with a wonderful teacher who was something of a god to me, a man named Sandy Meisner, who was part of the Group Theater. At the end of the two years I spent at his school, the Neighborhood Playhouse in New York, I was asked to come back as an assistant. I didn't want to teach

*Ron Silverman moderated this siminar. This transcript also contains segments from seminars Sydney Pollack gave at the American Film Institute on November 30, 1977, January 6, 1978, January 13, 1978, February 28, 1980, April 29, 1986, November 3, 1993, and December 19, 1995.

acting but was so honored and flattered at this invitation—I was nineteen years old at the time—that I took the job and spent four or five years teaching with him. I found I had a skill for teaching, and even started my own little studio with Wynn Handman. I began to get more jobs as an acting coach, because I had students who went out and started to work in plays in and around New York. Teachers are like security blankets. One of my students would get a job but not necessarily trust the director, and would call me and say, "Listen, would you meet me and go over this scene and make sure I'm doing it right?" It wasn't something I wanted to do or intended to do. I really wanted to be an actor. When somebody first suggested I direct, I took it as a terrible insult that I was a lousy actor or something.

It was really through the teaching that I accidentally got a job as dialogue director in 1960. John Frankenheimer was directing his first film, *The Young Savages,* with Burt Lancaster and Shelley Winters. He asked me to help him find and coach three new actors, so I held auditions in New York and found three actors for him. When Frankenheimer brought them out to California, he asked if I would come along and help with these kids. Eventually he said, "You know, you ought to direct." Burt Lancaster, who was at the height of his career in those days, was always kind of joking with me. "Hey, kid, what are you telling those guys? What do you say to them?" He would delight in embarrassing me. After a while I started to talk to him more and more about his own role. At the end of the picture I was packing my bags when I got a call from Lancaster's secretary. "Mr. Lancaster would like to see you." I went over to his offices and he said, "Listen, stop screwing around. You should become a director." I was really offended by this. At first I thought he meant that I would never become an actor. I said, "I haven't thought about it." Burt said, "I'm going to call a guy. I think you should stay in town and go see him." He proceeded to call the agent Lew Wasserman. I didn't even know who Wasserman was. So I went to a meeting with Wasserman, who clearly wasn't very interested in meeting with me, but was doing his friend Burt a favor. He said, "Well, what have you directed?" Nothing. "Where do you live?" New York. "Can you move here?" Yes. Then he said, "How much do you need to live here?" And like a schmuck I said, "A hundred dollars a week." I was married with a child at the time. He said, "Okay, I'm going to pay you a hundred dollars a week for six months. I'm going to put you under the wing of Dick Irving." Dick turned out to be a wonderful guy who produced a whole lot of fodder that was churned out for television every day. Chekhov it wasn't.

So I moved out here and spent time watching them make these shows. One of them was a half-hour western show that was shot in two days and was really awful. It was called *Shotgun Slade,* starring Scott Brady, and the gimmick was that Brady carried a sawn-off shotgun on his hip and the music was modern jazz. They had canceled the show, but there were maybe four more to shoot, and they knew I couldn't screw things up any worse than they already were, so they said I could direct one of them. They had nothing to lose. At this point I didn't even know which end of the camera to look through. I didn't know what a lens was, I didn't know how to stage a scene. I didn't know anything about the mechanics. I didn't know how to do the action stuff, and I was the laughingstock of the lot. I had broken down the script into beats and had made these impossible drawings of close-ups with feet in them. I had absolutely no sense of what to do, so it was a total mess, even though the one thing I was good at was working with the actors. It would be really raggedy until two characters got into a room together, and then the thing would settle down for a while. At first they couldn't even edit the show, but I ended up spending a lot of time in the cutting room with a wonderful editor who put it together for me. He blew up shots, flipped other shots over, and cut this poor mess together. Once I saw him trying to put this film together I got fascinated with the mechanics. So my training ground was five years of twenty television shows a year. I tried everything with a wide-angle lens and a close-up, without cuts, all in cuts, from a helicopter, only hand-held camera. In five years I did a hundred television shows, so by the time I got my first feature film I'd really spent time at film school learning about the mechanics.

Can you talk about your stylistic approach to shooting Jeremiah Johnson?

That area where we shot in Utah, where all the snow was, is the Sundance area that belongs to Bob Redford, and several of us have cabins up there, so I knew what it looked like in winter. Most of our mountains in this country are north-south ranges, because they're offshoots of the Rockies. North-south ranges in this country slope very gently. We have a couple of east-west ranges called the Wasatch and the Uintas. They run counter to the geography and are more alpine and more rugged. They aren't terribly high, but they're very picturesque and dramatic.

We took off in snow machines and tractors and went to out-of-the-way places. It's extremely difficult logistically to shoot a picture like that. You're looking at twenty feet of snow. The horses panic and won't walk in it. You're battling light reflected from the snow, so you have to use great arc lights, but try moving an arc light in those conditions. We had to make tractors and trailers, little snowmobiles, sleds that would pull the arc lights around. It was approached in a very simple way photographically. Necessity was the mother of invention, because I couldn't really move that much, except for zoom lenses. In other words, because I couldn't set up a lot of dolly tracks, because I couldn't do a lot of panning around, I shot the film with rather static, classically composed frames. The framing came from looking at Bierstadt paintings of the old West, seeing where the horizon is placed. It was the opposite from what I did on *They Shoot Horses, Don't They?*, where everything is deliberately messy and uncomposed, spilling out of the frame, like arbitrarily putting a cookie cutter into dough. I never wanted the audience to feel there was a complete picture within the frame. I wanted to get the sense that the picture was spilling out from all sides.

When we made *Jeremiah Johnson,* Redford was not who he is today. We made a deal at Warner Bros. to do this script called *Liver-Eating Johnson.* Shortly before this, Redford had bought Sundance, the ski area, and he needed money, so he took an advance on his salary and put it into the land up there. I gave them an estimate of what I thought the picture would cost based on nothing other than a roundhouse estimate on another western I had done in Mexico. I told them I thought the picture would cost about $3.5 million. The studio did a budget which came out to around $5.4 million. New management had just taken over at the studio, and this was going to be their first picture. They were mortified when they saw the budget of $5.4 million and said we needed to structure the thing so we could shoot mountain scenes on the backlot or in a studio. We even considered the Pyrenees between France and Spain because we thought it would be cheaper to shoot there. The budget for the backlot version came to $3.6 million, so I said to them, "If you give me the $3.6 million and don't ask me any questions I'll make the same picture as you budgeted for $5.4 million, but I can't make it through the studio. Just put the money in an account, put your own auditors on it, and I'll deliver you the picture." They said, "That's great, but you'll have to put up your salary and your house." So I signed over the lease to my house and gave them my salary.

I just had to get out there and shoot the thing, which wasn't easy. There was too much at stake. I had to shoot in all conditions, and as a result there are some grossly mismatched scenes. We would take shots one day and come back the next and it wasn't snowing. There was nothing I could do. About five months before we were to start filming I explained the situation to a good friend of mine at Panavision. I said it was my own money and that I was in trouble. From a union point of view I wasn't legally allowed to purchase and load film, but he was able to. Every Friday in the fall I'd get a call from Redford and he'd say, "The colors are fantastic! The leaves are turning." This was months before we started shooting, so I called my friend at Panavision and said, "Send me an Arriflex and a zoom and a tripod." The equipment would be delivered to my house with the magazines all loaded. I'd get on a Western Airlines flight to Salt Lake City, rent a station wagon, throw those crazy clothes on Redford and shoot all of the main-title shots when the leaves are turning and he's walking. If I had taken crews up there it would have been fabulous, but just too expensive. I shot it myself and we saved a fortune.

Obviously Redford knew about the financial problems behind the film, so he didn't take a trailer. He didn't have a car and driver, he didn't get any expense money. He lived in a motel room as I did and, quite honestly, we broke a lot of union rules. We didn't take a Hollywood projectionist to run dailies. We hired a local theater guy for five dollars a night to run the dailies instead of paying twelve hundred dollars a week, plus fringe benefits, plus transportation, plus food, plus everything to hire a union guy. I didn't even see dailies every night. I saw them twice a week, because it saved money. I remembered from my television days that Universal Studios had devised a system of punching film to save developing costs. Every bit of film you expose through the camera is expensive to develop. Universal had developed this way of drilling a hole in the back of a Mitchell camera and spring-loading a flat-headed punch which wouldn't puncture the film, just make a dimple on it. The camera operators were trained to punch after each take. You do take one, you punch once, you do take two, you would punch twice. At the end of the day if you wanted to print only takes three and eight, you could hire an editor, for scale, to come into the darkroom with a glove and roll down the negative until he felt the dimple. He could count the takes and cut the undeveloped negative so you would only develop the pieces you wanted printed. If you're willing to take the risk of ruining your negative, you save an enormous amount of money. I made the picture for $3.1 million, about $2.3 million less than what the studio had originally budgeted.

You take a crew on location and they get paid for six days of work but also for the seventh day sitting around in a motel. The seventh day is double time if you work them. The hot thing to do at night in Heber City, Utah, is go down to Chick's Famous Cafe and have some greasy scones.

You've got a crew that's as anxious to get out of Heber City as you are, so you sit down and say, "Hey, guys, let's say we go out every Sunday afternoon. I'll make a big picnic lunch and we'll shoot for two, three hours." This is totally against union rules, but we shot all of the animal stuff, all the buffalo hunts and the deer hunting and the grizzly bear and all that, on Sundays, and again saved a fortune. What the hell else did they have to do? Sit at the motel window and watch it snow?

There is a wonderful lack of verbalization between the characters in the film.

The mountain people and the Indians are stoical people. What these guys lived through was so unbelievable, the cold they endured, the physical discomfort. They were short on displaying emotion, otherwise they would just go around crying all the time. There's a whole other vocabulary to learn. You can't go out into that weather and say, "My toes are cold," because your toes are always cold. What did they say to each other when they say goodbye? "Watch your topknot." It's understated stuff like that. The dramatic situation is carrying everything for you, and you really don't need anyone saying anything. It's like the scene in *Three Days of the Condor* when Max von Sydow and Redford are riding down in the elevator together. You could have them say anything. It really doesn't matter, because the situation is doing it all for you. That's true in all good dramatic situations.

How do you feel about the character of Jeremiah Johnson?

I'm always moved by that sort of simple-minded courage. He reminds me of other characters I've dealt with, like the characters in *They Shoot Horses, Don't They?* who come out every time the siren rings. I find that moving. Those people are innocent of their plight. I would find the whole thing worthless if Johnson or any of the characters in *Horses* felt sorry for themselves. I found him a touching character, in a curious way, but for me he was also a metaphor for a dropout. Here was a guy who, instead of fixing things where he was, decided to adopt his own code and his own morality. Instead of making things work within society's ethical code he said, "To hell with that. I want to go where I'm responsible for my own destiny. I don't have to abide by anybody's code or morality but my own." But of course that doesn't work. It never does. It can't. It's a fallacy in a collective society, in a world as populated as we are. It's a myth. Maybe it was possible once, but no longer. So the problem became one of devising a way for his own morality to trap him there and destroy him. At a certain point I wanted to symbolize that visually by having him climb higher and higher into the mountains. I had a mythical ending where he just went higher and higher until he froze to death and became a monument to himself, alone on a mountain encased in ice. But it's one thing to think those thoughts and another thing to film them. I kept cutting and cutting the film and found that shot we used at the end where he puts his hand down. I don't know if it means peace or not, but a lot of people take it to mean peace and that's just fine with me. It just seemed like the right moment to end it. There wasn't any more story to tell. His adventure was over.

Could you talk about your work with Robert Redford over the years?

We met in 1960 when we were kids working together on a movie. It was his first film, so we were sort of drawn to each other. I was scared to death and I think he was too. Later I began to direct some television and didn't see too much of him. I directed him first in 1965, a film made from a Tennessee Williams one-act play called *This Property Is Condemned*. Natalie Wood was in the prime of her stardom, so she could dictate who her co-stars would be. She had seen Redford in the play *Barefoot in the Park* and chose him to be in the film. It was the second film I ever directed.

Pollack on location in Bay St. Louis, Mississippi, where he shot *This Property Is Condemned* (1966), with Robert Redford and Natalie Wood. The film was based on a one-act play by Tennessee Williams.

For the particular kind of love story that I do, Redford is a kind of archetype. There's something very American about him. He has a much darker inside than what one sees on the outside. He's prototypically American in that sense. America has this glamorous exterior and a rather troubled, dark interior. Redford has that. He's the kind of actor I particularly like in the sense that he's mysterious. Actors often feel they have to do a little acting here and there. The fact is there are very few of them who have the confidence to trust the audience and just be. One of the things that's most impressive in film acting is someone with enough confidence to do nothing, someone who as a human being is sufficiently interesting so that if he's behaving truthfully within a role, the audience will be satisfied and watch him. Redford has that quality. He creates a lot of interest by what he doesn't do, by the way he withholds things. He creates a need on the part of the audience to move toward him to find out more. He's not the kind of performer that leaps off the screen and grabs you by the nose and involves you. He prefers understatement, and starves audiences, but at the same time we're never bored. Audiences want more from him, whether it's vulnerability or extroverted emotion. To make an analogy, if he has ten dollars he'll spend three and keep seven in his back pocket. Everybody wants to get at the seven dollars in that pocket and they keep coming back to see him. He's a guy who wants to see if it's possible to be a part of something without giving up any of his individuality and finds, at least in all of the films that I've made with him, that it can't be done. But he keeps trying in the next film. In a certain way they're all the same character: a guy who leaves society and travels to an unexplored wilderness to try to preserve his own individuality, to see if he can live a life that's not beholden to any structured set of mores.

I know I'm being simplistic here, but a lot of people become actors because they need to fulfill a certain fantasy of who they are in opposition to who they really are, which means that the farther the reach of the character, the more comfortable they are playing it. Then there are other actors—the ones who become what we call movie stars—who are quite comfortable with their own persona and have a peculiar knack which the screen is very fond of, of just being able to sit while the camera is on them without finding it necessary to do something, to be acting. Now, some people are much more impressed with a certain kind of overt churning-up of emotion. That in itself, of course, is an accomplishment. It really depends on what's required in the role. But to my mind Redford is best in roles where the character is somewhat introverted, though still capable of a lot. His early television work, if you ever have an opportunity to see it, was all character work. He became a leading man quite late in his life. He was a crazy character actor. I remember a *Defenders* episode where he plays a psychotic escaped killer who traps E. G. Marshall in his office at gunpoint. I saw him playing a crazy Nazi on a *Playhouse 90* with Charles Laughton. Movie stars are, emotionally speaking, character actors in the bodies of leading men or leading women. Redford is essentially a character actor, regardless of what anybody says about him. Most people can't get past his looks, including the critics. Nobody had any idea he was going to be a big sex symbol. He was more surprised than anybody when he started to get cast in those roles, but one thing he always had in his acting was this sort of confidence to never do too much.

Generally I work with Redford much more directly than I do with other actors. By "directly," I mean I would say to Bob, "What are you doing? That's terrible . . . What are you doing? Do it again." I would never say that to another actor. I say it partially because he knows me well enough that he doesn't take it personally. It doesn't hurt his feelings. He's a very instinctive kind of an actor. Although he did have formal training, he's not an actor who likes to talk about it a lot and he doesn't like to rehearse a lot. He doesn't mind any number of takes as long as you give him something different on each take.

Would you talk about how you work with your editors?

Often when I speak at colleges, people ask, "Do you edit your own films?" That would be like saying to a painter, "Do you mix your own colors?" The answer is of course. You have to. When I was doing television I got lucky in that I found an editor at Universal Studios, a terrific guy who would let me stay all night editing with him. The shooting day would end at maybe five o'clock, and then I would work with him until six the next morning without the producer knowing. He would present his rough assembly to the producer, but I had already had some input. It was my way of learning about postproduction.

The only way I know how to work with an editor is really the simplest way. During filming I watch the dailies with him and give him notes. Let's say I print two takes. I might say, "The first half of take three and the second half of take four," and he makes a note. Or I might say, "Don't open the sequence on the master. Open on her close-up and stay on it for about four or five lines and then go to the master." I may not even say that much. What happens is that he starts to put together a rough assembly. I finish shooting and hope he's about two weeks behind me so I can take a vacation for a week, because I'm exhausted. I come back and look at the assembly. On the worst days it's just awful. Valium. I'm not joking. You wouldn't believe what any of these pictures look like in rough assembly. In *They Shoot Horses, Don't They?* we were suicidal. It was four and a half hours of garbage. I've never looked at a rough cut of any film of mine where I haven't been ready to give up the business or kill myself. It's gotten now so it's a joke.

Once the rough assembly is done, I go into the projection room with the first reel and, like anything else, start with the general and get more specific. Forward and back, forward and back. I tell the editor what to change in reel one. Then we go on to reel two. It takes about two and a half weeks to get through the picture this way, at which point I run it again and then go back and look through every outtake and every trim that's not in the picture, which might take me a month. If I find really good moments I cut them out and put them aside. Then we go back to the Moviola, starting with reel one, and I say, "Stop right there—put in that other close-up there." Then I start whittling and whittling. It never stops, which is one of the things they complain about, because I keep on cutting films right through the mixing, which means they have to change all the sound masters and the negative cuts.

I stay with the films after they've opened. I go to Europe and look at the theaters and the projection lenses and listen to the sound system. I run my finger across the screens and wash them if they're dirty, which they always are. You've put two years of your life into something and you give it to some jerk who's handling twenty films at the same time. The older I get, the longer it takes me to make a film, because I'm more reluctant to let them go. I stay with them.

Is there anybody else you bring in to consult on the cut?

I have an editor who I trust who'll sometimes say, "I don't like that very much." He doesn't say much. I know how he feels. I can tell if he's bored. I have a group of truth-telling friends who I bring in who tell me what they think. One thing to know is that uninitiated people don't understand the process. Something might feel repetitive to someone, but it's not easy to articulate exactly what the problem is. Working out what might be wrong with a rough cut when people complain about it is like trying to get a baby to tell you what's wrong when they're sick. Somebody might say "That scene is too long," when really it's the scene just before that's too long. The director is a doctor. He has to deduce things backwards. I'll show my wife, who is very smart and knows the business, a rough cut and she'll say, "You've got eighteen scenes where he's saying the same thing to her." I'll say, "What do you mean? There's just one scene." She'll say, "There are eighteen." Well, of course there aren't eighteen, but it feels to her like there are, so I have to work out what's making her think there are eighteen scenes when there's only one.

Do you like to preview your films to public audiences?

I'm too stubborn to preview. If I preview a picture, I'm making their picture instead of mine. If they don't like it, I cut it out. If they like it, I leave it in. Where's the satisfaction in that? I just don't believe in it.

When an actor asks you for information about his or her character, do you make that up yourself, or do you work it out with the writer beforehand?

The actor may not need to know everything or he may have thought about it himself, but the first person who really has to know things like that is me. In other words, the actor does his own filling in of where his character was before the first scene of the film took place, what the last couple of years of his life were, but I should be able to answer any questions at all. Maybe I should turn to the writer in cases like this, but often the writer isn't there. My dream would be to have the writer throughout on a film. I would love to have the luxury of having the writer with me

Sally Field plays a Miami newspaper reporter in *Absence of Malice* (1981). Pollack directed, and Paul Newman was the co-star.

when I pick locations and during shooting, which is when a lot of new ideas happen, and having him view the dailies, which is when you see the characters finally come to life and where things are clarified that you could never have originally envisaged. Often you realize that a single close-up means you can do away with a whole page of dialogue. I would love to have dinner with the writer every evening and talk about the work and what's to come, and keep refining and changing the screenplay.

But actually most writers couldn't help the actor with the kind of information they sometimes want, because facts are not what they're looking for. The actor doesn't need to know the biography of a character. What the actor needs are those things which translate directly into attitude or behavior, and there's a certain amount of practice that goes into knowing the difference. In other words, if I asked someone who is not an actor to tell me the background of a certain character in a film we had just seen, there would be a vast difference between the way they would tell it and the way I would tell it. "He was married once." Well, that doesn't mean anything. Was he married to a girl fourteen years younger than himself? Or was he married to a girl twenty-five years older? Was he married for a year and given custody of the children? The marriage doesn't mean anything without going another step. What kind of marriage was it? What kind of an attitude did he have at the end of the marriage? Did it wound him in some way? And how can the director give something to the actor so he or she can dig into the background of a character and arrive at a point where they really can pinpoint who that person is? You can throw any imaginary situation to a really good actor and they'll know how to respond to it, in character, because of a total grasp and understanding of the elements that were formative in that character's life. It's a good exercise for a director, because it means you also have a total grasp of the world of those characters.

Do you prefer scripts with nothing but dialogue and general descriptions of what you are supposed to shoot, or scripts full of specific shots?

I've read scripts that have been pretty much all dialogue and I've read scripts where every shot is laid out in graphic detail. I've never paid much attention to the latter. When you start reading things like "We begin on a tiny dot," you get very suspicious. It doesn't mean a good writer can't write a visual screenplay once in a while, but usually the guys that do all that shot work don't know what the hell they're talking about. It gets crazy: "The following shots will be six seconds apiece," or "The pace will accelerate rapidly until we are in a cacophony of blah blah blah." I just close the script. Professional writers will write in master shots and use a change of shot to describe the room, character, tone of the scene or whatever, and will occasionally write something like "Close-up on so-and-so." That's their province and it's all kosher, but a director doesn't want much beyond that.

Do you sit down with the actors before the shoot and do a read-through of the script?

To be honest with you, I don't rehearse much. I know that's blasphemy and I know there are a lot of wonderful directors whose films I admire enormously who do rehearse, but I've slowly moved farther away from it. I can't do things in the rehearsal that I can when I'm there on set filming, and neither can most of the actors I work with. There's a tendency to get very intellectual and experimental in rehearsal, but that's just a waste of time for me. If I'm on the set I can see what it looks like. I see the actors in costume and look through the camera and see the frame in two dimensions, and it becomes clear what the actors need to be doing. It's hard to sit around with a cup of coffee, talking, imagining what it's going to look like. For the most part I rehearse just before the take, and then shoot.

I've only rehearsed one movie my whole life with read-throughs, and that was *Bobby Deerfield*. I did it that way because Pacino insisted on it. Al gets more spontaneous the more he rehearses. The more secure he is in knowing everything, the freer that permits him to be. We did homework to construct a whole life for him which exists before the film starts and between scenes, and even after the film ends. Al works best by being able to create a total reality for himself. If there's an eight-page shot in a night-club, he wants to know if it's the first time they've been there. Is it Saturday night? What did they do during the day? Where are they going afterwards? Have they eaten dinner? Are they having drinks? How long has he been with the girl? Did she pick him up? Did she meet him at a racetrack? There are hundreds of things that give him clues about the nature of the relationship, so he's able to know exactly where, emotionally, the furniture is. Al is an actor who comes from the theater and really needs to feel secure. Other than that I've never rehearsed a picture in my life.

You've talked in the past about how directors often direct too much.

Pollack's last film, *The Interpreter* (2005), starred Sean Penn and Nicole
Kidman. Pollack gained unprecedented permission to shoot several scenes
inside the United Nations General Assembly in New York.

The final objective when it comes to directing is to get everyone to do
what you want. Sometimes you can do this without a lot of people knowing that's what you're doing, which is the best way. The people who strut
around all the time barking orders are usually the insecure ones. The trick
of directing is knowing when to shut up and when to stay out of the way
of what's working. If you've prepared properly and cast it properly, hired
the right people, you don't have to run around doing a lot of screaming.
You have to know when to let it work by itself. My hobby is flying. I have
a plane and fly everywhere in it. One of the first things you learn when
you're flying, and one of the most difficult things to learn, is that you land
an airplane by not letting it land. What you do is get it down close to the
ground and then hold it off as long as possible, and that's what makes it
touch down nicely. In the same way, directing is sometimes about not
directing. Some directors feel compelled to be directing all the time.
Everything's happening perfectly but they're still directing. There's nothing to do if it's going great. Just shut up and shoot it! I find that you make
an actor terribly anxious when you overdirect him. The fact is, you can
get very close to the precise vision you have by making the actor think
they thought it all up themselves. When that happens, they do it better
and feel more at home with it. Most beginning directors spend so much
time directing that they aren't seeing what the actors are really doing.

Technique is for when intuition fails. Quite often it's a blessing to get an untrained actor who won't overcomplicate things. By the same token, a well-schooled actor who knows and understands how to use his technique uses it only when necessary. But there's no reason to assume that an actor won't understand intuitively how to do something. There's no law that says the actor can't show up without saying a word and you roll the camera and it's perfect. The hardest thing in the world is just to walk away from it and say "print" and move on to the next one. As a rule I get to the set and send everybody out except the actors, so they don't feel self-conscious or that they're being watched. I want to see what the actors feel most comfortable doing. I say, "Okay, let's just do it once real easy," always letting them know that I don't expect to see a performance, that I want them to do it for themselves, to find out what it's about. I don't say anything. I give them a few minutes to find out where they are, where the furniture is. Let them try it a couple of ways, even if it's all wrong. If you're secure enough to know that eventually you're going to be in control, you don't have the need to jump on them each time they go off in a wrong direction. Let them go down the wrong alley. Even agree with them. "Yes, very interesting." "Terrific idea." "What if on top of that we had this?" Sometimes they get themselves in a position that I won't be able to shoot, in which case you say, "That's terrific, but instead of sitting there, if you walked over there and sat, then I'd get more distance between you. I really feel that you should be talking at her from here." You don't say, "Don't sit down there. Go over there instead."

It's always a very careful process. The key is making them feel confident and secure and relaxed. A relaxed actor can do anything. If he doesn't realize he's not doing what you want, say, "Try moving around a little bit. Maybe put something in your hand. Start playing with the knife. Fool with your belt buckle." Just lead them into that agitation. You don't have to start pushing them around with "You sit here and you sit there." You can get exactly what you want without that, and then you don't make them feel like dummies. You're turning them away from their idea, a little at a time. Never say, "No, that's all wrong. It's like this . . ." If you do that, you're inhibiting something essential to the process. I would suggest that with your mind you force the actors to do what you want them to do without verbalizing it all. That's what speech in film really is. It should be the last thing that happens. You have a certain impulse, and when you can't hold back anymore you might be forced to say something. In reality, eight times out of ten I don't have to do anything except call the cameraman in and say to the actors, "Okay, do what you just did." I just get everybody out there and let them play the scene for the first time, and then I start to jabber if I have to. But if I don't have to, I don't.

Are there any differences between acting on film and for the theater?

One thing I find interesting about rehearsing a stage play, as opposed to a film, is that you have to train the actors to perform without you. What you want in theater is an actor who is independent of the director. The stage actor has to understand at every moment what he or she is doing. The stage actor has the scene before as a springboard and the scene after as a follow-through, so there's an emotional map of where they need to go that helps them give a spontaneous and truthful performance every night. I can recall getting a part in a Broadway show, and during the first reading of the play we sat around a table. There was a marvelous nervous spontaneity during that first reading. We asked questions and the director began to discuss details with us. It was a process of breaking everything down. Slowly the performances grew back organically and, hopefully, retained the original spontaneity that we'd had instinctively. We tested that emotional map out in real time as we worked on the pace and shape of the story. But that's a four-week process, a luxury you don't have in film.

Film is the complete opposite. The only one who's going to be there when the performance gets put together is the director, sitting in the editing room. Hopefully by then you have what you need from everyone. If it doesn't work, it's the director's fault. Curiously, what you want in a film is a confused actor, a slightly unsettled actor, someone who's not quite certain about things, someone not so entrenched, an actor who is dependent on the director, because it's easier to influence them. In film, an actor doesn't have to understand anything. He just has to do it once and the camera has to be rolling. He doesn't necessarily have to understand how he gets from here to there, because he's not going to be performing it the way he would on stage and he's not going to have to repeat it, except perhaps for the close-ups. There is an intellectual level of understanding in a theater performance that doesn't need to be there in film, because the stage actor is playing the character over and over every night, going through the piece from beginning to middle to end. The film actor only gets to do everything once. It's easier to move a tree that doesn't have roots than it is to move a tree with established roots, and in the rehearsal process an actor is like a tree that slowly grows roots. I want them comfortable enough to act, but able to adjust to whatever it is I'm holding in my head as the director, because they're long gone by the time any of us are going to know whether it really works or not. You want the maximum degree of dependency on you when you're making the film. You want a lost actor.

Making a movie is like putting your hand on a record and slowing it down so it's unrecognizable. Then you ask, "Is this going to work?" There aren't a lot of people who know how to gauge that. That's really what you're doing as the director. You're out there for sixteen hours a day and come home with a minute and a half of film which is going to be cut together with a moment that you're not going to shoot for another month and a half. You're working out of continuity. You're dealing with a patchwork, and the way in which the patchwork comes together is fundamentally constructed upon the director's vision. Simply, you want the least amount of interference in that process as possible. You don't want a committee decision to be made about any aspect of the film. To my mind there is a feeling in *Jeremiah Johnson*—I call it a melancholy feeling, call it whatever you will—a kind of soulful, spiritual feeling to the movie. Now, this doesn't come from explaining the feeling to the actors. I can't say, "I want you to be soulful." An actor wouldn't know what to do with direction like that. You can't act soulful. Acting a mood is what bad actors do all the time. The mood has to be a by-product of what people are actually doing. Everything comes from one thing: the reality of doing.

With movies it's not so easy to rehearse from beginning to end, because often movie scripts don't read like plays. They're episodic. They have a half-scene in a room and then a cut to a street corner. It's not easy to sit down in a room and read that kind of stuff. With film you're moving at a very different speed, and as the director maybe you've had seven or eight months of working this all out in your head. The actors come in and want to go down all those blind alleys that you've already gone down. But I don't really want that. I don't want to take that time. I just want them to trust me and move this little bit when I need them to move, because it's the only way I can keep it fresh for them. You've got to roll the camera before everything starts questioning itself. This is why I do as little rehearsal as possible, unless I have enough time to move through the period of questioning and insecurity and then build it back up. Something wonderful happens when the actors aren't quite sure of what they're going to say next. Actually, it's often when they're really ready that you've got to be a little careful. For me the film is taking place while I'm shooting it. I'm not just photographing what we might have already created before the cameras are rolling.

Sidney Lumet is very much a stage-oriented director. He rehearses all his pictures for a couple of weeks and blocks everything with tape on the floor, in the shape of the set. As the people are moving around he's whispering to his cameraman, "Close-up." Then, when they get on the set, everybody knows what to do. The point is, if I tried to work like Sidney Lumet, I would walk around during filming with a splitting headache from guilt. I'd say, "Jesus, I'm not doing anything." But if Sidney Lumet saw me working he would say, "How can you go in when you don't have things worked out?" It just depends upon what's right for you. I tend to work more instinctively than intellectually. I often don't even know what the films are about when I'm doing them. I can envision a film better if it does something emotionally to me than if it does something intellectually. Afterwards I try to explain to myself what it means, so I can make it intellectually cohesive.

Please understand that this is a personal way of working. It's not necessarily right and it's not necessarily wrong; it's just my way. There isn't any methodology to creative work. We all do it differently. All creative work is personal, and I can't tell you that one method works any better than any other. You've each got to find your own way of doing things, and it could be exactly the opposite from what I do. For example, I do a lot of work to music. During preproduction on a picture, perhaps two months before shooting, when I don't have to map things out exactly, I sit in my living room, have a drink, get comfortable and put on some music, very loud—louder than my family likes, so I close all the doors—and think. My mind starts to wander and sometimes I see sequences and camera moves. Also, one of my ways of crystallizing a concept is talking about it. Sometimes you don't really understand something until you're forced to articulate it. I believe in doing a lot of talking when I'm working on a picture. I talk to my kids, I talk to my wife. I talk to any damn fool who'll listen to me. I say, "I'm doing this picture. Let me tell you what it's about." Each time I tell it, I tell it a little differently, and as I watch their faces I can see spots where it sags and can sense that this particular moment might not be a very good one. When I'm telling a story to someone, I know I'm in trouble if I clearly can't keep their interest.

Does your sense of how to direct actors in films get you into trouble?

A lot of actors perhaps think my way of working would turn them into second-class citizens. But nothing could be further from the truth. My pictures are rooted in the performances. But I do believe that actors and

directors operate on different levels, and there comes a point where it's
not only unnecessary but harmful to verbalize intellectually certain things
to an actor. A good example is what the film is about thematically. Every
good film has a spine. I think of this visually, like an armature in a piece of
sculpture. It's not something you ever see, it's the little bundle of wire that
gets balled up and then you put the clay on it. It's the hard center that
holds up the clay. It gives you parameters within which to work. It's something you can hold every scene up to and say, "Does this illustrate the
story's central idea?" Each character, each scene, is in some way either
helping to illuminate or disprove the central idea of the piece. I believe in
titling each scene. I write in the margin of the script my own titles for the
scene, like "Two aging champions at the end of the line," or "Nobody's
what they expected the other person to be," or "Tommy's last time to feel
young," something like that. These little titles mean something to me.
Title the scenes in a way that will lead you to a look or a feeling. They're
more poetic than factual. When two people are breaking up, for example,
it might be "How much is this costing them?" Doing this really helps me
know how to shoot the scene.

Once you've made it clear to yourself what the central idea is, once
you've found the right spine or armature, the right nerve of a scene, it dictates and determines everything, including the film's visual style. If you
can't use the spine to create a visual style, then you haven't found the right
armature and you're still being intellectual. The key questions are always
concerned with the emotional core of the story. If you know what that
core is, you start to arrive at what the film's visual style should be. Form
can never be entirely distinguished from content. In *The Way We Were,*
there was something nostalgic and romantic about those people. They
began with their best feet forward, full of aspiration and hope, the way
one remembers the best years of one's life. Then as they get to Hollywood
things get tougher and they begin to come to grips with the harshness of
life. I knew I wanted the image to look harder toward the end of the film
than it did in the early sections. The early part of the film was overexposed, which did two things: it cooled the colors down a little bit and it
bled the sky around the trees. It had a softer look. That kind of film stock
starts to look very dirty when you underexpose it. So if you take the story
of *The Way We Were,* on the simplest level, we overexposed college, we
exposed New York normally, and underexposed Hollywood. Then you
combine that with a way of moving the camera, your choice of lenses, and
an editorial rhythm of how it's cut and edited.

But knowing the spine of the picture is not necessarily going to help the actor at all. It sets intellect in motion, and essentially that's not the currency of the actor. There are some actors who have the impression that having a lot of information is going to help them, when in reality they don't understand how to put two wires together to translate that information—which is essentially intellectual—into physical behavior that can be seen and heard. That's finally what acting is about. You can meditate on what a scene means, but if you haven't found a way to turn that into something active, something that can be illustrated by behavior, it'll just be intellectual talk. A good actor is a person whose emotions are relatively close to the surface, who can activate him- or herself quickly and efficiently by knowing what buttons to press. Objectivity is poison to the actor. Why waste all this time analyzing a role? It's useful only insofar as it triggers emotion. Emotion is a product of the unconscious. You can never go after it directly. You have to find a task to perform or a thing to do, and the doing of that thing produces emotion. So intellect is in many ways an enemy of emotion. We use rational thought to keep ourselves from being emotional. Rational thought is not necessarily what you want from an actor. He doesn't have to understand or know why or how he did something. It's only necessary that the camera be rolling when he does it. So the focus of a film performance is different than that of a theater performance, even if the process of acting is the same. Good acting is good acting. But directorially speaking, the approach has to be very different. In film you try to create dependency and on the stage you try to get rid of dependency.

Are there any general techniques you use when working with actors?

The primary requisite is that the whole thing be done with a degree of truthfulness. You just nodded your head. Did you think about nodding your head? No. Why did you nod your head? Because you were listening to me, really listening, weren't you? You're biting your nail now. Now you're laughing. You don't have to think about any of that, so you and I have a sort of simple reality going. There's no character involved yet, but we have a basic truth which comes from the fact that you, for example, want something from me. You can't have acting without that. You want to understand what I'm explaining to you. Why? Because it's important to you, it's what you want to do with your career. You have a real reason for listening to me. So by listening to me, by wanting something and having a reason for wanting it, you have an objective. Who are you, what do you want, why do you want it? Those are the three basics that will create a simple reality. As it gets more complex you begin to create a character.

When amateur acting is bad, it's because the actors begin to play the characters. What they lose is the simple reality of the situation. Actors turn into rotten actors by indicating more emotion than they really have. What the director has to do is prevent them from doing that, but at the same time be able to increase the amount of emotion they really do have. Try to take the pressure off the actor by saying, "Don't give me any more than you have. Give me less. Have it, but don't show it. Don't go beyond what's good for you." The minute you say that, the minute you relax them, the reality of what they really have increases. If you make sure the actor knows he doesn't have to give you so much, it happens by itself.

One of the most useful things to do is watch *Candid Camera.* There's no better lesson in pure reality behavior. It's the only place you'll see that kind of truth on television. Do yourself a little experiment. Just click back and forth between *Candid Camera* and anything else on the channels where people are performing, and you'll see how misguided most acting is. You see a guy go into a gas station and the attendant doesn't know there's no engine in the car. You want to see how people behave when they're surprised? They don't do anything! If you can do nothing, with honesty, in a situation like that, then you've got the essence of good film acting. The camera can do so much of the acting for you through close-ups and movement. I think movie acting is easier because there are more subtleties possible, lots of tiny colors that would get lost on a stage.

When working with actors, at some point it's necessary to make a decision between the preconceived idea you might have and the quality of the performance you're going to get. When you see that the performance wants to go in another direction, you have to make a decision about whether or not you're going to insist that the performance move closer to your own intellectual concept and perhaps destroy some of the reality of the performance, or whether you as the director should accommodate more of the performance while still trying to keep your concept alive. I think the latter is best if you do films about people. It may not be the best, let's say, if you're doing horror films or action films. But if you're doing films about people, where it's the degree of reality and truth in each performance which ultimately are what make the film work—which is usually the case in my films—then you really must accommodate to the range of the actor.

What happens when you have an actor who takes a while to get going and another who is best on the first take?

That's exactly what happened on *The Way We Were.* Although Redford had formal training, he hates rehearsals and is a very instinctive actor who doesn't like to talk about things. He doesn't mind any number of takes so long as you give him something different on each take. Barbra Streisand, on the other hand, is very thorough and methodical, and likes to rehearse, so there was something of a problem with those two in a scene. What you're hoping for is that you get it on film before he starts to go downhill from being stale, but after she's already gotten up to speed.

Have you ever said, "I don't know," when someone asks you a question on set?

You do a lot of lying when you direct. If you're a captain who has to lead a platoon of guys to take a hill, and the night before you find an old friend from high school and sit down and start to drink and say to the guy, "You know, I'm scared to death," if he's smart he's not going to follow you. It's the same with actors. On the other hand you can say anything you like to an old pro like Burt Lancaster. He understands immediately when you know something and when you don't. Fact is, it's not a good idea to say that you don't know. You'll be stuck with honesty that doesn't do anyone any good.

How did you come to make Tootsie?

That project has a complicated history. A few years ago Don McGuire wrote an original script called *Calling Diana Darling,* the story of a female impersonator who wants to be taken seriously as an actor. Actually it's the story of this slob of an agent who really takes advantage of his clients. Buddy Hackett was going to play the lead. It was a completely different film to the one we eventually made. McGuire's script eventually changed its name to *Would I Lie to You?,* which was read by Dick Richards, a friend of Dustin Hoffman. Independently, Dustin had already decided that he wanted to play a woman, perhaps because it's the ultimate challenge for an actor. But he wanted to play it believably, not in a camp way, different from something like *La Cage aux folles.* Dustin was working on a script with his pal Murray Schisgal about a tennis player who wanted to be champ. He couldn't beat the men but could beat the women, so he decided to masquerade as a woman and become a tennis champ that way. In the meantime Dick Richards hired Bob Kaufman to rewrite the McGuire screenplay, but then he was fired. At this point Dustin's company owned the project with Columbia. The next writer was Murray Schisgal and the title was changed to *Tootsie*. Murray did three additional drafts and then Hal Ashby was hired, but he couldn't get free from editing a film he was making. Then Murray Schisgal was fired and Larry Gelbart was hired. By the time I came along, the script read as a residue of Don McGuire, Bob Kaufman, Murray Schisgal and Larry Gelbart. It was really a kind of drag comedy, which was not what I wanted to do. When I first read it, I turned it down.

Then I was asked to take a meeting with Larry and Dustin, and I explained to them what I didn't like about the project. They asked me to think about it. I still said no. I just thought it was silly and bawdy. It didn't have a spine or a serious idea behind it. It was just one gag, and the jokes were thin and repetitive, like him walking into the men's room wearing his dress. It didn't seem to be about anything. But there was one line that intrigued me. Somebody says to Michael, Dustin's character, "Being a woman has made you weird." I thought that if the line was "Being a woman has made a man out of you," I would know how to at least start the screenplay. That would be an interesting point of view. Then my agent, who is also Dustin's agent, came up with a very creative concept. He knew that I usually don't start with a finished script but spend time working on the script. He suggested I take two paid weeks and work with Larry and Dustin to see if we could come up with something. Of course that's the trap, because as soon as the juices start to flow you get caught up in it. You're hooked. So we met and restructured the story and fairly soon I could see a way it might work. The spine became the idea of a man who is forced, for reasons of survival, to put on a dress and by doing so becomes a better man. Once we had that spine, the jokes were hanging on something of substance, and the whole thing worked much better. It was a real human situation that was escalating toward something. We had to construct the most dismal possible world for this guy before he puts on the dress. There was a scene I cut out where his ex-wife shows up with her new husband. We didn't have what *Some Like It Hot* had, which is a gun. In that film there's a bunch of gangsters who want to kill Tony Curtis and Jack Lemmon. It's easy to understand why they put those dresses on. Dustin and I kept asking, "What the hell is going to make this guy put on a dress? What's the gun?" And by playing his agent who tells him he'll never work in New York again, I was the gun.

At that point Larry had worked on the film for over a year, and after four drafts he'd had enough. We hadn't had a woman's input on it, so I brought in Elaine May, who finished up with a polish on the script. My job was to take Larry's work and Elaine's contributions and blend them together. For example, she invented the roommate character, played by Bill Murray. He's really a structural device to give Dustin somebody to talk to about what he's going through when he's working on the soap opera. She also fleshed out the Teri Garr character and the soap-opera character played by George Gaynes. So those elements had to be integrated into Larry's already workable structure. I went to New York and sat in a room and pieced the script together, and then started myself to work through it from the start. Of course we continued to work on it during the shooting.

Is it true that Hoffman modeled the character of Dorothy Michaels on his mother?

That's what he said. His mother died about six months before the picture was made. But the character was pieced together through a series of tests. In the first tests he didn't look at all like a woman, he looked like a guy in drag. Originally in the script he was a nurse in the hospital. We put a nurse's uniform on him and it looked like a joke. Short sleeves, muscular hairy arms, a blond wig. He looked grotesque. We had to fix a lot of details, like shaving his eyebrows and then penciling them back in. The wig would make his head too big for his shoulders so we had to pad his shoulders out. He couldn't keep his brassiere straps up, so we had to stitch the thing together at the back. We learned, piece by piece, how to light him. We learned what clothes worked and what didn't. We learned what earrings were too heavy. We realized he needed glasses to disguise the size of his nose. And each time, when we would test the new thing, we would improvise. Dustin is a sensational actor and had to find this woman in himself. I kept trying to trap him by asking him the most difficult and personal questions I could. I wanted to take away the security of him knowing what the next moment would be. When you do that, there's a different level of concentration and connection with yourself that emerges. He would start by answering as Dustin and then find a way of transferring this and answering as the woman he was playing. How conscious this was in terms of his mother I don't know, and I don't think he knows.

We went down to New York University and sat down with a speech therapist and looked at the speech waves of a female voice pattern. Then

we put an instrument on his throat and he began to talk and we watched
the speech waves of his voice. We kept trying to get his voice congruent in
some way with the female voice. It's not easy. You can't just start talking
up high, because you'll strain your voice. Dustin didn't want to do a
falsetto because that's too campy. So he begged me to let him play the part
with a French accent. He has a trick where if he doesn't want anyone to
know he's home, he'll answer the phone in a French accent. "Allo? Who's
calling please? This is Mr. Offman's residence." He really does it well, but
it didn't sound right for the part. I knew what he was asking for, which is
a costume, something to hide behind. That's how we found the southern
accent. It was much easier for him to be less self-conscious about pushing
his voice up high. Slowly, with all my questions and his answers, the character got built up layer after layer.

The whole point is that we couldn't make this film work if the audience didn't accept him as a woman. What frightened me was if audiences
didn't believe it. When you look at rushes and stare at Dustin for hours,
you start seeing the beard. You say to yourself, "My God, this isn't going
to work. Absolutely not." *Tootsie* is very different to *Some Like It Hot*.
Those guys weren't women, they were clearly guys in drag, and most of
the fun was recognizing Tony Curtis and Jack Lemmon with wigs on.
That's different to what Dustin did, which was really quite difficult and
complicated.

Why did you play the part of the agent in the film?

Because Dustin drove me crazy until I said I'd do it. He got a bug about
me playing that part. I haven't done any acting in twenty years and have
no wish to act and direct at the same time, something I found uncomfortable. But it got to be really annoying because he really wanted me to
do it. Dustin said, "If a peer of mine tells me I'm never going to work
again, I'm not going to put on the dress. But if you tell me I'm never
going to work again, maybe I'll put on the dress, so you have to play the
part." I said, "Dustin, this is ridiculous. You're an actor. They're paying
you a lot of money to be an actor." He sent me two dozen roses and a
card: "Please be my agent. Love, Dorothy." Finally I said I'd do it. I found
it disconcerting to watch the camera and him and my own performance
at the same time. I blew a lot of takes because I was too busy observing
him so I'd know what to tell him once that take was over. I was okay in my
close-ups because I didn't have to watch him, but in the master shots my

primary responsibility was as a director. I had a lot of trouble surrendering that objectivity and trying to get subjective and get into the scene.

Were there any improvisations in the film?

You can sometimes use improvisation to solve a writing problem, and sometimes an acting problem. The party scene near the start was scripted, but it never worked and eventually everyone gave up trying to fix it. Elaine May said, "You'll just have to throw a party." You can't make it real on paper. So I called an ex-student of mine to bring his acting class to the set for the party scene. The only person who literally improvised was Bill Murray. You can't write that stuff. What I did was make a list of what had to happen in the scene. To Dustin and Bill I said, "What are your obligations here?" What do I, as director, want the audience to know by the end of the scene? One of the things, for example, is that Michael's roommate is a playwright who is so esoteric that his work is essentially unsalable, and that Michael is going to try and raise eight thousand dollars and produce his play. Another is that Michael has to be established as a chauvinist. This is a guy in his mid-forties, he's unmarried and lives with a roommate. He is incapable of treating women with any respect. This was important because it works against the change that happens by the end of the story. I went back to the spine of a man who becomes a better man for having been a woman. I wanted to set that up at the party and show how that character was not entirely wholesome. By the end of the film, we see how he's changed. We wanted to start him out as far away as possible from where we wanted him to end up. One of the ways was to show him dealing ineptly and uncaringly with a baby, and then we had him make passes at three different women using the same line with each of them.

I began to visualize the scene in two sets of three beats. Dustin and Bill have three beats each. The whole structure of the party is a series of intercuts between the two of them. For Bill I needed a table of people that slowly deserts him. I asked him, "Can you make up something that sounds dangerously close to being profound but is actually nonsense?" He said, "Sure, I can do that." I didn't know what he was going to say. With Bill Murray what you see in the film is the first take every time. The extras in the scene didn't know it was meant to be nonsense. I didn't tell them. Take one he says, "I wish I had a theater that was only open when it rains." As soon as take one was over, I told some of the extras to step out of the shot. I added some more empty beer bottles, messed up his hair, unbuttoned his shirt, and he was ready for the next take with "I don't like it when people come up to me and say they liked my play." The third is, "I did a thing about suicides of American Indians." With Dustin it was as simple as telling him to say the same thing to each girl: "You're an actress?"

What are your thoughts on the Actors Studio and the work of Lee Strasberg?

I think Lee is a lot like analysis. Now, there's nothing wrong with analysis, but his teaching methods are so psychological and sometimes so esoteric that they are misunderstood and abused by half the people who are exposed to them. Some people have turned themselves into total bores by making a cult out of analysis. It's impossible for them to be human beings or react spontaneously to anything. They find a hidden meaning in everything. That doesn't mean you should condemn analysis in general just because someone somewhere has abused it. I think what Lee does is essentially very valuable, but only when it's properly understood. The point is that it's difficult to understand Lee properly because he's made a science out of his work and ideas, and people have turned it into a cult. It's really just another way of defining the task of the actor. It gives him or her certain handles to grasp when approaching a role. The Method is not a religion. It's not an answer to everything. It won't make you great. It won't even always make you good. But if it's understood, it will be a help.

Do you have any advice for those of us who are screenwriters?

I think the single most helpful thing for working on a screenplay is learning something about acting. What is required at every moment of a script is the ability to generate truthful behavior within imaginary circumstances. When you start work as a screenwriter, one of the key principles to remember is, at any given moment, who wants what and why. I find that the single most deficient area in all training institutions having to do with film directing is that there's not enough emphasis put on understanding the acting process. I'm not talking about teaching you how to talk to an actor. That's the easy bit. It's about how to think about storytelling. There's a good reason for this deficiency: it's a very complex process. I can no more tell you how to deal with actors in a two-hour session like this than somebody could teach me to paint. I can make you aware of certain things, but that's all. I went to an acting school six and a half hours a day for two years before I began to scratch the surface. I thought I understood it, but I didn't really begin to until I spent another three years teaching. You need to spend a year with two people and two chairs.

Have you ever miscast a role?

Yes, and when that happens you may find yourself in a compromise position where the choice is: force him to follow your concept against his will, which will probably mean the quality of the performance will be worse than if you alter your concept and compromise with him. In other words, let him give a performance that is half yours and half his. The question is whether you want to go for the concept or the quality of the execution. How much can you bend the concept and still preserve the picture, as opposed to working with a reluctant actor giving a performance they don't really believe in but which fits your concept?

There are very few actors I've worked with who truly want to express themselves for the sake of expressing themselves, actors literally just wanting to have their way. Most actors enjoy being directed if they respect and accept the directions being given. That was certainly true of me when I was an actor. I welcomed someone giving me insight into a scene or clarifying a problem or opening a door to an easier or better way to approach a scene. It's true that sometimes you have disagreements, but in most cases if you get to the point of a real hard disagreement with an actor about a character, then you've made the wrong casting choice. It shouldn't happen, and if it does, it's your fault. If you're careful about casting, you're choosing someone whose instincts are ninety percent correct for what you want. The other ten percent you have to hope will come out of trust. If an actor has done his or her homework, there will be points along the way when they'll know better than you what's right for the character, which is when you as the director have to back off and accept their input. When it comes to situations like this, you have to make a very careful, calculated decision: how much are you going to beat the actor into submission, and how much will you compromise your concept in order to accommodate the actor doing it with real enthusiasm and conviction?

When you read a script, what is it that first draws you to wanting to make it into a film?

Sometimes it's just one scene that makes you want to do a picture. Usually what happens is, that you change the script that's been sent to you so it expresses something that you're personally concerned with. You see a glimmer of light or you connect with something in it which gives you the opportunity to make the film. I've never found a completed screenplay that I just cast and shot. For me it's never worked that way. It's always a case of rewriting or finding an idea that I've developed into something, or a book that turns into something else.

Doing an adaptation of Horace McCoy's novel *They Shoot Horses, Don't They?* is a completely different kind of problem than adapting Erich Maria Remarque's *Heaven Has No Favorites.* You commit to a project like *They Shoot Horses, Don't They?* because of what that book is about, while *Heaven Has No Favorites,* which became *Bobby Deerfield,* provided me with a springboard to deal with something quite different from what the book actually dealt with. The thing that interested me about *Bobby Deerfield* is the idea of a man who has denied his own past and, as a result of trying to construct an identity that isn't organic, has turned himself into a completely isolated individual. He is coming to terms with his own roots. Through the process of a relationship with a girl he learns to accept the reality of who he is. That, thematically, is what interested me about *Bobby Deerfield,* but that's not in any sense what the book is about. So at a certain point the picture begins to take on its own life, regardless of the book. As they say, at some point you send the model home and go ahead and finish your own painting.

On a major production you have a thousand people who come to you for the final decisions. How do you organize that? How do you pace yourself during the course of a day?

If somebody would ask me what is the most important thing about directing, I would say to be in good physical shape. The difference between how I feel now and how I felt ten years ago is enormous and very telling, to the point where I have begun, for the first time in my life, to understand directors who I thought were crazy when they would say, "I'm too old to do this film. Get a younger director." The fact is that directing a film is the most enormously grueling physical exercise you can go through, partly because there's so much emotional strain. It's not just a question of whether or not you solve the artistic problems, because for every moment that it takes you to solve the artistic problem, it's costing millions of dollars, and millions of dollars makes people behave badly. Grown men behave like five-year-olds. They cry. They threaten you. They get hysterical. Actors think you're going to destroy their career and they get crazy at three in the morning and call you. They won't come out of their trailer. Somebody comes to you every minute with a decision. What you do is just put it in gear. You can't permit yourself to give in to the anxiety that this kind of thing can create.

You start at six in the morning and you're wired all day. If you're also producing the film, after you watch the dailies in the evening you go into a production meeting about how much over budget you are. The trucks are costing money, and they won't give you permission to shoot on the street the day after tomorrow where, if you don't do it, you're already two million dollars over the budget. Then, before you can go to bed you have to eat and the first thing you reach for is a glass of scotch, and before you know it, you've creamed half a bottle. You fall into bed. You wake up in the morning hung over and you drink fifteen cups of coffee. Honestly, I'm not exaggerating. I train between pictures as hard as I can. By the time I finish a picture I'm in horrible shape, and during the editing period I try to jog, diet and quit smoking and drinking. I smoke four packs of cigarettes a day while shooting. You light a cigarette every time you say "Cut!" and the minute you say "Roll it!" you put one out.

I stand by what I've just said to you, and yet if you ever came on a set where I'm working you would go away and say, "My God! He's so calm." People say that to me all the time, as they'll say to any director, "You're so unruffled by all of this." But they don't know what's going on inside. You get very adept at the art of hiding whatever anxiety you have. Anybody who's directing a big-budget picture with major stars who tells you they aren't scared to death is a liar.

How important is crew morale?

Very. But I don't think you can do anything about it. The only thing you can do is to be good at your job. There's nothing that raises crew morale better than a professional director who knows what he's doing. It takes a crew one second to see through an unprofessional director who's trying to play the boss. You either are the boss or you aren't. You walk on a set and the crew knows. They're tough, cynical old hands—very savvy people. There's so much featherbedding in these unions that some of those guys have been sitting there holding cables for forty years. They've seen it all, and right away they can smell fear. You walk on a set and either have their respect or don't. You can behave like a star with the stars or you can behave like a crew member with the crew members. Doing the latter is not necessarily a guarantee that they'll respect you. Sometimes they'll disrespect you when you become a part of the crew. I don't ever take a trailer for myself and don't ever disappear. I'm always there, mostly because I don't trust them to do it right. If they're laying a dolly track, I'm going to watch them lay every board, because eight times out of ten they're going to be two inches off, four inches off or a foot off, and it will make a difference in the framing of the shot. If you catch them two or three times, they start to respect you. They know you aren't going to accept sloppy work. It's about knowing what you want technically, because these guys are impressed by technical knowledge. Saying "I want this shot to have a lyrical feeling" is very different from saying "I want to keep the camera moving; we have to set this up so it can be lit without eye-level lighting," because the minute they hear you talking like that they know they can't pull a fast one.

How important is the assistant director to you?

When he's good, he's invaluable. I can honestly say that I've worked with only one first-class AD, and I worked with him only once because I couldn't get him back again, and he's now a producer. This guy was so good on *The Way We Were,* he drove me crazy. He grabbed me the night before we were going to shoot the end sequence in front of the Plaza Hotel and said, "What are your shots for tomorrow?" "What are my shots? I don't know. I've got to shoot the sequence." "No. You've got to write down for me every shot." Well, he made me do it. So I said, "Okay, I have a crane here, and that can be the first shot," and so on. Then he took those shots and put them in the order in which they could be done most efficiently, which meant jumping around a lot in a difficult acting scene. I began the scene very loose and high on a crane. He made me shoot the beginning and ending first, and then made me shoot all of the medium shots. We had one day to get this done, because the Plaza Hotel is not going to tie up that whole entrance for another day, and neither would the New York Police Department block it off from cars. It was a cold winter day, so we were going to lose the light at four o'clock and I couldn't get started until nine. It was a tough scene. But if it hadn't been for him I wouldn't have gotten everything. Normally, left to my own devices, I would probably have shot in continuity as much as I could.

Can you give us an example of something that you saw clearly in your own mind, and after it was done you were pleased with a result that was quite different from what you had originally conceived?

Three Days of the Condor was faster-paced than I thought it would be and about less than I thought it would be. I thought that it was a more substantial story. When I first looked at the rough cut, I said, "That's it? All that work and that's all there is?" I don't know what I originally saw in my mind, but I think I saw something more than what the rough cut gave me. They all turn out differently to what I originally thought. It can only ever be that way, because one conception is a product of your own imagination and the other incorporates the weather and people and clothes and two dimensions instead of three and the film process and editing and sound.

I read that as a film director you have been influenced by dance.

When I was going to acting school one of the most influential classes I had was a class called Preclassic Dance Forms. I had a wonderful old man for a teacher who was known as the founder of modern dance. His name was Louis Horst. He was Martha Graham's mentor and a great old guy. None of us could dance a damn, but we took this class because we didn't really have to dance. He was teaching us form. We learned the structures of these classic dances: sarabande, allemande, gavotte, pavane. They all had different forms. If it had an eight-bar structure it would have, let's say, an A-B-A form, like a popular song. You'd get two of the eight bars to state a theme, and then six bars to develop it. Section A would be something like one-two-three-four, two-two-three-four, and then for the next six bars you could put together any combination of those things but you couldn't do anything you hadn't already introduced in the first two bars. That's when I got haunted by form. I began to see films in circles. So I can't work on a film without seeing it in terms of dance. The form I've worked with almost exclusively is an A-B-A form, where the characters almost always return to the beginning. I think of the T. S. Eliot poem, part of which says that the purpose of all our wanderings will be to arrive at the place where we started and know it for the first time. It seems so analogous to me and to what I believe.

I've seen three of your films and all of them have unhappy endings.

I don't know why they have those endings. I always get asked this question, and I don't know how to answer it, because I don't sit down and say, "I have to do a film with an unhappy ending." I look at material—screenplays and books—until I find something that interests me. For some reason or other a lot of them have unhappy endings. That worries me, but I don't know what to do about it. I can't just arbitrarily say, "Now I'm going to do a film with a happy ending." I believe in happy endings, I really do. I don't consider myself a pessimist or a nihilist. I don't believe that life is hopeless. I like films that make me feel good at the end, but I'm perverse enough that I feel good at the end of a lot of my pictures. I can't help it.

Do you feel that through your films you have articulated everything you've wanted to express over the years?

I don't think of myself as having anything to say, to be honest with you. I think of myself as wanting to live through certain things and give myself to those experiences. I'm not a philosopher in the sense of having a clear vision of the world that I'm anxious to impart. I think there are people gifted in that way, who see life in a certain way, and make films in order to illustrate that. I can't avoid giving you my own view of life, such as it is, when I make a film, but that's not the genesis for me. The genesis goes back to whether or not I care about these characters and about what's happening in the story.

Let me add that I don't think any work of art should articulate for you precisely what it is. The nature of it being art is that it's a discovery. In a film where two people sit down and talk about the theme of the picture, I go to sleep. Almost any successful piece of art is a metaphor. When you talk about a successful film, you talk about what has been successfully dramatized. Dramatized, not said. There's a difference. Here's a couple that gets married for all the wrong reasons, and the marriage finally collapses. You can't just sit them down and have one say to the other, "Well, we got married for all the wrong reasons." It's perhaps intelligent and psychological and true, but it has nothing to do with art. Art is the ability to take the two people and dramatize the fact that they should never have married in the first place. Now, that doesn't mean that I'm for obscurity as opposed to clarity. You can make the mistake of being too obscure. You see a film and say, "That's fine, Sydney, but it's all in your head. It's not on the screen. We just don't get it." Well, then I have to address it in another way. I didn't dramatize it successfully. But the way to fix that is not to sit down and have it articulated. The way to fix it is to find a better, clearer dramatization.

Films as Director

1965 *The Slender Thread*
1966 *This Property Is Condemned*
1968 *The Scalphunters*
    The Swimmer
1969 *Castle Keep*
    They Shoot Horses, Don't They?
      (also producer)
1972 *Jeremiah Johnson*
1973 *The Way We Were*
1975 *The Yakuza* (also producer)
    Three Days of the Condor
1977 *Bobby Deerfield* (also producer)
1979 *The Electric Horseman*

1981 *Absence of Malice*
1982 *Tootsie* (also producer)
1985 *Out of Africa* (also producer)
1990 *Havana* (also producer)
1993 *The Firm* (also producer)
1995 *Sabrina* (also producer)
1999 *Random Hearts* (also producer)
2005 *The Interpreter* (also executive
    producer)
    Sketches of Frank Gehry (also
    producer and
    cinematographer)

Pollack also directed television episodes including *Shotgun Slade*, 1961; *The Tall Man*, 1962; *The Defenders*, 1963; *The Alfred Hitchcock Hour*, 1962–63; *Ben Casey*, 1962–63; and *Bob Hope Presents the Chrysler Theater*, 1963–65. He produced numerous films that he did not direct.

Every one of you here, as part of a new generation of filmmakers, has a job to do. Film is a cultural form of great significance and the thoughts and images and ideas of the stories you tell will be transmitted into the heads of millions of people. You're about to embark on the best job in the world.

DAVID PUTTNAM
(Born in London, England, 1941)

David Puttnam is the only Hollywood studio head ever to become a member of the House of Lords. He started out during London's Swinging Sixties in advertising and as a photography agent, finding success for himself and his clients, who included David Bailey and Richard Avedon. When he was twenty-five he decided to take a run at the film business along with two colleagues from his advertising business, Ridley Scott and Alan Parker. He rose swiftly to the top of his new profession. He produced Scott's first film, *The Duellists,* then Parker's *Bugsy Malone* and *Midnight Express,* which won Oliver Stone his first Academy Award as a screenwriter. Puttnam won an Oscar for himself with *Chariots of Fire* in 1981. *Local Hero* and *The Killing Fields* followed, and then in 1986 he won the Palme d'Or at the Cannes Film Festival for *The Mission,* directed by Roland Joffé. A great believer in collaboration, Puttnam always strove to find the right team of director, writer and actors before launching a project. "Collective strengths are always far greater than individual strengths," he said, "something that's often overlooked in the scramble for success." He established a reputation for jump-starting the careers of writers and directors while making pictures that were commercially successful, received critical acclaim and won the big prizes.

In 1986 Coca-Cola, then the owner of Columbia Pictures, came to him with an offer to become chairman and chief executive of Columbia. Puttnam was intrigued and believed he could change the way Hollywood did business by bringing new filmmakers to the scene and curbing excessive spending. He quickly became controversial, challenging long-standing practices, canceling contracts and alienating many of the town's most powerful agents and stars. In his first year he donated Columbia's traditional fund for company Christmas gifts to charity, with a message urging studio employees to "enjoy a very happy

Producer David Puttnam, right, with director Bill Forsyth in Scotland during
the shooting of *Local Hero* (1983), which starred Burt Lancaster.

Christmas knowing that your generosity has made it possible for many less
privileged to feel cared for at this special time of year." He was reported to have
told the Coca-Cola board of directors, "I wouldn't make a *Rambo,* no matter
what the size of the built-in profit guarantee. If someone wrote me a check for
the total box-office gross, I wouldn't take it."

Columbia's experiment with Puttnam and his exploration of Hollywood
lasted less than two years. He was from the beginning caught in storms of
controversy, mostly of his own making: "I couldn't stop espousing the ideas
that I'd been talking about for years, so to a certain extent from the start I was
wandering into quicksand."

Puttnam returned to England and embarked upon an active and prominent public life. He served for ten years as chairman of the National Film and
Television School, became the first chancellor of the University of Sunder-
land and in 2007 chaired the Joint Parliamentary Committee on the Draft
Climate Change Bill. He was knighted in 1995 and made a life peer in 1997.

Puttnam came to the AFI on four occasions. He provided a unique perspective to the fellows with his strong point of view on the role of a producer,
his insights into the challenges of running a studio, and his bold articulation
of cinema as a cultural force with profound effect around the world. As he
told *Vanity Fair,* "The medium is too powerful and too important an influence on the way we live—the way we see ourselves—to be left *solely* to the
tyranny of the box office or reduced to the sum of the lowest common
denominator of public taste."

DAVID PUTTNAM

———

October 13, 1994*

How did you become a producer?

I was brought up with cinema and feel very lucky in that respect. We didn't have a television in our house until about 1958, so from the age of eleven I was a regular cinemagoer. I could walk to any one of five cinemas from my house in the suburbs of North London, where, if there was a double bill on, I could choose from sometimes six films. I spent an awful lot of time in the cinema, perhaps four times a week. My entire cinematic education really was American films. Many years later I became friendly with Sir Michael Balcon, who had run Ealing Studios in the forties and fifties, and I remember him saying to me, "I'll bet you saw lots of Ealing films as a kid." I had to admit that when it came to which films I would see any given week, there were only two basic criteria: first, whether it was in color, and second, if it was American. Only if there was nothing else playing would I see a British film. My diet of American cinema formed what might be called my ethical understanding of the world. American cinema was very influential at that period of time, films like Zinnemann's *The Search,* William Wyler's *The Best Years of Our Lives,* Stanley Kramer's *Inherit the Wind* and Kazan's *On the Waterfront,* as well as underrated figures like Robert Rossen. Their films were all about something, as well as being extremely well made. It was from films like this that just about

*Jean Firstenberg moderated this seminar. This transcript also contains segments from seminars David Puttnam gave at the American Film Institute on February 27, 1980, October 26, 1983, January 16–17, 1985, and January 4, 2002.

every tenet by which I've tried to live my life somehow evolved. I really do mean that. Many of these films were sharply critical of American society, but they also demonstrated a capacity for infinite happiness.

What formed in my mind was an image of America. This country was represented on screen as a nation of equality and fairness and openness, unlike the country I am from, which with its class-based society is an inherently unfair one. In short, as a child I was effectively blotting paper, with your films as the ink, looking at a society I had no direct knowledge of but still find utterly admirable in intent and purpose and tone. One of the most exciting moments of my life was arriving by air in 1963 for the first time in America. I actually felt I was coming home, to the font of all my hopes and aspirations. My dreams had been shaped here in Los Angeles, five and a half thousand miles from my childhood home.

I should say that I wasn't a cineaste as such, just someone who loved the experience of going to see films and the feeling I had when I walked out of them. I can still remember how it felt coming out of *Pinocchio,* which was probably the first film I ever saw, with the words of "When You Wish Upon a Star" ringing in my ears, and I distinctly remember saying to myself, "I want to make people feel exactly how I feel right now." One of the things I've tried to do with all my own films is give audiences this same sense I had fifty years ago. Because of this I've always felt the profound responsibility that comes along with the filmmaking process. The creation of these images and sounds is perhaps the principal means we have today of conveying knowledge and understanding, and is becoming ever more potent. Filmmakers really are tinkering around in people's minds, imprinting messages, emotions and ideas that might influence them for life.

I left school in 1958 and tried to get into the film business, but failed. It was a highly nepotistic business and I had no relatives in the industry. Plus at the time it was very much a studio-based industry, and geographically I lived in the wrong part of London, so I couldn't get to where the work was. Reluctantly I drifted into advertising, where I was extremely successful, and from there ended up running an agency that represented photographers. But at the age of twenty-five I had to decide whether I was going to spend the rest of my life in advertising or have another crack at the film business. For me this was the ultimate challenge. I was encouraged to make the move through the fact that I had a very talented group working around me, including a young writer named Alan Parker who also wanted to break into films. He didn't have the nerve to leave advertising, so he loved the idea of me trying it out and seeing how I might do. I also knew an art director who had studied at the Royal College of Art, who also realized his future wasn't in advertising, named Ridley Scott.

With the money I had made I invested in some screenplays and spent a year trying to raise money on the script we thought was our best shot. I was sitting in the office of the man I had convinced to put up money for this project. A chap from *Variety* came into the office to write up the press release, and we went through the important stuff like who was going to write it and direct it and star in it. Finally we came to the question of who was going to produce the film. I looked around at these two men, who were clearly starting to lose interest in all of this, and said, "Me." I swear that had either of them turned around and said, "Don't be silly," I would have said, "I'm just kidding." But nothing happened, and the reporter said, "How do you spell your name?" And that Friday I was a film producer, because it said so in *Variety*.

I knew nothing. To give you an idea of the depth of my ignorance, the one thing I did know how to do was sign checks. It made me look important, so it was something I made sure I did every week. Every Friday one check came up that said "Focus Puller." I noticed this sum of money varied every week, and it seemed to be going up and up. By week three or four I said to myself, "Clearly I must assert my control on this film." So I said, "I've had it with this focus-puller business. How can the same piece of equipment be costing different sums of money each week?" They just stared at me, and said, "He did more overtime." I said, "What?" They said, "Last week the focus puller did more overtime." I said, "The focus puller is a person? Not a piece of equipment?" I stopped asking questions after that.

Is there anything you learned in the advertising business that has been particularly useful to you as a film producer?

One crucial thing—that there needs to be someone out there who wants your product. I've always been disciplined about knowing what the markets are for the stories I want to tell. If the market is a small one, I'm well aware that I need to make that film as cheaply as possible. There are films you have to make for a million dollars, and other films you have to make for twenty million dollars. I can't remember working on anything I'm seriously proud of that wasn't very difficult to get made. Film is the art of the possible, and at the end of the day you deal the resources you have as best you can. You hope and pray and argue for the maximum of resources, but then work with what you're given. Strangely enough, I find that the ideal relationship between a director and a producer isn't a harmonious one. You can be friends. You can like each other, but if you're both doing your job properly you must be sparring. The director should be pushing me further than the resources that I actually have, and I should be saying, "I've gone as far as I can, so don't push me any further." And I really should have gone as far as I possibly can, otherwise I'm not doing my job properly.

Many young filmmakers today are victims of what the media's notion of a film director is. The media are wrong, plain and simple. When you're making a film, it's not art. It's not that it wouldn't be nice if it were art, it's just that rarely does it get the chance to be art. If you believe there's a person called a film director who walks onto the set every morning to "create art," you're asking for trouble. The best you can hope for is a student at the AFI watching your film and declaring that it is art.

What's interesting is that you and your colleagues seemed to stay together as a group for quite some time.

Sir Michael Balcon once gave us some important advice. When Hugh Hudson and Alan Parker, Ridley Scott and I started out, he told us to stick together. He said, "The things that bind you are more important than the competition that will drive you apart." The really great work that many of you in this audience will do doesn't separate you from other people; it supports and aids and assists them. Hugh's success, *Chariots of Fire,* made it possible for Roland Joffé to make *The Killing Fields.* But Hugh and I would never have made *Chariots* if it weren't for Alan Parker's success with *Midnight Express,* and Ridley would never have made *The Duellists* without Alan having made such a success of *Bugsy Malone.* And we got Alan off the ground with *Bugsy* because of the success Michael Apted had with *Stardust,* which was made because *That'll Be the Day* was a hit. Each of those directors could make their films because each passed the baton without dropping it.

Ridley Scott's first film, The Duellists, *is very accomplished. How did you get it made?*

What attracted me to Joseph Conrad's story *The Duel* is that I wanted to make a film about mindless violence. Most films have within them some reason for the violence that people perpetrate on each other. What's extraordinary about the Conrad story is that it's about violence for no reason. In fact it's about a man who manufactures reasons to justify his obsession for mindless and motiveless violence. I found this idea much more scary than any story involving violent acts that could be rationalized in some way. But Conrad's story doesn't create much emotional involvement with the characters, and we were dangerously close to ending up with a fascinating sixty-minute television film without a center, so we invented a subplot in order to spin it out into a legitimate ninety-minute film on a relatively small budget. Cut to the 1976 Cannes Film Festival. I had produced Alan Parker's *Bugsy Malone,* which had been an extraordinary success, but this was during a year when the films had been particularly violent. Tennessee Williams was the president of the jury and walked out halfway through the festival. We were the second-to-last film of the festival, and here was this quite well-made musical starring children that perfectly caught the mood of these crowds that had had enough of this blood and guts. I spoke with a studio executive who said, "This Alan Parker's very good. You got anyone else at home you want to work with?" I told him about Ridley, who caught a plane down there the next morning. We ran through our projects, and it was quite obvious this man was prepared to take a chance on us. He said he couldn't pay for the expensive films, but he was a Conrad fan and gave us a million dollars to make *The Duellists.* I had to raise a bit more money from the government. We used the best of the crews that Ridley had used on his commercials and I had used on my previous films. It was important to do that, because Ridley's commercials were about looks and style while my features had been about story, and though I wanted to make a stylish film, I didn't want it to wallow completely in style.

Were you concerned about the violence in Midnight Express?

I learned a big lesson making that film. There is an important sequence when Billy moves to the lunatic asylum from the prison. We didn't have enough time to create the narrative progression to justify it in the audience's mind, so that's where the idea came from of Billy doing something so crazy that the audience accepts the idea of him going mad. We had him bite another man's tongue out. Alan Parker wanted to do it in deep close-up. I wanted to do it from the other side of Malta. We compromised on a mid-shot. The idea was that the audience would see what's going on, become horrified, bury their heads in their hands, and when they look back up Billy is in a new environment. So, months later at the premiere in

New York, I'm sitting there and this sequence comes up. He bites the tongue and spits it out, and the whole audience gets up and cheers. I knew I was in a lot of trouble. I realized I'd been in the business for ten years but knew absolutely nothing about audiences. I was stunned by my arrogance and ignorance, and even ended up spending some time with a priest talking about the quandary I found myself in. *Chariots of Fire* and *Local Hero* are, to an extent, direct responses to that moment when I was so appalled by that collective response to such horrific violence. I had taken a wrong turn and almost overcorrected to get back on course.

Are you always on the sets of the films you produce?

I'm on the set as little as I can be, but I do show up early in the morning, because I think it's good for morale to demonstrate that I can wake up in the morning as early as everyone else, and that I'm part of the crew. I also reserve the right to close down production for the day. I feel the decision to go into overtime is a financial one, and that's something I have to decide on. That doesn't mean I'm arbitrary about it. It's a decision always made in conjunction with the director. The producer doesn't really have anything to do during a shoot unless there's a problem, so to a certain extent me not being there is a sign that everything's going smoothly. If a producer shows up day after day on set you just become too familiar a face and lose authority.

When you have a script, how do you decide which director to send it to?

The first thing I look for is the kind of person who has a similar vision to my own. I've never worked with a director who I knew couldn't direct the film better than I ever could. People think the term "casting" applies only to actors. It's the director who casts the actors, but the producer casts everyone else, including the crew. Just like with actors, if you get it wrong, you can get a lot of grief. The key is finding collaborators who see in their minds precisely the same film that you do. Imagine you meet a writer whose vision of the film is perhaps five percent different from your own. You think, "I can work with that." Then the two of you go meet a director whose vision is another ten percent off from your original conception. Again you might decide to go with him. Once the actors enter the picture, they might pull it another ten percent off, so before you know it, you're making a very different film from the one you had originally set out to make. This is why you can't afford any differentiation whatsoever between the film you're attempting to make and the one that each colleague believes he or she is making as they fulfill their obligations to the project. If that happens, you end up sitting at the premiere of a film you never wanted to make in the first place.

More often than not, the directors I admire turn out not to give too many directions. Years ago Marlon Brando told me that Elia Kazan was the only director whose direction had actually helped him as a performer. All the other directors he'd worked with basically just let him go. When I was presenting an award to David Lean, I did some preparation by talking to John Mills. I asked John what it was like working with David. He said, "I don't think in forty years he ever spoke to me once." And he wasn't joking. A friend of mine was the boom operator on *The Shining*. Stanley Kubrick used radio mikes throughout the film, and so my friend was able to hear everything Stanley said to the actors. There was one scene that was going badly, and everyone knew it wasn't working. In the end, Stanley said, "Let's have some tea and come back to it." My friend watched Stanley walk over to Jack Nicholson, so he grabs for his headphones, thinking he's going to hear a great director talk to his actor and solve this very real problem. What he said was, "All right, Jack?" "Sure. Everything's okay." "Hey, Jack, do you see the tits on that tea lady?" That's all they discussed, then went back and started again after the break.

How do you work with writers?

The genesis of the original idea dictates the manner of that relationship. Ten times out of ten the original idea is one I bring to the writer, which means I have the right to push him in certain directions. I can say, "No, that character wouldn't do that in scene nine." The writer can argue, but you as producer are entitled to say such things. If the writer brings an idea to you, the producer's rhetoric inevitably is different. Rather than saying, "No, he wouldn't do that," phrase it as a question. Ask him, "Can you please explain to me why the character does that in scene nine?" Some writers need real guidance and some balk at being told in what directions the story needs to move.

I can write, but I write poorly. I can direct, but there are better directors out there. People use this term "creative producer." I don't think I'm a creative producer. I think I'm a producer, plain and simple. That term suggests that there are a lot of producers out there who aren't creative. If I've done anything in my career, it is perhaps to widen the definition of a producer in the eyes of those people who might have said, "I don't want to be a producer, they're just money men." That's actually an imposition pro-ducers force upon themselves. Most studios would, I think, be delighted if the producers got more involved in the creative side of film production.

What about your relationship with the studios?

There can only be one line of communication from the studio to the director, and it has to be through the producer. You have to be absolute about this. You cannot allow them to talk to each other. Not because of what they might say, but because it puts you in no-man's-land. The instant an executive feels he can pick up the phone and speak to the direc-tor you're dead, because you can't then impose your own formula on the production of that film. Consider the plight of the studio executive. He knows he's got perhaps five, more likely three, years in the job. When, as inevitably happens, he's fired or leaves, what does he become? Not a film director, but an independent producer—and what possible value am I to him? I'm now a competitor. On the other hand, what relationship does he need? Clearly, good connections to directors all over town. So it's really not in his best interests to have a relationship with you. The producer really is an inconvenient factor in the equation of studio filmmaking. The thing is this: someone has to run the film, and it's not as if these people who want access to the director actually want to run the film. They want the power without the responsibility.

How involved are you in the editing of your films?

Very involved, although I only go into the editing room once the director and editor feel they have a workable cut. I'm obsessive about selecting the right editor. I would certainly delay a film if I can't get who I consider to be the right editor for the job. *The Killing Fields* was an excellent example of how much a good editor can bring to a film. Jim Clark told us he thought there was a problem with the second act, in the French embassy, because it didn't have a narrative theme running through it. It was a series of disparate sequences that were all generally about boredom and people waiting to be evacuated. He said, "We're going to need some subplot run-ning through to keep it going." He latched on to the idea of the photo-graph for Dith Pran's passport, and built it into a running sequence so that other things were happening in parallel to the boredom. There was now an imperative running through the entire sequence. In that respect Jim's contribution really was immense.

Generally the director and I try to hire an editor who is very much his own man with his own views and his own reputation to protect. Another point of view is vital, because sometimes the director can get too close to his material. The analogy I always make is being forced to watch other people's home movies. It's very important that the editor not be there just to throw together material as the producer and director dictate. In an ideal world we have a democratic system that works on a two-to-one basis. If the director and editor feel strongly about a cut, I'll back off. But equally, if the editor and I feel strongly about something, we expect the director to back off. That's done by agreement and considerable mutual regard, and sometimes painful debate. On *The Killing Fields* all three of us at different moments lost our absolutely favorite sequences from the film. All three had to concede defeat to the other two.

Do you have anything to say about your experiences here in Hollywood as head of Columbia Pictures?

I'm happy to tell you how it happened. I was approached by Columbia at exactly the moment when *The Mission* had won the Palme d'Or at Cannes. My films had competed at Cannes for years, but I'd never won the top prize. So my wife said, "What are you going to do now? You've won an Oscar and the Palme d'Or. Are you going to go around the track again?" Suddenly out of the blue came the offer from Columbia. She said, "Do what you need to do, but don't tell me when you get to be sixty how different life would have been if you had run a Hollywood studio." I remember her saying, "I don't think you're going to enjoy it, but get it out of your system." That led to a series of conversations with Columbia for about a month that culminated in a meeting in a New York hotel room with me, my lawyer and representatives of the studio. I was genuinely ambivalent and perhaps in my heart of hearts didn't want it to happen, but they agreed to everything. I remember getting in the elevator, and my lawyer was terribly excited. For him it was a big win. He said, "Every single thing we held out for they agreed to!" And I said, "I feel sick. I just made the biggest mistake of my life." I really felt I'd trapped myself. I suppose part of me was enjoying the excitement, but I really did feel sick.

What I then did was fly out to Los Angeles to tell the guys at Warner Bros., who I was under contract to, that I'd been offered the job of running Columbia. They said, "Look, don't do this. You're making a mistake. We'll match whatever they've offered you. And you're under contract to us. We can pick up the phone, call Columbia and explain that you still work for us. We'll get you off the hook." That was probably when I should have said, "Okay. I'll stick with you." The real problem was thinking I could bring my European sensibilities about cinema to Hollywood, and make them work over here.

Let me tell you a story. It's the scenario of all too many films that end up being produced here in Hollywood. A few years ago I was here doing postproduction on *Midnight Express* and was interested in doing a film about César Chávez. I knew enough about him to think there was a good film to be made. There was a fair amount of enthusiasm from United Artists, so I found a writer and started to develop a screenplay. It was going very well until we got a message that Robert Redford was also interested in making a film about Chávez. I was asked to meet with Redford to see if these two projects could be worked on as a single film. From the start I didn't like the idea because I knew, obviously, that we wanted a Mexican to play the lead. The executives at United Artists said, "Really? A Mexican? Why?" I said, rolling my eyes, "Because Chávez was Mexican." It's a perfect example of something that sooner or later you'll have to deal with, which is telling people what you really think of them. You don't want to argue at such an early stage of the process. After all, your script isn't finished, and it will end up not being any good, so why get into an argument now about the fact that they want Robert Redford to play the leader of the farm workers in California? Instead you say, "Interesting approach you're taking here. Let's talk about it." You don't actually say, "As long as I'm breathing air, Robert Redford will never play César Chávez in this film," which is what you should have said, but because the sun is shining and your salad tastes good and your wife is playing tennis with his wife, you just smile.

So now you get your screenplay finished and it's really good, and your studio-executive pal reminds you of the conversation you had about Redford. Without telling him, you check out Redford's availability and with immense relief discover he's not available for at least a year. So you go back to the studio and say, "Redford would be a great idea," knowing he'll never be able to do it. You leave their office and they say to each other, "This Puttnam's a good guy. Easy to get on with and open to the idea of Redford playing Chávez." But then they call you and say, "Remember that role of the friend, the lawyer? Redford could play him, no?" I say, "Sure, but it's a small part." They say, "So we'll build that part up and make it the story of Chávez and his lawyer friend." Now you've got this script that has to be changed to expand the role of the lawyer, but you know Redford's not available so you think you're going to win this battle anyway. But they come back to you and say, "We found out Redford's not available. But Jimmy Caan is! He's very keen on the film." Now you're in a lot of trouble, because you've agreed Redford would be good for the role and you've agreed to change the script and distort the story, so you stand there and say, "I suppose Jimmy Caan could be good."

Let me cut to nine months later. You're driving down Sunset Boulevard and you see your name on a billboard. You're the executive producer of a film about César Chávez's lawyer friend starring Larry Hagman. It has nothing whatsoever to do with the film you were originally developing, and yet it's there with your name on it. All you did was not be nasty. You never had a fight, you never took issue with anything anyone suggested. The film is made and released, and everyone's reasonably happy and they even want to talk to you about your next project. But the fact remains that you've just made an utterly terrible film. You didn't do anything wrong as such, but you also didn't do anything right.

There are no villains in stories like these. I can't say I've met genuinely awful or vindictive people at the studios. Some of them aren't terribly bright, but they have their way of seeing the world and their priorities and problems. You mustn't fool yourself that somewhere there's a middle ground where you'll both meet, clasp hands and make the movie that's exactly what you had in mind. You have to come up with other reasons for imposing your dream on them. My way of doing it is delivering a bargain to them. I go around the world collecting bits of money together so that when I ask them for the lump sum I need, it's a good buy for them. Asking Warner Bros. for five million dollars to make *The Killing Fields* was a good deal for them; but if I'd gone in and asked for half the budget, it wouldn't have gotten made.

Let's ask ourselves the underlying question: in whose interests here is it to make an inexpensive film? The studios say they want cheap films because they're not risking as much. But consider that as a studio executive you're paying several actors many millions of dollars to appear in films and several directors perhaps two million dollars for each film. With those figures it isn't difficult to make a case that you, the executive, should earn half a million dollars a year. If, however, things changed and no actor was earning more than half a million dollars and films cost less, the executives' salaries start to look sick. Add to this, once the executive is booted out of his job—and they always are, inevitably—he wants to be able to lay claims to independent-producing fees of four hundred thousand dollars per film. So what you've got is the entire industry working on a conveniently bloated structure, and it's hard to find a single individual in whose interests it is to bring those costs down.

You grew up on American films but have often spoken of being a distinctly British filmmaker.

What it really comes down to is that I need to work with people only to whom I can bring something. I once worked with Jacques Demy. We really got on together, but the film was a catastrophe because he was making one film and I was making another. Sometimes it's just not possible for me to make cultural jumps. If, tomorrow, someone introduced me to the thirty-five-year-old Luis Buñuel, much as I admire his talent and his work, the best thing I could do would be to introduce him to someone I thought could help him. I am absolutely a British filmmaker. Of course I love foreign cinema. But much as I adore Italian cinema, I can't imagine a situation where I could work successfully with an Italian director, or he with me. I say that with regret. The real problem is people making different films.

There is one final thing I'd very much like to say. It's related to the responsibility of the filmmaker. Every one of you here, as part of a new generation of filmmakers, has a job to do. Film is a cultural form of great significance and the thoughts and images and ideas of the stories you tell will be transmitted into the heads of millions of people. You're about to embark on the best job in the world. There's a moment in William Wyler's *The Best Years of Our Lives* when Fredric March comes home and the children see him first. He puts his hand over their mouths because he wants to creep up and surprise Myrna Loy. Everyone watching that film recognizes the humanity in that scene. If you get something like that right, your film is going to play in Burbank, London and Cairo. People recognize exactly what's going on between those characters. I once watched *Chariots of Fire* in China, without subtitles and with an audience that didn't speak English. I know they understood what was going on. Take a character with whom audiences can identify, put him or her through a moral crisis at the end of which they emerge with their dignity intact, whether or not they win their struggle, and audiences will respond. Human beings understand the emotions of other human beings. It's that simple.

Sadly, however, over the past few years filmmakers have failed to tap the real power and influence of cinema. Many have failed even to

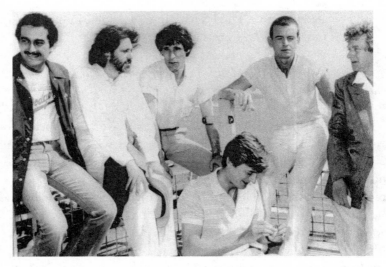

Puttnam with director Hugh Hudson (far right) and actors Ben Cross,
Ian Charleson and Nigel Havers on the set of *Chariots of Fire* (1981).

acknowledge the awesome responsibilities their job entails. There is an
underlying and pervasive poverty of ambition amongst too many people
in this industry. Simply claiming to be a purveyor of entertainment just
seems profoundly dishonest to me. Filmmakers have to decide for themselves what kind of society they want to be a part of, and then promote
that society through their work rather than take advantage of society's
weaknesses. But film is actually regressing back to the era of the fair-
ground spectacle, when all audiences demanded was the thrill of standing
in front of the Lumière brothers' screen as a train was rushing towards it.
The fact is that events portrayed on screen have real consequences in the
real world. Why do we rarely see what happens after the missile hits its
target or when the policeman falls from the highest building in town?
Present-day cinema has encouraged us to believe that we live in a world
without consequences and that violence is somehow a heroic end in itself.
Today's message is that good will always triumph over evil so long as sufficient blood is spilled. As thoughtful filmmakers, you have to decide
what side you're on.

Many years ago I found myself working for an extraordinarily gifted
taskmaster who I found all but impossible to please. One day I asked him,
"What do you want of me?" He said, "It's really very simple: amaze me.
You're here to do the things I can't. Go away and amaze me." Today I'm

putting the same challenge to you. Amaze me with your commitment. Amaze me with the subtlety and sophistication with which you excite and inform your audience. Amaze me with the ingenuity with which you persuade your finance and distribution partners to send out into the world the film—and the message—as you originally conceived it. Amaze me by telling stories in such a way as to allow people to feel understood and valued and never alone. Amaze me with the way you leave a distinctive mark on your own generation, not just in this country but around the world. And most of all amaze me with the maturity and wisdom and compassion with which you are prepared to address genuinely complex issues. However you look at it, filmmakers carry a very real responsibility in respect to the imaginative worlds they choose to portray and the manner in which they choose to portray them. Films reinforce or undermine the wider values of society. They reflect or damage our sense of identity as people and as nations. Never forget that this is not just a business.

Films as Producer

1971 *Peacemaking*
Melody
1972 *Bringing It All Back Home*
Glastonbury Fayre
The Pied Piper
1973 *Double Headed Eagle:*
Hitler's Rise to Power
1918–1933
Swastika
That'll Be the Day
The Last Days of Man on Earth
1974 *Radio Wonderful*
Mahler
Stardust
1975 *James Dean: The First American*
Teenager
Brother Can You Spare a Dime
Lisztomania
1976 *Bugsy Malone*
1977 *The Duellists*
1978 *Midnight Express*

1980 *Foxes*
1981 *Chariots of Fire*
1982 *P'tang, Yang, Kipperbang*
(television)
Experience Preferred . . . But Not
Essential
1983 *Forever Young*
Local Hero
Secrets
Red Monarch (television)
Those Glory Glory Days
(television)
1984 *Cal*
Arthur's Hallowed Ground
(television)
The Killing Fields
1985 *Defense of the Realm*
Mr. Love
1986 *The Frog Prince*
Winter Flight
The Mission

Knights & Emeralds
1990 *Memphis Belle*
1991 *The Josephine Baker Story*
(television)
*Without Warning: The James
Brady Story* (television)
Meeting Venus
1992 *A Dangerous Man: Lawrence
After Arabia* (television)

1994 *Being Human*
The Burning Season (television)
War of the Buttons
1995 *Le Confessional*
1999 *My Life So Far*
2004 *A Very Long Engagement*
2009 *We Are the People We've Been
Waiting For*

Ideally speaking, what the composer should contribute to the film is something that makes you see something in that film you couldn't have seen without the music.

LEONARD ROSENMAN
(Born in Brooklyn, New York, 1928—Died 2008)

Most of the great composers of the golden age were steeped in the classical traditions of Europe, a list that includes Max Steiner, Miklós Rózsa, Erich Korngold, Dimitri Tiomkin, and Franz Waxman. It took a young composer from New York to introduce avant-garde technique and twelve-tone music to motion-picture scores in Hollywood.

Leonard Rosenman wanted to be a painter as a child, but after serving in the Army Air Force in the Pacific during World War II he turned to music, seizing the opportunity to have lessons with the Austrian pioneer of modern composition, Arnold Schoenberg. Rosenman earned his degree in music at the University of California, Berkeley, then returned to New York, a struggling musician. He agreed to give piano lessons to a young actor, and the actor invited a director he was working with to a performance of Rosenman's compositions at the Museum of Modern Art. The actor was James Dean and the director was Elia Kazan. Kazan asked Rosenman to write the music for *East of Eden,* launching the composer's movie career and gaining a memorable score that combined Coplandesque Americana with Schoenberg-style dissonance.

John Houseman was impressed and asked the young musician, over the objections of the MGM music department, to write a score for a drama he was producing about patients in a mental hospital. Rosenman composed the first "serial" score written for a motion picture, *The Cobweb,* using the twelve-tone technique to evoke the inner neuroses of the characters. Rosenman would go on to write more than sixty scores. He won Oscars for *Barry Lyndon* and *Bound for Glory.* His other films include *Rebel Without a Cause, Edge of the City, Fantastic Voyage, Beneath the Planet of the Apes, A Man Called Horse, Star Trek IV* and *RoboCop 2.*

Leonard Rosenman was one of the first composers to use avant-garde
music in Hollywood film scores.

Rosenman had strong opinions and was quick to express them, often
clashing with directors and producers, whom he sometimes charged publicly
with musical ignorance. The producer who offered him *Fantastic Voyage*
asked him to write a jazz score, saying he wanted a hip science-fiction movie.
Rosenman told him, "That's a great idea for an advertising agency, but it
doesn't fit the film." Undaunted, the producer hired him, and Rosenman
wrote a memorable score for the story of miniaturized scientists who are
injected into the bloodstream of a wounded scientist to fix a blood clot in his
brain. One critic described the music as the "gentle shifting of orchestral colors, dissonant levels and textures, that intensify the otherworldliness by creating a sense of floating buoyancy."

A Hollywood composer's career depends on the pictures he is offered, and
Rosenman often felt shackled by the job offers that came his way. Yet he
proved that he could write lush traditional scores as well as the more innovative ones, and he was skilled at adapting the music of others. Ironically for an
innovator, his Oscars came from adapting the music of Handel and Schubert
for Stanley Kubrick on *Barry Lyndon* and adapting Woody Guthrie's songs
for Hal Ashby on *Bound for Glory.* In 1976 he went to the stage to accept his
second Oscar in as many years and reminded the Academy, "I write original
music, too, you know."

He wrote many scores for television series, including *The Defenders, Combat!, The Twilight Zone* and *Marcus Welby, M.D.,* and received Emmys for

Sybil and *Friendly Fire*. As time passed, the techniques he championed in the fifties came into common use among film composers. Rosenman relieved his frustrations with the movie industry by writing compositions for the concert stage, including numerous chamber works, two violin concertos, and a symphony.

Over four decades in Hollywood he wrestled with the question of how to communicate with directors. "The fact is, music is an abstract, magical, mystery medium to most filmmakers, because they don't understand it," he said. "They feel that it has the power to heal, to cure broken legs, to cure stuttering, to cure bad photography, bad acting—and I'm sorry to say it can't do any of that."

LEONARD ROSENMAN

—◆—

February 14, 1979*

Perhaps you could start by talking about what you think music does in film.

I think it's possible to learn about one medium through another. I've learned a great deal about music from film and a great deal about film from music. It's a question of what you take out of it and how you use it. You may think it's odd to hear composers talking about film, but I find film and music so analogous that, as I say, one medium can learn something from the other. In my estimation the greatest influence on twentieth-century avant-garde music is film. I'd like to tell you a little bit about what music does generally and then what film does. Let's investigate their properties.

I feel that music and film are similar simply because they are creative devices that move in time—both real and ontological time—and involve the use of the temporal lobe of the brain, which is to say they involve memory and interpretation. We perceive them both through the juxtaposition of certain details of the composition: cuts, rhythms, color. We're dealing here with two kinds of time. The first is the actual length of the film or piece of music, the second is our perception of such a thing. There may be two pieces of music that are five minutes long, yet one seems interminable and the other seems too short. It's the same with film. We can have the most arresting and gorgeous film in the world, but it might be either a bore or it's over too fast. A film that's two minutes long might seem like ten minutes and a piece of music that's ten minutes long might seem like it's only two minutes.

*James Powers moderated this seminar. This transcript also contains segments from seminars Leonard Rosenman gave at the American Film Institute on January 28, 1975, and August 8, 1980.

In Western culture there is nothing more vital in our experience than visual information. That's the strongest stimulus there is. The Chinese say that one picture is worth a thousand words. Well, if one picture is worth a thousand words, it most assuredly is worth a million notes. What they're saying is that pictures are more descriptive than anything else. Words are harder to comprehend because essentially they are symbols of pictures. Even more abstract, of course, are musical notes, which may represent words which may represent pictures which may represent experience, so we may be four times removed from literary experience. The result is that one medium—the medium that you're specializing in here, the visual medium—is tremendously powerful. Of course my interest has been in the visual and musical media, and what happens when these two things are married. The use of music in a film will change your perception of that film, and the use of film with music will change your perception of the music. We're dealing, after all, with audiences, and the success or failure of our endeavors in music and film has to do with the audience's response. One has to know how one medium functions with the other for it to become a catalyst for our emotions.

I feel—and this is perhaps the first statement of the day that might be considered controversial—that music has no emotions at all, whereas films have emotions because they deal with pictorialization. Let me qualify this and say I am talking about nonexperimental films dealing with the pictorialization of emotions that we feel and see and hear about in our everyday experiences. Music in itself has no emotion, but it does have the ability to engender emotions, and it's the emotion that you engender that can give a scene its raison d'être. Music is the catalyst that causes you to feel something. It's a series of vibrations, of sounds, organized rhythmically and aligned structurally in a way that tends to engender emotions in the audience. It's the nature of our own individual experiences with music that creates those emotions. Therefore I conclude—and Stravinsky felt the same way—that music really doesn't have any emotions of its own. It's just a series of vibrations and sounds. I could say that this young lady has lovely eyes, but if I took her eye out and put it on the table it would look like an oyster. It would have no expression at all. It's the context of the entire thing that causes something to be expressive or inexpressive. It's the context of your experiences and what you bring to the experience of listening to music that makes you feel it in an emotional way.

That particular ability not to express an emotion but to cause emotions to be felt has a great deal to do with the relationship between music and film. A piece of music, for example, will seem changed in the ear of the listener because it has been influenced by you having heard it earlier in the film. If you hear a theme, when it comes back later in the film it can be a tremendous thrill. Why? Because you remember it, and it connects you to the film. You have participated in the film to the extent that you remembered the theme, and having gone through these meandering journeys, it's a kick when it comes back. If you didn't remember the theme, if the music didn't go through the temporal lobe and affect your memory, it would feel as if you were watching just an isolated series of events. Likewise, if you have several analogous events in a film, if the hero returns in reel twelve, it's only exciting because you remember he left in reel one. If you don't perceive or remember the connection between one event and another, all of this becomes meaningless. You are utilizing your interpretive powers to participate in the experience.

Years ago I did a film called *The Outsider,* about the Indian who raised the flag on Iwo Jima and who died a drunk. There's a scene where you hear a tune that's been established earlier in the film relating to his best friend who was killed. You hear this tune in a kind of echoey way, and he looks around. You know that in some way he's hallucinating about his friend. The music means he doesn't have to say anything. We already know exactly what he's thinking. After all, films are pictures that move and not radio scripts transliterated to film. It's best to show it rather than say it, and that's where music can really help. I remember years ago I used to read the newspaper while I was watching television, because you didn't have to look at the set to know what was going on. Everyone was saying everything you needed to know. Then one day they played John Ford's *The Informer* on TV, and I started to read, and of course had to actually look at the screen because the thing is silent. Isn't that the name of the game?

When the heroine dies in La Bohème, *Puccini plays music from a happier moment in the story. That's what tears us apart.*

No question about it. Richard Strauss, who was a composer of the late nineteenth and early twentieth centuries, felt that music could express anything, including the gleam on silverware, the cows giving milk, you name it. That was his entire literary idea. He wrote things like the *Symphonia Domestica* which spoke about the butter on the table and the roast beef and people eating and so on, really kind of tranquil scenes. However, if you ask five people what that music was all about you'll hear five entirely different stories, each of which, by the way, happens to be exactly as valid as Richard Strauss' own ideas. This is an exemplar of the marriage that's necessary between the artist and the audience. The audience must participate. In the same way, the last twenty-five minutes of *2001* is really quite fantastic because in order to enjoy the film or empathize with it, it's necessary for you as the audience to make an interpretation. When you walk out and say, "I think the film was about so-and-so," and Arthur C. Clarke, who wrote the book, says, "Well, it wasn't really," it doesn't really matter. Your idea is as valid as Clarke's because it was necessary for you and me to interpret and participate in the film in order to understand it.

There's an old musical adage which I think also applies to film: the larger the work, the bigger the contrasts; the smaller the work, the smaller the contrasts. A perfect example musically of this was in postwar Germany where a composer was writing very tiny pieces, about a minute and a half or two minutes long, consisting of little tiny moments, almost like pointillism in painting. But the composers he influenced attempted to make pieces forty-five minutes long with these little tiny moments, and they didn't work. What happened with these long pieces with tiny contrasts is that diminishing returns and a sense of fatigue set in, and it all becomes a gray, homogenous mass. In other words, the totality is the sum total of the proportion of the parts to each other. This is a fundamental quality of both music and film. The proportion of these parts is achieved not merely by length but by contrast. We've all seen films in which there are a tremendous amount of very quick jump cuts for a long period of time. Eventually all these exciting little moments cease to become exciting, because there's no balance of contrasts. If you have a film that's an hour and a half long, and the contrasts are very short, all these things will even out, so that your film appears to have no contrasts at all. On the other hand, if you have a film that's an hour and a half and your contrasts are large, if the film is made up of ten-minute chunks, you'll be able to perceive the contrasts and the picture won't be boring. The film will appear to have hue and texture and variety, and it will remain interesting. In other words, there is some kind of a golden mean between the length of the contrast and the length of the overall piece.

I saw Kon Ichikawa's film *The Burmese Harp* on television last night. Aside from its tremendous content and the divine eye of the director, the film is particularly interesting in terms of contrasts. It's a tremendously long, sprawling film with contrasts that are very slow and very long. If, for example, he had utilized the kind of quick and jumpy cutting that someone like Billy Friedkin would use, the film would have seemed too long within the first half hour. So there's a paradox here. *The Burmese Harp* is a long and very slow film. You say to yourself, "That must be a bore." Actually not, because the relationship between the contrasts and the movement of this film, the physical size of the film, is so beautifully done. It's like a statue by Michelangelo. The proportions are so heroic because it's so large. The muscles may seem too large or the torso too large or the legs too small, but if it was any different the entire statue would seem out of balance, and that's the nature of *The Burmese Harp.*

If one is really a student of film, as one can be a student of music, you begin to see that the whole thing has to do with larger shapes. What makes this complicated is that understanding it all involves the two different kinds of time I mentioned previously. It involves the ability to hold your attention for short periods of time which the filmmaker wants to make long, and also for long periods of time which the filmmaker desires to make short. In other words, all art that moves in time has to do with manipulation of time, with time blocks, in accordance with the whole. Of course you might want to make a very short film with very long contrasts. I'm not saying that's bad necessarily, but I do think one should be conscious that these are the materials you're dealing with and then make a conscious choice about it. I'm talking about control, and in order to control what you have in art you have to understand the ingredients you're working with. If I have a yo-yo with a cord that stretches six miles, I have to be tremendously skilled to control it. It's easier if I start with a yo-yo with a cord that's only a couple feet long. Then, as my skill with the yo-yo evolves, my cord can get longer. It's all about practice. The skill needed to write a four-hour opera is the same as for a short film. The proportions of a short film are exactly the same as those in a long film, but they're in accordance with the shorter length of the film.

When music comes together with film, the music becomes an analogue of the film. It seems to take on the protective coloration of the film. If the film is disjunct, the music will seem disjunct. If the film is smooth, no matter what the music is, the music will take on this character, because the film is a much stronger stimulus than the music. On the other hand, another thing happens reciprocally. The music causes the film to seem slower or faster or smoother or more disjunct in some way, so there's an interaction between the two which influences your perception. A good case in point is Carol Reed's *The Third Man,* in which you had a film with a great deal of dramatic intensity, a tremendous amount of activity. There were chases and love scenes and killings and God knows what else, and yet the music was one theme played over and over again on one instrument, a pop tune which became famous at the time, and somehow this pop tune—not developed or elaborated but repeated over and over again—took on the same intensity as the scene. It was chase music or love music, but actually you were hearing exactly the same thing.

The problems that we face musically are not unanalogous to the problems you face as filmmakers. After all, here's a tremendous amount of footage that you're trying to organize in time. The whole process of cutting has to do with balance too, and also the idea that if one thing is too long and the other is too short, then the very point of the film may be vitiated. The same thing would happen if, in my estimation, event one is the most important event in a piece of music but happens to be shorter than event two, and event two is given undue emphasis. I would have in some way vitiated what I consider the major event of the piece, and people would misconstrue the entire emphasis of that piece. Elia Kazan, who directed the first film I did, *East of Eden,* told me, "The greatest flops among films are made up of a tremendous number of minor characters who are superbly delineated." He felt that the really successful films, from an artistic standpoint, were concerned with a single character throughout the whole story. He believed that a film should basically be about one thing and that it's not important to delineate everybody else. Everything else kind of fades into a sketchy oblivion. That's his interpretation, but it's an interesting point to consider, except that every rule is designed to be broken, like with Renoir's *The Rules of the Game,* a film that consists only of small, superbly delineated characters and happens to be a masterpiece.

What Kazan told me helped in my approach to films, because I always look for the spine of the story. This gives a sense of style to the film. It's not merely a matter of writing eighteenth-century music if the film is set during the eighteenth century. I'm talking about the dramatic style which basically helps establish the mood of the film. You can have each individual scene scored marvelously and the whole thing might not work. I think the power of a really good film score is in its cumulative aspect. Very often a filmmaker who doesn't understand this will come on the sound stage and hear a cue and say, "Jesus, it just doesn't work." I'll tell him he can always throw it out and suggest that he see how it fits with the rest of the film, after which he says, "Oh my gosh, it does work!" It's the same with a film. You might have made a film with three hundred scenes, each of which is exquisitely constructed, but the whole thing doesn't make any sense. One has to think of the entire story from beginning to end, and then aim at the end. That's why the Greek chorus came out at the beginning and told you what the end was going to be about. It was telling you that the author was aiming for a specific goal, that the seeds of the end were in the beginning.

There's an old saying that if you want to look for strictness, don't go to the masters, go to the disciples. The disciples are always very strict and the

Rosenman recalls that the year he did the score for *East of Eden* he had five major performances in New York. "The minute I did my first film I didn't have a performance in New York for twenty years. They wouldn't look at my works."

masters are very free. I think that's something to remember and then forget. What I'm trying to say is that all these rules are basically technical ideas of tremendous interest, like sixteenth-century counterpoint, which I had to study and then forget. It's good as a discipline, but then you forget it. In other words, all this accumulates in your consciousness, which we then express in our own particular way. We assimilate. It's the difference biologically between the properties of the living and the properties of the dead. The properties of the living grow by assimilation. They assimilate and change and spew out things in their own way. The dead—that is to say, stalactites and things of this kind—grow by accretion. They grow one on top of the other. Things don't change, they simply pile up on each other. So the whole process of learning is basically an assimilation. There is a conscious period of forgetting and then a period of remembering a different way. All this stuff I'm throwing out at you I ask you to eventually forget in the interest of creativity.

When I was working in theater we used to take arbitrary pieces of film and put them together with pieces of music that had no rational connection, and the results were often fantastic. I wonder if that arbitrary-associational thing is of value to you as a composer.

It's of value in an experimental sense. It's of value if you learn something from it. But I do think that the dereliction of control in art makes it less valuable art. I met a filmmaker the other day who has been given millions of dollars to make a film. He does an average of fifty takes for each shot and prints every take. I maintain that if you give three chimps three cameras and have them shoot anything, they're eventually going to come up with something if they shoot that much film. A lot of filmmakers these days have ideas about creativity that are diametrically opposed to what creativity actually is. They feel that creativity is improvisation, fooling around and getting as much material as possible and hoping that it works, as opposed to having some idea in your mind that you attempt to vivify technically.

I'm not saying there's no place for improvisation, because, after all, jazz and all popular music is based on improvisation, as well as the fact that in the eighteenth century it was a tremendous mode of musical expression. I also adore improvisational theater if it's really done well. But I think that the more control the artist has over his material, the closer to art it is. In film it really seems to me that if you look at it objectively, the more of a one-man show it is, the more artistic it is. Look at the greatest

filmmakers of all time—Fellini and Bergman and people of that kind—
and you know damn well there's no decision being made by committee in
those films, that they are the final arbiters of taste in their work. I knew
Fellini quite well, because I lived in Italy for four years, and even in the
scoring sessions he is in complete control of what goes on. It's his film. He
knows what he wants.

I think the idea of the compartmentalization of all art may perfect it in
some sense, but it perfects something in terms of industry and not in
terms of art. I'm not adjudicating here and saying that one is bad and one
is good. My colleagues keep saying, "You can't tell me I'm not writing
music." But I'm only saying that there's a difference in function between
marvelous wallpaper and Jackson Pollock. They function differently. Different processes create those two different things. In other words, the
propulsion of film music is not musical ideas, it's filmic and literary ideas.
Film music supports something which has been a priori established for it.
While it appears to have all the ingredients of music—counterpoint, har-
mony, themes, color and orchestration—in my estimation it really doesn't
fulfill the prime obligation or definition of music. It's the difference
between a high form of artisanship and art. Since the propulsion of film
music doesn't come from musical ideas but from film and literary ideas, it
is not real music.

It is, in its own nature, incomplete.

Yes. The process of the composition of film music is not the process of the
composition of music per se. The great difference between film music and
concert music which uses written texts, like opera, is that the composer of
opera voluntarily takes the text and alters it to adhere to musical principles. He has refashioned all the ingredients into a musical idea. It was his
choice and his manipulation of all things into a musical form. In film,
there's no way the composer manipulates the film except very indirectly,
by altering your perception of it. He fills in a rigid a priori construct in
terms of time. The film is finished, and indeed has to be in order for the
composer to be able to write a score. It must be frozen. He may be able,
by his music, to alter your perception of the time of that film. A scene, for
example, in real time that lasts for a minute and a half could be made to
seem like it lasts three minutes, or even twenty seconds. But he is impris-
oned, bound by the obligations of an a priori construct. The composer for
film is a cog in a process. He's adapting music to a film in very much the

same way that Wagner would take the story of Tristan and Isolde and adapt it to his music.

In other words, if you play a film score it shouldn't really make sense without the images behind it.

In my estimation, it doesn't. I did the first twelve-tone film score in 1955. It was a thing called *The Cobweb.* At that time Dimitri Mitropoulos was conductor of the New York Philharmonic and he saw the film and asked if I would like to have them play it in concert. I said I wouldn't because I felt that the music was composed for the film and that the amount of work it would take to refashion it as a concert piece would be such that I might as well have written a new piece. So I really don't believe in sound-track albums except as a commercial endeavor, which is fine if you've got a beautiful tune and it helps the box office. But in terms of absolutely straight money-on-the-table art I think it doesn't quite work. A sound-track is very truncated and disjunct and doesn't quite have the shape that a piece of music really needs. If a composer can contend with the ego problems attending those kinds of definitions, I think he'll work very well in films.

Let me just add here that when I say "soundtrack" I don't mean only music, I mean all the sounds in the film. Kazan said he felt I should take over the administration of the entire soundtrack of *East of Eden,* including the bird sounds and dubbing the actors' footfalls, to maintain the rhythm and make sure that the entire style of the film was consistent. That also meant the silences.

Going back to the statement you made that music has no emotion of its own . . .

That seems to have struck some kind of a nerve here.

What about when a composer uses singers in his music. Does it still have no emotion?

It's the same thing, unless you're communicating words with that music. What's happening is that you're communicating the emotions connected with the experience connected to the words. Words are much more directly connected to our experience than music is. If someone sings a love song and uses the verbal terminology of love in the song, then the emotions engendered obviously have to do with love, but they're telling you something about love in words, and clearly that's extramusical. If you use a love song with the words of love in connection with a murder scene, then you're really saying something else. It becomes more abstract. I maintain and stand by my contention that music expresses no emotion, that you the listener supply the emotion. If you put words to the music, then it's the words that are expressing the emotion. If you don't hear the words and just hear the chorus, that serves—for me anyway—exactly the same purpose as any other instrumental combination, except perhaps that it may be a little more dramatic.

It's all about subjective perception?

Absolutely. It's all your perception.

Isn't that true of every form of communication?

Yes, I think so. I had occasion to live for six months on the Rosebud Sioux Reservation, where I was doing research for a film. I found that the things I felt were love songs were actually battle hymns and the things I thought were battle hymns were love songs. There was absolutely no frame of reference. It was so weird. It was a total sense of disorientation. The only analogous situation is that once by mistake I put a dime in a vending machine at Universal Pictures thinking I was getting hot chocolate. I drank it and it turned out to be chicken soup.

I was interested in how you handled writing the score for the Woody Guthrie film, Bound for Glory?

I was brought in toward the end of the editing but before the film was absolutely finished. We had a lot of conversations about Woody Guthrie's music and the score of the film. I felt right from the beginning that it would be inopportune and rather tasteless to take these Woody Guthrie tunes, which musically are essentially rather simpleminded—after all, the motivational force behind those tunes was basically the words—and arrange them for a large orchestra. I didn't think that was my job. I felt the solution to the problem was that the orchestra should comment dramatically upon the action. The director, Hal Ashby, had originally laid a kind of dummy track onto the film which consisted entirely of Guthrie music, with the result, in my opinion, that the score tended to make the film too homogenized and didn't stress the drama of the story. It became a kind of fusion between a documentary and a drama. I felt it needed another dimension.

What are your thoughts about putting music under dialogue?

I honestly feel that if the actors are really interacting, really doing their jobs, it's a kind of chamber music of its own. You really understand the inner monologue of what's going on and you really don't need music. So generally I feel that good dialogue doesn't need musical accompaniment. If the actors aren't doing a good job, there's nothing that can help them. When I first started in films I worked at Warner Bros., and at that time their films had wall-to-wall music. If the film was an hour and a half long, the score was an hour and a half long. Historically this came from silent films, where the function of music was to add sound effects, and also cover up all kinds of realistic sounds, like popcorn, the toilet flushing, the projection machine and so on. The music helped remove the idea of reality so the audience would be able to suspend disbelief. Jack Warner evidently felt that music had this magical mystery power to make people feel things or make something palatable which didn't seem palatable. Basically they knew nothing about whether the product was good or bad, so they began to use music indiscriminately. Through the thirties and forties there was a transition whereby you had a film with sound, dialogue, special effects and everything else, but the filmmakers weren't quite sure about the role of music. It seemed to work in the silent films in a certain fashion, with wall-to-wall music, so they just continued to do it. They didn't realize that diminishing returns set in, and if you had music from frame alpha to frame omega, people wouldn't listen to it after a while. It was like an enema in the Jewish family tradition. The idea was that it couldn't hurt you. If you see an old Warner Bros. movie like *Anthony Adverse* or *Captains Courageous* with wall-to-wall music, after a while you're saying, "Stop the music!"

Did you think Gone With the Wind *was that way?*

Yes. Max Steiner, who scored *Gone With the Wind,* was the creator of a kind of Mickey Mouse style of music. If a man with a clubfoot walked into a shot, the music walked along with him with a clubfoot. Max is very important in our craft, because he wrote the first original score to a film, which was *King Kong.* He made an outstanding contribution to movies, and something like *Gone With the Wind* was a beautiful score in its time, but was basically lusterless because you had the first four bars arbitrarily at any given point throughout the film.

What kind of problems did you have in introducing twelve-tone music into film scores?

Alex North and I—he also worked with Kazan, on *A Streetcar Named Desire*—are credited with bringing film music into the twentieth century. When I came on the scene in 1954 to do *East of Eden,* I was an ex–college professor, and I had a reputation in the concert field as an avant-garde composer and concert pianist and conductor. I knew nothing about scor-

Rosenman, seated, with James Dean, standing, on the set of
Nicholas Ray's *Rebel Without a Cause* (1955).

ing films and nothing about movies except that I liked them. When I came on the scene, the big composers in this town were Max Steiner, Dimitri Tiomkin and Bernie Herrmann. Korngold was dying but he was still there. I found it difficult to get work. The kind of music that these composers wrote basically had its roots in the nineteenth century with the romantic music of Rachmaninoff, Tchaikovsky, Schumann and Brahms, the Russian and German Romantics. The result was if, for example, there was a single line of music in a film, that line wasn't played by, let's say, an oboe or a flute. The line was played by all the violins, all the trumpets, all the flutes, all the oboes, and all the clarinets. No one ever took any chances, with the result that if you listen to a lot of the scores from older films, the music has an incredible thickness to it. It's not a thickness of luster, it's a thickness of turgidity, a lack of profile, a lack of inner voices moving, a lack of counterpoint. It just sounds elephantine.

I remember when we recorded *Eden.* I had a solo flute play something and the flutist stopped in the middle and looked around. I said, "What's the problem?" He said, "There isn't anyone playing with me." I said, "No, I'm afraid you have to count." Having a large orchestra but using small chamber ensembles within that orchestra and using very few entire orchestra sections was an entirely new development. The result was that you had a different sound in film music. You had much more of a clear focus of drama and potentially a much greater palette of color in the score, because you had small groups as opposed to large groups playing, not some large, homogenous mess. For my second film I did *The Cobweb* for producer John Houseman, a very literate man who wanted me to write a score in my own style. I said, "Are you sure you know what you're saying?" He said, "Yes, I'll give you carte blanche. Do anything you want." When I finished I thought the score would be thrown out, but he said, "So be it, I'll fight for it." If I had written a consonant, conservative score with a few salt-and-pepper dissonances thrown in, it probably would have been thrown out, but the thing had absolutely no frame of reference whatsoever to anything that had gone before, and they knew so little about it. Actually I'm being charitable. They knew nothing about this kind of music and felt that, knowing nothing, if they made a wrong adjudication, they could be misjudged by others.

When I came here I thought that filmmakers were intruders on my culture. Then as I began to get my head on straight, I began to realize I was an intruder in their culture. It was remarkable that I was accepted the way I was and could make a living and try things out. I utilized films to buy time to write concert music. I used films as a laboratory for dealing with problems. That's not to say I didn't take it seriously, because if your name is on it, you do the best you can. It was felicitous because the film-maker would get something unusual and interesting and I was able to try out a lot of problematic areas in my own work and see what they sounded like. Other twelve-tone composers have come into town who were out to teach filmmakers a lesson and write an avant-garde score. But that's not the point. The schizophrenic nature of my kind of activity is that if I write a work on my own for the concert stage, there's nobody who stands between myself and my work, except the size of the orchestra and to some extent the commissioners. But when I work on a film, my prime objective is to serve the film. I think that most composers who work in films have a serious problem in that they don't write other kinds of music, which means their entire musical ego is tied up in film music. It's very easy to get confused as to what kind of music you're writing. That's never happened to me, because for a while I was the only composer in the United States with feet in both territories.

Has a film ever been cut to your music, rather than you scoring the finished film?

I prefer to see the film before it's finished so I can get some idea, because with a major feature film it's usually about a year between the writing of the script and the finished film. Nobody sets out to make a bad film, so let's consider at the outset that the people making the film are sincere and interested in making a good film. They spend about a year on it and then the composer comes in and is given about four weeks to match this con-ception. It's not fair to me or the director to ask me to crystallize in two weeks an impression of the film analogous to the director's. It's more ideal for the composer to have as much communication as he can with the filmmaker, and when I spot a film I try to see it as often as I can. Then at the spotting session I'll finally get it digested and find out what I want to do with it. Then I'll sit down with the filmmaker and we'll run the film on a stop-go projector, and I'll say, "I think the music should do this and that. I think it should go from here to there." Sometimes there'll be ques-tions or arguments. "I don't think it needs music there." "I would like to say so-and-so there." Let's say that a man and woman are kissing. "I'd like to show the poisonous element in this in some way, because three reels later he kills her." In other words, we talk about dramaturgy.

On *Eden* I worked along with Kazan right from the first day of shoot-ing. I wrote rough sketches, and when the film was in rough cut, so was the music. I played the music for the actors before they went out to do their scenes. In scenes where the music carries the rhythm of the scene rather than the dialogue, I asked Kazan if he would let me dictate the action of the scene by directing it with him, like an opera. To my amazement he said he had often wanted to work like that. It was a real collaboration between a filmmaker and a composer. I worked *Rebel Without a Cause* like that too. I even wrote part of the script, and we staged scenes for the music. I worked that way to some degree with Hal Ashby on *Bound for Glory,* and John Frankenheimer sometimes reshoots scenes because I have certain musical ideas for them, even though the whole film might be finished. In my opinion the music should be inextricable from the dramatic framework. Of course, television is different. I did *Marcus Welby* for six years. After the second year I was all alone. I'd record the thing and never even watch the show after that. It was all disease music. I'd score about thirteen shows and they would track the other twenty-seven from that. A brain-operation score became a mastectomy score. Television is the quintessential schlock medium.

For *The Savage Eye,* which is a kind of documentary of Los Angeles, I was shown about four hours of footage before it was cut and was commissioned to write a suite. Then they cut the film to the music, which is a piece of mine called Chamber Music One which has been performed in concert many times. Ordinarily I don't allow any score of mine to be played in performance. I keep that part of my life separate. I don't believe film music belongs on the concert stage, except for something like this, where the film was made post priori. There's a striptease sequence in the film I use when talking about how different kinds of music can alter your perception of the image. Students always ask me what I was thinking of when I wrote the music to the striptease scene, or how I tried to interpret it. I ask them what they think I felt when I was writing the music, and their answers are marvelous and all valid. There were things like, "Obviously you showed the whole thing to be terribly vulgar and that the dancer didn't want to be up there," and "You tried to bring out the erotic in the striptease." The truth of the matter is I felt nothing about the striptease while I wrote the music, because I had never seen it. I just wrote a piece of music and they put the striptease to it. Hopefully this gives you some idea about the arbitrariness of music in movies and the interesting change of perception with regards to the relationship of music and film. If I and some colleagues of mine had been asked to score that scene, you would have had a different interpretation from each of us, yet each interpretation would have been valid.

The composer for films is a dramatist in his own right, and it's how he sees the dramaturgy, or how he sees the mise-en-scène musically, in its larger sense, that determines whether something is going to work, or whether we're at least in the ballpark or not. What we're trying to develop is some sort of unified style. If we deal with many different kinds of things in a film, we try to see not where the differences are but where the similarities are in order to maintain a style: the photography, the narration, what the camera sees, what we're trying to say in the film. I think what the composer is trying to say should achieve the same consistency. Ideally, the composer should contribute something that makes you see something in that film you couldn't have seen without the music.

For example, supposing you have an opening shot. I'm sure you've seen a helicopter shot of New York many times. This helicopter goes down into the canyons of New York and you begin to see in this concrete jungle a lot of people rushing around and cars and traffic. The filmmaker has several options with the soundtrack. You have the option of having it silent, which would create a certain kind of mood. You have the option of the sound effects of the city, which would be a kind of documentary style. What you hear and what you see corroborate each other. Both tell us that the city is a busy, noisy place. You don't actually need a soundtrack to tell you that, because you can see it. Then you have the option of writing the kind of big-city music which you used to hear in the old films, a lot of xylophones, kind of Gershwin-type stuff, which is really only musical sound effects and again doesn't really add to anything you've seen on the screen, just reinforces it to some degree. It's basically just another form of naturalism, the aural component of the visual mise-en-scène. But suppose the filmmaker said, "Is there something I can say with music that you can't perceive from seeing the scene?" Can the music make a statement about the scene which you can't otherwise see or hear? Let's say that despite the hustle and bustle of the city, we want to convey the idea that the city is a very lonely place. If the composer used a lonely saxophone line with a lot of echo and played a long, slow, plaintive tune against this terrific mélange, you would get an idea of the city that you couldn't have gotten without that soundtrack. In other words, the soundtrack is entering into the story and telling you something about the scene that the image itself couldn't tell you. That has to do with the communication between the filmmaker and the composer. So to write film music you almost don't have to be a composer, you have to be a dramatist.

What if the director can't communicate to you the style he's looking for?

You simply have to hope the guy is going to trust you enough to leave you alone. The only advice I can offer to all potential filmmakers in regards to working with a composer, and here I have to resort to the language of the young, is that the vibes have to be very good. There has to be a mutual understanding of what the music is trying to say. The filmmaker has to relinquish some control or else he winds up using records. Most filmmakers don't know anything about music, and that's really too bad, because of any two arts that are similar, there is nothing more similar than film and music. I've known a tremendous number of filmmakers over the past twenty years and some of them are very literate guys, but they all seem to have no communication at all when it comes to music. They've never been to a concert and don't listen to classical music. I probably know as much popular music as they do, but they don't know anything of what I know. I think sometimes this is a product of their lack of imagination. The good composers, the ones with a real sense of dramaturgy, would probably be as good if not better filmmakers than most of the filmmakers they work for, because they have a real understanding of many aspects of life and art which filmmakers don't. That's why I think it's important for filmmakers to know art, painting, literature, music. Filmmaking is a marriage of all those arts, and that's why a filmmaker has to know everything if he wants to be an artist.

I did a main title for a series that became a tremendous hit for years called *The Defenders*. The guy in charge, a very bright guy, said, "I'd like the music to express the law." I said, "Well, music can't express the law. It can express the laws of music but it can't express the law. If you want the music to express majesty or something like that, it will only express majesty if what you have on the screen is majestic." Music can't open and shut doors. It can't make actors better. It can change your perception of things; it can help along certain things; it can say something about the scene that you couldn't have conceived of without music—but it cannot help a bad film.

In other words, the subject of all this talking we're doing is to bring to consciousness all the choices that you have as filmmakers. I think anything one does by conscious choice is fine. It's only when people do things out of a lack of choice and out of ignorance that you get into terrible trouble. It's not what you know that gets you into trouble, it's what you don't know. When something is in your consciousness, you have choices. The fact is, music is an abstract, magical, mystery medium to most filmmakers, because they don't understand it. They feel it has the power to heal, to cure broken legs, to cure stuttering, to cure bad photography, bad act-ing—and I'm sorry to say it can't do any of that. It's up to you. You have to make good films, and then the music will also appear to be better.

Films as Composer

1955 *East of Eden*	1971 *The Todd Killings*
Rebel Without a Cause	1973 *Battle for the Planet of the Apes*
The Cobweb	1975 *Barry Lyndon*
1956 *Edge of the City*	*Race with the Devil*
1957 *The Young Stranger*	1976 *Birch Interval*
The Big Land	*Bound for Glory*
Bombers B-52	1977 *The Car*
1958 *Lafayette Escadrille*	*September 30, 1955*
1959 *Pork Chop Hill*	1978 *An Enemy of the People*
1960 *The Bramble Bush*	*The Lord of the Rings*
The Rise and Fall of Legs Diamond	1979 *Prophecy*
The Plunders	*Promises in the Dark*
The Savage Eye	1980 *Hide in Plain Sight*
The Crowded Sky	*The Jazz Singer*
1962 *Convicts 4*	1982 *Making Love*
The Outsider	1983 *Cross Creek*
Hell Is for Heroes	*Miss Lonelyhearts*
The Chapman Report	1985 *Sylvia*
1966 *Fantastic Voyage*	1986 *Star Trek IV: The Voyage Home*
A Covenant With Death	1990 *RoboCop 2*
1968 *Countdown*	1991 *Ambition*
1969 *Hellfighters*	1997 *Levitation*
1970 *A Man Called Horse*	2005 *Tristram Shandy: A Cock and Bull Story*
Beneath the Planet of the Apes	

Rosenman's scores for television include *Combat*, 1962–67; *Garrison's Gorillas*, 1967–68; *The Virginian*, 1967–69; and *Marcus Welby, M.D.*, 1969–76.

Directing is a little bit like writing with a taximeter running, and every time it clicks that's another $50,000. So if you don't know what you're doing you start hearing those clicks really loudly.

JOHN SAYLES
(Born in Schenectady, New York, 1950)

John Sayles' visit to the Conservatory offered an example to AFI's aspiring filmmakers of a man who uses his talent as a writer to provide himself a measure of independence and control over his own work. In many instances people who refer to themselves as independent filmmakers are actually *dependent*—on financing, distributors, unions, agents and actors—but Sayles eliminated interference by studios and producers by using money he earned as a screenwriter to make his films.

After graduating from Williams College, where he participated in campus theater programs, Sayles hitchhiked around the United States finding work as a meat packer, medical orderly and day laborer, accumulating life experience that nourished his writing. His short stories "I-80 Nebraska M. 490–M. 205" and "Breed" won O. Henry Best Short Story prizes, and his novel *Union Dues* was nominated for the National Book Award in 1977.

Sayles went to Hollywood where Roger Corman hired him to write *Piranha,* a low-budget variation on *Jaws* directed by Joe Dante. He wrote two more pictures for Corman, *The Lady in Red* and *Battle Beyond the Stars,* before Dante asked him to do a rewrite for *The Howling.* Meanwhile Sayles leveraged the money he'd earned and the production experience he'd gained into fulfilling his own vision. He wrote *Return of the Secaucus Seven* and directed it on a $60,000 budget in New England, initiating a partnership with Maggie Renzi, who to this day is his producing partner. The film was successfully distributed, establishing Sayles' reputation, as well as a way of working independently that would be the template for his career.

He continued to mix screenwriting assignments with his own writing-directing projects, the latter representing a consistently high level of work marked by political and social awareness: *Lianna, The Brother from Another*

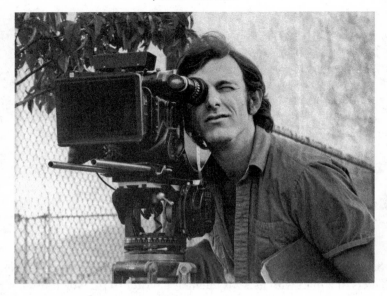

John Sayles uses his earnings as a screenwriter for hire to finance his
independent films. Here he is behind the camera on *Baby It's You* (1983),
which he wrote and directed.

*Planet, Matewan, Eight Men Out, City of Hope, Passion Fish, The Secret of
Roan Inish, Lone Star, Sunshine State, Silver City,* and *Honeydripper.* Sayles is a
man of many talents who took time between his pictures to write novels,
receive a MacArthur Fellowship "genius grant," craft the television series
Shannon's Deal, act in more than a dozen films, doctor the scripts for *Apollo 13*
and *The Fugitive,* and direct music videos for Bruce Springsteen.

"When I first went to Hollywood," Sayles told *Sight & Sound,* "I did
think it through: I want to write movies and I want to direct the movies I
write. How do I get to do this?" His career has been a matter of answering
that question year after year. "I'm not afraid of failure," he says. "I don't get
upset if people don't like it—I'm doing it because I'm interested."

JOHN SAYLES

——◆——

May 29, 1996*

How did you become a film director?

I was acting in a summer theater in New Hampshire. I realized I was surrounded by really good actors and wanted to make *Return of the Secaucus Seven*. I was interested in directing and had written some things for Roger Corman, though I knew it would be a long time before Roger would actually let me direct. I had written three movies for him that year and had some money, about forty thousand dollars, and wanted to spend it before the IRS could get to it. I said, "When am I next going to have that much money? I should spend it all on a movie. What kind of film can I make for this kind of money? Who are the actors I'll use? They're all around thirty years old. Where can I set the movie that's cheap? I'm not going to be able to move the camera very much or be able to do much visual storytelling, because that involves experienced people, equipment, time and money. What about *Nashville,* where you had a whole bunch of characters so there was always an excuse to cut to another conversation? Why don't I create situations where people are just talking to each other?"

I realized I might get to make only one film. I could have made a horror film or something like that, but I had never been dying to make a horror film, which might have broken me into the studios. Why not make something that I would want to see myself and that I wouldn't get to see if I didn't make it myself? As Mickey Spillane once said, "I write the kind

*Frank Pierson moderated this seminar. This transcript also contains segments from seminars John Sayles gave at the American Film Institute on December 10, 1985, December 11, 1985, and February 2, 2011.

of books I like to read." I figured I might never have this much control over a film again. I decided to make a film about a bunch of people having a hard time turning thirty. I had met a bunch of people who had been politically active years earlier and were still trying to be, but at the same time they were deciding whether to get married and have kids, and trying to make a living. The idea for *Return of the Secaucus Seven* evolved from that. I wrote it based on a couple of locations I knew I could get my hands on.

Do you think of yourself as a writer or director?

I think of myself as a storyteller. I've written short stories and novels and plays and movies for other people, and movies I've directed myself. I always say that I feel like the screenplay is the first draft, directing is the second and editing is the third. If you don't truly control all three of those drafts, the story could go anywhere. Many writers who control only the first draft ask "What happened to my story?" when they see it on the screen.

I do two basic kinds of screenwriting. One is when I know I'm going to direct the movie and one is screenwriting for other people, to make a living. The style of the writing is different. When I'm writing for myself, especially if I know I already have the money, the style of the screenplay is explicitly for me and the actors and the crew. But if I'm writing a screenplay that I want to direct that we're trying to sell to somebody, it's half screenplay and half sales tool. I try to make it as easy to read as possible. You have to get somebody excited enough so they'll put money into it. Writing for other people is more political than writing for yourself, and it changes the way the script looks on paper. If you read the script for *Brother from Another Planet,* where I already knew I had the money, it has very few stage directions. It's really only dialogue. But the things I write for other people have a lot more hype in them. When I wrote for Roger Corman I actually wrote shooting scripts that included details of every cut, because he knew he was going to make the movie. I never had to sell him on making it. Roger has directed so many films that he knows how to read a shooting script. Later, when I started working for studios, I discovered that most executives don't know how to read shooting scripts. It's confusing for them. If they see five pages of a script without any dialogue except screams and terror, they say, "We have to have something else in here." Someone like Roger knows it's only two minutes of screen time. There's too much direction in shooting scripts for people who don't know how to read them, too much to visualize. What I started doing is what William Goldman does, which is create some kind of expressionist script and give the reader the same feeling which hopefully the film will ultimately give them. At the end of *Butch Cassidy and the Sundance Kid* there is hardly any punctuation in Goldman's script. "Butch turns around and does this and Sundance does this and Butch pulls his gun." You know they're all cuts, but he's suggesting the rhythm of the scene. You may have an idea about the room that a character is walking into, but it will take you a half a page to describe it and the screenplay will get bogged down. There's a Raymond Chandler book where he doesn't really describe an office but has a line, something like "He gave me a drink of warm gin in a dirty glass." That's the only description of the office, but we see the room in our minds because of that one line. That's all the art director needs to do his work.

You are a member of a small cadre of American filmmakers who are able to tell your own stories in your own way.

I think if you have a movie that grosses over $100 million, or even one that comes close to that, you're going to get a couple more chances at the table and you can probably make whatever you want to make for a while. Altogether our movies haven't made $100 million or anywhere close to it, so we try to keep the budgets as low as possible. Almost every time out we've had a different distributor and a different way of bringing the money together, perhaps a studio or a video presale or my money or a combination of my money and some independent money.

When you talk about your money, do you really put your own money into your films?

Yes, and you're not supposed to say that in Hollywood, but I'm a screenwriter for hire and that's how I make a living. Over the years I've been able to make enough money writing screenplays so that sometimes I've been the sole investor in movies that are under $500,000, and I've often been a major investor in some of the other movies that we've pieced together. If you're going to ask somebody to have faith in you, you should at least have faith in yourself.

Your start with Roger Corman must have helped you learn how to make a buck stretch as far as you can.

Working for New World when Roger Corman owned it was very labor intensive. The good thing about Roger was that he would say, "It's up to you to make this as good as you can. I'm not going to get in your way. This is the movie you're making and this is the budget. Don't shoot a day over. Don't shoot a dollar over. If you shoot under I'll be even happier. And if you can make it a good film as well, that's your business and I'm not going to complain about it." He didn't interfere as long as you stayed on budget. He didn't worry about individual scenes so long as the basic structure was there. So then it's thrown back on the filmmaker, whereas very often in a studio situation you can go over budget as long as you make somebody happy. I've written movies where there were three different financial entities involved that wanted three different movies. One was European, one was an independent and one was a studio, and all three had to be kept happy. The director had to make all three movies and of course went over budget and got blamed for it. What they ended up with was a fight that continued into the editing room and press screenings. The great thing about Roger is that there was just Roger, who owned the company, and Francis Dole, who was his script supervisor. Only two people, not a committee. Roger had directed dozens of movies, produced hundreds, and together they gave you very specific script notes. It wasn't anything like, "We have problems with the second act," or "There's something wrong with the girl." That's really not helpful. It would be: "On page 58 we feel like this is too early to have another piranha attack. Can you delay it five pages? We think the audience needs a little bit more of a rest period." Very specific, useful things. With studios you get, "We have problems with the second act." So I ask, "What problems?" And they sit there and say, "I don't know. It just doesn't feel right." Sometimes it really comes down to the fact that they're paid to pick holes in things. Sometimes they aren't sure they want to make the film. And sometimes they know for sure they don't want to make it but have committed themselves to paying you for a draft, so they just go along with it, hoping that magic might strike and some big actor will see the script and want to do it.

Roger used to hire the cheapest caterer in Hollywood and eventually people would complain, and then the second week he would get another caterer. He might go through three or four, being responsive to the crew, but on the next movie he'd still hire that bad caterer for the first week because they were the cheapest caterer in Hollywood, and it took at least a week for people to feel so bad they would complain.

It sounds like you had fun there.

It was a lot of fun. Also, most of the movies in those days weren't getting reviewed much, so there wasn't a whole lot of pressure on the directors. And there's never that much pressure for the writers, because people never know who writes those kinds of films.

What was the first picture you did after breaking out of the Corman factory?

At first I didn't break out that far. I did three movies for Roger and then the next two movies I wrote were for directors I'd worked with when we were with Roger. I did *The Howling* with Joe Dante and *Alligator* with Louis Teague.

How did Lone Star *begin in your mind?*

I think it began when I was a kid and watched Fess Parker play Davey Crockett in the Disney shows. I got interested in Davey Crockett and the legend of the Alamo, and then as I got older I learned a little bit more about Texas history. I hitchhiked through Texas and around the border, and got to learn a little bit more about it. I could see it was a little more complex than the Alamo as just a simplistic, stirring story about these guys who gave their lives for liberty. I became fascinated with the Texas/Mexican border. With towns like El Paso and Laredo, Eagle Pass and Del Rio, it's not that the Anglos are up here and then there's a line with the Mexicans down here. In reality there are two communities who both speak Spanish, and somebody drew a line in the sand and said, "You're one kind of people and you're another kind of people." Over the years, Mexican-American and Mexican culture have drifted apart slightly, but the people on both sides of the border have much more in common with each other than anybody from those border towns has with somebody from San Antonio, or certainly Houston.

Lone Star came to me in part from an awareness of class. I'd say I was probably brought up middle class, and went to a school that had welfare kids, middle class kids, working-class kids and some kids who were almost upper class. I certainly recognized there was such a thing as class in America, which is something most Americans don't like to think about or just want to ignore. It's not as rigid as it still is in Britain, where you just say what university you went to and they've got you pegged, or you open your mouth and they say, "Oh, I know that accent. You're from so-and-so and you went to this-or-that public school." It's much more fluid in the United States, but it does exist, and it's something that should be dragged out into the light of day.

Much of my thinking about *Lone Star* came from the idea of borders as something we create to separate ourselves from other people, and those things that separate us in American culture. There's race, class, economics and sex. In the case of *Lone Star,* with the military story, there is also rank. These are all things that make us say, "I'm this way and I'm not that way. There are people like us and people like them." I'm always fascinated where people draw those lines in their lives and say, "This is where I end and someone else begins."

When did these ideas begin to crystallize into a screenplay?

We'd had a really hard time with our previous movie, *The Secret of Roan Inish.* It was one of these situations where we had some interest from people in financing part of the movie. I had some money of my own, so I plunged in and financed a third of the movie in the hope that somebody was going to put up the other two-thirds of the budget. We were two weeks into the shooting before the other people actually put the cash in the bank. So we were two weeks in, working on foreign soil, before I knew if I was going to have to pull the plug or not. Of course once I started spending my money I was over the proverbial barrel and they were able to keep changing the deal in their favor. I liked the people and I liked the movie, but the economic situation was so stressful, coming in from a day of shooting and then getting on the phone back to the United States and having people say, "We have to know your net worth and what your car and house are worth." I was really putting myself on the line. It's not like I'm Coppola. We're not talking about millions of dollars, but it was all the money I had.

The Secret of Roan Inish was a very hard movie to get released, but finally we made a deal with a small distribution company. The whole thing had been so tooth-and-nail that after it was over I didn't have another movie ready to go. I had to work for a lot of other people just to pay the rent. Then we got an invitation from a friend who lives in Texas to come down and sit on a houseboat for a couple days on Lake Amistad on the Mexican border. It's kind of neutral territory. I had three or four things in mind, but I just said, "Well, I've had this border idea for a long time. Why don't I do that next?" As often happens if I've been carrying something around for long enough, the first draft takes only two weeks. I sat down and wrote the script, and then did a little more research and wrote it again. I had been working for Castle Rock as a writer for Rob Reiner, so they knew me. They asked, "What are you going to do next? We'd like to read it." I think *Lone Star* is the first time when the first person who looked at something I've written said, "Yes, let's do it."

Your transitions in Lone Star *were very visually interesting.*

Lone Star moves from the present to the past. I wanted the past and the present not to be separate, even by a cut or a dissolve. Only in one situation, where I couldn't do it any other way, did I have a cut or a dissolve. Most of the time it's done in-camera. We just pan the camera over to one character and there you are in the past. Then you pan the camera again and there you are back in the present. It helped underscore how much the past is affecting how these people act in the present.

Are there any particular techniques you use when working with nonactors?

Generally we try to cast the smaller speaking parts from the area. Certainly in *Lone Star* I'd say of the fifty-five speaking parts, nearly twenty are from Texas. You don't ask nonactors to carry a film. They come in to play a character with certain qualities that the nonactor knows and understands. I find that people who are good storytellers very often have some acting ability. When we went to West Virginia to make *Matewan* we needed older actors, people over sixty. We had a very low budget, and one of the things that's very hard to do is to get an older established SAG actor to work for scale. If they're the lead that's one thing, but you're not going to get them to go down to West Virginia to work for a day in a movie directed by somebody they've never heard of. So we figured, "We'll cast them locally. They'll have the accent already." We found that many of the older people couldn't read, because their eyes weren't good enough, so they'd get bogged down on just seeing the letters on the script. Often we'd just get them telling stories about when they were a kid. We'd ask if they had any coal miners in the family and if they'd grown up in a coal camp, and eventually the people who were good storytellers started to act the part.

Also, if you haven't done any acting and you're sixty years old, you're going to freeze up when you see the camera and the boom. They've learned their lines but they don't know what to do with their hands, so I usually give them something physical to do. "The important thing about this scene is that you have to take three shovelfuls of the coal while you're talking. Get the coal into the bucket and then hold the shovel in your left hand. That's all I really need. Don't worry about the lines." They get so into the physical thing that they start to relax about the lines—they've dug a hole before, they've chopped down trees, they've hung laundry. I do this with kids very often. I just have them play the scene and say, "Okay, guys, here's the deal. You're going to play baseball, but we're not going to start the scene until he hits the ball." What happens is that the kids get so involved with playing the game that they put all their energy into it and think, "The most important thing is to hit the ball." It's even a good thing to do with professional actors who say, "This is emotional stuff. I want to underplay it. Give me something to do with my hands. Give me a car to drive. Give me a broom to hold."

You've acted for quite a number of other directors as well.

I just did a movie for Bertrand Tavernier. I'm basically a day player. I work for scale. I'm over six foot tall, so very often I play Cop Number 1. But a day-player gig is a fascinating thing. You learn so much because there's a lot of down time for an actor, so on the set I'm thinking: How am I being received? How do I feel coming on this set? How would I help these actors? I think it's a good thing even if you just want to be a director or a cinematographer to take some acting classes. Try to act, especially if you want to be a writer. As a screenwriter, one of the things I do after I finish a first draft is I go through and I play every part. Very often I feel like if I give this guy just a little something here, this actor and this character will become three-dimensional, they will have their own way of seeing the world, have their own rhythm of expressing themselves, so the characters all don't seem like they're written by the same guy.

How do you handle specific genres when you write a script?

When I've worked on genre films I've always felt there's a machine you have to feed, otherwise your story isn't going to be a genre film. With a monster movie, for example, I think that by the first twenty minutes people should know what the monster is. For *Alligator,* which is a monster movie, not a horror movie, I used the structure from the giant-ant movie *Them!* You introduce the thing without having the audience see it properly. Something kills somebody, so you realize there's something dangerous out there. If you've read the title of the movie, like with *Alligator*, it's pretty obvious what it is, but in the case of *Them!* you don't know. Then you meet the people who are going to deal with it, and by the end of the first half-hour you know who we'll be following through the movie. Within that first half-hour the monster manifests itself and we see it in all its glory, eating people or whatever it does. In the middle section there are a couple more encounters, but the most important thing is that our heroes have to bring together traditional forces, usually an army with state-of-the-art weaponry. They attack the thing but it doesn't do any good, and the thing disappears for a while. Toward the end of the first hour the girl and guy get interested in each other. It's usually the scientist's daughter and the newspaper man, something like that. Then in the last half-hour the thing goes on a rampage. "This is really out of control! Somebody has to stop this thing!" Somewhere in the last twenty minutes someone says, "I've got a wild, crazy idea, but I don't know if it's going to work." We thought of so many things to kill those piranhas.

With *Alligator* it was even more difficult because they only built one alligator, so the question became, "What can we do to this thing without damaging it?" They had signed it up for a publicity tour once the film was released. My first idea was dousing it in gasoline and lighting it so it could run around for a while, but they said no. They would have to build a whole new alligator. Eventually we just decided to blow it up because they could fake that. So the last twenty minutes are all about bumping off the creature. With generic movies like that you really have to follow the story as cleanly as possible. Look at *The Road Warrior*. George Miller, the director, said he saw some kids watching videos and they were fast-forwarding through all the talking sections and going straight to the action, so he said, "Aha! I'll make a movie that they don't have to fast-forward, because there won't be any talking." There isn't much complexity in the character of Mad Max. Very often when I'm writing a genre movie I'll try to visualize the entire story and write it through without any dialogue.

The films I've directed myself fit in between genres. When I write for myself I start with a bunch of characters that suggest a story. Then I plot the story and go back to the characters. I want the audience to spend time with the characters, and perhaps I'll put a plot in there, which makes it less like a genre film and more like a novel. With *Return of the Secaucus Seven* the structure is a three-day weekend. What do you do during a three-day weekend when you're getting together with friends? People come in from different directions. They're a little stiff with each other. You tell them where they're sleeping. They go out the first night, they wake up the next day and interact, and the next day they go home. That's the spine of the movie. I had that structure before I had anything else. The only reason to have those characters is because of something they want or need, and so by the end of the story we have to know if they feel the same by the end of the weekend. In that movie, each character has something they want. It might be something big or small, but they do all want something.

Apparently the director Allan Dwan, when he was working on a script, would mark out on a piece of paper all the characters and then draw lines between them. If he saw a character with only one line, he would dump that character. If a character is linked to several other characters, then they are cemented to the script. With *Return of the Secaucus Seven* I would ask, "What's his relationship with her? They don't have a scene together. Do they need a scene together? What would come out of a scene together? Is there tension? How would that change them and the people around them?"

What stage of the filmmaking process do you enjoy most?

Writing, directing and editing are three different things. Directing is a little bit like writing with a taximeter running, and every time it clicks that's another $50,000. So if you don't know what you're doing, you start hearing those clicks really loudly. That's why when electric typewriters first came out I didn't like them, because you can hear this humming noise and it's like someone is standing there saying, "Come on, come on!" Paper never does that. The part of directing I don't enjoy is all the logistical stuff. Sometimes it's like the scene in *On the Waterfront* where the actor has to say, "Kid, it's not your night." You have to go up to an actor and say, "Look, I know it would be nice to have two hours to do this scene, but you see where the sun is? Let's do our best and if it's terrible we'll try to find a way to come back, but let's see what we can do." You try to take that pressure off the actor, but he's standing there saying, "I have thirty minutes to do my three-page scene?" It's one reason why I do so much acting in my films and in other people's movies, because I'm always trying to work out how to take the pressure off the actors.

Presumably being in the actor's position is a big help in both writing and direction.

Even if you're no good at acting, you'll learn things from exploring that perspective. I was an actor before I was a writer or a director. I acted in summer stock, and one of the best lessons I ever had was when I was in two different productions of *Of Mice and Men*. In one of them I played Candy, the old-timer who had his hand cut off and doesn't have any Social Security and worries about whether they're going to let him stick around when he's old. In the other production I played Lenny, the big retarded guy. You walk into the same universe, into the same bunkhouse, the same exact lines are spoken, but your point of view is totally different. When I write a movie I play every part in my head and say, "Okay, do I have enough ammunition here to make this a three-dimensional character?" Tying them emotionally into the movie is one reason why the secondary characters in my movies sometimes move to the foreground. Each of those different people comes into the exact same room, into the same situation, but they all have a different back story. They all have things they want and don't want. Exploring that through the process of acting is fascinating and invaluable.

One of the things I try to do in my movies is be a reporter who really listens to what is being said to him. There are some documentary makers who have made the film in their head before they even get to the location. They impose their ideas on things. The other kind of documentary maker, the "reporter," goes to the location and says, "What do people really think? I'm going to do the legwork and find all that out."

In *Lone Star* you can enter the movie from a lot of different places. There's the guy who's trying to get his family across the border, and the woman who has been there for a generation and doesn't want any more people coming across.

How do you work when you're hired to write for someone else?

When you're writing for other people you are basically the carpenter. You're not the architect. They tell you the house they want and you say, "Okay, but if you point it in that direction you're not going to get any light until after two o'clock," and they say, "That's fine." That's what you do for them. I can't get as emotionally involved when I'm writing for other people. I'm helping them get their green light and tell their story. But you're using all the same muscles you use when you write your own stuff, so in a way it's great cross-training.

Can you talk about your work as a script doctor?

Too often when I'm asked to rewrite a script, I'm given an action-adventure thing where the hero is a jerk. The guy who wrote it has based this character on who he is or who he would like to be, and doesn't realize the hero is such a jerk. The girl is who he would like to have fall in love with him, but she's in no way a real person. The writer has dreamt a story where she'll fall into his arms. So there's one person who you're not crazy about, another person who isn't even a person, and then a lot of one-dimensional characters who speak alike in this bad-guy-ese or good-guy-ese, or grumpy-old-man-ese. The writer just hasn't thought it through and recognized that these characters actually need to be real people.

I was working on a film at MGM, a Loch Ness monster movie, which was actually really good. The studio said, "We have a problem with the girl. We want her to be likeable." Essentially, as written in the original draft script, she was too smart for them. I said, "I'll do what I can." I thought she was fine, a solid character, and really didn't want to change anything. But I kept throwing in lines throughout the first half of the script, things like "a likeable young woman," and "he looks at her and realizes that he likes her a lot." I took the script back to them and they said, "Wow! I don't know how you did it, but we really like the girl now."

What about how to begin and end scenes?

William Burroughs wrote something about him not being a travel agent. He wasn't interested in how people got into the room or how they get out. For him, if the audience doesn't know exactly where they are, tough luck. It's probably not that important anyway. I tend to try and start a scene after it's already started. Maybe the audience is lost for the first thirty seconds, but from the context of what's happening, and from what they bring to that scene from the movie thus far, most of them will understand what's going on. I've always been willing to take that risk of having the audience do some of the work themselves.

Writing scenes without stopping to give exposition or introduce characters really helps the momentum of a story. Cut from one scene to a character that you know talking to a character you've never met. Who is this new guy? Instead of showing the sign on the front of the door that reads "District Attorney," and then move inside with someone saying, "Hi, Mr. District Attorney, here is my plight," why not just cut to the scene with this unknown guy? Perhaps the phone rings and the district attorney says something, or we see something behind him or he plays with something on his desk that makes it clear who he is. You don't stop the story to explain things to the audience. In my films very often a scene will end with a question rather than an answer, whereas in a different kind of movie what you do is end things with an answer. "Aha! We need to go to Istanbul!" Cut to Istanbul. In my films it's more of a feeling than an answer; we see the characters thinking about what's happening.

Do you always work with the same cinematographer?

One of the most important things to consider when you're making a film is the speed-to-quality ratio, which means there are some great cinematographers who you're not going to ask to do a four-week movie in Harlem. They're not going to be happy or do good work. They'll wait for just the right light and I'll be thinking, "You can wait for the light for five minutes but then we have to start shooting this thing, because we've only got four weeks." Some cameramen won't be happy doing that. For others that's the challenge. I wouldn't have used Michael Ballhaus for *Eight Men Out*. He's German, he doesn't know baseball and he'd be saying, "Why can't they run straight down that line, it looks good." With *Brother from Another Planet* we were going to be filming in Harlem for four weeks on a $300,000 budget. I felt strongly about not wanting to be an invading army. I had seen a couple of big studio productions go into Harlem and rope off four blocks and repopulate it with actors who had been flown in to play the extras. I was really interested in the life of a black city and wanted to use some of the many underemployed black actors I knew. All the crew from New York could live at home and we didn't have to pay for board or dinner. I said, "Okay, let's try to be part of the community and hire as many local people as we can for the little jobs that we have, but also look for African-Americans who are starting out in the business." There weren't that many then, so it was a huge relief when Ernest Dickerson sent in the best collection of work. I gave him the job immediately.

Then there's the color philosophy for each film. With *Matewan* we asked ourselves, "When are we going to see red? There's not very much natural red in this mining town. Maybe we'll see a little when the Italians come on the scene, and we'll use it for blood and not much else." We didn't want to put a lot of filters on the lenses and make it look like *McCabe and Mrs. Miller*. There's a kind of weightlessness that comes with that kind of gauzy look that's nice in some movies, but *Matewan* is about working guys and coal, and everything on screen needed some weight. Instead of using filters we washed everything a million times, because in those coal camps there was acid dust in the air so they used lye to wash things, and nothing had any sheen to it. We wanted all the signs, all the houses, all the clothes so distressed and the colors so muted—and washing everything did the same job that a filter would have done.

Do you often work with the same editor?

I've edited most of the films myself. I tend to end up with a first cut that's only ten minutes longer than my final cut, because when you're making a low-budget movie, anything you shoot that you don't use you still have to schedule and pay for. You don't want to look back and say, "My God, we shot $300,000 worth of movie on an $800,000 budget." You want to do more of your cutting at the script stage.

Is music important to you?

I've worked with the same composer on almost all the movies, Mason Daring. We usually have a conversation about the philosophy of the music, the way I have a conversation with the cinematographer about what the look of the film should be. In the case of *Lone Star,* a lot of my research for the story came out of music. There is more Mexican-American history in traditional Mexican songs and "The Ballad of Gregorio Cortez" than there is in books, so a lot of my way into the story was through the music. I sat down for a week and just listened to music, and thought emotionally, subtextually, thematically about what music belonged where.

We decided that the musical vocabulary of *Matewan* would be the rhythm of a mountain ballad, so we wanted every instrument that you hear in so-called hillbilly music, except the banjo. For *The Secret of Roan Inish* we listened to a lot of Irish music so we'd know the difference between a ballad and a reel. What are the genres of Irish traditional music? What are the instruments? Then we basically sat down with traditional players, some in Boston, some in Dublin, and said, "Play us some stuff. We want a reel for this piece of the film. This is the rhythm it's cut to. . . . What was that third one that you played? . . . Ah, it's traditional music in the public domain, so we don't have to pay. That's great. Let's start to tailor that with the film. This time let's have only the bagpipe play, because the emotional feel is right for this moment." On *Matewan* we had John Hammond, Jr., who's like a walking encyclopedia of the harmonica blues styles. We said to him, "It's 1920. There are guys coming up from the Delta to West Virginia listening to country music and whatever else." We gave him a few specific things to do, but we just put the headphones on him and said, "Play to the movie." I cherry-picked little pieces here and there that fit emotionally.

Could you talk a little bit about studio involvement in your films?

The deals I make basically give me final cut, or else I won't do the movie. We let them do test screenings. We basically say, "A market screening is for marketing. Don't tell me how to cut the picture." Having said that, I'm interested in asking certain questions at those screenings, something like "Is there anything that confused you?" I'll have five or six points that I have a question mark about. "Did you get this? Did you need this? Did you understand this?" It's usually about clarity. I don't ask them, "Did you like this or did you not?" Studios always ask, "Is the film too long?" but that's like handing somebody a glass of milk and asking them if they think it's sour. I'm always pressuring them on these forms to ask if the movie is too short.

They did market testing on *Baby It's You* and what it told them is that boys between the ages of fourteen and twenty-four didn't like the movie. In the film the girl is smarter than the boy, and young men didn't want to deal with that at their age. The best test audience, women between the ages of twenty-four and thirty-four, loved it. The studio said, "But the people who go to movies the least are women between the ages of twenty-four and thirty-four, because they got kids or careers." I said, "Well, you'll just have to find a way to get them out of the house." It didn't happen, but I'm not going to change the movie because of that. My point is, if I wanted all those people contributing to the creative process I would have had them come over to my house when I was writing it and say, "Thumbs up or down? You want the dog to die? Okay, the dog dies."

The only time I've really had what I would consider a very bad experience with a studio was *Baby It's You,* where contractually I didn't have final cut. We made it as a negative pickup, which meant that the studio was not on the scene until we had done the first cut. In the meantime they had imagined another movie, partly because *Porky's* and *Fast Times at Ridgemont High* and *Valley Girl* had all done very well and so they had imagined we were making a high-school teen comedy. *Baby It's You* went from high school in the first half of the movie to college in the second, and there was some heavy-duty stuff that happened. Even though there were elements of high-school comedy, it was never going to be a real high-school comedy, which is what the studio wanted. Everything I wanted to do was in the exact opposite direction, and I was fired out of the editing room. By the time the movie was finished, the studio disliked the film and me so much that they just gave it a token release so they could get the ancillaries. It's known as "dumping" a film. At that time most of the major studios had deals with the cable companies so that anything they released would automatically earn a certain amount of money. They test-marketed their cut and it tested one point below mine, which had tested pretty well. Eventually they realized I wasn't kidding when I said I was going to take my name off the film as writer and director. They figured they weren't going to make money on it anyway, so they put me back on the picture and I got the cut I wanted. Of course, they ended up barely releasing it. A theater in Atlanta wanted to play the film and they said, "We're not opening it in Atlanta." The guy in Atlanta said, "Well, can you give me the film anyway? I want to open this picture." They said, "Okay, but we're not going to support it." So he got it without a poster and he hand-wrote "*Baby It's You* by John Sayles" on it and did six weeks of business. They never asked for the print back, and finally he sent it back on his own nickel because he had to get it out of the projection room. They never even asked for their cut of the money.

So you've pretty much stuck to independent financing?

Yes. Generally when you're working with a studio, unless you've recently made somebody $100 million, it's rare that you're going to get true final cut. You rarely have any muscle if there's a big star involved, because the movie is getting made only because that star agreed to do it. If you and that star are good friends, you might have clout to do whatever you want in the editing room, because they need the actor to do five cities of publicity. At the same time, half the independent movies made don't get final cut either. Some good old boy who made his money in supermarkets and who put up $2 million doesn't like this scene and does like that one and wants to tell you how to cut it.

I wonder if you plan in the future to extend your storytelling to a larger scale?

I think no matter what scale you work on, it's possible to tackle larger issues. Things can be extrapolated. To a certain extent when I was making *Lone Star* I was thinking about Yugoslavia. A lot of the emotional through-line when writing the script was based on the notion that one morning I can wake up and somebody hands me a gun and says, "Hey, you're a Serb, I'm a Serb. You know that guy across the street? He's a Croat. Let's shoot him." It was connected to this extraordinary historical moment when cultural ties that needed to be honored meant that people who had lived for years together in the same village were now killing each other. It couldn't be avoided. Even though *Lone Star* is a story of a small town on the Mexican border, you can extrapolate something big from it.

I can see parallels between *Do the Right Thing* and *City of Hope*, which is set in a very small, mythical but realistic New Jersey town. In *Do the Right Thing*, Spike Lee set his story on a block in Brooklyn, but you can extrapolate from that block to a much bigger story because it's so well written.

Have you ever considered adapting one of your novels to film?

My novels are even more complex than these movies are. In a film there might be three points of view. We see through the omniscient point of view and every once in a while through the eyes of a couple characters. In my novels there are sometimes twenty points of view, and chapters from multiple points of view. My last book, *Los Gusanos,* would make a good fifty-part miniseries, but to do it as one movie would be too reductive. I don't really like to make novels into movies unless you're expanding them.

Matewan is actually based partly on a four-page section in my second novel, *Union Dues.* A fifteen-year-old kid tells a story about his grandfather, and his grandfather is the fifteen-year-old kid in *Matewan.* But that four-page story when expanded was about two-thirds of a two-and-a-half-hour movie.

Do you start a story with the characters or the milieu and situation?

In the case of *Matewan* and *Eight Men Out* I felt that the stories were good metaphors for a much larger story theme or story. With *Matewan,* you've got a massacre with guys facing each other at high noon on a street with guns, but what a great vehicle to talk about a whole fifty-year period of labor history. This story encapsulates that whole thing. Sometimes I have a story but don't know where it's going to be set. I had the story of *Passion Fish* from the time that I saw *Persona* in college twenty years earlier. I had worked in hospitals, I'd been an orderly and thought it would be cool to make an American version of that. I knew who the characters would be and I carried them around until one morning I woke up in Lake Arthur, Louisiana, and the whole thing came together.

How do your visual ideas affect the story?

On the first couple of movies I knew we didn't have the money to explore the visuals as much as I'd have liked to, and realized we were going to have to make the movie actor-intensive. I asked myself, "What's the simplest way we can light and shoot this movie so that it looks good? We'll get the actors to do all the work." Over the years I've had more experienced crews and a little bit more time and money, and have been able to say, "I'll make notes as if I had to tell this movie without any dialogue, and think about what frames would I want to set up." On set very often the first thing you do in the morning or during lunch hour is say, "We had those thirteen shots we thought we were going to get today to tell this sequence, but we've only done three of them. We're not going to get ten shots from now until sundown. Can we combine some of these shots? What needs to be dropped? What are the five shots we need to tell the story?"

I can give you an example of how visual ideas connect directly with story. Joe Morton's character in *Lone Star* is very sure of himself, and the camera is always a little below his eye line. Filming from below is the strongest position in a wide-screen frame. He starts the film dead center in the frame. He's the colonel, talking down to the sergeants and enlisted guys. As he starts to have his crisis of faith, he starts moving toward the edges of the frame and we start shooting from above. Almost the exact opposite happens with Mercedes, Miriam Colón's character, who at first is seen out of focus in the background. She's just a lady at the cash register, but then as we get to know her character and know something about her past she gains stature. We move the camera down on her until finally in the last scene you see her when the people who have just waded through the river are asking her for help. You realize this is an incredible woman. She's gone through all this stuff and suddenly becomes a three-dimensional character. She's not just the lady who runs the cash register at the restaurant. Even the initial decision to shoot in wide screen means a lot. You have to ask yourself whether you're making a horizontal movie or not. For me, *Lone Star* was very much a wide-screen story because I wanted to show the horizon stretched out. The landscape in Texas isn't mountainous, it's long and flat, and shooting in wide screen gave the opportunity to isolate characters in the frame.

You raise a lot of epistemological issues in Lone Star. *The story is that of Sam, the sheriff, investigating the case of his father.*

You have to stop when your history, your legends, your religion, are not serving you as a community or as a person anymore. You have to stop and say, "Maybe this is a little too simplistic. Maybe we're leaving out half of our population?" Maybe we should look at the Alamo and say, "There are two sides here. Sure, there is something admirable about these guys who gave up their lives for this thing they believed in, but let's not pretend that theirs was a moral position. Taking Texas from Mexicans was also an economic issue. It was a land grab, among other things. Let's not be revisionist and just say everything that was good is bad and everything that we thought was bad is now good. Let's say it was complex."

Sam is somebody who starts out very much as an adolescent. When you're an adolescent you learn that your parents are sometimes hypocrites. To me that's what the sixties was about: a lot of middle-class and upper-middle-class kids who were brought up in the fifties, told this was an Ozzie and Harriet world, suddenly discovering that there was poverty and racism and that their parents and the government were lying to them. They had a typical adolescent reaction, which was to say, "These people are terrible. They're the worst people since Hitler. Maybe they're worse than Hitler." But of course it was more complex than that, and a lot of those people have grown up since saying, "Sure, there was a lot of bad stuff going on and I still don't accept it, but I understand where it was coming from and they weren't the worst people in the world since Hitler." That's where Sam ends up. He could have just stonewalled and said, "I don't care. I'm still going to besmirch my father's reputation." Instead he comes away a lot more mature, saying, "I'm not going to say he was a wonderful guy. I'm not going to say he was a terrible guy. I'm going to say that this is a complex story." That's why he can now go on with his life and doesn't feel the need to be sheriff any longer.

Any time you look into history you're asking, "Whose point of view is it from?" If you acknowledge that history should be told from different points of view, you're going to be in a very different universe than that of a generic movie with good guys and bad guys, where we know exactly where they're coming from. With *Lone Star* I was taking that idea and some other stories and ideas that I had and trying to work them out in a fairly complex way. The scene in the school where the people are fighting over how history is going to be taught may seem like a lump of sand in the middle of this movie, but every year when high-school textbooks are reviewed in Texas that very battle is hard fought. I was in El Paso recently and there was a huge fight over a mural that the city was putting up. It was supposed to show all the heroes from the different ethnic communities, and one of the people was Pancho Villa. There were people who were in their eighties who said, "Pancho Villa rode into my town in New Mexico and dragged my grandmother out in the street and put a bullet in her head." Then there are people from the Hispanic community who said, "Pancho Villa was a freedom fighter and one of our heroes. We want him up there." That stuff is so much in the air and it's so much about how we define ourselves.

I think political awareness is a very important thing. You see old movies made in the forties or fifties and say, "Look at the attitudes in that movie about sex or race or class. They could never get away with that today." That was a mainstream movie, not a political movie, so what you have to realize is that the movies so many of us go to today and don't think anything about are those same kinds of films. One of the most political movies I saw in the past ten years was *Adventures in Babysitting*.* I came away from that movie thinking, "My God, what a picture of our culture this is." It doesn't think it has a political thought in its head. It's politically unconscious, as opposed to politically conscious, and I think that's a very dangerous thing to be.

Films as Director

1980 *Return of the Secaucus Seven*

1983 *Lianna*

    Baby It's You

1984 *The Brother from Another Planet* (also screenplay and editor)

1987 *Matewan* (also screenplay)

1988 *Eight Men Out* (also screenplay)

1991 *City of Hope* (also screenplay and editor)

1992 *Passion Fish* (also screenplay and editor)

1994 *The Secret of Roan Inish* (also screenplay and editor)

1996 *Lone Star* (also screenplay and editor)

1997 *Men with Guns* (also screenplay and editor)

1999 *Limbo* (also screenplay and editor)

2002 *Sunshine State* (also screenplay and editor)

2003 *Casa de los Babys* (also screenplay and editor)

2004 *Silver City* (also producer, screenplay and editor)

2007 *Honeydripper* (also producer, screenplay and editor)

2011 *Amigo* (also screenplay and editor)

Sayles was screenwriter on numerous films he did not direct including *Piranha*, 1978; *The Lady in Red*, 1979; *Alligator*, 1980; *Battle Beyond the Stars*, 1980; *The Howling*, 1981; *The Challenge*, 1982; *Enormous Changes at the Last Minute*, 1983; *The Clan of the Cave Bear*, 1986; *Wild Thing*, 1987; *Breaking In*, 1989; *Men of War*, 1994; and *The Spiderwick Chronicles*, 2008.

*Adolescent fantasy film from 1987, directed by Chris Columbus.

When telling a good story to someone you should be able to get up in the middle to go take a bath or make some coffee, and they should run after you wanting to know what happens next.

PAUL SCHRADER
(Born in Grand Rapids, Michigan, 1946)

The first class at the AFI Conservatory in 1969 included seventeen fellows seeking careers as filmmakers and three "research fellows." My concept was that combining scholars and filmmakers would create a synergy of ideas and interests that would benefit both groups. I was proven wrong. The research fellows were resentful of the greater resources available to the filmmakers, and the filmmakers were put off by harsh critiques from the research fellows. The tensions grew to the extent that we eliminated the research component a few years later. If I had to select one person from the original class who seemed least likely to have a career as a Hollywood filmmaker, it might have been Paul Schrader, a research fellow in his early twenties. He came with interesting credentials. Raised in the Midwest, Schrader was a Dutch Calvinist who was not permitted to see films until his late teens. He studied film at UCLA, wrote criticism and devised an intellectual framework for thinking about cinema. He favored the films of Robert Bresson, Yasujiro Ozu and Carl Dreyer. With his heart set on being a film critic, he expressed no interest in making films.

The richest part of the AFI experience for Schrader was the seminar program with noted filmmakers where he met the three people he cites as his most important influences: Roberto Rossellini, Jean Renoir and Charles Eames. Pauline Kael was a friend and mentor to Schrader and arranged an offer for him to be the film critic at a Seattle newspaper, stressing that he had to decide immediately. Although broke, in need of a job and going through what he described as a painful divorce, Paul turned down the opportunity because he had started writing the story that became *Taxi Driver* and wanted to finish it. He was, in effect, throwing his hat over the wall and would follow the filmmaking path from that time on.

AFI graduate Paul Schrader's screenplay for *Taxi Driver,* 1976, led to the
Martin Scorsese classic that starred Robert De Niro. Scorsese (left) talks with
Schrader (center) and producer Michael Phillips on a New York street.

He wrote screenplays for *The Yakuza* with his brother Leonard, *Obsession,*
Raging Bull with Mardik Martin, *The Last Temptation of Christ,* *The Mosquito*
Coast and *Bringing Out the Dead.* He became a director in 1978 with *Blue*
Collar, which he followed with *Hardcore, American Gigolo, Cat People,*
Mishima, Patty Hearst, Affliction, Forever Mine and *Auto Focus.* In 2003 he
took over as the director of *Dominion: Prequel to "The Exorcist"* when John
Frankenheimer died, and later wrote and directed *The Walker* and *The Jesuit.*

Schrader never lost his enthusiasm for history and criticism. In 2006 he
published a lengthy essay entitled "Canon Fodder," in which he named what
he regards as the sixty essential films, the cinema equivalent of Harold

Bloom's *Western Canon* for literature. His introduction revealed his own complex relationship to cinema. "I have, perhaps, ten years of films left in me, and I'm perfectly content to ride the broken-down horse called movies into the cinematic sunset," he wrote. "But if I were starting out, I doubt I'd turn to films as defined by the twentieth century for personal expression."

PAUL SCHRADER

—◆—

April 28, 1976*

How did you come to write Taxi Driver?

I started out as a critic. I had been a divinity student in Michigan and one summer ran into Pauline Kael, who became a patron. She got me into UCLA Film School. There was a circle of us who were protégés of Pauline, including Roger Ebert, Steve Farber and David Denby. We would check in with her regularly. The phone would ring and she would say, "There's a film that we have to get behind and support." One of the great things about being a critic at that time was that criticism was part of the counterculture movement. The film critics in 1968 shut down the Cannes Film Festival. When you were a critic you were helping to carry the message to audiences and you felt a genuine sense of social belonging. That's all gone now, and criticism has really been relegated to a secondary activity as a form of consumer guidance. There's no ideological fervor left in that occupation, and the reasons film criticism seems uncommitted are the same that films themselves are uncommitted.

Anyway, Pauline had found a secure writing job for me in Seattle. Newspapers would call her and ask for recommendations. It was everything I seemed to want, to be in a film-oriented town and have an audience and work in a community. But there was part of me that said, "I'd like to try screenwriting." I asked her if I could have a week to decide. She said I couldn't, so I told her I didn't want the job. I left her house, and with the exception of one occasion, that was the last time I ever spoke to

*James Powers moderated this seminar. This transcript also contains segments from a seminar Paul Schrader gave at the American Film Institute on April 5, 1989.

her. I came out to Los Angeles and started writing. A series of personal problems swept over me and I ended up being more or less transient, and out of that experience came *Taxi Driver*. I didn't write it thinking it would be made, I wrote it because if I didn't put something down on paper I was going to end up doing something my protagonist was imagining. I wrote *Taxi Driver* years before it was made, before I knew Scorsese and De Niro. The script was written very fast, both drafts in ten days, and is essentially the same as you see it on the screen. Everything I've written has been done very fast.

Do you outline before you start writing?

You should do everything you can to avoid writing your story down until the last minute. I'm serious about that. When you have a vague story idea in your head, start by telling it to people. Watch them. It really doesn't matter what they say afterwards, because you need to watch their eyes and their ass. It's like being a stand-up comic. You'll know which parts of the story need more work. Maybe it's only five minutes long when you tell it for the first time, but you'll find that the next time you tell it, the story will be longer and the subplots more complex. Eventually you'll have to write it all down and you'll be making an outline. When telling a good story to someone, you should be able to get up in the middle, go take a bath or make some coffee, and they should run after you wanting to know what happens next.

At a certain point I write down all the scenes and how many pages I think each one should take, so I know the marks. You know when you're on page 30 or 40 if you're hitting the marks. You can check the outline as you go along. The scene says, "Travis buys guns—four pages." So you type out four pages of Travis buying guns. *Taxi Driver* was written in chapters, without camera instructions, and they were all named. The scene with him in the mirror was called "Foreplay to Gunplay." The scene where Peter Boyle talks was called "The Wizard Speaks." "The Pussy and the .44" is the scene with the guy in the backseat. They're all chapters and they were written that way.

I figured out how to write scripts by reading them, and I figured out how to do it in a very analytical way. I made a curve and charted the characters and the hundred minutes and all the elements of drama and comic relief. The screenplay I used to teach myself was a typically indulgent first script. It was about a man who finds out he's dying, so he goes back to his hometown in Michigan and takes a job as a pipeliner, and feels he has some kind of moral license to do what he wants, so he steals things, including his neighbor's wife. He creates havoc in this town before we discover he's not dying after all. It really was a first effort, and I wouldn't make it today if I had the chance.

How did Scorsese come to make Taxi Driver?

I was doing a review of De Palma's film *Sisters* and was interviewing him. It turned out he was looking for a chess partner, so I started playing chess with him. I told him about the script. He introduced me to Marty, who was editing *Mean Streets*. Michael and Julia Phillips, who had just done *The Sting*, lived nearby, so Brian told them he wanted to make the film. Then Michael and Julia and I saw a rough cut of *Mean Streets* and we realized that Marty and Bobby De Niro would be perfect for *Taxi Driver*. Then Bobby got an Oscar and *Alice Doesn't Live Here Anymore* was a hit, and Marty and Bobby looked more and more appealing.

In Taxi Driver, *was the Harvey Keitel character originally black or white?*

Well, you've gone right to the heart of the matter. The film is riddled with racism, and Travis, the main character, is a racist not by conviction but by fear. He is everything by fear. He has very few convictions about anything except immorality, but when you feel the pressure coming down, when you feel the world shrinking, one naturally looks for enemies, and what better enemies are there than people who are not like you?

Travis' enemies are people who are at ease. He hates people who are comfortable. He himself is extremely uncomfortable. He's not at ease anywhere, so he hates. Travis admires the politician but also hates him because the politician is at ease, especially in the world of women. This is where Travis' feelings about blacks emerge. He sees the blacks out there almost as animals. He sees them out there having fun, out there jiving with women. He sees them dancing and relaxed. He's so uptight himself and so constipated and attenuated that for him the blacks begin to be some kind of a focus for the thing he can't have, that relaxation he lacks. So the racism starts to run through the film. It starts to rear its head very overtly.

You see him looking at these people and you know it's not a matter of conviction, because he doesn't have any real beliefs or strong theories about blacks. It's just that he has this thing about people who are at ease. The logical conclusion of the film would have been that all the people he killed were black. It was in my mind when I wrote the script that he killed only black people, but that was just too much. Marty and I were just too terrified of it. I mean, the film explores the borders of bad taste as it is, and there is just so far you can go in the commercial cinema before people get up and throw stones at you. I think that if we had followed his racism to the natural conclusion, which is him killing three black guys, the audience would have just said, "Holy fuck, that's just too much." So we made them white, which is a thin cover. Somebody asked Pauline Kael if the film was racist, and she said, "No, it's not racist, because he doesn't kill black guys at the end." She missed the point completely. His actions are racist, and the only reason he doesn't kill black guys at the end is that we didn't want anybody stabbed in the theaters. That's my opinion. Marty may dress it up and put it in a different language, but the racism of the film really is quite clear. I think it's possible to distinguish between the racism of the main character and the racism of the filmmakers. I mean, Marty and I and De Niro are racists to the extent that all people are racists. I think it's part of the job of a writer or anybody worth his salt to explore his closets. We're all in the dirty-laundry business. An artist gets to a certain point where he says, "I'm not afraid to explore my Jewishness," "I'm not afraid to explore my homicidal tendencies," "I'm not afraid to explore my sexual deviations," "I'm not afraid to explore my racism."

I mean, the whole fucking film takes place in his head. New York consists of a lot more than Forty-second Street and Broadway. All you see of New York is his very peculiar vision of it, and he has a very sordid view of things. You only see blacks through his eyes, and the only exception is the black he works with, who he borrows money from. You are given no alternative view of reality. One of the rare things about *Taxi Driver* is that this character, Travis Bickle, has been in a lot of movies, but you've always been given another perspective on him. In *In Cold Blood* you see him through John Forsythe's eyes. In *Psycho* you see him through Martin Balsam's eyes. In *White Heat* you see him through Edmond O'Brien's eyes. But this is as though you see *White Heat* solely through Cagney's eyes, which makes for something very different, because Cagney is very mentally disturbed in that film. You have the same situation here. You're getting Travis' perceptions of the world, which are very distorted and unrealistic.

I remember Frank Capra saying that when Clark Gable took off his shirt in It Happened One Night *and he wasn't wearing an undershirt, the undershirt business went down. I'd hate to think that the gun business does well when people watch De Niro buying hot guns.*

This is a very legitimate argument, and let's explore it. The question is: will somebody walk out of *Taxi Driver* and emulate the film? It's a well-mounted moral argument and I take it very seriously. But I don't agree with it on a whole number of levels, first within the context of the film and then, too, just in terms of sociological studies. Within the context of the film, I've thought about this a number of times, because I was upset by hearing people say that people cheered during the slaughter at the end of the film. I've seen the film maybe ten times with audiences. I've seen it in Milwaukee, Chicago, New York and here in a couple different theaters. Marty said that he saw it with an audience that cheered, and it bothered him greatly. I haven't seen it with an audience that cheered.

To me, when you get to the shot of Travis and his Mohawk, that's it. This character has now passed beyond the pale of your identification. I don't mind the audience cheering all through the gun buying and the hitting of the black guy, because the movie is rolling. But all of a sudden when you see him and you realize that he has passed beyond the boundary of sanity and he's clearly an insane, psychopathic killer, then all of a sudden I find that every audience I've seen the film with just stops, and they watch the last fight in an almost detached, terrified kind of way, because you can't really identify with that character anymore. He is beyond identification, and I don't think audiences identify with him in the end. I think he's just too weird to identify with. At least, that was our intention.

At the same time, I think as many people walk out of *Fantasia* and commit murders as walk out of *Bonnie and Clyde* or *Death Wish*. To me, a film like *Taxi Driver,* which explores the hatred, the mental processes of this man, his antagonisms and angers and frustrations, is less pernicious than, say, television shows such as *Barnaby Jones* or *S.W.A.T.,* which just assume that the man with the gun is good and he's defending order. They did a study several years ago about what provoked sexual assaults, the immediate causes rather than the deep-seated causes. Obviously, the reason somebody goes out to kill someone is very deep-seated, and *Taxi Driver* would just be an immediate trigger. They did a study of triggers and analyzed sexual criminals, and they said that the primary trigger was any situation in which sexuality was veiled, such as walking past a window and seeing a woman in the window. That's the kind of thing that triggers. One of the things that was mentioned four or five times by guys who had committed rape was the Coppertone ad, which is now defunct, but at that time they had an ad with a dog ripping off the panties of a prepubescent blond girl of about nine or so. To me that seemed exactly right, because it's just the proper mixture of violence, innocence and sexuality to trigger a mind to move forward. To my mind, the deep-seated triggers of violence and sexual assault are much more innocent than we assume. A film like *Taxi Driver* has more of the satiating effect of pornography. You walk out worn out. I defy anybody to walk out of a porno film and commit sexual assault. It grinds you down. It eventually wears you out. It takes you a day to get your libido back in shape.

If you want us to see black people through the eyes of Travis, who has a distorted mind, it would seem to me that as an audience we would need to see some objective state of mind and then see the distortion. Only through some kind of comparison can we really understand Travis' state of mind. But we don't see any objective, human black person in your film.

You don't see any objective, human women, either. The film is just as sexist as it is racist.

I'm talking about racism now.

That's because you're black. You're not a woman.

I think you have a responsibility to this country, not just to me as a black person. Even in the scene with Scorsese in the back of the cab, where there is some objectivity, I kept asking myself, "Why does his wife have to be with a black person?" His wife could have been fucking somebody else, but you deliberately chose that she's with a black man.

Because I wanted to use a word the same way that the man in the store used the crowbar. I wanted to use the word "nigger" and hit the audience right over the head with it and make it hurt.

Black people are only niggers when they're bad, and that's all you show. We would understand the fact that he sees them as bad if we saw some good black folks in the picture, but in this film black people are always menacing and always bad and always wrong. That is the only reality for black audiences while we're in the film.

That's the operative phrase—"while we're in the film"—because the film is a very distorted, subterranean view of life.

It's your view, though.

No.

I take it away as your view.

It's the view of the film. If I were condemned to living that view, I wouldn't have written it. I've written other things, and the film I'm going to do next is as much in its way antiwhite as this is antiblack.

I don't care about that. I'm concerned with this picture that is out there now and influencing people. You're very smart and intellectual, but there are a lot of people who aren't as smart as you and don't say, "This guy is totally crazy and the way he perceives black folks is fucked up." They say, "Wow, look at those scary images. Yeah, black people are like that." I think you have a responsibility as an artist to pay attention to how you can affect people's minds, because film is a powerful medium.

This conversation is testament to that.

What you were trying to do was to show the disintegration of a mind on the screen, right?

Yes.

But Travis' mind is gone from the minute we see him. I saw no delineation between sanity and madness. I didn't feel as if I saw someone go crazy.

The question is: "Why don't we know more about him?" I think we know a lot. My feeling about the film is that symptoms are universal and causes are particular. The film deals with symptoms, it doesn't deal with many of the causes. It deals with causes as they are implied. The problem with dealing with causes directly in movies is that causes are so particular that they let the viewer off the hook. When you're watching *In Cold Blood* and seeing Perry Smith's father hitting him with his belt and pointing a gun at him, you say to yourself, "Oh, his father used to beat him. That's the reason he's like that. Boy, I'm glad my father didn't beat me. I'm not like Perry Smith." But I didn't want the audience to think for a second, "I'm not like Travis Bickle." The film deals with the symptoms, the things that we all share, which are frustration, anger, attenuation, alienation, a sense of being totally a nobody cut out of society. *Taxi Driver* lets the causes evolve in the viewer's consciousness, even though it does lay in a few hints. It's interesting to see which way viewers go. Some people see the movie and say, "He was in Vietnam." The movie doesn't say that, but it's implied. But if we had said in the movie, "Hey, it was Vietnam," you would immediately turn off from the movie, because you would say, "That's too superficial an explanation for his behavior." If we had said something about his parents and his upbringing or his religious background, you would say, "That's too superficial an explanation." It would let you off the hook. So to keep the audience right at the moment of pressure all the time, you have to just deal with the symptoms and not the causes.

I can explain to you what I think his problem is, which is that he has a view of morality in his head which has no relationship whatsoever to the world around him. He's attracted to this world and cannot make the connection between what he's been taught and believes, and what he feels. He's come from somewhere in the Midwest, where he was a freak, and an outcast, too, because there he was attracted to the underworld of wherever he was. So he felt uncomfortable and left home and came to New York, to the biggest sewer he could find, and he dove in. Yet all the while he's in this sewer he has this thing in his head that says, "I'm doing something wrong, I'm doing something wrong," and he can't reconcile what he is. He can't admit that he's actually going to those porno movies. The difference between the man in the backseat and the man in the front seat in that scene with Scorsese is that the man in the backseat would never kill anybody, because he's expressing the thoughts that are in his head—his jealousy, his sexual anger, his racism—by talking about them, and he will just go back to work the next day. The man in the front seat won't even admit that he's thinking the exact same thing as the man in the backseat. His mind can't even admit that, so in the end he's going to find a way out, and the way out is going to focus on something else, get his attention away from himself, and he's going to make society kill him, because he's coming to the inchoate realization that he should not, in fact, exist. He's too American and too uneducated, in a quintessential way, to solve his existential drama within the context of his own person. If this were a character in a French or a Japanese film, he would simply put a gun to his head and it would be the end of the movie. It would be like the end of Louis Malle's *Le Feu follet*. But this is an American film, and this man forces society to do what he can't admit he must do, which is kill himself. The irony is that society doesn't do it. There's a line in *The Yakuza*, a script that I wrote, where Richard Jordan says, "In Japan, if a man cracks up he closes the window and kills himself. In America, if a man cracks up he opens the window and kills somebody else." That's what's happening in this movie. He opens the window and kills somebody else to try to force society to punish him, because he knows he has to die. At the end of the film there are no bullets in the gun and he doesn't die, so he's still stuck and the movie has to start all over again. It all has to happen again. The drama has to be replayed. He'll have to start turning up the flame under his pressure cooker again. That's my idea of what is going on.

It's not in the film.

Some people have found it.

But surely the point of writing is that you reach the most people you can with whatever it is you're trying to say?

But you also have to maintain as high a level of quality as you can. At a certain level you have to sacrifice quality to popularity and vice versa. At a certain level, maybe, *Taxi Driver* does both. It's sacrificing quality to popularity at one level and at another level it's sacrificing popularity to quality.

The thing about him coming from the Midwest, coming from one sewer to another sewer, I never saw any of that in the film.

He doesn't seem like a New Yorker, does he?

You've given me that just now.

You watch the movie and realize that he's not a New Yorker.

But I'm saying that's all in my imagination.

But that's how the movie is supposed to work. It's supposed to make you think about such things.

But I would have him come from somewhere else.

That's why in the film we deal only with the symptoms, so you can supply the causes.

It seems to me that you're taking an internal situation and externalizing it on film, which is, from what I can tell, a very risky thing to do, because this isn't a novel. The audience isn't reading on the page about what's going on in his mind.

But it uses a novelistic technique. He does have a diary.

The problem seems to be that your concept of this character is precisely what you see in the film, whereas this may not be the perception of anyone else in the room here.

What can I say? It's the way I saw the story. I think the film is true enough to the way I saw and felt to have meaning to other people.

You do feel that the film is an accurate representation of what you wrote?

Yes.

Were there any other changes from the initial story to the way it ended up?

There were two scenes written at Marty's request. Both of them were written to expand roles for people he wanted in the film. He wanted a new scene for Albert Brooks and he wanted a new scene for Harvey. I objected to both the new scenes because they didn't take place from Travis' point of view. I wanted everything in the movie to be from Travis' point of view. We shot them. The one with Albert didn't get in the film because it wasn't good, and I was glad it didn't get in. The one with Harvey did get in, which is the dance scene, and it's the only scene that doesn't take place from Travis' point of view, and for that reason was perhaps a little risky. The immediate cause to put that scene in was that we had Harvey Keitel, who we liked and think is a very good actor, and we wanted to get him in the movie more. We had a second reason, which was that I wanted to show that the pimp could give the girl, the child, something that Travis couldn't give her, which was the illusion of love. Travis couldn't even give her the illusion. He couldn't do a thing for her. In a way, the pimp could do more for her than he could, with all his self-righteous ideas. Travis couldn't even touch her, and the pimp could at least hold her and give her an illusion. So that was the function of the scene.

There was no improvisation on the part of actors in the film?

Well, "improvisation" is a very tricky word, because I worked very closely with Marty. A lot of Marty's so-called improvisation is done before the shooting. I was in New York six weeks prior to the start date and we got together with all the actors and went through the scenes, and the actors would come out with a lot of improvisational stuff, like the stories the cabbies tell. We interviewed some cabbies and taped them and wrote the stories down. These became lines that you hear in the background that were actually written in that six-week period. Then you get on the set and a different magic takes over. I'm not of the school that believes the writer should be on the set. It's nice to have a writer there, and it's fun for the writer, but he's really a visitor, because when a movie starts rolling it belongs to the actors and the director, and they should be going with their feelings and with their sense of the emotion of the picture. A writer should only interfere if he's asked or if he feels that something has drastically gone awry. I saw Bobby making changes to Travis and never mentioned to him that he was deviating from what I considered to be the character. The character I wrote was far more linear and the character Bobby played is far more schizophrenic, but I considered that to be within the actor's province, because that's the kind of person Bobby is. The other level of improvisation occurs right on the set, where you're going through lines. The actors read them once or twice, and by the third time they become different. Then the writer goes into his trailer and gets to work. That's normal in every film.

So there was improvisation.

Well, yes. There is improvisation in every movie. If there's no improvisation, you're in trouble.

What is the responsibility of the filmmaker to the audience? Do you consider such things when you're writing?

Yes, obviously. The filmmaker has a responsibility to a number of people. Strangely enough, the filmmaker's first responsibility probably is to his backers. I know that's very vulgar, but somebody has put up $2 million, and it didn't come out of your daddy's back pocket. It came out of people who have worked for a living, and if the film fails, stock goes down and people lose their jobs. So that's a level of responsibility right there. You have to say, "Am I being honest and fair with the people who are putting up their money? Am I going to give them a chance to get it back?" That's one level. Another level of responsibility is to yourself. "Am I being honest and true to myself?" The third level of responsibility is, "What effect will this have on the audience?" All of those things have to be weighed. At a certain level your own pure anarchy may have to be toned down because you fear its effect on the audience.

If you considered the audience before making Taxi Driver, *what effect did you think the film would have?*

I thought it would wear them out, be very purging, very exhausting. I wanted people to come out of the theater completely worn out, like they'd been beat up, like they'd gone fifteen rounds with a pro. I wanted to really work them over. I wanted to make them feel the anger, make them feel frustrated, make them get right to the point where they say, "I could do that. I could become that cut off. I could go that crazy. I could get that close to those forbidden emotions." Marty had an argument with Joe Gelmis, the critic. Gelmis said, "*Taxi Driver* evokes in me emotions that I do not want evoked." Marty said to him, "That's your problem, not mine."

Did you ever think of having Travis move in any direction other than downhill? Why did Cybill Shepherd's character fall away so early on? After that moment I lost interest, because I saw where the film was going.

Well, you're starting at the very end of the process. You have to start at the beginning. I'm now teaching full-time at UCLA in one of the screenwriting courses, and the very first day I ask everybody to write on a piece of paper their most pressing personal problem. When I wrote *Taxi Driver* I took all my problems and wrote them down, because that's what it's about. That's where it starts. It starts with a problem. From there you move to film metaphors. You ask yourself, "How can I explore my problem through a metaphor?" What film metaphors can help me confront, deal with, explore, maybe solve—but probably not solve—the problem? One of the tragedies of life is that it affords us very few problems. It more often gives us dilemmas, and dilemmas don't have solutions, problems do. One of the great reasons that movies are attractive is that movies more often deal with problems than with dilemmas. Therefore a movie can pose a problem, solve it, and we walk out of the movie saying, "Gee, isn't life great? There was a problem and now it's over." But life isn't like that. Life gives us dilemmas that don't get solved. That's why I like movies that keep going, that play their last scene on the sidewalk, because the dilemma always remains and the movie doesn't ever really end.

The problem in this movie, for instance, is total attenuation, feeling totally cut off. The film metaphor for this is a taxi driver moving through the city, a man who lives in this car surrounded by people yet has no identity, a man in front of whom people would do or say anything. He is part of the machine. So you create a situation, a premise, in which the metaphor explores the problem. You get two people who represent both sides of the problem. You get the girl who he wants but can't have and the girl he can have but doesn't want. You see him enforcing his own problem, and as I structure it I say to myself, "I'm creating a movie in which he is the source of his problem." It's not the city that creates Travis. Cities don't create people. People create cities, and Travis creates his own problems. He chooses to focus on a woman he can't have, and when through luck he gets her, he puts her in a situation where she will have to reject him. He knows that once she sees what he's really like, once she goes into that theater with him, she will have to reject him because he's saying, "This is what I'm really like. You cannot like me." So he makes her reject him. Then he finds a girl—he doesn't focus on an eighteen-year-old hooker he can fuck, that doesn't attract him—he focuses on a twelve-year-old who he can't ideologically fuck. So he chooses these objects, which intensifies his problem, which forces him into a suicidal solution. To me it goes all the way back to the very origin of the problem, because when I started structuring the movie I started to realize that the problem was not loneliness per se, the problem was self-imposed loneliness, which is a different problem. It's self-torture, these mechanisms of self-destruction, of cutting yourself off rather than being cut off.

What I'm saying is that it would have been clearer if I had seen him do it to himself a couple of times.

You see him do it all over the place. The movie is riddled with it. He pushes the TV until it falls. He says, "I've got to take care of my body," and eats junk food. He chooses the wrong women. Everything he does is self-destructive. He says, "I can't sleep." So what does he do? He's speeding through the whole movie. He's lonely, so what does he do? He takes a job where he cuts himself off. The movie is filled with the mechanism of self-destruction. Everything he does has this equivalent at the narrative level.

I just think it would have been interesting if once or twice he was able to free himself from that.

He is able to free himself to the extent that he's able to get Cybill Shepherd to go out with him. Then he has to force her to reject him.

I'm just saying that one more like that would have made it more interesting for me.

One more like that and you'd be sitting there attacking me for being too explicit, too obvious.

Does the story really end for you at the moment when the car disappears in the night?

The script ends when the car drives away, though I do like the coda of the city that Marty added. The final credits are very beautiful.

Did you ever conceive of a continuation of Travis' story?

No.

It seems like the cycle starts again.

For him, but not for me. The cycle starts for Travis again, but I'm not going to write the script again. Actually I did write another version of the story which starts shooting in June. It's a very bloody film and I'll probably deserve the arrows I'll get for that one.* But no, for me it was never a gun. It was always only a typewriter.

Can we talk about The Yakuza, *which seems like a totally different kind of film?*

What happened is that I had written *Taxi Driver* on the kitchen table of the apartment of a girlfriend who had left me because I was too broke to leave her. It was her apartment. That was the situation when it was written. I was just drinking and driving and then I started to write it. As soon as I wrote it I left LA and was gone for six months. I just gave the script to

---

Rolling Thunder (1977), directed by John Flynn.

my friend and I left. It's not the kind of script you write to sell. I mean, you look at it and you wonder how the hell it got made. Then I was in North Carolina staying with a friend who lived in Winston-Salem and I got a letter from my brother, who had been a missionary in Kyoto until the church threw him out. He had taken to watching Japanese gangster movies and he wrote me saying Takakura Ken* was the greatest thing in the world, that this was a great genre. He said, "Wouldn't it be great if you could make an American movie and use that stuff?" So I called up my friend, and I said to him, "My brother wrote me this letter. What do you think?" He said, "I think it's a movie. If you guys want to write it I'll pay for both of you to come back to LA and live in an apartment until you finish it." So we came back and I wrote it. It's the same as *Taxi Driver* to the extent that it deals with a self-destructive ritual purification. Admittedly it doesn't fully work on the screen, but the whole idea of *The Yakuza* was to get the character to the point where he would take off part of his body and give it to another man in order to be forgiven. In a sense, *Taxi Driver* is just a larger case of that, of self-loathing to the extent that you start to punish yourself. It's not a particularly deep or unusual theme.

Seeing some of Travis' writing reminded me of Arthur Bremer and his diaries.

The script was written just after the Bremer shooting,[†] but the Wallace shooting did provide a focus. I had an idea that was moving to a self-destructive ending, and the character had to play this ending out on a stage, and when the Bremer shooting occurred I realized that the mass media was the logical stage on which to play out the ending of the story, so I wrote it that way. Bremer's diary had not come out at the time I wrote the script, and I read it with some trepidation when it was published. There was some very good stuff in there and I was tempted to put it in the script, but in the end didn't. We made a very strong point of leaving Travis' diary exactly as it was written, and registered the script before Bremer's diary appeared, so Bremer, who doesn't have much else to do, would have no reason to sue us.

Can you tell us about your next project?

---

*Japanese actor (b. 1931).
[†]Arthur Bremer (b. 1950) attempted to assassinate U.S. Democratic presidential candidate George Wallace in 1972.

I'm trying to fuck the system to the extent that I had an idea for a movie called *Blue Collar* that I wanted to make for two million dollars, and I wanted Richard Pryor and Harvey Keitel to star in it. I knew it was a good idea and that it would sell for a lot of money and immediately go out to stars like Cosby or Poitier instead of Pryor, who I heard likes *Taxi Driver* and even bought a print of it for himself. If you give the script to the studio, then you give them the power to cast it, and that can change a script entirely, because if they cast it with a certain person then that person will have the script rewritten. By choosing the actors yourself, the nature of the script is not fundamentally changed. I wanted the film to be about young, angry guys on the auto line. I'm trying to beat the system where the writer gives a script to a producer and the producer sells it to the studio and the producer gets twenty points and the writer gets five. I have a script and I've got my cast. I'm going to get a budget. I'm making a deal with a studio and I'm going to hire a producer for five points and keep the twenty for myself. Why should I be giving my ideas away if I am in a position to approach Harvey and Richard and tell them very honestly, "You come with me before we go to the studio and we'll have the power." We'll walk into the studio and say, "Here's the script, here's the director, here are the two guys, here's a budget, here's a producer. Take it or leave it." If they take it, then all the major creative decisions have already been made. It's a way of giving yourself power. It takes an act of faith on the part of Pryor and Keitel to say, "I will commit to you." Some actors won't do it. But if they do, then Harvey and Richard and I can sit in a room together and the power will reside with us, and we can make the film about the subject we want to make it about and deal with the racism at our level, and not have to listen to what a man thirty years our senior and cut off from the theme of the movie has to say. I mentioned the idea to a studio executive and knew the very first thing he was going to say. He said, "Two black guys and a white guy? Why isn't it two white guys and a black guy?" You've got to get around that because that is exactly where they're wrong. It's because it's two black guys and a white guy that gives it the edge, gives it push and energy and something new.

You think that's the best way to make a film in Hollywood?

The best way is the way that allows you to make a good film. Sometimes you have to admit that you're not the person to do it. At a certain point you have to say, "Wait. Maybe it should be rewritten by somebody else."

Writer-director Schrader and George C. Scott on the set of
Hardcore (1979). Scott played a strict Calvinist businessman
from Schrader's hometown of Grand Rapids, Michigan.

It's a strange thing, but sometimes it happens. Sometimes you say,
"Maybe another person should do this. It should be directed by somebody else." I have a script now which is going to be directed by someone
else. It's a script that is very close to me called *Hardcore,* about pornography, and Warren Beatty is producing and starring in it.* Through working with Beatty, whom I respect tremendously for his business acumen,
I've come to realize that this was probably a subject almost too close to me
for me to direct as a first film. In the same way, I probably would have
been wrong to have directed *Taxi Driver* as a first film, because I think it
needed Marty's sensuality to combat the script's native asceticism. So
every situation is different. You try to pull all the elements together. If,
after Scorsese and De Niro and I had put the thing together, I had been
offered a chance to direct the movie, I would have declined it in favor of

*Beatty withdrew and George C. Scott played the leading role with Schrader directing.

Marty. I'd come to believe that the three of us were the right three people to do that movie, So I would have said, "No, I think Marty is the right person. Let's stay with Marty."

Some of the most powerful parts of the film are images. Did you work closely with Scorsese?

I didn't work that closely with him. We all wanted to make the same picture, but I'm a writer, he's a director, and Bobby's an actor. Bobby did stuff in there that Marty hadn't planned. Scorsese gives De Niro enough room to work. If De Niro says, "Look, this is how it has to be," then Marty gives him the room, in the same way that I as a writer give Marty the room. You have to respect each other's talents. If you don't you're in bed with the wrong people. Some things that you think must have been done by Scorsese are in the script, and some things that you think must have been written by the writer were done by the actor and the director. There's no hard-and-fast rule.

Do you have any thoughts about being a writer and a director?

I just see being a director as a way of having more control over the thing one creates. It's like forming a vase and not owning the oven it's baked in.

Schrader (left) directed and wrote the screenplay for *American Gigolo,* (1980), in which Richard Gere plays a male prostitute.

Why not run the kiln too? Why not get more control, so finally when you take that thing and set it on the table you can say, "That's the way I wanted it to look."

Which particular aspect of directing will you be most curious to see if you can do?

Composition. That's what I feel less certain about. I think I have a good eye, but I don't know for sure.

What about working with actors?

I think I can get along with people, as long as I'm the boss. I don't get along very well when they're the boss. I've never held a job in my life.

What are your thoughts on film schools?

From the AFI, I went to UCLA where I now teach. Film school provides an environment that allows you to see films and where you can educate yourself. It also gives you a certain amount of dignity, because it's awfully hard to come to Los Angeles and just rent an apartment on Formosa Avenue and say, "Here I am." It takes a lot of guts to hang around and wait four or five years for something to happen, working for Chicken Delight and washing cars, which I did when I got out here. Saying "I'm a student at UCLA" gives you a kind of dignity and purpose. It allows you to grovel with style.

I remember reading that you said a script shouldn't have too many clever lines.

It applies not only to clever lines. I think a noncomedy should have about five good lines and about five great lines. Any more than that and it starts to become word-heavy and unrealistic. You start listening to all the words and you're not watching the movie.

What are the five great lines in Taxi Driver?

"I do not believe that one should devote his life to morbid self-attention" is my favorite line. That's one of the first things he says, and then he proceeds for the next hour and a half to do just that. There are a few other lines that stand out, but you have to run away from them, because if you let them hang in the air too long you're in trouble. You have to move right through them. You don't really realize you've heard a good line in a movie until the scene is over. I didn't write the best line in *Taxi Driver*, which is "You talkin' to me?" Bobby did.

Do you think about the premise of the story consciously every time you write a scene?

You go back to what caused you to write a script in the first place, the peculiar nature of the dilemma, the burr under your saddle, the piece of sand in your oyster, depending on what you consider to be the product. You go back to that. You analyze it and ask, "What am I doing? Does what I'm writing have anything to say about that?"

Do you do a lot of research before you write?

Research is often an excuse not to write. If you do enough research, you don't have to write. The curious thing is that in a movie you deal with real images, so that in the film of mine that De Palma directed I set a scene in a church that I'd read about in a tour guide book, only the tour guide was ten years old and when they got out there the church had been destroyed by a flood. They called me on the phone from Florence and said, "You've got a whole scene set in this church and it ain't here anymore." I said, "Oh, that's too bad." The point is that they're not going to rebuild the church. Obviously they're going to find another one. So if you write a scene which says, "The blue-and-white LAPD cruiser pulls up to the curb," you know they're not going to take a black-and-white and repaint it for you, they're just going to use a black-and-white and say, "Oh, he must have gotten them mixed up." At a certain level research doesn't make any difference, because a director and an art director have to go out to an actual location. If you describe a restaurant, they're not going to build that restaurant, they're going to try to find one. You can put in anything you want and they'll change it as reality evolves. The point is that you have to have enough research to make the reader think you know what you're talking about, that you have some authority.

So you're saying that the environment doesn't influence the characters much.

It does, but the psychological environment is more important, than the realistic environment. The psychological environment of a cab driver is inside his head, it's not New York City.

So the characters could be anywhere?

You choose an environment which is metaphorically representative of the psychological reality. An auto line is an environment representative of a certain monotonous anger, and pornography on Santa Monica Boulevard is metaphorical of a certain fantasy life or, in this case, fear of sex. With *Hardcore* I wanted to write a movie about fear of sex and set it in the nightmare world that the man is absolutely afraid of, the long dream that won't end, which is Santa Monica Boulevard.

Norman Mailer said he likes war because it brings out the essence of people. Is that why you send people out into their worst fears?

Yes. The writer takes two schizoid halves of his personality and has them meet. The villain and the protagonist are the same person, it's just that they've switched. Often when you're in trouble with a scene, that's what you do. Have a character express something he's worried about to someone else who thinks differently, and make them have an argument. In the same way, if I wrote a film about homosexuality, which I would love to do, I would work with my homosexual and straight sides. As a committed heterosexual I would do a film about the homosexual underground. There are no limits to that kind of exploration. Once you open yourself to that kind of exploration you have to accept the consequences of it, even if it means that people call you a fascist.

Do you think any of your metaphors in the future will reflect that kind of humanity?

As you may know, my two favorite directors are Ozu and Bresson. I wrote a book about Ozu, Bresson and Dreyer, a book of theological aesthetics. To me the final achievement in life is to make a film such as *A Man Escaped* or *Autumn Afternoon*. I mean, that's it. Once completed you can hang up your spurs and rest. I haven't reached that point. In many ways *Taxi Driver* is the struggling of a Bresson film through a Peckinpah kind of environment.

Do you feel that for dialogue to sound right you should know the way people in New York might talk or the way people in Detroit would talk?

You really write the way you talk or the way you hear, and you have to trust your actors to be good enough to adapt the script to their own style. You can write five characters who talk exactly alike in a movie, and if you cast them with five different actors you'll get five different performances. That's one of the reasons why obvious dialogue isn't good, because it reminds the viewer that characters are talking alike. When you see Lee Marvin and Paul Newman talking just alike in *Pocket Money*, you know the reason is that one person has written dialogue which is so peculiar and idiosyncratic that it stands out too much. You hear the writer's keys typing in the background. You shouldn't do that. You should let the viewer think that these people are just inventing the words as they go along.

In an interview you said you wanted to make films about adult problems as opposed to adolescent problems. Could you elaborate?

I hate movies where people lose their innocence. I think once you lose your innocence you have to accept certain realities and realize that you're not going to get out of this world alive. Your brain cells are dying at a phenomenal rate. Learn to accept those things and life then becomes more interesting. I think children are boring as hell. I mean, they're boring to the extent that they are adult versions of themselves. Children themselves are enormously interesting because they are not, in fact, children. They're just little tiny people, that's all. We understand the difference. It's the adult nostalgia that's so boring, the adult version of what it meant to be a child that I find uninteresting.

Films as Director

1978 *Blue Collar* (also screenplay)
1979 *Hardcore* (also screenplay)
1980 *American Gigolo* (also screenplay)
1982 *Cat People*
1985 *Mishima: A Life in Four Chapters* (also screenplay)
1987 *Light of Day* (also screenplay)

1988 *Patty Hearst*
1990 *The Comfort of Strangers*
1992 *Light Sleeper* (also screenplay)
1997 *Touch* (also screenplay)
1997 *Affliction* (also screenplay)
1999 *Forever Mine*
2002 *Auto Focus*

2005 *Dominion: Prequel to "The Exorcist"*

2007 *The Walker* (also screenplay)
2008 *Adam Resurrected*

Schrader was screenwriter on numerous films he did not direct including *The Yakuza*, 1974; *Taxi Driver*, 1976; *Obsession*, 1976; *Rolling Thunder*, 1977; *Old Boyfriends*, 1979; *Raging Bull*, 1980; *The Mosquito Coast*, 1986; *The Last Temptation of Christ*, 1988; *City Hall*, 1996; and *Bringing Out the Dead*, 1999.

> Some stories present themselves almost complete in my mind,
> because often they mirror some incident or experience in my life.

NEIL SIMON
(Born in New York City, 1927)

Neil Simon is a keen observer of the human condition and a master of the one-line gag, skills he has displayed in the theater, on television and in motion pictures. He is the most successful playwright of his time, crafting an unmatched run of Broadway hits that started in 1961 and stretches into the twenty-first century. Walter Kerr, the renowned *New York Times* critic, credited Simon with being one of the finest writers of comedy in American history.

Simon began writing with his older brother, Danny, selling jokes and sketches, and then gained a place on the staff of Sid Caesar's brilliant television series, *Your Show of Shows.* Simon was thrown in with the best comic minds of the day. In addition to Caesar there were Mel Brooks, Carl Reiner, Larry Gelbart and Woody Allen. "I knew when I walked into *Your Show of Shows,*" Simon said, "that this was the most talented group of writers that had ever been assembled."

Simon arrived at the point where he decided he had to write a play or else he'd be in television forever, so he wrote one about two brothers who don't want to take over their father's fruit business. *Come Blow Your Horn* was a success on Broadway and paved the way for *Barefoot in the Park, The Odd Couple, Plaza Suite, Last of the Red Hot Lovers* and *The Prisoner of Second Avenue,* all in the first decade of his playwriting career. *California Suite, Brighton Beach Memoirs, Biloxi Blues, Broadway Bound* and his Pulitzer Prize–winning *Lost in Yonkers* followed. Simon has been equally prolific in motion pictures with twenty-eight screenplays to his credit. He has seen most of his plays made into films, while also writing a dozen original screenplays, including *The Out-of-Towners, Murder by Death* and *The Goodbye Girl.* He

In 1983 a Broadway theater was named for Neil Simon
in recognition of his prolific career as a playwright.
Simon said, "It would be transparent and pointless for
me to act humble. When you turn that corner and see
your name a mile high, it leaves you speechless."

received Oscar nominations for *California Suite, The Goodbye Girl, Sweet Charity, The Sunshine Boys* and *The Odd Couple.*

Simon's stories are often drawn from the experiences of his own life and family. *The Odd Couple* was inspired by his brother Danny, who got divorced and moved in with another divorced man, and it became an entertainment trifecta: a Broadway triumph, a hit movie with Jack Lemmon and Walter Matthau, and a popular television series.

"If Broadway ever erects a monument to the patron saint of laughter," said *Time* magazine, "Neil Simon would have to be it." He has been a vibrant voice in American culture for nearly half a century, never hesitating to try a new path. As Neil himself put it, "If no one ever took risks, Michelangelo would have painted the Sistine floor."

NEIL SIMON

———⊱⊰———

November 15, 1977*

How old were you when you attempted your first play?

I was sixteen when I first started to write in high school, DeWitt Clinton
in the Bronx. I just kept writing anything, and then when I was nineteen
worked on a radio show. Eventually with my brother, Danny, I got jobs
working in television, and at the age of thirty I said to myself, "This is not
for me. I don't want to spend the rest of my life doing this. I think I can
do better things." That's when I started my first play. I guess it was my
own dissatisfaction with staying in the same place. I wanted change, and I
wanted something better. Not for my life, but in terms of my growth as,
hopefully, an aspiring artist. My biggest fear about being a playwright was
whether I could put together a hundred and twenty pages that made sense
in terms of a story and character. So I wrote *Come Blow Your Horn* as a test
play, an example for myself. I never thought I would have the stamina or
the wherewithal to write a full-length play, because I had been writing
mostly half-hour situation comedies like the "Bilko" show or sketches on
Your Show of Shows, so I wrote what I knew about best, which was my
own family life. The first version took about four or five months, but I
kept going over it and over it. I must have written twenty versions. The
play was shunted around from producer to producer. Every producer in
New York had a shot at it. They all liked it and said it was promising but
I had to do some rewrites. I'd do the rewrites and they would just lose
faith because a young unknown playwright was not the best gamble in the

*James Powers moderated this seminar. This transcript also contains segments from seminars
Neil Simon gave at the American Film Institute on March 16, 1978, and February 13, 1985.

world. Finally I tried the play out at the Bucks County Playhouse and it worked, but I said, "I don't think I'll ever write another play because I wouldn't have the energy to spend three years on each one." I discovered that each play took less and less time.

You worked on Your Show of Shows *and some of the other great comedy shows of the 1950s.*

These days I watch the credits at the end of, say, *The Carol Burnett Show* and they just go on and on and on. That's the way it was with us on *Your Show of Shows.* We had seven writers, among them myself and Mel Brooks, Larry Gelbart and a number of other first-class writers. Also in the room were Carl Reiner and Howard Morris, and the producer of the show, Max Liebman. So there were ten or eleven of us, starting each Monday morning, sitting around on sofas and chairs. If you didn't get there early, you didn't get a seat. It was very crowded, and it was pretty difficult to write under those conditions. Michael Stewart, who later wrote *Hello, Dolly!* and *Carnival* and a number of other Broadway successes, sat behind a typewriter. Sid Caesar was about the best comic editor I'd ever worked for—he knew what was right for him better than almost any other comedian—would sit opposite Michael, and we tossed ideas around for the sketches. Everybody would be pitching and throwing out ideas, and Sid would very mysteriously just seem to nod to Michael every once in a while, and Michael would type away. We never knew what he was typing, because we were all laughing and having terrific ideas. After about an hour and a half Sid would say, "All right, Michael, read it back," and there on the page would be a sketch that we had written. We didn't even realize we had written it, because Sid was giving Michael the signals for the little things he liked and Michael would pick up on them. After that we would generally break off into pairs and go into various rooms of the office to work on different sketches. Then we would all come back into the room with the material and tear it apart. We were ruthless. We'd all pitch in and work on it, and that's how the show got written. The show was live and we would all be there up until the dress rehearsal, at which time we were still editing and rewriting. We would have a small audience come for the dress rehearsal and make changes based on that. Then we'd go home to watch the show. I would sit there laughing, because I'd forgotten what I had written. My wife said, "That sounds like your joke," and I'd say, "I can't really remember because everybody was pitching their ideas so hard."

From there I went to "Sergeant Bilko" and worked on that for about two years. That was a completely different kind of writing because it wasn't group writing. There were two teams of writers, with two of us in each room. One team, Billy Friedburg and myself, would write one week's show, while the next team—in those days Coleman Jacoby and Arnie Rosen—would write the other week's show. We never gave the script to the other team for rewriting. Billy was the head of the staff and he would make editorial comments on their shows. But that was a much more difficult show to write, because even though it was a half-hour situation comedy the pace was so rapid, and Phil Silvers spoke so rapidly that we had to write fifteen pages more than on any other show. The plot twists and turns were so complicated that we would spend about four days plotting the show, then about three days putting in the dialogue. It took us eight days to write one show. The work was endless. But I learned more about the technique of writing for films than I did writing for *Your Show of Shows*. In between—or after, I never quite know the chronology—I worked on a series called *Max Liebman Presents,* which was an offshoot of *Your Show of Shows.* They were adaptations of Broadway musicals done for television. I worked on *Dearest Enemy,* which was a Rodgers and Hart show, and *Best Foot Forward,* and countless other Broadway musicals, updating them. Sometimes we put new songs into the shows, and I got to learn about doing Broadway musicals. So that's my background.

I'm interested in how you compare television of that period with television today.

I think some of the shows then were better than any of the shows today, like "Sergeant Bilko." I say that not because I worked on it, but because it was such a well-conceived show. I think *Your Show of Shows* and *The Ernie Kovacs Show* were terrific. I'm not crazy about most of the television situation-comedy shows of today. I just don't think it's possible, week in and week out, to do quality work, no matter who the writers are. If Shakespeare made a series out of *Hamlet,* by the fourth week it's going to be pretty awful.

I would advise anyone who aspires to write anything of quality to get out of television. It's a great medium to learn in when you're starting out, but after a while it does you in. I'm talking about both writers and actors. I see so many quality actors I knew in New York who go into television— and they're quite good in what they do in the situation comedies, they're better than anyone around—but they find it a hard adjustment to go back to acting in films or theater because the demands of television aren't nearly as high as they are in film. God knows, there are a lot of dreadful films and bad plays, but as a writer, if one aspires to do really good work, you really need to spend the time on the scripts. I spend up to a year on a play or a movie. I get to do it over and over and over, something you don't get working on a television show.

When you write, do you overwrite?

It happens as a natural sequence of events. When I write, I just write the story. For example, I just finished a screenplay and in my typing version it came to 105 pages. A normal screenplay is around 120 pages. I sent it to the typist and it came back 150 pages, so I had to cut about thirty pages. But I never consciously think about overwriting. I know when I write that it's only the first of many versions.

Do you start your stories with the story or the characters?

Generally they go hand in hand, but if I have a story and the characters are not quite up to that story, it won't work. Max Gordon, a famous old Broadway producer, gave me my first piece of advice as a playwright. He said, "You must have strong characters. It's the only thing that will get you through the play, because during rewrites, if your story isn't working, you'll always have these people to fall back on." People are the most interesting things to write about. If you woke me up in the middle of the night I'd be able to tell you how the characters speak and what the story is about. I really have to get those things firmly in my mind. The writing is never a problem if I have a good story and characters. It's like I can't wait to get to the office.

Do you feel pressured to be prolific now that so many people want your work?

Yes. Obviously the pressure comes from me because I could easily say no to things. I just enjoy it. I'm at my happiest when I'm alone in the office at the typewriter working. I'm fairly disciplined. I think of all those years that I trained working in television where I had to come up with a Bilko script every week.

I truly don't understand the writing process, though. It's all so instinctive with me. I really don't know what the next line is going to be. I rarely know what the next story point is going to be. One just sits there and it comes. You know, talking about writing is probably the hardest thing in the whole world. I've often thought about someone asking a baseball player, "How do you hit?" I imagine the answer would be, "They throw the ball and you swing at it." There are some people who are quite good at it. Occasionally I am, but as you asked your question I started to panic. Frankly, I panic whenever I sit down to write a play. I forget how to do it. I've written a good number now, but every time I start I want to call someone who has written one and say, "How do you do it?"

Often the stories you tell are at odds with the comic style of your writing.

There are certain things I'm sure are going to be funny but I'm often wrong, especially once it gets into the hands of the actors and the director. Often they have a completely different interpretation of something that I think is funny. They see something else in it. This goes back to the first day of rehearsal of *Barefoot in the Park* when we sat around and read the play. All of the actors and the crew, the producer, all laughed uproariously. When we had read through it once, Mike Nichols said, "Okay, now forget it's a comedy. We're doing *King Lear*." That was the approach. The same thing is true for me in the opposite way. When you're doing something dramatic, there should be humor in it. I have a certain oblique way of looking at things, and I'm able to find humor in things. I probably take life as seriously as anyone I know, but at the same time occasionally I'll say, "Prick the bubble and bring down some of the pomposity of life. Smile at some of it." Sometimes maybe I go too far, but when I've done really serious work, the critics come down on me. "No," they say. "Give us the other thing you do so well." So I give them the other thing and they say, "When is he going to write a serious play?"

For the most part I know when I'm writing something funny. Over the years I've discovered that if the audience doesn't like the characters or situation, no matter how witty the dialogue is, they won't respond the way you hoped they would. I've had lots of experiences where I've written scenes full of what I thought was the best dialogue I have ever written and there was no response from the audience, because they didn't like what was happening to the characters. On the other hand, when an audience does like the characters, they'll laugh at almost everything because they just don't want them to leave the stage. I found that out watching *The Goodbye Girl* with an audience. They watched from beginning to end with a smile on their face. At first I was alarmed because we weren't getting the huge laughs I was used to getting in some of the plays, but it's hard to laugh when you're smiling.

When you're writing, are you saying to yourself, "What's going to make these people laugh?"

No. The most important question is, what's going to make *me* laugh? I know a lot of people won't think it's funny, but I do it anyway. So I'm losing a large segment of the audience before I even start. I don't always know what's going to make people laugh, but I do know what I think is going to be funny for me.

Are read-throughs important for you as a writer?

Absolutely. The only real test for me is to sit down and read the play with the actors. All of us can tell right away. The best example is when we did the original play of *The Odd Couple*. Mike Nichols was directing. We had worked together before and I knew he knew what he was doing. I said, "Is there anything in the play you'd like to change, that you're unhappy about, that you feel we're in trouble with right now?" He said, "No, I feel quite good about it. Is there anything that you feel nervous about?" I said, "No. We've worked on the play together for months. I've read the play over and over for any little fault. I can't find any." Yet I was sure that the next day at eleven o'clock, an hour after we started the reading, we would all be in desperate trouble. The next day we start reading. The first act was sensational. We read the second act, and it was even better. It was so good that the producer got up and went home. He said, "You don't need me. It's a smash hit." And then we read the third act, and it was in the toilet. It was bad. None of us knew this until we'd read it, and suddenly those words started to come to life, and then lost their life. I had to go home and write an entire new third act.

It amazes me how people sit down on the set on the first day of filming, and read the script for the very first time, and say, "Hey, this doesn't work." I always wonder why they waited so long. It's like building an airplane and forgetting the engine. It's just dumb. Almost every time I do a film, and certainly every time I do a play, I've spent months before that first day of rehearsal hearing it and rewriting it.

How much of your stories are fantasy and how much is reality?

They're all a combination of both. I always say that I write about what has happened to me in the past, or what is happening to me now or what I feel is about to happen to me. Even when I think I'm not writing about myself, somehow I am. I think most writers do this. I try to become every single person that I write, even for a split second. I try and put myself in his or her position in life, then quickly switch and become the other person. If you only have one point of view, you're never really going to understand the conflict going on between two characters. One side will always overpower the other.

The characters generally come from people I've observed in life. Some are observed through a kind of osmosis. You aren't even really aware you are observing them, and you're certainly not doing this with the intention of writing a play about them. As a writer you have to be like absorbent litmus paper. The things you absorb will stay with you, sometimes for years. With the film I'm working on now, there are fragments of ideas that I've had in my head for seven or eight years that I've tried to work on and discarded. With this idea, they simply fell into place.

For me, writing is not just inspiration, walking around and waiting until this wonderful idea comes to you. What you do is just sit down and work. You have to discard and go over and over things until you find out what you want to write about. "What will I write? Who do I find interesting? What is it about their life that I don't know that I should find out about?" I don't mean that I do research into their life, but if one is much more observant than one usually is, you begin to understand who people are and what they're about. I look for the foibles of characters, their weaknesses and strengths. Of course, the two things go hand in hand.

Something like *The Star-Spangled Girl* was actually based on a real incident. I had a dinner party at my house in New York and one of the most prominent writers in America was there, a man I really have great respect for, a brilliant writer. A man in the space program and his wife were also there. It was a very eclectic group. The man's wife, who was very attractive, had the completely opposite points of view politically than my writer friend did, and the two of them got into this vehement argument. I just sat there watching it. They were really going at each other. I said to myself, "What would it be like if they were also very physically attracted to each other?" I used that as the basis of the play.

One of the things I'm most proud about is the third act of *California Suite*. It's about a British couple. The wife is up for an Academy Award and is coming to town with her husband, who is an antique dealer in London. Through the telling of the story—their conflict and their problems in working out their relationship—we discover he's bisexual. I thought it was one of the best pieces of writing I had ever done. The two characters are a composite of dozens of people—I can't tell you the names specifically—English actors I know, people who have been up for awards, people who are bisexual, people who have just normal sexual problems. They all seemed to come into my mind and I was able to add them to that weird process. You need not so much sensitive ears as sensitive antennae. It's not just listening to the words, it's what you keep in your mind, and what stays there. The other stuff falls out anyway, and the good stuff manages to stay there for you to draw upon the day you need it, even if it's years later.

When you sit down to write a story, do you ask yourself, "I wonder how this is going to end?"

It depends. Some stories present themselves almost complete in my mind, because often they mirror some incident or experience in my life. In the very beginning I had no idea about how to write a play, so I read all the books on playwriting and took some classes. Most of them said you have to make a very detailed outline of what the play is about and then try to write the play to conform to the outline. But when I did this the play became so constricted. I found in the writing that the characters started to move off in their own directions and I felt I had to force them back into the outline. I said, "No! You can't go there. You have to go where I already planned for you to go." With *Come Blow Your Horn* I outlined all three acts and then, when I started writing, realized that the acts didn't want to go in those directions at all. I found that the play was becoming very stilted and forced. Now I just let the characters go where they want. I don't think it pays to make detailed notes or an outline. It also takes the joy out of writing by knowing too specifically what's going to happen, because I want to be as surprised as you are. I have a vague idea of where it's going, but very often it changes along the way. When I start, all I want to know is what the basic idea is, what the opening scene is about, what one of the main conflicts is, and what the big scene in the story is. I'm writing a play now and haven't the vaguest idea where it's going, but the characters and the situation are enough to interest me to continue working on it and see where it goes.

I had an interesting experience with *Plaza Suite*, which is actually three one-act plays, three stories. The first is about a couple who have been married for twenty-three years. They go to a suite at the Plaza Hotel in New York because their house is being painted, but it's also their anniversary. The wife is trying to rekindle the flame that's dying out in their marriage. In the course of that evening we find out that the husband has just turned fifty and is having an affair with his secretary. By the end of the first act—I had originally planned it as a three-act play—the wife discovers the affair and the husband can't bear to be with his wife on their anniversary night because it's all too painful for everyone. He walks out just as the waiter comes in with a bottle of champagne that she had ordered. The waiter sees him go and says, "Is he coming back?" She says, "Funny you should ask that," and the curtain comes down. When I started writing the second act I thought, "What's the point? It's over." I don't think it's always the playwright's job to tell you what happened. It's his job to tell you what life is like and to present the facts as fairly and as clearly and as interestingly as possible. So having finished that one act I said, "What do I do with this?" Then I came up with the idea of writing two more one-act plays.

So you start writing without any kind of outline?

I have a general sense of what's going to happen. Sometimes I'm lucky and the whole play will come to me in one piece. *The Odd Couple* wasn't really my idea, it was my brother Danny's idea, because he literally lived that existence. He got divorced and moved in with his best friend to save money on alimony and they got into terrible fights because he was cooking the pot roast and the girls were coming in late. So Danny was going to write the play himself but couldn't because he's so used to working in collaboration. So I wrote it instead, and it presented itself to me in three complete acts. I had to construct the exposition, which is always the most difficult thing in a play, in order to tell the audience what's going on with the characters, who they are, where they came from, and what the situation is. This always has to be done entertainingly. It mustn't seem like exposition, as if you're giving the audience information. I felt the best way to do it was through the voices of other people, and the best way to do that was through a poker game. So the idea was to open up the first act with a poker game, where we find out what Oscar and Felix are like. The second act would also start with a poker game, but because of the changes in their lives—Felix having moved into Oscar's apartment and wreaked havoc on everyone—we see what the poker game has become. That's enough of an outline for me. Then I just sit down and start writing.

Have you ever written a part for a specific actor?

Rarely. It happened with *The Odd Couple.* I had finished an act and a half. I met Walter Matthau at a party and said, "Walter, I'm writing a play for you. Don't do anything next year." With film, one doesn't like to write for specific actors because chances are you won't get them, and then you have to rewrite the part to fit somebody else's characteristics. With a play you write the character essentially so that no matter who plays it they can fit the role.

Many of your plays are about two characters locked into a situation from which they can't escape, and the comedy or drama flows from that. Do you feel that the intrusion of other leading characters dilutes what is basically a successful formula?

No, I don't. As a matter of fact, I think I've been changing in the last few years, certainly in the movies. They're not just two characters anymore. *Chapter Two* is four characters. I've written plays with eight and ten characters. *The Odd Couple* is eight characters, though the main characters are just two people. I think that comes from working in television. But it just seems to be a formula I hit on, getting people of opposite interests and putting them in a state of conflict in a room or a house, or some untenable position. It has served me well for a number of years. But I think slowly I'm beginning to move away from that formula.

Could you make any generalizations about the difference between writing screenplays and stage plays?

There are certain lines that seem to be geared more to a live audience. Even though the dialogue may sound natural, it's bigger than life, because the actors are talking out loud for two thousand people in a theater. But when the camera moves in, someone just saying "Uh-huh" can be the most telling and important thing. When I'm adapting the plays I take out a lot of the dialogue. I'm certainly someone who works with words and ideas rather than pictures, so I don't lose the words entirely, but you also don't want it too talky. I really don't like adapting the plays. I do it because it's good to have some permanent record of the play. I don't want them to be gone forever. But I would much rather write original screenplays. It just seems like a fresher thing to do. It's more fun.

    When I'm writing a film I'm less conscious of writing for an audience. Despite the fact that there's an audience in the theater watching the film, they're watching it very privately. They could all leave the room and leave just one person there, and it would still work. If any one of you went to see any one of the plays, if you sat all by yourself in the theater, it just wouldn't work. It's not so much that the writing is geared to an audience, it's that I'm aware of the audience being there, and the audience is very much a part of the play. The very concept of live theater is that there is an audience. So in the screenplays there are less lines directed towards getting a laugh, even though that's subconscious on my part. With film I find that writing dialogue comes easier.

When you see *The Goodbye Girl* you'll see that the dialogue flows more easily than it does in a play, because in a play the audience disrupts the flow. In a film there's an enormous laugh and the film goes on. In a play there's an enormous laugh and the actors have to wait. One of the prime examples is in *The Odd Couple*. It came in a rewrite. In the third act, Oscar was detailing to Felix all of the things that Felix does that drive him crazy, like the sounds that he makes with his nose in the middle of the night and the way he cleans up the apartment. I wrote, "And then you leave me little notes on my pillow. 'We are all out of cornflakes.' " I wanted him to sign the note, so I said, "Felix." Well, that isn't funny. So I said, "Felix Unger." That isn't funny, either. So I put down the initials, "F.U." And I said, "Oh God, that's funny." Well, "F.U." got the biggest laugh that I had ever heard in the theater. It was enormous. The laugh was so enormous that Walter Matthau walks into the other room and out again, and the audience is still laughing. He gets himself a glass of water, and they're still laughing. He picks up a newspaper and starts to read, and they're still laughing. He can't get the next line out: "You signed it 'F.U.' and it took me three hours to figure out that 'F.U.' was Felix Unger." Those are the accommodations that live theater must make to a live audience, something that one doesn't have to do in films.

But I still prefer writing for the stage because I'm able to explore the characters much more in depth. I like the confinement of the room I'm writing about because there's nothing else for the audience to watch except those characters, whereas a film is all of those other things. Obviously when I write for the theater what I see in my mind is what the audience sees. But when I'm writing a movie all I see is the story, the characters in my mind. I have no idea what point of view the director is going to shoot from. I may see a very important moment on the face of the main character. The director may shoot it that way, but he might also shoot someone else's face, or something completely different. I'm always very lucky to get a director who'll interpret my point of view, rather than use me to interpret his point of view. That's why I get along so well with Herbert Ross, and why I think he's the best director today in films, from the writer's point of view. He always looks to support and enhance the writer, without losing any of his own creativity. Then once he gets into the editing room, he and the editor will choose the shots they feel are the most effective. So it's a waste of my time to try to write about the specific images that will be on the screen. Occasionally I do it and hope the director will follow it, but you never know where that camera's going to be. You never know what the set is going to look like. So I don't worry about that too much. I just worry about the story.

There's no modesty involved here, but it's true that the films would not be anything as good as they are without Herbert. On *The Goodbye Girl,* Herbert constantly came to me, as Mike Nichols has done in the past when it came to my theater work, and said, "This scene is not going to work. You need something else." That's all I need to know. It's enough, because in the past other directors have said, "Fine. Is this what you want me to shoot? I'll shoot whatever you want me to shoot." They go and shoot it and it's no good. So I need to collaborate with very competent people. Herb's work is as good as my work. It's just a different kind of work.

When we were doing the play of *Prisoner of Second Avenue* we had a run-through in New Haven, the night before we were going to open. The run-through seemed very good, the ending seemed okay to me, but Mike Nichols came to me and said, "The ending isn't going to work." I said, "Well, we'll find out tomorrow night." He said, "Why wait until tomorrow night? Let's go and talk about it." So we went back and sat in the lobby of the hotel, and neither one of us said a word for four hours, we just sat there. It was two o'clock in the morning and I started to think very carefully. I remembered that early on in the play there's a reference to a snowfall headed for New York. I said, "I've got it. At the end of the play the snow starts to come down, and the main character gets a shovel so he can throw snow on his hated enemy." That's all I said, and Mike stood up and said, "Good night." And it worked. It was a wonderful ending. But had Mike not pushed me, I wouldn't have thought of it, because one can't think of all these things. That's why I like working with good, solid directors.

Is film more of a collaborative process than theater?

I think so. In the theater, the playwright is king and it's the director's job to interpret what the writer has put down on paper. In film, the writer is there to interpret what the director wants to say. If he doesn't do this, the director will end up writing it himself. I don't enjoy writing for film as much, but it has its rewards, like the fact that you do a film only once and invariably you'll have the best possible cast, better than you may often get in the theater. But I like theater because of all the chances you get. During auditions I hear the material over and over again, and after I hear the actors speak the lines I go home and rewrite. Then during the weeks of rehearsal I'm constantly rewriting. On a film you might get two weeks of rehearsal, and a week of that is technical. That's all I get. So the first day of a film shoot is tantamount to opening night on Broadway. The best they'll do is recut it, but they'll rarely say, "Why don't you rewrite that scene and we'll reshoot it." With film you really need a director with a strong opinion who knows exactly what he wants.

Do you ever watch the films being made?

Yes, and that's one thing I think is terribly important. I'm on a set the same as I would be for a play. With a play I'm there constantly. I can see if something isn't working and I'll rewrite it, fix it up or talk it over with the actors or the director. I didn't do that with any of the first plays that were made into films, but on *Murder by Death, Heartbreak Kid, The Sunshine Boys* and *The Goodbye Girl* I was there every day, rewriting. I think that if a writer is any good, a director who doesn't want him on the set has got to be crazy. Some writers feel they should be paid for being on the set. I can't quite understand that. Their argument is that they're giving up their time when they could be working on something else. My feeling is that if you're on the set and you're making it better, you'll have a better film, which means you'll get more money the next time, which means you'll eventually be getting everything you want.

With *The Heartbreak Kid* I had it in my contract that no words could be changed until I was consulted. Elaine May, the director, could improvise as much as she wanted so long as the final material would be mine. In other words, I could take the improvisations and structure them. I'm not wedded to the words, but I do want to be in on the conversations about changing the dialogue, because otherwise it means that the actors or Elaine or the producer suddenly become my co-authors, and I don't want co-authors unless I'm there to coauthor it with them. The reason that film seems improvised is because that's the way Elaine May directs, and that's what was so wonderful about it. She would rehearse the words, and then throw out the words, and then just have them do the scene the way they wanted to, and then put back the words. It's her style of directing, and I found it wonderful.

Can you talk more about The Heartbreak Kid?

Bruce Jay Friedman wrote a four-page story called "A Change of Plan," about a man who goes down to Florida, meets a girl at the pool, starts to woo her, drops his wife, goes to Minnesota to marry again, and at the wedding reception starts to pursue the mother. In the story there's no background to the guy's marriage or whether the girl at the pool is prettier than his wife. There's none of that. It's a really interesting character study of a man who can never be satisfied with what he has. The grass is always greener. The basic idea appealed to me. It didn't really adhere to my background as a playwright or a person, but I thought I'd take a whack at it anyway. What I didn't want to do was write a story about a guy who's married to an unattractive girl who falls for an attractive girl. That's too simplistic. It has to be about this character who is never satisfied. Initially we wanted Diane Keaton for the role of the wife. I thought she was perfect because she's attractive, and it proved that it wasn't looks he was after. Unfortunately it didn't work out that way.

Originally I wanted a different ending for the film. My ending was closer to the original intent of the short story. The guy goes on a honeymoon with the girl, and he's ecstatically happy. They're making love and she's coming out with these words, "Oh yes, honey! Yes!" And he has a look on his face which is to say, "My God, I'm going to have to listen to this for the rest of my life." Suddenly you know it's going to happen all over again and he's going to be dissatisfied. The circle has been completed. But Elaine May had another idea, which was that his victory was hollow. He had won the girl that he wanted but was now living in a world he was totally unprepared for. It was an interesting idea, but I don't think audiences really zeroed in on what it was all about. That was the general reaction from people. I thought my ending made more sense and would have made a stronger impact with a general audience. If it had been a play, had I been working with Elaine or any other director, I would have said, "Tomorrow night let's try it my way and see how it goes."

Have you ever thought about directing a film or a play?

Yes, for about three minutes. I just have no affinity or liking for it. I don't like talking to the actors, because if I say, "I think you ought to move over there," and they ask, "Why?" I just want to say to them, "Leave me alone. I don't want to get into that." I just know it's better if they go over there. I have the best of both worlds, because as long as I can get top directors to direct my work, then I can stand over their shoulders. They think of so many things and embellish the writing. It's better to have two good minds than one cluttered mind directing the film.

How do you go about choosing what you're going to work on as your next project?

First I try to think of something that I myself would like to go see. I mean, the story has to interest me enough that I would want to go buy a ticket. If I were to write something saying, "I won't like this, though I assume they will," then I'm dead. But then, I never really know what works. I get excited every other day with what I think is a wonderful idea. Then I write six pages and realize it's terrible. I must have about fifty manuscripts

The first of Simon's many theater and film collaborations with Mike Nichols (right) was the Broadway production of *Barefoot in the Park,* 1963, which starred Robert Redford and Elizabeth Ashley.

ten or twenty pages long in my drawer at home. I've needed all of those attempts to find out what was wrong and to get on to something else. I don't have any unproduced plays. When I get past page thirty or forty then I know what it's going to become.

What I look for specifically is the Greek chorus in one character that will echo my own thoughts. It doesn't matter who that character is. If you look at my better plays there is always somebody who has pretty much my point of view, mirroring what I have to say. He can change drastically. He can be very neurotic in one play and very unneurotic in another. He doesn't have to be close to who I am physically and personally. He can be a woman or a child. I've written about myself many times. *Come Blow Your Horn* was about me leaving home at the age of twenty-one, and *Barefoot in the Park* was literally me and my first wife living in that Greenwich Village apartment, although I wrote about only one facet of it because it was a very lighthearted comedy and didn't really get into any depth. I saw myself as the Richard Dreyfuss character in *The Goodbye Girl* because in a sense it was a way for me to express all of the romantic things I would like to have done for my wife, Marsha Mason. *Chapter Two* is specifically autobiographical. It has to do with the death of my first wife and then meeting Marsha, and learning what it was to let go of the past in order to start a new relationship, which was the most difficult period of my life. Writing that play was a cathartic experience, something I really had to do.

What was the origin of The Goodbye Girl?

It's a fascinating story. Mike Nichols was looking to cast the lead in *The Graduate* and finds this obscure Off-Broadway actor called Dustin Hoffman. Dustin told me this story himself. He tested for the role again and again, and finally was at home with his wife and a phone call came. Both of them knew it was about whether or not he got the role. When he did get it, he said he knew his life was irrevocably changed, for good and for bad. I found that kind of monumental change in someone's life fascinating. So I wrote a script called *Bogart Slept Here.* Robert De Niro and Marsha were going to play the two leads, and Mike Nichols was going to direct. We actually shot about a week of it. De Niro had finished *Taxi Driver* on Friday and showed up Monday morning to start shooting. It took him a whole week to get Travis Bickle out of his system. The picture was not turning out the way we thought it should, so Mike very wisely and bravely said, "Let's stop. I don't think we can do it right. I've lost judgment on it. De Niro's brilliant, but I don't know where he's going with this picture." So we just called the whole thing off. But Ray Stark kept on at me, saying, "The love story of those two characters is really interesting." Eventually I started from the time this boy and girl meet. She's a dancer and he's an Off-Broadway actor, and *The Goodbye Girl* developed from there.

Do you have more than one piece of work going at the same time?

What happens is that I'll write a draft of something and then put it away. I might show it to the producer, the director, or the people involved if it's a play or a film. But I know it's not nearly ready to see the light of day, so I'll start work on something else, because with a play or a film it's not going to go into production for at least six months anyway while the cast is assembled. So during those six months, rather than just sit around and keep working on that project, because I'm too close to it, I'll work on something else. Then after about three months I'll start work on the second draft. Sometimes I might have the opportunity to do a third draft before the first reading. It's an old adage in the theater, and it's absolutely true, that plays are not written, they're rewritten. It's the rewriting that does it all. As far as I'm concerned, any first work is a blueprint for me. I can't rewrite a blank page, I can only rewrite the things that don't seem to work to me, and I have to read it over and over again.

Did you ever want to be an actor?

No. Unlike my good friends Mel Brooks and Woody Allen, I just don't think I have that ability to get up at the front of the stage. I'm much more introverted. I like the anonymity of being a writer, to be in the back of the house in the dark watching, because if it's no good you can always run out. The actors have to stay there. My heart goes out to any actor on opening night when that curtain goes up. I just don't know how they can do it. It's incredible.

When you are writing, how much do you stage the action in your head and then write the stage directions?

I put down as many directions as I think are important, but they don't have to use them. The stage directions aren't as important as the words, which I change constantly. Often they are there just to throw the actors into something, and often the directors will tell the actors not to pay attention to any of it. If something is important, I think I can write a direction that may help. I don't put directions in when they're not important. If it's arbitrary just to sit down and light a cigarette, I don't put it in. But going to the door to let somebody in, that has to be written. With screenplays it's the same thing, but again they're not used very much. The attitudes of the characters are the important things.

One piece of advice I have for you all. When you're writing a scene, don't end that day's writing with the end of the scene. If you do end the scene, it means the next day you have to start a new scene, and that can be tough. If you can go in the next day and have to finish a scene, you're immediately propelled into the rhythm of that scene, and perhaps the story as a whole. When I started writing plays I would write four or five pages, and the next day start by retyping those same four or five pages without making a single change. It made me remember what I was thinking and got me caught up in the rhythm again.

With a play like Chapter Two, *how do you step back from something like someone dying from cancer and write about it objectively?*

The thing is to be ruthlessly honest. You have to not be afraid of hurting anybody, including yourself. There are certain limits, of course, which is why I would never write the biography of a famous person. I write about people that I know and observe. Through the years I have become more and more ruthlessly honest. *Chapter Two* was the most painful play to write because I had to relive those experiences. I dealt with myself as honestly and as objectively as I could, and made myself not always very attractive, showing the neurotic behavior that I went through at certain times. My wife Marsha and I really did have a scene similar to one in the play. I wrote the scene paraphrasing her emotions about me still holding on to the past and threatening our marriage, because I was trying to push her to the brink in some strangely unconscious way. I was doing things to hurt us, until finally she came out with this incredible speech. And that was the end of it. There was no point in my bringing back the ghosts anymore. I was able to go on and say, "Okay, now we can start living our life." So that play was very important for me to write. I also felt instinctively that everybody else could benefit from that experience. We don't have to suffer through the deaths of our wives or our husbands, because we all suffer through some sort of loss. Any kind of loss, even if it's losing your job. I was just trying to tell others, "You don't have to be stuck. You're stuck as long as you want to be stuck. Sometimes we need the help of somebody else. You have to be fortunate enough to find that somebody, but you also have to be open." Writing the play wasn't easy, but it was worth it because it was a catharsis for me. It was a way for me to expel all of those ghosts and get over it. One never loses all the memories, but writing is one of the best ways of dealing with situations, even if you're not a writer. It's yelling at the world. You can't really stand on a rooftop and scream, but you can get it down on paper, and that's a terrific thing.

◆

Films and Television as Screenwriter

1963 *Come Blow Your Horn*

1966 *After the Fox*

1967 *Barefoot in the Park* (also producer)

1968 *The Odd Couple*

1970 *The Out-of-Towners*
The Odd Couple (television)

1971 *Plaza Suite*

1972 *Last of the Red Hot Lovers*
The Heartbreak Kid

1974 *The Prisoner of Second Avenue*

1975 *The Sunshine Boys*

1976 *Murder by Death*

1977 *The Goodbye Girl*

1978 *The Cheap Detective*
The Good Doctor (television)
California Suite

1979 *Chapter Two*

1980 *Seems Like Old Times*

1981 *Barefoot in the Park* (television)
Only When I Laugh (also producer)

1982 *I Ought to Be in Pictures* (also producer)
The New Odd Couple (television)

Sonny Boys (television)

1983 *Max Dugan Returns* (also producer)

1984 *The Lonely Guy*

1985 *The Slugger's Wife*

1986 *Brighton Beach Memoirs*

1987 *El bon doctor* (television)
Plaza Suite (television)

1988 *Biloxi Blues*

1991 *The Marrying Man* (also producer)

1992 *Broadway Bound* (television)

1993 *Lost in Yonkers*
The Odd Couple: Together Again (television)

1996 *The Sunshine Boys* (television)
Jake's Women (television)
London Suite (television)

1998 *The Odd Couple II* (television—also producer)

1999 *The Out-of-Towners*

2001 *Laughter on the 23rd Floor* (television—also producer)

2004 *The Goodbye Girl* (television— also producer)

2007 *The Heartbreak Kid*

Between 1950 and 1959 Simon wrote for television including *The Garry Moore Show, Your Show of Shows, Caesar's Hour* and *The Phil Silvers Show.*

You should be able to extract any scene in a picture and run it as a self-contained short. It's a little film in itself with a beginning, a middle and an end.

STEVEN SPIELBERG
(Born in Cincinnati, Ohio, 1946)

In 1975, a movie about a shark unexpectedly became a hit of mammoth proportions. It was the first film to gross $100 million, and altered the industry with a new and abiding concept: the summer blockbuster. During the making of *Jaws*—as has been the case with so many films that turn out to be cinematic landmarks—industry gossip and press reports signaled a disaster in progress, with ominous stories about a recalcitrant mechanical shark, 155 shooting days and an escalating budget. It is likely that thirty-year-old Steven Spielberg went to bed many nights in his Martha's Vineyard hotel room believing that his promising career was doomed. He said he never left the island during shooting because he was afraid he'd never come back.

Spielberg is the most financially successful director in history, with a creative legacy to match. His entrepreneurial talents are equal to his prodigious storytelling skill, a combination that has given him more power than any other filmmaker. He is perhaps the only person in his profession who can imagine an idea for a film and, with total confidence, know it will be made. The result over a near-fifty-year career is more than twenty films as director and many projects as a producer.

Spielberg grew up in Arizona fascinated by movies. His mother said, "He was my first, so I didn't know that everybody didn't have kids like him. I just hung on for dear life." Steven had no struggle deciding on a profession. He knew after his fourth 8mm film that this was a career, not a hobby. He shot his first film, *The Gunsmog,* at age twelve to earn a Boy Scout merit badge. "I've always thanked the Boy Scouts," Steven recalled, "because I made my first movie and stood back and looked at it and said, 'Hey, this is fun.' When the troop applauded, I liked the feeling. It felt real good on my heart."

At the age of twenty, Spielberg told the head of Universal it was very

Steven Spielberg (right) with David Lean at Heathrow Airport in 1985.
Spielberg, an ardent admirer, was for a time the executive producer of
Lean's *Nostromo*, a script based on the Joseph Conrad novel
that never went into production.

important to him that he direct something before he turned twenty-one. He
did just that, guiding Joan Crawford smoothly through an episode of *Rod
Serling's Night Gallery,* and he was off and running.

Any short list of Spielberg films is bound to leave out major works, but a
sampling of his successes speaks to his originality and vision: *Close Encounters
of the Third Kind, Raiders of the Lost Ark, E.T.: The Extra-Terrestrial, Empire of
the Sun, Jurassic Park, Schindler's List, Saving Private Ryan, Munich* and *War*

Horse. No director, or for that matter no producer or star or studio executive, has achieved a body of work comparable to his. Yet his friend Tom Hanks says, "Steven is still the audio-visual guy in junior high, the guy who brings the movie projectors around and knows how to thread them."

Spielberg combines visual imagination and surefire storytelling instincts with a grounded humanity that radiates in his best films, enabling him to engage audiences in all corners of the world. One of his heroes, David Lean, observed, "Steven has this extraordinary size of vision, a sweep that illuminates his films." His musical colleague on so many of his films, John Williams, put it another way. "He was twenty-four when I met him but his soul was eight hundred. And when Steve is eight hundred he'll be turning twenty-four."

STEVEN SPIELBERG

◆

May 24, 1978*

I never know how to start with you people. I really don't. This is a pressure cooker for a filmmaker, to be in front of the next generation, because I guess that's what some of you are going to become. The fourth wave.

Do you really think it works in generations?

Yes, it's like big waves. There have only been three major waves so far. I don't know what the longevity of the film business will be. It could be only a seven-wave set. I really don't know how it works. My generation and the one now coming up are completely different, because the generation now coming up is full of people who were raised even more on movies than I was. I discovered movies fairly late in life, but all my friends who are just beginning to make movies are incredibly well read. They are almost film historians. They can talk circles around me about who did what and who was the editor of Max Ophuls' films.

The business isn't exactly in the greatest shape it's ever been, and they're looking for new blood. The great thing about successful young filmmakers is that it gives the studios blind confidence in the other guys waiting in the wings. Ten years ago they wouldn't have hired anybody under thirty to make a picture, and now most of the life support for our business comes from young people.

Could you talk about how you got into directing?

*James Powers moderated this seminar. This transcript also contains segments from seminars Steven Spielberg gave at the American Film Institute on November 14, 1973, November 26, 1975, and September 28, 1977.

I got into directing by getting a little 8mm Kodak movie camera and making little movies. I used to just crank them out, little one-reelers, one after the other. They were just little dramatic exercises. It was a hobby and nothing more, although subconsciously I was beginning to take it seriously. I began to experiment and ran the gamut of what I now call the student film when I was about fourteen.

Did you splice footage or did you just edit in the camera?

I began editing in-camera and then I began splicing. White flashes would show on the film when you stopped the camera, so I edited the flashes out and that led me to a primitive revelation: if you put two pieces of film together with two people, one looking right and the other looking left, you've created a conversation. The films grew larger and larger until one day I made a feature that ran all of two and a half hours. I had the Eastman lab apply a sound strip and I rented a machine called a Bolex Sonorizer and post-synched the whole film. The actors came in and watched their lips move and went through one or two rehearsals before they spoke to themselves on the white screen sheet. It was my first feature, a science-fiction picture. I get a kick out of seeing it every now and again.

What happened to it?

It's in the left-hand drawer of my bureau at home. Four dusty little reels.

How much did it cost?

Five hundred dollars and a year of my time. I was at school, so I could only shoot on Saturday and Sunday. What really hurts is that all the films I made never helped me. They helped me to grow as a filmmaker but never to get a job. I used to tote these reels around, but I found it impossible to get anyone to spend five minutes in a screening room looking at my pictures. Then I had this idea: if I could get a general release, somebody would be in the theater and see the damn things. *Amblin'* was one of the first films I made in 35mm that went into release.

You studied at Cal State Long Beach?

Yes, but I'm not that knowledgeable when it comes to film history, because the one thing they didn't have at Cal State was a film history course. Of course there are filmmakers I admire, like William Wellman and John Ford. I admire Stanley Kubrick because he is so incredibly organized in his storytelling. Kubrick and John Ford love the behavior of people. They love perverse things that might pop out of a very staid, ordinary scene. Ford especially. If you look at some of Ford's films, in many scenes something in the behavior is unique. There's a strong sense of reality that seems agrammatical. It's the same with Polanski, who I think is a great behaviorist director. He gives his actors little gifts of business. Some people call him self-indulgent, but I love little asides that don't have anything to do with the story. At the most crucial point in the film, a character does something totally aberrant.

Most of what I've learned about cinema—and this sounds so pretentious—has been self-taught. My parents wouldn't let me see movies when I was very young. I had all of my television viewing censored. The first film I remember seeing was *Snow White and the Seven Dwarfs*, and after that I used to sneak in whenever I could. I came from a strict Jewish family and they didn't believe I should waste an afternoon in a movie theater eating popcorn.

How did you get the backing for Amblin'?

I happened to crash into somebody who wanted to be a producer, who gave me $15,000. We made it in ten days. I consider it my big break. It was based entirely on a five-page triple-spaced script. I made the movie in 35mm and flaming color because it's hard to make a producer or a studio head look at a film if it's not in 35mm. I was never totally satisfied with the resolution of the 16mm I was using, and was also tired of the 16mm black-and-white films I'd been pumping through the porno labs in downtown Hollywood. I had an arrangement with two porno houses to put my film on the end of their laboratory wash and it would just go through, and I would come in for dailies at ten o'clock in the morning and watch porno until twelve-thirty, and then my film would come on. You could count the grain in the porn, but I was using high-resolution black-and-white, and it was pretty neat to see them side by side.

I made *Amblin'* not because I was turned on to the story and not because I really had anything to say, I just wanted to get an Arriflex and run some 35mm color stock through it. In a way, that was the bug that bit me. I made the film in ten days, a very quick job. I had it out in eight weeks and it was seen by a lot of people in town one night when it showed at the Lytton Center. Everything snowballed after that. There were several folks in the audience who had connections with Universal Studios. They brought the picture over to show to some of the fellows in editorial. Chuck Silvers was the first man who saw it. He called Sid Sheinberg and made an appointment to show Sid the film. Sid saw the picture and had his secretary call to ask me to come over and have a meeting with him about maybe signing a seven-year contract. There was a lot of heavy word of mouth around the studio that said, "If you don't pick up on this film, Columbia or Paramount will." So for forty-eight hours there was a little bidding war. I was approached by Roy Silver and Bruce Campbell to do some work for Campbell-Silver-Cosby, who were just beginning *The Picasso Summer.* I signed the contract so fast it made their heads spin.

Could you tell us what a seven-year contract at Universal does to you?

In a way it's sort of like having filet mignon for dinner every night. You forget there's Nathan's on Ventura Boulevard, that there's Carl's Jr. and a host of junk-food places all over town. I thought Universal was the prime rib of movie studios. I kept remembering Orson Welles' famous line that a movie studio was the best toy a boy could ever have, and I began to function at Universal as if it were a giant sandbox. I used all the facilities, and being under contract meant that the agents were coming to me with television scripts. I spent a year trying to get some projects off the ground, but nothing happened. I discovered as much resistance among the house producers, even though I was under contract, as I did when I wasn't under contract. The only difference was that now they knew my name.

Were you doing episodic television at that time?

The first year I did the *Night Gallery* pilot. That was because Sid Sheinberg called up Bill Sackheim and said, "Bill, give him a job." Bill felt that because it was a trilogy, the center segment was expendable. He said, "Okay, Steve can do the center segment." This was without knowing that Joan Crawford was going to be a major contributor, which happened only later. I didn't cast Joan Crawford, I wanted Jo Van Fleet. They came to me and said, "We just made a deal with Joan Crawford. We're paying her $50,000 for this forty-five-minute episode. You've got a lot of responsibility now. Do a good job." Having to take her to dinner that night was the most frightening moment of my life.

Time went on, and my goal was to make features. Long before Universal offered me the contract, I'd had the opportunity to watch TV direc-

STEVEN SPIELBERG   599

tors work, and I thought it really was a Ford Motor Company operation. There was no real concern for the story because they had to do something like twenty-five shows a season, and they were put out one after another with certain prerequisites. The Joan Crawford show really didn't work out for me. It's not like the offers came pouring in after the show hit television. The phone didn't ring for weeks. I just sat there staring at blank pieces of paper in my typewriter and began writing some original screenplays. Even though I had a contract and was on the inside and people were coming up to me on the street and saying, "You've got it made! You're set for life," the fact is I couldn't get a job. I was just an observer on a weekly retainer. I was being paid $250 a week, which was less than the girl in *Amblin'*, Pam McMyler, was getting. We were both put under contract at the same time, but I felt it was just hopeless. I remember the day I went to Sid Sheinberg and said, "This experiment of ours isn't working out. I think it's time I went back to the independents." He said, "I won't let you out of your contract but I will give you a year off. Go see what kind of a cruel world it is out there." He let me go and I spent a year writing. I collaborated on a screenplay for *Ace Eli and Rodger of the Skies* and wrote the first treatment of *Sugarland Express,* after I read the newspaper story about this couple who took a policeman hostage. This was three years before I made the movie. I also accumulated a number of projects. One I almost got was called *Addie Pray,* which later became *Paper Moon,* the Bogdanovich film. I began reading books and really trying to get features off the ground. I had a lot of meetings, had a lot of people take me to lunch, put on a lot of weight, but nothing happened. I went back to Universal at the end of the year and said, "I give up, I surrender, I'll do *Marcus Welby.*" That was my start, when I began doing episodic television everything opened up.

One of the most interesting things I did was a show called *The Psychiatrist.* There were only six made and I did two of them. It was an interesting quality experiment that failed, I think because the stories were very vital and took issue with current events. I guess people don't want to watch Walter Cronkite and then an hour later suddenly see the news all over again. They like to turn on the TV and say, "I'm taking a four-hour Valium tonight." To me, most prime-time programming is a giant tranquilizer to soothe your day.

How do you look good when you're directing episodic television, so that somebody says, "Out of the fifty guys who are directing episodic television, this guy ought to get a shot at a feature"?

Sometimes it'll automatically happen, when you get a piece of material that's so bad you can only rise above it. I often felt I was a standby foreman, second banana to a lot of well-intentioned experts on the set who were all trying to help me. I felt I was losing my esteem and my reputation, which didn't even exist at that time. Also my professionalism, because everyone was rushing to my aid, and when fifty people rush to your aid with a hundred ideas it makes you back up and take a second look.

Television is a producer's medium. They run it. They can fire you right off the set if you're a day over schedule. I didn't want that to happen to me, so for my first year I was very careful. But at the same time I really felt this wasn't the business I wanted to be in. I didn't want to be pressured and felt I was cheating myself by wanting to please the producers. I felt very self-righteous, and pretty soon decided I would risk getting fired in order to do something brave. I had done about four or five bad shows when I finally gave in to my own impulses, at which point the shows got better.

I wanted to bring certain feature-film techniques to my television work. I didn't want to shoot everything from the chin to the forehead. I didn't want to shoot inserts. I didn't want the lighting to look like an operating theater where you can't even see a person's expression. I wanted to shoot using those film techniques I've always admired. I remember having a conversation with Sid Sheinberg. I said, "All your TV looks the same. Everything is in close-up, over-the-shoulder and master. It's all very predictable." Sid said, "How would you do it differently?" I said, "Look at any movie that plays on television—it isn't in close-up, over-the-shoulder and master. There's an idealism and ambition behind it." He said, "We're not restricting you to shooting in a certain style. Shoot any way you want to."

After your television work did you feel you were ready to do a feature?

I felt I was ready to do features even before I did *Amblin'*. I didn't have the technical expertise or a good story in mind, but I had a number of impulses—impulses without content or form—and I had a great urge just to get on a sound stage with a bare-bones story and create it as I went along. That was my dream about making movies, something that has certainly changed over the years. What episodic television did was give me the chance to pay my dues, which is very important when it comes to those guys over fifty who hire you to make the Movie of the Week. There are people in this business who are capable of giving you a film script that's quite good and saying, "Here, I want you to direct this movie." Most of them aren't going to say that until they see a body of work, and television for me created a body of work that allowed the financial experts to say, "He's worth $1.7 million for his first film," as opposed to someone else saying, "He's only worth half a million dollars." So it was really an education, a practical baptism in 35mm. I also began to learn about preparation and planning and sketching and storyboarding before I ever hit a sound stage, because you need to know exactly what you want.

So television directing is a good place for training?

Yes, because you're under the gun. You have to finish those hour-long shows in six days. You've got to finish those ninety-minute shows in ten days. If you're not prepared, you'll be left in a cloud of dust. The crew moves faster than you do.

The whole Joan Crawford show was frightening because I hadn't met the crew before I came on the set, and they thought it was a joke. They really thought it was a publicity stunt and I couldn't get anybody to take me seriously for two days because I was so young. It was very embarrassing. Joan could have been a problem, but instead she was the only person on the crew who treated me like I'd been working for fifty years. She was just sensational. She understood that I probably shouldn't have been there making that particular show, that I should have been doing something more out of my imagination, but she was very compassionate.

I knew how I wanted the show to look and felt I knew how to arrive at that look, but I just didn't have the time. My eyes were bigger than my stomach. I wasn't used to shooting ten pages a day. That means three interiors and four locations, traveling from one stage to the next, and then to the backlot. All in one day. I remember setting up a shot in *Night Gallery,* just a real gimmicky shot, and people were saying, "He won't be around much longer." I knew I only had eight days to do forty-five minutes, which was actually better than hour-long episodes where you only had six days. I would come to work in the morning with twenty-five shots stretched out and wind up getting maybe half those, so right there you have to be very quick on your feet and rewrite your own shots. By eleven o'clock we'd be only on the second shot of the day, and many times I wouldn't eat lunch. I'd go into a trailer with my shot list and try to rearrange things. I began working in long, continuous concept masters which weren't broken up as I had originally planned, without coverage, letting the camera follow the actors around.

I relied very heavily on Dick Batcheller, who was my cameraman on *Night Gallery.* He said, "Look, I've been doing TV for years now. Let me tell you, that shot list of yours is impossible. I can tell you right now, at eight o'clock in the morning, that what you planned last week and last night is impossible. Pick your best shots and we'll go with those." Of course he was absolutely right. I was saying, "Jesus, if that's going to help me get rid of these four shots, we'll do it." I admit that at that time I had a lot I needed to get out of my system, and that I wanted to be flashy for the sake of being flashy. I wasn't too concerned with the story and turned my back on the old-fashioned direct way of filming things. I wanted to sit down and plan shots that looked like Rembrandt. I wanted the lighting to be different from anything that had been on television up to that time. I wanted everything to be very low-key. I didn't realize that Joan Crawford had never been lit with less than four thousand-foot-candles. Believe me, Joan Crawford is sharp. She can look at a light and say, "Steven, that's F4, not F11." She knew. We had a couple of private discussions about the lighting and the staging of the scenes. You have to understand that here's a director putting his entire life into one show, emotionally speaking. Everything is planned. If I lose a shot I don't know what I'm going to do. It's sort of like losing your bishop on your second move, and here's Joan Crawford coming to me and saying, "I look better on this side. No high-hat shots from the floor." She would tell the cameraman, "Cut me across the forehead with a scrim, because my forehead is too high and my last cameraman always brought the shadows low to my forehead." Conceptually I had to rethink the entire show. By day two my dream was shattered by practicality. I realized you have to be something of an improvisational artist when you're working on even the best-planned pictures.

Another time I did a *Night Gallery* scene with three actors all in a room together. It was a five-page scene and I was under a lot of pressure. I got the whole scene in one shot. I took the camera all over the place. It went through two rooms, characters were going in and out of close-up, but never calling attention to the camera. It was plotted out in such a way that the audience really wasn't made aware of the moving camera—it was just conscious of these three men going at each other. Herb Schlosser at NBC saw it and it shook him up. I got a call. "Steven, Jeannot Szwarc is going to redo your whole show." At first I was really taken aback. I said, "You mean they're throwing out the whole show?" He said, "No, they're leaving three scenes in, but they're reshooting seven." I knew exactly what scenes they were reshooting. All the scenes they reshot were scenes with very little coverage and a great deal of energy among the actors, so much energy that at times you didn't hear exactly what they were saying, but you were still drawn into their situation. It was completely reshot out from under me with two over-the-shoulders, two close-ups and a master shot. It looked like typical episodic television.

When you talk about a concept master, what do you mean?

I think a scene in a movie should act like a short subject. You should be able to extract any scene in a picture and run it as a self-contained short. It's a little film in itself with a beginning, a middle and an end. That's what I mean by a concept master or a concept scene. Every scene is memorable, and when you talk about a movie you don't talk about the movie as a whole but rather all these exciting parts that made up the whole. When I see a picture, even something like *One Flew Over the Cuckoo's Nest,* there are many scenes that come to mind that are like concept scenes, like the first ensemble scene where they introduce McMurphy to the group.

When you were working out setups for the television shows, if an actor would come to you with a problem of motivation for the scene, how would you handle that?

That would sometimes happen because there was no rehearsal time. Television actors are usually paid not to ask questions, and it's funny how many actors just come to the set, do their job and go home at night. But there are some I've worked with who get wrapped up in the show. There's always time between setups to talk. My theory is that if the crew gets twenty minutes to light the set, why can't the director have twenty minutes to talk to the actors? What I would do is talk between takes and make corrections. I would average six or seven takes per major scene when I was directing television, and that was usually because the actor wasn't playing the scene right.

Was there anything that you enjoyed about working in television?

I enjoyed the discipline, and after a while I began to enjoy the spontaneity. When you have to make a decision quickly, magical accidents seem to happen. It comes down to the fact that everybody should make whatever movies they can, however they can, just to test who they are as filmmakers. There are people here who are going to hate me saying this, but I think television is probably the best proving ground in the world. It's like a hell that you're almost obligated to go through before you're given the bonus of a longer schedule and a lot more autonomy and a chance to really climb into the film and make the project more personal. I did some real good work when I wasn't particularly passionate about a particular television show, when I had to learn about a subject I knew nothing about. They said, "Here's a script of *Marcus Welby.* Do you know anything about hemophilia?" "No, but I'll research it." So suddenly I know all about hemophilia, while the network's telling me, "You can't show any blood."

I learned to accept each episode as a learning experience, until I realized that the most effective shows were the well-told stories and not the flashy ones. I think if I had gone the other way and made some low-budget films first, I wouldn't have gotten that flashiness out of my system. Something else that proved useful is that there are very few really good people working in television today. I'm not talking about the actors or even the writers, I'm talking about the directors. That means the really good television directors are noticed pretty quickly. It certainly shows when a director who's making fifty shows a year just wants to phone it in and then go on to something else. The industry is always nervous about rocking the boat by bringing in someone new, but if you can get in through television, it's the best way to distinguish yourself, to rise above the commonness and that look you get seven nights a week. From there you can make the break into feature films. You'll be surprised how quickly you can make that transition. I was turning down features while I was doing television. I was offered mainly exploitation films that I didn't want to do. The reason I waited so long was that I wanted to get *Sugarland* off the ground.

During your television days were you hustling to get on the shows you wanted or were they pretty much coming to you?

I had to hustle. I had to ask for work. Nobody would give me a job. After I did *Night Gallery,* I didn't get work for a year. Finally I asked for a *Marcus Welby* and I got it. I asked for an episode of *Owen Marshall* and got it. I was offered two *Psychiatrist* episodes from a friend of mine who was producing the show. After that—because the look went against the common denominator of those shows—they wouldn't use me anymore on *Marcus Welby* or *Owen Marshall.* But then the higher-quality shows that wanted some kind of individual look contacted me. I worked on *Columbo* and

The Name of the Game. Movies of the Week began coming to me. I was able to distinguish myself by doing things which led people in the feature-film world to say, "Stick with television." But in television they said, "Go make a feature."

Is that where Duel *came from?*

I had to ask for *Duel.* I read the Richard Matheson story in *Playboy* and talked the producer into hiring me. When I became involved, I tried to promote it as a theatrical feature at Universal. The studio said, "If you can get Gregory Peck, you have a feature commitment." He said no, and so we made it for television. $425,000 bought fourteen shooting days, though I went two days over schedule.

Were the voice-overs in Duel *scripted?*

If you ask me, "What would you do if you were to do *Duel* over again?" I'd say, "Take all the voice-overs out. Every one of them." They were in the script and I wanted to take them out, but the network forced us to leave them in. We won and lost a battle. The network forced us—actually ordered us—to put all of them back in, but our producer persuaded the network to let us cut some of it. There was about sixty percent more in the rough cut. I wish I could have cut the rest. I hated the inner mono-logue. We tried to get the distribution company to take out all the voice-overs and turn *Duel* into the first American silent movie of the last forty years.

I felt it might be more effective if the truck had been one of those new, shiny Macks. It might have been even eerier.

As a matter of fact the truck that I found, even though it was old, was in a casting session. The studio brought seven trucks to the backlot. They were all lined up. I drove up in the studio car and got out and walked around one of the trucks, kicking the tires. A feeling of enormous power. Trying the doors and sitting behind the wheel and playing all the games and saying, "This truck feels right, you know? It doesn't look good, but it feels right." All the trucks were shiny. They were brand-new. The Peterbilt we used was maybe six years old, but it was all shined up, so I had them spill oil over it. They painted it, put dead bugs on the window and stuck dead grasshoppers into the grill. I had them tie two big railway steel rails onto the bumper and added the license plates and the lights and a lot of stuff to personalize the thing. I added the big exhaust manifolds on both doors like gangrenous growths coming out of its ears. I tried to personalize the truck in the production design stage.

Did you do anything in particular to get all of those terrified expressions on Dennis Weaver's face?

Dennis comes naturally terrified. I think he's a wonderful actor. I'm a big fan of Orson Welles' film *Touch of Evil,* where he played the nighttime insomniac watchman. He was so great in that. When we met, I said to Dennis, "I want half of whatever you gave to Orson Welles." That's really the character he played. He played the night watchman, but cut the mania in half. I could have gone for a much more granite actor, but Dennis has a vulnerability about him. He can be strong and at the same time perfectly terrified and weak as a church mouse. That's what I like about him. He can go back and forth. There's nothing complicated about the character he was playing. I was determined to make him just a regular guy.

Dennis went from *McCloud* into *Duel* for sixteen days and then right back into *McCloud.* There wasn't much time to prepare. What we talked most about was how much driving Dennis was going to do as opposed to the stunt drivers, because Dennis insisted on doing all his own driving. He did about eighty percent of it. All the complicated stunts, the spinouts, that's actually Dennis in the car. He jumped out of the car and rolled right into close-up before the truck and car collide and catch fire. I think he wanted to get out of *McCloud.*

Was the sequence when the truck nearly pushes the car in the path of a train in the script?

We got a timetable and just waited for the train. The train was an hour late, and while we were waiting I found a junkyard of old jalopies, so I took a lot of montage shots of the wrecked cars, which the European critics called "bravely symbolic." I've traveled throughout Europe with *Duel* and everyone thinks the picture is about something else. It's remarkable what they've read into it. I had four critics in Rome walk out on a press conference when I refused to say this picture was really the battle between the upper classes and the working classes in America today.

What did Duel *teach you about storytelling?*

I've learned that audiences, especially people who go to the movies and appreciate them on a gut level, don't know a long lens from a wide-angle lens. They don't know good composition from bad. They're subconsciously and aesthetically pleased by things they can't articulate. For the most part, audiences are concerned with what the picture is about, who's in it, and whether or not it's entertaining.

Did you use storyboards?

Almost the entire movie was storyboarded. I had somebody in the art department at Universal draw a huge overhead map of the entire movie. The whole movie is one big road. I shot the movie not with a script but with this map that arched around the motel room. On Monday we'd do this much of the map and on Tuesday we'd do this much of the map. We shot in continuity and just about everything was planned. I think when you make an action film, especially a road picture, it's the best way to work, because it's very hard to pick up a script and sift through five hundred words of prose and then commit them to memory. *Duel* was more of a concept than a page-by-page description of what had to be shot. I felt that breaking the picture up and mapping it out would be easier for me.

Do you draw your own storyboards?

No, not like George Lucas or John Milius, who are artists. They paint and sketch and do charcoal and oils and things like that. What I do is make the best foreground-background stick figures in town. I can do horizons and hills and trees and perspective. I can put depth in drawings, but I can't draw. I pretty much outline the composition and the concept, and then hire a freelance artist to hang around with me for a few months. He takes the whole movie out of my head and puts it onto cards. I'm able to show those cards to anybody who has a job on the film. I also had the entire picture, every sequence, plotted on cards. I had them mounted on a bulletin board in my motel room, so rather than taking the script and opening it to a page, I would select, let's say, ten cards, and that would be the day's work. When I'd shot that particular sequence, I'd tear up the cards.

How did you get that shot which moves from behind Dennis Weaver's car and all the way to the front of the truck?

We had a little car, a made-over Corvette with all the body work taken off and all our camera mounts attached, built by Pat Hustis, a very famous driver in Hollywood, who had built the car which filmed the car chase in *Bullitt*. It was really just an engine and camera mounts, a moving dolly that can go sixty miles an hour. I shot the truck from a low angle for about a mile and at times said to Pat, "Slow down and let the truck gain on us a bit to give the feeling of it catching up with the car."

What about the one of the truck going over the cliff?

We had five cameras. I only used one shot, but there were four protection cameras. I had one buried underground, shooting straight up, hoping that the truck and car would land on the camera. We took a chance that the film would be spared. If we had told the production manager about this he wouldn't have allowed it, so we buried the camera and hid it under the brush where nobody could find it. The camera operators and I kept it to ourselves. I don't know why, but cameramen love to see their Arriflexes torn to pieces. In the end we turned the camera on and the truck missed it by forty feet. We didn't realize how much momentum the truck would have when it hit the car and went over. I did the shot in slow motion with consideration toward the poor viewer, who has had to endure this picture for the past ninety minutes. There had to be a payoff. You had to see each piece of that truck falling off the cliff.

Why do we never find out who is driving the truck?

I'm about to get sort of philosophical, but I always felt that if the driver was identified it would become a story about one man trying to kill another man, not a malevolent truck trying to run down a human being. At the last minute, with the close-up of the gears being shifted, you do see that the truck does, in fact, have a driver. I never really intended for anybody to believe that the truck was driving itself. I really tried not to get too esoteric with *Duel*. The movie really walks a fine line between logic and fantasy, and finally I wanted to tip the scales in favor of logic, even if the French thought the film was an allegory for many things.

What drew you to the story of The Sugarland Express?

When I first read the newspaper account, it was the most unique bit of Americana I had come across in a long time. It was so unique and so impossible that I made some calls to make sure it was true. When I found out it had actually happened, I was astounded that the police had made such a media event out of it, this roving circus that developed into the six o'clock evening news on wheels. I wanted to make the film because I felt it made an important statement about the Great American Dream Machine that can transform innocent people into celebrities. When I probed deeper, I realized there was a deeply affecting personal story about a dim-witted couple and a child they loved. A lot of *Sugarland* is actually fictitious. The opening of the picture should have read "This movie was inspired by a real event which happened in Texas in 1969" and not "This movie is based on a real event." The inspiration led to a rekindling of all of our imaginations. We had a great time sitting around inventing scenes that never took place in real life.

I added to the screenplay just to keep it lighter than the truth, because I don't think there's an audience anywhere for the kind of picture that tells the story as it really happened. It's a tragic fairy tale that really happened in Texas back in 1969. These two kids hijacked a police officer in his car. The whole state mobilized and eventually gunned them down. I wanted to make the beginning light because I didn't think I could sustain a grim movie without having a hundred walkouts from the audience. I wanted to begin the picture with hope and energy and fun and you're getting your money's worth for the first half-hour before you begin to sense where the picture is heading. Then you become involved in a very serious drama. It was a challenge to make a light picture at the beginning and a heavy picture at the end. The transition is very gradual, a blending of frivolity and distaste.

When I think of *Bonnie and Clyde* there are only two heavy moments in the film: when Gene Hackman is shot, which is about halfway through, and then of course at the end, which is totally a shock. Although you knew things were being set up, you refused to believe they were actually going to be gunned down. I wasn't tense until I saw C. W. Moss hiding in the hardware store and not coming out to the car where Bonnie and Clyde are waiting for him. The difference in *Sugarland* is that the tension comes at the midway point. A lot of elements begin to take shape, like the plan the cops are formulating. The audience is watching this trio, oblivious to what's about to happen to them, but we know it's a collision course. You're prepared for an ending that isn't happy, for the death of a sympathetic antihero and the girl never getting her baby back. It's all foreshadowed. It could only have ended that way.

Were you working with any visual concept when you made the film?

Sugarland begins with mounting tension, and all the exposition of the film is laid out in the first four minutes. The entire first chapter of the film is shot in close-ups. As the picture expands the camera begins to ease off until, by the twenty-five-minute point, you're really loose. You're just a spectator watching, from a comfortable distance, as this insane Dream Machine phenomenon unfolds. As the picture accelerates toward the inevitable climax, the camera starts moving in again. The biggest close-up of the entire film is Goldie Hawn at the beginning of the picture and contains the most important line in the movie, which either sells or doesn't sell what the picture's about. She says, "I want my baby back. Are you going to help me or not?" If you don't buy what she says to her husband, you'd better leave the theater.

Did you have technical problems when you were making the film because so much of it takes place in a car?

I realized you can't do that much in a car, and after you've exhausted everything it just becomes a redundant variation on the same theme. *Sugarland* is seventy percent inside a car, so I had to come up with new angles without getting gimmicky by scrunching low and shooting upwards. We would either subtly shoot the scene in one take, where you see everybody and you let the audience be the film editor, or break it up and cover the hell out of it.

Vilmos Zsigmond built a platform around the car so I could slide the camera on a dolly to the backseat. We also had a mount inside the car, on the front and back seats, which allowed me to make a 360-degree shot. I really didn't do that to be flashy, I did it to relieve the monotony of spending all those hours in that automobile. Every day I tended to use different lenses. Some days I shot entire scenes with a wide-angle lens without moving the camera, other days I broke it up in a number of ways. The big danger in *Sugarland,* with all that shooting inside the car, is you start wondering—and this is a problem I never worried about six years ago— whose point of view are these shots from? Exactly who is hanging by their fingers to the rolled-down window? But I didn't want to bore the audience, and felt that if I told a good story and had a lot of variety, visually, in and around the car, the film would carry itself to the end. In a way I had *Duel* to cut my teeth on. *Duel* had twice as many exteriors as interiors. It was an exercise in exterior, not interior, photography.

Would you change the way you did Sugarland Express *today?*

Only in the technique and the point of view. I would give more credence to the police forces and would probably tell the story from two points of view, inside the car, and behind the police lines through binoculars and telescopes. I think the story would have been less biased. If you'd been behind the police lines, seeing a car with two hijackers and their hostage—seen the same way I think Costa-Gavras saw *Z,* in a very documentary way—we would better understand why the police put an end to the life of this boy and, in a way, created a tragedy out of a frolic.

Do you think it's troublesome when a film has more than one point of view?

Not at all. It's worked in so many films, including *American Graffiti,* which really had four separate points of view. But in *Sugarland* it was important to have two points of view, and I didn't absolutely accomplish that.

Was Sugarland Express *popular?*

No, it wasn't a box-office success. It cost $1.8 million, but even with television sales it's barely going to break even. I averaged about four printed takes per shot, which meant we went over budget in raw stock and printing by $50,000. But it was important for Goldie, because she had never played a consistently dramatic role before, and I had to print a lot of takes to get rid of all her cutesy-pie crust, and then select the most subtle ones in the cutting room. I must say that she's totally different than she's ever been before. I wanted to do anything possible to keep the Goldie Hawn Tinkerbell-light away from her, and in the end she really did keep all that sugarplum stuff to a minimum. I even thought that if I shot the whole picture during overcast weather, the look of the shots would play against the lightness of the script and the fluffiness of Goldie's image. I think I was right.

There are many reasons why the film wasn't a success, not the least of which is that the Goldie Hawn fans didn't want to see her in that kind of movie and the non–Goldie Hawn fans weren't willing to give her a shot in a dramatic role. Audiences fell right through the cracks. I also have a feeling that the down ending turned a lot of people off, certainly in light of things like *American Graffiti* and *The Sting* and other films that premiered months before us that were kind of lighthearted and carefree. Audiences weren't expecting Goldie to be in a motion picture in which one of the major actors is shot and killed and the film ends on a low note. They wanted her to go off into the sunset.

Beyond that, the distribution wasn't good. The ad campaign sold Goldie Hawn with a smile on her face and a teddy bear next to her. It looked like a romp in the woods. When the film opened in New York there was a line of kids waiting to see the picture. The movie was misrepresented more than anything else, and when it came time for the studio to back up their mistake with money, that's when the distribution men at Universal got cold feet and said sort of *sotto voce*, "We'll allow it to play out its Easter run and let it close out." That's exactly what happened. The film opened and closed in three weeks. It was very disappointing for me. Later Universal rereleased the film, using another tactic that I wasn't amused with: "From the director of *Jaws.*" The film still didn't do well.

When did you first get hold of the Jaws *treatment?*

I shared an office with the production manager for Richard Zanuck and David Brown. Dick and David had produced *Sugarland Express* and had given me five projects they wanted me to direct, but I didn't care for any of them. Then they offered me a huge biopic about General MacArthur, but I didn't want to do that either, because it would have been two years out of my life, working in ten countries, getting a garden variety of dysentery in each one of them. I knew there was an opening for me to do whatever I wanted with Dick and David, and I picked up *Jaws*—I'd never heard of it, I thought it was a porno—and took it home with me to read over the weekend. I knew the minute I read it that I wanted to direct the movie, and I went to the office on Monday and said, "I just read this project of yours and I'd really like to do it." They said, "Of all the projects we have, *Jaws* is the only one with a director attached." So I said, "If anything changes, call me." They called eight days later and said, "He's out."

What did you think about Peter Benchley's novel? The film is considerably different.

That reflects how I felt about the novel. The book disturbed me but didn't really scare me. It began with a real burst of speed and all of a sudden the middle section got weighted down by this terrestrial sociology, this provincial moralizing about a town without pity. I didn't want to make any kind of moral value judgment with the movie. I wanted it to be pure entertainment, not in the sense of a disaster film but in the sense that the film would be all high points from beginning to end—suspense and high adventure. What I really wanted to make was *Captains Courageous*. The only time the book really frightened me was in the last hundred pages, when Benchley stopped describing what the shark looked like and began concentrating on how the barrels were moving through the water and hitting the boat. They could only see the barrels, not the shark, and that terrified me.

Your construction of suspense in Duel *and* Jaws *seem so similar that occasionally I saw teeth on the truck.*

It's probably a terrible thing to say, but there were so many similarities between *Duel* and *Jaws*. I felt *Jaws* would be the sequel to *Duel* in disguise. There were so many things I couldn't do in *Duel* because I only had sixteen shooting days and only three weeks to cut it and put it on television. I felt I could take all of the leftover ideas and quick-heat them in the microwave oven and stick them in *Jaws*. And that's exactly what I did.

There is certainly similar thematic material in *Duel* and in *Jaws*, like the technique I used to make the ocean come alive and to make the truck come alive. Both films are about a man who battles against all odds, against a really impossible challenge. Thematically the films seem to be almost the same story with different characters—at least that's how European journalists wrote about them. But the execution is totally dissimilar because I had a nemesis in the first film which was always visible on the horizon or in the shadows, and in *Jaws* I had to create a tension and a suspense from seeing absolutely nothing until sixty minutes into the picture. To me, *Jaws* was more challenging in that sense. I knew the minute I saw that truck I'd be using 20mm lenses placed lower than the front headlights at all times. I would never really be above the truck. I got up on a crane one day to look at the truck on the backlot and I said, "Not scary." It's also the truck coming around corners, peeking its eyes at you, and I felt that *Jaws* was much more challenging because I didn't have those raw materials to work with.

Can you talk about the casting?

I had always envisioned a strong, silent man like Roy Scheider who could play sort of a nebbish. I wanted someone who could always fall back on the strength of his character: glasses off, hair combed back away from forehead. In *Jaws,* Scheider has his hair combed over the forehead and glasses on, and he looks like a man who would have trouble living in New York for a week. That helped me a lot. I wanted to work with Roy because I loved him in the few films I'd seen him in, including *The French Connection,* but I was afraid he'd be too strong for the part. The moment I met him I said, "Would you play the part in glasses?" Once he had the glasses on he was cast without any alternative. He was my first and last choice, as was Richard Dreyfuss, who played Hooper. I wanted the Hooper character to be kind of a dilettante wise-ass. Having Richard on our team didn't hurt any. He brings a little bit of that neurotic edge to a part, and he's a very funny guy. All the funny lines that come out of Richard's mouth either happened on the set between him and me, or he came to me with some ideas and Carl Gottlieb enhanced them for the script, so a lot of Rick's funniest lines are sort of self-inflicted. Richard pretty well designed his own character as Matt Hooper. When he had a good idea, if it conformed to my overview of the whole movie, we would use it.

Quint was the only character that took a while to cast. I desperately wanted Lee Marvin. We called him and made him an offer, and he said, "I don't want to go out fishing for a mechanical fish. I want to go out to Hawaii and catch some real sharks." So he was out. The casting of Robert Shaw is interesting, because it exemplifies what happens in this business when your first choice turns you down and you begin going down a list of people. It's kind of like a tumbling effect. Once one person passes, everybody seems to pass. Half a dozen actors didn't want the role or weren't available. They just didn't want to play that kind of a caricature. Finally David Brown said, "We had a very successful relationship with Robert Shaw in *The Sting.* Why don't you take a look at some of his films? Look at *A Man for All Seasons* and *Figures in a Landscape.*" I looked at them and thought, "Terrific, let's get Robert Shaw." The more I got to know Robert on location, the more I liked him for the part and the more I wished he had been my first choice. He was reputed to be a very difficult man to deal with, but I thought he was funny and pleasant and helpful and grandiose.

What did you have to do to prepare the people on Martha's Vineyard for the shoot?

It was like sending commandos onto an occupied beachhead to soften the landing attempts. We sent in PR men, the production manager and the art director. Everyone wanted to make sure we would be accepted and welcome, so that when we finally landed on the island there wouldn't be any armed resistance. This continued for about three weeks. Once we were there we realized we didn't really have a hook into them. In fact, they had a hook into us Hollywood folk. We saw the prices of everything rising and rising. Inflation hit Martha's Vineyard like it's never hit any other area of this country, and we began paying tourist rates for everything in the middle of May. We were taken gross advantage of by just about every person who owned a boat, a pier or land in the area.

How did you shoot the first sequence with the girl being eaten by the shark?

It was all day for night, using heavy neutral density filters. We shot four mornings in a row between about six and eight o'clock. Bill Butler needed specific conditions in order to get true day for night. He needed black clouds on the horizon and the sun just above the black clouds so there was sparkle on the water, as a kind of moonlight effect. A white sky wouldn't do and a blue sky wouldn't do. We were very fortunate because for four days in a row we got great sunrises. Susan Backlinie played the part. She was a stunt girl we found through the Stuntmen's Association. She had a harness around her waist with ropes leading to shore, where two teams of ten men hung on each rope. When one team ran to a marker stake they had to stop at that stake so the other team of ten could continue to pull. They had to let the rope go slack at the stake. The danger was that if they didn't, she would have ten men pulling on each side and it would have snapped her back. We had to be really careful with twenty men running on sand and not making a mistake. If the timing was off, she would jerk once, stall, then jerk again. I didn't want this. I wanted a kind of pathetic back-and-forth-through-the-water motion, and that was tough to get. But she came through it.

How do you work with your cameramen?

The best situation I find is when cameramen like the same movies I like, or the same artwork. Vilmos and I looked at a lot of Norman Rockwell together before *Sugarland Express*. I like a cameraman who is open-minded and will try absolutely anything, and who can work fast, meaning I don't like to sit around when the actors are prepared and fired up to do a scene waiting while the cameraman lights a room this size. There are cameramen who would spend six hours lighting this room! Vilmos and Bill Butler, who shot *Jaws,* are both fast and very good. Vilmos and I had a very good relationship. He has one of the best eyes in town. We would share ideas: "Wouldn't it be better to shoot this scene in a master from forty feet back rather than break it up and cover it?" Sometimes I would agree, sometimes not, and every time I said "I prefer my idea to your idea," he would step down and do it my way. There was never any dissonance. I worked with Bill a little differently because we're old friends. I found myself being more autocratic, not because I trusted Bill any less than I trusted Vilmos, but because *Jaws* was such a personal responsibility that I really had to call every shot. Every day I had to say, "This is where the camera goes." I began working closely with cameras myself. To cut off the relationship between myself and the viewfinder would be like denying my existence to the film world.

I gather there were problems with the mechanical shark.

The shark was the first real prima-donna actor I ever worked with. He wouldn't do anything I told him to do. It was designed to jump out of the water like Flipper and work its jaws and roll its eyes and flap its tail and almost walk up on shore and shake your hand. As it turned out, the shark could barely make a right-hand turn and could never go left. When it submerged, bubbles came up. It's only through the magic of several cameras and film editing that the shark looks the way it does.

A typical day on *Jaws* would be me saying, "Okay, we'll get forty pages in one day! We're going to finish this movie on Tuesday! I know you might think we've got another four months—we'll be done tomorrow!" Sometimes I'd actually believe that. Let's say the first sequence of the day is the boat coming toward camera, making a turn and going away from the camera. Then suddenly the barrels come in, chasing the boat. "I'll do that by ten o'clock!" The second sequence is the barrels coming toward the camera and going underwater. That's a little bit of rigging with the five-thousand-pound weights, so I figure we get that ready by noon. Then we take half an hour for lunch and shoot the sequence where the shark rams the boat—we used an underwater cable to shift the boat about—and by five we're ready to set up a shot of the boat at dusk. What would actually happen is that I'd get to location about seven in the morning, fully enthused. From the beach, the water would look as calm as a lake. I'd make the trip four miles out to open sea, where the waves suddenly hit. I'd get out to the camera platform, rally everyone around, and then end up sitting all day doing virtually nothing. The camera crew and the actors would be all ready to go and we'd have to wait six hours for special effects. We had to wait for the shark to function, even float. Sometimes it was four hours just to get him to surface. He'd be under there with divers unclogging his hydraulic tubes. Suddenly it's five in the afternoon and we're still waiting for the first shot of the boat coming toward the camera, making that turn. That was a typical day. It was planning everything and getting nothing in the can.

I suppose this was because of a lack of proper preproduction time. We really needed a year to get our act together, but were given three and a half months because the actors were about to go on strike and the studio told us to start production before the strike began. I spent so much time on the screenplay that I had little time to work with the fellows who were building the shark, and when it came right down to it there was no time even to test the thing. We tested it for the first time during first-unit principal photography. It cruised along, and right in front of everybody sank thirty feet to the sandy bottom—and never came up. And that did it. I tell you, everybody looked at everybody else that day and we knew we'd be there till September. This was April 15. Everything began going downhill from there.

Most of *Jaws* was shot between the hours of four and six in the afternoon. Apart from the opening sequence with the girl, there was no scene in *Jaws* we ever got before ten o'clock in the morning, including interiors that were relatively easy to light. Subconsciously the company adopted an orbit of afternoon shooting. There was nothing that I or anybody else could do about this by talking to them or bribing them. The crew just slowed down. They were used to getting up in the morning and dawdling until eleven waiting for special effects. I think part of it was that the crew felt they weren't making a movie but that they were doing time. They were on an island with absolutely nothing to do at night. The whole island closes down at nine o'clock. They began to cat around but that didn't help very much, because none of the ladies showed up until June, because school wasn't out until the summer, so they just sat there and their brains began to fry. I think one of the main reasons for the morale deterioration was being kicked around on an aquatic earthquake every day. When you're out there on the water from seven in the morning until seven at night and you're being tossed back and forth, you just don't want to hammer those tie-down chains. You don't want to climb in your wet-suit and go down thirty feet and haul up anchors or position five-thousand-pound concrete weights with brass eyeholes. It was manual labor. It was like breaking rocks, and everybody was affected. People really went bonkers on that film. They went right off the deep end. It was like a bunch of inmates set adrift. It was like living out my worst nightmare. Even now, looking back on it, the hardest thing about *Jaws* is talking about the making of the movie. To tell you the truth, as much as I didn't want to put the dialogue voice-over in *Duel,* I wish I hadn't shown the shark in *Jaws* until maybe the very last moment when it eats Robert Shaw. I wish I had kept it out of the picture until then. I would have been home in August instead of November.

Did you ever consider whether it was possible to make the film without the shark?

The entire film could have been done without the shark, but it would have been an Antonioni picture and wouldn't have made half the money it did. It would have been a big hit in Europe but would have done no business here. It would be a lot more challenging too, letting you guess what the shark looked like, what was happening underwater, and playing with the phobia of the sea so many of us have. I'm much more terrified of things I don't see. Walt Disney frightened me more than any other film-maker. I think he's a master of horror. The only part of the book that really frightened me was when they see the barrels, and the minute the shark sank for the first time, I said, "Maybe the barrels would be just as scary popping up out of the water and going around in circles and coming at the boat."

Who wrote the script of Jaws?

I supervised every draft of *Jaws,* and just about every scene in the movie is from my own head, as set down on paper by five different people. I should have been brave and sat down and written the screenplay myself, but I felt I needed a sounding board, someone to come in and play with my ideas and make them better and give me ideas back that I never would have imagined myself. As such, *Jaws* had six screenplays and five writers, including three uncredited writers. The script changed daily. The actors really supplied most of their own dialogue. Scenes that were never in the screenplay were added that same day, like the autopsy scene and the scene at the billboard where the two men are trying to talk Murray Hamilton into closing down the beaches. That scene was written the night before it was shot by everybody sitting around in a room, with Carl Gottlieb taking notes, Rick Dreyfuss ad-libbing, Roy Scheider ad-libbing, me standing on the table, and Verna Fields, who edited the film, jumping up and down. If an actor has an idea that's much better than the idea I had a month ago at home writing the script, or a week before I plan the scenes, I'll change my plans. If it's a better idea and it makes it a better movie, I'll change on the spot. I didn't do that in the first week or two of *Jaws* because it was just such a difficult shoot, but once it was obvious that the film was an impossible movie to make according to the studio's ballpark shooting schedule, I was much looser to listen to the actors' ideas.

To be honest, it's very hard to tell who did what. It's hard to draw the line between what John Milius did and what Howard Sackler did and what Peter Benchley did and what Carl Gottlieb did. I had to take that jumble and sit with the actors, who also felt it was a jumble, and sift through every single page and distill it until we were certain that every scene made a point. If a scene didn't make a point, it didn't belong in the movie. I worked closely with my art director, Joe Alves, because it was Joe who designed the shark. Almost every Sunday the two of us would get together, and we wrote the third act together. "You mean the shark can do that? Great! In that case he can burst through the starboard windows." There are things in the movie that were never in the screenplay because as they were building the shark and testing it, I was seeing things I had never seen before. I spent a lot of time in the workshop and designed a lot of the third act to function around the capabilities of those three damn mechanical sharks.

To be a little more specific, Benchley did three drafts. Peter and I were agreed on most everything, except at a certain point he'd really had enough because he hates to fly and didn't want to make the trip out to Los Angeles anymore. He would only write in his New Jersey home, so we didn't have much communication except for the several times we'd meet here in Los Angeles. Then I hired Howard Sackler, not because he wrote *The Great White Hope,* but because he was a diver and a good friend of David Brown. We had a meeting and Howard came up with some simply marvelous ideas, one after the other, and together we totally rewrote the script in about three weeks. But I'm never really satisfied with anything. I'm always changing and needed somebody on the set every day with me to change the things. I needed a short-order cook, so I hired Carl Gottlieb, who was a friend of mine. He was there for about five weeks before Zanuck and Brown decided they'd paid him enough money and sent him back to Los Angeles. So for probably four and a half months we were left to our own devices, and the actors and I would sit in a room together almost every night and refine the dialogue and think of new moments and pieces of business. The movie took shape as we went along, but the structure was there from the fourth draft. In retrospect I should have hired only one writer and spent four months getting the screenplay to where I liked it, rather than being pressured into an early start date with a script I didn't care for and had to improvise my way through.

Interestingly, I've found from *Close Encounters* that I'm much more pig-headed when I'm the author and more collaborative when I haven't written the screenplay. I guess I feel if I'm violating the writer's version by directing, I should invite everybody to help violate him with me.

The Indianapolis *speech is beautifully done by Robert Shaw.*

The speech came from a book that Howard Sackler found in a library. He thought it was a great opportunity to have a flashback. I didn't want a flashback but thought it would work if we just had someone say it. So Howard wrote out about half a page and I brought it over to John Milius who loved it. He sat down, and faster than the pen could write had written nine pages at his dinner table. Later we cut it down to five pages and Robert Shaw revamped it so it would fit his own character, his own rhythm. He wanted it to be more to the point and less graphic. The speech was written for a MacArthur type, but Robert didn't feel his personality was as ostentatious as that. I thought the speech John wrote was absolutely brilliant, but I knew we had to sacrifice a lot of the words so that Robert would feel comfortable playing the part.

In the script it's written that Quint gets drunk before he talks about the *Indianapolis.* That's the only way he can break down enough to be personal with these two strangers he has aboard his boat. In the filming of the scene Robert asked me if he could really get drunk, and I said, "Yes." So Robert got a little blotto and the scene that timed out sober at six minutes ran about ten minutes, to the end of the magazine, and would have gone five minutes more if I hadn't tapped him on the shoulder to let him know we had run out of film. I discovered through this process—and Robert already knows from experience—that an actor, as good as he is, with all the tools available to him to make himself as much like another person as possible, above all has to have control. He has to know what he's doing at every moment. It was kind of scary to watch an actor get carried away like that. It was the most dangerous experiment of the film— something the two of us collaborated on. I was the only one who knew that Robert was going to drink four glasses of Jim Beam before he did the scene. To be honest, his drunk performance was better than his sober performance. It was absolutely riveting and brilliant. I have it and I show it every once in a while to friends. It's one of the best things I've ever seen him do, but it was very personal both to Robert Shaw as an actor and Robert Shaw as a person, and it didn't belong in *Jaws*. I really believe in controlling every aspect of a movie, especially an actor's performance, even when it comes to improvisation. So we reshot the scene the next day.

The idea for them to compare scars was mine. It was written one way by Howard Sackler and explained to me another way by John Milius. Then Carl Gottlieb had some ideas and I wound up rewriting the scene with a guy named Craig Kingsbury, a guy from Martha's Vineyard who wears no shoes, has been struck by lightning twice, gets drunk with oxen, and generally does strange things. This was the man who Robert Shaw mostly relied on for his salty dialogue. Robert would go over to Craig and say, "We're stuck. What would Quint say in this case?" And Craig would say, "Well, you know, I got in a big fight in an Okie bar in San Francisco celebrating my third wife's demise." That's a typical Craig Kingsburyism, and I'd write that down with Robert and we'd do it that day. Sometimes Craig came on the boat and just sat back listening. I'd say, "How'd you like the scene, Craig?" He'd say, "These guys are talking like West Coast Californians," and he'd come up with some good dialogue. Working that way is exciting, but you shouldn't do it on every picture or you won't live very long.

Is working with actors one of your foremost concerns?

There's nothing more exciting than getting five actors in a room who are all so concerned about the project that they're all helping each other. They're cross-pollinating their feelings about the characters. I spent two dutiful years in Jeff Corey's acting classes, though I wasn't studying to become an actor. If anything, it was to vent certain psychological frustrations. Today, one of my concerns is making sure the actors have a conception of the movie I want to make. Sometimes the actor entertains a totally different concept of the movie, and that's where many of the battles begin. I think the director's first accomplishment, if he ever accomplishes it, is to get the actor to understand his vision of the piece. It's important for everyone to agree that this is the story we all want to tell, or at least if I'm the one who wrote the screenplay then this is the story I want to tell. If the actor is unable to understand this, then the director shouldn't hire that actor.

Spielberg with Harrison Ford and Sean Connery on the set of
Indiana Jones and the Last Crusade (1989).

How much improvisation is in the finished film?

I'm enthusiastic about controlled improvisation. This means you rehearse
the improv, you don't just shoot it and then try to save it in the editing
room. With *Jaws* I worked with the actors using improvisation only with
the scenes that really stank, the ones that just lay there on paper. I'd have
the actors come over for dinner and we would get into heavy discussion
about things. Every actor really wanted to make his own part coherent. I
had promised Rick Dreyfuss I would make his role bigger, really make it
into something, including pieces of business like the squeezing of the Sty-
rofoam cup. I had that gag on my mind and couldn't find a place for it
until *Jaws*. I have a whole book of ideas, volumes of little notebooks. The
cup gag was number 440. Finally I found a place for it!

Compared to your other pictures Jaws *is a huge film. Did you ever feel its size got
in your way?*

No, and I'll tell you something: I always felt that *Jaws* was too small of a
movie. When I first began shooting and watching the dailies I said, "This
is a Movie of the Week. We've actually got a very thin story here. We're
banking on the unseen presence of the shark to carry this picture
through." I remember really worrying about that and going back and trying to get heavy, and the minute I tried to get heavy—meaning politically
heavy, with the mayor and the duplicity and the opening and closing of

the beaches—the whole feeling of the film seemed to bog down. Getting this film off the ground was like a scene from *Destination Moon,* where they had to take everything off the spaceship so they had enough thrust to reach Earth. Rather than adding things to make it a heavier film and a bigger epic, we began stripping the film down to its bare essentials. That was my main take on the picture. It had to be streamlined in order for it to fly.

I heard that after you saw a cut of the film, you decided to go back and get some pickup shots.

I spent six months in the cutting room putting the picture together, and when it was all done it played, but there were some things that didn't look complete to me. I discovered in postproduction how important certain inserts could be for getting out of a scene in seconds and speeding up the action. I wound up shooting two days of inserts after the film was cut, just for my own gratification, even though everybody else was happy with the film. I was the only person unsettled by the cut. One of the things we shot was for the Ben Gardner sequence where the two men go out in the fog and Rick Dreyfuss suits up and goes underwater to check out the boat. There was no reaction from the audience at an early preview. I sat down for two weeks trying to figure out why nobody screamed, until I realized I could pull a real cheap trick. Three days after the last preview we went to a swimming pool and got the shot of the head floating out of the boat. It gets the biggest scream in the picture.

What is it that you think made Jaws *so enormously successful?*

That's the one question no one can really answer. If they could, they'd make a hundred-million-dollar film every time. I can't answer that question myself except to say that I think if it had been a film about a crocodile, it wouldn't be as successful. When I first read the *Jaws* galleys I was amazed at how captivated I was by the ocean. I don't know anything about the ocean. Why did a shark attacking three men in a boat appeal to me? Apparently I was sucked into the same primal sensation that gripped all those people around the world who made the movie a success. I think there's something primeval within all of us that has to do with being eaten, being at the mercy of a shark when you're in its environment, a nonhuman, liquid environment. That kind of claustrophobia is damned scary. I think people are afraid of being on some other animal's food chain and being attacked in the water where they can't run and save themselves. It's like that nightmare we all have where something is chasing us and we can't move our legs.

I'm interested in making scary movies that are within the realm of plausibility. When you're talking about a sixty-foot ape you're really deep into fantasyland, but when you're talking about sharks, however big they are, you're close to home. I also think there are some other factors that are rather Freudian and kind of deep and rather silly to talk about. I'd rather hear it from the psychiatrists than have you guys hear it from me.

Are you going to produce your own movies from now on?

No, I don't think all of them. I think a good producer is essential for a director to free his mind, to go off and make the movie. Otherwise the director can't go to sleep. He would have to be on the telephone every day until midnight making sure everyone will show up the next day. On *Jaws,* for the first month and a half, the pressure was unbearable because we were slipping so far behind schedule. I should pay tribute to the producers, Dick and David, who blocked every tackle and didn't allow any penetration from the studio that they thought would depress me or make me do less than a good job. Any time somebody was screaming and making threats back in Hollywood, I wouldn't hear about it on Martha's Vineyard. That, to me, is the primary role of a good producer.

A lot of filmmakers over the last few years have tried to form their own companies so they could achieve some sort of independence.

I don't know about forming companies, because the fact is, the movie business is a real risk. I'd rather spend my money on real estate and maybe some small 16mm movies I make myself someday, operating the camera myself. I actually have a very grim attitude about reaching into your own pocket and spending your own money on motion pictures, even though I have a lot of respect for those who have the courage to do so. Times have really changed. Today it's the banks and not the studios. It's great to have friends who are directors, because you trade scripts and conversation and gossip and everything else. But when it comes to getting a business together, it gets so nasty. The attorneys move in and suddenly the person you used to call four nights a week, just to rap with, you can't talk to anymore because the attorneys have sort of put a restraining order on your conversation. I think it would just destroy my relationship with George

Lucas or Marty Scorsese or any of my directing friends if we formed a company. I wouldn't mind working for a director—or a producer who was once a director—who's going to form his own company, but the idea of getting five directors together in a room where all of us have to make one film every three years for that company, where we would all sort of share in the profits, seems to me a little inequitable. It's been tried and it hasn't worked. Look at Friedkin, Bogdanovich and Coppola with the Directors Company. I think once we begin making deals with each other and producing each other's movies and forming a company, you're asking for trouble. As close as we all are to each other, it's still a very competitive business.

Why were you so secretive about Close Encounters of the Third Kind?

The first reason was I knew it was going to be a two-and-a-half-year project, and in that time I didn't want television burning out the genre. I didn't mind if they did something on UFOs, but I was concerned that they didn't do my story. Television has a way of copying feature films almost verbatim, so I thought that if I at least kept the story line quiet and let people know it was a serious film about UFOs, then TV could do what it wanted, but at least it wouldn't have my story. The second reason was I really think it spoils the surprise when people feel they've seen your movie ten times before they've seen it once. *Rocky* opened in November, but I didn't see it until March and nothing surprised me beyond the last fifteen minutes of the film. Had I seen *Rocky* in the first screening at the Goldwyn Theater, I would have been much more excited by it.

When you wrote the script, did you start with the big ending?

With *Close Encounters,* the first thing that came to mind was the mountain. From there, everything followed. Actually one of the first things that came to my mind was the *Night on Bald Mountain* sequence from one of my favorite movies, *Fantasia.* I used the image of the mountain as the focus of the Dreyfuss character's journey. Then I just pulled out all the stops. I wrote the ending first, then went back to the beginning and wrote a story that would play out to the end. The mountain became the end of the movie. Everything moved toward the end, which is why there are problems with the first and second acts. It's a problem when you start with the end and have to work backwards, as opposed to telling a story naturally where the end writes itself.

What do you think the problems are?

There's a problem in how many clues you can give the audience. How many times did I have to remind people that he was being physically implanted? In the first draft of the screenplay nobody got it. There were one or two clues. I gave the screenplay to a lot of my friends, but very few of them understood the idea of him seeing the shape of the mountain everywhere he looks. I'd say, "It was there on page 30, and again on page 70. Didn't you see the thing he does with the shaving cream in his hand, and the way he dumps all the dirt on the rug?" And they said, "No, we just thought he was acting crazy." So that began to worry me. Then I added a clue on page 50 and one on page 80 then gave it to the same friends and they said, "You're beating us over the head with it." So I finally gave up and did what I wanted to do.

There were great difficulties in constructing a logical story around an idea that came out of a fantasy of mine, that of what a UFO experience is all about. It explores, in as realistic a fashion as possible, what UFOs are to the public psychology, the social psyche, to nonbelievers, to the government, and to this one man who has an experience that changes his life. It's sort of suburban science speculation.

When you wrote the script, did you have Richard Dreyfuss in mind?

I think the worst thing you can do is write a script for a personality, because if he doesn't do it then you not only have to change your thinking, but it's very hard to get a new perspective on the script. I actually wrote *Close Encounters* for a forty-five-year-old man, but Dreyfuss talked me into casting him. I didn't want Rick, and he knows that. Jack Nicholson was my first choice and he wanted to do the movie, but wanted me to wait two years until he'd finished directing a film. Richard heard me talking about the story all through *Jaws*. Every night. If I can talk a story out loud, I will, on my own, think of four or five good ideas, so everybody around has to listen to my movies. So Richard, who had dinner with me every night on *Jaws* for about 155 days, had to listen to about 155 days' worth of *Close Encounters,* and he contributed ideas and thoughts. Finally he just said, "Look, you fucker, cast me in this thing." And I did.

What is your favorite part of the film?

The opening, with the discovery of Flight 19. I think one reason is that it was photographed after the movie was cut together and shown to the executives. It was all ready to ship out to the theaters when, all of a sudden, I began cooking again, writing my second draft. It was interesting doing that when you already know a movie very well. I wish everybody could make a movie, then a year later have the luxury of remaking that same movie. I didn't remake the whole film, but I did add seven or eight scenes after the first cut. I think those additions really helped the film.

Was the sequence in India one of the added scenes?

No, that was part of the original concept and I could probably have deleted it. There were four sequences that took place in foreign territories, and I cut three of them. The airplane sequence originally took place in the Amazon. They had to cut through the jungle with machetes to get to these totally inaccessible airplanes, where the terrain had been flattened out by something, presumably a UFO. I had budgeted just that one sequence at about a million dollars, but in the end it was much easier to go out to El Mirage dry lake in the Mojave Desert and create a big sandstorm instead. Also in the original script they find a 410-foot ocean liner on its starboard side in the Gobi Desert, but it was such a giveaway. Right away when you see the ocean liner you say, "Well, it's a UFO for sure." There was no mystery once you saw the ocean liner listing in the sand.

How close did the finished film come to your original idea?

About seventy percent, which is good for me. The things I didn't do in *Close Encounters* I'll do in the sequel. But it was pretty much the movie I wanted to make. There were things I wanted to get on the screen that I didn't get. There is an ET encounter session on the cutting-room floor right now. I shot it but it didn't work. There was a sequence I committed to film where fifty extraterrestrials mass themselves around three or four technicians, touching and stroking and tugging at them. It was a beautiful idea but just didn't work on film. The first concept of the mother ship was terrible. It was an all-black, pie-shaped wedge with a little tip on the end, but all it did was blot out the stars. All you knew was that something darker than the sky was moving out from behind the mountain. I thought it was going to be terrifying, to see something so huge that it just blacked out the sky. No bulkhead, no rivets, nothing. Then at the last minute, it would turn on the lights and land. That was the concept, but when I saw the wedge they built for me I said, "This is the third act of my movie? After all this, a black wedge is going to come down?" I got the catharsis when we were filming in India. On the way to and from the Bombay location we passed a huge oil refinery with ten thousand inside pipes and tubes. It was amazing to see at night. I sketched it and when I was back in L.A., up on Mulholland Drive looking out over the city, I thought, "Wouldn't it be neat to take the lights of the San Fernando Valley and invert them beneath the oil-refinery concept from Bombay?" That's how the mother ship came into being. It's a distillation of both of those thoughts.

How did you get François Truffaut for Close Encounters?

I called him in Paris. I had never met him, but I've seen all his movies and know he's a frustrated actor because he put himself in several of his own films. I wrote the part for him, but didn't think he would ever do it. I was amazed when he said yes. He read the screenplay and said, "I do not understand the screenplay but I like the part. It doesn't matter, just talk to me about my character." He trusted me. He put himself in my hands. He was his own stand-in. He wouldn't let anybody stand in for him the first two weeks, and I asked him, "Why are you doing this? Why are you standing on that chalk mark?" He told me he was writing a book about actors and really wanted to feel what it was like. He wanted to watch an American crew work, so he stood in for himself until he was tired.

Truffaut was wonderful to work with because he's as simple as his films. I thought I was going to meet a very complicated man who had spoken down to cinema in order to make these tender, romantic, light, wonderful films about the human persona. Instead, he was exactly like his movies. I invited him to contribute anything he possibly could so he made some contributions where his character was concerned and several times suggested where to put the camera. He would say, "Why don't you put the camera over here? Wouldn't that look nicer?" On a couple of occasions I would walk over there and it *would* look nicer, so I put the camera over there.

In the time it took me to make *Close Encounters*—and this is a good lesson to all of us—Truffaut wrote a script and a novel, directed and cut a movie, and began a second film. It just shows that there are countries in the world today where you can be as productive as John Ford and Howard Hawks were when they were turning out three movies a year.

The young boy is wonderful. Could you give us any pointers about directing kids?

I love working with kids because there's just a kind of embryonic spontaneity that you can't possibly get from an adult. People grow up and go to acting classes and lose that spontaneity, then they go into therapy to try and recapture some of it. You have to let kids do what they want to do. You have to let them tell you what they want to do.

The little kid in *Close Encounters* really is remarkable. I think they left him down here on Earth for the movie, and once it opens he'll be gone again. He's three years old, and after a take he would say things like, "I'd like another one." I looked at two hundred children on videotape and saw about fifty in person in New York and Los Angeles. I wanted someone young enough to accept an experience like this, but who wouldn't dissect and intellectualize it and articulate it to his parents saying, "Mother, a man with thin arms and a thin neck just crawled through the doggie door." I wanted the kid to be about two years shy of being able to tell his parents about what he's experiencing in the role, so I needed a boy with bright eyes and a beatific look and a great awareness. I'd play tricks on him to get spontaneous reactions. I had large presents that I would slowly open off-camera, one ribbon at a time. I would take the paper off slowly, then take the lid off the box, then take off the cellophane wrapper and reach my hand in and pull out a police car with the siren going. His reactions were all on film, and I would take those close-ups and patch them into a scene where he's reacting to something happening in the sky.

I was torn between two kids, and by the first day of shooting I still couldn't make up my mind, so I shot an entire day with both kids. I'd shoot one take with the one, Cary, and then take him out and shoot with the other kid, and I decided I would make up my mind at the end of the day. After the first take Cary came over to me and said, "You're wasting your time. You're going to hire me for this." He told me dreams he had about flying saucers and how important it was that he was in this movie. There's a sequence that was really the acid test, where both kids had to react to something off-camera that the audience never sees. The kid has to watch it with his eyes and respond in several different ways, almost imitating what he's seeing. I played a little trick on both of them. I really shouldn't be telling you this, but I will. I sent away to a costume place in Hollywood and got a gorilla suit and a Mad Hatter's suit. I dressed up one of the AFI interns as the Mad Hatter and our makeup man as the gorilla, and brought in the first kid. As he walked in he looked at the floor when he was supposed to look up. When the gorilla walked out, the kid just stared the gorilla down. It was like nothing happened. The kid looked bored. Then Cary came in and the gorilla jumped out and Cary's reaction is on film. It's just priceless. He almost wet his pants.

Just as you didn't want to show the shark until the end of Jaws, *did you have any similar thoughts with the aliens in* Close Encounters?

I never had any doubts I would show the extraterrestrials until I began seeing the dailies, and then I said, "Kubrick's right." In *2001* he withheld things for a reason, but I decided to just be courageous, hold my breath, accept the criticism and show the ETs. They were always going to be humanoid, because that's what people report, and I was walking a fine line between the fantasy of my own imagination and what people have reported when they see a UFO and its occupants. They report small spindly creatures, not blobs on skateboards. It's really a human shape. Now, that might be the projection of our own ego, something that we wish would happen, but I really wanted to stay true to the extraterrestrial hypothesis here on earth.

We developed three kinds. First the ones with the large head, the large cranium on the small children. I cast girls to play the extraterrestrials. They were just completely mellifluous in their movements. Boys are tough and stand around, but girls are much more lithe and long-armed, so we had fifty little girls running around. The second ET was the marionette developed by the puppeteer Bob Baker, the one that raises his arms in a gesture of greeting. The third was a Carlo Rambaldi invention, which was a complete autoanimatronic creature. It was controlled off-camera with levers and wires, and had musculature under a secret formula of skin. Rambaldi can make skin like human skin. I went over and I kissed this ET on the cheek and it was like kissing a human. It was amazing. He was able to take little plastic strips and insert them underneath the skin and create musculature, so a lever would make the cheeks rise, preparatory to a smile, which a second lever would control, and the third lever would control a squint under the muscles of the eyes.

Isn't there a title in Close Encounters *that says, "Special effects conceived by Steven Spielberg"?*

No, it's "Visual Effects Concepts by . . . " It all begins with seeing a picture in your mind and wanting that picture exactly up on the screen. In some cases I knew how to do it myself and in other cases I had no idea how to do it, so I depended on others. Doug Trumbull was an extension of my vision. When you physically realize effects, all it really means is that you sit around with seven or eight people and a piece of paper and say, "That's what I want. How do I get it?" There are seven or eight different ideas, and the idea that's most readily available is the one that's tried out first. I can't tell you how many times on a major effect—let's say the mother ship or any of the small objects—we went back for ten or fifteen different takes because none of them were right. Sometimes the ship would wobble. Half the guys would say, "The audience won't see it," and I'd say, "I'll see it." We'd go back and do it over again until it was right.

So you had to conform your original thinking to what was technologically possible?

No, I had to spend a lot of money to conform the state of the art to my original thinking.

Did you shoot Close Encounters *in continuity, and how important do you think that is?*

I shot the home-life story in continuity, because it was important for Richard Dreyfuss' character to deteriorate emotionally in the way he did, otherwise he would have had to make some leaps that, as an actor, he might not have been able to cope with. It was also important for me to shoot in continuity because of my own understanding of the film. As I saw the dailies being assembled in the cutting room on location, I was able to add things and make improvements. Doing it that way means the film is growing and becoming alive as you move forward. Of course sometimes you can't do it like this. *Sugarland* was partially shot in continuity. *Jaws* was shot entirely out of continuity, which is why I had to go back in and get those shots.

If you had all the money in the world, what kind of movie would you make?

If I had all the money in the world I'd probably subdivide the money and make twenty movies. *Close Encounters* was my dream project long before *Jaws.* I got it off the ground before *Jaws,* then I put it aside to do *Jaws.* I even made *Close Encounters* in 8mm when I was sixteen. It was almost the exact story. So finally making the film is sort of a dream come true. You reach a point in your career and they say, "Now what do you want to do?

You can do anything you want." You say, "Give me twelve million bucks. I want to make a flying-saucer movie." But at the same time it's ironic how these things turn out. Sometimes it's the movie you never wanted to make that turns out to be your greatest film, and the film you waited all your life to make turns out to be the one where people say, "What? Flying saucers?"

Is there now a certain budget that you can be entrusted with?

It's scarier now, because now I can really hit the cement hard. I'm getting a ten-million-dollar budget for my next film, which means I have farther to fall. With a million and a half dollars you can walk away with a small lump on the back of your head, add a cold compress and you'll be fine in the morning. You hit your head on a ten-million-dollar picture and you go off to Europe and make a film like *The Passenger.*

Do you have any interest in doing documentaries?

I'm strictly, I think, a dramatic storyteller, even though there are so many documentaries I admire. I really admire Frederick Wiseman's work. I think he and Riefenstahl are the deans of documentaries. But I don't think I would really know how to make a documentary without wanting to stop it cold and rearrange it and rewrite it like I do with fiction film. Actually I think feature films *are* documentaries. I like the early Costa-Gavras films because they seem like documentaries where he makes life appear completely natural. Parts of *Paths of Glory* are to me as much documentary as is William Wyler's *Memphis Belle.* Certain films are like that, controlling drama in a way so you don't even realize it's dramatic. But I'll probably never make a documentary.

Do you have any interest in making a film that takes place in a house with a bunch of people?

I'd like to, but not until a story comes along that can arouse me as much as the films I've made so far. If a story happens to be about two people trapped in the metro somewhere, that's great. I can't wait to do it. I would love to make a picture like *Taxi Driver,* which I think is one of the most brilliant personal movies I've seen in the last three years. Absolutely outstanding. But look, I've only made a few films, and when you come right down to it I really shouldn't be sitting here talking to you for five more years. I don't really have a body of work with which to say, "This is who I am." I've done the kinds of films that have given me the opportunity to experiment and try things I might fail at. Now I've got the chance to make however many films the hate-love aspect of this business will allow me.

I think the toughest thing for a director is to know what you want. It's not about getting what you want, but just knowing what it is you want to do. So many people who make movies don't know what they want. They'll say, "I think I want this. I think I want the person to scream now," or, "I think I want you to act happy or . . . scared." I've heard it all before. But once you know what you want, if you have a very clear-cut idea, getting it isn't hard. It just takes time. It's why I'm so in love with animators. I think animation is the father of live-action cinema, because these people must have in their minds a precise and clear picture of how a chipmunk rolls over in the snow. They've got to know precisely what each side of that chipmunk looks like. They have to know how the fur moves and how the wind is blowing. They don't build model chipmunks and roll them over. No, they have to use their imagination and paint all those cels. That's why I think all directors should be animators first, because what they do is make their imaginations tangible.

Any final advice for us?

If you're a young, untested director, your first story should be boy-meets-girl. To free up the cash, you've got to let the bankers understand what you're going for, and all that takes is something that looks cut-and-dried on paper. A lot of first-time-out filmmakers try to tell their life stories and probe the depths of their personalities, but it's very hard to uproot the money when you're not making an audience movie. The kind of movie that tells us about you is something you should be doing three pictures from now, when you don't have to make excuses to anybody or ask anybody for money. When they come to you and say, "We liked your western—what do you have next?," that's the moment you say, "Well, I have a film I wanted to make when I got out of film school but I've kept it all these years, and now I want to do it." That's when they won't ask you any questions.

I picked up a lot of good advice from Henry Hathaway. One of the things he said is that you have to know what you're doing every single minute of the day. Even if you don't know what the hell you're doing, pretend you do. If I learned from all of my mistakes, which I never do, my

Spielberg on the set of *Catch Me If You Can* (2002), with Leonardo DiCaprio.

budgets would be lower each time and my enthusiasm would lessen each time and my movies would become smaller and smaller. Actually I think it's all the opposite. Every time I make a movie it really is like starting over again. When you make a film, and then you make your second film, you feel that you gain very little experience, except possibly public relations with your crew and your cast, learning how to deal with people better than you did the first time out. But every time I start a film, it's the same thing: that knot in the stomach, the nausea when you wake up in the morning, and the responsibility of spending somebody else's money. Honestly, every time I make a movie it's like going back to film school.

Films as Director

1974 *The Sugarland Express* (also story)

1975 *Jaws*

1977 *Close Encounters of the Third Kind* (also screenplay)

1979 *1941*

1981 *Raiders of the Lost Ark*

1982 *E.T. The Extra-Terrestrial* (also producer)

1983 *Twilight Zone: The Movie (segment 2)* (also producer)

1984 *Indiana Jones and the Temple of Doom*

1985 *The Color Purple* (also producer)

1987 *Empire of the Sun* (also producer)

1989 *Indiana Jones and the Last Crusade*

Always

1991 *Hook*

1993 *Jurassic Park*

Schindler's List (also producer)

1997 *The Lost World: Jurassic Park*

Amistad (also producer)

1998 *Saving Private Ryan* (also producer)

2001 *A.I. Artificial Intelligence* (also producer and screenplay)

2002 *Minority Report*

Catch Me If You Can (also producer)

2004 *The Terminal* (also producer)

2005 *War of the Worlds*

Munich (also producer)

2008 *Indiana Jones and the Kingdom of the Crystal Skull*

2011 *The Adventures of Tintin* (also producer)

War Horse (also producer)

Spielberg directed a number of short films including *Firelight*, 1964; and *Amblin'*, 1968. He directed episodes of television series including *Marcus Welby, M.D.*, 1970; *Rod Serling's Night Gallery*, 1969–71; *Columbo*, 1971; and the television movie *Duel*, 1971. He also produced many films and television programs that he did not direct.

> What enables you to do your best work as an actor is the trust of the director, and the feeling that whatever you come up with, he's going to seriously consider it, and weigh it, whether he agrees with the choice you've made in the scene or not—but he believes in you.

MERYL STREEP
(Born in Summit, New Jersey, 1949)

When a young actress named Meryl Streep made her screen debut in Fred Zinnemann's *Julia* in 1977, no one would have predicted that in the year she turned sixty she would be starring in two films and that the films would be written and directed by women: *Julie & Julia* by Nora Ephron, and *It's Complicated* by Nancy Meyers. Streep is the premier actress of her day and has sustained a career far beyond the "term limits" that normally apply to female stars. Her achievement is even more remarkable in light of Molly Haskell's observation that she has "amassed a body of work that's phenomenal any way you look at it, but especially in a filmmaking climate tyrannized by the male adolescent demographic."

Streep set her course to be an actress when she enrolled at the Yale School of Drama and gained experience in a wide range of plays with the Yale Repertory Theater. She was recognized as an actress of great promise, and Joseph Papp put her on stage at New York's Public Theater, which led to her opportunity in *Julia*, which in turn led to her Oscar nomination in *The Deer Hunter* and an Emmy for the miniseries *Holocaust*. Then Woody Allen cast her in *Manhattan* and Robert Benton in *Kramer vs. Kramer*, for which she won her first Academy Award.

Leading directors started offering her major roles: Karel Reisz in *The French Lieutenant's Woman*, Alan Pakula in *Sophie's Choice*, Sydney Pollack in *Out of Africa* and Mike Nichols in *Heartburn, Postcards from the Edge* and *Silkwood*. The directors admired her ability to disappear into the characters she created. She played a variety of stellar parts, winning awards and praise from the critics. At times when she fell out of favor she would find a way back, like when she showed up with her hair dyed brown to work with Clint Eastwood on *Bridges of Madison County* and earned one more Oscar nomination.

Meryl Streep in *Out of Africa* (1985).

Streep is the mother of four children and has made that a priority, turning down parts in important pictures that would take her away from her family. Yet she continues to command roles that display her range: *The Devil Wears Prada, Doubt, Mamma Mia!, Julie & Julia* and her portrayal of Margaret Thatcher in *The Iron Lady. The Iron Lady* brought her a record seventeenth Oscar nomination.

She occasionally performs with distinction on the stage, but family considerations limit her appearances, and she works in television when the right project comes along. In *Angels in America,* Tony Kushner's Pulitzer Prize–winning play, directed by Mike Nichols, she played three roles, Hannah Pitt, Ethel Rosenberg and an elderly male rabbi.

Nora Ephron enlisted Streep to portray Julia Child in *Julie & Julia* (2009), and Stanley Tucci to play her husband, Paul.

"If there's a heaven for directors," observed Alan Pakula, "it would be to direct Meryl Streep your whole life." For her part, Streep told *Daily Variety* that she was proud of the integrity of her career, of "this eccentric, quirky collection of movies I've done, all with their idiosyncratic pleasures. They've never said about my movies, 'What's the sequel?' and 'Can we merchandise this?' "

MERYL STREEP

May 16, 2004*

What got you interested in acting, and when did you think this was your profession?

I guess I got interested as a child. I liked play-acting and never grew out of it. But all along I thought I would be in the theater. I also had a concurrent desire not to be involved because I thought it was silly. And a lot of it is silly. But after a while it was like being coated in caramel—you just can't pull away. It's so sweet on so many levels.

When I was a kid I wanted to be older than I was. I was interested in what it felt like to be my mother, or my grandmother, or the lady up the street who was an Italian war bride. Her husband was a GI who brought her to New Jersey. She was very exotic to me, but also there was such a dignity to her. When they called me to do *Bridges of Madison County,* I had that lady and a love for her inside me. I was always interested in what it would be like to be somebody else.

You studied at Yale?

I was in the acting program, but Yale is a school for directors, writers, dramaturges, critics, playwrights and designers, so everybody's in the mix. It's a conservatory where everybody has their shot. But it's not really an egalitarian education for the actors, because each director gets to pick their ideal cast for their project, so certain actors were used over and over.

*Jon Avnet moderated this seminar. This transcript also contains segments from an interview Meryl Streep conducted in 2004 when she received the AFI Life Achievement Award.

Every year they would have a different acting guru who would come in and head the department. Then his whole gang would be thrown out and the next group would come in. So there was a lot of whining and bitching and I was right up there with everybody. At the same time there was an enormous opportunity to be exposed to a lot of different ways of doing what basically nobody really understands how they do—which is acting.

After you left Yale, you started working on stage in New York?

Yale got a lot of attention because Robert Brustein was running it. He had a theory called "No More Masterpieces," which was the idea that even if you do a classic play, if you were doing Shakespeare, you would never do it in Elizabethan dress. Or if you did, you'd have to deconstruct it in some way. It was sort of the beginning of looking at old material in a way that was relevant to the time and the context in which it found itself. The point was that Yale got a lot of attention, and people would come up and see productions we did there. It meant people knew who I was before I went to the city. I got a job at the O'Neill Playwrights Conference, which is a fantastic workshop for new writers. I was in a community of souls there—writers and actors. It was a way of entering this little network that existed in New York, which was a very fierce and exciting group of people, because at that time I graduated there were sixteen Broadway theaters dark—empty! So, everybody thinks their time is the worst—or the best.

How did Julia *come about? That was a very prestigious part.*

Juliet Taylor, who is the casting director for Woody Allen's movies, is a great, great, imaginative casting director. She would go to all the shows, so she saw me in the Phoenix Theatre production of an Arthur Miller one-act on the same bill with a Tennessee Williams one-act. I had gotten some good reviews so she asked me if I would like to fly to London and meet Fred Zinnemann. I was really stunned because it was to audition for the part of Julia. He is a great storyteller and he was interested in women and their inner lives, and was also, apparently, adventurous in casting. He said, as I walked in, "I've already decided to cast Vanessa Redgrave," and I said, "Well, you know, that's fine. I mean, I completely understand." He said, "Would you take a smaller role?" I mean, this was my first season in New York, my first year out of school. So I said, "I'd be at your feet and very grateful to do anything—I'll get coffee." So that's how I got my first role.

Your debut scene was with Jane Fonda. How do you walk into the set that day?

I still am in awe of people who can just walk in to a movie that's already started filming and shoot their one day and be confident. I didn't know how to begin. I didn't know "Action!" I thought maybe someone else was supposed to do something when they said that. Jane took me under her wing. She said, "That little line on the floor—don't look at it, that's where your toes are supposed to be. And that's how you'll be in the movie. If they're not there, you won't be in the movie." So that was a great education. It was a very heady experience to go off to England and shoot this film with Vanessa Redgrave and Jane Fonda and watch them work.

Shortly thereafter there was The Deer Hunter. *How did you put the character of Linda together?*

Well, I have the Ivy League thing but I also have the New Jersey thing. I went to public high school in New Jersey, and that's not that far from Norton, West Virginia. In fact, we used to drive across the state line to drink there. Linda is fairly reminiscent of a lot of girls who went to my high school. I think *The Deer Hunter* was beautifully cast straight down through the entire company—and I'm pretty sure I was cast by Robert De Niro based on a performance I did as the maid in *The Cherry Orchard* at Lincoln Center, where I had devised a thing where every time I came on stage, I would fall down at some point during the scene. What I love about Robert De Niro and his imagination is that he could see that shameless performance, which was just begging for laughs, and he could say, "That's Linda. That's her."

Did you know people like Linda?

I think of one girl in my high school who married a guy and he didn't come back. I always thought of Linda as someone who waited to be asked—to be asked to the prom, to be asked to dance. She waited for a phone call, waited for a boy to come home. She isn't a proactive female. It probably couldn't be further from me, but I really know that girl and I felt for her. In a way, I always thought I could have been that girl if I hadn't had the mother I had, or the temperament.

How did Kramer vs. Kramer *come to you?*

Dustin Hoffman wielded a lot of power and could sort of do whatever he wanted, and he insisted that I be seen for this part. Dustin had seen my work in the theater and in *Holocaust*. So I went in and met him and the director, Robert Benton, and Stanley Jaffe, the producer. I met them all at the same time and was cast.

No audition?

I don't think I read anything. I just met them. It was a very busy year because I was shooting Woody Allen's *Manhattan* at the same time, and I was in Central Park in *Taming of the Shrew*, which was a very energetic role. Stanley Jaffe only had one worry, that I wouldn't be able to do this work. They were saying, "Well, aren't you going to get the characters mixed up?" I tried to explain the whole idea of repertory theater, where you get ready for two or three different plays all at the same time, and during the week different plays are performed. It was really fun.

Can you talk about the character of Joanna Kramer?

There is a little bit of a teeny pattern in characters that I'm drawn to—not necessarily everything that I've ever done. I like to defend characters that

Woody Allen working with Streep on the set of *Manhattan*, 1979.

would otherwise be misconstrued or misunderstood. Joanna Kramer was one of the earliest ones, but certainly it goes further back. I remember when I grew up in my hometown, we knew the two people that had been divorced—it was very unusual that people would divorce. But then the sixties happened, the seventies, and then custody battles started being very intense. I didn't understand Joanna in the book. Her motivation wasn't clear to me. Robert Benton, who is a great soul and a compassionate human being, felt the same way. He was looking for a way not to explain Joanna, but understand her. I like the idea of being a translator of a person to people who wouldn't maybe cross the street to meet her. When *Kramer vs. Kramer* came out it was new, but now it seems like everybody comes from two families. Usually the courts awarded the mother custody, and then there was this huge backlash against that. *Kramer vs. Kramer* played into that rage. Most of the movie was about Dustin's relationship with his son, whom he had ignored for most of the first five years of his life.

I didn't know Dustin before we started working. On the first day working together, he slapped me as hard as he could across my face—it sort of set up the stakes. I remember going, "Is this supposed to be acting?" It was intense but I just reacted and that was easy. The second part was the courtroom stuff after Joanna has disappeared for most of the movie and then comes back and makes a plea to be reinvolved in her son's life. There was some question about the courtroom testimony—what to say—and everybody had their different ideas. Benton said, "Everybody write in a paragraph what you think she would say." Dustin was thrilled because he had very strong opinions about what she should say, and so did Benton and so did I. So we went into our little dressing rooms and wrote, and then we voted and I won. So I got to say what *I* wrote. It was a kind of unreal introduction to that kind of big Hollywood movie because they don't let you do that normally, but that was Benton's generosity and imagination.

The French Lieutenant's Woman *was like a triple role, very complicated. Can you talk about that?*

French Lieutenant's Woman was a special kind of weird challenge because it had that Pirandello effect, the play within a play. I found it really hard because I never really knew what reality I was in. I never knew if I was just being the French lieutenant's woman, or if I was the actress being the French lieutenant's woman, or if I was the actress being the actress being the French lieutenant's woman. So it was very confusing, and Harold Pinter was hilarious and completely not forthcoming as to what I was doing. My friend Karel Reisz, who was just one of the greatest directors I ever worked with, and a wonderful soul, really didn't want to say exactly where I was at any time. The geography was meant to be uncertain. That was the tension within the piece. I like to attach myself to an emotional truth and then sit there and believe in it. It was like experimental theater—always having the rug pulled out.

How did you deal with your character's foreign accent?

I had a wonderful teacher who helped me and gave me some tapes. Are we going to go into the whole accents thing? I mean, I've always called accents the auto mechanics of taking a trip. You can talk about the scenery and the way you felt when you came into this town, or you can talk about the carburetors and how they were firing. And to me talking about the accent is like talking about what's going on under the hood— I'm not interested in it.

Can you take about the film Silkwood?

That was an important movie because it was my first Mike Nichols film, the first time working with Nora Ephron and getting to know her and Ann Roth, a great costume designer; and new friendships, Kurt Russell and Cher. The character Joe Sommer plays, I think he's a union organizer in Washington, asks her, "Are you a stand-up girl?" When I read that I thought, yes, she is. She's a stand-up girl. Like a lot of people who stand up and make a noise, she was a pain in the butt, she antagonized people. Like some whistle blowers, maybe she had a thin skin. Thank God we have these people among us. She was the first real person that I'd ever played, so I felt a responsibility to her life and to her children.

What was the environment like on the set?

It was what I've come to know is the hallmark of a Mike Nichols set. The whole process is really fun because he's the scoutmaster who's got a great sense of humor, and it's very wry and you laugh a lot—even when he's giving you a direction. When you go home at night, you realize it was terribly insulting—you're laughing because he's very funny in how he insults you. All the actors loved him, and I had a great time.

Were you at all frightened by the character in Sophie's Choice?

I was not. I was deeply happy throughout the shoot, because I think Sophie was so happy and grateful to be alive and in love. It's a wonderful life-affirming feeling to have two men be in love with you. That's what kept her afloat. She didn't look at her back pages until she had to, and I didn't look at them until the night before I had to shoot them. I was intent on keeping her alive. I just thought she had appetite and desire, and all the qualities of people who have come through horrible things— they taste the day, it's so sweet to wake up in the morning. So I was happy all through the shoot, even when we went to shoot the camp stuff in Yugoslavia. That was a different story—it was sort of miserable. It was a whole European crew and cast, and all these crazy East German actors— because that was before the Wall came down—and they were so compli-cated and hard-drinking and interesting to talk to. But it was harsh and unrelenting, and not like the rest of the shoot in the Pink Palace on Tenth Avenue.

How was working with Alan Pakula?

Alan Pakula is like a rabbi. You know, every director runs his set such a dif-ferent way. I just think it's so amazing. Mike Nichols always expresses his anxiety about that. He said, "Well, how does Alan do this?" It's like every lover wants to know, "Is it as good as with . . . ?" But Alan's approach was almost psychoanalytic, and he loved to parse the minutiae of an event and talk about it a lot. I love those conversations, but I would sort of tune them out. I loved hearing him talking about all of this, not that it was anything that was going to really help, because the thing only happens when you're doing it. But he loved the story so much. He had written the adaptation himself—it was a five-hour movie that he reluctantly cut. He loved filming it and expressed that to us every day.

Certainly Sophie is one of the most haunted characters you've played.

Well, it's just imagination. I always say to young actors—my son is in act-ing school and I went and talked to his class—that I think everybody has everything in them, and that directors and casting people usually see so little of your potential. You have everybody in you. People who really want to act, and do it, can access all kinds of horrible things. That's what we ask actors to do. We want them to channel murderers because we have

Streep in the title role of *Sophie's Choice* (1982), based on William Styron's
novel, for which director Alan Pakula wrote the screenplay.

murderous feelings and we want to see that played out. That's the actor's
job. I just hate those meetings where you walk in, you sit down, and they
just want to "have a look at you." Well, then that's all they're going to
get—is a look, but a look at you is nothing. You've got to imagine and see
people's work, because people's work is where you'll find whether they can
open you up to the hidden world of a character, to the stuff that is never
explained but always layers your appreciation of the story. That's why
we're here, to serve this entire story.

I am answering your question, even though it seems like I've gone
wildly far afield. In *Kramer vs. Kramer* I hadn't had a baby yet, but I played
a woman who was leaving a child. I felt that in my body because I was
already, at the time, the mother that I would become. I was probably the
mother I would become at twelve. It was the same with *Sophie's Choice*. I
had one child when I shot that movie. The central moment of *Sophie's
Choice* is the idea that you have to choose between two children. I already
knew what that would feel like. A teenage boy reading *Sophie's Choice*
would know what that felt like—that's the power of literature, that's why
we ask these stories to translate us to each other. I read the scene once, and
I never ever thought about it again. I hadn't actually lived it until the end
of the film when we shot it. I already knew what it would feel like so I just
didn't want to read those two pages, and so I didn't until the night before
we shot it.

There's the question of how much rehearsal is enough. Some actors like more rehearsal.

Well, Robert De Niro does. I mean, talk about exhausting the possibilities! He really likes to rehearse, but I'm done on take four. That's it for me, but he wants to go twenty-two times. He keeps coming up with different weird things, and surprising us, and himself. I learn from him, and from everybody I work with. Some people don't want to touch rehearsals with a ten-foot pole. For Redford, it's just going to happen on screen—and it does, for him. So everybody's different, but I think whether to rehearse or not is all about the director's sensibility. There are some stars that exert their power, and they can impose their need to do more, more, more, or less, and less, and less. But I'm very flexible, I'll go with whoever wants to do whatever, because I don't want the process to be my enemy. Once you say, "I can't rehearse that many times, I'll lose it," or once you say, "If I don't rehearse, I'm not going to know where I am," then you're lost. Do you know what I mean? You're in an adversarial relationship to the process, and the process has to be your friend. You have to love being there, you have to love the chair you're in. My mantra is, "Be who you are, know what you know, feel where you are." That's all you have in the end.

Do you ever find yourself working with people who have different processes than you?

Definitely. The horrible, dirty secret of this business is that you really don't need actors. Actors bring amazing things if you want them, but you don't actually need them. You can find nonprofessionals and direct them in one movie and it will be real, but then they can't make a second and a third movie because they've given the thing they have.

Kids and nonactors don't know what they're doing but, boy, they're so powerful on screen. I always learn from working with babies. It's pretty humbling for an actor because they're so straight. When they're looking at you, they're really looking at you. And when they're not, they're not.

How was working with Redford on Out of Africa?

He's a very delicate actor. He's so subtle, I guess in the Spencer Tracy school. In the moment it feels glancing, but when it's on screen it really is so eloquent. I feel like the relationship in that film was very modern, this idea of a woman wanting a man to commit and him wanting to have his

cake here and his cake there. This is a very simple story, but it played out
on this huge backdrop of colonization in Africa and friendship between
cultures.

My kids were never really interested in watching my movies because
they didn't like me behaving weirdly. They want me to be me—and not
die—and I died in a lot of things, or fell down stairs, and things like that.
But my son watched *Out of Africa* when he was ten. I thought, "I want
him to know what I do!" I put him down in front of the television and he
watched it, and he got very engrossed. You know the scene where they're
burying Finch Hatton, and it's very, very sad? He was just watching and
watching, but when it came to the very end of the film where she said
goodbye to her friend at the train station, he was just pouring tears. Pour-

Meryl Streep in Nancy Meyers' *It's Complicated* (2009).

ing tears. He said, "She had to say goodbye to her friend." That was where it landed for him. It's a good movie if it has a lot of things going for a lot of different people. He didn't understand the romantic thing—but he *understood.*

What was the process with Sydney Pollack as a director?

Sydney complains a lot about the shooting, a lot of whining. "Oh, this is so hard," and "I can't drink during the week," and "I have fifty thousand people over here, and I have horses, and elephants, and it's all so hard." He just basically wants to get into the editing room. That's what he loves. Mike Nichols likes the party. He likes to be on the set, and he cries at the wrap party because he's got to go to the editing room and sit with the editor. "It's so *boring*," he says. Everybody's different. Sydney's remarkable because he would have these little contests with David Watkins, the cinematographer. The weather moves very fast across the sky in Africa and they would have these contests of what the F-stop was and when the cloud would finish moving. There were a lot of pissing contests like that. So adorable.

Was there rehearsal?

Yes, Sydney loves to rehearse because he's an actor. Redford didn't want to.

Is it a complicated relationship?

It's very complicated and I didn't want to get in the middle of it. But I just thought it was so pleasurable, and one of the earliest sequences is at the dinner table where Redford comes for dinner, and basically falls in love. Michael Kitchen is his compadre and they come and I tell a lot of stories. I was doing this and they were kind of glazing over after I would tell the same story, so I started making up other stories. Redford's very easy to crack up—he has no control. So that was fun. A lot of improvisation and stuff.

Was there a lot of improvisation in the scene?

No, only off-camera when Sydney wanted me to elicit certain reactions from the actors.

The Bridges of Madison County *was a very popular book. I read that Clint Eastwood said he made only one call about filling the role of Francesca Johnson.*

I was aware of the book and I'd heard they were going to make a movie. My agent said, "Are you interested?" and I said no, because I didn't really see the potential of the book. But then I got the call from Mr. Eastwood and I think he's accustomed to making only one call. He said, "The script is on your doorstep." I said, "Well, I already know about the book." He said, "Just read the script." He was right, the script was wonderful. Richard LaGravenese took this story and in a way reversed the emphasis from the sort of narcissism of the photographer and put it inside the head of the Italian farm wife. Her point of view was more realized than in the book and the trajectory of the story more beautiful. I read it and loved it and said yes immediately. I was an admirer of Clint's and I knew he was going to have an interesting point of view on it.

You mentioned the woman you knew in New Jersey who inspired some things about Francesca.

That woman, an Italian war bride, was on my street when I grew up in New Jersey. She didn't look like Francesca Johnson but there was something in her bearing. She had a very thick Italian accent, and she'd married a tall blond GI and had these three little blond children. She was very dark and exotic and had a beautiful way of speaking. She was very interesting to me, and I basically pulled her up for Francesca.

Was the scene when they first meet on the front porch done early in the shoot?

Yes, it was pretty much shot chronologically, so that was the first day of shooting. I have to hand it to Clint, he didn't know I was going to get off the plane and have dyed my hair brown and have this big thick accent. I mean, it doesn't necessarily call for that. He just went with it—and it's great when a director gives you that permission to make a big, big choice. All the padding—I thought of her as a voluptuous kind of woman, not the way she's described in the book, which is shirt tied up over the midriff and tight jeans. I wanted a kind of proper Italian, and that reserve was important.

Clint shoots with relatively few takes?

Yes, his crew really loves him and he has an effortless authority that he wins from all the other movies. He says, "Okay, let's do it. Let's shoot the rehearsal." The crew is ready. He says, "That's good, let's move on." He shot the rehearsal and didn't do a second take. He did that all the time. So his crew was really hyperalert—and terrified.

He's very canny about what his audience would accept from him. It's like Harrison Ford said, "They don't want me to act." And he's right. The guys do not want to see Clint cry. Even though he was so into the scene, and so committed, I said to him, "Here's the Academy Award, babe! What are you doing? You're turning away from the camera! You're not putting that shot in the movie!" He said, "No. I know what they can accept and what they won't." Maybe you never get to see what he's capable of, because he doesn't put it in. That's his choice. He's the director.

What about the powerful will-she-or-won't-she? moment in the rain, which I guess was the last day of shooting.

Yes, the whole film moves to that moment. It's good screenwriting when the paths have been well prepared towards this crossroad—literally a crossroad—a blinking light in the rain. The romance is all washed away, there's nothing but the choice, and the sadness of it and the finality of it.

I heard somebody say something on television the other day: "Give them emotion, give them action, but make them wait for it." Make the audience wait. And that's sort of the same as in *Kramer vs. Kramer*—there's a certain tension that you maintain all through that you've got to hold off till the end.

You've worked with so many talented directors. Which director did you enjoy working with the most?

I've enjoyed almost all the directors I've worked with. To separate out my favorites will put everybody's nose out of joint, and that whole thing. But you know, obviously, I've worked with Mike Nichols about 150 times, and I've really loved working with him. And Bob Benton and Sydney Pollack and Alan Pakula, and Clint, and I loved working with Spike Jonze, recently. Now see, I'm going to forget people that I loved working with.

What enables you to do your best work as an actor is the trust of the director, and the feeling that whatever you come up with, he's going to seriously consider it, and weigh it. Whether he agrees with the choice you've made in the scene or not, he believes in you. It's like being at the piano recital if your parents don't show up. If they're in the back and they're holding their breath, you feel better. The director is the parent. That is the dynamic, even when they're younger than you. Spike Jonze is a parent, because he gives you the trust and the regard and the mutuality of purpose with the other actors. For a director, I think one of the most important things is to have a story that you really need to tell with every fiber of your being, because then your cast will believe in you, and they'll do anything for you. It's the old "Go with your passion" thing. But it's really true.

There are actors who often say, "In the theater, I'm up on stage, and I can create the character."

I think that's true. Actors who come from the theater think holistically. They think of themselves as part of an ensemble. Theater actors probably are a big pain in the ass, because they want to know, "How does that lead into this?" and "How does that fit into what this person says in the beginning of the movie?" "Well, you're not in that scene." "I know, but they're *talking* about me." In film the director's the only one with the whole picture. I love directors who have an open-door policy and the collaborative spirit and all that, but I also love that it's his fault in the end. I don't have

Streep as the powerful fashion-magazine editor with Anne Hathaway in
The Devil Wears Prada (2006).

to think about it when I go home at night, but the director wears it for two years.

I come to every project thinking I don't know anything. "I don't know how to start. I should get out of the business. He's so good. How did he do that?" I don't make myself aware of what I do know. I *do* know a lot, but I don't think about it and, in fact, don't remember it a lot of times, because that serves me well. It serves me to begin blank and to try to forget the nine hundred other movies, and my reputation, and the training, or whatever horrible obstruction there is to creating a new character. I put myself in a panic of anxiety—to become blank and to start by starting.

Like every actor, at the end of a shoot I always think I'm never going to work again. I have no reason to think that there would be anything for a fifty-four-year-old woman. You just think, "Well, that's it. That's the end." I started saying that to my husband when I was forty. I said, "Well, *Postcards from the Edge,* that's it. That's the end. I mean, I'll be *forty-one*— I'll be the age Bette Davis was when she did *All About Eve.* Washed up." Now, today, I'm two years older than she was when she made *What Ever Happened to Baby Jane.* I just think it's a miracle. Actually, it's *not* just a miracle, it's because now women are running things at some studios, and that makes a big difference. There are a lot of women trying to break through into the managerial positions and make decisions about money. It's important because many of these stories are not interesting to men. They're not. Take my story, just on the face of it: *The Dilemma of a Fifty-four-Year-Old Woman*—already they don't want to see it! But the dilemma of a fifty-four-year-old man who's lost his wife in a plane crash and finds a young student who is sympathetic to him: "That's a very interesting movie, we'll go with that. That's a green light." So the world's not fair, we know that. The thing is, the sisters gotta do it for themselves.

Films as Actor

1977	*Julia*	1982	*Still of the Night*
1978	*Holocaust* (television)		*Sophie's Choice*
	The Deer Hunter	1983	*Silkwood*
1979	*Manhattan*	1984	*Falling in Love*
	The Seduction of Joe Tynan	1985	*Out of Africa*
	Kramer vs. Kramer		*Plenty*
1981	*The French Lieutenant's Woman*	1986	*Heartburn*

1987 *Ironweed*
1988 *A Cry in the Dark*
1989 *She-Devil*
1990 *Postcards from the Edge*
1991 *Defending Your Life*
1992 *Death Becomes Her*
1993 *The House of the Spirits*
1994 *The River Wild*
1995 *The Bridges of Madison County*
1996 *Before and After*
      Marvin's Room
1998 *Dancing at Lughnasa*
      One True Thing
1999 *Music of the Heart*
2002 *Adaptation*
      The Hours
2003 *Angels in America* (television)

2004 *The Manchurian Candidate*
      Lemony Snicket's A Series of
          Unfortunate Events
2005 *Prime*
2006 *A Prairie Home Companion*
      The Devil Wears Prada
2007 *Evening*
      Rendition
      Lions for Lambs
      Dark Matter
2008 *Mamma Mia!*
      Doubt
2009 *Julie & Julia*
      Fantastic Mr. Fox (voice)
      It's Complicated
2011 *The Iron Lady*

A director comes along, and beyond a certain point you recognize that a transference has to take place, and he has to conceive of your script as his film.

ROBERT TOWNE
(Born in Los Angeles, California, 1934

Robert Towne has as good an understanding of how films are made in Hollywood as anyone. He has been active since 1960 as a screenwriter, script doctor and director, and has observed from the inside how certain scripts become films and countless others lie on shelves unproduced. His keen understanding of how to tell stories on the screen has made him the man people call for help when a script isn't working, so it's hard to know exactly how many films he has contributed to beyond the ones for which he is the credited screenwriter.

Towne attended classes in Hollywood taught by Jeff Corey where he met others who were getting started, including Roger Corman and Jack Nicholson. His first script was for Corman, *The Last Woman on Earth,* and later he adapted an Edgar Allan Poe story for him, *The Tomb of Ligeia.* Towne had success as a television writer and became friends with Warren Beatty. When Beatty made *Bonnie and Clyde,* he asked Towne to get involved a few weeks before shooting began, and Towne was available on location during shooting. Towne's contribution to this landmark film is undefined and uncredited, but it was the beginning of a close association between the two men. Towne has spoken of the unique power of stars in the seventies: "You could be even bolder because you were backed by movie stars who were invested in the movie getting made. As long as they were on board, the film would get done."

During a three-year period in the seventies, Towne wrote three memorable screenplays that brought him Oscar nominations: *The Last Detail, Chinatown,* for which he received an Academy Award, and *Shampoo.* Major films that he contributed to without credit include *The Godfather, The Parallax View, The Missouri Breaks* and *Heaven Can Wait.* Towne has also written and

Robert Towne on the set of *Days of Thunder* (1990),
with Robert Duvall and Tom Cruise.

directed four films: *Personal Best, Tequila Sunrise, Without Limits* and *Ask the Dust.* He regards *Greystoke: The Legend of Tarzan* as his best screenplay and his greatest disappointment. Towne was planning to direct the picture after *Personal Best,* but the studio reneged on its commitment and turned it over to Hugh Hudson. Towne took his name off the picture and gave the screen credit to his dog, P. H. Vazak, who received a one-of-a-kind canine Oscar nomination.

He told Kenneth Turan, in a *New York Times* interview, of facing despair in 1982 over his separation from *Greystoke,* a painful divorce and the death of his dog, and how he walked out on a desolate Santa Monica beach feeling that he had nothing. "There was a guy on the beach with his wife who came up to me and said, 'Excuse me, but we made a mistake. We came out here but because of a bus strike, our transfer tickets don't work and we can't get back downtown. Can you help us?' I reached into my pocket and gave him all the money I had. I realized that was the best thing anybody could have done for me. I was feeling completely impotent, and here on this beach was one guy I could do something for. It made me feel that I was not completely useless, that somehow things would be okay."

Towne rebounded, and he and Tom Cruise began a successful collaboration with *Days of Thunder.* Towne went on to write *Mission: Impossible* and *Mission: Impossible II* for Cruise. Towne's own words seem to best describe his distinctive value to the film community. He said, "I help get movies made."

ROBERT TOWNE

October 13, 1976*

The Last Detail was an adaptation and Chinatown and Shampoo were originals. As a writer, what are the differences between the two?

There is a peculiar kind of difference. It's more frightening to do an original because it's easier to face somebody else's mediocre material than your own mediocre material. You don't have the kind of writing inhibitions you have when it comes to an original. You can sometimes write very easily and fluidly when adapting something, and you learn things you don't learn doing your own material. In a strange way it releases your writing abilities, and in some cases you might actually do better work because you don't have to take full responsibility for it. I think it takes more courage, more stupidity, whatever you want to call it, to deal with original material. I have mixed feelings. I think there are circumstances under which it's possible to end up having more affection for an adopted child than for a natural child.

Was Shampoo *your own idea?*

It's a very convoluted history, but I had done a draft of an original screenplay on the subject which I never finished. Then Warren Beatty and I were talking about what would be a contemporary adaptation of *The Country Wife,* Wycherley's Restoration comedy. It's a wonderful play about a man called Horner who lets it be known throughout all of social

*James Powers moderated this seminar. This transcript also contains segments from seminars Robert Towne gave at the American Film Institute on September 12, 1994, and January 22, 1975.

London that his doctor, Dr. Quack, has rendered him a eunuch, so he is
no longer able to cuckold men. Consequently all the husbands trust
Horner with their wives, which is a big mistake. He's actually in fine
shape. Warren and I were talking about it and he said, "What would be
the contemporary equivalent? An actor?" I said, "No, it would be a hairdresser." I'd been thinking about it for some time, and he said, "You're
right."

You must know a fascinating hairdresser somewhere.

I've known a few, and I've known girls who have known a few, which was
what got me interested. I've known ladies who went out with hairdressers.
Very attractive ladies. It was a long time ago, but it was a big revelation to
me. A hairdresser is in an incredible position. Think of the degree of
instant intimacy. You've got your fingers in their hair. Also, they are sort of
crude Pygmalions. They make women pretty. They know what the flaws
are and they cover them up. For a lot of women it might be the most tender and intimate contact they have.

Beatty's character looks weary all the time. Was that written or was that something
Beatty developed himself?

It was very much on his mind that this character was meant to be weary,
exhausted, tired, more passive than active. If you think about it, he never
really seduces anybody, it just happens. It's just gotten totally out of hand.
He's a guy who in a weird way, without quite being aware of it, is under-
going a breakdown over two or three days. Beatty was also emotionally
and physically exhausted by the time we started the picture. There was a
great deal of uncertainty about who was going to finance it. Columbia
had agreed to a deal and preproduction was underway. Stars with sizeable
salaries like Julie Christie and Goldie Hawn and a director like Hal Ashby
had been committed to. Then it appeared as if there were some sort of
misunderstanding about how the picture was going to be financed and
exactly how much it was to cost, so there was a period where it looked as
if there was no deal. Up until a week or so before we started shooting,
Warren had literally assumed the burden of the picture himself. At that
point, because of very complex difficulties with Columbia, it appeared as
if he was going to have to pay personally for a $4 million movie, and this
was a very tiring thought to him. He got weary just thinking about it.

How do you feel about critics who criticize your scripts when they've never in fact read them and have seen only the finished film?

The issue here is not just about the script but about the whole process of moviemaking, about assigning credit or blame to cameramen, actors, directors, writers and producers. You can say whether you like a movie or whether you don't like it, but it's very chancy when you start saying, "So-and-so's script was responsible for this," because you never know what happened unless you were there, and very often the people who were there never know themselves. I feel it's foolish. Trying to pinpoint what specific things the director did is a very convenient way of writing history, but it really has very little to do with the event itself.

I was expecting an explosive moment in The Last Detail. *I had the feeling that this story and these characters could have developed more cataclysmically.*

I really don't understand what you mean. I think there *is* an explosion of sorts in the film. When Buddusky, the Jack Nicholson character, chases after the kid, there really is a great rage in him. He beats the kid up badly when he catches him in the snow. Part of the point of the picture is that there really is no resolution to this situation. Buddusky gets angry and beats up the kid partly because he is being forced to take him to jail. He was that mad about it. It was self-loathing, it was guilt, it was rage, it was fear of fucking up the detail. It was a lot of complicated things, so all he could say at the end of the picture was, "I know my job." I felt, without saying it or trying to be pushy about it in terms of the film, that by inference we're all lifers in the Navy, and we go along and are helpful to people if our kindness or our courtesy doesn't cost us too much and if it flatters our vanity. So we'll get this kid laid, we'll buy him a few beers, we'll let him have a good time if that makes him think more of us, but we won't risk our necks. All we'll do is feel a little guilty and cover it up by saying, "I hate this chicken-shit detail." That's it. In the original book Nicholson's character is sort of an intellectual who secretly reads Camus and has a beautiful wife in New York. He's an atypical sailor with a kind of Whitmanesque appreciation of the sea, but I wanted to tell a story about typical people and I felt he should be a regular sailor.

People always hide behind their jobs when they have to do something unpleasant, whether it's the massacre at My Lai or taking this kid to jail, or cutting down a row of trees in the Valley in front of somebody's house.

They say, "Well, it's my job." We cop out or cop a plea and say, "The king asked me to do this, so I guess I have to do it." For me, that was the point of the story. These two men were no better than they ought to be really, and no worse. But they were not particularly courageous. Nobody is. That's why there's so much swearing in the service. It's really a sign of their own impotence. All they can do is express their anger, like little children yelling about what the old man made them do. That's the extent of their action. I thought it would be dishonest to think they would let this guy off or feel so badly they would get themselves killed or do anything like that. It also lets the audience off the hook. The audience says, "Gee, we're not so bad, because we let the guy go," or, "We felt so bad, we killed ourselves." But you don't. You just go along and say, "Well, the kid was crazy anyway."

How did Chinatown *come about? Was it your conception?*

Yes. It came about because Columbia wasn't going to do *The Last Detail* for a long time. Right after I had written the script there was a reaction to the permissiveness of film. They were frightened of anything where the language was socially taboo or the scenes were sexually explicit. I wouldn't change the language, and I had a peculiar kind of leverage at Columbia simply because at that moment Jack would go along with whatever I wanted to do, and Columbia knew it. It was kind of a Mexican standoff. Normally a writer never has any leverage, but I had a little bit, so I conceived a detective story. I thought that no matter how bad a director I was, at least I could tell the story and hopefully keep people interested. But I didn't want to do just any detective movie, I wanted to do something that interested me. Once you say you want to do a detective movie you start thinking about what crime means to you, what you think is really a horrible crime, what angers you, and so I thought, "I don't want to do a crime story about the kind of things that don't anger me." I wanted to do something that really infuriates me, and the destruction of the land and the destruction of that community was something that I thought was hideous. It was kind of doubly significant because it was really the way Los Angeles was created.

I read an article about Robert Evans that suggested there was tremendous chaos on the set of Chinatown, *that no one really knew what was going on.*

That's not true. Everybody knew what was going on. There's no point in rehashing it, but Roman and I had a lot of arguments and disagreements.

Basically he would get his way, because once you hire Roman either you take him as he is, or you fire him. He's gifted but very difficult. Clearly he's a great director and in command of more disciplines probably than almost any other director in the world. Roman has probably taught me more about filmmaking than any other director I've worked with. I think he did a very good job, and the most important thing he did was take a complex story and be determined to tell it lucidly in the way that he knew best, which would not necessarily have been the way I would have done it. Let me give you one example of a disagreement I had with him, because I can quarrel with the movie in every single scene if I want to, and yet I think it's a very good movie. I think Faye Dunaway did an extraordinary job and handled the most difficult revelatory scene in a way that made it utterly credible. However, it was always my idea that her character not be so lacquered and not look as ostensibly neurotic as Roman wanted Faye to look. I always saw her as sort of a California Yankee, just peaches and cream, infuriatingly healthy, no makeup, nothing wrong with her. It's the tale of a lower-class guy who's made to feel like a pimp and a creep in her presence and is driven mad with the thought that there has to be something wrong with her, and is having a hard time finding it while becoming more and more fascinated with her. He actually falls in love with her. Then he finds out that there really is something wrong with her, that she's been fucking her father. I wanted all that to come out of left field. I wanted there to be a patina of health and not of neuroses in her character, so we argued over her makeup. "Everybody dressed that way. Everybody wore their makeup that way," Roman would say. I'd yell, "No, they didn't, Roman!" But there was no confusion about the story. The script was completely set about a week before the shooting began and was never deviated from, other than a few sequences which were shot and subsequently cut because they didn't play well or weren't necessary. You can't imagine the number of things you can disagree with on a movie and, if there is a central vision, which Roman had, still have it turn out well, even though it isn't necessarily what you originally wanted.

I don't mean this unkindly, but I think it was impossible for Roman to come back to Los Angeles and not end his movie with an attractive blond lady being murdered.* In the original script the last scene didn't take place in Chinatown. That was another argument we had. I always felt it was really pushing the metaphor to end up at the physical location, to actually be in Chinatown. In a way, the point was that it wasn't a location but a

*Towne is referring to the murder of Polanski's wife Sharon Tate in August 1969.

state of mind. At one level Chinatown is meant to suggest a place where a guy thinks he knows the rules of the game, but discovers that he doesn't; that appearances and reality are not the same, no matter what he thinks. At a deeper level it's meant to suggest the futility of good intentions. No matter what he does, it's wrong. Whether he does something or does nothing, it's wrong.

There was one horrible day about two weeks before shooting when somebody said, "My God, there's no scene in Chinatown, and the film is called *Chinatown*!" It was one of those insane sessions where somebody said, "Maybe if the girl liked Chinese food we could get her over there?" Finally out of this meeting, where some normally very bright people sort of lost their heads, it was collectively agreed upon—not by me, but by everyone else—that there should be a scene in Chinatown. Originally I had Evelyn kill her father and the detective try and stop her. He didn't trust her and had an instinctive distrust of women because of the nature of his work, so he put his trust in the law first, but he was too late and couldn't prevent her from killing her father. In the first and second drafts he gets her daughter out of the country and the thing ends with you knowing that she's going to have to stand trial and not be able to say why she killed her father. The child is the one person who is not tainted, and all Evelyn is trying to do is protect her daughter. She has the purest action in the whole story. She really is acting out of mother love. But they get away with the larger crime, the crime against the whole community. In a sense that was my point, that there are some crimes for which you get punished, and killing her father was a crime for which she could be punished, and so she would be. Then there are some crimes that our society isn't equipped to punish, so we reward them. You displace a whole community and take their land, and there's really nothing you can do but put their names on plaques in City Hall and give them a financial reward one way or another, and make them pillars of the community. In order to find that balance, I wanted to end the film that way. The very last shot of the screenplay was Gittes on top of what in the script had been called Alta Vista Road, looking out on this pastoral valley which changed, as you saw it, into the valley of today. Then you get closer and closer to all its contemporary jack-in-the-box ugliness. For me, that was the end of the film.

What was the nature of the interaction that caused you to change it? Or did you write the ending?

I wrote the ending more or less that way. I was arguing while I was doing it, but a very tricky thing happens when you're making a film. A director comes along, and beyond a certain point you recognize that a transference has to take place, and he has to conceive of your script as his film. You just hope that your visions will complement and be consistent with each other, and in that case they were. But Roman wanted to try it the other way, and I said okay, hoping that when Nicholson came back from doing his film with Antonioni he'd look at this idea and say, "Jesus, this is really terrible. Let's go back to the other way." But he didn't, so it ended up Roman's way. My own feeling about it was that something seems even more relentlessly bleak if there's a little light there, just to underscore the bleakness. If you show something decent happening, it makes what's bad even worse.

I was intrigued by what I thought was the familiarity of the characters. I'd seen them a hundred times in other places: the hard-boiled detective, the manicured rich client, the floozy secretary. They all struck me as coming directly out of Raymond Chandler and writers of that genre. Was that Polanski's interpretation?

Roman's characterizations were funnier, more foolish. He went more towards what you could call stereotypes. Roman would have called them archetypes. He was determined to take a story which was not the usual detective-genre story, and tell it as a detective story. There's no question that the story was heavily influenced by Chandler, but Chandler was also heavily influenced by people who lived here at the time. This was a city that bred that kind of thing. *Chinatown* is not about the kind of crime that involves jewels, or the petty political or cop corruption that Chandler dealt with, but a different kind of crime.

Was Gittes a compilation of several different people?

Most detectives in the movies I've seen, particularly older ones—and if you read Chandler or Hammett—are always very down on divorce work. It's like, "If you want to do that, go down the block." But I knew that was practically all they ever did. That's how they made their money. There were some notorious divorce detectives here in L.A. who were colorful and very successful and vulgar and enjoyed the publicity. I thought about taking a guy like that who was kind of venal and crude, and getting him involved with a crime that was really bad, and allowing him to experience the implications. I wanted to tell the story from his point of view. I drew on a lot of things that I knew about Jack. Jack is kind of a clotheshorse. He always wanted to do all that stuff, so I just fantasized about that aspect of his personality and things I knew about him. Philip Marlowe is a kind of knight. His ethics were above reproach, and the Gittes character is kind of a reaction against that, even though I found it wasn't easy to get away from wanting a character like that, in a detective story, to have fundamentally decent instincts. Gittes is a fundamentally decent character. He's very persistent and insatiably curious, and capable within certain limits.

Did you write Chinatown *knowing that Jack Nicholson was going to play the part?*

Jack and I have known each other for years. We were in Jeff Corey's acting class together, and I saw him work two or three times a week for several years. I saw him improvise and got to know him extremely well. This all had an influence on the way I wrote scenes in the script. I love to write for Jack. I find it useful to have an actor in mind when I write.

I gather that the original screenplay was much more political.

Yes, and that was another argument Roman and I had. The story originally tackled the politics behind the water distribution of Los Angeles much more than the final movie did, but maybe it was too complicated. The fact is, we weren't doing a documentary on the Owens Valley. Maybe there is as much of that history in the film as the story could bear. In the original screenplay there was a lot more about the orange groves, but those deletions were partly due to the way Roman shot it. That stuff in the orange groves was some of the first sequences that were shot, but he didn't like it and there was no way of going back and reshooting. We ended up replacing the cameraman, Stanley Cortez, two weeks into the picture. He just didn't work as fast in color as he did with black and white, so they replaced him with John Alonzo. It wasn't anything other than that.

Were any of the scenes that Cortez shot in the picture?

There were a couple. The scene in the restaurant was Stanley Cortez, but when they went outside the restaurant that's John Alonzo. If you look at the picture closely you'll see there's a big difference in the way Faye looks.

Faye looks great outside the restaurant and looks a little like Margaret Dumont inside the restaurant. I'm exaggerating. But she looked wonderful outside. Alonzo was a good guy for the film.

You used Carey McWilliams' book Southern California Country *as a starting point?*

I started with McWilliams' book, which is probably still the best book about California and Los Angeles ever written, and still relevant today. Then I read some of the Department of Water and Power's accounts. I actually picked up the history everywhere. I must have read accounts of it in at least a dozen different places, including Mary Austin's *The Land of Little Rain.* The film is pretty accurate. Wells were poisoned and blown up. Frederick Eaton, the mayor of Los Angeles, and a consortium of people decided to buy up land secretly and bring the water down to the valley and create an artificial drought so they could float a bond issue to build an aqueduct. There was a tremendous amount of resistance from the farmers of the Owens Valley, who had settled in California long before anyone else and built up the beautiful farmland. They could have preserved the Owens Valley, but if they had done that they would have tipped their hand about what they were actually doing with the water.

It was actually an article from 1969, in *Old West* magazine, that really triggered the story. It was called "Chandler's L.A." and had contemporary photographs of Los Angeles with accompanying prose. I was suddenly filled with a tremendous sense of loss about what the city had been. Looking at these photographs, I saw little pockets of time that threw me right back into the past. I realized it was possible to photograph the city in such a way as to re-create that moment in time, thirty-five years ago. The article provoked my willingness to slog through a very complicated story that, at various points along the way, I thought was insane to stick with.

Did you always intend to tell the story from Gittes' point of view?

No. That was something Roman wanted, in keeping with classic detective stories. I felt that because the story was complex and because I wanted to dwell longer on the relationship between Evelyn and Gittes, I should break the point of view, and rather than break it somewhere in the middle I wanted to break it at the beginning, so I started the story with Mulwray. In the original script it opened in the riverbed with Mulwray alone, being watched, and then moved to Gittes.

Did you have Chinatown *completely mapped out before you started writing?*

Not totally. One of the biggest single structural problems in working it out, although right now it seems obvious, is that there is a story which takes place in the present, which is this land-and-water scandal, and there is a story which takes place in the past, which is the story of Evelyn, her father and Mulwray, and there is a point at which they dovetail. At a certain point in working out the story, I was actually dealing with the past before I was dealing with the present. Then I realized the past had to bubble up through this simple story about what the hell was happening with this water, and once I had gotten that notion right, then I had worked out about seventy percent of the structure. I tried it about five or six different ways and couldn't get quite through to the end of the story, although I knew roughly what the end was. Finally, after making ten or more attempts to tell the story to myself, and never being able to get all the way through to the end, I said, "This is far enough. I know how it's going to end. Now I'll just devote myself to the problem of writing it."

Do you normally map out the story before you start on the screenplay?

Usually I have a pretty clear idea of where it's going to end up, even if I don't know every step of the way. Generally it's a combination. You have to pretty much know where you want to go with it and then allow yourself enough latitude for surprises, because the characters will change things once they come alive.

What steps should a young screenwriter take to ensure that his script stays intact? Are there instances where a new screenwriter should have his name taken off a picture?

I think there are instances when you should definitely have your name taken off a picture. To answer your first question, I don't think you can ensure yourself. It might be possible if you're fortunate enough to be a screenwriter who has a friend who is a director and you work together so you more or less agree from the beginning. As far as taking your name off movies is concerned, I've done it twice. When you feel that what you've written has been violated, you owe it to yourself to take your name off. I mean, what else have you got?

Was The Yakuza *one of those pieces that you took your name off?*

No. I felt I had to bear the credit or the blame for that one myself. I wasn't happy with the movie, but I did feel I was sufficiently to blame. I felt I was responsible and my name should be on it. One of the movies I did take my name off was *The New Centurions.* I only saw the first twenty minutes of it and was physically ill, and asked to have my name taken off. It's a horrible movie, although ironically it was successful. I felt that my work had been violated at many different levels, and what I would have liked to have done with the material I was never able to do. So I felt that I should take my name off. It was an expensive move for me, because it meant the loss of $20,000 or so when it was sold to television, and I didn't have any money at that point, but I felt it was personally damaging to have my name on it. I just couldn't live with myself. I didn't feel I was to blame for the badness of the film. There was another instance with a film that wasn't uninteresting, a respectable movie called *Cisco Pike,* but there were so many changes that I didn't want to deal with, so I took my name off. I think you take your name off movies that you feel you can neither take credit nor blame for.

What was the problem with The Yakuza?

The script had an interesting problem, which was to make this fairy tale credible at some level, and I thought, "This would be an interesting thing to try." I think the fatal mistake was the casting of Robert Mitchum. This isn't to say that I don't think Mitchum is a wonderful actor, but the story is a soap opera, as all Yakuza Japanese films are. These kind of hangdog soap operas where they cry and beat their breasts and kill a bunch of people. Yakuza are Japanese gangsters and in Japan Yakuza films are sort of B movies. If you took our soap operas on daily television and our B gangster movies and mashed them together, you'd get a Yakuza film. All these gangsters are stricken with this terrible sense of duty and obligation, that they're obliged to do these things, so they end up killing 25,000 people, or themselves, or both, or mutilating themselves. It's really quite interesting, but because I was unfamiliar with Yakuza films and even less familiar with the Japanese style of acting, I didn't realize that casting Mitchum left you no contrast. You have a bunch of Japanese actors walking around wringing their hands and looking glum and bleak, but so was Mitchum. You really needed someone who was buoyant, very American, asking, "What is this shit that's going on over here?" You needed some real contrast to make the film work, a character who had no patience with that kind of silliness. I mean, Mitchum—who had already been cast—was more

Japanese than the Japanese. The man was a wreck, a complete mess. He was in more pain than Takakura Ken, if that's possible, so it just was a lot of very anguished people. When you have Japanese actors who are having a hell of a time with the language, and you have Mitchum, who's not quick that way, everything just became too slow.

Is there anything you haven't done because you thought it was too controversial to get made?

I've always had the feeling that anything I write can be made into a movie. I think you have to have that feeling. It's not entirely realistic, but I think you have to think that you can write anything. I've never consciously censored an idea that I thought would be good for a movie because I thought it couldn't be made. Basically I think it's possible to get anything made that somebody thinks will make money, and very often controversial movies do make money.

You mentioned earlier that if there is some hope in a situation, it makes a bad situation even worse. Ideas like that must have come out of a long process of work.

We could examine *The Last Detail* that way. If you know it's going to end up badly, along the way you want to show a certain amount of

Towne wrote three consecutive Oscar nominees: *The Last Detail* (1973), *Chinatown* (1974), and *Shampoo* (1975). A quarter of a century later he pursued his fascination with Los Angeles with *Into the Dust* (2002), which he wrote and directed, starring Colin Farrell (right).

warmth, affection and concern for each other—friendship, good times, people being decent. It accentuates the fact that in the end, all those things go by the boards. In a melodrama, if there are confrontations between good and evil, your ability to identify with evil is lessened if evil is always triumphant. Its victory should be qualified. I'm making no direct comparison to anything I've done, but if you take a great tragedy like *King Lear,* what makes it so effective is all the little kindnesses along the way from the Fool and Cordelia, the virtuous daughter. Ultimately so much of this is destroyed, but it all gives weight to the presence of evil. If evil seems to take place in a vacuum, if it's just so relentlessly cruel, it's not so effective.

Who would you like to have seen direct The Last Detail, Chinatown *and* Shampoo?

I wouldn't answer that question because I think all three pictures were well directed. Every writer has quarrels with directors, and I had more quarrels with Roman than I've had with other directors. However, I guess I'd have to say I would have wanted to direct *Chinatown* myself.

I probably will direct at some point. I'm thinking about directing what I'm writing now. The prospect frightens me, but I'm still thinking about it. I was originally going to direct *Chinatown,* but halfway through writing it I became desperately broke, and when I sold an option on it I really knew I was giving up the opportunity to direct it. But I needed to finish it more than anything else at that point.

I read that in the beginning of your career you worked for Roger Corman. I wonder how you managed to convince somebody that you could write.

It wasn't hard to convince Roger of anything because he was paying so little for movies in those days and they were so inexpensive. It was literally, "You want to do it? Go ahead." He would pay a few hundred dollars, figuring it was worth it to see what somebody could come up with. Roger was making movies that literally cost $50,000, so it wasn't much of a gamble. "How'd you like to write a movie?" he said. I said, "Fine." Roger would let anybody do anything, no matter how bad you did it. Everyone I know got their start with Roger.

Could you talk about any techniques you have for maintaining a strong dramatic narrative?

It's a very hard question to answer in the abstract because I think strong narrative lines are dictated, at least to some extent, by characters with whom you are very familiar. You need to know what those characters want and what they don't want, what they're afraid of and what they're not afraid of. Once you're clear on that, you just have to ask yourself what specific scenes are really about, and that involves a lot of rewriting. Sometimes you never realize what a scene is about until after you've written it, and then when you realize what you think it should have been about, it's too vague, so you try to clarify it. That process of clarification, trying to keep it lucid, is really what I think makes for strong or clear narrative. Clear narrative comes from familiarity with characters that are clear in your mind. I know that's vague, but it's an impossible question to answer in the abstract. I gave you an example of the problem with *Chinatown* on what comes first: present or past. It didn't occur to me for a long time, but once it occurred to me I then reworked things along that line. The thing about movies that's frustrating, and also very satisfying, is that you never encounter the same problem twice.

That said, there are certain principles to consider. Generally speaking, scripts are too talky. When there's a problem, it's usually because the story lacks clarity, not having a clear idea about where he's going. It's muddy thinking that messes people up. Very often when creative people are insecure, they can get deliberately esoteric. One of the great things about Roman—and I'm really not in love with Roman on any level—is that he is one who will strive to be understood. He will strive for that lucidity. I think that's the mark of anybody who's really terrific. They strive to make the story clear.

Speaking of clarity, I watched Chinatown *and couldn't piece it all together until after the film was finished.*

Some people say they can follow it; other people say they had difficulty with it. I do think it's as lucid an exposition of that kind of convoluted story as you're going to get.

Do you structure your scripts into three acts?

There's vague talk sometimes about three acts. Most screenplays run about a hundred and twenty pages. The first forty pages are the first act, and at about page eighty you go into the end action of the piece. But even that's kind of up in the air. I don't really try to break it down that way. You keep it in mind in a vague sort of way. I believe in the build of a soft opening, leading the audience into it, so by the end you don't have to explain things. Things carry themselves along. I almost like it when a movie's a little boring in the beginning, because it establishes a kind of credibility that you can build on. It's sort of ballast if you're going to do more and more implausible things and lead them down the garden path.

It's almost impossible to lose an audience in the first ten minutes, but almost inevitable in the last ten minutes if you haven't laid the groundwork at the beginning. In other words, it's not like television. You don't have to grab them. In a movie with a very fast opening you inevitably end up paying for it somewhere along the way, by explaining what happened in this fast-and-furious action sequence at the start.

You have a reputation as a script doctor. When you're called in on that type of assignment, how do you deal with it?

I'll give you a specific case which is fairly well known. With *The Godfather* it became an interesting problem because of the tension involved in the shooting of that movie. It was about six weeks into production and the word from the studio was that Francis Coppola was behind schedule and it was a complete disaster and it was a terrible movie. Fred Roos called me one afternoon and said, "Would you read this script? There's no scene in the book between Michael Corleone and his father toward the end of their relationship, and we've got to have something there. Francis is tired." He was under tremendous pressure and couldn't write under those conditions. He was just trying to hold on. Fred said, "I want a scene where they say they love each other." I said, "Send me the script and I'll read it." Obviously the job wasn't to write a scene about two people literally saying they love each other. It had to be about something else, something specific, an action. So I read Mario's original script and then Francis' rewrite of Mario's script, which is really the screenplay. I said I'd give it a shot. I was flown to New York and I looked at the first hour of the footage they had assembled. I wrote one version, which Marlon didn't like. Then I met with Marlon and Al Pacino and Francis and we talked, and nobody quite knew what to do at that point.

Marlon was leaving the next day and they didn't want to pay him beyond that day, so I went home and finally wrote the scene in one night. I worked on it all night long, and it became a scene about the succession of power. It's the scene in the garden between Al and Marlon where Marlon seems a little senile, and says, "Have you taken care of everything?" Al

says, "I told you I'd take care of it." Marlon says, "Oh, I've forgotten." Al
says, "What's worrying you?" and Marlon says, in effect, "I never really
wanted this for you." It's about a guy who's apologizing for his life but not
apologizing for it. It really becomes a scene about the succession of power
and the feeling of ambivalence that the father has toward both relinquish-
ing power and laying all the problems on to his son. Through that
wrestling with the problem, I felt it would be apparent that they cared a
great deal for one another. I came in the next morning and Marlon was
sitting in makeup. He said, "Read it." He insisted I read it. I did both
parts in front of him, which was very scary. He was very careful in his
response. He wanted to know exactly what I thought, and that's why he
had me read it. Both Marlon and Al liked the scene, and Francis too.
Then I worked with them as they rehearsed, which is somewhat unusual,
but because of my relationship with Francis and because they felt the
scene was going to work very well, we rehearsed all morning and they shot
it that day. That was the end of it.

Was there any question of your getting involved in the sequel to The Godfather?

Not really. There was a little talk about it, but I didn't do it. I saw the original cut along with a bunch of other friends of Francis', and we talked
about it and made suggestions the way everybody did, but I wasn't
involved.

   This is a business where people very often have got some kind of project going and it isn't working and they call you up. People—all people,
writers included—tend to follow the path of least resistance. As a rule it's
tough to start with nothing. To start from the idea, through the various
drafts, and then all that's involved right through to the end is an exhausting experience. It takes a lot of passion or energy or insane devotion to see
it all the way through.

On the subject of doctoring, what was your responsibility on Bonnie and Clyde?

That was a lot more complicated. It was a long process. I was on the film
all the way through, from about three weeks before shooting started.

The script is credited to David Newman and Robert Benton.

I don't know what would have happened if it had been arbitrated by the
Writers Guild. There was a certain feeling of guilt because Benton and

Newman were not asked to come down while the shooting was going on. Probably none of it would have ever been examined so closely if the film hadn't enjoyed the success it had. I did make some structural changes. I thought it was a terrific script when I first read it, but it was kind of unformed. It was long and centered around a ménage à trois between Bonnie, Clyde and C.W., in which Clyde was not just impotent, he was sort of a homosexual involved with C.W.—or W.D., as he was originally called. It was kind of funny, but at the time I think there were two considerations. One was that I don't know if Warner Bros. would have made it that way. The other is that, in a funny way, it got static. It got to be like a series of vaudeville routines: now they're in bed with so-and-so, now they're in bed with so-and-so. It would be pretty hard to resolve those relationships in any serious way unless you did a whole movie about that. I mean, *Jules and Jim* takes a whole movie to resolve relationships between three people. So in a strange way, although those scenes were very amusing, ultimately they didn't go anywhere.

Arthur Penn and Warren thought the script was in trouble, so I was asked to come in and made some minor structural changes. You always knew they were going to die. You knew it before you went to see the movie, and if you didn't, you knew it early on, so the real suspense in that film was not if they were going to die, but how, and if something was going to be resolved between the two of them before their deaths. In order to do that you had to structure their relationship so it moved inevitably toward their particular fate, which was death at the end of the road they were traveling on. Remember the scene with the undertaker and Velma? It's a terrific scene which was in the original script, and is probably the one scene that wasn't touched at all. After that scene, after they've been clowning around and having hamburgers and getting very cozy with each other, Clyde or Bonnie or somebody asks Eugene what he does and he says he's an undertaker, and Bonnie says, "Get him out of here." Now, that scene took place after she'd seen her mother, and the first structural change I made was to put that scene before she'd seen her mother, so that this scene brings home the fact that she's afraid of dying and wants to see her mother. I put the family reunion scene after that and then, rather than have the family reunion kind of happy, as it was, I had Clyde saying, "We don't want to live more than three miles away," and Bonnie's mother says, "If you try and live three miles from me, you won't live long." All these avenues that Bonnie thought of as still being open were slowly being closed, and the two of them were being thrown more and more back on themselves, on that peculiar kind of intimacy they had.

I was working on scenes every day and they'd say, "Try it this way." My overall impression was feeling like a fool because I was asked to rewrite scenes so many times—I mean, not just rewrite what was originally on the page, but also rewrite myself. I thought, "Jeez, I must be terrible," because they'd keep asking me to do it again and again. Then I realized that Arthur was really using me the way a good director uses an actor: "Try the scene this way, try the scene that way." It was very intelligent of him. After I saw what he was doing, I didn't feel so bad and went along with it.

Can you describe the process of reading a script to discover what might be wrong with it, and how you might improve it?

What I've tended to do when I'm actually rewriting either my own material or somebody else's is try to ask myself what the scene is really about. Not what the events are, but what's underneath it, what's the subtext of the scene, and try to do it as simply as possible and see how my single-sentence description of what the scene is trying to achieve really squares with the scene itself. Is the scene really doing what it should?

As far as trying to see what's wrong with somebody else's material, or how you go about reworking somebody else's material, I just read the script like somebody going into a movie to watch it, trying to enjoy it. My responses at that level are very emotional—for example, being disturbed because a character didn't do something that I wanted her to do. Then I try and analyze my own emotional responses. I generally don't try to rewrite something unless I have that emotional response to it. It has happened where somebody has said, "Will you help me with this?" and I've agreed because it was a friend of mine, but to get involved in rewriting something, I generally like to have a feeling about it before I do it. In one way the key to successful rewriting is the key to what Houdini used to do. He never got himself in the box until he had a pretty good idea of how to get out of the box. I think I need a pretty good idea about what keys I need to get out of the problem before I would tackle it.

What I'm really trying to get you to talk about is to what degree you think the process of screenwriting can be understood, or to what degree you think a writer just has to go on impulse.

I think movies take the form of dreams and fantasies that you'd like to have, or anxieties you'd like to purge from yourself. They tend to go forwards and backwards in time. They fill your mind the way a dream does. In terms of understanding the process, I can only tell you what has been useful to me, which is that seeing my work made into a film is probably the single most useful tool for understanding the process, because you always have an idea when you're writing of what it's going to look like blown up on a screen, and this idea is constantly being challenged when you see the movie itself. It has to do with either the similarity or the difference between what you thought it was going to be and what it actually is. The most useful thing is for you to see your writing filmed as you've conceived it. This allows you to understand a little more clearly what that transference process involves, what really happens to the material. I think that's been the single most useful thing to me. I don't think there's any systematic formula. A lot of it is experiential.

In the context of your dream life, how did Chinatown *originate? Did you have an image or a situation?*

Let me start with just the notion of a detective movie. In a detective movie, more than in most movies where there's a protagonist, whether you never waver from his point of view or you occasionally break it, he's someone moving through situations where there are puzzles, where there are things he doesn't understand, things he's trying to solve. You watch him and your identification with him is usually stronger than it is in most movies, because he's leading you through the maze, much the way in which you watch yourself moving through a dream. The detective becomes a sort of surrogate for the viewer or the dreamer. He is trying to unravel mysteries, which is what happens when you dream. When you take apart a dream, it's very similar to a detective movie. You're trying to figure out the pieces to the puzzle. When it came to *Chinatown,* things just occurred to me from so many sources. I remembered images from my past as a child, places I'd been. I don't know that you could say they were responsible for the narrative, but they were certainly responsible for things that provoked the narrative. Once that framework is established, other things are done in a more systematic and more analytical way. I'm sorry but I can't really be more specific than that.

I gather you turned down The Great Gatsby. *Was that because of something specific about* Gatsby *or is it just a general idea of yours that you shouldn't adapt literary classics?*

It was both. I think at that point in my life—it was around 1972—I felt
that I had nothing to gain by doing it. I had worked on *The Godfather* and
they had liked that and they wanted me to do *Gatsby*, but I felt that it was
a very chancy thing to attempt. A lot of what was in the novel was by suggestion. So much of it was in prose and so much of it was utterly untrans-
latable, and even if you could translate it, I thought it would be a
thankless task and you'd just be some Hollywood hack who fucked up a
classic. I felt that I had a lot to lose and very little to gain. That whole
book is a mirage.

Do you try to stay on the set while a film is being shot?

I think it's an abdication of your responsibility not to. I think you should
be there as much as you possibly can. The writer's function on the set is
going to be determined to a great extent by the people he works with and
how much they're willing or able to allow another voice in an ongoing dialogue as the movie is being made. I think it's very valuable to have a writer
on the set. A director who is willing to invest a year of his life in a screenplay should have enough respect for the writer to want to continue working with him as the film is being made, and I think that a writer should
have enough respect for his own work to want to be on the set, even if it's
emotionally costly, financially unrewarding and occasionally humiliating.
The writer is another eye on the set, someone obliged to be supportive of
the director as much as possible because he's in a highly vulnerable position. That doesn't mean agreeing with him all the time. In fact, I think it
means clashing where you feel it's essential and trying to guide him where
you feel it's useful to him. Hopefully he'll do the same for you.

It's certainly difficult for some directors to have the writers around. I
worked with Philippe de Broca for a couple of weeks and remember coming up with something. He said, "Oh, Bobby! That's just great, but you
must allow me to think I thought of it myself." Certain directors have to
feel that they came up with all the ideas. Some directors can't abide the
sight of someone who might be involved at a very elemental level in the
creation of something. Others are much more mature or shrewd about it
and invite collaboration and exploit it for their own ends. Coppola is
wonderful in his ability to maintain his own vision and at the same time
take from other people. He's incredible that way because you never feel he
doesn't have his own idea of what he wants. He's able to take from other
people who have something to offer, whereas there are others who are so

threatened by this that they tend to shut it off. Obviously it's valuable to have close relations with colleagues, because any conflict that arises is not necessarily viewed as disrespect or questioning the talent of the director, it's just a group of people who care about each other and are working toward a common goal. Film is a collaborative medium and the two most important people on any project, in terms of influencing its conception and execution, are the writer and the director. In an ideal world you want them both to be strong. When Alexander was dying, his generals asked him to whom the empire belonged. He said, "The strongest."

What I like about a lot of the films from your screenplays is that they aren't what I call theater films or talking heads.

The process of writing a screenplay is figuring out how to keep the dialogue as spare as possible, and how to advance the narrative as much as possible with the images.

I'm curious as to what you're doing now.

Right now I'm working on *Tarzan*. It's a screenplay based on the first sixty pages of the original Burroughs novel. After that I sort of go off on my own. Tarzan is basically a story about a child who is raised by animals, and the heart of the story is an attempt to imagine and describe and dramatize a child raised by a troop of apes from the age of eleven months to the age of about eighteen. That's the heart of the story, but the narrative goes beyond that as he encounters civilization. Needless to say, you can't use dialogue because apes don't talk and he wouldn't either, so it involved a lot of challenging problems. It's complicated to take a child from eleven months and show all that interaction without having people talking. It has to be done completely visually.

I got interested in the story, oddly enough, because I read Jane Goodall's book *In the Shadow of Man* and thought it might really be possible for a child to be raised by apes. Today we know so much more than Burroughs did and can be so much more specific about the behavior of apes and what would happen to the child under those conditions. I got Warner Bros. to pay the money to the Burroughs estate to get the option.

Have you seen The Wild Child, *the Truffaut film which deals with a child being brought up by animals?*

I have seen the movie and liked it enormously. But that film was about a child who was probably raised in isolation. Nowhere is there any indication that the child was raised by animals. He was raised in isolation, having been abandoned probably at the age of eighteen months to two or three years. He had a wound across his throat, which may have been an attempt to kill this unwanted child, but somehow he survived. There have been fairly well-documented cases of children raised by animals, the most famous being the wolf-children of Indapur, the two girls who were raised by wolves and found by hunters. The wolf-mother was killed, the cubs were sold, and the children were turned over to an Indian missionary. That's much more what I'm dealing with. Truffaut's film is dealing with an attempt to socialize the child, not dealing with a child from, so to speak, an alien culture.

Some people have a theory that certain actors have an understanding of the writing process.

It's why I did some acting. There was a period when I was getting started when Jeff Corey, who was then virtually the only teacher out here, had a workshop for actors and directors and producers where we all improvised. I did that for years and I think it was extremely valuable. The great thing I took away from those classes was that dialogue, in a certain sense, is insignificant. I think that's important when it comes to all forms of dramatic writing, but probably even more important for screenwriting, because the overwhelming size of the picture conveys so much information that it's almost impossible for dialogue to add anything to it. If you want to move the story along, what a character says has to be different from what they do. I was never a good actor, but I figure that if I can say something, then a good actor can say it. It was probably the single most useful thing I ever did. Actually it's where I met Roger Corman, who said, "Kid, I hear you want to write."

Do you ever improvise with actors?

I don't remember a scene coming out of improvisation. Contrary to what a lot of people think, a lot of actors are capable of thinking intelligently, and no matter how hard you work on a script, if you give it to a good actor he's going to know moment-to-moment what his character is going to do, better than you are. He knows it's going to be his face up there and he doesn't want to look like a schmuck, so he's going to know at every moment if there's something that's awkward or inconsistent.

Could you give some advice for people who are trying to become writers in terms of how to sell a script?

It's almost as simple as writing a script that somebody wants to buy. People are sufficiently hungry for material, and if somebody thinks your idea will make a movie and you want to sell it, I don't think there's a problem. Writing the script is always the big problem. But beyond that, I think the thing to do is to find your contemporaries. If you're not interested in directing, find someone you like and respect who is and try to put it together at that level. I would find friends that I love talking with about film, that I like being with, that I like working with, that stimulate me, excite me, and I would try to work with them.

What kind of work habits do you have?

I think my work habits come from my time as a fisherman. When I'm writing, that's pretty much all I do until I drop and sleep and get up and do it again until it's finished. There really is an analogy to be made here with fishing. A fisherman goes out every day. The ocean covers up the fish pretty well, so it's kind of an act of faith. You throw your line in the water and hope there are fish down there. There were yesterday, so you figure there'll be something down there today. As a writer, you're doing the same thing. You think there's something under there and you've got to fish it out. I always thought that Hemingway's *The Old Man and the Sea* was about the creative process. The old man was good enough to hook the big fish, but wasn't strong enough to reel it in. That's the tragedy of it. He could conceive of a great novel but couldn't complete it, and eventually he blew his brains out.

Do you have a particular vision of mankind?

You phrase it in such a way that it makes it hard for me to give an answer, because I think everybody has a vision of mankind, of life, of whatever it is. Part of the process of writing is not so much to explain your vision but to discover it. I think that's what you do when you write: you find out what you think.

Films as Screenwriter

1960 *The Last Woman on Earth*
1964 *The Tomb of Ligeia*
1968 *Villa Rides*
1971 *Drive, He Said*
1973 *The Last Detail*
1974 *Chinatown*
1975 *The Yakuza*
Shampoo
1982 *Personal Best* (also producer and director)
1984 *Greystoke: The Legend of Tarzan, Lord of the Apes* (as P. H. Vazak)

1987 *The Bedroom Window* (also producer)
1988 *Tequila Sunrise* (also director)
1990 *Days of Thunder*
The Two Jakes
1993 *The Firm*
1994 *Love Affair*
1996 *Mission: Impossible*
1998 *Without Limits* (also director)
2000 *Mission: Impossible II*
2006 *Ask the Dust* (also director)

It's the idea that one goes into a movie house to seek a sense of security. One looks for something that is better organized than the world in which we live, and if one goes back to see the same film over and over, it's because one wants to live in a world where everything is predictable.

FRANÇOIS TRUFFAUT
(Born in Paris, France, 1932—Died 1984)

François Truffaut was the most influential film figure of his generation. He led the band of French critics who redefined world cinema in the fifties and became one of the most original directors of his time. He was a proponent of the auteur theory, declaring that the creative vision of the director defined a film, and in his writing celebrated America's Golden Age directors, especially Ford, Hawks and Hitchcock. His book *Hitchcock/Truffaut* became a bible of articulated film technique and craft.

I was in Cannes the night *The 400 Blows* premiered in 1959 and remember it as a watershed moment. Truffaut's first feature-length directorial effort earned him the directing prize and launched the New Wave that brought film critics Claude Chabrol, Jean-Luc Godard, Jacques Rivette, Alain Resnais and Eric Rohmer to the world's screens as directors.

Truffaut was born to an unmarried mother and an unknown father. He later adopted the surname of his stepfather, but lived a lonely and rebellious childhood, being confined for a time in a juvenile detention center. He wrote home with a request: "Jam, and my files on Orson Welles and Charlie Chaplin." He decided that he would educate himself by seeing three films a day and reading three books a week. In his twenties he worked at film magazines in Paris but became lonely and enlisted in the French army, then deserted and was sent to prison in Germany. On his return to Paris, critic André Bazin gave him a job at *Cahiers du Cinéma* where he wrote nearly two hundred articles and reviews, including a revolutionary condemnation of established French cinema. "The film of tomorrow appears to me as even more personal than an individual and autobiographical novel, like a confession or a diary."

Over the next twenty-five years Truffaut fulfilled that forecast in his own work. Antoine Doinel, the boy in *The 400 Blows* played by Jean-Pierre Léaud,

François Truffaut at an AFI seminar, 1975.

became the director's alter ego in *Antoine and Colette, Stolen Kisses, Bed and Board* and *Love on the Run,* films that were seen as Truffaut's search for a lost childhood. His other work ranged from his vibrant homage to moviemaking, *Day for Night,* his masterpieces, *Jules and Jim* and *Shoot the Piano Player,* and a mixture of stories that show his far-ranging interests and versatility, *The Story of Adèle H., The Soft Skin, Two English Girls, Mississippi Mermaid, The Last Metro* and *The Wild Child,* in which he played an eighteenth-century doctor helping a boy adapt from the forest to society.

Truffaut was diagnosed with a brain tumor in 1983 and died a year later, at fifty-two. He was philosophical at the end, telling his biographer Annette Insdorf that the New Wave had been a return to the origins of cinema. "Those who had made silent films in California were under thirty. Later, the industry became so financially heavy that filmmaking belonged to old men. The New Wave turned the meter back to zero, and people under thirty could be heard once again."

Asked whether the New Wave had any negative effects on filmmaking, Truffaut—whose youthful attack on the French establishment argued that they were hamstrung by polished and literary screenplays—candidly responded, "In certain cases, yes: neglect vis-à-vis the screenplay or the laws of dramatic progression."

FRANÇOIS TRUFFAUT

February 28, 1979*

Is there anything you'd like to say before the questions?

Only that I'm terrified. Usually I communicate better with one person at a time. It's only through my films that I communicate with lots of people, and even then I hide behind my films, just as I intend to hide myself a little bit here today.

How did you come to make Les Mistons?

Before *Les Mistons* I made a 16mm film but abandoned it because it wasn't very good. Alain Resnais wanted to see the film and kindly offered to re-edit it. He did a much better job but the film was lost soon afterwards. *Les Mistons* was my next project. I wanted to make a film about children that would include five or six stories. The thing about the story of *Les Mistons* is that there isn't a single scene that takes place indoors, so I didn't need lighting. We were able to shoot it without direct sound and synchronized it all afterwards. I shot the film thanks to someone who had camera equipment, and the film was made for the cost of the celluloid. I should say that I wasn't very happy about it. I did something I don't think should be done with children in films: they are used in the service of a story that is really about adults. I felt it would be better to leave *Les Mistons* as a short and involve myself in *The 400 Blows*. Actually, in its original form *The 400 Blows* was also twenty minutes long. It was the story of a child who plays hooky and who tells his teacher that his mother has died. His lie is discovered and he spends the night in Paris wandering. Eventually I developed it into a feature-length film.

*James Powers moderated this seminar. This transcript also contains segments from a seminar François Truffaut gave at the American Film Institute on December 30, 1975.

Would you ever make a film here?

I would really like to do a film in French here. I receive one or two scripts every month from Hollywood. I always read them, or someone helps me read them, and some of them interest me because it's not my usual kind of material. Had I received, for example, the screenplay for *Paper Moon,* I think I would have wanted to say yes, because I really liked the relationship between the little girl and her father. Unfortunately, they send me stories on Prohibition and Zelda Fitzgerald.

With your interest in films on children, have you ever thought of doing Salinger's The Catcher in the Rye?

No. That really belongs only to Salinger, and you really shouldn't make a film of it. I feel the same about Proust. There are some books which I think should remain books, when one is almost sure that the film could not be better or even as good.

Where do you get your ideas?

From newspapers or books. *The Story of Adèle H.* came from new information on the Hugo family.* When I make films about children, they usually are subjects I've been thinking about for a long time. I could make a film on children every year because I feel it's an inexhaustible subject, but I hold back because I don't want to become specialized.

Do you follow the practice of attaching a videotape camera to your 35mm camera in order to see rushes immediately?

No, I have never done that. It bothers me a bit. It's like Polaroid pictures. I like to take pictures of my children and go pick them up fifteen days later at the store.

How important is the dialogue versus the image for you?

I don't see any competition between image and dialogue in my films.

And in other people's films?

---

*The film is based on the diaries of Adèle Hugo, the daughter of Victor Hugo.

I don't know. Bergman's films, for example, are very interesting visually and there is often a lot of dialogue. I don't think that films are purer when the characters stop talking. One of my favorite Hitchcock films is *Dial M for Murder*, and people speak throughout it, while the mise-en-scène is also fantastic.

But in general, dialogue does seem to be sacrificed to image.

Yes, especially in karate films. But that's an extreme case.

Do you do much preparation before shooting?

I don't work very much before the filming. In general I'm in my office reading *Le Monde*. I think one has to prepare a lot more now that films are in color. Before color films you could go to a place you hadn't seen before and still get good shots, but now I go to the location with my set decorator, my assistant, Suzanne Schiffman, and my director of photography, Nestor Almendros. Basically I work very little before shooting, which means a lot is left to chance. At the same time I always like to achieve some kind of perfection, which is impossible to obtain in film even when you work a lot. So there is a contradiction here. When I have finished a film, my greatest desire wouldn't be to start all over again, but to do a remake of the film. With some stories I could do a remake after three years and no one could tell it was a remake. With others I know I couldn't do a remake for at least fifteen years. For example, I would really like to redo *Day for Night*, but I can't. I think *Day for Night* said a lot of things about filmmaking, but it didn't say enough about acting.

Because of the film's special nature, did you have less of a script for Day for Night *than your other films?*

The outline was already there before shooting, but the dialogue was written each week on Sunday, just like the scene in the film where I'm with the script girl.

Why did you act in Day for Night?

Probably to play the part of a director who is something like me.

Did your dual roles create any problems?

Truffaut directs Jean-Pierre Léaud and Jacqueline Bisset in his elegy to
moviemaking, *Day for Night* (1973). The character played by Truffaut says,
"Shooting a movie is like a stagecoach trip. At first you hope for a nice ride.
Then you just hope to reach your destination."

No, it wasn't too difficult. It made me feel more playful. The problem was
that sometimes after I had finished acting I would say "Cut!" too soon.
After a while I told Suzanne to say it for me. It's a fact that actors are
always impatient, eager to finish.

What is the nature of your collaboration with Suzanne Schiffman?

Suzanne Schiffman studied in Chicago. She was a continuity girl starting
with Jacques Rivette's first film, *Paris nous appartient,* on all of Godard's
films starting with *Le Petit Soldat* and in all of mine starting with *Shoot the
Piano Player.* Since I spoke much more with her than with the rest of the
crew, the first assistant was always unhappy, so starting with *The Wild
Child* I asked her to be my assistant. After that, because she would help
me on Sundays in redoing scripts, she became my script writer. She
remains with me through the shooting and even into the editing, and
often she knows me so well that she'll say, "I really don't think you want
this scene to take place in the courtyard. Don't you think it should be on
the stairs?" I think she even knows in advance which days I'm going to be
in a good mood and which days I won't. She knows, in any case, the

things that will frighten me and the situations that I'll be able to get out of more easily.

What were the first reactions to the New Wave films that you, Godard and others presented?

During the first year the public, and then the public and reviewers together, thought that the New Wave films were great. Then the next year everyone thought they were all bad. Virtually every first film from our group, if you can call it a group, was well received. The problem always came with the second film. I was less anxious making my second film because I felt I had been accepted as a director. But it was that second film, *Shoot the Piano Player,* which presented a lot of difficulties, because it took me six months to get it shown. The tone of the film wasn't understood. It was finally better understood here than over there. It was better understood by foreigners.

Jules and Jim *has always been one of my favorite films. How much of it was tailored to Jeanne Moreau?*

I wasn't thinking of her when I originally wanted to do the film. It happened gradually. But I think I was able to do the film thanks to her, because it was a subject that frightened me very much. I could have done it as a first film. I could have done it as a second film. But something was always making me postpone. Every once in a while Jeanne Moreau would come to see me and very discreetly ask, "What's happening with this book you showed me that was so good?"

If you weren't thinking of Jeanne Moreau at first, did you have a different image of the person who was to play the part?

At first I thought it was necessary to have a Scandinavian or German woman.

How do you work with actors, before and during shooting?

There are no set rules. I don't think there are two actors you can speak to in the same way. Some need to know a lot of things; others need purely physical hints, like how to lift their arms or breathe.

You don't have rehearsals?

Never. It seems to me that the actor will perhaps act differently if the stage is small, if it's big, if there are doors, windows, if the walls are black, if the walls are light-colored. You can't know all of this ahead of time. I have almost no rehearsals, or I'll have isolated rehearsals, working individually with actors, but not together. I notice that when I rehearse with someone, if I know the dialogue by heart, I don't hear what the actor is saying. One needs to discover things at the last minute, while you're shooting.

I think cinema work is much more intimate than theater work. I never wanted to be a theater director precisely because I can't stand talking to a lot of people at once. What I love in the cinema is that you talk to people one by one. For example, in the films with Jean-Pierre Léaud, often if he has to do a scene with a young woman he likes, he gets very childlike and timid. If the young woman has never acted before, she is intimidated, so I take each one out separately and say to both of them, "You are the one who is strong and mature here." Maybe one could say the same thing to both of them at once, but I'm not sure.

How do you work with children?

There is a very clear division among children. Not between boys and girls, but between those who are less than five years old and those who are more than five years old. Those who are more than five can be considered to be collaborators in the film. They know they are working and helping you, and having fun too, but under five years of age it's not voluntary acting. There is a kind of theft taking place. I think that with children you cannot write their dialogue. You have to give them an idea and tell them what you expect. You can give them the dialogue, but only orally. Then they repeat it, but not always with the words in the right order. No learning by heart. Maybe one can get good results in other ways. I suppose Tatum O'Neal had specific dialogue in *Paper Moon,* and I thought that was a great performance.

Could you talk about casting Jean-Pierre Léaud and how your relationship has developed over the years?

He came to be screen-tested at the age of thirteen and a half. I had asked for a letter and photo from each boy, and in the photo he sent me he looked much too sweet. Then he arrived and was so different that I didn't even recognize him. He was even rather aggressive and very different than the other children. Many of the others had been sent by their parents, and they came to make them happy, whereas Jean-Pierre Léaud really wanted that part. There were other children who were closer to the character I had thought of, but he was more intense. I soon realized he himself was a more interesting character than the one in the script, so I chose to change the story a little in order to make it more closely resemble him. For a time after *The 400 Blows* and the short we made a few years later of Antoine and Colette, he wanted to become an assistant director and then a director, but that didn't work out, and he realized he wanted only to be an actor.

Has your relationship with Léaud changed?

He is an actor now. What I mean is that he no longer acts as he did in *The 400 Blows*. He didn't know fear then. He acted because it was fun.

How completely scripted are you when you go into production, and how much do you rely upon the actor's spontaneity to influence the script?

I'm not enthusiastic about letting actors write their own dialogue. Well, perhaps if they write their dialogue, but not if they improvise it as they go along. I have made films in which the dialogue was completely written in advance, like *Adèle H.* or *Fahrenheit 451,* but probably the films in which I took the most pleasure were the ones where the construction was solid but the dialogue hadn't been written before shooting. This is the case of *Day for Night,* where every Sunday we wrote dialogue for the rest of the week. This works when the actors aren't too nervous about memorizing lines. It allows you to write dialogue while keeping in mind what you've just seen in the rushes. There is always a positive element in disorder. The fact that you're not shooting in chronological order will give you these wonderful, enriching moments from time to time. If an actor did a certain scene with more emotion than was anticipated, you write something that precedes it which will provide a counterpoint to that scene.

Is it dangerous for an actor to really identify with his part?

I would prefer it if he wouldn't, but maybe that's not a courageous answer.

As a director, you don't see any advantage to it?

There's a risk that working with the actor will become more difficult.

Which directors influenced The 400 Blows?

When I was a lover of films, after the German occupation of France, I was formed by the American cinema. When I met Rossellini, he was violently anti-American, for good and bad reasons. Some of them were simply questions of private life or morality, but he found all of us at *Cahiers du Cinéma* simply intoxicated with American cinema and he wanted to clean out our brains a little. From Rossellini came this idea of following a character throughout the film. There are no flashbacks and no complicated constructions in the scenario. The screenplay of *The 400 Blows* was very intimate for me, so in a sense I didn't need that much craft to write it.

Let me talk now of Hitchcock. There is a scene in the film that I completely ruined, where the little boy, Antoine, is playing hooky with his friend instead of being in class, and all of a sudden, in the middle of the street, he sees his mother kissing another man. His mother sees him. When I got into the editing room, I didn't have satisfactory material. It was a question of a very brief scene, but the editor needed much more material in order to go back and forth between the two of them. In a rather childlike way I had neglected to plan the shots, and realized that in order to do the scene right I should have thought of Hitchcock. Three weeks later I was shooting an important scene in the classroom where Antoine, pretending that his mother has died, sees that the teacher has been called out by the director into the hallway. His parents have shown up at school and he is going to get slapped in the face in front of the class. But before shooting this scene I really thought of Hitchcock. I expanded the waiting, all the exchanges of looks that were necessary between them. There were little boxes inside the window at the door to the classroom. I had the ones on the bottom painted white, so that when the mother arrives you see only the top half of her face. Also, when Antoine is called and he goes towards the door, you have a subjective traveling shot that precedes him. So in this particular case Hitchcock helped me a great deal.

After shooting *Jules and Jim* I felt like doing something special, so I approached Hitchcock and said I wanted to do a book about him because I had spent six or seven months at the editing table with the film and had started to realize that there must be laws of directing that are never really expressed, and that Hitchcock was the one who had created his laws and that it was with him I had to speak. I can give you another simple example, the kind of thing you notice on an editing table. When the camera is filming a car that is passing by the side of the road, the following scene will be inside the car. What many films will do is that first you see the car arriving from a point in the distance. It gets larger and larger until it passes the camera and gets smaller again. Only then you jump into the car. I realized it was much better to cut when the car was at the largest point on the screen—in other words, when it was right in front of the camera. This is the kind of thing that led me to want to talk to Hitchcock.

Do you think it's possible to psychoanalyze a director from seeing his films?

Yes, certainly, especially when the film's subject matter is of an emotional nature. I think, for example, that Hitchcock's and Bergman's films are very valuable for psychoanalysts. Buñuel's, too.

Do you think that people will someday look back at your films and find them dated, particularly in acting styles?

Oh, yes. They do that already. But this is normal. Films have successive lives. A film made ten years ago shocks us because it seems old-fashioned, and twenty years later it doesn't shock us because we accept it as a piece of history, like a statement on that period. In respect to form and the meaning of form, Hitchcock's films have aged the least. You can make any film you want on a train today, but you could never do it as well as *The Lady Vanishes.*

When Ingmar Bergman was here, he said that if you have nothing personal to say, don't make films. What do you think?

I think that everyone has something personal to say but sometimes they don't dare. It is thought, for example, that original scripts are more difficult than adaptations. One has to overcome this anxiety because in reality an original script is easier to write than an adaptation. In any case, the result on the screen, in the case of an original script, is always more coherent than with an adaptation. But with so much taking of ideas from oneself, you get a lot of doubts, and once in a while you would like an idea to come from outside.

In your latest film, Love on the Run, *you reference your work of twenty years ago. When you sit down to look at your old films, does it make you aware of how you have changed over the years?*

No, not really. The progress one makes is really very minor. In all honesty, the work I am doing now is not necessarily any better than what I was doing twenty years ago. Perhaps I am more competent at handling the more difficult shots. For example, twenty years ago I don't think I could have succeeded with a film like *The Wild Child*, because the material was too limited. Or I wouldn't have been able to make *Day for Night*, because there are too many characters.

Could you talk about the contribution the New Wave movement has made to American films?

That is really a question for a historian. I think the films that have really influenced contemporary American filmmakers are those that have been great box-office successes, like *A Man and a Woman* and *Z*. *A Man and a Woman* is a film that I like very much, but I was afraid it would have a very bad influence in America because Claude Lelouch made the film with a camera on his shoulder, all by himself. When I came over here I began to see in American films a sad kind of influence. The best cinematographers in the world started to film things a little out of focus so that it would look like *A Man and a Woman*. For example, *In the Heat of the Night* was filmed by Haskell Wexler, one of the greatest cinematographers, but the camerawork was rather awful. This has now changed thanks to the generation that followed, with people like Coppola. In reality this new generation is not so much influenced by European cinema but by American cinema. Maybe it's better that way. Perhaps the influence of one continent on another is not always positive. What we do less well in Europe is try to imitate American thrillers.

Are you precise in setting up the mise-en-scène, in the Hitchcock sense?

I've never used storyboards. In every film there is a part that you visualize very strongly before you start and another part that you leave to chance, but very often it reverses itself, and the things you visualized most strongly become disappointing and those you left to chance become the strongest and most precise. In general, I think if you visualize the entire film you will necessarily be disappointed.

Could you discuss the difference of production methods between working in France, and in the United States with Steven Spielberg on Close Encounters of the Third Kind?

In reality, I don't think Spielberg works in a manner so different from French directors. Obviously, on the set of *Close Encounters of the Third Kind* in Alabama, there were two hundred of us. In France it would have been twenty or twenty-five, but often the crew didn't know what was going to be done the next day. All that counted was on a small piece of paper in Steven's pocket. This surprised me, but in another sense I thought it was very similar to the French method of working. He pretty much had everybody waiting at his disposal all the time. In France we would have been more careful with the budget. For example, there were often extras that were brought to the set but were not used in the shot.

Could you speak about the difference between working in black and white and in color? It seems that you speak about your black-and-white films with a certain nostalgia, and I wonder if you'll ever make a black-and-white film again.

I have to talk about black-and-white cinema with nostalgia, because not all black-and-white films were masterpieces, but they were rarely ugly. It is certain that in nine films out of ten, color introduced a certain ugliness. One could say this is an aesthetic and subjective judgment, but I think it is more serious than this. I think that color ruins the effectiveness of the illusion. It pulls fiction into documentary. In other words, I think, a comic scene in color is less comic than in black and white, and the same is true with emotional scenes. I think color is here and we have to work with it, but I am for struggling against it. I consider it something to overcome.

When did you start acting in your own films?

The first time was in *The Wild Child*. I felt that there shouldn't be a well-known actor in the film. On the other hand, if I gave the role to an actor who was unknown, he would take advantage of that and ignore the child. Children act with a great deal of purity. For example, they never worry about where the camera is positioned, while professional actors do. The other thing is that I was a little jealous of who was going to play that part, because I knew he would take care of the child. The child was deaf and dumb, so it was going to be necessary to take him by the hand and lead him here and there, and for me this is an extension of directing. Finally I decided to do it myself and enjoyed it very much. I discovered how to direct from the other side of the camera, instead of being behind it trying to figure out how everything would happen.

Do you have a particular technique when it comes to screenwriting?

In order to feel good about making a film, I have to believe that the general concept is a strong one. When I was a journalist years ago, I noticed everyone usually reworked the first things they wrote, and then rushed the rest, which was inevitably flawed. I decided always to do the contrary. I begin a film only if I'm positive that the last fifteen minutes are going to be good. Even when I start the editing, I begin by working on the last two reels. After all, it's towards the end of a film that an audience is more demanding. I often have very laborious exposition in my films and recently have been trying to begin a film right in the middle of the action to avoid the exposition, but it remains difficult. On the other hand, the audience is very nice about the first twenty minutes of a film. They accept that it's going to take a little bit of time for the story to get under way, but by the fifth reel these things have to come together.

Many of the scripts of my films are ideas that I've been thinking about for a few years. Those which remain longest in my head are those that are most difficult to make, like *Adèle H.* or *The Green Room.* These things stay in my head for six or seven years before I even decide to make the film. But those years are never lost, because once a year I'll get a sudden great idea about one of the stories.

Would you like to direct a film in English in this country?

When I heard that *Fahrenheit 451* was going to be in English I wanted to do it almost completely silent. It lasts a hundred minutes, and there are sixty minutes without dialogue. But luckily, with the music of Bernard Herrmann, we ended up, little by little, making an opera on book burning.

Am I correct in assuming that you think women are more mature than men?

It's very delicate to talk about these things today. What I think is that in questions of love, women are professionals, whereas men are amateurs. I think women live their love stories in a double sense. They experience them and reflect on them at the same time. Men do not take the time to reflect upon what they are feeling. They reflect on it when it's too late.

Do you think storytelling in cinema has changed over the years?

What I've been thinking about these last few years, besides color, is that the variety of visual elements that used to be enriching to a film no longer are. You remember that in films twenty years ago there were love scenes, chase scenes, scenes out in the country. They tried to give the audience a variety of elements. They thought variety was a positive thing, and I thought so, too. I'm talking about the time when people went to the same movie house every week, no matter what was playing. But I think since television has assumed such an important role in our lives, variety is no longer a value to be desired. Very simply, if you watch the news for a half an hour, within that news broadcast you already have all the forms of cinema that exist. You have interviews, reportage, you have candid camera, you have a clip from a film that has opened in town, you have a few commercials that cost a fortune to make and are perfectly executed. So it seems to me, by contrast, when you go into a movie theater, you want to see something more rigorous. It's in this spirit that I made films like *Adèle H.* Fifteen years ago, in a film like that, I would have shown all kinds of detail of the period itself, but I enclosed the film around Isabelle Adjani. It was a close-up of her, an attempt to construct emotion through unity.

In the past, variety was a kind of insurance against boredom. If people don't like this part, at least they'll like the following scene. I don't know if you agree with me, but if you see films from thirty or forty years ago, the films that remain most solid are the ones that give the impression of being closed. In other words, they are films in which there are no natural elements. There is something claustrophobic about them. There are certain films in which if a bicycle passes by when you are shooting, that bicycle remains in the film. But you don't have bicycles in the films of Dreyer or Eisenstein, and not in Hitchcock's films, either. I think a film that remains as fantastic thirty years later is *The Big Sleep* by Howard Hawks. Or *Rear Window,* in which there wasn't a single natural thing in the film. Or *Sunrise* by Murnau. It seems to me that the films that hold up best are artificial ones, rather than the ones that try to stay close to life.

But in your own films you pursue a more open style of filmmaking, far less closed than many of the people you admire. You seem to prefer location shooting to filming in studios and depend far less on control of all the elements in the frame.

I was speaking of what I like, and not what I do. If you're making a film with thirty or forty kids, you cannot make a closed film. In the case of *Small Change,* I made it as a reaction to the preceding film, *Adèle H.* In other words, I relax from the discipline I impose on myself in one film by going in another direction when I make the next one.

What do you think of the ideas of the theorist Christian Metz, who considers cinema from a grammatical and linguistic point of view?

I don't want to be ironic, because filmmakers in general are rather sarcastic about this, but if you spend time in an editing room, you realize pretty quickly that things happen in unanticipated ways. Simply, accidents happen. Something which you intended to have a certain meaning may acquire a new meaning. Linguistics is a science, but for me it's in the editing room where one discovers his mistakes and the desire to fix them, and in turn draws from that process a law or rule for the next time.

There are people who think that in the future we will have a language of film that equals our written language. Do you think we are evolving in this direction?

Yes, that's probable. There's already a clear phenomenon in America that troubles me a bit, the way young people are planted in front of a television set. Television habituates them to a spectacle that is interrupted every five minutes. I am troubled to see that even the most successful American films are ones whose narration is interrupted every few minutes too. There are very few American films left, like William Wyler's *The Best Years of Our Lives,* that tell a story for two hours from beginning to end. Instead you have a song or dance or special effects that interrupt the story every few minutes. I wonder if there isn't a kind of degradation of tension taking place here, or to be more optimistic, a transformation of vision.

Music plays an important role in your films. Can you say something about how you work with composers?

It's difficult for a filmmaker who doesn't know music well to explain to a composer what he wants. It takes a long time to reach an understanding. Inversely, when the composer plays a piece of music for the filmmaker, it's very hard to figure out what that is eventually going to sound like in the finished film. Logically, the best way for a filmmaker and a composer to work would be to listen to records of pre-existing music, but that isn't easy, because composers tend to want to begin at zero, as if they are starting with something completely fresh. I've had the great pleasure in my recent films of working with a composer who has been dead for thirty-five years. He was the greatest composer we ever had in French cinema, Maurice Jaubert, who died in the first few days of the war in 1940. Between 1930 and 1940 he wrote the scores for Jean Vigo's two films, *Zéro de conduite* and *L'Atalante*. For René Clair he wrote *À nous la liberté*, and *Quai des brumes* for Carné. I read a book about him and realized I could involve myself in music that had already been written. We found scores he had written for documentaries, symphonies and things outside cinema. We rerecorded them, respecting the orchestration that had been done at that time. Beginning with *Adèle H.*, we created a kind of cinema that adjusted itself to this prerecorded music. We had the music during the shooting, which helped Isabelle Adjani a great deal, because most of the time she's alone in the film.

Do you find yourself uncomfortable with the prospect of working with big budgets?

I would not make an expensive film very well. I wouldn't be very good at handling large sums of money, because I concentrate on human relations.

Have you had any problems finding money to make your recent films?

Two-thirds of my films have been made in collaboration with American producers. I think I have an advantage in being a French film director because I give my completed screenplay to the office in Paris. They make a four-page summary and send it to New York, where someone says yes or no. On the other hand, if you're an American director you have to send the entire script to New York, and they begin to discuss it and ask questions. We're lucky in foreign countries because America needs a few foreign films a year.

The photographic style of Jules and Jim *is different from your other films. You start on one character, then do a quick pan onto another character, and then perhaps go back to a third.*

Jules and Jim is a film where everything is being connected all the time. This wasn't deliberate when we started, but it imposed itself during the shooting. We were forced to respect the rhythms of the characters, their way of life. We had a woman who was loved by two men, but this wasn't a situation that involved adultery, so we didn't want to separate the characters. There are no isolated shots of the characters. Their behavior was so intimately connected with the environment that we had to shoot the characters with the natural exteriors behind them. I'm saying this now as a rationalization after the fact, but during the shooting it was all instinctive.

Have you ever thought why you love film so passionately?

Film lovers are sick people. I don't know if this means that once one becomes a director one is cured. It has often been said, and I think it's true, that you need a nervous tension to arrive at the point where you can make films. It's the idea that one goes into a movie house to seek a sense of security. One looks for something that is better organized than the world in which we live, and if one goes back to see the same film over and over, it's because one wants to live in a world where everything is predictable.

Films as Director

1955 *Une Visite* (also screenplay)

1957 *Les Mistons*

1959 *The 400 Blows* (also screenplay)

1960 *Shoot the Piano Player* (also screenplay)

  The Army Game (also screenplay)

1961 *The Story of Water* (also screenplay)

1962 *Antoine et Colette*

  Jules and Jim (also screenplay)

  Love at Twenty (also screenplay)

1964 *The Soft Skin* (also screenplay)

1966 *Fahrenheit 451* (also screenplay)

1968 *The Bride Wore Black* (also screenplay)

  Stolen Kisses (also screenplay)

1969 *Mississippi Mermaid* (also screenplay)

1970 *The Wild Child* (also screenplay)

  Bed & Board (also screenplay)

1971 *Les Deux Anglaises et le continent* (also screenplay)

1972 *Une Belle Fille comme moi* (also screenplay)

1973 *Day for Night* (also screenplay)

1975 *The Story of Adèle H.* (also screenplay)

1976 *Small Change* (also screenplay)

1977 *The Man Who Loved Women* (also screenplay)

1978 *The Green Room* (also screenplay)

1979 *Love on the Run* (also screenplay)

1980 *The Last Metro* (also screenplay)

1981 *The Woman Next Door* (also screenplay)

1983 *Confidentially Yours* (also screenplay)

Acknowledgments

I am blessed with friends and colleagues who helped make this book come to life.

Paul Cronin is a film scholar and a filmmaker with a law degree who combines restless energy with a keen intellect. He is a valued collaborator, and I thank him for his diligence, insight and advice, all of which contributed to this book.

Dottie McCarthy has worked at my side for over twenty years. She serves as associate producer on the Kennedy Center Honors and our company's other productions, yet still made time to shepherd this book along, offering wise counsel while making certain that every detail was attended to.

Victoria Wilson is the ideal editor. She encourages the author to take on the project, provides support along the way and carries out her editorial role with insight, imagination and taste.

There is no better agent or friend in New York than Lynn Nesbit.

Jess Morgan, my business manager for over forty years, and his colleague Deidre Baxter are graceful and exacting in carrying out the necessary legal and administrative tasks.

AFI's president, Bob Gazzale, has provided thoughtful advice and was helpful—along with members of his staff, including Pat Hanson, Sara Clothier, Chris Merrill, Seth Pierson and Mike Pepin—in making the resources of AFI available to this project. Adrian Borneman, who came to work with me when AFI was founded in 1967, was one of the institute's most dedicated workers until her retirement in 2010. Adrian can always find unique pieces of AFI history at a moment's notice.

And, as always, my thanks to Liz Stevens, whose love, patience and encouragement enable me to face the many good challenges that come my way, as does the love of my accomplished children, Caroline, Michael and David, and their children.

I have taken care in editing these seminars to keep the thoughts of the filmmakers true to what they said, while smoothing syntax and removing repetition. In many instances filmmakers visited AFI more than once and passages from multiple seminars have been used. And in some cases the film-makers have been interviewed for clarification.

The filmmakers whose seminars comprise this book gave generously of their time to come to AFI and meet with the fellows. It is their insight and their ideas that give this book its value.

Illustrations

Sources

Baltake, Joe. *The Films of Jack Lemmon.* Citadel Press, 1977.

Biskind, Peter. *Easy Riders, Raging Bulls: How the Sex–Drugs–and–Rock-'n'-Roll Generation Saved Hollywood.* Simon and Schuster, 1998.

———. *Down and Dirty Pictures: Miramax, Sundance, and the Rise of Independent Films.* Simon and Schuster, 2004.

Brown, Jared. *Alan J. Pakula: His Films and His Life.* Back Stage Books, 2005.

Carson, Diane, ed. *John Sayles: Interviews.* University Press of Mississippi, 1999.

Clagett, Thomas D. *William Friedkin: Films of Aberration, Obsession and Reality.* Silman-James Press, 2003.

Friedman, Lester, and Brent Notbohm, eds. *Steven Spielberg Interviews.* University Press of Mississippi, 2000.

Grobel, Lawrence. *Endangered Species: Writers Talk About Their Craft, Their Visions, Their Lives.* Da Capo Press, 2001.

Heston, Charlton. *In the Arena.* Simon & Schuster, 1995.

———. *The Actor's Life: Journals 1956–1976.* E. P. Dutton, 1976.

Insdorf, Annette. *François Truffaut.* Cambridge University Press, 1994.

Jackson, Kevin, ed. *Schrader on Schrader & Other Writings.* Faber and Faber, 1990.

Kline, Sally, ed. *George Lucas: Interviews.* University Press of Mississippi, 1999.

Munn, Michael. *Charlton Heston: A Biography.* St. Martin's Press, 1986.

O'Connell, Sean. *filmcritic.com,* November 29, 2010, "Q&A: *Black Swan*'s Natalie Portman and Darren Aronofsky on Bad Coffee and Brutal Ballet."

Simon, Neil. *Rewrites: A Memoir.* Simon and Schuster, 1996.

Smith, Gavin, ed. *Sayles on Sayles.* Faber and Faber, 1998.

Thomson, David. *The Whole Equation: A History of Hollywood.* Alfred A. Knopf, 2005.

Truffaut, François. *The Films in My Life.* Simon and Schuster, 1978.

Index

Page numbers in *italics* refer to illustrations.

A Note on the Type

This book was set in Adobe Garamond.
Designed for the Adobe Corporation by Robert
Slimbach, the fonts are based on types first cut by Claude
Garamond (c. 1480–1561). Garamond was a pupil of
Geoffrey Tory and is believed to have followed the
Venetian models, although he introduced a number of
important differences, and it is to him that we owe the
letter we now know as "old style." He gave to his letters
a certain elegance and feeling of movement that won
their creator and immediate reputation and
the patronage of Francis I of France.

Composed by North Market Street Graphics,
Lancaster, Pennsylvania
Printed and bound by Berryville Graphics,
Berryville, Virginia
Typography based on a design
by Anthea Lingeman